The English Legal System

Cavendish
Publishing
Limited

London • Sydney

The English
Legal System

Fourth Edition

Gary Slapper, LLB, LLM, PhD
Director of the Law Programme, The Open University

David Kelly, BA, BA (Law), PhD
Principal Lecturer in Law, Staffordshire University

Cavendish
Publishing
Limited

London • Sydney

Fourth edition first published in Great Britain 1999 by Cavendish Publishing Limited, The Glass House, Wharton Street, London WC1X 9PX, United Kingdom.

Telephone: +44 (0) 20 7278 8000   Facsimile: +44 (0) 20 7278 8080

E-mail: info@cavendishpublishing.com

Visit our Home Page on http://www.cavendishpublishing.com

This title was previously published under the Principles of Law series.

© Slapper, G and Kelly, D 1999

First edition   1994
Second edition   1995
Third edition   1997
Fourth edition   1999

British Library Cataloguing Data

Slapper, Gary
English Legal System – 4th ed
1. Law – England 2. Law – Wales
I. Title II. Kelly, David, 1950 Aug 16
347.4'2

ISBN 1 85941 466 4

Printed and bound in Great Britain

PREFACE

A good comprehension of the English legal system requires knowledge and skill in a number of disciplines. The system itself is the result of developments in law, economy, politics, sociological change, and the theories which feed all these bodies of knowledge. A detailed knowledge of several areas of law is indispensable but students are also expected to appreciate the historical development of many legal institutions, and the social and political debates which surround legal issues. It is important to understand the legal theory which is behind policies on matters as diverse as the law relating to arrest, search and seizure; the distribution of work among different types of court; the structure of legal services; judicial review of administrative discretion; the operation of the doctrines of precedent and statutory interpretation; plea bargaining, contingency fees and legal aid. Being proficient in this subject also means being familiar with contemporary changes and proposed changes. This book aims to assist students of the English legal system in the achievement of a good understanding of the law, its institutions and processes. It is also our aim to help cultivate in students of the system a critical approach to current legal issues and problems.

Much has changed within the English legal system since the third edition of this book in 1997. Taken together, the changes probably amount to the most significant period of systemic, structural and procedural legal reformation in the last century.

In the Woolf reforms, we see a major redesign of the whole of civil procedure, and use of the civil courts. The Access to Justice Act 1999 has fundamentally altered the provision of legal services with the introduction of the Legal Services Commission, the Community Legal Service, and the Criminal Defence Service. The changes the Act has brought to the system of conditional fee arrangements, the magistrates' courts system, rights of audience and appeals are also of major importance. There have been substantial changes in EU law, the considerable changes as a consequence of the Human Rights Act 1998, and new law and practice in the fields of civil liberties, and Alternative Dispute Resolution. Apart from these concrete changes, there is an appreciable change in public attitude to lawyers, judges, the law and its operation. Lively public debate has followed the publication of the Macpherson Report into the killing of Stephen Lawrence, and governmental proposals to alter rights to trial by jury.

We have endeavoured to state the law as at 15 August 1999.

Gary Slapper
David Kelly
August 1999

ACKNOWLEDGMENTS

We are very grateful to many people for their assistance, counsel, expertise, good humour and patience, all of which have contributed to the writing of this book. We are especially indebted to Suzanne, Hannah, Emily, Charlotte, Jane and Michael.

Thanks to Marilyn Lannigan for her assiduous research, and to Jo Reddy for her dedication, lynx eye and lawyer's tenacity; thanks to Sonny Leong for his idea to re-style the text, and to Professor Hazel Genn, Liz Rodgers, Michael Fealy, Steve Greenfield and David Stott for their comments on parts of the draft text. Thanks also to Miceal Bardén, Janice Richardson, Doreen and Ivor Slapper, David and Julie Whight, the OUBS Research Committee, Frances Gibb at *The Times*, Carol Howells, Raie Schwartz, Alison Morris, and Hugh McLaughlan.

CONTENTS

TABLE OF CASES

Table of Cases

TABLE OF STATUTES

TABLE OF STATUTORY INSTRUMENTS

TABLE OF EC TREATIES

TABLE OF ABBREVIATIONS

AA	Arbitration Act 1950/1979/1996
ABWOR	Assistance by way of representation
ACLEC	Advisory Committee on Legal Education and Conduct
ADR	Alternative dispute resolution
AJA	Administration of Justice Act 1985
BA	Bail Act 1976
BIS	Bail Information Schemes
British J of Criminology	British Journal of Criminology
British JLS	British Journal of Law and Society
CA	Children Act 1989
CAA	Criminal Appeal Act 1968/1995
CCR	County Court Rules
CCRC	Criminal Cases Review Commission
CDS	Criminal Defence Service
CEO	Civilian enforcement officers
CJA	Criminal Justice Act 1967/1972/1982/1987/1988/1991/1994
CJPOA	Criminal Justice and Public Order Act 1964/1984/1994
CJR	Civil Justice Review
CLC	Citizens' Law Centre
CLS	Community Legal Service
CLSP	Community Legal Service Partnership
CLSA	Courts and Legal Services Act 1990
CPIA	Criminal Procedure and Investigations Act 1996
CPR	Civil Procedure Rules 1998
CPS	Crown Prosecution Service
Crim LR	Criminal Law Review
CSA	Child Support Agency
DCOA	Deregulation and Contracting Out Act 1994
DGFT	Director General of Fair Trading
DPMCA	Domestic Proceedings and Magistrates' Courts Act 1978
DPP	Director of Public Prosecutions
ECHR	European Court of Human Rights

ECJ	European Court of Justice
EEC	European Economic Community
EL Rev	European Law Review
EP(C)A	Employment Protection (Consolidation) Act 1978
EU	European Union
Howard J	Howard Journal
Howard J of Criminal Justice	Howard Journal of Criminal Justice
HRA	Human Rights Act 1998
JA	Juries Act 1974
JCE	Justices' chief executive
JdA	Judicature Act 1873
JLS	Journal of Law and Society
JP	Justice of the Peace
JPA	Justices of the Peace Act 1979
JSB	Judicial Studies Board
JSPTL	Journal of Society of Public Teachers of Law
LAA	Legal Advice and Assistance
LAdA	Legal Aid Act 1988
LAG	Legal Action Group
Law Soc Gazette	Law Society Gazette
LCD	Lord Chancellor's Department
LPC	Legal Practice Course
LQR	Law Quarterly Review
LSO	Legal Services Ombudsman
MCA	Magistrates' Courts Act 1980
MCC	Magistrates' Courts Committee
MDP	Multi-disciplinary partnerships
MLR	Modern Law Review
MNP	Multi-national partnerships
NCC	National Consumer Council
NILQ	Northern Ireland Legal Quarterly

NLJ	New Law Journal
OSS	Office for the Supervision of Solicitors
PACE	Police and Criminal Evidence Act 1984/1994
PAP	Pre-action protocol
PCA	Parliamentary Commissioner for Administration
PCCC	Professional Conduct and Complaints Committee
POA	Prosecution of Offences Act 1985
QC	Queen's Counsel
RSC	Rules of the Supreme Court
SJ	Solicitors Journal
SLR	Student Law Review
SFO	Serious Fraud Office
SEA	Single European Act 1986/1987

CHAPTER 1

LAW AND LEGAL STUDY

1.1   Introduction

There are a number of possible approaches to the study of law. One such is the traditional/formalistic approach. This approach to law is posited on the existence of a discrete legal universe as the object of study. It is concerned with establishing a knowledge of the specific rules, both substantive and procedural, which derive from statute and common law, and which regulate social activity. The essential point in relation to this approach is that study is restricted to the sphere of the legal without reference to the social activity to which the legal rules are applied. In the past, most traditional law courses, and the majority of law textbooks, adopted this 'black letter' approach. Their object was the provision of information on what the current rules and principles of law were, and how to use those rules and principles to solve what were by definition *legal* problems. Traditionally, English legal system courses have focused attention on the institutions of the law, predominantly the courts, in which legal rules and principles are put into operation, and here, too, the underlying assumption has been as to the closed nature of the legal world; its distinctiveness and separateness from normal every day activity. This book continues that tradition to a degree but also recognises, and has tried to accommodate, the dissatisfaction with such an approach that has been increasingly evident among law teachers and examiners in this area. To that end, the authors have tried not simply to produce a purely expository text but have attempted to introduce an element of critical awareness and assessment into the areas considered. *Potential examination candidates should appreciate that it is just such critical, analytical thought that distinguishes the good student from the mundane one.*

Additionally, however, this book goes further than traditional texts on the English legal system by directly questioning the claims to distinctiveness made by, and on behalf of, the legal system and considering law as a socio-political institution. It is the view of the authors that the legal system cannot be studied without a consideration of the values that law reflects and supports, and again students should be aware that it is in such areas that the truly first class students demonstrate their awareness and ability.

1.2   The nature of law

One of the most obvious and most central characteristics of all societies is that they must possess some degree of order to permit the members to interact over a sustained period of time. Different societies, however, have different forms of order. Some societies are highly regimented with strictly enforced social rules whereas others continue to function in what outsiders might consider a very unstructured manner with apparently few strict rules being enforced.

Order is therefore necessary, but the form through which order is maintained is certainly not universal as many anthropological studies have shown (see Mansell and Meteyard, *A Critical Introduction to Law*, 2nd edn, 1999).

In our society, law plays an important part in the creation and maintenance of social order. We must be aware, however, that law, as we know it, is not the only means of creating order. Even in our society, order is not solely dependent on law, but also involves questions of a more general moral and political character. This book is not concerned with providing a general explanation of the form of order. It is concerned, more particularly, with describing and explaining the key institutional aspects of that particular form of order that is *legal* order.

The most obvious way in which law contributes to the maintenance of social order is the way in which it deals with disorder or conflict. This book, therefore, is particularly concerned with the institutions and procedures, both civil and criminal, through which law operates to ensure a particular form of social order by dealing with various conflicts when they arise.

Law is a *formal* mechanism of social control and as such it is essential that the student of law be fully aware of the nature of that formal structure. There are, however, other aspects to law that are less immediately apparent, but of no less importance, such as the inescapable political nature of law. Some textbooks focus more on this particular aspect of law than others and these differences become evident in the particular approach adopted by the authors. The approach favoured by the authors of this book is to recognise that studying the English legal system is not just about learning legal rules but is also about considering a social institution of fundamental importance.

1.3   Categories of law

There are various ways of categorising law which initially tend to confuse the non-lawyer and the new student of law. What follows will set out these categorisations in their usual dual form whilst at the same time trying to overcome the confusion inherent in such duality. It is impossible to avoid the confusing repetition of the same terms to mean different things and indeed the purpose of this section is to make sure that students are aware of the fact that the same words can have different meanings depending upon the context in which they are used.

1.3.1   Common law and civil law

In this particular juxtaposition, these terms are used to distinguish two distinct legal systems and approaches to law. The use of the term common law in this context refers to all those legal systems which have adopted the historic English legal system. Foremost amongst these is, of course, the United States but many other Commonwealth, and former Commonwealth, countries retain a common law system. The term 'civil law' refers to those other jurisdictions which have adopted the European continental system of law derived essentially from ancient Roman law, but owing much to the Germanic tradition.

The usual distinction to be made between the two systems is that the former, common law system, tends to be case centred and hence judge centred, allowing scope for a discretionary, ad hoc, pragmatic approach to the particular problems that appear before the courts; whereas the latter, civil law system, tends to be a codified body of general abstract principles which control the exercise of judicial discretion. In reality, both of these views are extremes, with the former over-emphasising the extent to which the common law judge can impose his discretion and the latter under-estimating the extent to which continental judges have the power to exercise judicial discretion. It is perhaps worth mentioning at this point that the European Court of Justice, established, in theory, on civil law principles, is, in practice, increasingly recognising the benefits of establishing a body of case law.

It has to be recognised, and indeed the English courts do so, that, although the European Court of Justice is not bound by the operation of the doctrine of stare decisis (see 2.3), it still does not decide individual cases on an ad hoc basis, and, therefore, in the light of a perfectly clear decision of the European Court, national courts will be reluctant to refer similar cases to its jurisdiction. Thus, after the ECJ decided, in *Grant v South West Trains Ltd* (1998), that Community law did not cover discrimination on grounds of sexual orientation, the High Court withdrew a similar reference in *R v Secretary of State for Defence ex p Perkins (No 2)* (1998) (see 13.3.6 for a detailed consideration of the ECJ).

1.3.2   Common law and equity

In this particular juxtaposition, the terms refer to a particular division within the English legal system.

The common law has been romantically and inaccurately described as the law of the common people of England. In fact, the common law emerged as the product of a particular struggle for political power. Prior to the Norman Conquest of England in 1066, there was no unitary, national legal system. The emergence of the common law represents the imposition of such a unitary system under the auspices and control of a centralised power in the form of a sovereign king; and, in that respect, it represented the assertion and affirmation of that central sovereign power.

Traditionally, much play is made about the circuit of judges travelling round the country establishing the 'King's peace' and, in so doing, selecting the best local customs and making them the basis of the law of England in a piecemeal but totally altruistic procedure. The reality of this process was that the judges were asserting the authority of the central State and its legal forms and institutions, over the disparate and fragmented State and legal forms of the earlier feudal period. Hence the common law was common *to* all in application but certainly was not common *from* all. (The contemporary meaning and relevance and operation of the common law will be considered in more detail later in this chapter and in Chapter 2.)

By the end of the 13th century, the central authority had established its precedence at least partly through the establishment of the common law. Originally, courts had been no more than an adjunct of the King's Council, the *Curia Regis*, but gradually the common law courts began to take on a distinct institutional existence in the form of the courts of Exchequer, Common Pleas and King's Bench. With this institutional autonomy, however, there developed an institutional sclerosis, typified by a reluctance to deal with matters that were not or could not be processed in the proper *form of action*. Such a refusal to deal with substantive injustices, because they did not fall within the particular parameters of procedural and formal constraints, by necessity led to injustice and the need to remedy the perceived weaknesses in the common law system. The response was the development of *equity*.

Plaintiffs unable to gain access to the three common law courts might directly appeal to the sovereign, and such pleas would be passed for consideration and decision to the Lord Chancellor who acted as the King's conscience. As the common law courts became more formalistic and more inaccessible, pleas to the Chancellor correspondingly increased and eventually this resulted in the emergence of a specific court constituted to deliver 'equitable' or 'fair' decisions in cases which the common law courts declined to deal with. As had happened with the common law, the decisions of the Courts of Equity established principles which were used to decide later cases, so it should not be thought that the use of equity meant that judges had discretion to decide cases on the basis of their personal idea of what was just in each case.

The division between the common law courts and the Courts of Equity continued until they were eventually combined by the Judicature Acts (JdA) 1873–75. Prior to this legislation, it was essential for a party to raise their action in the appropriate court, for example, the courts of law would not implement equitable principles; the Acts, however, provided that every court had the power and the duty to decide cases in line with common law and equity, with the latter being paramount in the final analysis.

Some would say that, as equity was never anything other than a gloss on common law, it is perhaps appropriate, if not ironic, that now both systems have been effectively subsumed under the one term: common law.

Common law remedies are available as of right. Remedies in equity are discretionary, in other words, they are awarded at the will of the court, and depend on the behaviour, and situation, of the party claiming such remedies This means that, in effect, the court does not have to award an equitable remedy where it considers the conduct of the party seeking such an award does not deserve such an award (*D and C Builders v Rees* (1965)). The usual equitable remedies are:

- *injunction* – this is a court order requiring someone to do something or, alternatively, to stop doing something (*Warner Bros v Nelson* (1937));

- *specific performance* – this is a court order requiring one of the parties to a contractual agreement to complete their part of the contract. It is usually only awarded in respect of contracts relating to specific individual articles, such as land, and will not be awarded where the court cannot supervise the operation of its order (*Ryan v Mutual Tontine Westminster Chambers Association* (1893));

- *rectification* – relates to the alteration, under extremely limited circumstances, of contractual documents (*Jocscelyne v Nissen* (1970));

- *rescission* – this order returns parties to a contractual agreement to the position they were in before the agreement was entered into. It is essential to distinguish this award from the common law award of damages, which is intended to place the parties in the position they would have been in had the contract been completed.

1.3.3 Common law and statute law

This particular conjunction follows on from the immediately preceding section in that the common law here refers to the substantive law and procedural rules that have been created by the judiciary through the decisions in the cases they have heard. Statute law, on the other hand, refers to law that has been created by Parliament in the form of legislation. Although there has been a significant increase in statute law in the 20th century, the courts still have an important role to play in creating and operating law generally and in determining the operation of legislation in particular. The relationship of this pair of concepts is of central importance and is considered in more detail in Chapters 2 and 5.

1.3.4 Private law and public law

There are two different ways of understanding the division between private and public law.

At one level, the division relates specifically to actions of the State and its functionaries vis à vis the individual citizen, and the legal manner in which, and form of law through which, such relationships are regulated: that is, public law. In the 19th century, it was at least possible to claim as such as AV Dicey did that there was no such thing as public law, in this distinct administrative sense, and that the powers of the State with regard to individuals was governed by the ordinary law of the land, operating through the normal courts. Whether such a claim was accurate or not when it was made, and it is unlikely, there certainly can be no doubt now that public law constitutes a distinct, and growing, area of law in its own right. The growth of public law, in this sense, has mirrored the growth and increased activity of the contemporary State, and has seen its role as seeking to regulate such activity. The crucial role of judicial review in relation to public law will be considered in some detail in Chapter 6.

There is, however, a second aspect to the division between private and public law. One corollary of the divide is that matters located within the private sphere are seen as purely a matter for individuals themselves to regulate, without the interference of the State, whose role is limited to the provision of the forum for deciding contentious issues and mechanisms for the enforcement of such decisions. Matters within the public sphere, however, are seen as issues relating to the interest of the State and general public, and, as such, to be protected and prosecuted by the State. It can be seen, therefore, that the category to which any dispute is allocated is of crucial importance to how it is dealt with. Contract may be thought of as the classic example of private law, but the extent to which this purely private legal area has been subjected to the regulation of public law, in such areas as consumer protection, should not be underestimated. Equally, the most obvious example of public law in this context would be criminal law. Feminists have argued, however, that the allocation of domestic matters to the sphere of private law has led to a denial of a general interest in the treatment and protection of women. By defining domestic matters as private, the State, and its functionaries, have denied women access to its power to protect themselves from abuse. In doing so, it is suggested that, in fact, such categorisation has reflected and maintained the social domination of men over women

1.3.5 Civil law and criminal law

Civil law is a form of private law and involves the relationships between individual citizens. It is the legal mechanism through which individuals can assert claims against others and have those rights adjudicated and enforced. The purpose of civil law is to settle disputes between individuals and to provide remedies; it is not concerned with punishment as such. The role of the State in relation to civil law is to establish the general framework of legal rules and to provide the legal institutions for operating those rights, but the activation of the civil law is strictly a matter for the individuals concerned. Contract, tort and property law are generally aspects of civil law.

Criminal law, on the other hand, is an aspect of public law and relates to conduct which the State considers with disapproval and which it seeks to control and/or eradicate. Criminal law involves the *enforcement* of particular forms of behaviour, and the State, as the representative of society, acts positively to ensure compliance. Thus, criminal cases are brought by the State in the name of the Crown and cases are reported in the form of *Regina v ...* (*Regina* is simply Latin for queen and case references are usually abbreviated to *R v ...*), whereas civil cases are referred to by the names of the parties involved in the dispute, for example, *Smith v Jones*.

A crucial distinction between criminal and civil law is the level of proof required in the different types of cases. In the criminal case, the prosecution is required to prove that the defendant is guilty beyond reasonable doubt, whereas, in a civil case, the degree of proof is much lower, and has only to be on the balance of probabilities. This difference in the level of proof raises the possibility of someone being able to succeed in a civil case, although there may not be sufficient evidence for a criminal prosecution. And indeed, this strategy has been used successfully in a number of cases against the police where the Crown Prosecution has considered there to be insufficient evidence to support a criminal conviction for assault.

It should also be noted that the distinction between civil and criminal responsibility is further blurred in cases involving what may be described as hybrid offences. These are situations where a court awards a civil order against an individual, on the balance of probabilities, but with the attached sanction that any breach of the order will be subject to punishment as a criminal offence. As examples of this procedure may be cited the Protection from Harassment Act 1997 and the new provision for the making of Anti Social Behaviour Orders available under s 1(i) of the Crime and Disorder Act 1998. Both of these provisions are of considerable interest and deserve some attention in their own right. The Protection from Harassment Act was introduced as a measure to deal with 'stalking', the harassment of individuals by people continuously following them, and allowed the victim of harassment to get a court order to prevent the stalking. Whereas stalking may have been the high profile source of the Act, it is possible, however, that its most useful provision, if it is used appropriately, may actually lie in providing more protection for women, who are subject to assault and harassment from their partners, than is available under alternative criminal or civil law procedures. The newly instituted Anti Social Behaviour Orders, available against individuals aged 10 or over on the application of the police or local authority, may be made in situations where there has been: intimidation through threats, violence and a mixture of unpleasant actions; persistent unruly behaviour by a small group on an estate; families who resort to abuse when complaints are made to them; vandalism;

serious and persistent organised bullying of children; persistent racial or homophobic harassment; persistent antisocial behaviour as a result of drug or alcohol abuse (Home Office Guidance Document 1999).

Whereas these Acts may seem initially to offer a welcome additional protection to the innocent individual, it has to be recognised that such advantage is achieved, in effect by criminalising what was, and remains, in other circumstance, non-criminal behaviour, and deciding its applicability on the basis of the lower civil law burden of proof.

Nor should it be forgotten that, although prosecution of criminal offences is usually the prerogative of the State, it remains open to the private individual to initiate a private prosecution in relation to a criminal offence. It has to be remembered, however, that, even in the private prosecution, the test of the burden of proof remains the criminal one requiring the facts to be proved beyond reasonable doubt. An example of the problems inherent in such private actions can be seen in the case of Stephen Lawrence, the young black man who was gratuitously stabbed to death by a gang of white racists whilst standing at a bus stop in London. Although there was strong suspicion, and indeed evidence, against particular individuals, the Crown Prosecution Service declined to press the charges against them on the basis of insufficiency of evidence. When the lawyers of the Lawrence family mounted a private prosecution against the suspects, the action failed for want of sufficient evidence to convict. As a consequence of the failure of the private prosecution, the rule against double jeopardy meant that the accused could not be re-tried for the same offence at any time in the future, even if the police subsequently acquired sufficient new evidence to support a conviction. (The Macpherson Inquiry, into the manner in which the police dealt with the Stephen Lawrence case, recommended the removal of the double jeopardy rule, but this particular recommendation is not likely to be implemented on grounds of civil liberties.) To conclude at this stage, however, it has been reported that the Lawrence family are to initiate a private law action against the suspects – the point for now being that the burden of proof will be lower.

In considering the relationship between civil law and criminal law, it is sometimes thought that criminal law is the more important in maintaining social order, but it is at least arguable that, in reality, the reverse is the case. For the most part, people come into contact with the criminal law infrequently, whereas everyone is continuously involved with civil law, even if it is only the use of contract law to make some purchase. The criminal law of theft, for example, may be seen as simply the cutting edge of the wider and more fundamental rights established by general property law. In any case, there remains the fact that civil and criminal law each has its own distinct legal system. The nature of these systems will be considered in detail in later chapters.

1.4   The separation of powers

Although the idea of the separation of powers can be traced back to ancient Greek philosophy, it was advocated in early modern times by the English philosopher *Locke* and the later French philosopher *Montesquieu* and found its practical expression in the constitution of the United States. The idea of the separation of powers is posited on the existence of three distinct functions of government, the legislative, executive and judicial functions, and the conviction that these functions should be kept apart in order to prevent the centralisation of too much power. Establishing the appropriate relationship between the actions of the State and the legal control over those actions crucially involves a consideration of whether there is any absolute limit on the authority of the government of the day. Answering that question inevitably involves an examination of the general constitutional structure of the United Kingdom, and, in particular, the inter-relationship of two doctrines: parliamentary sovereignty; and judicial independence.

1.4.1   Parliamentary sovereignty

As a consequence of the victory of the parliamentary forces in the English revolutionary struggles of the 17th century, Parliament became the sovereign power in the land. The independence of the judiciary was secured, however, in the Act of Settlement 1701. The centrality of the independence of the judges and the legal system from direct control or interference from the State in the newly established constitution was emphasised in the writing of John Locke who saw it as one of the essential reasons for, and justifications of, the Social Contract on which the social structure was assumed to be based. It is generally accepted that the inspiration for Montesquieu's *Spirit of Law (De L'Esprit des Lois)* was the English constitution but, if that is truly the case, then his doctrine of the separation of powers was based on a misunderstanding of that constitution as it failed to take account of the express *superiority of Parliament* in all matters, including its relationship with the judiciary and the legal system.

It is interesting that some Conservative thinkers have recently suggested that the whole notion of parliamentary sovereignty is itself a product of the self-denying ordinance of the common law. Consequently, they have suggested that it is open to a subsequent, more robust, judiciary, confident in its own position and powers within the developing constitution, to reassert its equality with the other two elements. When, however, it is recalled that when the Conservative party was in power, it was to no little extent embarrassed by, and not too understanding of, the actions of recalcitrant judges, it is at least a moot point whether such a proposition reflects a real commitment to judicial equality with the executive, or merely represents the gall of a defeated executive, hoping to enlist the judges in their oppositional role. It does not require an uncritical commitment to the role of the judiciary to recognise that powerful executives, which exercise effective control over acquiescent legislatures, do not take too well to the interference of an active judiciary.

Given the existence of the doctrine of parliamentary sovereignty, which effectively means that Parliament, as the ultimate source of law, can make such law as it determines, the exact extent to which the doctrine of the separation of powers operates in the United Kingdom is a matter of some debate. For example, the position of the Lord Chancellor, who is at the same time a member of the government and the most senior judge in the land with control over judicial appointments, is not unproblematic (this will be considered in detail in Chapter 6). There is, however, high judicial authority for claiming that the separation of powers is an essential element in the constitution of the United Kingdom (see *R v Hinds* (1977) in which Lord Diplock, whilst considering the nature of different Commonwealth constitutions in a Privy Council case, stated that 'It is taken for granted that the basic principle of the separation of powers will apply ...' (at p 212)). In any case, the point of considering the doctrine at this juncture is simply to highlight the distinction, and relationship, between the executive and the judiciary and to indicate the possibility of conflict between the two elements of the constitution. This relationship assumes crucial importance if one accepts, as some have suggested, that it is no longer possible to distinguish the executive from the legislature as, through its control of its majority in the House of Commons, the executive, that is, the government, can legislate as it wishes, and, in so doing, can provide the most arbitrary of party political decisions with the form of legality. The question to be considered here is to what extent the judiciary can legitimately oppose the wishes of the government expressed in the form of legislation, or the extent to which it can interfere with the pursuit of those wishes.

1.4.2 Judicial independence

The exact meaning of 'judicial independence' became a matter of debate when some members and ex-members of the senior judiciary suggested that the former Lord Chancellor, Lord Mackay of Clashfern, had adopted a too restrictive interpretation of the term which had reduced it to the mere absence of interference by the executive in the trial of individual cases. They asserted the right of the legal system to operate independently, as an autonomous system apart from the general control of the State, with the judiciary controlling its operation, or at least being free from the dictates and strictures of central control.

According to Lord Mackay, in the first of his series of Hamlyn lectures entitled 'The Administration of Justice' (1994):

The fact that the executive and judiciary meet in the person of the Lord Chancellor should symbolise what I believe is necessary for the administration of justice in a country like ours, namely, a realisation that both the judiciary and the executive are parts of the total government of the country with functions that are distinct but which must work together in a proper relationship if the country is to be properly governed ... It seems more likely that the interests of the judiciary in matters within the concerns covered by the Treasury are more likely to be advanced if they can be pursued within government by a person with a lifetime of work in law and an understanding of the needs and concerns of the judiciary and who has responsibility as Head of the Judiciary, than if they were to be left within government as the responsibility of a minister with no such connection with the judiciary.

There is, however, some concern within the judiciary as to whether the relationship between the executive and the judiciary is proper and doubts have been raised as to the Lord Chancellor's positioning between the two institutions. Fears have been expressed that rather than representing the interests of the judiciary within the government, the current Lord Chancellor, Lord Irvine of Lairg, is actually pursuing and implementing policies that are driven by the economic dictates of the Treasury and which are having a severely detrimental impact on the operation of the whole justice system. Rather than being the voice of the judiciary in Cabinet, he is suspected by some, as was his predecessor, of being the voice of the Cabinet in the judiciary.

In a paper presented to the Bar Conference and subsequently published in the *New Law Journal* ((1994) NLJ, 30 September), Sir Francis Purchas claimed that the second half of the 20th century had seen the executive make substantial inroads into the independence of the judiciary and warned against the dangers of an executive-centred court system in which the judges have no effective protection against executive interference and in which the disposal of cases took priority over the attainment of justice. In his view:

The quality and extent of justice available has been reduced, and the access to that justice has been curtailed. Generally speaking, this has arisen as a succession of legislative acts, orders or provisions brought into being by the executive, or a policy of inaction followed in pursuance of the Treasury ethos of market forces and competition policy ...

In relation to the situation of the Lord Chancellor, Sir Francis stated that:

... when the Lord Chancellor is an active member of the Cabinet charged with the introduction of measures which he knows will be opposed by the judges and in many respects by the professions, the inadequacy of the traditional structure is fatally exposed. In the present context of acute confrontation with an all-powerful executive pursuing a market-forces ethos which is wholly inapplicable to the provision of justice, the judiciary may well require a more powerful and representative body through which their independence may be preserved so as to be an effective check on the executive.

Does this suggest that the Lord Chancellor should be replaced by a judicial trade union? If it does, it is ironic, coming from the body who have traditionally been the enemies of trade unions, although always ready to defend the closed-shop interests of the Bar from which they came.

The tension inherent in the relationship between the courts and the executive government has taken on an even more fundamental constitutional aspect in relation to the development of the process of judicial review by means of which the courts assert the right to subject the actions and operations of the executive to the gaze and control of the law in such a way as to prevent the executive from abusing its power. In the United States, with its written constitution, the judiciary have the power to declare the Acts of the legislature to be unconstitutional and, therefore, unlawful.

As Roger Smith observed, in an article, 'Politics and the judiciary', in the *New Law Journal* ((1993) 143 NLJ 1486):

> Judicial review ... is pushing our political system towards a greater separation of powers. The judiciary is disengaging itself from its earlier subservience to the legislature and the executive. There are, doubtless, various strands to this which include the influence of the United States of Europe. However, another important element must be the failure in recent years of the usual checks and balance of democracy. Britain is in danger of becoming a one-party State ... Other parts of the constitution are forced into the opposition role, particularly when their interests and perceptions are offended.

It is of no little interest to note that Parliament, in the form of the House of Commons, reasserted its ultimate authority in relation to the recommendations of the Committee on Standards in Public Life, which was established, under the chairmanship of the senior Judge Lord Nolan. The committee was set up to consider, amongst other things, ways in which either actual or perceived corruption within the legislative body could be controlled. The committee's recommendation that an independent Parliamentary Commissioner for Public Standards, an Ombudsman, should be appointed to enforce controls over the activities of MPs was resisted by some members of the Commons on the grounds that nobody outside of Parliament could be given the authority to regulate Parliament. The fact that such an assertion might be seen as protecting the right of particular members to engage in 'sleaze' was portrayed as being of secondary importance to the constitutional question as to the sovereignty of Parliament. The fact that this argument was almost completely spurious, in that any such Ombudsman would be acting for Parliament and representing the authority of Parliament, was recognised and Sir Gordon Downey was appointed to fill the office of Commissioner for Public Standards, responsible to the Commons Committee on Standards and Privileges. Much of Sir Gordon's work has related to what has become known as the 'cash for questions' scandal. This affair refers to the fact that a number of Members of Parliament have been accused of, and some have admitted, being paid for asking questions in the House. The payment was made by Mohamed Al Fayed, the chairman of the House of Fraser group which owns Harrods, and was organised through the offices of the parliamentary lobbyist Ian Greer. In July 1997, Sir Gordon Downey issued a three volume report on the allegations of sleaze made against certain MPs ((1997) *The Times*; *The Guardian*, 4 July). Although five MPs were censured in the report with a severity which would have required them to be expelled from the House of Commons, they were still MPs. In the event, however, all those condemned in the report had either not stood as candidates at the General Election on 1 May 1997 or were defeated on that occasion. Geoffrey Robertson QC, who acted in the Downey Inquiry, stated after publication of the report:

> The real lesson of the Downey Report is that never again should MPs be regarded – or regard themselves – as above the law ... Self-regulation is not enough: it is time to follow the lead of Parliaments in the Commonwealth which have established an independent commission against corruption headed by a judge, to investigate and report allegations against ministers, MPs and public servants ((1997) *The Guardian*, 4 July).

The sensitive relationship between the judiciary and Parliament was highlighted in two cases. In *R v Parliamentary Commissioner for Standards ex p Al Fayed* (1997), it was held that the operation of the Parliamentary Commissioner for Public Standards was not open to judicial review, as he dealt with matters relating to the internal operation of Parliament. The operation of the Parliamentary Commissioner for Administration (the Ombudsman, see 8.4) is subject to judicial review, however, because his is an external, rather than an internal, parliamentary role (*R v Parliamentary Commissioner for Administration ex p Balchin* (1997)).

Judicial review and its political implications will be considered in detail in Chapter 6, but at this point it should be noted that any general treatment of the relationship of the judiciary and executive must consider the particular meaning and scope of the doctrine known as the 'Rule of Law' and its relationship to human rights.

1.5   The Rule of Law

The Rule of Law represents a symbolic ideal against which proponents of widely divergent political persuasions measure and criticise the shortcomings of contemporary State practice. This varied recourse to the Rule of Law is, of course, only possible because of the lack of precision in the actual meaning of the concept; its meaning tending to change over time and, as will be seen below, to change in direct correspondence with the beliefs of those who claim its support and claim, in turn, to support it. It is undeniable that the form and content of law and legal procedure have changed substantially in the course of the 20th century. It is usual to explain such changes as being a consequence of the way in which, and the increased extent to which, the modern State intervenes in everyday life, be it economic or social. As the State increasingly took over the regulation of many areas of social activity, it delegated wide ranging discretionary powers to various people and bodies in an attempt to ensure the successful implementation of its policies. The assumption and delegation of such power on the part of the State brought it into potential conflict with previous understandings of the Rule of Law which had entailed a strictly limited ambit of State activity. The impact of this on the understanding and operation of the principle of the Rule of Law and its implications in relation to the judiciary are traced out below and will be returned to in Chapter 6.

1.5.1   AV Dicey

According to AV Dicey, in *Introduction to the Study of the Law of the Constitution* (1885), the United Kingdom had no such thing as administrative law as distinct from the ordinary law of the land. Whether he was correct or not when he expressed this opinion, and there are substantial grounds for doubting the accuracy of his claim even at the time he made it, it can no longer be denied that there is now a large area of law that can be properly called administrative, that is, related to the pursuit and application of particular State policies usually within a framework of statutory powers.

According to the notoriously chauvinistic Dicey, the Rule of Law was one of the key features which distinguished the English Constitution from its continental counterparts. Whereas foreigners were subject to the exercise of arbitrary power, the Englishman was secure within the protection of the Rule of Law. Dicey suggested the existence of three distinct elements which together made for the Rule of Law as he understood it:

- *An absence of arbitrary power* on the part of the State. The extent of the State's power, and the way in which it exercises such power, is limited and controlled by law. Such control is aimed at preventing the State from acquiring and using wide discretionary powers, for, as Dicey correctly recognised, the problem with discretion is that it can be exercised in an arbitrary manner; and that above all else is to be feared, at least as Dicey would have us believe.

- *Equality before the law*. The fact that no person is above the law, irrespective of rank or class. This was linked with the fact that functionaries of the State are subject to the same law and legal procedures as private citizens.

- *Supremacy of ordinary law*. This related to the fact that the English Constitution was the outcome of the ordinary law of the land and was based on the provision of remedies by the courts rather than on the declaration of rights in the form of a written constitution.

It is essential to recognise that Dicey was writing at a particular historical period, but perhaps more importantly he was writing from a particular political perspective that saw the maintenance of *individual* property and *individual* freedom to use that property as one chose, as paramount. He was opposed to any increase in State activity in the pursuit of collective interests. In analysing Dicey's version of the Rule of Law, it can be seen that it venerated *formal* equality at the expense of *substantive* equality. In other words, he thought that the law, and the State, should be blind to the real concrete differences that exist between people, in terms of wealth or power or connection, and should treat them all the same, as possessors of *abstract* rights and duties.

There is an unaddressed, and certainly unresolved, tension in Dicey's work. The Rule of Law was only one of two fundamental elements of the English polity; the other was parliamentary sovereignty. Where, however, the government controls the legislative process, the sovereignty of Parliament is reduced to the undisputed supremacy of central government. The tension arises from the fact that, whereas the Rule of Law was aimed at controlling arbitrary power, Parliament could, within this constitutional structure, make provision for the granting of such arbitrary power by passing appropriate legislation.

This tension between the Rule of Law and parliamentary sovereignty is peculiar to the British version of liberal government. Where similar versions of government emerged on the continent, and particularly in Germany, the power of the legislature was itself subject to the Rule of Law. This subordinate relationship of State to law is encapsulated in the concept of the *Rechsstaat*. This idea of the *Rechsstaat* meant that the State itself was controlled by notions of law which limited its sphere of legitimate activity. Broadly speaking, the State was required to institute *general* law and could not make laws aimed at particular people.

The fact that this strong *Rechsstaat* version of the Rule of Law never existed in England reflects its particular history. The revolutionary struggles of the 17th century had delivered effective control of the English State machinery to the bourgeois class who exercised that power through Parliament. After the 17th century, the English bourgeoisie was never faced with a threatening State against which it had to protect itself: it effectively was the State. On the continent, such was not the case and the emergent bourgeoisie had to assert its power against, and safeguard itself from, the power of a State machinery that it did not control. The development of *Rechsstaat* theory, as a means of limiting the power of the State, can be seen as one of the ways in which the continental bourgeoisie attempted to safeguard its position. In England, however, there was not the same need in the 18th and 19th centuries for the bourgeoisie to protect themselves behind a *Rechsstaat* version of the Rule of Law. In England, those who benefited from the enactment and implementation of general laws as required by *Rechsstaat* theory, the middle classes, also effectively controlled

Parliament and could benefit just as well from its particular enactments. Thus, in terms of 19th century England, as Franz Neumann stated, the doctrines of parliamentary sovereignty and the Rule of Law were not antagonistic, but complementary.

1.5.2 FA von Hayek

FA von Hayek followed Dicey in seeing the essential component of the Rule of Law as being the absence of arbitrary power in the hands of the State. As Hayek expressed it in his book *The Road to Serfdom* (1971):

> Stripped of all technicalities the Rule of Law means that government in all its actions is bound by rules fixed and announced beforehand.

Hayek, however, went further than Dicey in setting out the form and, at least in a negative way, the content that legal rules had to comply with in order for them to be considered as compatible with the Rule of Law. As Hayek expressed it:

> The Rule of Law implies limits on the scope of legislation, it restricts it to the kind of general rules known as formal law; and excludes legislation directly aimed at particular people.

This means that law should not be particular in content or application, but should be general in nature; applying to all and benefiting none in particular. Nor should law be aimed at achieving particular goals; its function is to set the boundaries of personal action, not to dictate the course of such action.

Hayek was a severe critic of the interventionist State in all its guises; from the fascist right wing to the authoritarian left wing and encompassing the contemporary welfare State in the middle. His criticism was founded on two bases:

- *Efficiency*. From the micro-economic perspective, and Hayek was an economist, only the person concerned can fully know all the circumstances of their situation. The State cannot fully understand any individual's situation and should, therefore, as a matter of efficiency, leave it to the individuals concerned to make their own decisions about what they want, or how they choose to achieve what they want, so long as it is achieved in a legal way.

- *Morality*. From this perspective, to the extent that the State leaves the individual less room to make individual decisions, it reduces their freedom.

It is apparent, and not surprising considering his Austrian background, that Hayek adopted a *Rechsstaat* view of the Rule of Law. He believed that the meaning of the Rule of Law as it was currently understood in contemporary English jurisprudence represented a narrowing from its original meaning which he believed had more in common with *Rechsstaat* than it presently did. As he pointed out, the ultimate conclusion of the current weaker version of the Rule of Law was that, so long as the actions of the State were duly authorised by legislation, any such act was lawful, and thus a claim to the preservation of the Rule of Law could be maintained. It should be noted that Hayek did not suggest at any time that rules enacted in other than a general form are not laws; they are legal, as long as they are enacted through the appropriate and proper mechanisms, they simply are not in accord with the Rule of Law as he understood that principle.

Hayek disapproved of the change he claimed to have seen in the meaning of the Rule of Law. It is clear, however, that, as with Dicey, his views on law, and the meaning of the Rule of Law, were informed by a particular political perspective. It is equally clear that what he regretted most was the replacement of a free market economy by a planned economy, regulated by an interventionist State. The contemporary State no longer simply provided a legal framework for the conduct of economic activity but was actively involved in the direct co-ordination and regulation of economic activity in the pursuit of the goals that it set. This had a profound effect on the form of law. Clearly stated and fixed general laws were replaced by open-textured discretionary legislation. Also, whereas the Diceyan version of the Rule of Law had operated in terms of abstract rights and duties, formal equality and formal justice, the new version addressed concrete issues and addressed questions of substantive equality and justice.

1.5.3   EP Thompson

The Rule of Law is a mixture of implied promise and convenient vagueness. It is vagueness at the core of the concept that permits the general idea of the Rule of Law to be appropriated by people with apparently irreconcilable political agendas in support of their particular political positions. So far, consideration has been given to Dicey and Hayek, two theorists on the right of the political spectrum who saw themselves as proponents and defenders of the Rule of Law; but a similar claim can be made from the left. The case in point is EP Thompson, a Marxist historian, who also saw the Rule of Law as a protection against, and under attack from, the encroaching power of the modern State.

Thompson shared Hayek's distrust of the encroachments of the modern State and he was equally critical of the extent to which the contemporary State has intervened in the day to day lives of its citizens. From Thompson's perspective, however, the problem arises not so much from the fact that the State is undermining the operation of the market economy, but from the way in which the State has used its control over the legislative process to undermine civil liberties in the pursuit of its own concept of public interest.

In *Whigs and Hunters* (1975), a study of the manipulation of law by the landed classes in the 18th century, Thompson concludes that the Rule of Law is not just a necessary means of limiting the potential abuse of power but that:

> ... the Rule of Law, itself, the imposing of effective inhibitions upon power and the defence of the citizen from power's all-intrusive claims, seems to me an unqualified human good.

In reaching such a conclusion, Thompson clearly concurs with Hayek's view that there is more to the Rule of Law than the requirement that law be processed through the appropriate legal institutions. He, too, argues that the core meaning of the Rule of Law involves more than mere procedural propriety and suggests that the other essential element is the way, and the extent to which, it places limits on the exercise of State power.

1.5.4 Joseph Raz

Some legal philosophers have recognised the need for State intervention in contemporary society and have provided ways of understanding the Rule of Law as a means of controlling discretion without attempting to eradicate it completely. Joseph Raz ('The Rule of Law and its virtue' (1977) 93 LQR 195), for example, recognises the need for the government of men as well as laws, and that the pursuit of social goals may require the enactment of particular as well as general laws. Indeed, he suggests that it would be impossible in practical terms for law to consist solely of general rules. Raz has even criticised Hayek for disguising a political argument as a legal one in order to attack policies which he did not approve of. Yet at the same time, Raz also sees the Rule of Law as essentially a negative value, acting to minimise the danger that can follow the exercise of discretionary power in an arbitrary way. In that respect, of seeking to control the exercise of discretion, he shares common ground with Thompson, Hayek and Dicey.

Raz claims that the basic requirement from which the wider idea of the Rule of Law emerges is the requirement that the law must be capable of guiding the individual's behaviour. He states some of the most important principles that may be derived from this general idea:

- laws should be prospective rather than retroactive. People cannot be guided by or expected to obey laws which have not as yet been introduced. Laws should also be open and clear to enable people to understand them and guide their actions in line with them;

- laws should be stable and should not be changed too frequently as this might lead to confusion as to what was actually covered by the law;

- there should be clear rules and procedures for making laws;

- the independence of the judiciary has to be guaranteed to ensure that they are free to decide cases in line with the law and not in response to any external pressure;

- the principles of natural justice should be observed, requiring an open and fair hearing to be given to all parties to proceedings;

- the courts should have the power to review the way in which the other principles are implemented to ensure that they are being operated as demanded by the Rule of Law;

- the courts should be easily accessible as they remain at the heart of the idea of making discretion subject to legal control;

- the discretion of the crime preventing agencies should not be allowed to pervert the law.

It is evident that Raz sees the Rule of Law being complied with if the procedural rules of law making are complied with, subject to a number of safeguards. It is of no little interest that Raz sees the courts as having an essential part to play in his version of the Rule of Law. This point will be considered further in Chapter 6 in relation to judicial review.

1.5.5 Roberto Unger

In *Law and Modern Society* (1976), the American critical legal theorist Roberto Unger sets out a typology of social order, one category of which is essentially the Rule of Law system. Unger distinguishes this form of social order from others on the basis of two particular and unique characteristics. The first of these is *autonomy*; the fact that law has its own sphere of authority and operates independently within that sphere without reference to any external controlling factor. Unger distinguishes four distinct aspects of legal autonomy which may be enumerated as follows:

- *substantive autonomy*. This refers to the fact that law is not explainable in other, non-legal terms. To use the tautological cliché – the law is the law. In other words, law is self-referential, it is not about something else; it cannot be reduced to the level of a mere means to an end, it is an end in itself;

- *institutional autonomy*. This refers to the fact that the legal institutions such as the courts are separate from other State institutions and is highlighted in the fundamental principle of judicial independence;

- *methodological autonomy*. This refers to the fact that law has, or at least lays claim to having, its own distinct form of reasoning and justifications for its decisions;

- *occupational autonomy*. This refers to the fact that access to law is not immediate but is gained through the legal professions who act as gatekeepers and who exercise a large degree of independent control over the working of the legal system.

The second distinguishing feature of legal order, according to Unger, is its *generality*: the fact that it applies to all people without personal or class favouritism. Everyone is equal under the law and is treated in the same manner.

In putting forward this typology of social order, Unger recognises the advantages inherent in a Rule of Law system over a system that operates on the basis of arbitrary power; but he is ultimately sceptical as to the reality of the equality that such a system supports and questions its future continuation. The point of major interest for this book, however, is the way in which each of the four distinct areas of supposed autonomy are increasingly being challenged and undermined, as will be considered at the end of the next section.

1.5.6   Max Weber

Unger sees the development of the Rule of Law as a product of Western capitalist society and, in highlighting the distinct nature of the form of law under that system, he may be seen as following the German sociologist Max Weber. Weber's general goal was to examine and explain the structure and development of Western capitalist society. In so doing, he was concerned with those unique aspects of that society which distinguished it from other social formations. One such distinguishing characteristic was the form of law which he characterised as a formally rational system, that prefigured Unger's notion of legal autonomy. (See Weber, *Wirtschaft und Gemeinschaft* (trans 1968).)

Weber's autonomous legal system was accompanied by a State which limited itself to establishing a clear framework of social order and left individuals to determine their own destinies in a free market system. In the course of the 20th century, however, the move from a free market to a basically planned economy, with the State playing an active part in economic activity, brought about a major change in both the form and function of law.

While the State remained apart from civil society, its functions could be restricted within a limited sphere of activity circumscribed within the doctrine of the Rule of Law. However, as the State became increasingly involved in actually regulating economic activity, the form of law had by necessity to change. To deal with problems, as and when they arose, the State had to assume discretionary powers rather than be governed by fixed pre-determined rules. Such discretion, however, is antithetical to the traditional idea of the Rule of Law which was posited on the fact of limiting the State's discretion. Thus emerged the tension between the Rule of Law and the requirements of regulating social activity that FA von Hayek, for one, saw as a fundamental change for the worse in our society.

With specific regard to the effect of this change on law's previous autonomy, there is clear agreement amongst academic writers that there has been a fundamental alteration in the nature of law. Whereas legislation previously took the form of fixed and precisely stated rules, now legislation tends be open-textured and to grant wide discretionary powers to particular State functionaries, resulting in a corresponding reduction in the power of the courts to control such activity. The courts have resisted this process to a degree, through the expansion of the procedure for judicial review, but their role in the area relating to administration remains at best questionable. The growth of delegated legislation, in which Parliament simply passes enabling Acts empowering ministers of State to make regulations as they consider necessary, is a prime example of this process (considered in detail in Chapter 2). In addition, once made, such regulations tend not to be general but highly particular, even technocratic in their detail.

The increased use of tribunals with the participation of non-legal experts rather than courts to decide disputes, with the underlying implication that the law is not capable of resolving the problem adequately, also represents a diminishment in law's previous power; as does the use of planning procedures as opposed to fixed rules of law in determining decisions. (Tribunals will be considered in Chapter 8.)

Legislation also increasingly pursues substantive justice rather than merely limiting itself to the provision of formal justice as required under the Rule of Law. As examples of this, consumer law can be cited; thus, in the Unfair Contract Terms Act 1977, it states that terms are to be evaluated on the basis of reasonableness; and, under the Consumer Credit Act 1974, agreements can be rejected on the basis of their being extortionate or unconscionable. Such provisions actually override the market assumptions as to formal equality in an endeavour to provide a measure of substantive justice.

All the foregoing examples of a change can be characterised as involving a change from 'law as end in itself' to 'law as means to an end'. In Weberian terms, this change in law represents a change from *formal rationality*, in which law determined outcomes to problems stated in the form of legal terms through the application of abstract legal concepts and principles, to a system of *substantive rationality* where law is simply a mechanism to achieve a goal set outside of law.

In other words, law is no longer seen as completely autonomous as it once was. Increasingly, it is seen as merely instrumental in the achievement of some wider purpose which the State, acting as the embodiment representative of general interest, sets. Paradoxically, as will be seen later, even when the law attempts to intervene in this process, as it does through judicial review, it does so in a way that undermines its autonomy and reveals it to be simply another aspect of political activity.

1.6 Human rights discourse and the Rule of Law

In an article published in the *London Review of Books* and *The Guardian* newspaper, in May 1995, the High Court judge, as he then was, Sir Stephen Sedley, made explicit the links and tensions between the doctrine of the Rule of Law and the relationship of the courts and the executive, and the implications for the use of judicial review as a means of controlling the exercise of executive power. In his view:

> Our agenda for the 21st century is not necessarily confined to choice between a 'rights instrument' interpreted by a judiciary with a long record of illiberal adjudication, and rejection of any rights instrument in favour of Parliamentary government. The better government becomes, the less scope there will be for judicial review of it.

> But, for the foreseeable future, we have a problem: how to ensure that as a society we are governed within a law which has internalised the notion of fundamental human rights. Although this means adopting the Rule of Law, like democracy, as a higher-order principle, we do have the social consensus which alone can accord it that primacy. And, if in our own society the Rule of Law is to mean much, *it must at least mean that it is the obligation of the courts to articulate and uphold the ground rules of ethical social existence which we dignify as fundamental human rights* ... There is a potential tension between the principle of democratic government and the principle of equality before the law ... The notion that the prime function of human rights and indeed the Rule of Law is to protect the weak against the strong is not mere sentimentality. It is the child of an era of history in which equality of treatment and opportunity has become perceived ... as an unqualified good, and of a significant recognition that you do not achieve equality merely by proclaiming it ... fundamental human rights to be real, have to steer towards outcomes which invert those inequalities of power that mock the principle of equality before the law.

Such talk of fundamental human rights denies the absolute sovereignty of Parliament in its recognition of areas that are beyond the legitimate exercise of State power. It also recognises, however, that notions of the Rule of Law cannot be satisfied by the provision of merely formal equality as Dicey and Hayek would have it and previous legal safeguards would have provided. For Sedley, the Rule of Law clearly imports, and is based on, ideas of substantive equality, that market systems and legal formalism cannot provide, and in fact undermine. His version of the Rule of Law clearly involves a reconsideration of the relationship of the executive and the judiciary and involve the latter in a further reconsideration of their own previous beliefs and functions.

1.7 The Human Rights Act 1998

As is evident in the previous quotation from Sir Stephen Sedley, some judges, at least, saw their role in maintaining the Rule of Law as providing protection for fundamental human rights. In attempting to achieve this end, they faced a particular problem in relation to the way in which the unwritten English constitution was understood, and was understood to operate. The freedom of individual action in English law was not based on ideas of positive human rights, which could not be taken away, but on negative liberties: that is, individual subjects were entitled to do whatever was not forbidden by the law. This was particularly problematic when it was linked to the doctrine of the sovereignty of Parliament, which, in effect, meant that Parliament was free to restrict, or indeed remove, individual liberties at any time, merely by passing the necessary legislation.

It is generally accepted that the courts developed the procedure of judicial review, as an aspect of the Rule of Law, in an attempt to protect individuals from the excesses of an over-powerful executive (see 6.10, for a detailed consideration). But, in so doing, they were limited in what they could achieve by the very nature of the procedure available to them. They could not directly question the laws produced by Parliament on the basis of substance, as constitutional courts in other systems could, but were restricted, essentially, to questioning the formal or procedural proprieties of such legislation. There was, however, an alternative forum capable of challenging the substance of English law; and one that was based on the assumption of positive rights, rather than negative liberties. That forum was the European Court of Human Rights (ECHR).

It has to be established, and emphasised, from the outset that the substance of this section has absolutely nothing to do with the European Union as such; the Council of Europe is a completely distinct organisation and, although membership of the two organisations overlap, they are not the same. The Council of Europe is concerned not with economic matters but with the protection of civil rights and freedoms (the nature of these institutions and the operation of the ECHR will be considered in detail in Chapter 13).

The United Kingdom was one of the initial signatories to the European Convention on Human Rights in 1950, which was established in post-war Europe as a means of establishing and enforcing essential human rights. In 1966, it recognised the power of the European Commission on Human Rights to hear complaints from individual United Kingdom citizens, and, at the same time, recognised the authority of the European Court of Human Rights to adjudicate in such matters. It did not, however, at that time, incorporate the European Convention into United Kingdom law.

The consequences of non-incorporation was that the Convention could not be directly enforced in English courts. In *R v Secretary of State for the Home Department ex p Brind* (1991), the Court of Appeal decided that ministerial directives did not have to be construed in line with the European Convention on Human Rights as that would be tantamount to introducing the Convention into English law without the necessary legislation. United Kingdom citizens were, therefore, in the position of having to pursue rights, which the State endorsed, in an external forum rather than through their own court system; and, in addition, having to exhaust the domestic judicial procedure before they could gain access to that external forum. Such a situation was extremely unsatisfactory, and not just for complainants under the Convention. Many members of the judiciary, including the present Lord Chief Justice Lord Bingham, were in favour of incorporation, not merely on general moral grounds, but equally on the ground that they resented having to make decisions, in line with UK law, which they knew full well would be overturned on appeal to the European Court. Equally, there was some discontent that the decisions in the European Court were being taken, and its general jurisprudence was being developed without the direct input of the UK legal system. The courts, however, were not completely bound to decide cases in presumed ignorance the Convention, and did what they could to decide cases in line with it. For example, where domestic statutes were enacted to fulfil Convention obligations, the courts could, of course, construe the meaning of the statute in the light of the Convention. It was also possible that, due to the relationship of the Convention to European Community law, the courts could find themselves applying the former in considering the latter. More indirectly, however, where the common law was uncertain, unclear or incomplete, the courts ruled, wherever possible, in a manner which conformed with the Convention. Or, where statute was found to be ambiguous, they presumed that Parliament intended to legislate in conformity with the United Kingdom's international obligations under the Convention. As Lord Bingham himself put it:

> In these ways, the Convention made a clandestine entry into British law by the back door, being forbidden to enter by the front (Earl Grey Memorial Lecture, http://webjcli.ncl.ac.uk/1998/issue1/bingham1.html).

But, even allowing for this degree of judicial manoeuvering, the situation still remained unsatisfactory. Pressure groups did agitate for the incorporation of the Convention into the UK legal system but, when, in 1995, a Private Members' Bill moving for incorporation was introduced in the House of Lords, the Home Office minister, Lady Blatch, expressed the then government's view that such incorporation was 'undesirable and unnecessary, both in principle and practice'. The opposition (the Labour Party), however, was committed to the incorporation of the Convention into United Kingdom law and, when it gained office in 1997, it immediately set about the process of incorporation. This process resulted in the Human Rights Act 1998 (HRA).

The Articles incorporated into UK law, and listed in Sched 1 of the Act, cover the following matters:

- the right to life (Art 1);

- prohibition of torture (Art 3);

- prohibition of slavery and forced labour (Art 4);

- the right to liberty and security (Art 5);

- the right to a fair trial (Art 6);

- the general prohibition of the enactment of retrospective criminal offences (Art 7);

- the right to respect for private and family life (Art 8);

- freedom of thought, conscience and religion (Art 9);

- freedom of expression (Art 10);

- freedom of assembly and association (Art 11);

- the right to marry (Art 12);

- prohibition of discrimination (Art 14);

- no restrictions on the political activity of aliens (Art 16).

The above list of rights are not all seen in the same way. Some are absolute and inalienable and cannot be interfered with by the State. Others are merely contingent and are subject to derogation, that is, signatory States can opt out of them in particular circumstances. The absolute rights are those provided for in Arts 2, 3, 4, 7 and 14. All the others are subject to potential limitations; and, in particular, the rights provided for under Arts 8, 9, 10 and 11 are subject to legal restrictions, such as are:

> ... necessary in a democratic society in the interests of national security or public safety, for the prevention of crime, for the protection of health or morals or the protection of the rights and freedoms of others (Art 11(2)).

In deciding the legality of any derogation, courts are required not just to be convinced that there is a need for the derogation, but they must also be sure that the State's action has been proportionate to that need. In other words, the State must not overreact to a perceived problem by removing more rights than is necessary to effect the solution. With further regard to the possibility of derogation, s 19 of the Act requires a minister, responsible for the passage of any Bill through Parliament, either to make a written declaration that it is compatible the Convention or, alternatively, to declare that, although it may not be compatible, it is still the government's wish to proceed with it.

The Human Rights Act has profound implications for the operation of the English legal system. Section 2 of the Act requires future courts to take into account any previous decision of the ECHR. This provision impacts on the operation of the doctrine of precedent within the English legal system, as it effectively sanctions the overruling of any pervious English authority that was in conflict with a decision of the ECHR. Also, s 3, requiring all legislation to be read so far as possible to give effect to the rights provided under the Convention, has the potential to invalidate previously accepted interpretations of statutes which were made, by necessity, without recourse to the Convention.

Section 6 declares it unlawful for any public authority to act in a way which is incompatible with the Convention, and s 7 allows the 'victim of the unlawful act' to bring proceedings against the public authority in breach. Section 8 empowers the court to grant such relief or remedy against the public authority in breach of the Act as it considers just and appropriate.

To understand the structure of the HRA, it is essential to be to aware of the nature of the changes introduced by the Act, especially in the apparent passing of such fundamental powers to the judiciary. Under the doctrine of parliamentary sovereignty, the legislature could pass such laws at it saw fit, even to the extent of removing the rights of its citizens. The new Act reflects a move towards the entrenchment of rights recognised under the Convention, but, given the sensitivity of the relationship between the elected Parliament and the unelected judiciary, it has been thought expedient to minimise the change in the constitutional relationship of Parliament and the judiciary. To that effect, the Act expressly states that the courts cannot invalidate any primary legislation, essentially Acts of Parliament, which are found to be incompatible with the Convention: they can only make a declaration of such incompatibility, and leave it to the legislature to remedy the situation through new legislation (s 4). Where a public authority is acting under the instructions of some primary legislation which is itself incompatible with the Convention, the public authority will not be liable under s 6.

The Act does provide for the provision of remedial legislation through a fast track procedure which gives a Minister of the Crown the power to alter such primary legislation by way of statutory instrument. It is significant that legislation proceeding from the newly elected Scottish Parliament is not deemed to be primary legislation, and therefore is open to the full rigour of the HRA procedures, with its legislation being capable of being invalidated by the courts.

Reactions to the introduction of the Human Rights Act have been broadly welcoming, but some important criticisms have been raised. First, the Convention is a rather old document, and does not address some of the issues that contemporary citizens might consider as equally fundamental to those rights actually contained in the document. For example, it is silent on the rights to substantive equality relating to such issues as welfare and access to resources. Also, the actual provisions of the Convention are uncertain in the extent of their application, or perhaps more crucially in the area where they can be derogated from; and at least to a degree they are contradictory. The most obvious difficulty arises from the need to reconcile Art 8's right to privacy, with

Art 10's freedom of expression. Newspapers have already expressed their concern in relation to this particular issue, and fear the development, at the hands of the court, of an overly limiting law of privacy which would prevent investigative journalism. This leads to a further difficulty – the potential politicisation, together with a significant enhancement in the power, of the judiciary. Although this factor has been significantly played down by those concerned, notably Lord Bingham (Earl Grey lecture, 1998) and Lord Woolf (Neil lecture, 1998), it is certainly true that it has not gone without criticism, especially from those on the left of the political spectrum, who are concerned about what they see as the shift in power to an unelected, unrepresentative, and unaccountable judiciary (this issue is further discussed in Chapter 6).

Perhaps the most serious criticism of the Human Rights Act is the fact that the government has not seen fit to establish a Human Rights Commission, to publicise, and facilitate, the operation of its procedures. Many have seen the setting up of such a body as a necessary step in raising human rights awareness and assisting individuals, who might otherwise be unable to use the Act, to enforce their rights.

Apart from s 19, which is already in force, the bulk of the HRA 1998 will not be brought into effect until 3 October 2000. The reason for the substantial time delay is the need to train all members of the judiciary from the highest Law Lord to the humblest magistrate, and the Lord Chancellor's Department has already allocated some £4.5 million for that purpose. However, even if the Act has not officially been brought into effect, it is already having an impact on decisions. Thus, in *R v DPP ex p Kebilene* ((1999) *The Times*, 31 March), Lord Bingham, with whom the other members of the Divisional Court concurred, declared that those sections of the Prevention of Terrorism Act 1989 which reversed the normal burden of proof in criminal trials were contrary to Art 6 of the Convention. Although the Human Rights Act was not yet in force, Lord Bingham held that the Director of Public Prosecutions should have taken into account the fact that any conviction against the defendant under the present law would in all likelihood be quashed when the HRA came into force. The Lord Chief Justice granted leave to appeal to the House of Lords, in recognition that the High Court's decision had such 'potentially far reaching implications'; which it certainly has in respect of the 100 or so convictions gained in Northern Ireland under the same provisions.

LAW AND LEGAL STUDY

Studying law

The study of law is not just a matter of learning rules. It is a general misconception that learning the law is about learning a mass of legal rules. Critical, analytical thought should inform the work of the good student.

The nature of law

Legal systems are particular ways of establishing and maintaining social order. Law is a formal mechanism of social control. Studying the English legal system involves considering a fundamental institution in our society.

Categories of law

Law can be categorised in a number of ways, although the various categories are not mutually exclusive.

Common law and civil law relate to distinct legal systems. The English legal system is a common law one as opposed to continental systems which are based on civil law.

Common law and equity distinguish the two historical sources and systems of English law. Common law emerged in the process of establishing a single legal system throughout the country. Equity was developed later to soften the formal rigour of the common law. The two systems are now united but in the final analysis equity should prevail.

Common law and statute relate to the source of law. Common law is judge made: statute law is produced by Parliament.

Private law and public law relate to whom the law is addressed. Private law relates to individual citizens whereas public law relates to institutions of government.

Civil law and criminal law distinguish between law whose purpose it is to facilitate the interaction of individuals and law that is aimed at enforcing particular standards of behaviour.

Separation of powers

The judges and the executive in the separation of powers have distinct but interrelated roles in the constitution. The question arises as to the extent to which the courts can act to control the activities of the executive through the operation of judicial review. The position of the present Lord Chancellor as judge and member of the government has been questioned by some.

The Rule of Law

Various writers have different understandings of what the concept actually means, but see it essentially as involving a control of arbitrary power – Dicey; Hayek; Thompson; Raz; Unger; Weber.

The essential question is whether the United Kingdom is still governed under the Rule of Law, and of course the conclusion depends on the original understanding of the Rule of Law: Hayek and Thompson would have said not; Raz would say it was. Sir Stephen Sedley has a view as to the continued operation of the Rule of Law which is based on substantive equality and challenges previous legal thought.

The Human Rights Act 1998

The Human Rights Act 1998 incorporates the European Convention on Human Rights into domestic UK law. The Articles of the Convention cover the following matters:

- the right to life (Art 1);
- prohibition of torture (Art 3);
- prohibition of slavery and forced labour (Art 4);
- the right to liberty and security (Art 5);
- the right to a fair trial (Art 6);
- the general prohibition of the enactment of retrospective criminal offences (Art 7);
- the right to respect for private and family life (Art 8);
- freedom of thought, conscience and religion (Art 9);
- freedom of expression (Art 10);
- freedom of assembly and association (Art 11);
- the right to marry (Art 12);

- prohibition of discrimination (Art 14);
- no restrictions on the political activity of aliens (Art 16).

The incorporation of the Convention into UK law means that UK courts can decide cases in line with the above Articles. This has the potential to create friction between the judiciary and the executive/legislature.

CHAPTER 2

SOURCES OF LAW

2.1 European Community

Ever since the United Kingdom joined the European Economic Community, now the European Community ('Union' in some legal contexts), it has progressively, but effectively, passed the power to create laws which have effect in this country to the wider European institutions. In effect, the United Kingdom's legislative, executive and judicial powers are now controlled by, and can only be operated within, the framework of European Community law. It is essential, therefore, even in a text that is primarily concerned with the English legal system, that the contemporary law student be aware of the operation of the legislative processes of the European Community. Chapter 13 of this book will consider the European Community and its institutions in some detail, and the remainder of this chapter will concentrate on internal sources of law.

2.2 Legislation

If the institutions of the European Community are sovereign within its boundaries, then within the more limited boundaries of the United Kingdom the sovereign power to make law lies with Parliament. Under United Kingdom constitutional law, it is recognised that Parliament has the power to enact, revoke or alter such, and any, law as it sees fit. Coupled to this wide power is the convention that no one Parliament can bind its successors in such a way as to limit their absolute legislative powers.

This absolute power is a consequence of the historical struggle between Parliament and the Stuart monarchy in the 17th century. In its struggle with the Crown, Parliament claimed the power of making law as its sole right. In so doing, Parliament curtailed the royal prerogative and limited the monarchy to a purely formal role in the legislative procedure. Prerogative powers still exist and remain important, but are now exercised by the government in the name of the Crown, rather than by the Crown itself. In this struggle for ultimate power, the courts sided with Parliament and, in return, Parliament recognised the independence of the courts from its control.

Although we still refer to our legal system as a common law one and although the courts still have an important role to play in the interpretation of statutes, it has to be recognised that legislation is the predominant method of law-making in contemporary times. It is necessary therefore to have a knowledge of the workings of the legislative process.

2.2.1 The pre-parliamentary process

Any consideration of the legislative process must be placed in the context of the political nature of Parliament. Most statutes are the outcome of the policy decisions taken by government and the actual policies pursued will of course depend upon the political persuasion and imperatives of the government of the day. Thus, a great deal of law creation and reform can be seen as the implementation of party political policies. Examples of this type of legal reform are the changes in trade union law, or education law, or the financing of local services introduced by the previous Conservative administrations.

It also has to be recognised that the current Labour Party Government, elected in May 1997, has introduced considerable constitutional changes as proposed in its election manifesto. Thus, the Scottish Parliament and the Welsh Assembly have been instituted, and the first elections have taken pace for both bodies; and moves are well afoot for the removal of the hereditary peerage from the House of Lords, although it is not as yet certain what is to replace that forum (this latter issue gives rise to a particular difficulty in relation to the judiciary in the House of Lords (see later, 6.1)).

As, by convention, the government is drawn from the party controlling a majority in the House of Commons, it can effectively decide what policies it wishes to implement and trust to its majority to ensure that its proposals become law. Accusations have been made that, when governments have substantial majorities, they are able to operate without taking into account the consideration of their own party members, let alone the views of opposition members. It is claimed that their control over the day to day procedure of the House of Commons backed with their majority voting power, effectively reduces the role of Parliament to that of merely rubber-stamping their proposals.

It is certainly true, as the experience of the previous Conservative administration in the United Kingdom demonstrated, that governments with small majorities, if not actually in a minority, have to be circumspect in the policies they pursue through Parliament. The fact that the May 1997 parliamentary elections returned the Labour Party to power, with a much larger majority than, even they, expected, has raised, once again, the prospect of an over powerful executive forcing its will through a politically quiescent parliament.

The government generates most of the legislation that finds its way into the statute book but individual members of Parliament may also propose legislation in the form of Private Members' Bills.

There are in fact three ways in which an individual member of Parliament can propose legislation:

- through the ballot procedure by means of which 20 back-bench members get the right to propose legislation on the 10 or so Fridays in each parliamentary session specifically set aside to consider such proposals;

- under Standing Order 39 which permits any member to present a Bill after the 20 balloted Bills have been presented;

- under Standing Rule 13, the 10-minute rule procedure, which allows a member to make a speech of up to 10 minutes in length in favour of introducing a particular piece of legislation.

Of these procedures, however, only the first has any real chance of success and even then success will depend on securing a high place in the ballot and on its not being too contentious. As examples of this can be cited the Abortion Act 1967 which was introduced as a Private Members' Bill to liberalise the provision of abortion; and the various attempts that have subsequently been made by Private Members' Bills to restrict the original provision. In relation to particular reforms, external pressure groups or interested parties may very often be the original moving force behind them; and, when individual members of Parliament are fortunate enough to find themselves at the top of the ballot for Private Members' Bills, they may well find themselves the focus of attention from such pressure groups proffering pre-packaged law reform proposals in their own particular areas of interest.

The decision as to which Bills are to be placed before Parliament in any session is under the effective control of two cabinet committees:

- the *Future Legislation Committee* determines which Bills will be presented to Parliament in the *following* parliamentary session;

- the *Legislation Committee* is responsible for the legislative programme conducted in the *immediate* parliamentary session. It is the responsibility of this committee to draw up the legislative programme announced in the Queen's Speech delivered at the opening of the parliamentary session.

Green Papers are consultation documents issued by the government which set out and invite comments from interested parties on particular proposals for legislation. After considering any response, the government may publish a second document in the form of a White Paper in which it sets out its firm proposals for legislation.

2.2.2 The legislative process

Parliament consists of three distinct elements; the House of Commons, the House of Lords and the Monarch. Before any legislative proposal, known at that stage as a Bill, can become an Act of Parliament it must proceed through and be approved by both Houses of Parliament and must receive the Royal Assent. The ultimate location of power, however, is the House of Commons which has the authority of being a democratically elected institution.

A Bill must be given three readings in both the House of Commons and the House of Lords before it can be presented for the Royal Assent. It is possible to commence the procedure in either House although Money Bills must be placed before the Commons in the first instance.

When a Bill is introduced in the Commons, it undergoes five distinct procedures:

- *First reading*. This is purely a formal procedure in which its title is read and a date set for its second reading.

- *Second reading*. At this stage, the general principles of the Bill are subject to extensive debate. The second reading is the critical point in the process of a Bill. At the end, a vote may be taken on its merits and, if it is approved, it is likely that it will eventually find a place in the statute book.

- *Committee stage*. After its second reading, the Bill is passed to a standing committee whose job is to consider the provisions of the Bill in detail, clause by clause. The committee has the power to amend it in such a way as to ensure that it conforms with the general approval given by the House at its second reading.

- *Report stage*. At this point, the standing committee reports the Bill back to the House for consideration of any amendments made during the committee stage.

- *Third reading*. Further debate may take place during this stage, but it is restricted to matters relating to the content of the Bill and questions relating to the general principles of the Bill cannot be raised.

When a Bill has passed all these stages, it is passed to the *House of Lords* for its consideration. After consideration by the Lords, the Bill is passed back to the Commons which must then consider any amendments to the Bill that might have been introduced by the Lords. Where one House refuses to agree to the amendments made by the other, Bills can be repeatedly passed between them but, as Bills must complete their process within the life of a particular parliamentary session, a failure to reach agreement within that period might lead to the total loss of the Bill.

Since the Parliament Acts of 1911 and 1949, the blocking power of the House of Lords has been restricted as follows:

- a 'Money Bill', that is, one containing only financial provisions, can be enacted without the approval of the House of Lords after a delay of one month;

- any other Bill can be delayed by one year by the House of Lords.

The House of Lords, no doubt, has used its reforming and delaying powers to good effect, but its inbuilt Conservative/conservative majority has also been deployed for less than totally praiseworthy campaigns. The latest of these involves the procedure of equalising the age of sexual consent between homosexuals at 16, as it is with heterosexuals. In 1998, the House of Lords managed to avoid an equalisation of the age of consent by threatening the government's major Criminal Justice Bill, subsequently, the Crime and Disorder Act 1998. In order to get the Bill through Parliament before the end of the session, the Home Secretary removed the provision. However, the House of Lords has maintained its resistance and has still refused to pass the proposal, now contained in the Sexual Offences (Amendment) Bill. The Government has expressed the intention to use the Parliament Acts to ensure that this legislative provision reaches the statute book, in spite of the House of Lords' objections.

The Royal Assent is required before any Bill can become law. There is no constitutional rule requiring the monarch to assent to any Act passed by Parliament. There is, however, a convention to that effect; and refusal to grant the Royal Assent to legislation passed by Parliament would place the constitutional position of the monarchy in jeopardy. The procedural nature of the Royal Assent was highlighted by the Royal Assent Act 1967 which reduced the process of acquiring Royal Assent to a formal reading out of the short title of any Act in both Houses of Parliament.

An Act of Parliament comes into effect on the date of the Royal Assent, unless there is any provision to the contrary in the Act itself.

2.2.3 The drafting of legislation

In 1975, in response to criticisms of the language and style of legislation, the Renton Committee on the Preparation of Legislation (1975, Cmnd 6053) examined the form in which legislation was presented. Representations were made to the Committee by a variety of people ranging from the judiciary to the lay public. The Committee divided complaints about statutes into four main headings relating to:

- obscurity of language used;

- over-elaboration of provisions;

- illogicality of structure;

- confusion arising from the amendment of existing provisions.

It was suggested that the drafters of legislation tended to adopt a stylised archaic legalism in their language and employed a grammatical structure that was too complex and convoluted to be clear, certainly to the layperson and even, on occasion, to legal experts. These criticisms, however, have to be considered in the context of the whole process of drafting legislation and weighed against the various other purposes to be achieved by statutes.

The actual drafting of legislation is the work of parliamentary counsel to the Treasury who specialise in this task. The first duty of the drafters must be to give effect to the intention of the department instructing them, and do so in as clear and precise a manner as is possible. These aims, however, have to be achieved under pressure, and sometimes extreme pressure, of time. An insight into the various difficulties faced in drafting legislation was provided by a former parliamentary draftsman, Francis Bennion in an article entitled 'Statute law obscurity and drafting parameters' ((1978) British JLS 235). He listed nine specific parameters which the drafter of legislation had to take into account. These parameters are:

- *Legal effectiveness*. This is the need for the drafters to translate the political wishes of those instructing them into appropriate legal language and form.

- *Procedural legitimacy*. This refers to the fact that the legislation must conform with certain formal requirements if it is to be enacted. For example, it is a requirement that Acts be divided into clauses and Bills not assuming this form would not be considered by Parliament.

- *Timeliness*. This refers to the requirement for legislation to be drawn up within particularly pressing time constraints. The effect of such pressure can be poorly drafted and defective provisions.

- *Certainty*. It is of the utmost importance that the law be clearly set down so that individuals can know its scope and effect and can guide their actions within its provisions. The very nature of language, however, tends to act against this desire for certainty. In pursuit of certainty, the temptation is for the person drafting the legislation to produce extremely long and complex sentences, consisting of a series of limiting and refining subclauses. This process in turn, however, tends merely to increase the obscurity of meaning.

- *Comprehensibility*. Ideally, legislation should be comprehensible to the lay person, but given the complex nature of the situation that the legislature is dealing with such an ideal is probably beyond attainment in practice. Nonetheless, legislative provisions certainly should be open to the comprehension of the members of Parliament who are asked to vote on it and they certainly should not be beyond the comprehension of the legal profession who have to construe it for their clients. Unfortunately, some legislation fails on both these counts.

- *Acceptability*. This refers to the fact that legislation is expected to be couched in uncontentious language and using a traditional prose style.

- *Brevity*. This refers to the fact that legislative provisions should be as short as is compatible with the attainment of the legislative purpose. The search for brevity in legislation can run counter to the wish for certainty in, and acceptability of, the language used.

- *Debatability*. This refers to the fact that legislation is supposed to be structured in such a way as to permit it and the policies that lie behind it to be debated in Parliament.

- *Legal compatibility*. This refers to the need for any new provision to fit in with already existing provisions. Where the new provision alters or repeals existing provisions, it is expected that such effect should be clearly indicated.

A consideration of these various desired characteristics shows that they are not necessarily compatible and indeed some of them, such as the desire for clarity and brevity, may well be contradictory. The point remains that those people charged with the responsibility for drafting legislation should always bear the above factors in mind when producing draft legislation but if one principle is to be pursued above others it is surely the need for clarity of expression and meaning.

2.2.4 Types of legislation

Legislation can be categorised in a number of ways. For example, distinctions can be drawn between:

Public Acts which relate to matters affecting the general public. These can be further subdivided into either government Bills or Private Members' Bills.

Private Acts, on the other hand, relate to the powers and interests of particular individuals or institutions, although the provision of statutory powers to particular institutions can have a major effect on the general public. For example, companies may be given the power to appropriate private property through compulsory purchase orders.

Enabling legislation gives power to a particular person or body to oversee the production of the specific details required for the implementation of the general purposes stated in the parent Act. These specifics are achieved through the enactment of Statutory Instruments. (See 2.2.5, below, for a consideration of delegated legislation.)

Acts of Parliament can also be distinguished on the basis of the function they are designed to carry out. Some are unprecedented and cover new areas of activity previously not governed by legal rules, but other Acts are aimed at rationalising or amending existing legislative provisions.

Consolidating legislation is designed to bring together provisions previously contained in a number of different Acts, without actually altering them. The Companies Act of 1985 is an example of a consolidation Act. It brought together provisions contained in numerous amending Acts which had been introduced since the previous Consolidation Act of 1948.

Codifying legislation seeks not just to bring existing statutory provisions under one Act, but also looks to give statutory expression to common law rules.

The classic examples of such legislation are the Partnership Act of 1890 and the Sale of Goods Act 1893, now 1979.

Amending legislation is designed to alter some existing legal provision. Amendment of an existing legislative provision can take two forms:

- a *textual amendment* is one where the new provision substitutes new words for existing ones in a legislative text or introduces completely new words into that text. Altering legislation by means of textual amendment has one major drawback in that the new provisions make very little sense on their own without the contextual reference of the original provision it is designed to alter;

- *non-textual amendments* do not alter the actual wording of the existing text but alter the operation or effect of those words. Non-textual amendments may have more immediate meaning than textual alterations but they too suffer from the problem that because they do not alter the original provisions the two provisions have to be read together to establish the legislative intention.

Neither method of amendment is completely satisfactory but the Renton Committee on the Preparation of Legislation favoured textual amendments over non-textual amendments.

2.2.5   Delegated legislation

Delegated legislation is of particular importance. Generally speaking, delegated legislation is law made by some person or body to whom Parliament has delegated its general law making power. A validly enacted piece of delegated legislation has the same legal force and effect as the Act of Parliament under which it is enacted; but equally it only has effect to the extent that its enabling Act authorises it.

The Deregulation and Contracting Out Act (DCOA) 1994 is an example of the wide ranging power that enabling legislation can extend to ministers. The Act gives ministers the authority to amend legislation by means of statutory instruments, where they consider such legislation to impose unnecessary burdens on any trade, business, or profession. Although the DCOA 1994 imposes the requirement that ministers should consult with interested parties to any proposed alteration, it nonetheless gives them extremely wide powers to alter primary legislation without the necessity of having to follow the same procedure as was required to enact that legislation in the first place. An example of the effect of the DCOA 1994 may be seen in the Deregulation (Resolutions of Private Companies) Order 1996 (SI 1996/1471), which simplifies the procedures which private companies have to comply with in passing resolutions. The effect of this statutory instrument was to introduce new sections into the Companies Act 1985 relaxing the previous provisions in the area in question. A second example is the Deregulation (Model Appeal Provisions) Order 1996 (SI 1996/1678), which set out a model structure for appeals against enforcement actions in business disputes.

The output of delegated legislation in any year greatly exceeds the output of Acts of Parliament as may be seen from the 1998 statistics which reveal that although just over 49 general public Acts were passed, no less than 3,321 statutory instruments were made.

In statistical terms, therefore, it is at least arguable that delegated legislation is actually more significant than primary Acts of Parliament.

There are various types of delegated legislation:

- *Orders in Council* permit the government through the Privy Council to make law. The Privy Council is nominally a non-party-political body of eminent parliamentarians but in effect it is simply a means through which the government, in the form of a committee of ministers, can introduce legislation without the need to go through the full parliamentary process. Although it is usual to cite situations of State emergency as exemplifying occasions when the government will resort to the use of Orders in Council, in actual fact, a great number of Acts are brought into operation through Orders in Council. Perhaps the widest scope for Orders in Council is to be found in relation to European Community law, for, under s 2(2) of the European Communities Act 1972, ministers can give effect to provisions of the Community which do not have direct effect.

- *Statutory Instruments* are the means through which government ministers introduce particular regulations under powers delegated to them by Parliament in enabling legislation. Examples have already been considered in relation to the DCOA 1994.

- *Bye-laws* are the means through which local authorities and other public bodies can make legally binding rules. Bye-laws may be made by local authorities under such enabling legislation as the Local Government Act 1972.

- *Court Rule Committees* are empowered to make the rules which govern procedure in the particular courts over which they have delegated authority under such Acts as the Supreme Court Act 1981, the County Courts Act 1984, and the Magistrates' Courts Act 1980.

- *Professional regulations* governing particular occupations may be given the force of law under provisions delegating legislative authority to certain professional bodies who are empowered to regulate the conduct of their members. An example is the power given to The Law Society, under the Solicitors' Act 1974, to control the conduct of practising solicitors.

2.2.6 Advantages in the use of delegated legislation

The advantages of delegated legislation include:

- *Time saving*

  Delegated legislation can be introduced quickly where necessary in particular cases and permits rules to be changed in response to emergencies or unforeseen problems.

  The use of delegated legislation, however, also saves parliamentary time generally. Given the pressure on debating time in Parliament and the highly detailed nature of typical delegated legislation, not to mention its sheer volume, Parliament would not have time to consider each individual piece of law that is enacted in the form of delegated legislation. It is considered of more benefit for Parliament to spend its time in a thorough consideration of the principles of the enabling Act, leaving the appropriate minister or body to establish the working detail under its authority.

- *Access to particular expertise*

  Related to the first advantage is the fact that the majority of members of Parliament simply do not have sufficient expertise to consider such provisions effectively. Given the highly specialised and extremely technical nature of many of the regulations that are introduced through delegated legislation, it is necessary that those authorised to introduce the legislation should have access to the necessary external expertise required to formulate such regulations. With regard to bye-laws, it practically goes without saying that local and specialist knowledge should give rise to more appropriate rules than reliance on the general enactments of Parliament.

- *Flexibility*

  The use of delegated legislation permits ministers to respond on an ad hoc basis to particular problems as and when they arise and provides greater flexibility in the regulation of activity subject to the minister's overview.

2.2.7 Disadvantages in the prevalence of delegated legislation

The disadvantages in the use of delegated legislation include:

- *Accountability*

  A key issue involved in the use of delegated legislation concerns the question of accountability and erosion of the constitutional role of Parliament.

Parliament is presumed to be the source of legislation but with respect to delegated legislation the individual members are not the source of the law. Certain people, notably government ministers and the civil servants who work under them to produce the detailed provisions of delegated legislation, are the real source of such regulations. Even allowing for the fact that they are, in effect, operating on powers delegated to them from Parliament, it is not beyond questioning whether this procedure does not give them more power than might be thought appropriate, or indeed constitutionally correct, whilst at the same time disempowering and discrediting Parliament as a body.

- *Scrutiny*

  The question of general accountability raises the need for effective scrutiny, but the very form of delegated legislation makes it extremely difficult for ordinary members of Parliament to fully understand what is being enacted and to monitor it effectively. This difficulty arises in part from the tendency for such regulations to be highly specific, detailed and technical. This problem of comprehension and control is compounded by the fact that regulations appear outside the context of their enabling legislation but only have any real meaning in that context.

- *Bulk*

  The problems faced by ordinary members of Parliament in effectively keeping abreast of delegated legislation is further increased by the sheer mass of such legislation. And, if parliamentarians cannot keep up with the flow of delegated legislation, how can the general public be expected to do so?

  These difficulties and potential shortcomings in the use of delegated legislation are, at least to a degree, mitigated by the fact that specific controls have been established to oversee it.

- *Parliamentary control over delegated legislation*

  Power to make delegated legislation is ultimately dependent upon the authority of Parliament and Parliament retains general control over the procedure for enacting such law.

  New regulations in the form of delegated legislation are required to be laid before Parliament. This procedure takes two forms depending on the provision of the enabling legislation. Some regulations require a positive resolution of one or both of the Houses of Parliament before they become law. Most Acts, however, simply require that regulations made under their auspices be placed before Parliament. They automatically become law after a period of 40 days unless a resolution to annul them is passed.

The problem with the negative resolution procedure is that it relies on members of Parliament being sufficiently aware of the content, meaning, and effect of the detailed provisions laid before them. Given the nature of such statutory legislation, such reliance is unlikely to prove secure.

Since 1973, there has been a *Joint Select Committee on Statutory Instruments* whose function it is to consider Statutory Instruments. This committee scrutinises Statutory Instruments from a technical point of view as regards drafting and has no power to question the substantive content or the policy implications of the regulation. Its effectiveness as a general control is therefore limited. European Community legislation is overseen by a specific committee and local authority bye-laws are usually subject to the approval of the Department of the Environment.

- *Judicial control of delegated legislation*

It is possible for delegated legislation to be challenged, through the procedure of judicial review, on the basis that the person or body to whom Parliament has delegated its authority has acted in a way that exceeds the limited powers delegated to them. Any provision outside this authority is *ultra vires* and is void. Additionally, there is a presumption that any power delegated by Parliament is to be used in a reasonable manner and the courts may on occasion hold particular delegated legislation to be void on the basis that it is unreasonable. The process of judicial review will be considered in more detail in Chapter 6 of this book. However, an interesting example of this procedure may illuminate the point. In January 1997, the Lord Chancellor raised court fees and, at the same time, restricted the circumstances in which a litigant can be exempted from paying such fees. In March, a Mr John Witham, who previously would have been exempted from paying court fees, successfully challenged the Lord Chancellor's action. In a judicial review, it was held that Lord Mackay had exceeded the statutory powers given to him by Parliament. One of the judges, Rose LJ, stated that there was nothing to suggest that Parliament ever intended 'a power for the Lord Chancellor to prescribe fees so as to preclude the poor from access to the courts'.

2.3 Case law

Case law refers to the creation and refinement of law in the course of judicial decisions. The foregoing has highlighted the increased importance of legislation in its various guises in today's society but, even allowing for this, and the fact that case law can be overturned by legislation, the United Kingdom is still a common law system and the importance and effectiveness of judicial creativity and common law principles and practices cannot be discounted.

2.3.1   Precedent

The doctrine of binding precedent, or *stare decisis,* lies at the heart of the English legal system. The doctrine refers to the fact that, within the hierarchical structure of the English courts, a decision of a higher court will be binding on a court lower than it in that hierarchy. In general terms, this means that when judges try cases they will check to see if a similar situation has come before a court previously. If the precedent was set by a court of equal or higher status to the court deciding the new case, then the judge in the present case should follow the rule of law established in the earlier case. Where the precedent is from a lower court in the hierarchy, the judge in the new case may not follow but will certainly consider it. (The structure of the civil courts will be considered in detail in Chapter 3 and that of the criminal courts in Chapter 4.)

It can be seen that the operation of the doctrine of binding precedent depends on the existence of an extensive reporting service to provide access to previous judicial decisions. The earliest summaries of cases appeared in the *Year Books* but, since 1865, cases have been reported by the Council of Law Reporting, established as a corporate body in 1870, which produces the authoritative reports of cases. Modern technology has resulted in the establishment of the *Lexis* computer based storage of cases. It should be noted, however, that whilst over 200,000 legal cases are dealt with in the courts each year, only about 25,000 get reported.

The most authoritative case reports are those provided in the *Law Reports.* These contain very useful summaries of the submissions made to the court by counsel in the case and also have the distinct advantage of the actual judgments being revised by the judges involved.

For reference purposes, the most commonly referenced law reports are cited as:

Law Reports:

Appeal Cases	(AC)
Chancery Division	(Ch D)
Family Division	(Fam)
Kings/Queens Bench	(KB/QB)

Other general series of reports:

All England Law Reports	(All ER)
Weekly Law Reports	(WLR)
Solicitors Journal	(SJ or Sol Jo)
European Court Reports	(ECR)

Various series of private reports have been collected together in the 178 volume collection of English Reports. The last two volumes are indexes to enable researchers to find their way through the other 176 volumes of cases.

There are a number of specialist reports. Indeed, there are too many of these to list all of them but amongst the most important are:

Industrial Relations Law Reports   (IRLR)

Knight's Local Government Reports   (LGR)

Lloyd's Law Reports   (Lloyd's Rep)

Reports on Tax Cases   (TC or Tax Cas)

Criminal Appeal Reports   (Cr App R)

2.3.2 The hierarchy of the courts

The structure of the court system is treated in more detail in Chapters 3 and 4. The *House of Lords* stands at the summit of the English court structure and its decisions are binding on all courts below it in the hierarchy. Up until 1966, the House of Lords regarded itself as bound by its previous decisions. In a *Practice Statement* of that year (1966), however, Lord Gardiner indicated that the House of Lords would in future regard itself as free to depart from its previous decisions where it appeared right to do so. Given the potentially destabilising effect on existing legal practice based on previous decisions of the House of Lords, this is not a discretion that the House of Lords exercises lightly. For example, in *Food Corp of India v Antclizo Shipping Corp* (1988), it was stated that the House of Lords would only review its previous decisions in cases where, not only was it of the opinion that there might be a general justification for reconsidering the accuracy of existing precedents, but such a consideration must also be necessary for and capable of deciding the particular case in point. In the *Food Corp of India* case, although the general point was made, the particular point failed on the facts of the case. There have been a number of cases, however, in which the House of Lords has overruled or amended its own earlier decisions. For example, in *Conway v Rimmer* (1968), the previous decision in *Duncan v Cammell Laird & Co* (1942), that an affidavit sworn by a government minister was sufficient to preclude the courts from examining documents on the ground of Crown privilege, was overturned to allow judges the final say in whether such documents should be considered or not. In *Herrington v British Rail Board* (1972), the House of Lords extended the previous ambit of occupiers' liability to include non-intentional, non-reckless injury sustained by a child trespassing on property. In *Miliangos v George Frank (Textiles) Ltd* (1976), they decided, contrary to their own existing authority that damages could be paid in currency other that sterling and, in *R v Shivpuri* (1986), the House bravely, if surprisingly, took the decision to overrule a previous decision in relation to 'criminal attempts' made only some 12 months previously.

The *Court of Appeal*. In civil cases, the Court of Appeal is generally bound by previous decisions of the House of Lords. Although the Court of Appeal, notably under the aegis of Lord Denning, attempted, on a number of occasions,

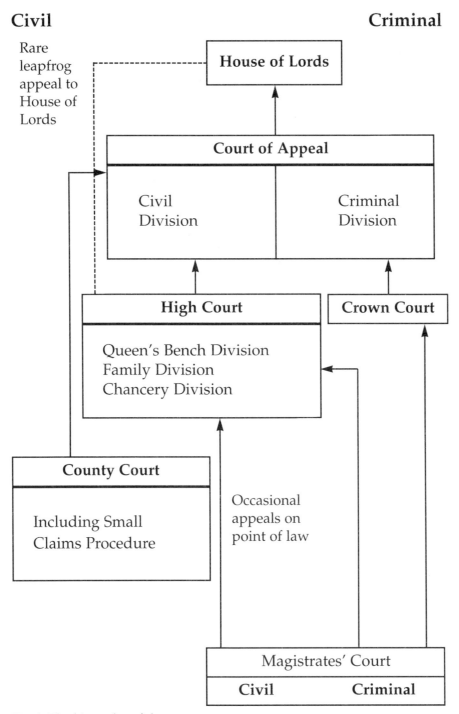

Fig 1: The hierarchy of the courts

to escape from the constraints of *stare decisis*, the House of Lords repeatedly reasserted the binding nature of its decisions on the Court of Appeal.

The Court of Appeal generally is also bound by its own previous decisions in civil cases. There are, however, a number of exceptions to this general rule. Lord Greene MR listed these exceptions in *Young v Bristol Aeroplane Co Ltd* (1944). The exceptions arise where:

- there is a conflict between two previous decisions of the Court of Appeal. In this situation, the later court must decide which decision to follow and as a corollary which to overrule. Such a situation arose in *Tiverton Estates Ltd v Wearwell Ltd* (1974). In that case, which dealt with the meaning of s 40 of the Law of Property Act 1925 (subsequently repealed), the court elected to follow older precedents rather than follow the inconsistent decision in *Law v Jones* (1974);

- a previous decision of the Court of Appeal has been overruled, either expressly or impliedly, by the House of Lords. In this situation, the Court of Appeal is required to follow the decision of the House of Lords. Thus, in *Family Housing Association v Jones* (1990), the Court of Appeal felt obliged to ignore its own precedents on the distinction between a licence and a tenancy in property law where, although they had not been expressly overruled, they were implicitly in conflict with a later decisions of the House of Lords;

- the previous decision was given *per incuriam* or, in other words, that previous decision was taken in ignorance of some authority, either statutory or case law, that would have led to a different conclusion. In this situation, the later court can ignore the previous decision in question. An example of this may be seen in *Williams v Fawcett* (1985) in which the Court of Appeal found exceptional circumstances under which it could treat its previous decisions as having been made *per incuriam*. Of importance amongst these circumstances was the fact that the case would be unlikely to go to the House for their final determination of the legal situation.

There is also the possibility that, as a consequence of s 3 of the European Communities Act, the Court of Appeal can ignore a previous decision of its own which is inconsistent with European Community law or with a later decision of the European Court.

Although, on the basis of *R v Spencer* (1985), it would appear that there is no difference in principle between the operation of the doctrine of *stare decisis* between the criminal and civil divisions of the Court of Appeal, it is generally accepted that, in practice, precedent is not followed as strictly in the former as it is in the latter. Courts in the criminal division are not bound to follow their own previous decisions which they subsequently consider to have been based on either a misunderstanding or a misapplication of the law. The reason for this is that the criminal courts deal with matters involving individual liberty and therefore require greater discretion to prevent injustice.

The *Divisional Courts,* each located within the three divisions of the High Court, hear appeals from courts and tribunals below them in the hierarchy. They are bound by the doctrine of *stare decisis* in the normal way and must follow decisions of the House of Lords and the Court of Appeal. It is also normally bound by its own previous decisions, although in civil cases it may make use of the exceptions open to the Court of Appeal in *Young v Bristol Aeroplane Co Ltd* (1944), and, in criminal appeal cases, the Queen's Bench Divisional Court may refuse to follow its own earlier decisions where it feels the earlier decision to have been made wrongly.

The *High Court* is also bound by the decisions of superior courts. Decisions by individual High Court judges are binding on courts inferior in the hierarchy, but such decisions are not binding on other High Court judges although they are of strong persuasive authority and tend to be followed in practice.

Crown Courts cannot create precedent and their decisions can never amount to more than persuasive authority.

County courts and *magistrates' courts* do not create precedents.

It has to be particularly noted that the Human Rights Act 1998 now requires courts in the United Kingdom to take into consideration all previous decisions of the European Court of Human Rights, which now become precedents for the UK courts to follow. This is the case even where the ECHR decision was in conflict with previous UK law. Equally, any English precedent which was in conflict with a decision of the ECHR is now invalidated.

2.3.3 Binding precedent

Not everything in a case report sets a precedent. The contents of a report can be divided into two categories:

- *Ratio decidendi*

  It is important to establish that it is not the actual decision in a case that sets the precedent; that is set by the rule of law on which the decision is founded. This rule, which is an abstraction from the facts of the case, is known as the *ratio decidendi* of the case. The *ratio decidendi* of a case may be understood as the statement of the law applied in deciding the legal problem raised by the concrete facts of the case.

- *Obiter dictum*

  Any statement of law that is not an essential part of the *ratio decidendi* is, strictly speaking, superfluous; and any such statement is referred to as *obiter dictum* (*obiter dicta* in the plural), that is, said by the way. Although *obiter dicta* statements do not form part of the binding precedent, they are persuasive authority and can be taken into consideration in later cases, if the judge in the later case considers it appropriate to do so.

The division of cases into these two distinct parts is a theoretical procedure. Unfortunately, judges do not actually separate their judgments into the two clearly defined categories and it is up to the person reading the case to determine what the *ratio* is. In some cases, this is no easy matter, and it may be made even more difficult in appellate cases where each of the judges may deliver their own lengthy judgments with no clear single *ratio*. (The potential implications of the way in which later courts effectively determine the *ratio* in any particular case will be considered below and in Chapter 5.) Students should always read cases fully; although it is tempting to rely on the headnote at the start of the case report, it should be remembered that this is a summary provided by the case reporter and merely reflects what he or she thinks the *ratio* is. It is not unknown for headnotes to miss an essential point in a case.

Example

Carlill v Carbolic Smoke Ball Co Ltd (1892)

FACTS

Mrs Carlill made a retail purchase of one of the defendant's medicinal products: the 'Carbolic Smoke Ball'. It was supposed to prevent people who used it in a specified way (three times a day for at least two weeks) from catching influenza. The company was very confident about its product and placed an advertisement in a paper, *The Pall Mall Gazette*, which praised the effectiveness of the Smoke Ball and promised to pay £100 (a huge sum of money at that time) to:

... any person who contracts the increasing epidemic influenza, colds, or any disease caused by taking cold, having used the ball three times daily for two weeks according to the printed directions supplied with each ball.

The advertisement went on to explain that the company had deposited £1,000 with the Alliance Bank, Regent Street, London, as a sign of its sincerity in the matter. Any proper claimants could get their payment from that sum. On the faith of the advertisement, Mrs Carlill bought one of the balls at the chemists and used it as directed but still caught the 'flu. She claimed £100 from the company but was refused it so she sued for breach of contract. The company said there was no contract for several reasons but mainly because:

(a)   the advert was too vague to amount to the basis of a contract – there was no time limit and no way of checking the way the customer used the ball;

(b)   the plaintiff did not give any legally recognised value to the company;

(c)   one cannot legally make an offer to the whole world so the advert was not a proper offer;

(d)   even if the advert could be seen as an offer, Mrs Carlill had not given a legal acceptance of that offer because she had not notified the company that she was accepting;

(e)   the advert was a 'mere puff', that is, a piece of insincere sales talk not meant to be taken seriously.

DECISION

The Court of Appeal found that there was a legally enforceable agreement, a contract between Mrs Carlill and the company. The company would have to pay damages to the plaintiff.

RATIO DECIDENDI

The three Lord Justices of Appeal who gave judgments in this case all decided in favour of Mrs Carlill. Each, however, uses slightly different reasoning, arguments and examples. The process, therefore, of distilling the 'reason for the decision' of the court is quite a delicate art. The *ratio* of the case can be put as follows.

Offers must be sufficiently clear to allow the courts to enforce agreements that follow from them. The offer here was 'a distinct promise expressed in language which is perfectly unmistakable'. It could not be a 'mere puff' in view of the £1,000 deposited specially to show good faith. An offer may be made to the world at large and the advert was such an offer. It was accepted by any person, like Mrs Carlill, who bought the product and used it in the prescribed manner. Mrs Carlill had accepted the offer by her conduct when she did as she was invited to do and started to use the smoke ball. She had not been asked to let the company know that she was using it.

OBITER DICTUM

In the course of his reasoning, Bowen LJ gave the legal answer to a set of facts which were not in issue in this case. They are, thus, *obiter dicta*. He did this because it assisted him in clarifying the answer to Mrs Carlill's case. He said:

> If I advertise to the world that my dog is lost, and that anybody who brings the dog to a particular place will be paid some money, are all the police or other persons whose business it is to find lost dogs to be expected to sit down and write me a note saying that they have accepted my proposal? Why, of course, they at once look [for] the dog, and as soon as they find the dog they have performed the condition.

If such facts were ever subsequently in issue in a court case, then the words of Bowen LJ could be used by counsel as persuasive precedent.

This decision has affected the outcome of many cases. The information system LEXIS, for example, lists 70 cases in which *Carlill* is cited. It was *applied* in *Peck v Lateu* (1973), and *distinguished* in *AM Satterthwaite & Co v New Zealand Shipping Co* (1972).

2.3.4 Evaluation

The foregoing has set out the doctrine of binding precedent as it operates in theory to control and indeed limit the ambit of judicial discretion. It has to be recognised, however, that the doctrine does not operate as stringently as it appears at first sight and that there are particular shortcomings in the system that have to be addressed in weighing up the undoubted advantages with the equally undoubted disadvantages.

2.3.5 Advantages of case law

There are numerous perceived advantages of the doctrine of *stare decisis*; amongst which are:

- *Consistency*. This refers to the fact that like cases are decided on a like basis and are not apparently subject to the whim of the individual judge deciding the case in question. This aspect of formal justice is important in justifying the decisions taken in particular cases.

- *Certainty*. This follows from, and indeed is presupposed by, the previous item. Lawyers and their clients are able to predict what the likely outcome of a particular legal question is likely to be in the light of previous judicial decisions. Also, once the legal rule has been established in one case, individuals can orient their behaviour with regard to that rule relatively secure in the knowledge that it will not be changed by some later court.

- *Efficiency*. This refers to the fact that it saves the time of the judiciary, lawyers and their clients for the reason that cases do not have to be re-argued. In respect of potential litigants, it saves them money in court expenses because they can apply to their solicitor/barrister for guidance as to how their particular case is likely to be decided in the light of previous cases on the same or similar points. (It should of course be recognised that the vast bulk of cases are argued and decided on their facts rather than on principles of law, but that does not detract from the relevance of this issue, and is a point that will be taken up later in Chapter 4 of this book.)

- *Flexibility*. This refers to the fact that the various mechanisms by means of which the judges can manipulate the common law provide them with an opportunity to develop law in particular areas without waiting for Parliament to enact legislation.

  In practice, flexibility is achieved through the possibility of previous decisions being either overruled, or distinguished, or the possibility of a later court extending or modifying the effective ambit of a precedent. (It should be re-emphasised that it is not the decision in any case which is binding, but the *ratio decidendi*. It is correspondingly and equally incorrect to refer to a decision being overruled.)

This apparently small measure of discretion, in relationship to whether later judges are minded to accept the validity of *obiter* statements in precedent cases, opens up the possibility that judges in later cases have a much wider degree of discretion than is originally apparent in the traditional view of *stare decisis*. It is important in this respect to realise that it is the judges in the later cases who actually determine the *ratio decidendi* of previous cases.

Judges, as has been noted previously, in delivering judgments in cases, do not separate and highlight the *ratio decidendi* from the rest of their judgment and this can lead to a lack of certainty in determining the *ratio decidendi*. This uncertainty is compounded by the fact that reports of decisions in cases may run to considerable length; and where there are a number of separate judgments, although the judges involved may agree on the decision of a case, they may not agree on the legal basis of the decision reached. This difficulty is further compounded where there are a number of dissenting judgments. In the final analysis, it is for the judge deciding the case in which a precedent has been cited to determine the *ratio* of the authority and thus to determine whether he is bound by the case or not. This factor provides later courts with a considerable degree of discretion in electing whether to be bound or not by a particular authority.

The main mechanisms through which judges alter or avoid precedents are:

• *Overruling*

This is the procedure whereby a court higher up in the hierarchy sets aside a legal ruling established in a previous case.

It is somewhat anomalous that, within the system of *stare decisis*, precedents gain increased authority with the passage of time. As a consequence, courts tend to be reluctant to overrule long standing authorities even though they may no longer accurately reflect contemporary practices or morals. In addition to the wish to maintain a high degree of certainty in the law, the main reason for judicial reluctance to overrule old decisions would appear to be the fact that overruling operates retrospectively with the effect that the principle of law being overruled is held never to have been law. Overruling a precedent might, therefore, have the consequence of disturbing important financial arrangements made in line with what were thought to be settled rules of law. It might even, in certain circumstances, lead to the imposition of criminal liability on previously lawful behaviour. It has to be emphasised, however, that the courts will not shrink from overruling authorities where they see them as no longer representing an appropriate statement of law.

The decision in *R v R* (1992) to recognise the possibility of rape within marriage may be seen as an example of this, although, even here, the House of Lords felt constrained to state that they were not actually altering the law but were merely removing a misconception as to the true meaning and effect of the law. As this demonstrates, the courts are rarely ready to challenge the legislative prerogative of Parliament in an overt way. For example, in *Curry v DPP* (1994), the Court of Appeal attempted to remove the presumption that children between the ages of 10 and 14 who were charged with a criminal offence did not know that what they did was seriously wrong and that the prosecution had to provide evidence to rebut that presumption. Mann LJ justified reversing the presumption by claiming that, although it had often been assumed to be the law, it had never actually been specifically considered by earlier courts. On such reasoning, he felt justified in departing from previous decisions of the Court of Appeal which otherwise would have bound him. The House of Lords subsequently restored the previous presumption. Although they recognised the problem, and indeed appeared to sympathise with Mann LJ's view, they nonetheless thought that such a significant change was a matter for parliamentary action rather than judicial intervention. The doctrine of *doli incapax* was finally removed by s 34 of the Crime and Disorder Act 1998. Of perhaps even greater concern is the fact that s 35 extended s 35 of the Criminal Justice and Public Order Act 1994 to cover all persons aged 10 or over. Thus, courts are now entitled to draw (adverse) inferences from the failure of such children to either give evidence or answer questions at their trial.

Overruling should not be confused with *reversing* which is the procedure whereby a superior court in the hierarchy reverses the decision of a lower court in the same case.

• *Distinguishing*

In comparison to the mechanism of overruling which is rarely used, the main device for avoiding binding precedents is that of distinguishing. As has been previously stated, the *ratio decidendi* of any case is an abstraction from, and is based upon, the material facts of the case. This opens up the possibility that a court may regard the facts of the case before it as significantly different from the facts of a cited precedent and thus consequentially it will not find itself bound to follow that precedent. Judges use the device of distinguishing where, for some reason, they are unwilling to follow a particular precedent and the law reports provide many examples of strained distinctions where a court has quite evidently not wanted to follow an authority that it would otherwise have been bound by.

2.3.6 Disadvantages of case law

It should be noted that the advantage of flexibility, at least, potentially contradicts the alternative advantage of certainty, but there are other disadvantages in the doctrine which have to be considered. Amongst these are:

- *Uncertainty*

  This refers to the fact that the degree of certainty provided by the doctrine of *stare decisis* is undermined by the absolute number of cases that have been reported and can be cited as authorities. This uncertainty is increased by the ability of the judiciary to select which authority to follow through use of the mechanism of distinguishing cases on their facts. A further element leading to uncertainty has been highlighted by James Richardson, the editor of *Archbold* (1995), the leading practitioners' text on criminal law, who has claimed that the lack of practical experience of some judges in the Criminal Appeal Court is:

  ... compounded by an apparent willingness, on occasion, to set aside principle in order to do what the court feels to be right (either way) in the individual case.

  As Richardson suggests:

  In the long run, this can only undermine a system which claims to operate on the basis of a hierarchy of binding precedent.

- *Fixity*

  This refers to the possibility that the law in relation to any particular area may become ossified on the basis of an unjust precedent with the consequence that previous injustices are perpetuated. An example of this is the long delay in the recognition of the possibility of rape within marriage, which has only relatively recently, given its long history, been recognised (*R v R* (1992)).

- *Unconstitutionality*

  This is a fundamental question that refers to the fact that the judiciary are overstepping their theoretical constitutional role by actually *making law* rather than restricting themselves to the role of simply applying it. This possibility requires a close examination of the role of the courts in the process of law making.

The traditional *declaratory theory of law* claims that judges do not make law, they simply state what it is. This view, however, gives rise to two particular conceptual difficulties:

- *Innovation*

Legal rules, as social institutions and creations, cannot be subject to infinite regression: they must have had a beginning at some time in the past when some person or group of people made or recognised them. Every common law rule must have had an origin. To put this in a simpler way, if a particular law was not created by statute, it must have been created by a judge; even if the level of creative activity was no more than recognising the legitimacy, or otherwise, of the practice in question, as was the role of the original circuit judges. Where an issue arises before a court for the first time, it follows, as a matter of course, that there can be no precedent for the court to follow, and, given the rapid change in contemporary society, it can only be suggested that such innovations and potentially innovatory court cases, are increasingly likely. In such novel circumstances, courts are faced with the choice of either refusing to decide a case, or stating what the law should be. In earlier times, judges did not shirk from this task and, even in modern times, courts are required on occasion to consider situations for the first time. Such cases are described as cases of first impression and inevitably involve judges in the creation of new law.

- *Reform*

The question arises as to how the law is to develop and change to cater for changed circumstances if cases are always to be decided according to precedent.

These considerations raise the question that if the law, as represented in either common law or statute law, is out of line with current social beliefs and practices, then should it not be incumbent upon the judiciary to decide cases in line with the currently prevailing standards, even if this means ignoring previous decisions and interpretations? Not to do so leaves the judges open to the charge of being out of touch with social reality. To overtly change the law, however, opens them up to the alternative charge of acting beyond their powers and of usurping the role and function of the legislature. Opinions on this matter range from those that would deny completely the right of judges to make or change the law, to those that would grant the judges the right to mould the law in line with their conception of justice. Others would recognise the fact that the common law was judge made and restrict judicial creativity; to the development of established common law principles. There is an important corollary to this latter position which links it with those who limit judicial creativity, for the implicit assertion is that judges have no place in reforming statutory provisions. They may signal the ineffectiveness of such provisions and call for their repeal or reform, but it would be a usurpation of the legislature's function and power for the courts to engage in such general reform.

In any case, this question unavoidably raises the issue of the actual extent of judicial creativity. (Compare and contrast *R v R* and *DPP v C* above in this light.) The previous consideration of *distinguishing* has demonstrated how the doctrine of *stare decisis* can be avoided by the judiciary. A further way in which judges have a creative impact on the law is in the way in which they adapt and extend precedent in instant cases. In addition, judicial reasoning, which will be considered in detail in a later chapter, tends to be carried out on the basis of analogy and judges have a large degree of discretion in selecting what are to be considered as analogous cases. They also have a tendency to extend, continuously, existing precedents to fit new situations, as the history evolution of the tort of negligence will show.

It is now probably a commonplace of legal theory that judges do make law. Perhaps the more interesting question is not whether judges make law but why they deny that they do so. In spite of the protestations of the judiciary, law and judicial decision making is a political process to the extent that it is deciding about which values are to be given priority within society. Through their choice of values the judiciary sanction or prohibit particular forms of behaviour. Due to their position in the constitution, however, judges have to be circumspect in the way in which and the extent to which they use their powers to create law and impose values. To overtly assert or exercise the power would be to challenge the power of the legislature. For an unelected body to challenge a politically supreme Parliament would be unwise, to say the least. It is for that reason that the courts on occasion take refuge behind the cloak of a naïve declaratory theory of law. (The political nature of judicial action will be considered further in Chapter 7.)

2.4   Books of authority

When a court is unable to locate a precise or analogous precedent, it may refer to legal textbooks for guidance. Such books are subdivided, depending on when they were written. In strict terms, only certain works are actually treated as authoritative sources of law. Amongst the most important of these works are those by Glanvill from the 12th century, Bracton from the 13th century, Coke from the 17th century and Blackstone from the 18th century. When cases such as *R v R* are borne in mind, then it might be claimed, with justification, that the authority of such ancient texts may be respected more in the breach than in the performance. Given the societal change that has occurred in the intervening time, one can only say that such a refusal to fetishise ancient texts is a positive, and indeed necessary, recognition of the need for law to change in order to keep up with its contemporary sphere of operation. Legal works produced after Blackstone's *Commentaries* of 1765 are considered to be of recent origin, and they cannot be treated as authoritative sources. The courts, however, will look at the most eminent works by accepted experts in particular fields in order to help determine what the law is or should be. For example, in the sphere of company law, the work of Professor LCB Gower has been referred to by the courts in order to help to elucidate some abstruse legal principles, as has Sir William Wade and Anthony Bradley's work in the sphere of public law. For a recent example, see the citation of Shetreet's, *Judges on Trial*, and De Smith, Wolf and Jowell, *Judicial Review of Administrative Action*, in Lord Browne-Wilkinson's decision in *Re Pinochet* (1999).

2.5 Custom

There is some academic debate about the exact relationship of custom and law. Some claim that law is simply the extension of custom and that with the passage of time customs develop into laws. From this point of view, law may be seen as the redefinition of custom for the purposes of clarity and enforcement by the legal institutions. The State institutions are seen as merely refining the existing customary behaviour of society. Others deny this evolutionary link and claim that law and custom are in fact contradictory, with law emerging in opposition to, and replacing, customary forms of behaviour. From this perspective, law is seen as being a new form of regulation handed down by the State rather than emerging from society as a whole.

The traditional view of the development of the common law tends to adopt the first of these views. This overly romantic view of the common law represents its emergence as no more than the crystallisation of common customs. This distillation is accomplished by the judiciary in the course of their historic travels round the land. This view, however, tends to play down the political process that gave rise to the procedure. The imposition of a common system of law represented the political victory of a State that had fought to establish and assert its central authority. Viewed in that light, the emergence of the common law can be seen actually to support the second of the two approaches suggested above.

Although some of the common law may have had its basis in general custom, a large proportion of these so called customs were invented by the judges themselves and represented what *they* wanted the law to be, rather than what people generally thought it was.

One source of customary practice that undoubtedly did find expression in the form of law was business and commercial practice. These customs and practices originally were constituted in the distinct form of the Law Merchant but gradually this became subsumed under the control of the common law courts and ceased to exist apart from the common law.

Notwithstanding the foregoing, it is still possible for specific local customs to operate as a source of law. In certain circumstances, parties may assert the existence of customary practices in order to support their case. Such local custom may run counter to the strict application of the common law and, where they are found to be legitimate, they will effectively replace the common law. Even in this respect, however, reliance on customary law as opposed to common law, although not impossible, is made unlikely by the stringent tests that have to be satisfied. The requirements that a local custom must satisfy in order to be recognised are that:

- it must have existed from 'time immemorial', that is, 1189;

- it must have been exercised continuously within that period;

- it must have been exercised peaceably without opposition;

- it must also have been felt as obligatory;

- it must be capable of precise definition;

- it must have been consistent with other customs;

- it must be reasonable.

Given this list of requirements, it can be seen why local custom is not an important source of law. However, the courts will have recourse to custom where they see it as appropriate as may be seen in *Egerton v Harding* (1974), in which the courts upheld a customary duty to fence land against cattle straying from an area of common land.

2.6 Law reform

At one level, law reform is either a product of parliamentary or judicial activity as has been considered previously. Parliament tends, however, to be concerned with particularities of law reform and the judiciary are constitutionally and practically disbarred from reforming the law in other than an opportunistic and piecemeal basis. Therefore, there remains a need for the question of law reform to be considered generally and a requirement that such consideration be conducted in an informed but disinterested manner.

Reference has already been made to the use of consultative Green Papers by the government as a mechanism for gauging the opinions of interested parties to particular reforms. More formal advice may be provided through various advisory standing committees. Amongst these is the *Law Reform Committee*. The function of this Committee is to consider the desirability of changes to the civil law which the Lord Chancellor may refer to it. The *Criminal Law Revision Committee* performs similar functions in relation to criminal law.

Royal Commissions may be constituted to consider the need for law reform in specific areas. The Commission on Criminal Procedure (1980) led to the enactment of the Police and Criminal Evidence Act 1984, and the recommendation of the 1993 Royal Commission on Criminal Justice (Runciman Commission) are still making their way into current legislation.

Committees may be set up in order to review the operation of particular areas of law. The most significant of these being the Woolf review of the operation of the civil justice system. Detailed analysis of the consequences flowing from the implementation of the recommendations of the Woolf Report will be considered subsequently.

If a criticism is to be levelled at these committees and commissions, it is that they are all ad hoc bodies. Their remit is limited and they do not have the power either to widen the ambit of their investigation or initiate reform proposals.

The *Law Commission* fulfils the need for some institution to concern itself more generally with the question of law reform. Its general function is to keep the law as a whole under review and to make recommendations for its systematic reform. The Commission continuously keeps under review the need to remove antiquated and/or anachronistic laws from the statute book, whose continued existence make it subject to derision if they do not bring it into disrepute. To that end, 14 Statute Law Repeal Acts have been enacted since 1969, and following a 1995 Law Commission Report (No 230), the Law Reform (Year and a Day Rule) Act was was introduced in 1996. This Act removed the ancient rule which prevented killers being convicted of murder or manslaughter if their victim survived for a year and a day after the original offence.

The Commission is a purely advisory body and its scope is limited to those areas set out in its current programme of law reform. It recommends reform after it has undertaken an extensive process of consultation with informed and/or interested parties. At the conclusion of a project, a report is submitted to the Lord Chancellor and Parliament for their consideration and action.

The annual report of the Law Commission for 1996 reveals that eight of its reports were, in whole or in part, implemented by Parliament. These reports related to family law, criminal law, property law amongst others and the notable legislation that the Law Commission could rightly claim credit for in the year in question were the Theft (Amendment) Act 1996 and the Family Law Act 1996. The report is, however, refreshingly if surprisingly open as to its disappointment in the lack of legislative action that has been taken in pursuance of its reports and recommendations. As its chair, Mrs Justice Arden, stated in the introduction to the annual report:

> It is a striking fact, worthy of repetition, that the public do not obtain the benefit of our work until it is implemented. There are nearly 20 Law Commission reports listed in this Report which the government has either accepted but not implemented, or to which it has not yet given its response ... Our widely welcomed Report on Offences Against the Person would modernise and

rationalise an area of the criminal law in constant use. Yet this remains neither accepted, rejected nor implemented – a public asset from which the public is not getting any benefit ... We hope that ... greater priority will be given by governments to implementing our law reform recommendations ...

The 1997 annual report evidences the continued activity of the Commission, but again its chair, still Mary Arden, had to report a lack of statutory outcome, this time due to the newly elected government's own heavy legislative programme. A new chair, the Honourable Mr Justice Carnwath, was appointed in February 1999.

Current judicial review procedures are very much the consequence of a 1976 Law Commission report and a review of their operation and proposals for reform was issued in October 1994. This report and its recommendations will be considered in detail in Chapter 7.

The establishment within the Lord Chancellor's Department of a division, one of whose tasks is to promote law reform, may signal an increased recognition of the importance of the process of law reform; alternatively, it may signal a move to marginalise the role of the Law Commission by bringing the law reform process more directly under the control of the Lord Chancellor.

Mention should also be made of the relatively new Civil Justice Council, established under the Civil Procedure Act 1997. The remit of this committee, which is made up a variety of judges, lawyers, academics and those representing the interests of consumers and others, under the chair of Lord Woolf, is to:

- keep the civil justice system under review;

- consider how to make the civil justice system more accessible, fair and efficient;

- advise the Lord Chancellor and the judiciary on the development of the civil justice system;

- refer proposals for change to the civil justice system to the Lord Chancellor and the Civil Procedure Rule Committee;

- make proposals for research.

Given the massive upheaval that has resulted from the implementation of Lord Woolf's recent review of the civil justice system, it is to be hoped that this new committee will function effectively to bring about smaller alterations in the system as soon as they become necessary.

SOURCES OF LAW

The European Community is increasingly a source of law for the United Kingdom.

Legislation

Legislation is law produced through the parliamentary system. Government is responsible for most Acts but individual members of Parliament do have a chance to sponsor Private Members' Bills. The passage of a Bill through each House of Parliament involves five distinct stages; first reading, second reading, committee stage, report stage, and third reading. Then it is given Royal Assent. The House of Lords only has limited scope to delay legislation.

Amongst the problems of drafting Acts is the need to reconcile such contradictory demands as brevity and precision. Legislation can be split into different categories: Public Acts affect the general public; Private Acts relate to particular individuals; Consolidation Acts bring various provisions together; Codification Acts give statutory form to common law principles; Amending Acts alter existing laws and amendments may be textual, which alters the actual wording of a statute or non-textual in which case the operation rather than the wording of the existing law is changed.

Delegated legislation

Delegated legislation appears in the form of: Orders in Council; Statutory Instruments; bye-laws; professional regulations.

The main advantages of delegated legislation relate to: speed of implementation; the saving of parliamentary time; access to expertise; flexibility.

The main disadvantages relate to: the lack of accountability of those making such law; the lack of scrutiny of proposals for such legislation; the sheer amount of delegated legislation.

Controls over delegated legislation are: in Parliament, the Joint Select Committee on Statutory Instruments; and, in the courts, *ultra vires* provisions may be challenged through judicial review.

Case law

Case law is that law created by judges in the course of deciding cases. The doctrine of *stare decisis* or binding precedent refers to the fact that courts are bound by previous decisions of courts equal to or above them in the court hierarchy. The House of Lords can now overrule its own previous rules; the Court of Appeal cannot.

It is the reason for a decision, the *ratio decidendi,* that binds. Everything else is *obiter dictum* and not bound to be followed.

Judges avoid precedents through either overruling or distinguishing them.

The advantages of the doctrine relate to: saving the time of all parties concerned; certainty; flexibility; the meeting of the requirements of formal justice.

The disadvantages relate to: uncertainty; fixity; unconstitutionality.

Custom

Custom is of arguable historic importance as a source of law and is of very limited importance as a contemporary source.

Law reform

Law reform in particular areas is considered by various standing committees particularly established for that purpose, and Royal Commissions may also be established for such purposes. The Law Commission, however, exists to consider the need for the general and systematic reform of the law.

CHAPTER 3

THE CIVIL COURT STRUCTURE

This chapter looks at the structure of the civil courts. You need to know which type of cases are heard in which trial courts; the rules relating to transfer of case from one level of court to another; the system of appeals and the criticisms which have been made of the various aspects of these systems.

What is the difference between a criminal and civil case? There are several key distinctions.

- Criminal cases are brought by the State against individual or corporate defendants whereas civil cases are brought by one citizen or body against another such party. The State here involves the police (or possibly customs and excise officers or tax inspectors) who investigate the crime and collect the evidence; and the Crown Prosecution Service which prepares the Crown's case. In civil cases, the State is not involved here except in so far as it provides the courts and personnel so that the litigation can be judged. If a party refuses, for example, to be bound by the order a court makes in a civil case then that party may be found in contempt of court and punished, that is, imprisoned or fined.

- The outcomes of civil and criminal cases are different. If a criminal case is successful from the point of view of the person bringing it (*the prosecutor*) because the magistrate or jury finds *the defendant* (sometimes called *the accused*) guilty as charged, then the result will be a sentence. There is a wide range of sentences available, from absolute or conditional discharges (where the convicted defendant is free to go without any conditions or with some requirement, for example, that the defendant undertakes never to visit a particular place), to life imprisonment. Criminal sentences, or 'sanctions', are to mark the State's disapproval of the defendant's crime. Sometimes, the State loses financially in imposing a punishment, for example, with custodial sentences: in 1999, the prison population rose to over 63,000 with very high costs to the State. It costs £34,000 to keep a prisoner in Brixton prison for one year and £32,000 to keep a woman in Holloway for one year. On the other hand, fines (the most common sentence or 'disposal') can often bring revenue to the State. In any event, however, the victim of a crime never gains from the sanction imposed on the criminal. A criminal court can order a convicted person to pay the victim compensation but this will be in addition to and separate from the sentence for the crime.

- If a civil case is successful from the point of view of the person bringing the action (the *claimant*), then the outcome will be one of a number of civil remedies which are designed to benefit the *claimant* and in which the State, or wider community, has no direct interest. Civil remedies include damages, and court orders like injunctions, orders of prohibition and specific performance. So, in civil proceedings, the *claimant* will sue the *defendant* and a successful action will result in *judgment for the claimant*. In matrimonial cases, the party who brings an action is called the *petitioner* and the other party is known as the *respondent*.

- Civil and criminal cases are processed differently by the English legal system. They use different procedures, vocabulary and they are dealt with, on the whole, by different courts. It is very important not to confuse the vocabularies of the different systems and speak, for example, about a claimant 'prosecuting' a company for breach of contract. The law of contract is civil law so the defendant would be 'sued' or 'litigated against' or have 'an action' taken against it by the plaintiff.

The question then arises 'what is the difference between a crime and a civil wrong; how am I to tell into which category a particular wrong falls?'. The answer is simply by building up a general legal knowledge. There is nothing inherent in any particular conduct which makes it criminal. One cannot say, for example, that serious wrongs are crimes and that lesser transgressions will be civil wrongs: some crimes are comparatively trivial, like some parking offences, whilst some civil wrongs can have enormously harmful consequences as where a company in breach of a contract causes financial harm to hundreds or thousands of people.

Sometimes, a single event can be both a crime and a civil wrong. If you drive at 50 mph in a 30 mph zone and crash into another vehicle, killing a passenger, you may be prosecuted by the State for causing death by dangerous driving and, if convicted, imprisoned or fined. Additionally, you may be sued for negligence (a tortious civil wrong) by a dependant of the killed passenger and the driver.

The organisation of the civil courts is currently undergoing a period of relatively rapid change. A highly detailed study of the business of the civil courts was undertaken by the Civil Justice Review which was instituted by Lord Hailsham, then Lord Chancellor, in 1985. The purpose of the review was to improve the machinery of civil justice by means of reforms in jurisdiction, procedure and court administration. In particular, the review was concerned with ways of reducing delays, costs and complexity of process. The report of the review was based on a study of five areas of civil action: personal injury, small claims, the commercial court, the process of debt enforcement and housing cases. In each area, a fact-finding research project was commissioned mostly from management consultants. The Lord Chancellor's Department then published five discussion papers on these areas. A *General Issues Paper* was published in 1987 in which problems common to civil process were discussed. The Review's final report was published a year later and largely implemented in the Courts and Legal Services Act (CLSA) 1990.

'High quality justice' had been identified in the *General Issues Paper* as the main objective in all parts of the civil court process. This included fair procedures, methods of adjudication so that each party was given proper opportunity to present his case and to have it judged impartially within a setting of consistency of judicial decisions. The primary aim was not, however, to be paramount. It had to be balanced against the aim of keeping parties' costs, delay and the cost to the State in proportion to the subject matter in dispute. This aim of efficiency included time targets for the handling of cases by the courts; effective deployment of judges, court staff and court facilities; the appropriate matching of the complexity of case to the level of experience of the judge; the adoption of streamlined procedures for simple cases; limiting the costs to the parties and to the court service.

An additional aim was expressed as the need for the courts to be 'effective', that is, court locations and hours that were convenient to litigants, the use of simple rules regarding jurisdiction and procedure.

Generally, the Review recommended that much of the case work previously dealt with by the High Court should be moved to the county courts as they were more numerous, relatively cheap and used simpler procedure. This has been carried out by the Courts and Legal Services Act and by Statutory Instruments, as we shall see later in this chapter.

Since the introduction of the Civil Procedure Act 1997 and the new Civil Procedure Rules (CPR) 1998, the operation of the civil courts has undergone yet another series of major changes. The implications of these changes are dealt with in Chapter 7.

3.1   The Court Service

From April 1995, a new executive agency was established to run all the courts except the magistrates' courts and the coroners' courts, both of which remain under the control of local authorities. The Court Service, which was previously controlled by the Lord Chancellor's Department, now has overall management responsibility for the law courts. Statements from the agency that it aims at 'reducing the unit cost of production per court hour' have attracted criticism that judges may thus be put under pressure to wind up cases more quickly. The agency is introducing court fees for litigants (for example, £200 per day for the county courts), and its longer term aim is to move to recovering the full costs of the civil courts, including the judges, from fees charged to litigants.

3.2   Magistrates' courts

Magistrates' courts have a significant civil jurisdiction. They hear family proceedings under the Domestic Proceedings and Magistrates' Courts Act (DPMCA) 1978 and the Children Act (CA) 1989. Here, the court is termed a 'family proceedings court'. A family proceedings court must normally be composed of not more than three justices, including, as far as is practicable, both a man and a woman. Justices who sit on such benches must be members of the 'family panel' which comprises people specially appointed to deal with family matters. The magistrates' court deals with adoption proceedings, applications for residence and contact orders (CA 1989) and maintenance relating to spouses and children. Under the DPMCA 1978, the court also has the power to make personal protection orders and exclusion orders in cases of matrimonial violence. They have powers of recovery in relation to the community charge and the council tax and charges for water, gas and electricity. Magistrates grant, renew and revoke licences for selling liquor.

3.3   County courts

The county courts were introduced in 1846 to provide local, accessible fora for the adjudication of relatively small scale litigation. There are 240 county courts. These courts are served by 539 circuit judges and 337 district judges, the latter appointed by the Lord Chancellor from persons who have a seven year qualification (s 71 of the CLSA 1990).

Before the 1999 civil justice reforms, jurisdiction of the county courts was separated from that of the High Court on a strict financial limit basis, for example, a district judge heard cases where the amount was £5,000 or less. The new Civil Procedure Rules, which we examine in Chapter 7, operate the same process irrespective of whether the case forum is the High Court or the county court. Broadly, county courts will hear small claims and fast track cases while the more challenging multi-track cases will be heard in the High Court.

The new civil justice reforms (see Chapter 7) are likely to put a considerable burden of work on the county courts. One question is, however, how much busier can the county courts become without a significant improvement in their resources? In 1990, whilst a combined total of 417,000 actions were commenced in the QBD and Chancery courts of the High Court, 3.5 million cases were commenced in the county courts. The profile of county court work is changing. Whereas the number of full trials has been relatively constant during recent years, the number of small claims arbitrations has risen sharply. In 1989, there were 22,267 trials and 49,829 arbitrations, whereas, in 1994, the comparable figures were 24,219, and 87,885. This reflects the doubling of the small claims limit from £500 to £1,000 in 1989. The trebling of this limit to £3,000 in 1996 resulted in the numbers of small claims rising to over 95,000 in 1998. The following complaints by practitioners working in the county courts are cited in Smith (ed), *Achieving Civil Justice* (1996):

- inconsistent practice between different courts;
- too many judges without specialist knowledge of relevant areas of law, like housing;
- inadequate use of new technology, lost files, and judges without access to computer assistance;
- overloading of case lists, for example, 40–50 housing possession cases listed for hearing within one hour.

A *Practice Direction* (1991) states that certain types of actions set down for trial in the High Court are considered too important for transfer to a county court. These are cases involving:

- professional negligence;
- fatal accidents;
- allegations of fraud or undue influence;
- defamation;
- malicious prosecution or false imprisonment;
- claims against the police.

The county court jurisdiction also involves probate, property cases, tort, contract, bankruptcy, insolvency, and relations. Regarding remedies, the county court cannot grant the prerogative remedies of *mandamus*, prohibition and *certiorari*. (See 6.10.2.) They cannot grant *Anton Piller* orders (an interlocutory mandatory injunction, obtained *ex parte* to prevent the defendant from removing, concealing or destroying evidence in the form of documents or moveable property) and neither, generally, can they grant *Mareva* injunctions (as for an *Anton Piller* order but to prevent the defendant from removing his assets out of the jurisdiction of the English courts or dissipating them). For recent authoritative guidance of both of these orders, see *Practice Direction ex p Mareva injunctions and Anton Piller Orders* (1994).

The nomenclature for cases beginning after April 1999 has altered under the Civil Procedure Rules. Henceforward, *ex parte* actions are simply actions without notice (being given to the other side); an Anton Piller order becomes an order to search premises; and a Mareva injunction becomes an order to freeze a company's assets.

Lord Woolf's Interim Report in 1995 recommended that the limit claims in the small claims court should be raised from £1,000 to £3,000, and this was brought into effect for all claims except personal injury claims in 1996. The Final

Report of Lord Woolf, *Access to Justice*, 1996, recommended (Recommendation 274) that, except for personal injury claims, the financial limit of the small claims jurisdiction should be eventually extended to £5,000.

From April 1999, the small claims limit rose from £3,000 to £5,000, except for personal injury claims which will be limited to £1,000. The small claims procedure has been seen my many as a major success of the civil justice system. Over 90,000 cases are disposed of this way (known as 'arbitration') by small claims courts annually. The procedure's speed, simplicity and relative inexpensiveness makes it attractive to many users. In 1999, the average time between the issue of summons and the start of the hearing was 21 weeks.

The government believes that extension of the small claims regime to a wider band of cases will enable more people to benefit from this quick and effective means of securing their rights.

One problem with the system, however, is that a significant proportion of successful small claimants are unable to recover the monies awarded them by the court. Following a National Audit Office report in 1997, the Court Service has been working on proposals to improve the efficiency and effectiveness of county court bailiffs.

The main advantage to litigants using the small claims process is the fact that, if sued, they can defend without fear of incurring huge legal costs, since the costs that the winning party can claim are strictly limited. Although successful plaintiffs are unable to recover costs of legal representation, the small claims procedure does not exclude litigants from seeking legal advice or engaging such legal representation. If a litigant is unrepresented, the District judge may assist him or her by putting questions to witnesses or to the other party, and by explaining any legal terms or expressions.

A litigant simply needs to complete a claim form, available from any county court, and send it to the court with the issue fee appropriate to the amount claimed (ranging £10 to £80, depending on the value of the claim). If the case is defended, it will be dealt with at an informal hearing, sitting around a table in the district judge's office. This avoids the need for a trial in open court, which many litigants find daunting.

A successful claimant can reclaim the issue fee from the defendant, and the judge may also award up to £50 for loss of earnings in attending court, any reasonable travelling expenses incurred in getting to court, up to £200 towards the fees of an expert's report, and up to £260 for advice and assistance in preparing or defending a claim which includes a claim for an injunction or an order for specific performance or similar relief. Where the case involves a relatively complex matter of fact or law, the judge would be able to transfer it out of the small claims procedure and into the fast track.

The working of the small claims system is looked at in greater detail in Chapter 8.

3.4   The High Court of Justice

The High Court was created in 1873 as a part of the Supreme Court of Judicature. It now has three administrative divisions: the Court of Chancery, the Queen's Bench Division and the Family Division (Divorce and Admiralty and Exchequer and Common Pleas were merged with the QBD in 1880 and 1970). High Court judges sit mainly in the Courts of Justice in the Strand, London, although it is possible for the High Court to sit anywhere in England or Wales. Current directions from the Lord Chancellor mean that the court sits in 27 provincial cities and towns.

The High Court judiciary comprises the Lord Chancellor (who is technically president of the Chancery Division but never sits, the Vice Chancellor usually sits); the Lord Chief Justice who presides over the QBD; the President, who presides over the Family Division; the Senior Presiding Judge (s 72 of the CLSA 1990); and up to 96 High Court judges or *'puisne* judges'* (pronounced 'pewnee' and meaning 'lesser').

To be qualified for appointment as a *puisne* judge, a person must have 10 years' qualification within the meaning of s 71 of the CLSA 1990 – essentially, someone who has had a general right of audience on all matters in that court for at least 10 years. (See Chapter 11.) These judges are appointed by the Queen on the advice of the Lord Chancellor. There is particular controversy about these appointments as they are made by invitation without any advertisement. The Lord Chancellor consults opinion he thinks relevant and reads a secret dossier on each possible appointee. Although the Lord Chancellor agreed in 1993 to appoint District judges using advertisements and conventional appointment procedures, he declined to use such methods in the appointment of High Court judges. High Court judges are appointed to a particular division although they can, if required by the Lord Chancellor, be asked to sit in another division when the volume of work dictates such transfer.

3.4.1   The Queen's Bench Division

The Queen's Bench Division, the main common law court, takes its name from the original judicial part of the general royal court which used to sit on a bench in the Palace of Westminster. It is the division with the largest workload and has some criminal jurisdiction (see 4.5.1 and 4.5.2, on criminal courts) and appellate jurisdiction. The main civil work of this court is in contract and tort cases. The Commercial Court is part of this division, being served by up to 10 judges with specialist experience in commercial law and presiding over cases concerning banking and insurance matters. The formal rules of evidence can be abandoned here, with the consent of the parties, to allow testimony and documentation which would normally be inadmissible. This informality can be of considerable benefit to the business keen to settle their dispute as quickly and easily as possible. The QBD also includes an Admiralty Court to deal with the often esoteric issues of law relating to shipping. Commercial Court judges are sometimes appointed as arbitrators.

The Restrictive Practices Court, established by the Restrictive Practices Act 1956, hears cases relating to the area of commercial law concerned with whether an agreement is unlawful owing to the extent to which it restricts the trading capabilities of one of the parties. One QBD judge sits with specialist lay persons to hear these cases. The Employment Appeal Tribunal is presided over by similar panels, hearing appeals from Industrial Tribunals. These courts are not part of the High Court but are termed superior courts of record.

It is important to remember that most civil actions are settled out of court; only about 1% of cases where writs are issued result in civil trials.

3.4.2 The Queen's Bench Divisional Court

The nomenclature can be puzzling here. This court, as distinct from the QBD, exercises appellate jurisdiction. Here, two, or sometimes three, judges sit to hear appeals in the following circumstances:

- appeals on a point of law by way of case stated from magistrates' courts, tribunals and the Crown Court;

- by exercising judicial review of the decisions made by governmental and public authorities, inferior courts and tribunals. Leave to apply for judicial review is granted or refused by a single judge. Civil judicial reviews can be heard by a single judge;

- applications for the writ of habeas corpus from persons who claim they are being unlawfully detained.

3.4.3 The Chancery Division

The Chancery Division is the modern successor to the old Court of Chancery, the Lord Chancellor's court from which equity was developed. Its jurisdiction includes matters relating to:

- the sale or partition of land and the raising of charges on land;

- the redemption or foreclosure of mortgages;

- the execution or declaration of trusts;

- the administration of the estates of the dead;

- bankruptcy;

- contentious probate business, for example, the validity and interpretation of wills;

- company law;
- partnerships;
- revenue law.

Like the QBD, Chancery contains specialist courts; these are the Patents Court and the Companies Court. The Chancery Division hears its cases in London or in one of eight designated provincial High Court centres. The work is very specialised and there is a Chancery Bar for barristers who practise in this area. Chancery judges are normally appointed from this Bar.

3.4.4 The Chancery Divisional Court

Comprising one or two Chancery judges, this appellate court hears appeals from the Commissioners of Inland Revenue on income tax cases, and from county courts on certain matters like bankruptcy.

3.4.5 The Family Division

The Family Division of the High Court was created by the Administration of Justice Act 1970. It deals with:

- all matrimonial matters both first instance and on appeal;
- matters relating to minors, proceedings under the Children Act 1989;
- legitimacy;
- adoption;
- proceedings under the Domestic Violence and Matrimonial Proceedings Act 1976 and s 30 of the Human Fertilisation and Embryology Act 1990.

3.4.6 The Family Divisional Court

The Family Divisional Court, consisting of two High Court judges, hears appeals from decisions of magistrates' courts and county courts in family matters. Commonly these involve appeals against orders made about financial provision under the DPMCA 1978.

3.5 Appeals from the High Court

Appeals from decisions made by a judge in one of the three High Court Divisions will go to the Court of Appeal (Civil Division). An exception to this rule allows an appeal to miss out or 'leapfrog' a visit to the Court of Appeal and go straight to the House of Lords (ss 12–15 of the Administration of

Justice Act 1969). In order for this to happen, the trial judge must grant a 'certificate of satisfaction' and the House of Lords must give leave to appeal. For the judge to grant a certificate he or she must be satisfied that the case involves a point of law of general public importance either concerned mainly with statutory interpretation or one where he or she was bound by a Court of Appeal or House of Lords' decision. Also, both parties must consent to the procedure. There are usually fewer than six leapfrog procedures a year.

3.6 The Court of Appeal (Civil Division)

The Court of Appeal was established by the Judicature Act (JdA) 1873. Together with the High Court of Justice, the Court of Appeal forms the Supreme Court of Judicature. Why is it called 'Supreme' if the House of Lords is a superior court? The answer is that the JdA 1873 abolished the House of Lords in its appellate capacity, hence the Court of Appeal became part of the Supreme Court but, after a change of government, the House of Lords was reinstated as the final Court of Appeal by the Appellate Jurisdiction Act 1876.

The Court of Appeal is served by senior judges, currently 35, termed Lords Justices of Appeal. Additionally, the Lord Chancellor, the President of the Family Division of the High Court, the Vice Chancellor of the Chancery Division, and High Court judges can sit. The court hears appeals from the three divisions of the High Court; the divisional courts; the county courts; the Employment Appeal Tribunal; the Lands Tribunal and the Transport Tribunal. The most senior judge is the Master of the Rolls. Usually, three judges will sit to hear an appeal although for very important cases five may sit. In the interests of business efficiency, some matters can be heard by two judges. These include:

- applications for leave to appeal;
- an appeal where all parties have consented to the matter being heard by just two judges;
- any appeal against an interlocutory order or judgment (that is, one which is provisional).

Where such a court is evenly divided, the case must be reheard by three or five judges before it can be further appealed to the House of Lords.

There may be four or five divisions of the court sitting on any given day. The court has a heavy workload dealing with about 1,000 cases a year in contrast to the 50 or so disposed of by the House of Lords. In cases of great urgency, this court is often *de facto* the final Court of Appeal so that a party can act in reliance on its decision without waiting to see the outcome of any possible appeal to the Lords. In *C v S and Others* (1987), a case concerning a putative father's right to prevent a prospective mother from having an abortion, the woman was between 18 and 21 weeks' pregnant and her termination, if it was to be carried out, had to be performed within days of the Court of Appeal's decision. The hospital concerned was reluctant to carry out the operation in case the father appealed to the Lords and they favoured his case. To have earlier terminated the pregnancy might then, the hospital believed, have been the crime of infanticide. Leave to appeal to the Lords was refused and the termination was performed but, in the Court of Appeal, Sir John Donaldson MR said:

> It is a fact that some thousand appeals are heard by this court every year, of which about 50 go to the House of Lords ... So, in practical terms, in the every day life of this country, this court is the final court of appeal and it must always be the final court of appeal in cases of real urgency. In those circumstances, no one could be blamed in any way, *a fortiori* could they as a practical matter be prosecuted, for acting on a judgment of this court. If that be wrong, which it is not, the life of the country in many respects would grind to a halt. The purpose of any supreme court, including the House of Lords, is to review historically and on a broad front; it is not to decide matters of great urgency which have to be decided once and for all.

3.6.1   The Bowman Report 1998

The Report of the Review of the Court of Appeal (Civil Division) undertaken by Sir Jeffrey Bowman was published in 1998. The report contains important recommendations for reducing the number of cases coming to the Court of Appeal and for improving practice and procedures in the Civil Appeals Office and in the court itself.

In 1995, the then Master of the Rolls said:

> The delay in hearing certain categories of appeal in the Civil Division of the Court of Appeal has reached a level which is inconsistent with the due administration of justice. On current projections, there is every reason to think that, over the next few years, the situation will (if nothing effective is done) get worse and not better.

Based on averages, the time between setting down and final disposal of 70% of appeals in 1996 was 14 months. Thirty per cent of appeals took over 14 months, and, at the end of 1996, there were some appeals that had been outstanding for over five years. This is even more disturbing when you take into account that the time between the end of the first instance trial and the setting down of the appeal in the CA is not included in the periods mentioned above.

The Review's major recommendations included:

- that certain appeals which now reach the Court of Appeal Civil Division (CA) should be heard at a lower level – the largest category of such cases being appeals against decisions in fast track cases;

- that it should still be possible for appeals which would normally to be heard in a lower court to reach the CA in certain circumstances. In particular, an appeal could be considered if it raises an important point of principle or practice or one which for some other special reason should be considered by the CA;

- that the requirement for leave to appeal should be extended to all cases coming to the CA except for adoption cases, child abduction cases; and appeals against committal orders or refusals to grant habeas corpus;

- that there should be an increasing role for appropriate judicial case management;

- that there should be more focused procedures: cases should be better prepared at a much earlier stage in the process and realistic timetables should be set, which must be strictly observed;

- that the CA should impose appropriate time limits on oral argument on appeals the balance of judicial time should lean more towards reading and less towards sitting in court;

- that the courts should make greater use of information technology to support the other recommendations of this Review;

- information for litigants in person about the appeal process and what it can deliver must be available at an early stage. The information must be easily understandable and delivered in a range of different ways.

Some of the report's more controversial recommendations are in Chapter 5, which concerns the way Court of Appeal is constituted. The following recommendations will doubtless draw much debate:

34   There should be a power to appoint lawyers of outstanding distinction as academics or practitioners to sit as members of the Court of Appeal on occasions.

35   There should be a discretion to list cases before a single member of the Court of Appeal ...

37   Where specialist knowledge of law, procedure or subject matter is an advantage: the constitution [of the CA] should usually include one or two members with the appropriate specialist knowledge; but the constitution should not usually consist solely of specialist members.

38   Where a constitution contains specialist members, as many cases as possible within the particular specialist area should be listed before them.

In different ways, these proposals suggest radical departures from the accepted underlying principles of judicial justice, that is, that only practising lawyers can become senior judges, that judges are not appointed for their expertise in any given area of law, and, to hear a case, it is not necessary or preferred that a judge be an expert in the area of law of subject matter of the case.

The number of appeals set down has risen steadily over recent years. The latest set of *Judicial Statistics* (HMSO, 1996) show 1,853 civil appeals were set down for a hearing in 1995. Unburdening the CA of many of these cases will achieve the reformers aims of improved efficiency at this level but the question will then be: how will the lower courts which will have to deal with the extra cases cascading down to them cope without extra personnel and resources?

Sir Jeffrey Bowman states:

> We believe that the quality of justice will be improved by these changes. The elimination of delays in the Court of Appeal and the facility for simpler appeals to be heard more locally should yield substantial benefits to all litigants and will allow the Lords Justices of Appeal to devote their valuable time and skills to the most important issues.

The issue will be whether the full quantity of appeals is dealt with expeditiously, irrespective of how that number of cases is distributed between the Court of Appeal and other courts.

3.7 The Access to Justice Act 1999 – reforms to the appeal process

Part IV of the Access to Justice Act 1999 deals with aspects of reforms for the system for appeals in civil and family cases:

- it establishes the principles that should underlie the jurisdiction of the civil courts to hear appeals;

- it gives the Lord Chancellor power to define the venue for appeal in different categories of case;

- it changes the law relating to the constitution of the Civil Division of the Court of Appeal.

The intention is to ensure that the appellate system reflects the principle, which underlies the government's wider programme of civil justice reforms, that cases should be dealt with in a way that is proportionate to the issue at stake.

Background

In his 1994–95 Annual Report on the Court of Appeal, the then Master of the Rolls, Lord Bingham, stated that 'the delay in hearing certain categories of appeal in the Civil Division of the Court of Appeal has reached a level which is inconsistent with the due administration of justice'.

In his report, *Access to Justice* (July 1996), Lord Woolf set out his proposals for the reform of the civil justice system. At the heart of his proposals was the allocation of civil cases to 'tracks', which would determine the degree of judicial case management. Broadly speaking, cases would be allocated to the small claims track, the fast track or to the multi-track, depending upon the value and complexity of the claim. Those proposals have now been implemented in the The Civil Procedure Act 1997 and the Civil Procedure Rules 1998 (see Chapter 7). The principle that underlies this system of tracks is the need to ensure that resources devoted to managing and hearing a case are proportional to the weight and substance of that case. In order that the benefits arising from these reforms should not be weakened on appeal, Lord Woolf recommended that an effective system of appeals should be based on similar principles.

In 1996, Sir Jeffery Bowman chaired a Review of the Civil Division of the Court of Appeal (Review of the Court of Appeal (Civil Division) – Report to the Lord Chancellor, September 1997). He identified a number of problems besetting the Court of Appeal. In particular, he noted that the court was being asked to consider numerous appeals which were not of sufficient weight or complexity for two or three of the country's most senior judges, and which had sometimes already been through one or more levels of appeal. Additionally, he concluded that existing provisions concerning the constitution of the court were too inflexible to deal appropriately with its workload. To redress this situation, Sir Jeffery Bowman's Report included recommendations to alter the jurisdiction and constitution of the Court of Appeal. The Lord Chancellor consulted on proposals to effect certain of these changes (Reform of the Court of Appeal (Civil Division): *Proposals for Change to Constitution and Jurisdiction*, LCD, July 1998).

Due to the complex nature of routes of appeal in family matters, Sir Jeffery Bowman's report recommended that a specialist committee should examine this area with a view to rationalising the arrangements for appeals in family cases and bringing them in line with the underlying principles for civil appeals. The Family Appeal Review Group, chaired by Lord Justice Thorpe, published recommendations in July 1998 aimed at simplifying the current appeals procedure in family cases, applying the principles outlined in Sir Jeffery Bowman's Report.

The provisions enabling certain matters to be heard by a single High Court judge have the same objective of ensuring that the most appropriate use is made of judicial resources. The provision about the High Court's powers to deal with appeals by way of case stated from the Crown Court follows a recommendation by the Law Commission in its 1994 Report *Administrative Law: Judicial Review and Statutory Appeals*.

Changes made by the Access to Justice Act 1999 (Pt IV)

In relation to civil appeals, the 1999 Act will make the following changes, which are expected to come into effect in 2000:

- provide for permission to appeal to be obtained at all levels in the system (s 54);

- provide that, in normal circumstances, there will be only one level of appeal to the courts (s 55);

- introduce an order making power to enable the Lord Chancellor to vary appeal routes in secondary legislation, with a view to ensuring that appeals generally go to the lowest appropriate level of judge (s 56);

- ensure that cases which merit the consideration of the Court of Appeal reach that court (s 57);

- give the Civil Division of the Court of Appeal flexibility to exercise its jurisdiction in courts of one, two or more judges (s 59).

Together, these proposals are intended to ensure that appeals are heard at the right level, and dealt with in a way which is proportionate to their weight and complexity; that the appeals system can adapt quickly to other developments in the civil justice system; and that existing resources are used efficiently, enabling the Court of Appeal (Civil Division) to tackle its workload more expeditiously.

The provisions relating to the High Court (ss 61–65):

- allow judicial review applications, appeals by way of case stated and applications for habeas corpus which are related to criminal matters, together with appeals from inferior courts and tribunals in contempt of court cases, to be routinely heard by a single judge in the High Court, rather than, as at present, by a Divisional Court of two or more judges;

- place on a statutory footing the powers of the High Court to deal with appeals by way of case stated coming from the Crown Court.

Right to appeal

The Act provides for rights of appeal to be exercised only with the permission of the court, as prescribed by rules of court. Previously, permission was required for most cases going to the Civil Division of the Court of Appeal, but not elsewhere. For the future, it is proposed that, with three exceptions, rules will require permission to appeal to be obtained in all appeals to the county courts, High Court or Civil Division of the Court of Appeal. The exceptions are appeals against committal to prison, appeals against a refusal to grant habeas corpus, and appeals against the making of secure accommodation orders under s 25 of the Children Act 1989 (a form of custodial 'sentence' for recalcitrant children). There will be no appeal against a decision of the court to give or refuse permission, but this does not affect any right under rules of court to make a further application for permission to the same or another court.

The Act provides that, where the county court or High Court has already reached a decision in a case brought on appeal, there will be no further possibility of an appeal of that decision to the Court of Appeal, unless (s 55) the Court of Appeal considers that the appeal would raise an important point of principle or practice, or there is some other compelling reason for the Court of Appeal to hear it.

Destination of appeals

Section 56 of the Access to Justice Act 1999 enables the Lord Chancellor to vary, by order, the routes of appeal for appeals to and within the county courts, the High Court, and the Civil Division of the Court of Appeal. Before making an order, the Lord Chancellor will be required to consult the Heads of Division, and any order will be subject to the affirmative resolution procedure. The present intention of the government is that the following appeal routes will be specified by order:

- in fast track cases heard by a district judge, appeals will be to a circuit judge;

- in fast track cases heard by a circuit judge, appeals will be to a High Court judge;

- in multi-track cases, appeals of interlocutory decisions made at first instance by a district judge will be to a circuit judge, by a master or circuit judge to a High Court judge, and by a High Court judge to the Court of Appeal; and

- in multi-track cases, appeals of final orders regardless of the court of first instance, will be to the Court of Appeal;

- the Heads of Division are the Lord Chief Justice, the Master of the Rolls, the President of the Family Division, and the Vice Chancellor;

- a decision is interlocutory where it does not determine the final outcome of the case.

The legislation provides for the Master of the Rolls, or a lower court, to direct that an appeal that would normally be heard by a lower court be heard instead by the Court of Appeal. This power would be used where the appeal raises an important point of principle or practice, or is a case which for some other compelling reason should be considered by the Court of Appeal.

Civil Division of Court of Appeal

The Act makes flexible provision for the number of judges of which a court must be constituted in order for the Court of Appeal to be able to hear appeals. Section 54 of the Supreme Court Act 1981 provided that the Court of Appeal was constituted to exercise any of its jurisdiction if it consisted of an uneven number of judges not less than three. In limited circumstances, it provided that a court could be properly constituted with two judges. The 1999 Act allows the Master of the Rolls, with the concurrence of the Lord Chancellor, to give directions about the minimum number of judges of which a court must consist for given types of proceedings. Subject to any directions, the Act also allows the Master of the Rolls, or a Lord Justice of Appeal designated by him for the purpose, to determine the number of judges who will sit to hear any particular appeal.

Jurisdiction of single judge of High Court

The 1999 Act allows certain applications to be routinely heard by a single judge of the High Court. It does this by removing an obstacle that exists in the current legislation by which the route of appeal for these cases is to the House of Lords, but the Administration of Justice Act 1960 provides that the House of Lords will only hear appeals in these matters from a Divisional Court (that is, more than one judge) of the High Court. The 1999 Act amends the 1960 Act, so that the House of Lords can hear appeals from a single High Court judge. It will then be possible to make rules of court to provide for these cases to be heard by a single judge, while enabling the judge to refer particularly complex cases to a Divisional Court.

The cases in question are:

- judicial reviews and appeals by way of case stated in criminal causes and matters;

- appeals from inferior (civil and criminal) courts and tribunals in contempt of court cases;

- criminal applications for habeas corpus.

Another change made by the 1999 Act concerns appeals from the Crown Court for opinion of High Court. The Supreme Court Act 1981 gives the High Court specific powers of disposal over appeals by way of case stated coming from a magistrates' court. However, it does not do the same for cases coming from the Crown Court. Section 61 of the Access to Justice Act 1999 provides a statutory footing for the powers of the High Court to deal with appeals by way of case stated coming from the Crown Court.

3.8 The House of Lords

Acting in its judicial capacity, as opposed to its legislative one, the House of Lords is the final Court of Appeal in civil as well as criminal law. Its judgments govern the courts in England, Wales and Northern Ireland. They can also govern civil law in Scotland. Most appeals reaching the House of Lords come from English civil cases. In 1997, the Lords pronounced on 62 cases of which 44 came from England and only six were criminal. There is also a 'leapfrog' procedure, introduced by ss 12–15 of the Administration of Justice Act 1969, by which an appeal may go to the Lords direct from the High Court if the High Court judge certificates the case as being suitable for the Lords to hear and the House of Lords gives leave to appeal. All the parties must consent and the case must be one which involves a point of general public importance about a matter of statutory interpretation (sometimes called statutory 'construction' from the verb to *construe* meaning to interpret) or where the contentious issue is one on which the trial judge is bound by a precedent of the Court of Appeal or House of Lords.

The appeals are heard by Lords of Appeal in Ordinary of whom there are currently 12. Two of these must be from Scotland and one from Northern Ireland. Other senior judges like the Lord Chancellor sometimes sit to hear appeals. It is customary for only peers with distinguished legal and judicial careers to become Lords of Appeal in Ordinary. These judges are known journalistically as 'Law Lords'.

For most cases, five Lords will sit to hear the appeal but seven are sometimes convened to hear very important cases. The House of Lords' decision which abolished the 250 year old rule against convicting a husband for rape of his wife (*R v R* (1991)) is such a case. Cases are heard in relative informality in a committee room in the Palace of Westminster. The Appellate Committee of the House of Lords, as it is technically termed, sits with its members in suits, not judicial robes. Counsel, however, do wear wigs and robes. Unlike criminal cases (s 33 of the Criminal Appeal Act (CAA) 1968, there is no requirement that the appeal is on a point of law of general public importance. An appeal from the Court of Appeal to the House of Lords must have 'leave' (that is, permission) of either court.

The judges may deliver their judgments termed 'opinions' as speeches in the Parliamentary chamber. A majority decides the case. Sometimes, however, where a case has been heard at three levels of the civil process, the final outcome is not determined, overall, by a majority of what could be described as senior judges. Consider the case of *Gillick v West Norfolk and Wisbech Area Health Authority* (1985), a case in which the plaintiff, Mrs Gillick, sought a ruling that the defendant's policy to allow contraceptive advice to be given to girls under 16 in some circumstances was illegal. Her argument was rejected by the judge hearing the case in the High Court; accepted unanimously by the three Lords Justice in the Court of Appeal and then rejected in the House of Lords by three votes to two. Thus, overall, a majority of the eight senior judges who heard her case accepted it (five out of eight) but she lost her case because she lost in the final court.

3.9 The European Court of Justice

As we shall see in detail in Chapter 13, the Treaty of Amsterdam 1997 introduced a completely new system for numbering the Articles of the European Community treaties. In order to try to avoid confusion when readers consult other, already existing authorities which will refer to the old numbering, this book will refer to both the new and the previous numbering.

The function of the European Court of Justice, which sits in Luxembourg, is to 'ensure that in the interpretation and application of this Treaty [the EEC Treaty 1957] the law is observed' (Art 200, formerly 164). The court is the ultimate authority on European law. As the Treaty is often composed in general terms, the court is often called upon to provide the necessary detail for European law to operate. By virtue of the European Communities Act 1972, European law has been enacted into English law so the decisions of the court have direct authority in the English jurisdiction.

The court hears disputes between nations and between nations and European institutions like the European Commission. An individual, however, can only bring an action if he is challenging a decision which affects him.

The Treaty states in Art 234, formerly 177, that any judicial or quasi-judicial body, however low ranking, may refer a question to the European Court if it considers that 'a decision on that question is necessary to enable it to give judgment' and that such a reference must be made in a national court from which there is no further appeal. So, the High Court would have a discretion as to whether to refer a point but the House of Lords would not. The system was installed to try and ensure uniformity of interpretation of European law across all the Member States. Without such a mechanism, it would be possible for the English courts to be interpreting a point of European law one way while the Spanish courts were treating it as meaning something different.

Lord Denning formulated guidelines in *Bulmer v Bollinger* (1974) as to when an inferior court should refer a case to the Court of Justice for a preliminary ruling. He offered four guidelines to determine whether the reference was 'necessary' within the meaning of Art 234, formerly 177:

- the decision on the point of European law must be conclusive of the case;

- the national court may choose to follow a previous ruling of the European Court on the same point of Community law, but it may choose to refer the same point of law to the court again in the hope that it will give a different ruling;

- the national court may not make a reference on the grounds of *acte clair* where the point is reasonably clear and free from doubt;

- 'in general, it is best to decide the facts first' before determining whether it is necessary to refer the point of Community law.

If a national court decides that a reference is necessary, it still has the discretion (unlike the highest court) as to whether to refer the point. Lord Denning then listed some factors to help courts decide whether to refer; for example: bear in mind the expense to parties of a reference and do not send points unless they are difficult and important.

These guidelines have been influential in a number of subsequent cases. It is possible, however, for an appeal to be made against a decision of a court of first instance to refer a case to the European Court for a preliminary ruling under Art 234, formerly 177. The appellate court will interfere with the discretion of the trial judge who referred the case but only if the decision was 'plainly wrong': *Bulmer v Bollinger* (1974).

The language of Art 234, formerly 177, is imperative, saying that courts or tribunals against whose judgments there is no appeal *must* refer a point of Community law. This does not apply where the point has already been ruled on by the European Court. Equally, it does not apply where the national court has ruled that the issue in question is not one which requires the application of Community law. In *R v London Boroughs Transport Committee* (1992), the House of Lords decided that the case did not involve any community law issues because it concerned the regulation of local traffic, even though the Court of Appeal had held unanimously that United Kingdom legislation was in breach of certain community directives.

The European Court of Justice is a court of reference: the ruling the Court makes is preliminary in the sense that the case is then remitted to the national court for it to apply the law to the facts. The Court only addresses itself to points arising from actual cases; it will not consider hypothetical problems.

Lord Diplock (*R v Henn* (1981)) has characterised the Court's work in the following way:

> The European Court, in contrast to English courts, applies teleological rather than historical methods to the interpretation of the Treaties and other Community legislation. It seeks to give effect to what it conceives to be the spirit rather than the letter of the Treaties; sometimes, indeed, to an English judge, it may seem to the exclusion of the letter. It views the Communities as living and expanding organisms and the interpretation of the provisions of the Treaties as changing to match their growth.

The Court is made up from senior judges from each Member State (15) and a President of the Court, assisted by nine Advocates General. The latter are 'persons whose independence is beyond doubt' (Art 223, formerly 167) and their task is to give to the Court a detailed analysis of all the relevant legal and factual issues along with recommendations. The recommendations are not necessarily followed by the Court but they can be used on later occasions as persuasive precedent. The Court attempts to ensure consistency in its decisions but is not bound by precedent to the same extent as a court in England.

The Court of First Instance was set up to ease the mounting workload of the Court of Justice. It began work in 1989 and has a jurisdiction which is limited to hearing disputes between the community and its staff, cases involving EU competition law (excluding Art 234, formerly 177, references) and some matters involving the European Coal and Steel Community.

3.10   The European Court of Human Rights

The European Court of Human Rights (ECHR) does not arise from the EU. It arises from the 1950 European Convention on Human Rights, signed by 21 European States including the United Kingdom, and deals with matters relating to human and political rights. The court sits in Strasbourg and comprises of a judge from each Member State. The signatory States undertook to ensure a range of human and political rights to the citizens within their jurisdictions.

See 13.4 for further treatment of the ECHR.

3.11   Judicial Committee of the Privy Council

The Judicial Committee of the Privy Council was created by the Judicial Committee Act 1833. Under the Act, a special committee of the Privy Council was set up to hear appeals from the dominions. The cases are heard by the judges (without wigs or robes) in a committee room in London. The committee's decision is not a judgment but an 'advice' to the Monarch, who is counselled that the appeal be allowed or dismissed.

The Committee is the final court of appeal for certain Commonwealth countries which have retained this option and from some independent members and associate members of the Commonwealth. The Committee comprises Privy Councillors who hold (or have held) high judicial office. In most cases, which come from places such as the Cayman Islands and Jamaica, the Committee comprises five Lords of Appeal in Ordinary, sometimes assisted by a judge from the country concerned. The decisions of the Privy Council are very influential in English courts because they concern points of law that are applicable in this jurisdiction and they are pronounced upon by Lords of Appeal in Ordinary, in a way which is thus tantamount to a House of Lords' ruling. These decisions, however, are technically of persuasive precedent only although they are normally followed by English courts; see, for example, the tort case *The Wagon Mound* (1963), a case in which the Privy Council ruled, on an appeal from Australia, that, in negligence actions, a defendant is liable only for the reasonably foreseeable consequences of his tortious conduct. A total of 73 appeals were registered in 1997. The Committee is also the final appeal court for the Professional Conduct and Health Committees of the General Medical Council and the General Dental Council.

3.12   Civil court fees

As from 15 January 1997, a new scale of court fees for civil cases came into effect. The aim of the new fee scales is to raise £50 million and to make the civil courts self-financing. The fee for setting down a county court action doubles from £50 to £100. Filing a divorce petition, previously carrying an £80 cost has risen to £150. Issuing a High Court writ, previously requiring a £150 fee, will now cost £300 where the value of the claim is £50,000 to £100,000, and £500 where the value of the claim is over £100,000. The full court fee for pursuing a sizeable court fee could, henceforward, easily exceed £1,500. The principle of running the civil courts according to business principles is highly controversial. The innovation, announced by the Lord Chancellor, was denounced by Sir Richard Scott, head of the Chancery division of the High Court. He warned that justice should be reasonably accessible and without excessive cost. He stated that:

> The policy fails to recognise that the civil justice system is, like the criminal justice system, the bulwark of a civilised State and the maintenance of order within that State. People have to use the civil courts. They can't engage in self-help in a way which would lead to chaos.

Under the new scheme, people on legal aid would still have their court fees paid, but many unaided people can only just afford to litigate and the raised fees would be turn a difficult hurdle into an insurmountable barrier. The policy of making litigants pay for judges and courtrooms – for that is the essence of this new court fee structure – is a highly controversial policy. Many litigants would believe that they and others, as taxpayers, have already contributed to the funding of the legal system.

The cost of civil business in the courts (including judicial salaries, accommodation, staff, and administration) is over £335 million a year, of which £78 million is met by the taxpayer. The rest is recouped from court fees. In a debate in the House of Lords (*Hansard*, 1997, Vol 581, cols 863–81), the Lord Chancellor revisited the theme of at what rate, if at all, citizens should be charged fees for using the civil courts. He stated that he did not accept that all citizens had a constitutional right to go to law in the civil courts freely at the point of use. To do that, he observed, it would be necessary to find the money currently supporting the system from court fees (£257m paid by citizens) from somewhere else. He would have to cut that amount from somewhere else in his budget. He raised the possibilities of ending criminal legal aid, or ending legal aid for family proceedings. The Lord Chancellor said:

> Those who argue for free access to courts for all are really arguing that the government should charge taxpayers an additional £257m and then increase my budget by that amount. The Secretary of State for Health might argue that with that money he could provide several new acute hospitals. The Secretary of State for Education might argue that with that money he could provide 30 extra secondary schools.

Many theoretical questions about 'justice' and the legal system quickly reduce to matters of political economy. The issue of court fees is a good illustration. Is the provision of free access to court services for all (including many who could easily afford to pay court fees) more important than the provision of schools and hospitals?

The Court Service has issued a consultation paper proposing that fees for taking cases to civil courts are updated to reflect more closely the costs that are involved.

The principle idea here is that where people can afford to pay the costs involved in their bringing a legal action the taxpayer should not be expected to pay for them.

Nonetheless, it seems likely there will be a subsidy for costs associated with some family proceedings. This would be to put as few barriers as possible in the way of people using the courts to protect themselves from violence or harassment, or trying to resolve disputes on the care of children.

Under the new proposals, people on low incomes would continue to be exempted from all court fees. Automatic exemptions to the fees would apply to people in receipt of Income Support, Family Credit, Disability Working Allowance and Income based Jobseeker's Allowance.

Should fees be payable by those wishing to use the courts? Some observers point out that payments are not made by members of the public at the point of use in the education and health systems, and that justice can be seen as being just as important as those services. On the other hand, the Lord Chancellor has pointed out that were the courts to become free at the point of use, the money needed to pay for this would have to come from closing down large parts of the civil legal aid or shutting schools or hospitals. Thus, legal policy is inextricably bound up with social policy in general.

THE CIVIL COURT STRUCTURE

The differences between civil and criminal law

There is no such thing as inherently criminal conduct. A crime is whatever the State has forbidden on pain of legal punishment. The conduct which attracts criminal sanctions changes over time and according to different social systems. The terminology and outcomes of the two systems are different. In criminal cases, the *prosecutor prosecutes the defendant* (or *accused*); in civil cases, the *claimant sues the defendant*.

The Court Service

The courts (except for the magistrates' courts and coroners' courts) are now run by the Court Service, an executive agency, formerly part of the Lord Chancellor's Department.

Magistrates' courts

Magistrates' courts have a significant civil jurisdiction, especially under the CA 1989 as 'family proceedings courts'.

County courts

There are about 240 county courts in England and Wales. They are presided over by district judges and circuit judges. County courts hear small claims, that is, those whose value is £5,000 or under, and fast track cases. The civil justice reforms are likely to put a considerable burden of work on the county courts under the new system. The main advantage to litigants using the small claims process is the fact that, if sued, they can defend without fear of incurring huge legal costs, since the costs the winning party can claim are strictly limited.

The High Court

The High Court's judicial composition should be noted and the meaning of the 10 year qualification according to s 71 of the CLSA 1990. The High Court is under considerable pressure of work, hence the CLSA1990 provisions to ease its workload. The QBD deals with contract and tort, etc; its Divisional Court deals with judicial review and criminal appeals from Magistrates' and Crown Courts. Chancery deals with cases involving land, mortgages and bankruptcy and probate, etc; its Divisional Court hears taxation appeals. The Family Division hears matrimonial and child-related matters and its Divisional Court hears appeals from magistrates' and county courts on these issues.

The Court of Appeal (Civil Division)

The Court of Appeal (Civil Division) usually has three judges whose decision is by majority. For many purposes it is the *de facto* final Appeal Court (*C v S and Others* (1987)).

The Bowman Report 1998

The Report contained important recommendations for reducing the number of cases coming to the Court of Appeal and for improving practice and procedures in the Civil Appeals Office. The review's major recommendations included:

Certain appeals which previously reached the Court of Appeal (Civil Division) should be heard at a low level, and that the requirement for leave to appeal should be extended to all cases coming to the Court of Appeal except for adoption cases, child abduction cases and appeals against committal orders or refusal to grant habeas corpus. The *Access to Justice Act 1999* reforms the appeal process by establishing the principle that there is the need for permission to appeal at all levels in the system. The Act provides that, in normal circumstances, there will be only one level of appeal to the courts and it gives to the Civil Division of the Court of Appeal flexibility to exercise its jurisdiction in courts of one, two or more judges. Taken together, these proposals are intended to ensure that appeals are heard at the right level and in a way which is proportionate to their weight and complexity.

Civil court fees

A new scale of court fees for people using the civil courts came into effect in 1997. The aim of the new fees is to make the civil court self-financing. This change raises matters of importance in legal, social and economic debates. There are those who argue, for example, that the courts should, like the National Health Service, be free to people at the point of use, and financed by general taxation. There are others who argue that some payments should be made at the point of use. The Lord Chancellor has pointed out that, were the courts to become free in this way, the money needed to pay for this would have to come from closing down large parts of the civil legal aid system or closing schools or hospitals.

The House of Lords

In most of its 50 or so cases, five Law Lords sit. They hear cases of general public importance concerning points of law, for example, *R v R* (1991) changing a 250 year old rule and allowing prosecutions for marital rape.

The European Court of Justice

The ECJ sits in Luxembourg to ensure that the interpretation and application of the EEC 'Treaty of Rome' is observed consistently by all Member States. Note the importance of Art 234, formerly 177, and the guidance provided by *Bulmer v Bollinger* (1974).

The European Court of Human Rights

The ECHR sits in Strasbourg and arose from the 1950 European Convention on Human Rights. It has no mechanism for enforcement other than of a political nature. Its effect can be illustrated by cases like *Malone v UK* (1984).

As a consequence of the Human Rights Act 1998, the decisions of the European Court of Human Rights are now precedents for, and binding on, domestic UK courts. In terms of human rights issues, therefore, it is superior to the House of Lords.

The Judicial Committee of the Privy Council

The Judicial Committee of the Privy Council acts as a final Appeal Court for some Commonwealth countries and, because it comprises senior judges from the English legal system, it gives decisions which are persuasive precedent in English law.

CHAPTER 4

THE CRIMINAL COURT STRUCTURE

This chapter looks at the structure of the criminal courts. You need to know which type of cases are heard in which trial courts; the procedures of summary hearings, either way offences, transfers for trial, Crown Court trials and the rules governing the transfer of proceedings; the system of appeals and the criticisms which have been made of the various aspects of these systems.

4.1   Coroners' courts

The coroners' courts are one of the most ancient parts of the English legal system, dating back to at least 1194. They are not, in modern function, part of the criminal courts but because of historical associations, it makes more sense to classify them with the courts in this chapter than that dealing with civil courts. Coroners were originally appointed as *custos placitorum coronae*, keepers of the pleas of the Crown. They had responsibility for criminal cases in which the Crown had an interest, particularly a financial interest.

Today, there are 157 coroners' courts, of which 21 sit full time. Coroners are usually lawyers (with at least a five year qualification within s 71 of the Courts and Legal Services Act (CLSA) 1990), although about 25% are medical doctors with a legal qualification. The main jurisdiction of the coroner today concerns unnatural and violent deaths, although treasure trove is also something occasionally dealt with in these courts.

The classifying of types of death is clearly of critical importance, not just to the State, politicians and policy makers, but also to the sort of campaign groups that exist in a constitutional democracy to monitor suicides, drug-related deaths, deaths in police custody and prison, accidental deaths, deaths in hospitals, and through industrial diseases.

In 1998, there were 600,000 registered deaths in England and Wales. Deaths must be reported to a coroner if they seem unnatural or violent; the coroner will order a postmortem and this may reveal a natural cause of death which can be duly registered. If not, or in certain other circumstances, such as where the death occurred in prison or police custody, or if the cause is unknown, then there will be an inquest. There were 196,000 deaths reported to coroners in 1998 resulting in 124,400 post-mortem examinations and 23,600 inquests (*Statistics of Deaths Reported to Coroners in England and Wales*, Government Statistical Service, April 1999).

Most inquests (96%) are held without juries but the State has been insistent that certain types of case must be heard by a jury in order to promote public faith in government. When, in 1926, legislation for the first time permitted inquests to be held without juries, certain types of death were deliberately marked off as still requiring jury scrutiny, and these included deaths in police custody, deaths resulting from the actions of a police officer on duty, and deaths in prison. This was seen as a very important way of fostering public trust in potentially oppressive aspects of the State. In 1971, the Brodrick Committee Report on the coronial system saw the coroner's jury as having a symbolic significance and thought that it was a useful way to legitimate the decision of the coroner.

The coroner's court is unique in using an inquisitorial process. There are no 'sides' in an inquest. There may be representation for people like the relatives of the deceased, insurance companies, prison officers, car drivers, companies (whose policies are possibly implicated in the death), and train drivers, etc, but all the witnesses are the coroner's witnesses. It is the coroner who decides who shall be summoned as witnesses and in what order they shall be called.

Historically, an inquest jury could decide that a deceased had been unlawfully killed and then commit a suspect for trial at the local assizes. When this power was taken away in 1926, the main bridge over to the criminal justice system was removed. There then followed, in stages, an attempt to prevent inquest verdicts from impinging on the jurisdictions of the ordinary civil and criminal courts. Now, an inquest jury is exclusively concerned with determining who the deceased was, and 'how, when and where he came by his death'. The court is forbidden to make any wider comment on the death and must not determine or appear to determine criminal liability 'on the part of a named person'.

Nevertheless, the jury may still now properly decide that a death was unlawful (that is, crime). The verdict 'unlawful killing' is on a list of options (including 'suicide', 'accidental death', and 'open verdict') made under legislation and approved by the Home Office.

4.2 The criminal trial courts

There are over 7,000 different criminal offences in English law. These offences can be classified in different ways. You could, for example, classify them according to whether they are offences against people or property; again, you could classify them according to the type of mental element (*mens rea*) required for the offence, for example, 'intention' or 'recklessness'. One other type of classification, and the one to concern us here, is whether the offence is triable *summarily* in a magistrates' court (for relatively trivial offences like traffic offences) or is an *indictable* offence (the more serious offences like murder and rape) triable in front of a judge and jury in a Crown Court.

From the mid-19th century, magistrates were empowered to hear some indictable cases in certain circumstances. Today, there is still a class of offence which is triable 'either way', that is summarily or in a jury trial. A typical example would be a potentially serious offence like theft but one which has been committed in a minor way as in the theft of a milk bottle. These offences now account for about 80% of those tried in Crown Courts. Most defendants, however, opt for summary trial. Where several defendants are charged together with either way offences, each defendant's choice can be exercised separately so if one elects for trial in the Crown Court the others may still be tried summarily if the magistrates agree (*R v Brentwood Justices ex p Nicholls* (1991)).

Which types of case should be dealt with in which courts? This question was investigated by the James Committee which reported in 1975 on *The Distribution of Business between the Crown Court and Magistrates' Courts*. It found that for similar cases, Crown Court trials were three times more expensive than summary hearings. It concluded that the division of work between the different levels of court should reflect the public view as to what are the more serious offences justifying full trials and those which should be dealt with by magistrates. The committee also proposed a category of cases triable either way.

In all offences triable either way, the defendant has the right of trial by jury. If the defendant elects for summary trial the magistrates (and, in some cases, the prosecution) still have the right to remit the case for trial at the Crown Court if they think trial there would be more suitable.

4.3 Magistrates' courts

The office of magistrate or Justice of the Peace dates from 1195 when Richard I first appointed 'keepers of the peace' to deal with those who were accused of breaking 'the King's peace'. The JP's originally acted as local administrators for the King in addition to their judicial responsibilities. Apart from the 29,000 lay justices who sit in some 700 courts, there are also 92 stipendiary magistrates who sit in cities and larger towns. They are qualified, experienced lawyers who are salaried justices. Where a magistrates' court commits a person for trial of offences in classes one to three (see 4.4, below), the most convenient location of the Crown Court where a High Court judge regularly sits should be specified, and for offences in class four, the most convenient location of the Crown Court. These matters are confirmed in the *Practice Directions on the Allocation of Crown Court Business* (1995).

4.3.1 Summary trial

Summary offences are created and defined by statute. There are thousands of different summary offences. They include traffic offences, common assault, taking a motor vehicle without consent and driving whilst disqualified. Ninety eight per cent of all criminal cases are dealt with by the courts summarily.

Cases are heard in the court for the district in which the offence is alleged to have been committed. In most cases, the defendant will be in court but it is possible for the accused in road traffic offences to plead guilty by post and not to attend court.

The cases will be heard by two or three magistrates whose powers of sentencing are limited by the Acts which govern the offences in question. A stipendiary magistrate may sit without lay magistrates. The maximum sentence that magistrates can impose, however, is a £5,000 fine and/or a six month prison sentence. The maximum sentences for many summary offences are much less than these limits. Where a defendant is convicted of two or more offences at the same hearing, consecutive sentences amounting to more than six months are not permitted although this can rise to 12 months in cases involving offences triable 'either way' (s 133 of the Magistrates' Courts Act (MCA) 1980). Many statutory offences are now given particular 'levels' according to their seriousness. This means that if a government minister wishes to raise fines (say to be in line with inflation) he or she does not have to go through hundreds of different offences altering the maximum fine in relation to each one separately; the maxima for each level are simply altered. The current figures (from the Criminal Justice Act (CJA) 1991) are as follows: Level 5 up to £5,000; Level 4 up to £2,500; Level 3 up to £1,000; Level 2 up to £500 and Level 1 up to £200.

The Criminal Justice Act (CJA) 1991 provided for a new system of fining in magistrates' courts: the 'unit fine' system. Under this system, fines were linked to the offender's income. The idea was that the rich should pay more than the poor for the same offence. Crimes were graded from one to 10 and the level of crime was then multiplied by the offender's weekly disposable income. The system's figures, however, resulted in many anomalies and it was eventually abolished. Nevertheless, in fixing the appropriate amount for a convicted defendant's fine, the magistrates will still take into account his or her income. Other sentences that the court may use include absolute discharge, conditional discharge, probation, community service orders and compensation orders. This latter order is enjoying progressively wider use and is designed to save the victim of the crime suing the defendant in a civil court for damages. Whereas a fine goes to the State, the compensation goes to the victim. This system is governed by s 35 of the Powers of the Criminal Courts Act 1973. Their use has been encouraged by the amendment made by the CJA 1988.

After a conviction, the magistrates will hear whether the defendant has a criminal record and if so for what offences. This is to enable them to pass an appropriate sentence. If, after hearing that record, they feel that their powers of sanction are insufficient to deal with the defendant then he or she may be sent to the Crown Court for sentencing.

A bench of lay magistrates is legally advised by a justices' clerk who is legally qualified and guides the justices on matters of law, sentencing and procedure. The justices' clerk may give advice even when not specifically invited to do so. It is an established principle of English law that 'justice should not only be done but manifestly and undoubtedly be seen to be done' (*R v Sussex Justices ex p McCarthy* (1924) *per* Lord Hewart CJ). The magistrates are independent of the clerks and, according to the principle, the clerks should not *instruct* the magistrates what decision to make on any point nor should they appear to be doing so. The clerk should not, therefore, normally retire with the justices when they go to consider their verdict in any case although he or she may be called by them to give advice on any point. The clerk should not give any judgment on matters of fact.

The court is required in certain cases to consider a compensation order and to give reasons if it decides not to make such an order. As amended, s 35 states that a court before which a person is convicted, in addition to dealing with him in any other way may make a compensation order. The order is to compensate personal injury, loss or damage resulting from the offence in question or any other one 'taken into consideration' (that is, admitted by the defendant) by the court. The defendant can also be ordered to make payments for funeral expenses or bereavement in respect of a death resulting from an offence committed by the defendant (other than a death due to a motor accident). The court, s 35(1) states, 'shall give reasons, on passing sentence, if it does not make such an order in a case where this section empowers it to do so'. In 1994, the Crown Court issued compensation orders in 9% of cases where the accused was sentenced – a total of 6,600 orders. The magistrates' courts issued over 88,000 orders.

A new system of funding the magistrates' courts was introduced in 1991. The system links the amount of money given to a court to the number of cases it processes. One survey (for *File on Four*) found that 74% of clerks felt these changes put justice at risk. Clerks have reported that the changes have put pressure on the courts to give priority to 'quick' cases such as television licence prosecutions and traffic offences. Courts are allocated points for each case processed but a complex case may attract the same points as a simple one. The government has contended that, under good management, 'efficiency is the handmaiden of justice'. Anthony Scrivener QC, Chairman of the Bar Council when the system was introduced, stated that courts were not 'canning factories, their most important function is to dispense justice and this cannot be measured statistically'. Cost-conscious courts could be pressured into making poor decisions.

4.3.2 Offences triable 'either way'

The procedure for determining the mode of trial in cases triable 'either way' is set out in ss 18–26 of the MCA 1980. The justices (although it can be just one for this function) must decide whether the offence is more suitable for summary trial or trial on indictment. The court must consider (a) the nature of the case; (b) whether the circumstances make the offence one of a serious character; (c) whether the punishment that the magistrates' court could impose would be adequate; and (d) any representations made about the mode of trial made by the prosecution and defence. Further guidelines appear in a *Practice Note* (1990). The gist of this guidance is that 'either way' offences should be tried summarily unless a case has one or more aggravating features *and* the court considers that its sentencing powers are inadequate. Prosecutions conducted by the Attorney General, the Solicitor General or the Director of Public Prosecutions must be tried on indictment if so requested by the prosecutor. In 1995, these guidelines (the National Mode of Trial Guidelines) were revised by the Secretariat of the Criminal Justice Consultative Committee. The guidelines set out general principles. They explain features, for example, which would make trial on indictment appropriate for certain offences like burglary, criminal damage, dangerous driving, drugs offences, indecent assault, fraud and offences of violence. The guidelines say, for instance, that trial in the Crown Court is appropriate in the case of burglary where it has been committed in the daytime when the occupier or another person was at home; or where entry was at night into a house normally occupied; or where the offence has professional hallmarks.

If, after considering all the relevant matters, the court decides that summary trial is more suitable, it must explain its decision to the accused in ordinary language and then ask him whether he consents to such trial or wishes to be tried by a jury. The accused must also be told that if he is tried summarily and convicted, he may be committed for sentence to the Crown Court if the magistrates, having had information about his 'character and antecedents', think that greater punishment should be imposed than they have the power to use. Section 29 of the CJA 1991 amended the MCA and provided that an offence is not to be regarded as more serious for sentencing purposes by reason of a person's previous convictions or his failure to respond to previous sentences. During the first six months of this provision's operation (October 1992–March 1993), there was widespread opposition to this rule from the magistracy, the judiciary and the police. Thirty magistrates resigned in protest, stating that it restricted their powers to give deterrent sentences on young offenders who continued to commit petty offences. Section 66 of the CJA 1993 restored the previous position. The court is now allowed to take into account any failures to respond to previous sentences when sentencing a defendant.

As amended by s 1(2) of the CJA 1993, s 1(2) of the CJA 1991 now provides that the court shall not pass a custodial sentence on an offender unless it is of the opinion that:

(a)   the offence or the combination of the offence and one or more offences associated with it, was so serious that only such a sentence can be justified for the offence; or

(b)   where the offence is a violent or sexual offence, that only such a sentence would be adequate to protect the public from serious harm from him.

The section's import is that if a non-custodial sentence can be 'justified' then custody should not be imposed. To be given as a sentence, custody must be seen as the only suitable option. In *Cox* (1992), it was suggested that a non-custodial sentence would not be justified if the offence was:

> ... the kind of offence ... which would make all right thinking members of the public, knowing all the facts, feel that justice had not been done by the passing of any sentence other than a custodial one.

When the court comes to assess the phrase 'so serious' in s 1, it must carry out a very similar test to the one it carried out before the CJA 1993 except that it may now consider the offence together with one or more associated offences. An 'associated offence' (s 31(2)) is one for which the offender is to be sentenced if he is convicted of it in the same proceedings, or sentenced for it at the same time, or one he asks to be taken into consideration.

If the accused consents to summary trial, then the magistrates proceed to summary trial. If he does not consent, the magistrates proceed as examining magistrates.

Where a magistrates' court has started to try an 'either way' case summarily, it may, before the conclusion of the prosecution evidence, change (without the consent of the accused) from a summary trial to transfer proceedings (under s 44 of the Criminal Justice and Public Order Act (CJPOA) 1994). If the bench finds that the evidence does not support the 'either way' offence with which the accused is charged but does allow for a conviction for a summary offence, they may proceed to try the lesser offence.

These procedures apply where the accused is 17 or older. Children (aged 10 to under 14)) and young persons (aged 14 to 16) appearing before magistrates on an indictable charge must normally be tried summarily except (a) where the charge is homicide, or (b) in the case of a young person, where the offence is one for which an adult could be sentenced to 14 years imprisonment or more, or (c) where a child or young person is charged jointly with an adult and the magistrates consider it necessary in the interests of justice that they be transferred for trial to the Crown Court (s 44 and Sched 4, Pt II, para 36 of the CJPOA 1994).

If the defendant does not consent to be tried summarily, then the magistrates proceed to initiate the transfer for trial procedure. If, though, after considering all the relevant matters, the court decides that trial on indictment is more suitable, this decision is final.

A defendant charged with an 'either way' offence who has elected for trial at the Crown Court will first have his case subject to committal proceedings. (A person charged with an indictable only offence now goes direct to the Crown Court: see 4.3.4.) These proceedings used to take the form of 'old style' committals (small trials) or 'new style' committals (or 'paper trials' where the evidence was just documentary). Following a recommendation by the Royal

Commission on Criminal Justice (1993, Cm 2263), committal proceedings were abolished by s 44 of the CJPOA 1994. The new system, however, of 'transfers for trial', which would have expedited the process of deciding whether a defendant should stand trial, encountered great difficulties in being implemented and was never brought into force. Section 44 of the Criminal Procedure and Investigations Act (CPIA) 1996 repeals s 44 of the CJPOA 1994, and, in effect, introduces a new, streamlined version of committal proceedings in which no oral evidence can be given.

The new system of committals is governed by s 47 and Sched 1 of the CPIA 1996. The effect of the new law is to abolish the 'old style' mini-trial committals and the right of the defendant to have witnesses called and cross-examined at the magistrates' court. Now, defendants may only use written evidence at committal stage like witness statements and depositions from the prosecution. Exhibits may also be considered. Both sides can make oral representations to the magistrates as to whether the defendant should be sent for trial or discharged.

The system thus remains largely unchanged with the exception of the exclusion of witness testimony. This will save witnesses from having to go through the ordeal of giving evidence twice. Time and money will also be saved. There can no longer be any unmeritorious requests for 'old style' committals made in the hope that witnesses will not turn up. Nevertheless, the new system also means that the defence will be deprived of the opportunity of testing the evidence and having the defendant discharged early during the proceedings if the witnesses do not come up to proof.

In a few limited circumstances, a case can reach the Crown Court without having passed through committal proceedings. This applies to serious fraud cases (s 4 of the CJA 1987) where the case complexity demands that it be managed from the outset by a Crown Court. The by-pass procedure also exists for certain cases involving children where there has been alleged violence, cruelty or a sexual element (s 53 of the CJA 1991).

Old style committal proceedings were expensive, and the proportion of all committals that they occupied rose from 8% in 1981 to 13% in 1986. The effectiveness of the sifting procedure designed to weed out very weak cases was called into doubt by the high acquittal rate in jury trials. How far the new system will be an improvement upon the old remains to be seen.

Either way offences: venue for trial

There has been great debate about changing the rules in relation to who should choose the venue for trial (magistrates or defendants), and a government Consultation Paper, *Determining Mode of Trial in Either way Cases* (August 1998), added further heat to the public discussion.

As noted above, the decision as to where an 'either way' case should be heard is made at a hearing before the magistrates. Where a defendant pleads guilty, the magistrates will proceed to convict, otherwise they will go on to determine the mode of trial. They may consider it is more appropriate for the case to be tried at the Crown Court, in which case they will decline jurisdiction and direct it there. If they decide to try it themselves, the defendant has the right to refuse and choose to be tried at the Crown Court.

Approximately 22,000 defendants charged with either way offences elected to be tried in the Crown Court in 1998. Crown Court trials cost the State about £8,000 per day, whereas a magistrates' court hearing costs less than £2,000.

In practice, a common problem is where the nature of the charge is very serious (for example, theft) so a conviction for it could be ruinous for a defendant, but the actual facts of the case are not so serious (for example, alleged theft of a milk bottle). Is such a case relatively trivial? Well, not, perhaps to the defendant! Now, the defendant can elect for trial at the Crown Court (which is much more expensive and prolonged).

At the heart of the debate is the possibility that people on potentially serious criminal charges will be denied a jury trial in front of their peers if magistrates decide that the matter should be dealt with by them, and that the only justification for such a sweeping change in legal procedure is to save money.

One of the options in the new paper would, if implemented, give magistrates the final say as to where some offenders are tried.

The government paper presents four possible options for reform of the current system in triable either way cases, which allows defendants to elect for a jury trial at the Crown Court if they wish to do so, even after magistrates have indicated that they are happy to hear their case.

The options are:

(1) maintaining the status quo defendants who are charged with offences that are triable either way can elect for trial by jury if they wish;

(2) reclassification of particular offences. Particular either way offences such as minor theft could be reclassified as triable only in the magistrates court;

(3) outright abolition of election for trial:

   (i) if parties cannot agree on a venue for trial, magistrates would decide where the case should be heard. Following representations from the defence, they would have regard to such considerations as the complexity of the case and the effect of conviction on the defendant for example.

   This approach was favoured by the Royal Commission on Criminal Justice which reported in 1993;

   (ii) the decision on venue for trial should rest entirely with magistrates after having listened to representations from the prosecutor and the defence.

This approach was favoured by the Narey Review of Delay in the Criminal Justice System published in 1997;

(4) removal of the right to elect for jury trial in certain cases the right of a defendant to elect for a jury trial would be removed where they have been prosecuted for an offence which is similar in nature to an earlier conviction.

The Narey Review of Delay in the Criminal Justice System indicated that there is considerable support for a change to the current system, although the general public were not consulted about this, and it is a matter of speculation what response would be drawn by a plebiscite on the issue. In 1999, the Home Secretary, Jack Straw, announced the government's intention to legislate in accordance with 3(ii) (above) (see (1999) *The Times*, 19 May; see Chapter 10).

4.3.3   Youth courts

Magistrates sit in these courts to try children and young persons. A child is someone who has not reached his 14th birthday. These private tribunals sit separately from the ordinary magistrates' court in order to protect the young defendants from publicity. There jurisdiction was enlarged by the CJA 1991, to include 17 year olds. There must be three justices to hear such a case, of whom a least one must be a man and one a woman. The public do not have access to such a court. The CJA 1991 allowed for parents to be required to attend in any case and it is mandatory in the case of a child or young person under the age of 16 unless such requirement would be unreasonable in the circumstances. The name or photograph of any person under 17 appearing in the case must not be printed in any newspaper or broadcast without the authority of the court or Home Secretary.

Apart from these arrangements which aim to keep young people out of the criminal environment of the ordinary courts, there are special provisions relating to punishments for this age group. The current maximum fine for a child is £250 and £1,000 for a young person. Members of both age groups may be made the subject of care orders, supervision orders, and compensation orders. A sentence in a young offender institution is possible for anyone with a minimum age of 15 years. The minimum age for imprisonment is 21. No criminal prosecution can be brought against someone under 10. Such people are irrebuttably presumed to be incapable of committing crime. Such a child who committed a crime could be brought before a youth court in care proceedings in which he or she could be made the subject of a care order.

4.3.4   Indictable offences – committal proceedings

Where the magistrates decide that an offence triable either way should be tried in the Crown Court, they hold committal proceedings (as described above).

Section 51 of the Crime and Disorder Act 1998

These proceedings were also held where the defendant was charged with, an indictable-only offence (for example, murder). If, having read the papers, the magistrates took the view that there was a *prima facie* case to answer, they had to transfer the defendant to the Crown Court for trial; if not, they had to discharge the defendant. Now, however, s 51 of the Crime and Disorder Act 1998 states that, where an adult is charged with an offence triable only on indictment, the court shall send him directly to the Crown Court for trial. Where he is also charged with an either way offence or a summary offence, he may be sent directly to trail for that as well, provided the magistrates believe that it is related to the indictable offence and, in the case of a summary offence, it is punishable with imprisonment or involves obligatory or discretionary disqualification from driving. This system is being piloted in some courts in 1999 with a view to extension nationally in due course.

- *Reporting committal proceedings*

   In the old-style committal proceedings, it was generally only the prosecution that would give evidence, with the defence reserving its arguments. Until 1967, this prosecution case was frequently reported on in the press so that it was virtually impossible to find an unbiased jury for the trial. A notorious instance of this was the case of Dr John Bodkin Adams in 1957. During the committal, deaths of patients other than the one for which he was to stand trial were referred to but were not afterwards part of the evidence at the trial. The law on reporting was eventually changed in the CJA 1967 and is now in the MCA 1980, as amended by the CJPOA 1994. There are restrictions now on any application for dismissal put in by the defence. It is thus an offence to report on any aspect of the case if reporting restrictions have not been lifted by the bench. The bare matters which may as a matter of course be reported are:
   - the identity of the court and the names of the examining magistrates;
   - the names, ages, addresses and occupations of the accused and witnesses;
   - the offence charged;
   - the names of the lawyers engaged in the case;
   - the decision of the court whether to commit or not and, if so, details of the committal, for example, to which court;
   - any arrangements for bail;
   - whether legal aid was granted.

   These restrictions, however, must be lifted by the magistrates if requested to do so by the accused. Where there are two or more accused and one objects to the reporting restrictions being lifted then the magistrates must not lift them unless they regard it to be in the interests of justice to do so.

- *Effectiveness*

Full committal proceedings were protracted and expensive. A government research project in 1987 found that their average duration was one hour and 15 minutes as opposed to 6.7 minutes for new-style 'paper' committals. The overall cost for committals was about £4 million a year (excluding the costs of the CPS and Legal Aid) of which £2.7 million was spent on full committals. That this system does not effectively achieve what it aims to do – act as a filter against cases with insufficient evidence – is testified to by the high acquittal rate on the direction of the judge in the High Court: of all those acquitted in Crown Court trials after pleading not guilty in 1990, for example, 16% were acquitted on the direction of the judge (mainly because the prosecution case was inadequate) and 42% of those acquitted were discharged by the judge because, for instance, the prosecution offered no evidence. The lists for Crown Court cases are growing relentlessly and there has been strong criticism of magistrates that they are unnecessarily reluctant to refuse to commit defendants in old-style committals. It now remains to be seen how effective the new system of transfers is.

- *Consistency of sentencing*

Concern is often expressed at the sometimes quite notable discrepancies in sentencing practices employed by different benches of magistrates. It might be that these variations are unavoidable in circumstances where the rigidity of fixed penalties is unacceptable for most offences and regional differences in types of prevalent crime prompt justices to have certain attitudes to particular offences. There are several research surveys which demonstrate the discrepancies in magistrates' sentencing. Tarling, for example (*Sentencing and Practice in Magistrates' Courts*, 1979, Home Office Study 98), showed that in the 30 courts he surveyed the use of probation varied between one and 12%, suspended sentences between four and 16%, and fines between 46 and 76%. There is a Home Office book, *The Sentence of the Court*, which explains desirable sentencing practice but its guidance cannot form the basis of an appeal and it is rather outdated, the latest edition being one from 1986.

- *Independence*

Magistrates' courts were often called 'police courts' from the time when they were situated in the same building, or adjacent to the local police station. There is criticism that as the magistrates still hear local police officers giving evidence so regularly, they become too credulous and trusting of the officers' evidence. There is also criticism that many magistrates are too suggestible under the influence of their clerks.

- *The future*

  The current system has the twin advantages of being relatively inexpensive to run (as the 29,000 lay justices are unsalaried) and allows for lay participation (albeit from a narrow social band) in a crucially important part of the criminal justice system. Any change to a system involving fully paid, legally qualified inferior judges or inquisitors would entail great expense for the exchequer.

4.3.5 The Access to Justice Act 1999 – magistrates' courts

Important changes to the magistrates' court system have been made by Pt V of the Access to Justice Act 1999.

Part V contains a range of provisions relating to magistrates and magistrates' courts:

- it provides for various changes to the organisation and management of magistrates' courts;

- it unifies the provincial and metropolitan stipendiary magistrates into a single bench;

- it removes the requirement for magistrates to sit on cases committed to the Crown Court for sentence; and enables the Crown Court, rather than a magistrates' court, to deal with breaches of community sentences imposed by the Crown Court;

- it extends and clarifies the powers of civilians to execute warrants; this is intended to enable this function to be transferred from the police to the magistrates' courts.

The government's objective is to develop a magistrates' court service which is effectively and efficiently managed, at a local level by local people, within a consistent national framework. The government announced its plans for developing this new framework in statements to both Houses of Parliament on 29 October 1997 (*Hansard*: House of Lords col 1057–67; House of Commons, col 901–14). As part of this programme of reform, the Act includes provisions to:

- Reform the organisation and management of the magistrates' courts by:
  - creating more flexible powers to alter the various territorial units that make up the magistrates' court service, and to allow summary cases to be heard outside the commission area in which they arose;
  - expanding the potential membership of magistrates' courts committees by removing the limit on co-opted members;
  - establishing a single authority to manage the magistrates' courts service in London;

- o   removing the requirement for justices' chief executives to be qualified lawyers, and transferring responsibility for certain administrative functions from justices' clerks to justices' chief executives; and

- o   giving the Lord Chancellor power to require all MCCs to procure common goods and services, where he considers this will lead to more effective or efficient administration;

- Unify the Provincial and Metropolitan stipendiary benches into a single bench of District Judge (Magistrates' Courts), able to sit in any magistrates' court in the country.

- Remove the requirement for lay magistrates to sit as judges in the Crown Court on committals for sentence.

- Extend and clarify the powers of civilians to execute warrants.

The new powers to change organisational units reflect the government's intention to develop a more coherent geographical structure for the criminal justice system as a whole. Common boundaries should enable the various criminal justice agencies to co-operate more effectively.

The administration of the magistrates' courts service is based on three organisational units – the magistrates' courts committee (MCC) area, the commission area and the petty sessions area. The MCC area is the unit on which the administration and organisation of the courts is based. MCCs are the bodies responsible for the administration of the magistrates' courts service. There are currently 96 MCCs in England and Wales. Each MCC appoints a justices' chief executive to manage the courts in its area.

The Justices of the Peace Act 1997 already provides power to change the boundaries of MCC areas. The government believes that a structure with fewer and larger areas would be more efficient and effective. The number of MCCs has been reduced in recent years by a series of amalgamations; this trend is likely to continue in future, as part of the policy of a greater alignment of boundaries between criminal justice agencies. The commission area is the unit on which the appointment of magistrates and the jurisdiction of the magistrates' courts to hear summary cases is based. Magistrates are appointed to a particular commission area, on the basis of where they reside; and most summary offences must be tried in the commission area where the alleged offence took place.

Historically, MCC and commission areas have aligned with one another and with county and metropolitan county borders. However, most commission areas are defined in primary legislation, and can be changed by secondary legislation only to reflect changes in local government boundaries. Increasingly, there are MCCs which cover two or more commission areas. These MCCs cannot transfer magistrates or cases between areas. The ability to change commission area boundaries is intended to enable MCCs to allocate cases, and deploy magistrates, between the courts in their MCC area more effectively and efficiently.

Most MCC areas are broken down into smaller areas, called petty sessions areas. These are the benches, the basic unit of local court organisation. Petty sessions areas are defined in terms of local authority boundaries. This can limit an MCC's ability to organise its structure effectively, particularly where amalgamation has occurred. As a result, the full benefits of amalgamation may not be realised.

The Act redefines the basis of these units, to allow MCCs to decide the most appropriate and efficient structure for their area. The Act also removes the artificial distinction between a petty sessions area and a 'petty sessional division' – a distinction which currently exists solely for the purposes of geographical identification.

Constitution of MCCs

Each MCC comprises up to 12 members and is composed primarily of lay magistrates, appointed by their peers, who undertake the task in addition to their magisterial duties. Individuals are appointed to the MCC on the basis of their skills and experience.

Where an MCC believes that additional skills are required which cannot be found amongst the applicants for membership of the MCC, they may co-opt individuals, who need not be magistrates.

Currently, the number of co-options is limited to two. These may be in addition to the maximum membership of 12. In addition, the Lord Chancellor may appoint up to two individuals to an MCC.

Neither lay magistrates nor co-opted and appointed non-magistrates receive remuneration for their committee work. The Act removes the limit on the number of co-opted and appointed members, and provides power for MCCs to remunerate those members.

MCCs are the bodies responsible for the administration of the magistrates' court service. Local authorities are responsible for providing the accommodation needed by an MCC and for paying the expenses it incurs. Local authorities recoup 80% of the net cost from the Lord Chancellor's Department in the form of specific grant. In cases where an MCC area encompasses two or more authorities, the costs and accommodation are divided equitably between the authorities, but a 'lead' authority is appointed to receive the grant and pay the expenses.

A single authority for London

The Greater London area comprises a significantly larger number of MCCs (22) and local authorities (33) than any other area. The consequences of this, for issues such as funding and accommodation, are such that amalgamation under the provisions of the Justices of the Peace 1997 is not practical. The Act provides for the establishment of a Greater London Magistrates' Courts Authority, with special provision for its funding, accommodation, constitution and other necessary powers to enable the existing MCCs to be amalgamated effectively.

Justices' clerks and justices' chief executives

Most cases in magistrates' courts are heard by magistrates who are not qualified lawyers. They rely heavily on the legal advice of justices' clerks and their deputies, acting as court clerks. All justices' clerks are legally qualified and may have certain powers of a single magistrate delegated to them.

The post of justices' chief executive (JCE) was introduced in 1994, and every MCC has appointed a JCE. The JCE supports the MCC in planning and managing the efficient and effective administration of the courts within the area of the MCC. At present, however, justices' clerks continue to be responsible in statute for many administrative matters. In practice, many of these tasks are delegated to administrators. In 1998, the government published a Consultation Paper which considered the functions of justices' clerks (*The Future Role of Justices' Clerks*, Lord Chancellor's Department, September 1998).

The provisions in the Act relating to the qualifications and functions of justices' chief executives are intended to clarify the role of the JCE and the lines of responsibility and accountability between the JCE, the MCC and the other staff of the MCC; and to achieve a clearer distinction between the roles of JCEs and justices' clerks. The primary function of justices' clerks will continue to be the giving of legal advice to lay magistrates. Under the new management structure, JCE will be able to delegate any administrative function to any staff, including the justices' clerks, depending on local needs.

Unification of the stipendiary bench

The Act unifies the stipendiary bench, establishing the 92 stipendiary magistrates as a unified bench of professional judges with a new judicial title – District Judge (Magistrates' Courts). In April 1998, the government published a Consultation Paper about creating a unified stipendiary bench with national jurisdiction (*Unification of the Stipendiary Bench: Consultation Paper*, Lord Chancellor's Department, April 1998), with the intention of increasing the efficiency of the administration of justice at summary level.

The effect of this provision is to create a unified national bench, headed by a single judge, which can be deployed anywhere in the country to deal with fluctuations in workload as and when they occur, or with particularly complex cases that arise. The new District Judges (Magistrates' Courts) will be able to exercise jurisdiction in every commission area of England and Wales. The new title is intended to recognise more fully the status of stipendiaries as members of the professional judiciary. The new law has amended ss 11–22 of the Justices of the Peace Act 1997.

The main differences from the old law are as follows.

- Appointments are to be made without reference to any specific Commission area within England and Wales. A District Judge (Magistrates' Courts) has jurisdiction for every commission area);

- A Senior District Judge (Chief Magistrate) will be appointed as a national head of all District Judges (Magistrates' Courts). Previously, there was a Chief Metropolitan Stipendiary Magistrate, but no equivalent head of the provincial stipendiary bench;

- The Lord Chancellor will be able to remove one of these judges from office on the grounds of 'incapacity or misbehaviour'. Previously, the Lord Chancellor could remove a metropolitan stipendiary from office on the grounds of 'inability or misbehaviour'. Provincial stipendiaries could only be removed from office on the Lord Chancellor's recommendation, but no criteria were specified in statute (s 11(3)(b) of the JPA 1997).

  The test and procedure for removal have been unified to remove the inconsistency. 'Incapacity' has replaced 'inability' to reflect a similar change relating to Circuit Judges under the Courts Act 1971. The change of language brings these judicial posts into line;

- The Lord Chancellor may appoint Deputy District Judges (Magistrates' Courts) (new s 10B(1)). Unlike the appointment of acting stipendiary magistrates under the previous provisions, these appointments are not limited to three months duration, or solely permitted for the purpose of avoiding delays in the administration of justice:

  - s 10A(1): the 'seven year general qualification' is defined in the Courts and Legal Services Act 1990 as 'a right of audience in any class of proceedings in the county courts or magistrates' courts';

  - s 10D(2): this provision maintains specific exclusions of the rule codified under the Stipendiary Magistrates Act 1858, which allowed a single stipendiary to exercise the jurisdiction of two lay justices. Any express provision to the contrary made after that Act came into force survives by virtue of this section;

  - s 10D(6): s 65 of the Magistrates' Courts Act 1980 defines family proceedings. A stipendiary magistrate may hear these cases, subject to any rules and statutes specific to family proceedings (for example, the Children Act 1989).

Committals for sentence

Currently, cases committed to the Crown Court for sentence must be heard in the Crown Court by a bench composed of a High Court Judge, Circuit Judge or Recorder sitting with between two and four justices of the peace. In October 1997, a new procedure was implemented by which defendants are required to indicate whether they intend to plead guilty or not guilty, before the decision is made about whether the case should be heard in the magistrates' court or the Crown Court (s 17A of the Magistrates' Courts Act 1980, as amended by s 49 of the Criminal Procedure and Investigations Act 1996). This has led to a significant increase in the number of cases committed to the Crown Court solely for sentence, and an increase in the seriousness of the cases being committed for sentence. (Previously, all more serious cases were committed for trial, although many defendants subsequently pleaded guilty.)

The change in procedure has meant that magistrates are dealing in the Crown Court with cases which are outside their normal range of experience. In 1999, the government issued a consultation paper (*Magistrates sitting as judges in the Crown Court*, Lord Chancellor's Department, August 1998) which examined the role of magistrates in the Crown Court. The majority of responses agreed that the requirement for magistrates to sit on committals for sentence should be removed.

Warrant execution

Until now, the police have been primarily responsible for arresting fine defaulters and those in breach of community sentences. Increasingly, however, some police forces have given this work a low priority. The government therefore intends to transfer responsibility for the execution of warrants from the police to the magistrates' courts. The intention is to ensure that fines and community sentences are seen as credible and effective punishments, by ensuring that they can be effectively enforced.

A number of MCCs already employ civilian enforcement officers (CEOs), who work with the police under local arrangements. However, under current legislation, the powers of CEOs are unclear in a number of respects. In order to enable the courts to take on this new function effectively, the Act contains provisions to clarify and extend the powers of appropriate civilians to execute certain kinds of warrant issued by a magistrates' court.

The provisions relating to warrants are intended to enhance the credibility of fines and community sentences, by improving the effectiveness of their enforcement. This involves a transfer of resources from the police to magistrates' courts. The government has stated its intention to consult individual MCCs about the additional resources they require to implement the transfer, but no significant change in overall public expenditure on this function is expected. Over time, it is hoped to achieve an increase in the proportion of fines collected of at least 5%. (In 1996–97, the courts imposed over one million fines, worth £144 million in total. In the same period, unpaid fines to the value of £52 million, mostly imposed in previous years, had to be written off.)

The Act extends and clarifies the range of warrants issued by a magistrates' court which may be executed by civilian enforcement officers (CEOs), employed by MCCs, local authorities or police authorities.

The warrants in question will be listed in an order made jointly by the Lord Chancellor and the Home Secretary. It is intended that the list should include warrants of distress, commitment, arrest or detention in connection with the payment of any sum, and also warrants of arrest issued in connection with breaches of a range of non-financial penalties. A list of the warrants that the government intends CEOs to be able to execute includes warrants made under the Child Support Act 1991 and the Council Tax (Administration and Enforcement) Regulations 1992.

The Act allows MCCs to approve and appoint private enforcement agencies to execute certain kinds of warrant. Some MCCs already use private enforcement agencies or bailiffs to execute distress warrants. However, there is presently some uncertainty about whether a warrant can be 'directed' to such a person within the meaning of s 125(2) of the Magistrates' Courts Act 1980 unless it refers to him by name. The Act clarifies the law, so that warrants can be addressed to approved agencies for the area concerned, rather than just to an individual, named, bailiff. In future, the authorised employees of approved enforcement agencies will be able to execute the same range of warrants as CEOs anywhere in England and Wales.

These provisions significantly enlarge the use of private commercial agencies to perform what many would see as proper matters for only properly trained and accountable police officers or officials to perform. Is this enlargement of the private and for-profit sector within the criminal justice system a desirable development? It can be argued that, without it, the criminal justice system would come under unnecessary and severe strain as police officers, much-needed on patrol and responding to dangerous crime, would be occupied in chasing debtors. On the other hand, the entry of private commercial companies into the criminal justice system has been marked by periodic crises. In November 1998, for example, there was public scandal at the extent of injury to prison officers and trainers, and criminal damage at Britain's first private penal institution for young offenders. Riots at the Medway Secure Training Centre in Kent caused £100,000 of damage and the police were called in to deal with the rampaging 12–14 year olds ((1998) *The Times*, 13 November).

4.4   The Crown Court

Until 1971, the main criminal courts were the Assizes and the Quarter Sessions. These courts did not sit continuously and were not held in locations which corresponded with centres of population as had been the case when they developed. The system was very inefficient as circuit judges wasted much time simply travelling from one town on the circuit to the next and many defendants spent long periods in jail awaiting trial.

Change was made following the *Report of the Beeching Royal Commission on Assizes and Quarter Sessions* (1969). The Courts Act 1971 abolished the Assizes and Quarter Sessions. These were replaced by a single Crown Court, a part of the Supreme Court of Judicature. The Crown Court is not a local court like the magistrates' court but a single court which sits in over 90 centres. England and Wales are divided into six circuits each with its own headquarters and staff. The centres are divided into three tiers. In first-tier centres, High Court judges hear civil and criminal cases whereas circuit judges and recorders hear only criminal cases. Second-tier centres are served by the same types of judge but hear criminal cases only. At third-tier centres, recorders and circuit judges hear just criminal cases.

Criminal offences are divided into four classes according to their gravity. Class 1 offences are the most serious, including treason and murder and are usually tried by a High Court judge; exceptionally he may transfer a murder case (including attempts) to be heard by a circuit judge approved for this purpose by the Lord Chief Justice. Class 2 offences include manslaughter and rape and are subject to similar provisions. Class 3 offences include all remaining offences triable only on indictment and are usually tried by a High Court judge although releases of cases to circuit judges are more common here. Class 4 offences include robbery, grievous bodily harm and all offences triable 'either way' and are not normally tried by a High Court judge.

4.4.1 The judges

The High Court judges are usually from the Queen's Bench Division. Circuit judges are full time appointments made by the Queen on the advice of the Lord Chancellor. They are drawn from advocates with at least 10 years' experience of Crown Court practice (s 71 of the CLSA 1990) or lawyers who have been recorders. Appointment is also possible for someone who has had three years' experience in a number of other quasi-judicial offices like that of the stipendiary magistrate. Circuit judges retire at the age of 72, or 75 if the Lord Chancellor thinks it in the public interest.

A circuit judge may be removed from office by the Lord Chancellor on the grounds of incapacity or misbehaviour (s 17(4) of the Courts Act 1971). This right has not been exercised since 1983 when Judge Bruce Campbell, an Old Bailey judge, was removed from office a week after being convicted of two charges of smuggling.

To qualify for appointment as a recorder, a person must have 10 years' experience of advocacy in the Crown or county courts. Justices of the Peace may also sit in the Crown Court, provided they are with one of the types of judge mentioned above. It is mandatory for between two and four JPs to sit when the Crown Court is hearing an appeal or dealing with persons committed for sentence by a magistrates' court.

4.4.2 Jurisdiction

The Crown Court hears all cases involving trial on indictment. It also hears appeals from those convicted summarily in the magistrates' courts. At the conclusion of the hearing, it has the power to confirm, reverse or vary any part of the decision under appeal (s 48(2) of the Supreme Court Act 1981). If the appeal is decided against the accused, the Crown Court has the power to impose any sentence which the magistrates could have imposed, including one which is harsher than the one originally imposed on the defendant.

4.4.3   Delay

Defendants committed to the Crown Court to be tried will have to wait an average of three months for their case to come to trial. This wait is sometimes in custody. Ever since the Streatfield Committee Report recommended in 1961 that the maximum time a defendant should have to wait after committal for trial should be eight weeks, there have been many schemes to help achieve this aim but none has been particularly successful. Since 1985, for example, a person charged with an offence triable 'either way' can request the prosecution to furnish him with information (in the form of witness statements, a summary of the case, etc) of the case against him. This was aimed at increasing the number of guilty pleas by showing to the defendant at an early stage the strength of the prosecution's case.

The slowness of the trial procedure, the increasing number of annual trials and the relatively small number of judges to hear the cases all contribute to this problem. In 1990, the Crown Court dealt with 119,828 defendants, of whom 33,000 elected for trial before a jury on a plea of not guilty. These cases were to be heard by just 420 circuit judges and about 750 part time recorders. When one remembers that the average time to try a case on a plea of not guilty is about seven hours (one and a half court days), the burden of work on the courts becomes clear. The consequent delay has very serious repercussions on the criminal justice system: justice delayed is justice denied. The accuracy of testimony becomes less reliable the longer the gap between the original reception of the data by a witness and his or her account of it in court. Also important is the stress and pain for those innocent defendants who have to wait so long before their case can be put to a jury.

The largest ever study of Crown Court cases, undertaken by Zander and Henderson for the Runciman Commission, made some worrying findings. Their research was based on responses to questionnaires by more than 22,000 people involved in 3,000 Crown Court cases. The views of lawyers, judges, clerks, jurors, police and defendants were all canvassed. There were convictions in 8% of cases that defence lawyers thought weak, 6% that prosecution barristers thought weak and 4% that judges thought weak – suggesting that innocent people were still being convicted in significant numbers. Further, 31 defendants said that they had pleaded guilty to offences they had not committed. Their reasons were varied: to avoid a trial; to gain a less severe sentence or because they had been advised to do so by their lawyers.

Another worrying discovery, since poor defence lawyers have recently been cited as contributing to miscarriages of justice, is the large number of Crown Court cases (about one-third) that were being dealt with by clerks rather than by trained, qualified solicitors. Some defendants met with their barrister for the first time on the morning of their trial and for about one-third of these cases the conference lasted for just 15 minutes. In about one-third of all cases, the barristers only received their instructions the day before the trial.

4.4.4 Magistrates' courts v Crown Courts

For offences triable 'either way', there has been much debate about the merits of each venue. Each year, about 25,000 defendants elect for trial at the Crown Court only to enter a guilty plea at the last moment and this costs the Crown Prosecution Service about £7 million in wasted preparation. One of the reasons defendants do this is that prosecution cases often fall apart during the delay before a Crown Court hearing, allowing the defendant to go free. (See 10.3.4, below.) Another is that juries cannot be compelled to give reasons for convicting, unlike magistrates, who can be required to justify their reasons in writing for review in the High Court which can overturn convictions or acquittals. Thus, there is a greater chance with jury convictions that an appeal court will regard a conviction (should there be one) as unsafe and unsatisfactory because the jury's reasons for having convicted will not be known. Thus, a defendant who suspects that he might be convicted can reasonably prefer to be convicted by a jury than by a magistrate because the former do not and cannot give reasons for their verdicts and are therefore perhaps easier to appeal. Jury verdicts are arguably more likely to be regarded as unsafe on appeal because it will not be known whether some improper factor (like a judge's misdirection) had entered their deliberation. The reports of the Court of Appeal (Criminal Division) contain many cases where the court states that a conviction should be quashed because the jury might have been influenced by a misleading statement from the judge. It might be said that a defendant should prefer the magistrates' court as the sentencing is generally lower but when the defendants antecedents are known (after a conviction) he can still be committed to the Crown Court for sentence, so the magistrates' courts are not really preferable to a defendant with a criminal record who fears another conviction is likely.

4.5 Criminal appeals

The process of appeal depends upon how a case was originally tried, whether summarily or on indictment.

4.5.1 Appeals from magistrates' courts

Two routes of appeal are possible. The first route allows only a defendant to appeal. The appeal is to a judge and between two and four magistrates sitting in the Crown Court and can be (a) against conviction (only if the defendant pleaded not guilty) on points of fact or law, or (b) against sentence. Such an appeal will take the form of a new trial (a trial *de novo*).

Alternatively, the defendant can appeal 'by way of case stated' to the High Court (the Divisional Court of the Queen's Bench Division). This court consists of two or more judges (usually two) of whom one will be a Lord Justice of Appeal. Here, either the defence or the prosecution may appeal but the grounds are limited to: (a) a point of law; or (b) that the magistrates acted beyond their jurisdiction. If the prosecution succeeds on appeal the court can direct the magistrates to convict and pass the appropriate sentence. There is also an appeal by way of case stated from the Crown Court to the Divisional Court when the Crown Court has heard an appeal from the magistrates' court.

Appeal from the Divisional Court is to the House of Lords. Either side may appeal but only on a point of law and only if the Divisional Court certifies the point to be one of general public importance. Leave to appeal must also be granted either by the Court of Appeal or the House of Lords.

4.5.2 Appeals from the Crown Court

Appeals from the Crown Court lie to the Court of Appeal (Criminal Division) which hears appeals against conviction and sentence. This court, replacing the Court of Criminal Appeal, was established in 1966. The Division usually sits in at least two courts: one composed of the Lord Chief Justice sitting with two judges of the Queen's Bench Division and the other of a Lord Justice of Appeal and two Queen's Bench judges. The court hears about 8,000 criminal appeals and applications per year. In 1997, it heard 8,675 cases, 2,318 of which were appeals against conviction and 6,357 of which concerned sentence.

Until 1996, s 2 of the Criminal Appeal Act read:

2(1) Except as provided by this Act, the Court of Appeal shall allow an appeal against conviction if they think:

(a)   that the verdict of the jury should be set aside on the ground that, under all the circumstances of the case, it is unsatisfactory or unsafe; or

(b)   that the judgment of the court of trial should be set aside on the ground of a wrong decision of any question of law; or

(c)   that there was a material irregularity in the course of the trial,

and in any other case shall dismiss the appeal:

provided that the court may, notwithstanding that they are of opinion that the point raised in the appeal might be decided in favour of the appellant, dismiss the appeal if they consider that no miscarriage of justice has actually occurred.

January 1996 saw the introduction of the many sections of the Criminal Appeal Act (CAA) 1995. The introduction of ss 1, 2 and 4 of the Act bring particularly significant changes to the criminal appeal system.

Section 1 amends the CAA 1968 so as to bring an appeal against conviction, an appeal against a verdict of not guilty by reason of insanity, and an appeal against a finding of disability, *on a question of law alone* into line with other appeals against conviction and sentence (that is, those involving questions of fact, or mixtures of law and fact). Now, all appeals against conviction and sentence must first have leave of the Court of Appeal or a certificate of fitness for appeal from the trial judge before the appeal can be taken. Before the new Act came into force, it was possible to appeal without the consent of the trial judge or Court of Appeal on a point of law alone. In Parliament, the reason for this change was given as the need to 'provide a filter mechanism for appeals on a ground of law alone which are wholly without merit' (HC Official Report, SC B (Criminal Appeal Bill) Col 6, 21 March 1995).

Section 2 changes the grounds for allowing an appeal under the CAA 1968. Under the old law, the Court of Appeal was required to allow an appeal where: (1) the conviction, verdict or finding should have been set aside on the ground that, under all the circumstances, it was unsafe or unsatisfactory; or (2) that the judgment of the court of trial or the order of the court giving effect to the verdict or finding should be set aside on the ground of a wrong decision of law; or (3) that there was a material irregularity in the course of the trial. In all three situations, the Court of Appeal was allowed to dismiss the appeal if it considered that no miscarriage of justice had actually occurred. The law now requires the Court of Appeal to allow an appeal against conviction under s 1 of the CAA 1968, an appeal against verdict under s 12 (insanity) or an appeal against a finding (disability) if it thinks that the conviction, verdict or finding is 'unsafe' (as opposed to the old law which used the 'unsafe or *unsatisfactory*' formula).

During the parliamentary passage of the Act, there was much heated debate about whether the new provisions were designed to narrow the grounds of appeal. That would amount to a tilt in favour of the State, in that it would make it harder for (wrongly) convicted people to appeal. Government ministers insisted that the effect of the new law was simply to re-state or consolidate the practice of the Court of Appeal. One government spokesman said that:

In dispensing with the word 'unsatisfactory', we agree with the Royal Commission on criminal justice that there is no real difference between 'unsafe' and 'unsatisfactory'; the Court of Appeal does not distinguish between the two.

Retaining the word 'unsatisfactory' would imply that we thought there was a real difference and would only lead to confusion.

There were many attempts during the legislation's passage to insert the words 'or may be unsafe' after the word 'unsafe'. The Law Society, the Bar, Liberty, and JUSTICE called on the government to make such a change. Also opposed to the use of the single word 'unsafe' was the eminent criminal law expert Professor JC Smith. He has argued cogently that there are many cases where a conviction has been seen as 'unsatisfactory' rather than 'unsafe', so there is a need for both words. Sometimes, the Court of Appeal might be convinced that the defendant is guilty (so the conviction is 'safe') but still wish to allow the appeal because fair play according to the rules must be seen to be done. Accepting improperly extracted confessions (violating s 76 of Police and Criminal Evidence Act (PACE) 1984) simply because it might seem obvious that the confessor is guilty will promote undesirable interrogation practices because police officers would think that even if they break the rules any resulting confession will nevertheless be allowed as evidence.

Professor Smith has given the example ([1995] NLJ 534) of where there has been a serious breach of the rules of evidence. In *Algar* (1954), the former wife of the defendant testified against him about matters during the marriage. The Court of Appeal allowed his appeal against conviction but Lord Goddard said: 'Do not think that we are doing this because we think that you are an innocent man. We do not. We think that you are a scoundrel.' The idea behind such remarks is that rules are rules, and the rules of evidence must be obeyed in order to ensure justice. Once you start to accept breaches of the rule as being justified by outcome (ends justifying means), then the whole law of evidence could begin to collapse.

The proposal to include 'or might be unsafe' was rejected for the reason probably best summarised by Lord Taylor, the then Lord Chief Justice, who argued in the Lords, that there was no merit in including the words 'or may be unsafe' as the implication of such doubt is already inherent in the word 'unsafe'.

Section 4 provides a unified test for the receipt of fresh evidence in the Court of Appeal. Under the old law, the Court of Appeal had a discretion under s 23(1)(c) of the CAA 1968 to receive fresh evidence of any witness if it was thought necessary or expedient in the interests of justice. Section 23(2) added a duty to receive new evidence which was relevant, credible, and admissible, and which could not reasonably have been adduced at the original trial. There was often much argument about whether new evidence should be received under the court's discretion or its duty. Gradually, the 'duty' principles came to be merged into the 'discretion' principles. The aim of the latest amendment is to reflect the current practice of the court. The general discretion under s 23(1) has been retained, but the 'duty' principle has been replaced with a set of criteria which the court must consider. They are:

- whether the evidence appears to the court to be capable of belief;

- whether it appears to the court that the evidence may afford any ground for allowing the appeal;

- whether the evidence would have been admissible at the trial on the issue under appeal; and

- whether there is a reasonable explanation for the failure to adduce the evidence at trial.

Only the accused may appeal. No leave to appeal is required if the appeal is against conviction on a point of law but it is needed for appeals on points of fact or mixed fact and law. Leave is also required for appeals against sentence.

Under s 36 of the CJA 1972, the Attorney General can refer a case which has resulted in an acquittal to the Court of Appeal where he believes the decision to have been questionably lenient on a point of law. The Court of Appeal deals just with the point of law and the defendant's acquittal is not affected even if the court decides the point against the defendant. It merely clarifies the law for future cases.

The CJA 1988 (ss 35–36) allows the Attorney General to refer indictable-only cases to the Court of Appeal where the sentence at trial is regarded as unduly lenient. The court can impose a harsher sentence.

Following the determination of an appeal by the Court of Appeal or by the Divisional Court, either the prosecution or the defence may appeal to the House of Lords. Leave from the court below or the House of Lords must be obtained and two other conditions fulfilled according to s 33 if the CAA 1968:

- the court below must certify that a point of law of general public importance is involved; and

- either the court below or the House of Lords must be satisfied that the point of law is one which ought to be considered by the House of Lords.

In the wake of a string of notorious miscarriages of justice coming to light in the late 1980s and early 1990s, and its remit to investigate how these occurred and how they could best be avoided, the Runciman Commission made a number of recommendations that are relevant to our discussion here. It suggested that s 2(1) of the CAA 1968 should be redrafted and the grounds of appeal should be reduced to a single broad ground which would give the court greater flexibility. The law, it states, should be made clear that the court can allow an appeal even if there is no new evidence and where the jury were properly directed by the trial judge if, after reviewing the case, the court concludes the verdict is or may be unsafe. Recommendation 320 of the Commission's report says that in considering whether to receive fresh evidence, the Court of Appeal should take a broad approach to the question whether the fresh evidence was available to the trial court. This, coupled with Recommendation 321, could afford a significant change to appellants who have been disadvantaged by poor defence lawyers. The latter recommendation says that where an appeal is based on an alleged error by trial lawyers, the test to be applied by the Court of Appeal should not be confined to whether there was 'flagrantly incompetent advocacy'. The test to be applied to fresh evidence is (Recommendation 322) 'whether it is capable of disbelief'.

The High Court can quash tainted acquittals under s 54 of the Criminal Procedure and Investigations Act 1996. An acquittal is 'tainted' where someone has since been convicted of conspiring to pervert the course of justice in the case by interfering with the jury.

4.5.3   The Access to Justice Act 1999 – jurisdiction

Section 61 of the Access to Justice Act 1999 establishes the jurisdiction of the High Court to hear cases stated by the Crown Court for an opinion of the High Court. This part of the Act (Pt IV) enables these and certain other applications to the High Court to be listed before a single judge. It provides for the appointment of a Vice President of the Queen's Bench Division. It also prohibits the publication of material likely to identify a child involved in proceedings under the Children Act 1989 before the High Court or a county court; and allows for under 14 year olds to attend criminal trials.

Jurisdiction of single judge of High Court

The Act allows certain applications to be routinely heard by a single judge of the High Court. It does this by removing an obstacle that exists in the current legislation by which the route of appeal for these cases is to the House of Lords, but the Administration of Justice Act 1960 provides that the House of Lords will only hear appeals in these matters from a Divisional Court (that is, more than one judge) of the High Court. The 1999 Act (ss 63–65) amends the 1960 Act, so that the House of Lords can hear appeals from a single High Court judge. It will then be possible to make rules of court to provide for these cases to be heard by a single judge, while enabling the judge to refer particularly complex cases to a Divisional Court.

The cases in question include:

- appeals by way of case stated in criminal causes and matters;

- appeals from inferior (civil and criminal) courts and tribunals in contempt of court cases;

- criminal applications for habeas corpus.

4.5.4   Judicial Committee of the Privy Council

The Judicial Committee of the Privy Council was created by the Judicial Committee Act 1833. Under the Act, a special committee of the Privy Council was set up to hear appeals from the dominions. The cases are heard by the judges (without wigs or robes) in a committee room in London. The committee's decision is not a judgment but an 'advice' to the Monarch, who is counselled that the appeal be allowed or dismissed.

The Committee is the final court of appeal for certain Commonwealth countries which have retained this option and from some independent members and associate members of the Commonwealth. The committee comprises Privy Councillors who hold (or have held) high judicial office. In most cases, which come from places such as Hong Kong and Jamaica, the Committee comprises five Lords of Appeal in Ordinary, sometimes assisted by a judge from the country concerned.

Most of the appeals heard by the Committee are civil cases. In the rare criminal cases, it is only on matters involving legal questions that appeals are heard. The Committee does not hear appeals against criminal sentence.

The decisions of the Privy Council are very influential in English courts because they concern points of law that are applicable in this jurisdiction and they are pronounced upon by Lords of Appeal in Ordinary, in a way which is thus tantamount to a House of Lords' ruling. These decisions, however, are, technically, of persuasive precedent only although they are normally followed by English courts; see, for example, the Criminal Appeal case *Abbot v R* (1977). This was an appeal from Trinidad and Tobago. The Privy Council ruled that duress is no defence to the perpetrator of murder.

4.5.5   Royal Commission on Criminal Justice

Research undertaken for the Royal Commission by Kate Malleson of the London School of Economics found that judges' mistakes are by far the most common ground for successful appeals against conviction. The research discovered that in about 80% of cases where convictions were quashed, there had been an error at the trial; in most instances it was judicial error.

Of 300 appeals in 1990, just over one-third were successful. Of those appealing, almost two-thirds of defendants appealed against conviction on the ground that the trial judge had made a crucial mistake and, of those, 43% succeeded in having their convictions quashed. Sixteen defendants were vindicated by the Court of Appeal in claims that the judge's summing up to the jury was biased or poor; a further 42 convictions were quashed because the judge was wrong about the law or evidence.

This research was critical of the way the Court of Appeal failed to consider cases where fresh evidence had emerged since the trial or where there was a 'lurking doubt' about the conviction. The Report urges that the court is given a new role allowing it to investigate the events leading up to a conviction.

The Royal Commission was set up, under the chairmanship of Viscount Runciman, in March 1991, after the release of the Birmingham Six (an important case in a series of notorious miscarriages of justice in which people were found to have been wrongly convicted and sentenced for serious crimes). It reported in July 1993 with 352 recommendations, largely designed to prevent wrongful conviction. Several of the recommendations are relevant to discussion of the criminal courts. The numbers here refer to those of the recommendations in the Report.

The Commission recommended (331) that the Home Secretary's power to refer cases to the Court of Appeal under s 17 of the CAA 1968 should be removed and a new body, the Criminal Cases Review Authority, should be set up to consider allegations (332) that a miscarriage of justice might have occurred. The authority should have 'operational independence' (333) with a chairman appointed by the Queen on the advice of the Prime Minister. The authority should be independent of the court structure (336) and should refer meritorious cases directly to the Court of Appeal. There should be neither a right of appeal nor a right to judicial review (340) in relation to decisions reached by the authority. The authority should consist of both lawyers and lay people, should be supported by a staff of lawyers and (344) should devise its own rules and procedures. It should be able to discuss cases direct with applicants (345) and should have powers (347) to direct its own investigations. These recommendations were largely met by the terms of the CAA 1995.

The CAA 1995 legislates for the new Criminal Cases Review Commission (CCRC) which was established in 1997. The CCRC took over the Home Secretary's power (under s 17 of the CAA 1968) to reinvestigate already unsuccessfully appealed cases and refer back to Court of Appeal cases of suspected miscarriage of justice. The organisation Justice has expressed doubts about the independence of the CCRC as its members are to be government appointees. The wide power to reinvestigate cases where there appears to be a 'real possibility' (s 13) of miscarriage has been generally greeted with approval but it is a matter of regret in some quarters that those reinvestigating cases will not be CCRC investigators but, usually, police officers (s 19). As many allegations of injustice involve accusations against the police, there is a school of thought suggesting that a manifestly impartial, outside body should be responsible for the reinvestigation. In *R v Secretary of State for the Home Department ex p Hickey* (1994), it was held that when the Home Secretary, on receiving a petition from somebody wishing to have his case referred back to the Court of Appeal, makes inquiries and thereby obtains fresh evidence, fairness requires that he must disclose this new evidence to the petitioner. It is assumed this principle of openness will now also apply to the CCRC.

4.5.6   Criminal Cases Review Commission

The Criminal Cases Review Commission (CCRC) is an independent body set up under the Criminal Appeal Act 1995. The CCRC came into being on 1 January 1997. It is responsible for investigating suspected miscarriages of criminal justice in England, Wales and Northern Ireland. This function was previously carried out through the office of the Home Secretary. He would make occasional referrals of cases back to the Court of Appeal when a unit of civil servants in the Home Office evaluated a case (which had otherwise exhausted the formal court appeal system) as warranting further consideration. Over 250 cases were transferred from the Home Office around 31 March 1997, when the Commission took over responsibility for casework.

There are 14 CCRC members from a wide variety of backgrounds. Any decision to refer a case to the relevant court of appeal (the Court of Appeal (Criminal Division) or the High Court) has to be taken by a committee of at least three members. The CCRC considers whether or not there is a real possibility that the conviction, finding, verdict or sentence would not be upheld were a reference to be made.

In order to establish that there is a real possibility of an appeal succeeding regarding a conviction, there has to be:

- an argument or evidence which has not been raised during the trial or at appeal; or

• exceptional circumstances.

In order to establish that there is a real possibility of an appeal succeeding against a sentence, there has to be a legal argument or information about the individual, or the offence, which was not raised in court during the trial or at appeal.

Other than in exceptional circumstances, the Commission can only consider cases in which an appeal through the ordinary judicial appeal process has failed and, once a decision is taken to refer a case to the relevant court of appeal, the Commission has no other involvement.

The CCRC referred the notorious case of Derek William Bentley to the Court of Appeal. Mr Bentley was convicted of the murder of PC Sidney Miles at the Central Criminal Court on 11 December 1952. Mr Bentley did not actually shoot the officer. The gun was fired by his accomplice in a failed burglary attempt but Mr Bentley was convicted under the principles of 'joint enterprise', even though he was being held by a police officer under arrest metres away from where his accomplice fired the pistol. An appeal against conviction was heard by the Court of Criminal Appeal on 13 January 1953 and dismissed. Mr Bentley was hanged on 28 January 1953.

Bentley's conviction and sentence were the subject of numerous representations to the Home Office. In July 1993, on the recommendation of the Home Secretary, Her Majesty The Queen, in the exercise of the Royal Prerogative of Mercy, granted to Mr Bentley a posthumous pardon limited to sentence.

Following submissions from the applicants' solicitors and the completion of its own inquiries, the CCRC concluded that Mr Bentley's conviction should be reconsidered by the Court of Appeal. The trial was seen as unfair in a number of respects, for example, the fact that, although 18, Bentley had a mental age of 11 was kept a secret from the jury, and the judge's summing up to the jury was astonishingly biased in favour of the police. In August 1998, on a momentous day in legal history, the Court of Appeal cleared Bentley of the murder for which he was hanged 46 years earlier. In giving judgment, the Lord Chief Justice, Lord Bingham, said: '... the summing up in this case was such as to deny the appellant that fair trial which is the birthright of every British citizen.'

The CCRC cannot overturn a conviction or change a sentence. In those cases where specific criteria are met (essentially where there is new evidence or new argument), the Commission can refer a case to the Court of Appeal (in the case of Crown Court convictions) or the Crown Court (in the case of magistrates' court convictions). Only about 5% of new cases received by the Commission since 1997 have been against summary convictions.

The CCRC Annual Report for 1999 notes that 44 cases had been referred to the Court of Appeal by 31 March 1999, of which 13 had been heard resulting in 10 convictions or sentences being quashed and three upheld. By July 1999, the CCRC had received a total of 2,605 applications of which 961 cases had been completed.

Assessing the success of the CCRC thus far is difficult. The volume of documents it has to deal with (albeit electronically) is formidable, averaging around 2,000 pages per case. In the 1999 Report, the Chairman of the CCRC warns that more staff are needed to reduce the accumulation of cases awaiting review and deal with the numbers of new cases received – currently around four every working day.

Ultimately, the test of success for the CCRC will be the same one as that which was apparently failed by its predecessor – carrying the confidence of the general public and of politicians – that it represents a safe, quick and impartial method of dealing with cases not given justice in the ordinary courts.

4.6 A miscarriage of justice

One of the English legal system's worst miscarriages of justice cases in recent history was exposed in the Court of Appeal in February 1998. In 1979, Vincent Hickey, Michael Hickey, Jimmy Robertson and Pat Molloy, who became known as the Bridgewater Four, were convicted of the murder of a 13 year old boy, Carl Bridgewater. Although the men were not angelic characters (and had two serious criminal records), they strenuously protested that they were not guilty of the horrific child murder.

Eighteen years later, and after two earlier failed visits to the Court of Appeal and seven police investigations, three of the men were released on 21 February on unconditional bail in anticipation of an appeal hearing in April. The fourth defendant, Mr Molloy, died in jail in 1981. The appeal was eventually allowed.

The Crown has conceded that the case against the men was 'flawed' by evidence falsified and fabricated by police officers. There has also come to light significant fingerprint evidence, tending to exonerate the four which was not disclosed to the defence by the prosecution. Mr Molloy was questioned for 10 days without access to a solicitor, and a fabricated statement from Vincent Hickey was used to persuade Mr Molloy to confess to the crime. Before he died, Mr Molloy claimed he had been beaten by police officers in the course of his interrogation. The former police officers alleged to have falsified the evidence are now under investigation.

The case was given extensive coverage in the print and broadcast media in February 1997 and made a significant impact upon public consciousness. How far it will negatively affect public confidence in the criminal justice system remains to be judged. This major case raises many points germane to the operation of the criminal justice system. The following are of particular importance:

- The case was originally investigated in 1978, before the PACE 1984 had been passed. The requirements under the PACE 1984 for suspects to be given access to legal advice (s 58, Code C) and for interviews to be recorded (s 60, Code E) may have reduced or eliminated the opportunity for police malpractice of the sort which occurred in the *Bridgewater* case.

- Although the criminal justice system ultimately corrected an injustice, this result was achieved primarily through the indefatigable efforts of a few dedicated family members, campaigning journalists and members of Parliament who would not let the issue disappear from the public forum. The case attracted attention because of the terrible nature of the crime – a child murder. It is quite possible that many other unjust convictions in cases with more mundane facts are never propelled into public discussion or overturned.

- Miscarriages of justice cases involve two types of insult to notions of legal fairness: (a) the wrongly imprisoned endure years of incarceration; (b) the real culprits (a child killer in the *Bridgewater* case) are never identified and could well go on to commit other offences.

- The men were released due to the discovery of evidence which had been fabricated and falsified, yet the CPIA 1996 will in future restrict defence access to prosecution evidence.

- The CCRC has been established to re-evaluate alleged cases of miscarriages of justice. One criticism of it has been that it does not have its own independent investigators but will rely on police officers to re-examine cases. How far this new body will be able to succeed in its mission statement, and carry public confidence, remains to be seen.

- The jury is only as good as the information and arguments put before it allow it to be. After the prosecution's case had been devastated by the discovery of new scientific evidence in 1993 (a forensic psychiatrist showed that Molloy's 'confession' used language the suspect would not have used), the foreman of the jury from the 1979 trial risked prosecution for contempt of court by issuing a statement to say that he thought that the men were not guilty. He, along with another juror, said they regretted that they had not been given all the evidence that was available at the time of the trial.

THE CRIMINAL COURT STRUCTURE

Criminal courts

The trial courts are the magistrates' courts and Crown Courts. In serious offences, known as *indictable offences,* the defendant is tried by a jury in a Crown Court, for *summary offences* he or she is tried by magistrates and for 'either way' offences the defendant can be tried by magistrates if they agree but he or she may elect for jury trial. Note the new 'transfer for trial' procedure, and the contention from some groups that this could facilitate miscarriages of justice.

The main issues here concern the distribution of business between the magistrates' court and Crown Courts: what are the advantages of trial in the magistrates' court (a) for the State; and (b) for the defendant? Conversely, what are the disadvantages?

In 1999, the government announced its intention to introduce a change concerning the way decisions are made about where a defendant is to be tried. Under the new system proposed by the government, a defendant charged with an 'either way' offence would be able to make representations to magistrates that he or she wished to be tried in the Crown Court before a judge and jury, but the magistrates would have power to override the desire of the defendant and try the case themselves if they thought they were properly suited to this task, even against the wishes of the defendant.

Certain changes concerning the magistrates' courts have been made by the Access to Justice Act 1999. The 1999 Act provides for various changes to the organisation and management of the magistrates' courts. For example, the Act redefines the basis of the unit of Magistrates' Courts Committees (MCCs). The Act also unifies the provisional and metropolitan stipendiary magistrates into a single bench, and it removes the requirement for magistrates to sit on cases committed to the county court for sentence. The Act also makes some controversial changes in relation to warrant execution, by allowing MCCs to approve and appoint private enforcement agencies to execute certain kinds of warrant.

Criminal appeals from the magistrates go to the Crown Court or to the QBD Divisional Court 'by way of case stated' on a point of law or that the JPs went beyond their proper powers. If the prosecution succeeds on appeal, the court can direct the magistrates to convict and pass the appropriate sentence. There is also an appeal by way of case stated from the Crown Court to the Divisional Court when the Crown Court has heard an appeal from the magistrates' court.

From the Crown Court, appeals against conviction and sentence lie to the Court of Appeal (Criminal Division). Note the powers of the Attorney Relational Justice General under s 36 of the CJA 1972; and his powers under ss 35 and 36 of the CJA 1988.

Part IV of the Access to Justice Act 1999 establishes the High Courts' jurisdiction to hear cases stated by the Crown Court for an opinion. It enables these cases stated to be heard by a single judge.

The Judicial Committee of the Privy Council hears final appeals from some Commonwealth countries and its decisions are of persuasive precedent in English law.

Runciman Royal Commission recommendations

The Runciman Royal Commission recommendations cover a wide range of issues. Note, in particular, the commission recommended:

- that the Home Secretary's power to refer cases to the Court of Appeal under s 17 of the CAA 1968 should be removed and a new body, the Criminal Cases Review Authority ('the authority'), should be set up to consider allegations that a miscarriage of justice might have occurred. The authority should have 'operational independence' with a chairman appointed by the Queen on the advice of the Prime Minister. The authority should be independent of the court structure and should refer meritorious cases directly to the Court of Appeal. The authority was established under the Criminal Appeal Act 1995: see 4.5.6;

- the abolition of committal proceedings (now abolished by s 44 of the CPIA 1996 – see above);

- the curtailment of the right to jury trial.

CHAPTER 5

JUDICIAL REASONING

5.1 Introduction

The popular perception of the judicial process is described by David Kairys as government by law, not people; together with the understanding that law is separate from, and superior to, politics, economics, culture and the values and preferences of judges. This ruling perception is based on particular attributes of the decision making process itself, which Kairys suggests comprises, amongst other things, the judicial recognition of their subservient role in constitutional theory, their passive role in the operation of the doctrine of precedent, their subordinate role in the determination and interpretation of legislation, and the *'quasi-scientific*, objective nature of legal analysis, and *technical* expertise of judges and lawyers' (*The Politics of Law: A Progressive Critique* (1982)). To the extent that law is generally portrayed as quasi-scientific, the operation of objective, technical, and hence supposedly neutral rules, to what degree are the actual decisions that judges make accepted as legitimate by the public? It is necessary, therefore, to consider the nature of reasoning in general and the extent to which judges make use of such reasoning, before considering the social location of the judges. It is only on the basis of the non-existence of distinct and strictly applied principles of legal reasoning that the *existence* of judicial creativity and the *possibility* of judicial bias come into consideration.

5.1.1 Law and logic

There is a long running controversy as to the relationship of law and logic and the actual extent to which legal decisions are the outcome of, and limited by, logical processes. At times, lawyers have sought to reject what is seen as the rigid inflexibility inherent in logical reasoning in favour of flexibility and discretion. As the American Supreme Court Judge, eminent legal writer, and proponent of *Legal Realism*, Oliver Wendel Holmes, expressed it: 'The life of the law has not been logic, it has been experience' (*The Common Law* (1881)).

The implication of this position is that the law is no more than a mechanism for solving particular problems and that judges should operate in such a way as to ensure the best possible result, even if this means ignoring previously established legal rules.

At other times, however, the courts have appeared to base and justify their decisions on the working out of deterministic formal rules of law, categorised in such phrases as, 'The Law is the Law' and 'the Law must run its course'. The suggestion behind such expressions of the *Declaratory Theory of Law* is that the judge is no more than the voice of an autonomous legal system that he, through his legal training, is able to gain access to but is in no way able to influence. If, as the declaratory theory of law maintains, judges do no more than give expression to already existing legal principles and rules, then the particular views, opinions, or prejudices of the judiciary are of absolutely no consequence. If such a representation were accurate, then the logical conclusion would be that judges could be replaced by a computerised *expert system* which could be programmed to make decisions on the basis of a strict application of general rules. It is doubtful, however, if anyone would actually accept such a suggestion. It cannot be denied that the bulk of cases are decided on the simple application of the legal rules to the particular facts of the case with little or no consideration of the legal principles. In other cases, however, the straightforward and automatic application of a legal rule might lead to the possibility of injustice.

(For those particularly interested in the possibility of developing computer models of judicial reasoning and decision making, see Allen, Aikenhead and Widdison, 'Computer simulation of judicial behaviour', www.webjcli.ncl.ac.uk /1998/issue3allen3.html.)

Hard cases are decided on the basis of judicial reaction to the immediate facts of the case. Such a situation, however, is clearly antithetical to the declaratory theory of law.

These *hard cases* demand a consideration of the legal principles involved in order to achieve a just result. They may therefore be decided other than on the strict application of the law as it had been previously expressed. It should be pointed out that such cases are usually the province of the higher courts and of particularly active judges within those courts. The old maxim/cliché that '*hard cases make bad law*' should also be borne in mind. (The career of Lord Denning might be cited as an example of this procedure and its shortcomings. Reference should be made to material covered previously in Chapter 2 of this book for a more detailed consideration of the problems inherent in judicial law making and reform.)

5.2 Reasoning in general

In order to assess this apparent tension, if not divergence, of approach to the question whether legal reasoning is logical or not, it is necessary first of all to engage, at least minimally, in a consideration of what is to be understood by reasoning generally and logical reasoning in particular.

5.2.1 Deductive reasoning

As regards reasoning in general, there is a division between deductive and inductive reasoning. *Deductive reasoning* may be categorised as reasoning from the whole to the part; from the general to the particular. Deductive reasoning finds its simplest and yet most powerful expression in the Aristotelian syllogism. The syllogism takes the following form:

Major premise:	A = B	for example, Socrates is a man.
Minor premise:	B = C	for example, All men are mortal.
Conclusion: therefore	A = C	that is, Socrates is mortal.

The power of the syllogism lies in its certainty. If the premises are true, then the conclusion cannot be false. The reason for this is that the conclusion is actually contained in the premises and amounts to no more than a restatement of those premises.

With regard to syllogisms, however, it is important to distinguish between *validity* of form and *truth* of content. It is quite possible for a syllogism to be logically valid but false. An example of this would be:

Major premise:	A = B	for example, Socrates is a man.
Minor premise:	B = C	for example, All men are pigs.
Conclusion: therefore	A = C	that is, Socrates is a pig.

The logical form of this argument, as represented in alphabetical terms is valid, but the conclusion is not true. The reason for this is obviously that the minor premise is false: the statement that all men are pigs is simply not true.

It is also possible for a syllogism to be both true and valid yet still be based on a false premise. An example of this would be:

Major premise:	A = B	for example, Socrates is a man.
Minor premise:	B = C	for example, All men are Greek.
Conclusion: therefore	A = C	that is, Socrates is Greek.

Once again, the logical form expressed in alphabetical terms is valid, and once again the minor premise is false. On this occasion, however, the conclusion is true.

To reiterate the essential point, all that the syllogistic form of reasoning maintains is that, *if the premises are true then the conclusion cannot be false*; in itself, it states nothing as to the truth of those premises or the truth of the conclusion derived from them. As will be considered below much legal argument is about the truth of particular premises rather than the validity of the logical form being operated.

Deductive reasoning can take another form as follows:

If X then Y:	If it rains, you will get wet.
X:	It is raining.
Therefore, Y:	You will get wet.

Again, the conclusion is contained in the premises, but, equally again, if the premises are false, the conclusion may also be false.

5.2.2 Inductive reasoning

The second classic form of reasoning, *inductive reasoning*, may be described as arguing from the part to the whole; from the particular to the general. Inductive reasoning differs from deductive reasoning in two major respects:

- it reaches a conclusion which is *not* simply a restatement of what is already contained in the basic premises;

- it is *less certain* in its conclusions than deductive logic.

An example of this type of reasoning would be:

The sun has always risen in the East;

Therefore, the sun will rise in the East tomorrow.

If the premise is true, then the conclusion is probably true but not 100% necessarily so because the conclusion is not contained in the premise but is a projection from it. On the basis of past experience, we can reasonably expect the sun to rise in the east tomorrow but there is the possibility, no matter how remote it might be, that something might happen to the sun, or indeed the earth, to prevent its appearance tomorrow. The point is that we cannot predict with 100% accuracy what will happen in the future just because it happened in the past. Because the inductive argument goes beyond the content of its premises, it provides the power to predict events but it gives predictive power at the expense of certainty in its conclusion.

An alternative example of this type of inductive reasoning would be:

John is lying dead with a bullet in his head.

Jane is standing over him with a smoking gun in her hand.

Therefore, it can be concluded that Jane shot John.

Now, the conclusion may be reasonable under the circumstances but there are other possible explanations for the scene. Jane may have simply picked up the gun after someone else had shot John. We cannot actually tell who killed John but we may reasonably suspect Jane of the crime and she would be the first person to be questioned to confirm either her guilt or innocence. The investigation of this event would use a form of reasoning equivalent to scientific reasoning. From available data, a hypothesis would be formed; in this case, that Jane killed John. Investigations would then be undertaken to test the validity of the hypothesis. Depending on the outcome of the investigation, the original hypothesis would be either accepted, rejected or refined.

5.2.3 Reasoning by analogy

A third type of reasoning is *reasoning by example or analogy.* If deductive reasoning involves reasoning from the whole to the part, and inductive reasoning involves reasoning from the part to the whole, then reasoning by analogy involves reasoning from part to part.

An example of this type of reasoning would be:

Wood floats on water.

Plastic is like wood.

Therefore, plastic floats on water.

Or similarly:

Wood floats on water.

Stone is like wood.

Therefore, stone floats on water.

It can be seen that the truth of the conclusion depends completely on the accuracy of the analogy. The connection between the two objects that are being compared depends on weighing up and assessing their similarities and their differences. Only some characteristics are similar and the question is whether those are more important than the differences between the two objects. If the analogy is valid, then the conclusion may very well be equally valid, although not necessarily correct, but, if it is not valid, then the conclusion will certainly be wrong, as the above examples demonstrate.

5.3 Judicial reasoning

It is now appropriate to determine whether or to what extent judges use logical reasoning in reaching their decisions in particular cases and to determine which forms, if any, they make use of.

5.3.1 The syllogism in law

Some statutory provisions and also some common law rules can be expressed in the form of a syllogism. For example, the offence of theft may be reduced into such a formulation:

If A dishonestly appropriates B's property with the intention of permanently depriving B of it, *then* A is guilty of theft.

A has done this.

Therefore, A is guilty of theft.

This, however, represents an oversimplification of the structure of statute but, more importantly, the effect of concentrating on the logical form of the offence tends to marginalise the key issues in the relation to its actual application. As has been stated previously, the great majority of cases are decided on the *truth* of the premises rather than the formal *validity* of the argument used. In other words, argument will concentrate primarily on whether A actually did the act or not, and, secondly, on whether A appropriated the property either 'dishonestly' or 'with the intention of permanently depriving' B of it. Those are questions of fact not logic.

5.3.2 The logical form of precedent

The operation of the rules of precedent appears, at first sight, to involve a similar operation of deductive logic to that applied in statute law: the judge merely applies the legal principle established in the precedent to the facts in hand to determine the outcome of the case. Thus:

Precedent: in case X involving particular circumstances, legal principle Y was applied leading to conclusion Z.

Instant case: in case W similar circumstances to those in X have occurred.

Therefore: principle Y must be applied to reach a conclusion similar to Z.

A closer consideration of the actual procedure involved in precedent, however, will reveal that it is not totally accurate to categorise precedent as a form of deductive reasoning.

In looking for a precedent on which to base a decision, judges are faced with a large number of cases from which to select. It is extremely unlikely that judges will find an authority which corresponds precisely to the facts of the case before them. What they have to do is to find an analogous case and use its reasoning to decide the case before them. This use of analogy to decide cases is prone to the same shortcomings as were revealed in the previous consideration of reasoning from analogy in general. The major difficulty is the need to ensure the validity of the analogy made, if the conclusion drawn is to be valid. There is, no doubt, considerable merit in the wish for similar cases to be treated similarly but given the lack of precision that is inherent in the process of reasoning by analogy it is not altogether certain that such a wish will be met.

A further reason why the operation of precedent cannot simply be considered as an example of deductive reasoning relates to the process through which the precedent is actually determined once an analogous case has been selected. The binding element in any precedent is the *ratio decidendi* of the decision. In delivering his decision, the judge does not separate the *ratio* of the case from other *obiter* comments. As has been considered previously, the *ratio* is a legal abstraction from the concrete facts of the case in which it appears and, in practice, it is for judges in subsequent cases to determine the *ratio* of any authority. The determination of the *ratio* and thus the precedent in a previous case may be seen as a process of *inductive reasoning*, in that the judge in the present case derives the *general* principle of the *ratio* from the *particular* facts of the previous case. This move from the particular to the general is by its nature inductive. The point to be remembered here is that, as was considered in relation to reasoning in general, the use of inductive reasoning cannot claim the certainty inherent in the use of deductive reasoning. The introduction of this increased element of uncertainty is inescapable and unconscious but it is also appropriate to note that the determination of precedent by later courts gives the later judges scope to *consciously* manipulate precedents. This is achieved by the later judges formulating the *ratio* of a previous case in the light of their opinion as to what it *should* have been, rather than what it might actually have been. In other words, they have the scope to substitute their version of the *ratio* even if it contradicts what the original judge thought the *ratio* was.

Thus, the apparent deductive certainty of the use of precedent is revealed to be based on the much less certain use of inductive reasoning and reasoning by analogy, with even the possibility of personal views of the judges playing some part in deciding cases. This latter factor introduces the possibility that judges do not in fact use any form of logical reasoning to decide their cases but simply deliver decisions on the basis of an intuitive response to the facts of the case and the situation of the parties involved. The suggestion has been made that the judges decide the outcome of the case first of all, and only then seek some *post hoc* legal justification for their decision; and given the huge number of precedents from which they are able to choose, they have no great difficulty in finding such support as they require. The process of logical reasoning can be compared to the links in a chain, but a more fitting metaphor for judicial reasoning would be to compare it with the legs of a chair: forced into place to support the weight of a conclusion reached *a priori*. Some critics have even gone so far as to deny the existence of legal reasoning altogether as a method of determining decisions and have suggested that references to such is no more than a means of justifying the social and political decisions that judges are called upon to make.

In conclusion, however, it is not suggested that legal reasoning does not employ the use of logic but neither can it be asserted that it is only a matter of logic. Perhaps the only conclusion that can be reached is that legal reasoning as exercised by the judiciary is an amalgam; part deductive, part inductive, part reasoning by analogy with an added mixture of personal intuition not to say personal prejudice.

5.4 Statutory interpretation

A particular aspect of legal reasoning, and one which also raises questions as to the political persuasion of judges and the scope they have to exercise that persuasion in their decisions, relates specifically to the manner in which the judges interpret statutes when they are called upon to do so.

5.4.1 Problems in interpreting legislation

The accepted view is that the constitutional role of the judiciary is simply to *apply* the law. The function of creating law is the prerogative of Parliament. As has already been seen, such a view is simplistic to the extent that it ignores the potential for judicial creativity in relation to the operation of the common law and the doctrine of judicial precedent. Equally, however, it ignores the extent to which the judiciary have a measure of discretion and creative power in the manner in which they interpret the legislation that comes before them.

Chapter 2 has already considered the general difficulties involved in drafting legislation from the point of view of the person carrying out the drafting; but equally, it has to be recognised that determining the actual meaning of legislation presents judges with a practical difficulty. In order to *apply* legislation, judges must ascertain the meaning of the legislation, and in order to ascertain the meaning they are faced with the difficulty of interpreting the legislation.

Before considering the way in which judges interpret legislation, it is pertinent to emphasise that, in spite of the best endeavours of those who draft legislation to be precise in communicating the meaning of what they produce, the process of interpretation is inescapable and arises from the nature of language itself. Legislation can be seen as a form of linguistic communication. It represents and passes on to the judiciary what Parliament has determined the law should be in relation to a particular situation. Legislation, therefore, shares the general problem of uncertainty inherent in any mode of communication. One of the essential attributes of language is its fluidity, the fact that words can have more than one meaning and that the meaning of a word can change depending on its context. In such circumstances, it is immediately apparent that understanding is an active process. Faced with ambiguity, the recipient of information has to decide which of various meanings to assign to specific words, depending upon the context in which they are used.

Legislation gives rise to additional problems in terms of communication. One of the essential requirements of legislation is generality of application, the need for it to be written in such a way as to ensure that it can be effectively applied in various circumstances without the need to detail those situations individually. This requirement, however, gives rise to particular problems of interpretation; for, as has been pointed out in Chapter 2, the need for generality can only really be achieved at the expense of clarity and precision of language. A further possibility, that is not as uncommon as it should be, is that the legislation under consideration is obscure, ambiguous, or indeed is meaningless or fails to achieve the end at which it is aimed, simply through being badly drafted. The task facing the judge in such circumstances is to provide the legislation with some effective meaning.

Legislation, therefore, involves an inescapable measure of uncertainty that can only be made certain through judicial interpretation. To the extent, however, that the interpretation of legislative provisions is an active process, it is equally a creative process; and inevitably it involves the judiciary in creating law through determining meaning and effect to be given to any particular piece of legislation. There is a further possibility that has to be considered: that judges might actually abuse their role as necessary interpreters of legislation in such a way as to insinuate their own particular personal views and prejudices into their interpretations, and in so doing misapply the legislation and subvert the wishes of the legislature.

5.4.2 Approaches to statutory interpretation

Having considered the problems of interpreting language generally and the difficulties in interpreting legislation in particular, it is appropriate to consider in detail the methods and mechanisms which judges bring to bear on legislation in order to determine its meaning. There are, essentially, two contrasting views as to how judges should go about determining the meaning of a statute; the restrictive, literal approach and the more permissive, purposive one.

- *The literal approach*

  The literal approach is dominant in the English legal system, although it is not without critics and devices do exist for circumventing it when it is seen as too restrictive. This view of judicial interpretation holds that the judge should look primarily to the words of the legislation in order to construe its meaning and, except in the very limited circumstances considered below, should not look outside of, or behind, the legislation in an attempt to find its meaning.

- *The purposive approach*

  The purposive approach rejects the limitation of the judges' search for meaning to a literal construction of the words of legislation itself. It suggests that the interpretive role of the judge should include, where necessary, the power to look beyond the words of statute in pursuit of the reason for its enactment; and that meaning should be construed in the light of that purpose and so as to give it effect. This purposive approach is typical of civil law systems. In these jurisdictions, legislation tends to set out general principles and leaves the fine details to be filled in later by the judges, who are expected to make decisions in the furtherance of those general principles.

European Community legislation tends to be drafted in the continental manner. Its detailed effect, therefore, can only be determined on the basis of a purposive approach to its interpretation. This requirement, however, runs counter to the literal approach that is the dominant approach in the English system. The need to interpret such legislation, however, has forced a change in that approach in relation to Community legislation and even with respect to domestic legislation designed to implement Community legislation. Thus, in *Pickstone v Freemans plc* (1988), the House of Lords held that it was permissible, and indeed necessary, for the court to read words into inadequate domestic legislation in order to give effect to Community law in relation to provisions relating to equal pay for work of equal value. (For a similar approach, see, also, the House of Lords' decision in *Lister v Forth Dry Dock* (1989) and the decision in *Three Rivers District Council v Bank of England (No 2)* (1996) considered below at 5.4.4).)

The advent of purposive interpretation for Community law has not dislodged the primacy of literal interpretation for non-Community domestic legislation. It should be pointed out, however, that the traditional restrictive approach has not gone unchallenged and it should not be surprising to find that Lord Denning was involved in the attack. As in other areas, his unorthodox approach was rejected by the House of Lords (see *Nothman v London Borough of Barnet* (1988)).

In advocating the adoption of a purposive approach, Lord Denning was, in fact, merely expressing the earlier view of the Law Commission which, as early as 1969, had recommended such a change without success.

It is now clearly established that judges can only adopt the purposive approach where they can discover a clear statement of the purpose of the legislation expressed either in the statute itself, or in extrinsic material to which they may legitimately refer for guidance as to meaning (*Shah v Barnet LBC* (1983)). The effect of *Pepper v Hart* (1993), considered below, permitting access to *Hansard* remains to be seen but, for the moment, it is still the case that the judges remain subject to the established rules of interpretation of which there are three primary rules of statutory interpretation, together with a variety of other secondary aids to construction.

5.4.3 Rules of interpretation

What follows in this and the following two sections should be read within the context of the Human Right Act 1998, which requires all legislation to be construed in such a way as, if at all possible, to bring it within the ambit of the European Convention on Human Rights.

The three rules of statutory interpretation are as follows:

* *The literal rule*

    Under this rule, the judge is required to consider what the legislation actually says rather than considering what it might mean. In order to achieve this end, the judge should give words in legislation their literal meaning – that is, heir plain, ordinary, everyday meaning – even if the effect of this is to produce what might be considered an otherwise unjust or undesirable outcome. The literal rule appears at first sight to be the least problematic method of interpreting legislation. Under this rule, the courts most obviously appear to be recognising their limitations by following the wishes of Parliament as expressed in the words of the legislation under consideration. When, however, the difficulties of assigning a fixed and unchallengeable meaning to any word is recalled, the use of the literal rule becomes less uncontroversial and a consideration of the cases reveals examples where the literal rule has been used as a justification for what otherwise might appear as partial judgments on the part of the court concerned in the case.

A classic example of this approach from the area of contract law is *Fisher v Bell* (1961) where, in line with the general contract law principles, it was decided that the placing of an article in a window did not amount to offering but was merely an invitation to treat, and thus the shopkeeper could not be charged with 'offering the goods for sale'. In this case, the court chose to follow the contract law literal interpretation of the meaning of offer in the Act in question and declined to consider the usual non-legal literal interpretation of the word offer. (The executive's attitude to the courts' legal-literal interpretation in *Fisher v Bell* (1961), and the related case of *Partridge v Crittenden* (1968), can be surmised from the fact that later legislation, such as the Trade Descriptions Act 1968, has effectively legislated that invitations to treat are to be treated in the same way as offers for sale.)

A further problem in relation to the literal rule, relating to the difficulty judges face in determining the literal meaning of even the commonest of terms, can be seen in *R v Maginnis* (1987). The defendant had been charged under the Misuse of Drugs Act 1971, with having drugs in his possession and *with intent to supply them*. He claimed that, as he had intended to return the drugs to a friend who had left them in his car, he could not be guilty of *supplying* as charged. In this case, the judges, from first instance, through the Court of Appeal, to the House of Lords, disagreed as to the literal meaning of the common word 'supply'. Even in the House of Lords, Lord Goff, in his dissenting judgment, was able to cite a dictionary definition to support his interpretation of the word. It is tempting to suggest that the majority of judges in the House of Lords operated in a totally disingenuous way by justifying their decision on the literal interpretation of the law whilst, at the same time, fixing on a non-literal meaning for the word under consideration. In actual fact, in *R v Maginnis*, each of the meanings for 'supply' proposed by the various judges could be supported by dictionary entries. That fact, however, only highlights the essential weakness of the literal rule, and that is that it wrongly assumes that there is such a thing as a single uncontentious literal understanding of words. *Bromley LBC v GLC*

(1983) may be cited as an instance where the courts arguably took a covert politic decision under the guise of applying the literal meaning of a particular word in a piece of legislation.

- *The golden rule*

This rule is generally considered to be an extension of the literal rule. In its general expression, it is applied in circumstances where the application of the literal rule is likely to result in what appears to the court to be an obviously absurd result. It should be emphasised, however, that the court is not at liberty to ignore, or replace, legislative provisions simply on the basis that it considers them absurd; it must find *genuine* difficulties before it declines to use the literal rule in favour of the golden one. How one determines or defines genuine difficulty is of course a matter of discretion, and therefore dispute.

It is sometimes stated that there are in fact two versions of the golden rule:

(a) The narrow meaning

This is used where there are two apparently contradictory meanings to a particular word used in a legislative provision or the provision is simply ambiguous in its effect. In such a situation, the golden rule operates to ensure that preference is given to the meaning which does not result in the provision being an absurdity. An example of the application of the golden rule in this narrow sense is *Adler v George* (1964). The defendant had been charged, under the Official Secrets Act 1920, with obstruction 'in the vicinity of' a prohibited area whereas she had actually carried out the obstruction 'inside' the area. The court preferred not to restrict itself to the literal wording of the Act and found the defendant guilty as charged.

(b) The wider meaning

This version of the golden rule is resorted to where, although there is only one possible meaning to a provision, the court is of the opinion that to adopt such a literal interpretation will result in an absurdity. The classic example of this approach is to be found in *Re Sigsworth* (1935) in which the court introduced common law rules into legislative provisions, which were silent on the matter, to prevent the estate of a murderer from benefiting from the property of the party he had murdered.

Another example of this approach is found in *R v National Insurance Commissioner ex p Connor* (1981) in which the court held, in spite of silence in the actual legislation, that Connor was not entitled to a widow's pension, on the grounds that she had been the actual cause of her widowed status by killing her husband.

If it is not irrefutable, it is almost unarguable that matters relating to public policy issues are involved in cases in which the golden rule is employed. Subsequent to the *Connor* case, for example, the Forfeiture Act 1982 was passed giving courts the discretionary power to ignore 'the rule of *public policy* which precludes a person who has unlawfully killed another from acquiring a benefit in consequence of the killing'. This provision, however, merely serves to emphasise the extent to which such judicial decisions on points of law are based on wider considerations of public policy in the first place. In doing so, it immediately raises the question of the judges understanding of, and right to determine, public policy, which questions will be considered later in the next section of this chapter.

- *The mischief rule*

At one level, the mischief rule is clearly the most flexible rule of interpretation but in its traditional expression it is limited by being restricted to using previous common law rules in order to decide the operation of contemporary legislation. It is also, at least somewhat, paradoxical that this most venerable rule, originally set out in *Heydon's Case* (1584), is also the one which most obviously reveals the socio-political nature of judicial decisions.

In *Heydon's Case*, it was stated that in making use of the mischief rule the court should consider the following four things:

- what was the common law before the passing of the statute?;
- what was the mischief in the law which the common law did not adequately deal with?;
- what remedy for that mischief had Parliament intended to provide?;
- what was the reason for Parliament adopting that remedy?

It has to be remembered that, when *Heydon's Case* was decided, it was the practice to cite in the preamble of legislation the purpose for its enactment, including the mischief at which it was aimed. (An example where the preamble made more sense than the actual body of the legislation is the infamous Bubble Act of 1720.) Judges in this earlier time did not therefore have to go beyond the legislative provision itself to implement the mischief rule. With the disappearance of such explanatory preambles, the question arises as to the extent to which judges can make use of the rule in *Heydon's Case* to justify their examination of the policy issues that underlie particular legislative provisions. Contemporary practice is to go beyond the actual body of the legislation. This, however, raises the question as to what courts can legitimately consider in their endeavour to determine the purpose and meaning of legislation, which will be considered, separately, below.

The example usually cited of the use of the mischief rule is *Corkery v Carpenter* (1950), in which a man was found guilty of being drunk in charge of a 'carriage' although he was in fact only in charge of a bicycle. A much more controversial application of the rule is to be found in *Royal College of Nursing v DHSS* (1981), where the courts had to decide whether the medical induction of premature labour to effect abortion, under the supervision of nursing staff, was lawful. In this particularly sensitive area, whether one agrees with the ultimate majority decision of the House of Lords, in favour of the legality of the procedure, or not, probably depends on one's view of abortion. This fact simply serves to highlight the socio-political nature of the question that was finally determined by the House of Lords under the guise of merely determining the legal meaning of a piece of legislation.

From one point of view, the mischief rule serves a very positive purpose by providing courts with the authority to go behind the actual wording of statutes in order to consider the problem that those statutes are aimed at remedying. Alternatively, it is possible to see the mischief rule as justifying the court's interference in the areas of public policy that are, strictly speaking, beyond the realm of their powers and competence. It is equally relevant to point out that in cases such as *Royal College of Nursing v DHSS* such decisions are forced on the courts, whether they like it or not. It is only to be hoped that they make proper and socially acceptable decisions: but such questions remain to be considered below.

It is sometimes suggested that the rules of interpretation form a hierarchical order. On that basis, the first rule that should be applied is the literal rule, and that rule only cedes to the golden rule, in particular circumstances where ambiguity arises from the application of the literal rule. The third rule, the mischief rule, it is suggested, is only brought into use where there is a perceived failure of the other two rules to deliver an appropriate result. On consideration, however, it becomes obvious that no such hierarchy exists. The literal rule is supposed to be used unless it leads to a manifest absurdity in which case it will give way to the golden rule. The immediate question this supposition gives rise to is what is to be considered as an absurdity in any particular case, other than the view of the judge deciding the case. The three rules are contradictory, at least to a degree, and there is no way in which the outsider can determine in advance which of them the courts will make use of to decide the meaning of a particular statute. Perhaps it would be better if the 1969 recommendation of the Law Commission was given effect and judges were expressly permitted to adopt a purposive approach to statutory interpretation. At least, then, judicial creativity in this regard would be out in the open.

5.4.4 Aids to construction

In addition to the three main rules of interpretation, there are a number of secondary aids to construction. These can be categorised as either intrinsic or extrinsic in nature.

- *Intrinsic assistance*

  Intrinsic assistance is derived from the statute which is the object of interpretation; the judge uses the full statute to understand the meaning of a particular part of it.

  The *title*, either long or short, of the Act under consideration may be referred to for guidance (*Royal College of Nursing v DHSS* (1981)).

  It should be noted, however, that a general intention derived from the title cannot overrule a clear statement to the contrary in the text of the Act.

  It was a feature of older statutes that they contained a *preamble*, which was a statement, preceding the actual provisions of the Act, setting out its purposes in some detail, and to which reference could be made for purposes of interpretation. Again, however, any general intention derived from the preamble could not stand in the face of express provision to the contrary within the Act.

  Whereas preambles preceded the main body of an Act, schedules appear as additions at the end of the main body of the legislation. They are, however, an essential part of the Act and may be referred to in order to make sense of the main text.

  Some statutes contain section headings and yet others contain marginal notes relating to particular sections. The extent to which either of these may be used is uncertain although *DPP v Schildkamp* (1969) does provide authority for the use of the former as an aid to interpretation.

  Finally, in regard to intrinsic aids to interpretation, it is now recognised that punctuation has an effect on the meaning of words and can be taken into account in determining the meaning of a provision.

- *Extrinsic assistance*

  Extrinsic assistance, that is, reference to sources outside of the Act itself, may on occasion be resorted to in determining the meaning of legislation; but which sources? Some external sources are unproblematic. For example, judges have always been entitled to refer to *dictionaries* in order to find the meaning of non-legal words. They also have been able to look into *textbooks* for guidance in relation to particular points of law; and in using the mischief rule, they have been able to refer to *earlier statutes* to determine the precise mischief at which the statute they are trying to construe is aimed. The Interpretation Act 1978 is also available for consultation with regard to particular difficulties. Unfortunately, its title is somewhat misleading in that it does not give general instructions for interpreting legislation but simply defines particular terms that are found in various statutes.

Other extrinsic sources, however, are more controversial. In Chapter 2, the various processes involved in the production of legislation were considered. As was seen, there are many distinct stages in the preparation of legislation. Statutes may arise as a result of reports submitted by a variety of commissions. In addition, the preparation of the precise structure of legislation is subject to consideration in working papers, known as *travaux preparatoires*. Nor should it be forgotten that in its progress through Parliament a Bill is the object of discussion and debate in Parliament, both on the floor of the Houses of Parliament and in committee. Verbatim accounts of debates are recorded and published in *Hansard*.

Each of these procedures provides a potential source from which a judge might discover the specific purpose of a piece of legislation or the real meaning of any provision within it. The question is: which of these sources are the courts entitled to have access to?

Historically, English courts have adopted a restrictive approach to what they are entitled to take into consideration. This restrictive approach has been gradually relaxed, however, to the extent that judges are allowed to use extrinsic sources to determine the mischief at which particular legislation is aimed. Thus, they have been entitled to look at Law Commission reports, Royal Commission reports, and the reports of other official commissions. Until very recently, however, *Hansard* literally remained a closed book to the courts, but in the landmark decision in *Pepper v Hart* the House of Lords decided to overturn the previous rule. The issue in the case was the tax liability owed by teachers at Malvern College, a fee paying school. Employees were entitled to have their sons educated at the school whilst paying only 20% of the usual fees. The question was as to the precise level at which this benefit in kind was to be taxed. In a majority decision, it was held that, where the precise meaning of legislation was uncertain or ambiguous or where the literal meaning of an Act would lead to a manifest absurdity, the courts could refer to *Hansard's* reports of parliamentary debates and proceedings as an aid to construing the meaning of the legislation.

The operation of the principle in *Pepper v Hart* was extended, in *Three Rivers District Council v Bank of England (No 2)* (1996), to cover situations where the legislation under question was not in itself ambiguous, but might be ineffective in its intention to give effect to some particular European Community directive. Applying the wider purposive powers of interpretation open to it in such circumstances (see 5.4.2), the court held that it was permissible to refer to *Hansard* in order to determine the actual purpose of the statute. The *Pepper v Hart* principle only applies to statements made by ministers at the time of the passage of legislation, and the courts have declined to extent it to cover situations where ministers subsequently make some statement as to what they consider the effect of a particular Act to be (*Melluish (Inspector of Taxes) v BMI (No 3) Ltd* (1995)).

It is essential to bear in mind that *Pepper v Hart* is not intended to introduce a general purposive approach to the interpretation of non-European Community legislation. Recourse to *Hansard* is to be made only in the context of the mischief rule, as a further method of finding out the mischief at which the particular legislation is aimed.

An additional restriction is that it is likely that only statements made by a government minister, or some other sponsor, responsible for the legislation will be considered as authoritative in setting out the mischief. It is of some interest to note that the dissenting judgment of the Lord Chancellor, Lord Mackay, considered that a relaxation of the previous procedure would merely serve to increase the expense of litigation.

5.4.5 Presumptions

In addition to the rules of interpretation, the courts may also make use of certain presumptions. As with all presumptions they are rebuttable. The presumptions operate:

- *against the alteration of the common law*. Parliament is sovereign and can alter the common law whenever it decides to do so. In order to do this, however, Parliament must expressly enact legislation to that end. If there is no express intention to that effect, it is assumed that statute does not make any fundamental change to the common law. With regard to particular provisions, if there are alternative interpretations, one of which will maintain the existing common law situation, then that interpretation will be preferred;

- *in favour of the requirement that mens rea be a requirement in any criminal offence*. The classic example of this presumption is *Sweet v Parsley* (1969) in which a school teacher had been found guilty of allowing her premises to be used for the purpose of taking drugs contrary to the Misuse of Drugs Act 1971. As she had no idea whatsoever of what her tenants were doing, the House of Lords decided that she could not be convicted. Her lack of knowledge meant she had no intention of committing the offence alleged and therefore did not possess the required *mens rea*. This presumption can be rebutted expressly by the wording of the legislation. Offences which do not require the presence of *mens rea* are referred to as *strict liability* offences, and they usually involve aspects relating to the enforcement of public policy issues, rather than offences of a truly criminal nature. The presumption as to the need for *mens rea* may also be impliedly rebutted, on the basis of the judge's interpretation of the statute in question;

- *against retrospective application*. It is open to Parliament to expressly enact legislation contrary to this presumption. Although this is usually done in relation to areas such as tax law, the War Crimes Act 1990 shows that Parliament can impose criminal responsibility retrospectively, where particular and extremely unusual circumstances dictate the need to do so;

- *against the deprivation of an individual's liberty, property or rights*. Once again, the presumption can be rebutted by express provision and it is not uncommon for legislation to deprive people of their rights to enjoy particular benefits. Nor is it unusual for individuals to be deprived of their liberty under the Mental Health Act 1983;

- *against application to the Crown*. Unless the legislation contains a clear statement to the contrary, it is presumed not to apply to the Crown;

- *against breaking international law*. Where possible, legislation should be interpreted in such a way as to give effect to existing international legal obligations;

- *in favour of words taking their meaning from the context in which they are used*. This final presumption refers back to, and operates in conjunction with, the major rules for interpreting legislation considered previously. The general presumption appears as three distinct sub-rules, each of which carries a Latin tag. The *noscitur a sociis* rule is applied where statutory provisions include a list of examples of what is covered by the legislation. It is presumed that the words used have a related meaning and are to be interpreted in relation to each other. (See *IRC v Frere* (1969) in which the House of Lords decided which of two possible meanings of the word 'interest' was to be preferred by reference to the words location within a statute.) The *ejusdem generis* rule applies in situations where general words are appended to the end of a list of specific examples. The presumption is that the general words have to be interpreted in line with the prior restrictive examples. Thus, a provision which referred to a list that included, 'horses, cattle, sheep and other animals' would be unlikely to apply to domestic animals such as cats and dogs (see *Powell v Kempton Park Racecourse* (1899) in which it was held that, because a statute prohibited betting in a specified number of *indoor* places, it could not cover an *outdoor* location). The *expressio unius exclusio alterius* rule simply means that where a statute seeks to establish a list of what is covered by its provisions, then anything not expressly included in that list is specifically excluded (see *R v Inhabitants of Sedgley* (1831) where rates expressly stated to be payable on *coal* mines were held not to be payable in relation to *limestone* mines).

5.5   Legal reasoning and rhetoric

Following on from the previous questioning of the logical nature of legal reasoning, it might be valuable to consider further the claim that legal decisions are not the outcome of a process of logical reasoning but are in fact the products of a completely different form of communication. According to Peter Goodrich (*Reading the Law* (1986)):

> ... the legal art is an art of interpretation; it is concerned not with a necessary or scientific logic, but with probable arguments, with evaluative reasoning and not with absolute certainty. Rhetoric is the discipline which most explicitly studies the techniques relevant to presenting and evaluating, affirming or refuting, such probable arguments ... rhetoric, here, is defined as the reading of legal texts as acts of communication, as discourse designed to influence, to persuade and to induce action.

Goodrich has analysed the use of rhetoric in law, from ancient Greece until the present time, in Chapter 6 of his book. In so doing, he has revealed the specific rhetorical devices which judges bring to bear in their decisions in order to persuade their audience as to the objective validity of their decisions.

The question, however, is as to who constitutes the audience that the judiciary address. In the case of summings up to juries the answer is obvious, but there is still an audience being addressed when the judge delivers a judgment in any case. That audience, it is suggested, is the community at large, but the community not as an active participant in the legal process, but as a passive body that merely has to be persuaded of the inherent and unquestionable validity of the judge's decision in any particular case.

As Goodrich points out:

> The language of the legal decision strives for the appearance of objectivity and the exclusion of dialogue in favour of monologue. Its principal aim and function is that of achieving an image of incontestable authority and of correct legal meanings. Such a task is, essentially, a rhetorical one: the monologue is the language-usage of authority, it precludes dialogue or any questioning of the meanings given, and it closes legal discourse by privileging the voice of the judicial author as the supreme arbiter of meanings.

Rather than being presented as a particular individual's opinion, the legal text is typically expressed as in the language of objectivity. The use of such terms as 'thus, because, for the reason that, in spite of ... ' indicates the voice of necessity, not of choice. When this is combined with the use of terms, such as 'therefore or consequently', the outcome is to reinforce the impression that the judge is merely engaged in a working out and presentation of the formal operation of the objective system that is law. In this fashion, the language of apparently objective, and logically determined, legal categories is revealed to be a mere rhetorical device marshalled by judges to provide their particular decisions with the justification of pseudo-objectivity. This process is complemented by the use of axioms; unquestioned, and apparently unquestionable, self-evident truths, to which the judiciary frequently have recourse in order to validate, without justifying, their own assumptions and presumptions. One should be on one's guard when one reads judges referring to principles that are 'so fundamental that they need not be debated' or where conclusions follow 'as a matter of course' on the basis of 'well settled principle'. The question is whether such claims merely appeal to uncorroborated precedents and unsubstantiated prejudices.

One further aspect of the rhetorical nature of the judicial presentation directly relates to the inherently political nature of judicial decision making. It is almost a commonplace in the most politically sensitive cases that the judges involved will ritually intone the mantra to the effect that 'it is fortunate that the court does not have to consider the political aspects of this case ... ' before going on to make what cannot but be a political decision. As this book maintains, all judicial decisions are political in that they reflect a disposition as to where power should be located in any particular situation.

Judgments, and judicial presentations to juries, therefore, are not merely statements of law; they are equally if not more fundamentally exercises in rhetoric. To read a judgment in this way is to see it in a new revelatory light which shows the justificatory, if not manipulative, use of language and linguistic devices that are an essential element of the judgment. It has to be pointed out, however, that the nature and use of rhetoric has changed over time. The difference between the operation of rhetoric in the ancient world and its use by the judiciary today is that whereas in the ancient world it was used as a means of *persuading* an audience to reach a particular decision, its contemporary role is that of justifying the decision that the judge has taken. The judge speaks, the audience listens and is persuaded: the role of the audience as a participant has been removed and now merely exists as the passive receiver of the court's decision.

JUDICIAL REASONING

Reasoning in general

Deductive reasoning is reasoning from the whole to the part; from the general to the particular. The syllogism is a form of deductive reasoning.

Inductive reasoning is reasoning from the part to the whole; from the particular to the general.

Reasoning by analogy is reasoning from part to part.

Judicial reasoning

Laws can be presented in the form of syllogisms but do not actually focus on questions of deductive reasoning.

The doctrine of judicial precedent appears at first sight to involve deductive reasoning but is in fact based on the much less certain use of inductive reasoning and reasoning by analogy.

Statutory interpretation

Communication is inherently uncertain, but legislation has particular problems that arise from the contradictory nature of the various ends it tries to achieve.

Judges have to interpret legislation to give it effect – the question is do they give it the effect that Parliament intended?

Approaches to statutory interpretation

The literal approach, theoretically at least, limits judges to simply deciding the meaning of the words of the statute. It is the main approach in the English legal system, apart from cases involving European Community law.

The purposive approach allows judges to go behind the words of the statute to seek to give effect to its purpose but it is only recognised in relation to Community law.

The rules of interpretation

The literal rule gives words in legislation their plain, ordinary, everyday meaning, even if this leads to an apparent injustice.

The golden rule is used in circumstances where the application of the literal rule is likely to result in an obviously absurd result. In such circumstances, the court will not apply the literal meaning but will instead interpret the provision in such a way as to avoid the absurdity.

The mischief rule permits the court to go beyond the words of the statute in question to consider the mischief at which it was aimed. This is the nearest the English system comes to openly acknowledging the purposive approach to statutory interpretation but its ambit of operation is not nearly so wide.

Aids to construction

Intrinsic assistance relies on such internal evidence as the statute under consideration can provide through reference to the following: the title of the Act, any preamble, or any schedules to it.

Extrinsic assistance permits the judge to go beyond the Act in question in order to ascertain its meaning. Amongst possible sources are dictionaries, textbooks, other statutes including the Interpretation Act, 1978, reports, other parliamentary papers, and, since *Pepper v Hart* (1993), *Hansard* may also be consulted.

Presumptions

In addition to the rules of interpretation, there are also various presumptions that will be applied, unless rebutted. The most important of these are presumptions against the alteration of the common law; against retrospective application; against the deprivation of an individual's liberty, property or rights; and against application to the Crown. In addition, there are presumptions in favour of the requirement for *mens rea* in relation to criminal offences; and deriving the meaning of words from their contexts.

Rhetoric

Judgments, and judicial submissions to juries, are not merely statements of law; they are also exercises in persuasion and justification through the use of language and linguistic devices.

CHAPTER 6

THE JUDICIARY

6.1   The constitutional role of the judiciary

Central to the general idea of the Rule of Law is the specific proposition that it involves the rule of *law* rather than the rule of *people*. Judges hold a position of central importance in relation to the concept of the Rule of Law. They are expected to deliver judgment in a completely impartial manner through a strict application of the law, without allowing their personal preference, or fear or favour of any of the parties to the action, to affect their decision in any way.

This desire for impartiality is reflected in the constitutional position of the judges. In line with Montesquieu's classical exposition of the separation of powers, the judiciary occupy a situation apart from the legislative and executive arms of the State; and operate independently of them. Prior to the English revolutionary struggles of the 17th century between Parliament and the Monarch, judges held office at the King's pleasure. Not only did this mean that judges could be dismissed when the Monarch so decided but it highlighted the lack of independence of the law from the State in the form, and person, of the Monarch. With the victory of Parliament and the establishment of a State based on popular sovereignty, and limited in its powers, the independence of the judiciary was confirmed in the Act of Settlement 1701. The centrality of the independence of the judges and the legal system from direct control or interference from the State in the newly established constitution was emphasised in the writing of the English philosopher John Locke who saw it as one of the essential reasons for, and justifications of, the Social Contract on which the social structure was assumed to be based.

In order to buttress the independence of the judiciary, and remove them from the danger of being subjected to political pressure, it has been made particularly difficult to remove senior judges once they have been appointed. Their independence of thought and opinion is also protected by the doctrine of judicial immunity. Both of these principles will be considered in more detail below.

6.1.1   The constitutional role of the Lord Chancellor

It should be noted that the Lord Chancellor holds an anomalous position in respect of the separation of powers in the contemporary State, in that the holder of that position plays a key role in each of the three elements of the

State. The Lord Chancellor is the most senior judge in the English court structure, sitting as he does in the House of Lords. At the same time, however, the Lord Chancellorship is a party political appointment, and the occupant of the office owes his preferment to the Prime Minister of the day. Not only is the incumbent a member of the executive, having a seat in the Cabinet, but he is also responsible for the operation of his own government department. In addition to these roles, it should not be overlooked that the Chancellor is also the Speaker of the House of Lords in its general role as a legislative forum. The peculiar situation of the Lord Chancellor is also reflected in the fact that the incumbent can be dismissed, or persuaded to resign, by the Prime Minster and may cease to hold office on the election of a new government.

The present Lord Chancellor, Lord Irvine of Lairg and his immediate predecessor, Lord Mackay, have not gone without criticism from within the legal profession generally, and the judiciary in particular. The suggestion has been made that these Lord Chancellors have represented the interests of their political masters, at the expense of the interests of their legal colleagues. For some time, the legal professions have argued that economic imperatives have driven the machinery of the justice system, rather than the wish to provide the best possible service. Lord Mackay's motives and actions were continuously open to such suspicions. As Lord Steyn, one the Lords of Appeal in Ordinary in the House of Lords, was quoted as saying:

> The Lord Chancellor is always a spokesman for the government in furtherance of its party political agenda ([1997] PL 84).

However, for the moment at least, a truce appears to have been declared between the judges and the (relatively) new Lord Chancellor as is evident from the words of the Master of the Rolls, Lord Woolf:

> I do not forget that there was a period of confrontation between some of the judiciary and the former Lord Chancellor, Lord Mackay, but that was primarily concerned with reforms relating to the professions, including rights of audience for solicitors, and not the role of the judiciary in the administration of the courts. There was also the concern over the shortage of judges in 1994–95. However, after powerful and frank speeches by the then Lord Chief Justice and Master of the Rolls, a much needed injection of additional judges was provided. The present Lord Chancellor, Lord Irvine of Lairg, is also proposing far reaching changes to the rights of audience, but these are unlikely to meet with the same hostility ((1998) 114 LQR 579, p 585).

Whether this truce survives Lord Irvine's proposals in the White Paper *Modernising Justice* (1998), and what many see as the ironically titled, Access to Justice Act 1999, remains to be seen.

In addition to difficulties arising directly from their responsibility for implementing political policies in relation to the legal system, the question of the Lord Chancellor's judicial role has also come into question. As a consequence of the fact that the appointment of the Lord Chancellor is a purely political one, there is no requirement that the incumbent should have held any prior judicial office. Indeed, in the case of Lord Irvine, he has never served in any judicial capacity, making his reputation as a highly successful barrister, at one time, having both the present Prime Minister and his wife in his chambers. Nonetheless, as Lord Chancellor, he is the most senior judge and is entitled to sit, as he deems appropriate (see 6.3.2 for further observations about the Lord Chancellor's residual powers).

There is, however, a much more fundamental issue relating to the manner in which the Lord Chancellor's multi-functional role may be seen as breaching the doctrine of the separation of powers. There cannot but be doubts as to the suitability, not to say propriety, of a member of the executive functioning as a member of the judiciary. Given the heightened sensitivity in relation to impartiality, generated by Lord Hoffman's participation in the *Pinochet* case (see below), the Lord Chancellor himself withdrew from sitting in a case in March 1999, in which he recognised the possibility of a conflict of interest. That case involved an action by the family of a man who had died in police custody. The suggestion was made that the Lord Chancellor's participation in the judicial panel raised doubts as to whether the case would be decided by an independent and impartial tribunal. Given his recent guidelines warning the judiciary about the need to be sensitive to issues of conflict of interest, the Lord Chancellor clearly felt himself required to stand down from hearing the case. Such action on his part, however, merely raises the question as to in which cases can a Lord Chancellor sit, without having a political interest? The Lord Chancellor's position with regard to this mixture of political and judicial functions has been further questioned by Lord Steyn, in a paper written for the Constitution Unit at University College London in May 1999.

In any event, considerations of this nature may be forestalled by the European Court of Human Rights' decision relating to the operation of the constitution on the island of Guernsey (*McGonnell v UK* (1998)). The Bailiff of Guernsey has a similar mixture of administrative, legislative and judicial roles as has the Lord Chancellor. In a case brought by a Guernsey resident against a judicial decision of the Bailiff, the European Commission on Human Rights held that it was inappropriate for the Bailiff to take such decisions. In the view of the Commission:

> It is incompatible with the requisite appearances of independence and impartiality for a judge to have legislative and executive functions as substantial as those carried out by the Bailiff.

If the decision of the Commission is confirmed by the Court, as appropriate for the microcosm of Guernsey, it is equally applicable for the macrocosm of the United Kingdom. It is even possible that, under the Human Rights Act 1998, the Lord Chancellor's judicial position will be invalidated by the other judges. It should of course be recognised, perhaps with no little degree of irony, that it was Lord Irvine who was instrumental in bringing the European Convention into UK law, through the Human Rights Act 1998.

It might be preferable if the position of the Lord Chancellor were considered afresh. To do so would require a complete reassessment of the present structure of the English legal system, but this possibility is not without merit, as will be considered below.

6.1.2 The Constitution and the role of the House of Lords

A number of issues have come together to raise questions about the operation of the House of Lords as the final court of appeal in the English legal system. Amongst these are the devolution of parliamentary power to the new Scottish Parliament and Welsh Assembly; the proposed abolition of the rights of hereditary peers to vote in the House of Lords; the enactment of the Human Rights Act; and the role of the House of Lords itself in the *Pinochet* case. It is almost incontrovertible that changes will be required in the future and perhaps this time of large constitutional change presents the best opportunity for a considered revision of the operation of the senior judiciary and their courts.

In other constitutional systems, both civil, as in France, or common law, as in the United States of America, not only is there a clear separation of powers between the judiciary, the executive and the legislature, but there is also a distinct Constitutional Court, which deals with such issues. The English Constitution provides for neither of these. The anomalous position of the Lord Chancellor has already been commented on, as has the doctrine of the supremacy of Parliament (see 1.4), but it remains to to be considered whether either of these can continue to exist as they have, under the changed circumstances of the contemporary constitution. Equally, the potential role of the courts as Constitutional Courts, and the existing position of the House of Lords as a court within the legislative body, must come into issue.

It is a commonplace of politics that the devolution of power from the United Kingdom Parliament in London, particularly to the Scottish Parliament in Edinburgh, will give rise to disputes as to the relationship between the two bodies. Eventually, such issues will have to be resolved in the courts. Equally, the Human Rights Act will, for the first time, give the courts clear power to declare the United Kingdom Parliament's legislative provision to be contrary to essential human rights (see 1.7). Moreover, as a result of the secondary nature of the legislation produced by the Scottish Parliament, the courts will have the power to quash such Acts as invalid for lack of compatibility with the European Convention on Human Rights. Even allowing for the fact that the Human Rights Act has been introduced in such a way as to maintain the theory of parliamentary sovereignty, in practice, the courts will inevitably become involved in political/constitutional issues. Once the courts are required to act in constitutional matters, it is surely a mere matter of time before they become Constitutional Courts, as distinct from ordinary courts, with specialist judges with particular expertise in such matters. Once a Constitutional Court develops, the position of the Lord Chancellor will become untenable as a judge, as his political roles would automatically place him in a position of conflict of interest. He would have to give up his position as head of the judiciary, probably, as some have already proposed, to the Lord Chief Justice.

A further problematic consequence of such a development would be the continued location of the Constitutional Court within the House of Lords. If the existing House of Lords were to be replaced by an elected body, then questions would have to be asked about the situation of unelected members, such as bishops and judges; but, even if it were replaced by an appointed second chamber, the separation of powers would surely demand that the Constitutional Court be separate from it.

Membership of such a court could also be an issue. The present situation, where panels of five Law Lords, or seven as in the third *Pinochet* hearing, are selected from the full complement of 12, has been criticised as introducing an element of lottery into the judicial procedure. The question arises, would the decision in any case have been different, had a different body of judges been empanelled? In the *Pinochet* case, the second panel of seven reached the same decision as the previous five member court, but for different reasons. The *Pinochet* proceedings brought the House of Lords, no doubt unwelcome, publicity, and may have revealed the need for its internal reform. Already, suggestions have been made that the court should sit as a full court, involving all its members; but that, in turn, must bring into question the actual appointment procedures of these most senior judges, especially if it were to develop into a Constitutional Court. For the question has to be asked as to what expertise in constitutional matters generally, and human rights in particular, do the commercial lawyers who make up a significant number of the highest judicial posts have? And, if expertise in such issues is to be seen as the criterion for appointment to the Constitutional Court, then should not membership of the court be open to non-practitioners, such as academics? For the moment, such issues remain purely hypothetical, but for how much longer can this remain the case?

In his May 1999 paper, Lord Steyn, in commenting on the fact that the current royal commission on reform of the House of Lords will consider the position of the Law Lords, but will not be asked to consider the situation of the Lord Chancellor, expressed the view that:

> The strategic thinking behind this coyness may be that turning the searchlight on the Lord Chancellor's position may expose the fragility of the supposed pragmatic justifications for the present arrangement.

It is worth noting that the case set out in the above two sections for the reform of the Lord Chancellor's position and against the location of the most senior judges in the House of Lords was presented, in essence, to the commission examining the reform of the House of Lords by Justice, the civil rights organisation. Both aspects of the challenges were strongly rejected by Lord Chancellor Irvine in a speech to the Third Worldwide Common Law Judiciary Conference in Edinburgh, delivered on 5 July 1999

(www.open.gov.uk/lcd/speeches/1999/5-7-99).

6.1.3   The case of General Pinochet

No consideration of the operation of the judiciary generally, and the House of Lords in particular, can be complete without a detailed consideration of what can only be called the *Pinochet* case (the various cases are actually cited as *R v Bartle* and *R v Evans* (House of Lords' first hearing); *Re Pinochet* (House of Lords' appeal against Lord Hoffman); *R v Bartle* and *R v Evans* (final House of Lords' decision)). There will undoubtedly be other cases relating to the extradition of the ex-dictator, but the foregoing are the ones that established that his office as Head of State gave him no general immunity to extradition for offences against the United Nations Convention Against Torture, since the date it was incorporated into United Kingdom law by the Criminal Justice Act 1988.

In September 1973, the democratically elected government of Chile was overthrown in a violent army coup led by the then General, Augusto Pinochet Ugarte; the president, Salvador Allende, and many others were killed in the fighting. Subsequently, in the words of Lord Browne-Wilkinson, in the final House of Lords' hearing:

> There is no doubt that, during the period of the Senator Pinochet regime, appalling acts of barbarism were committed in Chile and elsewhere in the world: torture, murder and the unexplained disappearance of individuals on a large scale.

Although it was not suggested that Pinochet had committed these acts personally, it was claimed that he was fully aware of them and conspired to have them undertaken.

In 1998, General Pinochet, by now Senator for life and recipient of a Chilean amnesty for his actions (extracted as the price for his returning his country to democracy), came to England for medical treatment. Although he was initially welcomed, he was subsequently arrested, on an extradition warrant issued in Spain, for the crimes of torture, murder and conspiracy to murder allegedly orchestrated by him in Chile during the 1970s. Spain issued the international warrants, but Pinochet was actually arrested on warrants issued by the metropolitan stipendiary magistrate under s 8(1)(b) of the

Extradition Act. The legal question for the English courts was whether General Pinochet, as Head of State at the time when the crimes were committed, enjoyed diplomatic immunity. In November 1998, the House of Lords rejected Pinochet's claim by a 3:2 majority, Lord Hoffman voting with the majority but declining to submit a reasoned judgment.

Prior to the hearing in the House of Lords, Amnesty International, which campaigns against such things as state mass murder, torture and political imprisonment, and in favour of general civil and political liberties, had been granted leave to intervene in the proceedings, and had made representations through its counsel, Geoffrey Bindman QC. After the *Pinochet* decision, it was revealed, although it was hardly a secret, that Lord Hoffman was an unpaid director of the Amnesty International Charitable Trust, and that his wife also worked for Amnesty. On that basis, Pinochet's lawyers initiated a very peculiar action: they petitioned the House of Lords, about a House of Lords' decision: for the first time, the highest court in the land was to be subject to review, but to itself; only itself differently constituted. So, in January 1999, another panel of Law Lords set aside the decision of the earlier hearing on the basis that Lord Hoffman's involvement had invalidated the previous hearing. The decision as to whether Pinochet had immunity or not would have to be heard by a new, and differently constituted, committee of Law Lords.

It has to be stated in favour of this decision that the English legal system is famously rigorous in controlling conflicts of interest which might be seen to affect what should be a neutral decision making process. The rule, which applies across the board to trustees, company directors and other fiduciaries as well as judges, is so strict that the mere possibility of a conflict of interest is sufficient to invalidate any decision so made, even if in reality the individual concerned was completely unaffected by their own interest in coming to the decision. In the words of the famous *dictum* of Lord Hewart, it is of fundamental importance that 'justice must not only be done but should manifestly and undoubtedly be seen to be done' (*R v Sussex Justices ex p McCarthy* (1924)). With regard to the judicial process, it has been a long established rule that no one may be a judge in his or her own cause, that is, they cannot judge a case in which they have an interest. This is sometimes known by the phrase *nemo judex in causa sua*. Thus, for example, judges who are shareholders in a company appearing before the court as a litigant must decline to hear the case (*Dimes v Grand Junction Canal* (1852)). It is, therefore, astonishing that Lord Hoffman did not withdraw from the case, or at least declare his interest in Amnesty when it was joined to the proceedings. The only possible justification is that Hoffman assumed that all of those involved in the case, including the Pinochet team of lawyers, were aware of the connection. Alternatively, he might have thought that his support for a charitable body aimed at promoting civil and political liberties was so worthy in itself as to be unimpeachable: could not, and indeed should not, every English judge subscribe, for example, to cl 3(c) of the Amnesty International

Charitable Trust memorandum, which provides that one of its objects is 'to procure the abolition of torture, extra-judicial execution and disappearance'?

In either case, Lord Hoffman was wrong.

Once it was shown that Lord Hoffman had a relevant interest in its subject matter, he was disqualified without any investigation into whether there was a likelihood or suspicion of bias. The mere fact of his interest was sufficient to disqualify him unless he had made sufficient disclosure. Hitherto, only pecuniary or proprietary interests had led to automatic disqualification. But, as Lord Browne-Wilkinson stated, Amnesty, and hence Lord Hoffman, plainly had a non-pecuniary interest, sufficient to give rise to an automatic disqualification for those involved with it.

It is important not to overstate what was decided in *Re Pinochet*. The facts of that case were exceptional and it is unlikely that it will lead to a mass withdrawal of judges from cases; however, there might well be other cases in which the judge would be well advised to disclose a possible interest. Finally, with regard to *Re Pinochet*, whatever one's views about the merits, sagacity or neutrality of the current judiciary, there is considerable evidence to support the proposition that, historically, judges have often been biased towards certain causes and social classes. For example, JAG Griffith's book, *The Politics of the Judiciary* (1997) (see 6.11.1, below), is brimming with concrete examples of judges who have shown distinctly conservative and illiberal opinions in cases involving workers, trade unions, civil liberties, Northern Ireland, police powers, religion and other matters. Lord Hoffman was wrong, but it is nonetheless ironic that the first senior judge to have action taken against him for possible political bias is someone whose agenda was nothing more than being against torture and unjudicial killings. It will be very interesting now to see what other 'associations' are declared by presiding judges in the wake of the Lords' decision.

The House of Lords, therefore, decided that Lord Hoffman had been wrong, but it remained for the House of Lords to extricate itself, with whatever dignity it could manage, from the situation it, through Lord Hoffman, had got itself into. This it endeavoured to do by reconstituting the original hearing with a specially extended committee of seven members. Political and legal speculation was rife before the decision of that court. It was suggested that the new committee could hardly go against the decision of the previous one, without bringing the whole House of Lords' procedures into disrepute, yet the earlier court had actually contained the most liberal, and civil liberties minded, of the Lords. It was assumed that the new hearing would endorse the earlier decision, if with reluctance, but what was not expected was the way in which it would actually do so.

In reaching the decision that General Pinochet could be extradited, the House of Lords relied on, and established, Pinochet's potential responsibility for the alleged crimes, from the date on which the United Kingdom incorporated the United Nations Convention on Torture into its domestic law, through the Criminal Justice Act 1988 – 29 September 1988. Consequently, he could not be held responsible for any crimes committed before then, but was potentially liable for any offences after that date. Thus, although the later House of Lords' decision provided the same decision as the first one, it did so on significantly different, and much more limited, grounds to those on which Lords Steyn and Nicholls, with the support of Lord Hoffman, relied. Such a conclusion is neither satisfactory in law, nor political practice, and does nothing to deflect the unflattering glare of unwonted publicity that has been visited on the House of Lords.

6.2   Judicial offices

Although not required to know the names of present incumbents, students should be at least aware of the various titles of judges and equally know which courts they operate in:

- *Lord Chancellor*. The peculiar nature of this office has already been commented on, but it should be pointed out that, as well as being the senior judge in the House of Lords, the Lord Chancellor is formally the most senior judge in the Court of Appeal, and holds the position of President of the Chancery Division. On the announcement of the general election of 1997, the serving Lord Chancellor, Lord Mackay, announced his intention to resign from office, and the incoming Labour administration appointed Lord Irvine in his place. The present Lord Chancellor, therefore, is Lord Irvine of Lairg and he is referred to in reports as Lord Irvine LC.

- *Lord Chief Justice*. The holder of this position is second only to the Lord Chancellor in eminence. The Lord Chief Justice is the President of the Criminal Division of the Court of Appeal and is formally the senior judge in the Queen's Bench Division of the High Court. The present incumbent is Lord Bingham CJ.

- *Master of the Rolls*. The holder of this office is President of the Civil Division of the Court of Appeal. At present, this position is held by Lord Woolf MR.

- *President of the Family Division of the High Court of Justice*. This person is the senior judge in the Family Division and is responsible for organising the operation of the court. The current president is Sir Stephen Brown P.

- *Vice Chancellor*. Although the Lord Chancellor is nominally the head of the Chancery Division of the High Court, the actual function of organising the Chancery Division falls to the Vice Chancellor. The current incumbent is Sir Richard Scott VC.

- *Senior Presiding Judge for England and Wales.* The Courts and Legal Services Act 1990 recognised the existing system and required that each of the six separate Crown Court circuits should operate under the administration of two Presiding Judges appointed from the High Court. In addition, a Senior Presiding Judge is appointed from the Lords Justices of Appeal (see 6.2.1, below).

6.2.1   Judicial hierarchy

The foregoing are specific judicial offices. In addition, the various judges who function at the various levels within the judicial hierarchy are referred to in the following terms:

- *Lords of Appeal in Ordinary.* These are the people who are normally referred to as the Law Lords for the simple reason that they sit in the House of Lords and are ennobled when they are appointed to their positions. There can be between seven and 12 Law Lords, although the maximum number is subject to alteration by Order in Council. The function of the House of Lords, as the highest domestic court in the United Kingdom, is considered elsewhere but the legislative role of the Law Lords deserves some mention. Although the claim that the Law Lords do not take part in the party political debate in the House of Lords is correct, it is no longer accurate, as is sometimes claimed, that the Law Lords refrain from controversy in their contributions to debate. A comparatively recent example can be cited in the controversial debate that took place with regard to the reform of the legal profession. In that particular situation, some of the Law Lords were not shy of engaging in the debate to express their disapprobation with the proposals in a fairly controversial manner. (The increased willingness of the judiciary generally, and the senior judiciary in particular, to engage in overt political criticism of the government will be considered in more detail in the following chapter.)

  The qualifications for the position of Lord of Appeal in Ordinary will be considered later. They are referred to by their specific titles.

- *Lords Justices of Appeal.* This category, of which there may be up to 35 individuals, constitutes the majority of the judges in the Court of Appeal, although the other specific office holders considered previously may also sit in that court, as may High Court judges specifically requested so to do. They all used to be known as Lord Justice, even if they were female. The one present female member of the Court of Appeal, Elizabeth Butler-Sloss, had to be referred to by the male title because the Supreme Court Act 1981 had not considered the possibility of a woman holding such high judicial office. Now, however, the rules have been changed to permit her to be referred to as Lady Justice Butler-Sloss.

- *High Court judges*. These latter are sometimes referred to as *'puisne'* (pronounced 'pewnee') judges, in reference to their junior status in relation to those of superior status in the Supreme Court. There may be up to 98 such judges appointed. Judges are appointed to particular divisions depending on the amount of work needing to be conducted by that division, although they may be required to hear cases in different divisions and may be transferred from one division to another by the Lord Chancellor. Others, such as former High Court and Court of Appeal judges, or former circuit judges, or recorders, may be requested to sit as judges in the High Court. High Court judges are referred to by their name followed by the initial 'J'.

- The Lord Chancellor may also appoint *deputy judges* of the High Court on a purely temporary basis in order to speed up the hearing of cases and to reduce any backlog that may have built up. The Heilbron Report on the operation of the civil justice system was critical of the use of deputy judges and recommended that more permanent High Court judges should be appointed if necessary. The maximum numbers were subsequently increased to their present level, but the use of deputy judges has continued to provide grounds for criticism of the operation of the legal system, and has led to suggestions that the use of 'second rate' judges might eventually debase the whole judicial currency. This situation has to be considered within the context of the general arguments about the financial limitations within which the operation of the legal system is increasingly being required to operate, to the dismay and anger of many senior members of the judiciary.

- *Circuit judges*. Although there is only one Crown Court, it is divided into six distinct circuits which are serviced, in the main, by circuit judges who also sit as county court judges to hear civil cases. There are currently 562 circuit judges – such judges are addressed as 'Your Honour'.

- *Recorders* are part time judges appointed to assist circuit judges in their functions in relation to criminal and civil law cases.

- *District judges*. This category of judge, previously referred to as registrars, are appointed on a full time and part time basis to hear civil cases in the county court.

- The situation of *magistrates* will be considered separately below and the situation of *Chairmen of Tribunals* will be considered in a later chapter.

6.2.2   Legal offices

In addition to these judicial positions, there are three legal offices which should be noted:

- The *Attorney General*, like the Lord Chancellor, is a political appointee whose role is to act as the legal adviser to the government. The Attorney General alone has the authority to prosecute in certain circumstances and appears for the Crown in important cases. The *Solicitor General* is the Attorney General's deputy.

- The *Director of Public Prosecution* is the head of the national independent Crown Prosecution Service established under the Prosecution of Offences Act 1985 to oversee the prosecution of criminal offences.

6.3   Appointment of judiciary

In the first of his Hamlyn lectures of 1993, the then Lord Chancellor, Lord Mackay, stated that the pre-eminent qualities required by a judge are:

> ... good sound judgment based upon knowledge of the law, a willingness to study all sides of an argument with an acceptable degree of openness, and an ability to reach a firm conclusion and to articulate clearly the reasons for the conclusion.

Although the principal qualification for judicial office was experience of advocacy, Lord Mackay recognised that some people who have not practised advocacy may well have these necessary qualities to a great degree, as is reflected in the appointment of an academic and member of the Law Commission, Professor Brenda Hoggett, to the High Court in December 1993. Professor Hoggett, who sits as Mrs Justice Hale, is the first High Court judge not to have had a career as a practising barrister, although she qualified as a barrister in 1969 and was made a QC in 1989.

The Courts and Legal Services Act (CLSA) 1990 introduced major changes into the qualifications required for filling the positions of judges. Judicial appointment is still essentially dependent upon the rights of audience in the higher courts; but, at the same time as the CLSA 1990, effectively demolished the monopoly of the Bar to rights of audience in such courts, it opened up the possibility of achieving judicial office to legal practitioners other than barristers.

6.3.1   Qualifications

The main qualifications for appointment are as follows (the CLSA 1990 is dealt with in detail in Chapter 11 at 11.7):

- *Lord of Appeal in Ordinary*

    (a) the holding of high judicial office for two years; or

    (b) possession of a 15 year Supreme Court qualification under the CLSA 1990.

- *Lord Justice of Appeal*

  (a) the holding of a post as a High Court judge; or

  (b) possession of a 10 year High Court qualification under the CLSA 1990.

- *High Court judges*

  (a) the holding of a post as a circuit judge for two years;

  (b) possession of a 10 year High Court qualification under the CLSA 1990.

- *Deputy judges* must be qualified in the same way as permanent High Court judges.

- *Circuit judges*

  (a) the holding of a post as a recorder;

  (b) possession of a either 10 year Crown Court qualification or a 10 year county court qualification under the CLSA 1990;

  (c) the holding of certain offices, such as district judge, Social Security Commissioner, chairman of an industrial tribunal, stipendiary magistrate for three years.

- *Recorders*

  (a) candidates must possess a 10 year Crown Court or county court qualification under the CLSA 1990.

- *District judges*

  (a) require a seven year general qualification under the CLSA 1990.

6.3.2   Selection of judges

The foregoing has concentrated on the specific requirements for those wishing to fulfil the role of judge; but it remains to consider the more general question relating to the general process whereby people are deemed suitable and selected for such office. All judicial appointments remain, theoretically, at the hands of the Crown. The Crown, however, is guided, if not actually dictated to, in regard to its appointment by the government of the day. Thus, as has been seen, the Lord Chancellor is a direct political appointment. The Prime Minister also advises the Crown on the appointment of other senior judicial office holders and the Law Lords, and Appeal Court judges. Such apparent scope for patronage in the hands of the Prime Minister has not gone without criticism. It has been suggested that the former Master of the Rolls, Sir John Donaldson, owed either his elevation or his previous failure to achieve such high office, at least in part, to his service in the Industrial Relations Court instituted by a former Conservative government in 1971 to pursue its trade union policies. It has also been suggested that Prime Ministers have vetoed recommendations made by Lord Chancellors.

Judges at the level of High Court judges and Circuit Bench are appointed by the Crown on the advice of the Lord Chancellor and the Lord Chancellor personally appoints district judges, lay magistrates and the members of some tribunals. This system has not gone without challenge either, the question being raised as to how the Chancellor actually reaches his decision to recommend or appoint individuals to judicial offices. It is accepted that the Lord Chancellor's recommendations are made on the basis of the opinions of the existing judiciary as to the suitability of the potential candidates. Although the Lord Chancellor's Department published a guidance booklet entitled *Judicial Appointments*, the problem, or at least the suspicion shared by both the Bar and The Law Society, with the system is reflected in the widespread belief that it is over-secretive and leads to a highly conservative appointment policy. Judges are suspected, perhaps not unnaturally, of favouring those candidates who have not been 'troublesome' in their previous cases and who have shown themselves to share the views and approaches of the existing office holders.

In his 1993 Hamlyn lecture, Lord Mackay stated that the arrangements in the United Kingdom for the collection of data about candidates for the judiciary are comparatively well developed and provide those who have to take the decisions, essentially the Lord Chancellor himself, with fuller information than would otherwise be available to them. The reasoning behind this claim would appear to be that, because the procedure is secret and limited, people commenting on the suitability of candidates are willing to be more frank and open than would otherwise be the case were the references open to wider inspection. Such spurious justification is worrying in its complacency and its refusal to recognise that the secretive nature of the process might permit referees to make unsubstantiated derogatory comments that they would otherwise not feel free to make.

In 1994, advertisements were used, for the first time, to recruit likely candidates from the professions for the positions of assistant recorder, deputy district judge and circuit judge. In 1998, advertising was extended to appointments to the High Court Bench.

The first of such advertisements stated:

> The Lord Chancellor will recommend for appointment the candidates who appear to him to be best qualified regardless of ethnic origin, gender, marital status, sexual orientation, political affiliation, religion or (subject to the physical requirements of the office) disability.

This was seen as a practical step to address the matter of gender and race imbalance amongst the present judicial body. Currently, there are no women in the House of Lords, and only one in the Court of Appeal. In the High Court, the number is seven out of 98, and, of 562 circuit judges, 36 are women. At the level of recorders, there are 80 women from a total of 880; and, at district judge level, the number is 52 from 379 (February 1999, LCD;

www.open.gov.uk/lcd/judicial/senjud.htm).

Statistics relating to the ethnic origin of judges are more difficult to locate, but a survey carried out in 1997 estimated that only 1% of judges came from a non-white background, and all of those were sitting as circuit judges (Labour Research, July 1997).

Lord Irvine has continued this policy of encouraging women and people from ethnic backgrounds, or other minorities, to apply for judicial positions, encapsulated in his sound bite 'Don't be shy! Apply!'. As he admitted:

> Yes, it is true that many judges today are white, Oxbridge educated men. But, it is also true that they were appointed on merit, from the then available pool, at the time the vacancies arose ... It does not mean that the social composition of the judiciary is immutably fixed. For too long barristers were drawn from a narrow social background. As this changes over time, I would expect the composition of the Bench to change too. That is inherent in the merit principle (speech to the Association of Women Barristers, February 1998).

The 1997 Labour Research survey referred to previously, although admittedly carried out when Lord Irvine was only in his new job for two months, found that, in fact:

> ... even greater proportions of the judiciary attended Oxbridge universities than a decade earlier ...

Still, Lord Irvine remains optimistic, not to say bullish, about the way things are changing. As he points out:

> ... things are already on the move. In December 1994, 7.6% of the main tiers of the judiciary ... were women. It is now a little over 9%. Not a meteoric rise, true, but a steady one.

Accepting Lord Irvine's statistics, one certainly would have to agree that the change is not meteoric; in fact, at the rate he quotes, it would take 90 years for women to hold 50% of judicial offices.

A report on the judiciary carried out in 1992 by Justice, the British section of the International Commission of Jurists, recommended that a Judicial Commission should be established as the best way of reducing the strain on the administration of justice. It was suggested that such a Commission should operate independently of the judiciary and should be responsible for: all judicial appointments, including lay magistrates and tribunals; all judicial training; the career development of all judges; the maintenance of levels of performance and dealing with complaints.

In September 1994, the Labour Party peer and spokesman on legal affairs, and former chairman of the Bar Council, Lord Williams of Mostyn, attacked the reforms introduced by Lord Mackay, categorising them as merely 'cosmetic tinkering to no lasting or sensible purpose ... offer[ing] nothing which is likely to improve either judicial performance or public confidence in the judiciary'. His article presented a powerful indictment of the system of judicial appointment, claiming that:

> The present system, barely touched by the new changes, is secretive and ineffective. The first step is to apply to become an assistant recorder. That is, when the lock on the secret file creaks open. There is a file on every applicant. You cannot look at your file. You cannot ask who has commented on you. The cruellest error can remain unknown and uncorrected. The new system leaves all that firmly in place. The final decision about appointment remain in the hands of the Lord Chancellor ((1994) *The Guardian*).

Lord Williams maintained that a more fundamental reform of the judicial appointments procedure was called for and his preferred course of action would be for the Judicial Studies Board, which currently is responsible for training the judiciary, to be elevated to the level of a full judicial commission with responsibility for appointment as well as training.

Such proposals did not find favour with the then Lord Chancellor. In his Hamlyn lecture, Lord Mackay indicated that he would not consider the introduction of an independent Judicial Appointments Commission, although he somewhat inconsistently admitted that:

> ... if one were to consider the establishment of a new system for the judiciary, such a body might be regarded as appropriate.

If such a body would be appropriate if a scheme were to be instituted de novo, then why should it not be introduced as a reform of the existing system? The answer could only lie in the Lord Chancellor's faith in, and conviction as to the success of, the operation of the existing procedure. It is suggested that such faith approached the level of wilful blindness and the conviction is unsafe, Somewhat surprisingly, Lord Irvine seems to have come round to a similar opinion. One of his earliest actions was to declare the government's intention to inquire into the merits of establishing a Judicial Appointments Commission, as Lord Mostyn had previously proposed. This now seems to have been dropped during the turbulent time when the highly contentious Access to Justice Act 1999 was being taken through Parliament.

As this book was being written, it looked as if secrecy surrounding the way in which judicial and other legal offices are filled was about to be opened up to scrutiny, to the dismay and discomfort of all of those involved. When the government appointed a new 'treasury devil' in 1998, that is, their chief advocate in the civil courts, senior members of the judiciary were consulted about the suitability of the candidates on the usual secret basis. However, when the appointment went to a male member of the Lord Chancellor's ex-chambers, a woman candidate registered a claim for sex discrimination in relation to the appointment. As result of this action, the then Attorney General, John Morris, who made the appointment, would have been required to disclose details of the process leading to the decision, which included representations made by senior judges. The soundings were actually taken by the Attorney General's deputy, the Solicitor General, Lord Falconer at the time. Lord Falconer, however, was himself a close personal friend of the Prime Minister and his wife, who were both, once, members of the Lord Chancellor's chambers. It would at least appear, therefore, that there was a measure of the legitimate dubiety about the procedure, especially when it is alleged that all of the people sounded out were men, including the Lord Chancellor, and at least two others were intimates of the Blairs and the Lord Chancellor. This case merely compounded the Lord Chancellor's misfortune in his and/or his department's appointment policy, in that he had already been found to have appointed a member of staff in breach of the sex discrimination legislation. Fortunately for all those involved, although not for those who wished to see the appointment procedures opened up to scrutiny, the matter was resolved, and the case dropped, when the Attorney General agreed to pay £5,000 to a charity promoting the rights of women. (For further observations on the Lord Chancellor's powers, see 6.1.1.)

A different approach, following the example of the United States, might be for the holders of the higher judicial offices to be subjected to confirmation hearings by, for example, a select committee of the House of Commons. Lord Mackay dismissed any such possibility as follows:

> The tendency of prior examination ... is to discover and analyse the previous opinions of the individual in detail. *I question whether the standing of the judiciary in our country, or the public's confidence in it, would be enhanced by such an inquiry,* or whether any wider public interest would be served by it [emphasis added].

It is perhaps unfortunate that the italicised words in the above passage can be interpreted in a way that no doubt Lord Mackay did not intend but which, nonetheless, could suggest a cover up of the dubious opinions of those appointed to judicial office.

An even more radical alternative would be to open judicial office holding to election as they also do in the United States, although in this case one might well agree with Lord Mackay that:

> The British people would not feel that this was a very satisfactory method of appointing the professional judiciary.

Alternatively, and following Lord Mackay's emphasis on the professional nature of the judiciary, the United Kingdom could follow continental examples and provide the judiciary with a distinct professional career structure as an alternative to legal practice. (For a consideration of the way in which other jurisdictions appoint their judges, readers are referred to a 1991 Law Society Research Study No 5 entitled *Judicial Appointments* by Eleni Skordaki.)

Such alternative suggestions would not eradicate all questions of the judge's impartiality but they would certainly be an improvement on the existing system. For, as things stand at present, the lack of transparency in the appointment procedure merely clouds a more fundamental question, which can be posed in two forms: first, whether the best people are being selected from the available pool of talent; or, alternatively, and more radically, whether the present procedure ensures the appointment of the wrong type of judge generally.

6.4   Training of the judiciary

All judicial training, from the induction of new magistrates (see 6.8.3, below) to the honing of the skills of the judges in the House of Lords, is the responsibility of the Judicial Studies Board (JSB). Prior to the establishment of the JSB, the training of judges in the United Kingdom was almost minimal; especially when considered in the light of the Continental practice, where being a judge, rather than practising as an advocate, is a specific, and early, career choice which leads to specialist and extensive training.

The JSB provides training and instruction to all part time and full time judges in judicial skills. An essential element of the philosophy of the JSB is that the training is provided by judges for judges. The training requirements of the different jurisdictions are the responsibility of five committees (Criminal, Civil, Tribunals, Family and Magisterial). Another Committee, the Equal Treatment Advisory Committee, provides advice and support for all five committees. The JSB membership is drawn mainly from the judiciary, but also includes some leading academics and other professionals. The Board enjoys considerable autonomy from its parent department, the Lord Chancellor's Department, in deciding the need for and nature of judicial training

Assistant recorders are required to attend seminars on procedure and sentencing before they can sit on their own in the Crown Court. Later, training takes the form of further, intermittent seminars focusing primarily on sentencing. Those sitting in the Crown Court benefit specifically from the advice contained in the Crown Court Bench Book of Specimen Directions, which, as Lord Bingham states in the foreword to the most recent edition, 1997, 'are likely to provide useful source material which will in turn assist in the resolution of the problem under consideration'. The specific nature of the Specimen Directions is a delicate matter, as they do not, and indeed cannot, represent an unconditional statement of what the law, and judicial practice, is. They always have to be adapted by the judges to fit particular circumstances. Such a fact has to be recognised, and, indeed, it is enforced by an injunction not to reproduce the directions as a part of any commercial activity. Nonetheless, it is made available on the Internet at:

www.cix.co.uk/~jsb/specdir/index.htm.

The topic of judicial training raises the related question of the general competence of judges to decide particular cases when they may have been appointed to courts having jurisdiction in areas where they have had no previous practical experience and very little knowledge. That such appointments are made is a common enough practice, but its deleterious effect was highlighted by PJ Richardson in the preface to the 1995 edition of *Archbold*, the leading work on criminal procedure, in which he claimed that:

> Some of those who sit hearing criminal appeals have little or no practical experience of criminal law ... [consequently] the judgments get longer; authorities of apparent relevance are not cited or are overlooked.

The seriousness of the situation is emphasised in Richardson's prescription to remedy the problem:

> ... the identification of a nucleus of judges with experience of practice in the criminal courts and a common understanding of the principles of criminal liability, the rules of procedure and evidence and the considerations relevant to sentencing discretion.

If those hearing criminal appeals do not presently have such basic understanding, then the situation is certainly grave and requires immediate remedial action.

Also, as has been pointed out earlier in this chapter, doubts have been raised as to the knowledge and competence of the senior judiciary with specific regard to issues relating to human rights and civil liberties. Such doubts become pressing, with the introduction of the Human Rights Act 1998, and the potential development of the House of Lords as a Constitutional Court.

It should be noted, however, that today judicial training has probably never been of greater public concern nor been executed with such rigour since the JSB was established in 1979. A number of factors have precipitated this change. As we note in the preface to this book, the machinery and processes of law have undergone great change during the last few years. Consequently, the judiciary has been subject to thorough re-training in the new civil procedure (see Chapter 7). This training has included residential seminars for all full time and part time judges dealing with civil work, local training, and conferences held at various national locations. Similarly, following the incorporation of the European Convention on Human Rights into English law by the Human Rights Act 1998, the government set aside £4.5 million for human rights judicial training during 1999–2000. This budget for this enormous project included £1.6 million for the JSB, and £1 million for the Court Service to provide cover for judges who were in training.

Another consideration here should be the growth of consumer awareness. Frances Gibb has argued this point ('Rude judges must mind their language' (1999) *The Times*, 29 June). She notes that we inhabit an era of litigants who know their rights and expect good service, and that judges are under greater scrutiny than in previous times. In April 1999, the Lord Chancellor's Department (LCD) published figures showing that, from August 1998 (when data was first collected), 2,109 complaints were made against judges. Most, however, were against the actual judicial decision which the Lord Chancellor cannot investigate without violating the principle of the independence of the judiciary. Only 183 cases were investigated because they involved serious allegations about the conduct of the judge. Following that, five judges were sent letters by the LCD. The Director of Studies at the JSB, Judge Paul Collins, observes that, as there are over 5,000 full time and part time judges making hundreds of decisions, the number of complaints upheld is relatively small ((1999) *The Times*, 29 June).

In 1988, there were 2,000 judicial training days (days when any one judge is training not sitting). In 1999, the number will be more than 10,000 (Judicial Studies Board, Annual Report, 1999, London: HMSO). In 1999, for the first time, JSB training will include new guidance for all judges on equal treatment issues such as disability, gender and sexual orientation, and litigants-in-person. Equal treatment training is now integral to all induction courses. Lord Justice Waller's (chairman of the JSB) attitude is encouraging:

> There is absolutely no room for complacency in these areas. And I am not going to say – just because someone has been on our course, they will be perfect, but I hope that, as result, judges are better equipped to do their jobs ((1999) *The Times*, 13 July).

6.4.1 Runciman Commission's recommendations

The nature of the training undergone by barristers and judges was one of the issues considered by the Runciman Commission (1993). In relation to the judiciary, the Commission made several recommendations:

- that substantially *more resources* be allocated to judicial training in general;

- that training courses should involve a mixture of people from *different agencies and disciplines* within the criminal justice system and should not just be judge focused;

- that experienced judges should monitor the performance of those judges undergoing training;

- that judges should be required to attend *refresher training courses* every three years;

- that assistant recorders should receive their first refresher training two years after their initial training.

In particular, emphasis was placed on the need to ensure that judges were conscious of their situation in a multi-ethnic society, and it was specifically recommended:

- that there should be an increased effort to improve and extend the existing training of judges in the awareness of *race issues*;

- the question of judicial attitudes to women was apparently not as crucial in the view of the committee, as is evident in its recommendation that consideration should be given to extending such training to cover an awareness of *gender issues*;

- a further contentious suggestion of the committee was that judges should be subject to appraisal. Thus, it recommended that the Lord Chancellor should look to establishing a formal system of performance appraisal with presiding and resident judges having a leading role in the procedure; and

- that members of the Bar should be able to comment on the performance of judges.

It is gratifying to note that the Judicial Studies Board, in recognising the need for, and in implementing the provision of, necessary training, has gone a long way to accommodate the recommendations of Runciman.

6.4.2   Judicial reaction to race awareness training

The Judicial Studies Board has instituted seminars for training part time and circuit judges in racial awareness, for example, reminding them that, in a multi-cultural/multi-faith society, it is offensive to ask for people's 'Christian' names, as well as warning them as to the dangers of even more crassly offensive language and racial stereotyping that appears to be so much a part of the English use of metaphor. It has been reported, however, that such training has met with resistance. Lincoln Crawford, a barrister, part time judge, Bar Council member and former member of the Commission for Racial Equality, has commented on the existence of such resistance, in *Counsel* (1994, February), the journal of the Bar. In his article, he lists a number of reasons why judges are opposed to the training. First, there is the belief that judges apply the law fairly and do not need to be trained in race awareness for the simple reason that they are not racist in their outlook or practice. Such an assertion sits uncomfortably, however, with the documented research that reveals that black defendants found guilty of offences are treated more harshly than equivalent white defendants. Secondly, this initial approach is supported by an attitude that considers it to be an affront to the independence of their judgments to require judges to try to take account of the different cultural backgrounds of those black and Asian people who come before them. (One white judge actually remarked that he had been called 'nigger' at his school and that it had not caused him any harm.) Thirdly, Crawford claims, there is a bloody-mindedness amongst the judiciary, representing the view that they operate the British legal system and that anyone within the jurisdiction should take the law as they find it, even if it is partial and discriminatory in its lack of sympathy for other cultural values. The fourth justification for resistance to race awareness training is the view that it smacks of interference with the impartiality and independence of the judiciary, the implication being that judges should not be held to account even when they are operating in a questionable if not a patently discriminatory manner.

All of the foregoing supposed justifications are completely spurious and represent a denial of the cultural existence of a large section of British society. As Lincoln Crawford puts it:

> A judiciary which fears and feels nervous about plurality and diversity runs the danger of becoming closed, narrow and brittle.

It also runs the danger of completely alienating large sections of the population over which it exercises its power and, when law is reduced to the level of mere power rather than legitimate authority, its effectiveness is correspondingly reduced.

There was a surge of public resentment when a truly shocking example of judicial insensitivity, not to say stupidity, came to light. At the annual dinner of the Criminal Bar Association, High Court judge Graham Boal told a joke, much more offensive than it was funny, which was, at one and the same time, sexist, homophobic, racist and antagonistic to measures being taken to address such prejudices within the legal profession and the judiciary. When the circumstances were leaked to the newspapers by those at the dinner who were genuinely shocked by his behaviour, the consequent uproar resulted in the Lord Chancellor writing a strong letter of rebuke to Boal, warning him as to his future conduct. Lord Justice Waller, the chairman of the JSB, suggests that such incidents are becoming fewer as a result of judicial training.

He contends that remarks such as those of Judge Boal will be:

> ... picked up and brandished across the headlines and, in one sense, the judge deserves it. Yet, the rest of the judiciary is doing its job perfectly well. Most judges in this modern day are courteous and sensitive – their predecessors were not ((1999) *The Times*, 13 July).

But, of continuing concern is the fact that some of the audience actually laughed at his attempt at humour. Following the finding of 'institutionalised racism' within the police force by the Macpherson Inquiry into the murder of Stephen Lawrence, such behaviour cannot but raise questions as to the institutional culture of the bench, and the legal profession generally. The removal of rights to jury trial in relation to each way offences, in the light of contrary representations made by and on behalf of the black community, by such people as Courtney Griffiths QC, would seem merely to emphasise the perceived, even if unsubstantiated, doubts about the extent of racism within that culture.

6.5   Retirement of judges

All judges are now required to retire at 70, although they may continue in office at the discretion of the Lord Chancellor. The Judicial Pensions and Retirement Act 1993 reduced the retirement age from the previous 75 years for High Court judges and 72 years for other judges.

The reduction of the retirement age may have been designed to reduce the average age of the judiciary, but of perhaps even more significance in this respect is the change that was introduced at the same time in judicial pensions. The new provision requires judges to have served for 20 years, rather than the previous 15, before they qualify for full pension rights. This effectively means that, if judges are to benefit from full pension rights, they will have to take up their appointments by the time they are 50. Given that judges are predominantly appointed from the ranks of high earning QCs, this will either reduce their potential earnings at the Bar or reduce their pay package as judges by approximately 7.5%. This measure led to a great deal of resentment within both the Bar and the judiciary, Lord Chief Justice Taylor referring to its unfairness and meanness; and was one of the issues that fuelled the antagonism between Lord Mackay and the other members of the judiciary.

In any event, according to the statistics provided by the Lord Chancellor's Department, the average age for the Law Lords is 65.5, with Lord Slynn being the oldest at 69, and Lord Hope the youngest at 60. In the Court of Appeal, the average age is almost 62, with youngest being Sir John Laws at 53 and the oldest, Sir Alexander Beldam, at 74. Apart from Lord Irvine, who is a mere 58, the average age of the four other Heads of Division in the High Court is 67, this being considerably raised by Sir Stephen Brown who is 74.

6.6   Removal of judges

Reference has already been made to the need, with of course the exception of the Lord Chancellorship, to protect the independence of the judiciary, by making it difficult for a discomforted government to remove judges from their positions on merely political grounds. The actual provision is that judges of the House of Lords, the Court of Appeal and the High Court hold their office during good behaviour, subject to the proviso that they can be removed by the Crown on the presentation of an address by both Houses of Parliament. In actual fact, this procedure has never been used in relation to an English judge, although it was once used in 1830 to remove an Irish judge who was found guilty of misappropriating funds.

Judges below the level of the High Court do not share the same degree of security of tenure as their more senior colleagues, and can be removed, on grounds of misbehaviour or incapacity, by the action of the Lord Chancellor who does not require the sanction of Parliament. Although the famous/infamous Judge Pickles was notoriously the object of the displeasure of the Lord Chancellor in the mid- to late-1980s, he was never actually dismissed and, as yet, the only judge to be removed for misbehaviour remains the circuit judge who, in 1983, was found guilty of smuggling cigarettes and alcohol.

In a letter circulated in July 1994, Lord Mackay asked that judges inform him immediately if they are ever charged with any criminal offence, other than parking or speeding violations. The Lord Chancellor stated that he wished to make it clear that a conviction for drunk driving would amount, *prima facie*, to misbehaviour. Causing offence on racial or religious grounds could also be seen as misbehaviour, as could sexual harassment.

The discretionary power of the Lord Chancellor not to extend the appointment of a recorder, without the need to explain or justify his action, has previously provided grounds for criticism of, and accusations of political interference on the part of, the Lord Chancellor.

Stipendiary magistrates are subject to removal by the Crown on the recommendation of the Lord Chancellor and lay magistrates are subject to removal by the Lord Chancellor without cause or explanation.

6.7   Judicial immunity from suit

A fundamental measure to ensure the independence of the judiciary is the rule that they cannot be sued in relation to things said or acts done in their judicial capacity in good faith. The effect of this may be seen in *Sirros v Moore* (1975) in which a judge wrongly ordered someone's detention. It was subsequently held by the Court of Appeal that, although the detention had been unlawful, no action could be taken against the judge as he had acted in good faith in his judicial capacity. Although some judges, on occasion, may be accused of abusing this privilege, it is nonetheless essential if judges are to operate as independent representatives of the law, for it is unlikely that judges would be able to express their honest opinions of the law and the situations in which it is being applied, if they were to be subject to suits from disgruntled participants.

Given the increased use of the doctrine of *ultra vires* to justify legal action by way of judicial review against members of the executive, it is satisfyingly ironic that at least one judge, Stephen Sedley, sees the possibility of a similar *ultra vires* action providing grounds for an action against judges in spite of their previously assumed legal immunity. As he expresses the point, in the *London Review of Books* of April 1994:

> Judges have no authority to act maliciously or corruptly. It would be rational to hold that such acts take them outside their jurisdiction and so do not attract judicial immunity.

No doubt, such a suggestion would be anathema to the great majority of the judiciary, but the point remains: why should judges be at liberty to abuse their position of authority in a way that no other public servant can?

Before 1991, magistrates could be liable for damages for actions done in excess of their actual authority but the CLSA 1990 extended the existing immunity from the superior courts to cover the inferior courts, so magistrates now share the same protection as other judges.

It is worth stating at this point that this immunity during court proceedings also extends as far as advocates and witnesses, and of course jurors; although the controls of *perjury* and *contempt of court* are always available to control what is said or done in the course of court proceedings.

Related to, although distinct from, the principle of immunity from suit is the convention that individual judges should not be subject to criticism in parliamentary debate, unless subject to an address for their removal: legal principles and the law in general can be criticised but not judges.

6.8   Magistrates

The foregoing has concentrated attention on the professional and legally qualified judges. There are, however, some 30,000 unpaid part time lay magistrates and 92 full time professional stipendiary magistrates operating within some 700 or so magistrates' courts in England. These magistrates are empowered to hear and decide a wide variety of legal matters and the amount and importance of the work they do should not be underestimated: 97% of all criminal cases are dealt with by the magistrates' court.

6.8.1   Powers

Magistrates' courts have considerable power in relation to both criminal and civil procedure.

- *Criminal law*

    Magistrates are empowered to try summary cases, that is, cases which are triable without a jury. Additionally, however, they may deal with *cases triable 'either way'*, that is, cases which can either be tried summarily by the magistrates, or which can be tried on indictment before a jury in the Crown Court. (See, also, 4.3 and 10.8.)

    In relation to *summary offences*, the maximum prison sentence magistrates can impose is six months, even in relation to consecutive sentences in relation to more than one offence (Magistrates' Courts Act 1980). The maximum fine that can be imposed for a summary offence is £1,000 under the Criminal Justice Act 1991.

The above represent general maxima and particular statutes may impose a lesser maximum penalty; nor should it be forgotten that magistrates can impose alternative sentences, such as community service orders, or probation orders. They can also discharge offenders either conditionally or absolutely.

In relation to *offences triable 'either way'*, magistrates' courts have increased sentencing powers. In these circumstances, although the maximum prison sentence that can be awarded in relation to a single offence is still six months, they can, in cases where more than one offence is involved, impose consecutive prison sentences up to a maximum of 12 months. They may also impose a maximum fine of £5,000.

In addition to the foregoing sentences, magistrates can issue compensation orders. Such orders are not used as a means of punishing the offender but as a way of compensating the victims of the offender without them having to sue the offender in the civil courts. Compensation orders can, however, be issued without the imposition of any other sentence. The maximum payment under any such order is £5,000.

It should also be recalled, as mentioned at 4.3.3, that the magistrates' court also sits as a youth court, with its members drawn from a special panel of JPs, to hear criminal cases involving individuals below the age of 18.

- *Civil law*

Magistrates' most significant area of civil law jurisdiction is in family law cases, particularly under the Children Act 1989 and the Domestic Proceedings and Magistrates' Courts Act 1978. In such cases, they sit as a *family proceedings court*.

They also have powers relating to the collection of such civil debts as water, gas and electricity charges and for the council tax, the replacement for the former community charge or poll tax. They also sit as a licensing court and consider applications for the provision of liquor licences.

- *Crime and Disorder Act 1998*

Since April 1999, the magistrates' courts now have an important new role in awarding Anti Social Behaviour Orders under the Crime and Disorder Act 1998 (see 1.3.5).

According to the Home Office guide to the Act, its intention are to: introduce measures designed to reduce delays by bringing cases to court promptly, but, on closer examination, it looks suspiciously like another economy driven measure in relation to the criminal justice system. Section

48 allows metropolitan stipendiary magistrates to sit alone in youth courts. Section 49 allows specific powers of magistrates' courts to be exercised by single magistrates or, indeed, and perhaps of even more concern, by magistrates clerks. Clerks, however, will not be allowed to remand accused into custody, or decide disputes in relation to bail. Section 53 provides that members of the CPS, who are not Crown Prosecutors, may be designated by the Director of Public Prosecutions to perform the functions of prosecutors in magistrates' courts. This power is only intended to be used in relation to straightforward guilty pleas and proof in absence in motoring cases. It specifically does not apply in relation to: contested trials; indictable only cases; and cases where the magistrates have declined jurisdiction or the defendant has elected for jury trial.

6.8.2   District Judges (Magistrates' Courts)

Stipendiary magistrates, so called because they are paid a salary, are legally qualified, being required under the Justices of the Peace Act 1997 to be barristers or solicitors of at least seven years standing. Following the Access to Justice Act 1999 (s 78), stipendiary magistrates are to be called District Judges (Magistrates' Courts).

There are currently 92 such magistrates sitting in London and other urban centres. The advantage of the stipendiaries over the lay magistrates, apart from the obvious fact that they are legally qualified, is that they are full time and sit alone. This allows for a potentially greater through-put of cases; but advantages in efficiency have to be weighed against corresponding professionalisation of the judicial process and the loss in terms of the democratising effect of the lay magistracy. However, given the apparent lack of confidence that exists in the lay magistracy, perhaps such increased professionalisation would be no bad thing, although it would only come at a price, and an expensive one at that. The Runciman Report made two specific recommendations in relation to stipendiary magistrates:

- that there should be a more 'systematic' approach to the role of stipendiary magistrates in order to make best use of their special skills and qualifications;

- that the whole administration of the stipendiary magistrates system be overhauled.

The Access to Justice Act 1999 (s 78) amends the Justice of the Peace Act 1997, to unify the Metropolitan and Provincial salaried magistrates benches so that we now have just one bench of District Judges (Magistrates' Courts). This is not an entirely uncontroversial change because whereas local magistrates were once regarded (like police forces) as being intrinsically local and beyond the reach of central governmental powers, the new arrangement can be seen as increasing the potential influence of the Lord Chancellor's Department over local justice. Another viewpoint, however, and the reason advanced by the government for the change, is that a single bench will improve the geographic consistency of sentencing.

6.8.3 Qualifications and training

There is no requirement for lay magistrates to have any legal qualifications. On being accepted onto the bench, however, magistrates undertake a training process, under the auspices of the Judicial Studies Board. Magistrates are required to attend training courses, with a special emphasis being placed on Equal Treatment Training. The way in which the training programme seeks to overcome conceptions as to the politically limited nature of the magistracy is evident in the content of the extensive training materials produced for the magistrates. These include modules on: raising awareness and challenging discrimination; discretion and decision making; prejudice and stereotype; so the overall emphasis may be seen to be on equality of people, and equality of treatment. There is, however, a new emphasis on the practical skills involved in performing the duties placed on magistrates, and, consequently, much of the training will actually be based on sitting as a magistrate, with the input of specially trained monitors to give guidance and advice on how the new magistrate performs their tasks, and fulfils their role.

The training course is designed to give new magistrates an understanding of the functions and powers of the bench generally and to locate that understanding within the context of national practice, particularly with regard to sentencing. On the topic of discretion and sentencing, Lord Irvine provided the magistrates with the following strong advice/not to say warning:

> You ... must exercise your discretion in individual cases with great care within a system that needs to secure continuing public confidence. This is what makes the sentencing guidelines produced by the Magistrates' Association so important. They are guidelines – they do not curtail your independent discretion to impose sentences you think are right, case by case. But the guidelines exist to help you in that process, to give you more information in reaching your decision. And they help to assist the magistracy, to maintain an overall consistency of approach ... I urge you to follow the guidelines, which are drawn up for your benefit and the magistracy as a whole (speech to the Council of Magistrates' Association, March 1999).

Although particular key legal issues may be considered in the course of the training, it is not the intention to provide the magistrate with a complete grasp of substantive law and legal practice. Indeed, to expect such would be to misunderstand both the role of the magistrates and the division of responsibility within the magistrates' court. Every bench of magistrates has a legally qualified justices' clerk, whose function it is to advise the bench on questions of law, practice, and procedure; leaving matters of fact to magistrates to decide upon (see 4.3.1).

6.8.4   Appointment

Under the Justices of the Peace Act 1997, magistrates are appointed to, and indeed removed from, office by the Lord Chancellor, on behalf of the Queen, after consultation with local advisory committees. There are currently 111 such advisory committees, and 134 subcommittees within the UK. Section 50 of the Employment Rights Act 1996 provides that employers are obliged to release their employees, for such time as is reasonable, to permit them to serve as magistrates. In the event of an employer refusing to sanction absence from work to perform magistrate's duties, the employee can take the matter before an employment tribunal. Understandably, there is no statutory requirement for the employer to pay their employees in their absence, but magistrates are entitled to claim expenses for loss of earnings in the exercise of their office.

Proposals for office tend to be generated by local interest groups, such as political parties, trade unions, chambers of commerce and such like bodies, and this limited constituency may give rise to the view that the magistracy only represents the attitudes of a limited section of society. In a multi-cultural, multi-racial society, it is essential that the magistrates' court should reflect the composition of the wider society, and the rules relating to the appointment, and training, of magistrates do, at least in theory, support this conclusion. Nonetheless, there remains a lingering doubt, at least in the minds of particular constituencies, that the magistracy still represents the values, both moral and political, of a limited section of society. A further significant step towards opening up the whole procedure of appointing magistrates was taken when local advisory committees were granted the power to advertise for people to put themselves forward for selection. As the chairman of the Mid-Staffordshire Magistrates' Bench stated in a local newspaper, although previously rank and social position were the main qualifications, nowadays:

> ... it is important a bench has a balance of sexes, professions and political allegiances.

Given the current proposal to increase the cases to be decided by magistrates, it is to be hoped that the appointment and training procedures will give the general public more confidence in the much vaunted representational function of the magistrates' courts.

According to former Lord Chancellor Lord Mackay, in the first of his 1993 Hamlyn lectures, magistrates should possess qualities of fairness, a judicial temperament and a willingness to hear both sides of a case. These desired attributes are supported by the current guidance notes to the application form for becoming a magistrate, which set out six key qualities to be looked for in an applicant:

- good character;

- understanding and communication;

- social awareness;

- maturity and sound temperament;

- sound judgment; and

- commitment and reliability.

Once candidates of a suitable quality have been identified, the local advisory committee is placed under the injunction to have regard to the need to ensure that the composition of the bench broadly reflects the community which it serves, in terms of gender, ethnic origin, geographical spread, occupation and political affiliation. It may even be that individuals, who are otherwise suitably qualified, may not be appointed, if their presence would exacerbate a perceived imbalance in the existing bench. However, in 1998, the Lord Chancellor's Department issued a consultation paper relating to the political balance in the lay magistracy (*Political Balance in the Magistracy*, www.open.gov.uk/lcd/consult/general/jp-pol.htm). The paper suggested that political affiliation is no longer a major issue, and therefore may not have to be controlled in relation to the make up of benches of magistrates. As support for its suggestion, the consultancy document makes three points. First, that actually ensuring a political balance on the bench raises:

> ... the danger of creating a perception that politics do play a part in the administration of justice, notwithstanding that it is agreed on all sides that, in a mature democracy, politics have no place in the court room.

Secondly, that advisory committees:

> ... have increasingly found that many magistrates have declined to provide the information [relating to their political allegiance] or classed themselves as 'uncommitted'.

Thirdly, it claimed that, in any case, 'geodemographic classification schemes', based on an analysis of particular personal attributes, such as ethnicity, gender, marital status, occupation, home ownership, car owning status, are much more sensitive indicators for achieving social balance on benches than stated political allegiance.

This may well represent the emergence of the truly classless society. Alternatively, it might represent a worrying denial of the importance of political attitudes within law generally, and the magistrates bench in particular.

The report of the Runciman Commission recommended that magistrates be given the power to decide more cases by taking away the defendant's right to elect for a trial on indictment in certain situations. This recommendation was subsequently adopted by the current Home Secretary, Jack Straw. In support of its recommendation, the Commission referred to research that revealed that, for offences that could be tried either way, that is, by either the magistrates' court or before a jury in the Crown Court, the chances of acquittal are substantially higher in the Crown Court (57%) than in the magistrates' courts (30%). The report of the Commission stated that defendants should not be entitled to choose a particular mode of trial just because they thought it offered them a better chance of acquittal. The question that has to be asked in response to this is: why not? Because Crown Courts acquit more defendants than magistrates' courts does not necessarily mean that the Crown Court procedure is inappropriate. The problem may lie not with the Crown Court, but with the magistrates' courts. This matter will be considered in more detail in Chapter 10, but, for the present, it has to be recognised that the Runciman Report did nothing to address the fact that the magistrates' courts are more likely than the Crown Court to convict, and that this gives rise to, at least, the perception of the Crown Court being a fairer forum in which to decide cases; or, alternatively, the suspicion that the magistrates' courts are not as just as they might be.

6.9 Politics and the judiciary

Law is an inherently and inescapably political process. Even assertions as to the substantive autonomy of law (see Chapter 1) merely disguise the fact that, in making legal decisions, judges decide where the weight of public approval is to be placed and which forms of behaviour are to be sanctioned (see, for example, *R v Brown* (1993) where the House of Lords criminalised the sexual activities of consenting sado-masochists, arguably without fully comprehending some aspects of what was going on).

There is, however, an increasingly apparent tendency for contemporary judges to become actively, directly and openly engaged in more overtly political activity. The 1955 Kilmuir rules, named after the Lord Chancellor who introduced them, were designed to control the instances when the judiciary could express opinion in the media. The rules were abrogated in 1987 by Lord Mackay and, since then, the judiciary have been more forthcoming in expressing their views, not just on matters strictly related to their judicial functions but also in wider political matters.

An example of this process can be cited in the concerted action of the judiciary in response to the pronouncements of the then Home Secretary, Michael Howard, at the Conservative Party Conference in Autumn 1993 in which he asserted the success of prison as a means of dealing with crime and declared his commitment to sending more offenders to prison. First of all, Lord Woolf, architect of the government's prison reform programme and who was conducting an investigation into the operation of the whole civil law process, responded by making reference to:

> ... a fashion, not confined to the totally uninformed, to indulge in rhetoric advocating increased sentences across the board in a way which will be counter productive ...

and he was quoted in the *Guardian* newspaper as stating that such talk was 'shortsighted and irresponsible'.

Perhaps the really surprising aspect of this difference of opinion was not that Lord Woolf disagreed with the Home Secretary but that he was supported in his views by seven other judges in a series of interviews in *The Observer*, 17 October 1993, including the then Law Lord, Lord Ackner, and the chairman of the Judicial Studies Board, Lord Justice Farquharson.

Lord Ackner was prominent in taking Lord Mackay to task for his various interventions in the operation of the legal system. He also warned the Home Secretary that he was in danger of acting illegally by introducing a new system of criminal injuries compensation (see 6.10.7, below), but he has not been alone. For example, in January 1994, Lord Taylor, the then Lord Chief Justice, made an outspoken attack on the then government's criminal justice policy both in the House of Lords and in a public lecture, suggesting that government legislation might tend to undermine judicial impartiality.

The Home Secretary's approach to sentencing policy, and particularly his wish to impose minimum sentences for criminals convicted of certain offences or repeat convictions, consistently came under attack from the judiciary. As early as October 1995, when Michael Howard announced his intention to introduce such policies, the then Lord Chief Justice Lord Taylor took a mere two hours to issue a withering challenge to the Home Secretary's policy statement. According to Lord Taylor:

> Judges apply the [sentencing] framework conscientiously, but must be free to fit the particular punishment to the particular crime if justice is to be done. Minimum sentences are inconsistent with doing justice according to the circumstances of each case. Instead of limiting judicial discretion by introducing unnecessary constraints on sentencing, the police should be provided with the resources they need to bring criminals before the courts in the first place.

When the proposals were eventually issued in a White Paper in April 1996, they were commented on with severe scorn by the former Master of the Rolls, Lord Donaldson, in an article in *The Guardian* newspaper. Lord Donaldson stated that the objectives of sentencing policy should 'have nothing to do with the election of particular politicians or particular parties' and that the proposals 'would require the judge to pass what he believed to be an unjust sentence in any case in which, taking account of the circumstances of the crime and the offender, he would otherwise have passed a lighter sentence'.

Lord Taylor's replacement as Lord Chief Justice, Lord Bingham, took the opportunity of a television interview in November 1996 to express his opinion that the problems with the Home Secretary's proposals would only be mitigated if judges were not obliged to give mandatory sentences where they considered it unjust to do so. In his view, 'that, at least, would enable him to give effect to his sense of the justice of the case'.

Lord Ackner then took up the attack on the proposals, which then were contained in the Crime (Sentencing) Bill, in another article in *The Guardian* in November 1996 in which he compared the action of the government with the action of the government in the former Soviet Union.

In the event, the early dissolution of Parliament in advance of the General Election in May 1997 ensured that, in order to get the majority of the Bill through Parliament, the Home Secretary was required to reach a compromise and accept the retention of judicial discretion as proposed in an amendment to the Bill in the House of Lords.

However, perhaps the most vital area in which the judges play an active political role is in the relation to the operation of judicial review. As was stated in Chapter 1, judicial review subjects the executive arm of the State to the overview of the judges in such a way as to raise fundamental questions about the structure of the British Constitution and the role of the judges therein.

6.10   Judicial review

The recent growth in applications for judicial review is truly startling. The statistical records show that, in 1980, there were only 525 applications for judicial review; in 1996, 4,586; in 1997, 4,636 such applications; and, in 1998, 5,201. In recognition of the growth in applications for judicial review, 40% of which originate from outside London, the Heilbron Report recommended that such applications should not have to be made in London, but should be capable of being heard by circuit judges.

The remedies open to anyone challenging the decisions or actions of administrative institutions or public authorities can be divided into *private* or *public* law remedies.

6.10.1 Private law remedies

There are three private law remedies:

- *Declaration*

  This is a definitive statement, by the High Court or county court, of what the law is in a particular area. The procedure may be used by an individual or body to clarify a particular contentious situation. It is a common remedy in private law but it also has an important part to play in regard to individuals' relations with administrative institutions, as can be seen, for example, in *Congreve v Home Office* (1976), where the Court of Appeal stated that it would be unlawful for the Home Office to revoke yearly television licences after only eight months because they had been bought in anticipation of an announced price rise but before the expiry of existing licences.

  Declarations, however, cannot be enforced either directly or indirectly through the contempt of court procedure. Public authorities are, as a matter of course, expected to abide by them.

- *Injunctions*

  Usually, an injunction seeks to restrain a person from breaking the law; alternatively, however, a mandatory injunction may instruct someone to undo what they have previously done, or alternatively to stop doing what they are doing. Both types of injunction may be sought against a public authority. See *Attorney General v Fulham Corporation* (1921) in which a local authority was ordered to stop running a laundry service where it only had the power to establish laundries for people to wash their own clothes.

- *Damages*

  Damages cannot be awarded on their own in relation to administrative misconduct but may be claimed in addition where one of the other remedies, considered above, is sought, as, for example, in *Cooper v Wandsworth Board of Works* (1863). In this case, a builder had put up a building without informing the Board of Works as he was required to do. When the Board demolished the building, he nonetheless recovered damages against them on the basis that the Board had exceeded its powers by not allowing him to defend or explain his actions.

In order to seek one of these private law remedies, an individual merely had to issue a writ against a public authority in their own name. They did not require the approval of the court.

6.10.2 The prerogative orders

The prerogative orders are so called because they were originally the means whereby sovereigns controlled the operation of their officials. As a consequence, the prerogative orders cannot be used against the Crown, but they can be used against individual ministers of State and, since *R v Secretary of State for the Home Department ex p Fire Brigades Union* (1995), considered at 6.10.7, below, it is clear that ministers cannot avoid judicial review by hiding behind the cloak of prerogative powers.

- *Certiorari* is the mechanism by means of which decisions of inferior courts, tribunals and other authoritative bodies are brought before the High Court to have their validity examined. Where any such decision is found to be invalid, it may be set aside. An example of this can be seen in *Ridge v Baldwin* (1964). Here, the plaintiff had been dismissed from his position as Chief Constable without having had the opportunity to present any case for his defence. The House of Lords held that the committee which had taken the decision had acted in breach of the requirements of natural justice and granted a declaration that his dismissal was null and void.

- *Prohibition* is similar to certiorari in that it relates to invalid acts of public authorities, but it is different to the extent that it is pre-emptive and prescriptive in regard to any such activity and operates to prevent the authority from taking invalid decisions in the first place. An example of the use of the prohibition order arose in *R v Telford Justices ex p Badham* (1991). In this case, an order was issued to stop committal proceedings in relation to an alleged rape that had not been reported until some 14 years after the alleged incident. The delay meant that the defendant would have been unable to prepare a proper defence against the charge.

- *Mandamus* may be seen as the obverse of prohibition, in that it is an order issued by the High Court instructing an inferior court or some other public authority to carry out a duty laid on them. Such an order is frequently issued in conjunction with an order of *certiorari*, to the effect that a public body is held to be using its powers improperly and is instructed to use them in a proper fashion. In *R v Poplar Borough Council (Nos 1 and 2)* (1922), the court ordered the borough council to pay over money due to the county council and to levy a rate to raise the money if necessary. Failure to comply with the order led to the imprisonment of some of the borough councillors.

Access to these public law remedies was not directly open to individuals. They had to apply to the court for judicial review under Ord 53 of the Rules of the Supreme Court (RSC).

The present procedure for applying for remedies against public authorities was established in 1977 when the old RSC were altered by a new Ord 53.

(Subsequently, the procedural changes introduced in 1977 were given statutory effect by s 31 of the Supreme Court Act 1981.) In order to avail oneself of the prerogative orders, an application had to be made under the procedure established in RSC Ord 53; there was normally a time limit of three months for applications (*R v Aston University Senate ex p Roffey* (1969)). The non-prerogative orders, however, continued to exist as distinct remedies in private law, apart from Ord 53. The judicial review procedure was not compulsory in order to enforce private rights against public authorities, although Ord 53 permitted that procedure to be used.

Before the introduction of the present procedure, an applicant had to apply for a specific remedy or remedies. If, for some reason, they failed to obtain the remedy sought, the court was not at liberty to grant an alternative which would have been available had the applicant sought it in the first place. Under the present procedure, an applicant may seek more than one remedy, either jointly or alternatively, and may even seek the courts' leave to amend their application at the hearing. Initially, it appeared that the new procedure had merely simplified the procedure for obtaining judicial review and, although it permitted the use of Ord 53 to get access to the private remedies, those remedies still could be sought by the issuing of a writ.

In *O'Reilly v Mackman* (1982), however, the House of Lords decided that issues relating to *public* rights could *only* be enforced by means of the judicial review procedure, and that it would be an abuse of process for an applicant to seek a declaration by writ in relation to an alleged breach of a public duty or responsibility by a public authority. In deciding the case in this way, the House of Lords did much to demarcate and emphasise the role of judicial review as the method of challenging public authorities in their performance of their powers and duties in public law.

6.10.3 *Locus standi* – standing

The right to make an application for judicial review is not automatic. There is an initial stage which involves a party making an *ex parte* application to a judge stating the facts of the case, the remedy sought and the reason for the remedy. This initial stage is sometimes seen as a filtering process in which baseless causes are rejected. The party seeking judicial review must show that they have, at least, an arguable case and that judicial review is the appropriate mechanism for dealing with it.

They must also show that they have sufficient *locus standi* in the matter and are not just officious bystanders with no real interest. In order to show *locus standi*, they must have 'sufficient interest in the matter to which the application relates' to justify their taking it on themselves to pursue it. Whether a person has such an interest or not is a matter for the court to determine as decided in *IRC v National Federation of Self-Employed and Small Businesses Ltd* (1981). (See, further, 6.10.6.)

Standing to seek judicial review was extended to pressure groups with a particular interest in the matter at issue in *R v HM Inspector of Pollution ex p Greenpeace* (1994) and *R v Secretary of State for Foreign Affairs ex p World Development Movement* (1995), considered in detail below.

6.10.4 Grounds for application for judicial review

The grounds of application can be considered under two heads: *procedural ultra vires* and *substantive ultra vires*:

- *Procedural ultra vires*, as its name suggests, relates to the failure of a person or body, provided with specific authority, to follow the procedure established for using that power. It also covers instances where a body exercising a judicial function fails to follow the requirements of natural justice, by acting as prosecutor and judge in the same case or not permitting the accused person to make representations to the panel deciding the case.

- *Substantive ultra vires* occurs where someone does something that is not actually authorised by the enabling legislation. And, in *Associated Provincial Picture House v Wednesbury Corporation* (1947), Lord Greene MR established the possibility of challenging discretionary decisions on the basis of unreasonableness.

Lord Greene's approach was endorsed and refined by Lord Diplock in *Council of Civil Service Unions v Minister for the Civil Service* (1984) in which he set out the three recognised grounds for judicial review, namely:

- illegality;

- irrationality;

- procedural impropriety.

Lord Diplock, however, introduced the possibility of a much more wide ranging reason for challenging administrative decisions: namely, the doctrine of *proportionality*. Behind this doctrine is the requirement that there should be a reasonable relation between a decision, and its objectives. It requires the achievement of particular ends by means that are not more oppressive than they need be to attain those ends. The potentially innovative aspect of this doctrine is the extent to which it looks to the substance of the decisions rather than simply focusing on the way in which they are reached.

Lord Diplock's listing of proportionality within the grounds for judicial review was controversial, if not at the very least, arguably, mistaken. Proportionality, however, is a key principle within the jurisdiction of the European Court of Human Rights, and is used frequently to assess the validity of State action which interferes with individual rights protected under the Convention. Consequently, as the Human Rights Act 1998 has incorporated the European Convention into UK law, proportionality will be a part of UK jurisprudence and legal practice; at least, in cases which fall within the scope of the Human Rights Act. Although Human Rights Act cases and judicial review are different and distinct procedures, nonetheless, it is surely a mere matter of time before the doctrine of proportionality is applied by the judges in judicial review cases unrelated to the Convention.

6.10.5 The exclusion of judicial review

As will be considered in Chapter 8, one of the reasons for the setting up of extensive systems of administrative tribunals was precisely the wish to curb the power of the judges. It was felt that judges, and indeed the common law itself, tended to be more supportive of *individual* rights and freedoms as opposed to *collective* notions of welfare pursued by post-war governments, and that they would not administer such policies sympathetically. The judges, however, asserted their ultimate control over such tribunals generally, through the use of judicial review. There have been various attempts by parliamentary drafters to exclude the judiciary from certain areas by wording provisions in such a way as to deny the possibility of judicial review. These attempts, however, have mainly proved to be in vain and have been rendered ineffective by the refusal of the courts to recognise their declared effect. Examples are:

- *'Finality' or 'ouster' clauses*

  There are a variety of possible wordings for these clauses. For example, the legislation might provide that 'the minister's (or the tribunal's) decision shall be final', or alternatively it might attempt to emphasise the point by stating that the decision in question 'shall be final and conclusive' or it might even provide that 'it shall be final, conclusive and shall not be questioned in any legal proceedings whatsoever'. Unfortunately for the drafter of the legislation and the minister or tribunal in question, all three formulations are equally likely to be ineffective. The courts have tended to interpret such phrases in a narrow way, so as to recognise the exclusion of an appeal procedure but to introduce the possibility of judicial review, as distinct from appeal. The classic case on this point is *R v Medical Appeal Tribunal ex p Gilmore* (1957), in which Lord Denning stated that 'The word "final" ... does not mean without recourse to certiorari'. This, however, raised the point of provisions which expressly sought to exclude certiorari.

  In *South East Asia Fire Bricks Sdn Bhd v Non-Metallic Mineral Products Manufacturing Employees Union* (1980), the Privy Council decided that a Malaysian statute was sufficiently detailed in its wording to effectively exclude certiorari *for an error of law on the face of the record*. The Privy Council pointed out, however, that the exclusion could not be effective to prevent judicial review where the institution in question had acted *ultra vires* or in breach of natural justice.

- *Partial exclusion clauses*

    Where legislation has provided for a limited time period within which parties have to apply for judicial review, then applications outside of the period will not be successful. In *Smith v East Elloe Rural District Council* (1956), the House of Lords, although only by three to two majority, recognised the effectiveness of a six week limitation clause in the Acquisition of Land (Authorisation Procedure) Act 1946. Although that case was subject to criticism in *Anisminic Ltd v Foreign Compensation Commission* (1969), it was explained and followed in *R v Secretary of State for the Environment ex p Ostler* (1976).

In response to the Franks Committee's recommendation that judicial review should not be subject to exclusion, s 14(1) of the Tribunals and Inquiries Act 1971 was enacted to that end. Unfortunately, it only applies to pre-1958 legislation.

The current Immigration and Asylum Bill, whilst not in any way seeking to ban the possibility of judicial review in law, contains provisions which will, in effect, punish people who attempt to make use of it. The proposal in the Bill is that any asylum seeker who challenges a decision made by the Home Office, by way of judicial review, will automatically lose the right to State support.

6.10.6 Law Commission's Report on judicial review

In October 1994, the Law Commission published a report, *Administrative Law: Judicial Review and Statutory Appeals, No 226*, on the current operation of judicial review and made recommendations as to its future. The major proposals for the reform are:

- inappropriately commenced writ actions should be allowed to be converted into proceedings for judicial review;

- a preliminary consideration stage, to be conducted on paper, should be introduced and the test for whether a case should proceed should be *whether there is a serious issue which ought to de determined* rather than the present test which requires the case to be arguable;

- claims for restitution, debt and interest should be available in judicial review;

- the court should be able to grant interim relief before the conclusion of the preliminary consideration, and should be able to grant interim and advisory declarations;

- *locus standi* should be determined on the basis that the applicant *has been or would be adversely affected* by the action complained of or even more widely that *it is in the public interest*, and unincorporated associations such as pressure groups should be given standing. This latter recommendation follows the practice established in such cases as *R v HM Inspectorate of Pollution ex p Greenpeace* (1993) and *R v Secretary of State for Foreign Affairs ex p World Development Movement Ltd* (1995);

- legal aid should be available where an issue of general public interest is involved and costs should be available from central funds in such instances.

The Woolf Report has also had several implications for the operation of judicial review:

- judicial review should be seen as a last resort and parties are to be encouraged to use other mechanisms, such as ombudsmen, to resolve their difficulties;

- the first stage of the process, the currently named 'leave stage', is renamed the 'preliminary consideration stage';

- the preliminary consideration stage will be considered in writing;

- interim relief may be granted before the preliminary stage;

- right of action, standing, will be decided either, on the basis that the claimant will be adversely affected by the decision to be reviewed, or, on grounds of public interest;

- cases will be held outside London where appropriate; and

- judges from other than the Queens Bench Divisional Court will be used where appropriate.

6.10.7 The politics of judicial review

The relationship of the executive and the judiciary and the role of judicial review in establishing that relationship has been highlighted in a number of cases.

In *M v Home Office* (1993), the House of Lords decided that the court has jurisdiction in judicial review proceedings to grant interim and final injunctions against officers of the Crown and to make a finding of contempt of court against a government department or a minister of the Crown in either his personal *or his official capacity*.

M v Home Office is of signal importance in establishing the powers of the courts in relation to the executive. It is also interesting to note that in delivering the leading speech Lord Woolf quoted extensively from, and clearly supported, Dicey's view of the Rule of Law as involving the subjection of all, including State officials, to the ordinary law of the land (see Chapter 1).

In November 1994, the government suffered two damaging blows from the judiciary. In *R v Secretary of State for Foreign Affairs ex p World Development Movement Ltd* (1995), the Queens Bench Divisional Court held that the Secretary of State had acted beyond his powers in granting aid to the Malaysian Government in relation to the Pergau Dam project. The financial assistance was given not for the promotion of development *per se* as authorised by s 1 of the Overseas Development and Cooperation Act 1980, but in order to facilitate certain arms' sales. As Rose LJ stated:

> Whatever the Secretary of State's intention or purpose may have been, it is, as it seems to me, a matter for the courts and not for the Secretary of State to determine whether, on the evidence before the court, the particular conduct was, or was not, within the statutory purpose.

In *R v Secretary of State for the Home Department ex p Fire Brigades Union*, the Court of Appeal held that the Home Secretary had committed an abuse of power in implementing a scheme designed to cut the level of payments made to the subjects of criminal injuries. The court held that he was under an obligation, under the CJA 1988, to put the previous non-statutory scheme on a statutory basis. It was not open for the Secretary of State to use his prerogative powers to introduce a completely new tariff scheme contrary to the intention of Parliament as expressed in the CJA 1988. The decision of the Court of Appeal was confirmed by a 3:2 majority in the House of Lords in April 1995, the majority holding that the Secretary of State had exceeded, or abused, powers granted to him by Parliament. It is of interest to note that in his minority judgment Lord Keith warned that to dismiss the Home Secretary's appeal would be:

> ... an unwarrantable intrusion into the political field and a usurpation of the function of Parliament.

In 1997, in *R v Secretary of State ex p Venables and Thompson*, the House of Lords decided that the Home Secretary had misused his powers in relation to two juveniles who had been sentenced to detention during her Majesty's pleasure. The case, known generally to as the Jamie Bulger case, related to the killing of a small child by the two other children. The unusual nature of the case had caused a general furore and, when the two accused were found guilty, a tabloid newspaper started a public petition in an endeavour to ensure that they were locked up for life. In the light of such representations, the Home Secretary decided that the minimum period the two should spend in custody should be 15 years. On judicial review of the Home Secretary's decision, the House of Lords held that he should not have treated the children in this case in same way as adult prisoners sentenced to life imprisonment, and that he had a duty to review their sentence to ensure its continued appropriateness. The House of Lords also stated that, in acting in a quasi-judicial manner, the Home Secretary should not allow himself to be swayed by irrelevant considerations such as public petitions.

Even Lord Chancellors have not escaped the unwanted control of judicial review and, in March 1997, John Witham successfully argued that the Lord Chancellor had exceeded his statutory powers in removing exemptions from court fees for those in receipt of State income support. The exemptions had been removed as part of a wider measure to increase court income by raising fee levels, but Lord Justice Rose and Mr Justice Laws held that Lord Mackay had exceeded the statutory powers given to him by Parliament. Rose LJ stated that there was nothing to suggest that Parliament ever intended 'a power for the Lord Chancellor to prescribe fees so as to preclude the poor from access to the courts'. Mr Justice Laws on the other hand stated that: 'Access to the courts is a constitutional right; it can only be denied by the government if it persuades Parliament to pass legislation which specifically permits the executive to turn people away. That has not been done in this case' (*R v Lord Chancellor ex p Witham* (1997)).

It can be seen from the foregoing that the judiciary have at their disposal the means for addressing the potential for abuse that has followed on from the growth of discretionary power in the hands of the modern State, through the mechanism of judicial review, particularly if it is operated on the basis of the doctrine of proportionality. There are also significant indications that the higher judiciary may well be attempting to assert just such a measure of control over the executive. For example, the former Master of the Rolls and now Lord Chief Justice, Sir Thomas Bingham, was quoted in *The Observer* newspaper of 9 May 1993 as saying that:

> Slowly, the constitutional balance is tilting towards the judiciary. The courts have reacted to the increase in powers claimed by the government by being more active themselves.

Judicial review is a delicate exercise and by necessity draws the judiciary into the political arena, using the word political in its widest, non-party sense. That the judges are aware of this, is evident from the words of Lord Woolf in the same article. As he recognised:

> Judicial review is all about balance: between the rights of the individual and his need to be treated fairly, and the rights of government at local and national level to do what it has been elected to do. There is a very sensitive and political decision to be made.

However, another current Law Lord, Lord Browne-Wilkinson, as observed, admirably before his elevation to the House of Lords, on a BBC radio programme, that a great void was apparent in the political system, deriving from the fact that no government had a true popular majority and yet all governments were able to carry Parliament in support of anything they wanted. He went on to express the view that Parliament was not a place where it was easy to get accountability for abuse or misuse of powers. According to Sir Nicholas, while judicial review could not overcome the will of Parliament, judges had a special role because *democracy was defective*. He then asked a rhetorical question as to who else but the judges could ensure that executive action is taken in accordance with law, *and not abused by growingly polarised political stances*.

Such thinking has continued amongst the judiciary as can be seen from Mr Justice, as he was then, Stephen Sedley's article in the May 1995 edition of the *London Review of Books* in which he asserted that, after decades of passivity, there is a new 'culture of judicial assertiveness to compensate for, and in places repair, dysfunctions in the democratic process', and that the last three decades of the 20th century may have seen the British Constitution being refashioned by judges 'with sufficient popular support to mute political opposition'.

These manifestations of almost judicial triumphalism should at least give people cause for thought. The fact that the judges increasingly see it as incumbent upon them to use judicial review as the means of questioning and controlling what they see as the abuse of executive power does, at the very least, raise very serious questions in relation to their suitability for such a role. These doubts can be set out in terms of:

- *Competence*

  This refers to the question whether the judges are sufficiently competent to participate in deciding the substantive issues that they have been invited to consider under the guise of judicial review and may be entitled to consider under the HRA. Judges are experts in law; they are not experts in the various and highly specialised areas of policy that by definition tend to be involved in judicial review cases. They may disagree with particular decisions but it has to be, at least, doubted that they are qualified to take such policy decisions. A classic example of this difficulty were the 'fares' fair' cases (*Bromley LBC v GLC* (1983) and, later, *R v London Transport Executive ex p GLC* (1983)) in which the courts got involved in deciding issues relating to transport policy for London on the pretext that it was judicially defining the meaning of particular words in a statute. As was considered in Chapter 5, the apparently technocratic, and hence neutral, application of rules of interpretation simply serve to disguise a political procedure and, in these cases, the policy issue concerned was certainly beyond the scope of the judges to determine.

- *Constitutionality*

  This refers to the wider point that the separation of powers applies equally to the judiciary as it does to the executive. In interfering with substantive decisions and involving themselves in political matters, albeit in the pretence of merely deciding points of law, the judiciary may be seen to be exceeding their constitutional powers. It has to be remembered that judges are unelected and unaccountable.

- *Partiality*

   This refers to the possibility of individual and indeed corporate bias within the judiciary as will be considered in the following section.

The foregoing has indicated that the relationship between the State and the courts may, on occasion, involve a measure of tension, with the courts attempting to rein in the activities of the State. The relationship between the judiciary and the executive is well summed up in the words of Lord Justice Farquharson, again taken from an *Observer* article:

> We have to be very careful: the executive is elected. We have a role in the Constitution but, if we go too far, there will be a reaction. The Constitution only works if the different organs trust each other. If the judges start getting too frisky, there would be retaliation, renewed attempts to curb the judiciary.

It should also be borne in mind that many of the judicial statements above were made during the time of a large Conservative majority in the House of Commons pursuing policies that were seen by the judiciary as certainly inimical to its own interests and those of the Bar from whence they came; and which policies were portrayed as likely to undermine the whole justice system. The question remains to be asked whether this increased political activity on the part of the judiciary represented a truly disinterested pursuit of the rule of law or whether it is the product of a disgruntled judiciary intent on retaliating against an executive which has undermined its operation and situation?

   The judicial statements above were made during the time of a large Conservative majority in the House of Commons pursuing policies that were seen by the judiciary as certainly inimical to its own interests, and those of the Bar from whence they came. A time characterised by Lord Woolf MR as 'a period when the other checks on government were not operating as effectively as they usually do' ('Judicial review – the tensions between the executive and the judiciary' (1998) 114 LQR 579).

   That Conservative majority has now been replaced by a similarly large Labour majority. The number of judicial review cases continues to grow, and there have been judicial decisions against the government. For example, both the Home Secretary and the Secretary of State for Social Security have lost cases in some, although by no means the majority of, decisions in asylum cases (for example, *R v Secretary of State for Social Security ex p Joint Council for the Welfare of Immigrants* (1997), and the Health Secretary has been found wanting in his initial decision to limit supply of the impotency drug Viagra ((1999) *The Times*, 27 May)). It has to be said, however, that the judiciary do not appear as overtly antagonistic as they did during the previous administration.

   As was suggested in the passage from Lord Woolf's article, quoted in Chapter 1, it appears that a truce has been called between the judiciary and the executive. Perhaps they are being more circumspect because they realise that changes in the constitution, such as the Human Rights Act, must have an impact on, and increase the importance of, the judges' role. Given these changes, and the fiasco that was the *Pinochet* case, perhaps a period of judicial quietness, and self-reflection, is more in keeping than suggestions of expansionism or triumphalism. Although no longer in force, the Kilmuir rules did have a valid point to make:

> ... the overriding consideration ... is the importance of keeping the judiciary in this country isolated from the controversies of the day. So long as a judge keeps silent, his reputation for wisdom and impartiality remains unassailable; but every utterance which he makes in public ... must necessarily bring him within the focus of criticism.

6.11 Politics of the judiciary

When considering the role which the judiciary plays in the process of applying the law or indeed the process, already adverted to in Chapter 2, whereby the judiciary actually make the law, criticism is usually levelled at the particular race, class and gender position of the majority of the judges. It is an objective and well documented fact that the majority of judges are 'white, middle class, middle aged to elderly men': but the question that has to be considered is whether this *necessarily* leads to the conclusion that judges reach inherently biased decisions. It is always possible, indeed, the newspapers make it relatively easy, to provide anecdotal evidence which apparently confirms either the bias, or the lack of social awareness, of the judiciary; but the fundamental question remains as to whether these cases are exceptional or whether they represent the norm.

Why should judges' class/race/gender placement make them less objective arbiters of the law? It is worth considering the fact that *unsupported* general assertions as to the inherently partial approach of the judiciary is itself partial. Simon Lee, not totally fatuously, has highlighted the logical flaw in what he refers to as the 'Tony Benn thesis' (Benn is the left wing, Labour Party member of Parliament who created history by being the first hereditary peer to renounce his peerage in order to remain in the House of Commons). Just because judges are old, white, rich, upper middle class, educated at public school and Oxbridge does not mean that they all necessarily think the same way; after all, Benn was a product of the same social circumstances. There is, of course, the point that people from that particular background *generally* tend to be conservative in outlook, and the apparent validity of Lee's argument is clearly the product of logic-chopping that reverses the accepted relationship and uses the exception as the rule rather than seeing the exception as proving/testing the rule. Nevertheless, Lee's point remains true; that proof of judicial bias is needed.

As the previous chapter of this book pointed out, if law were completely beyond the scope of judges to manipulate to their own ends, then the race, class, and gender placement of individual judges would be immaterial, as they would not be in any position to influence the operation of the law. That chapter also demonstrated, however, the way in which the doctrines which set the limits within which the judiciary operate are by no means as rigid and restrictive as they might first appear. It was seen that, although judges are supposed merely to apply, rather than create, law, they possess a large measure of discretion in determining which laws to apply, what those laws mean, and how they should be applied. In the light of this potential capacity to create law, it is essential to ensure that the judiciary satisfactorily represents society at large in relation to which it has so much power, and to ensure further that it does not merely represent the views and attitudes of a self-perpetuating élite.

The limited class background of the judiciary was confirmed in figures issued by the Lord Chancellor's office on 17 May 1995 which revealed that 80% of Lords of Appeal, Heads of Division, Lord Justices of Appeal and High Court Justices were educated at Oxford or Cambridge. In justifying the figures, the Lord Chancellor's Permanent Secretary, Sir Thomas Legg, showing insouciance to the level of arrogance, simply stated that: 'It is not the function of the professional judiciary to be representative of the community.' Such a response, if it is true, or even acceptable, must surely undermine the right of such an unrepresentative body to take action in the name of the majority, as the courts do in their use of judicial review.

Unfortunately, the continuing social imbalance amongst the senior judiciary was further confirmed in a report on judicial appointments by the Commons Home Affairs Committee presented in June 1996. It revealed that four-fifths of judges went to both public schools and Oxbridge colleges, that only seven out of 96 High Court judges were women, and that only five out of the 517 circuit judges were black or Asian. Nevertheless, the Committee rejected proposals for positive discrimination or even for the establishment of a judicial appointments committee to replace the present informal system under the control of the Lord Chancellor.

Instead of things improving, if one actually has the temerity to consider it an improvement to have fewer Oxbridge men on the bench, a Labour Research investigation found that things were actually getting worse in terms of the wider representational make up of the judiciary (as has been considered above at 6.3.2). Still, Lord Irvine holds fast to appointment solely on merit, which appears wholly commendable; but, as has been stated before, who decides on merit, and what are they actually measuring?

6.11.1 Criticisms

Given the central position of judges in the operation of law and the legal system, particularly with regard to the growth in judicial review and their new role in relation to giving effect to the Human Rights Act, the question these reports raise is whether the social placement of the judiciary leads to any perceptible shortfall in the provision of justice. The pre-eminent critic of the way in which the judiciary permit their shared background, attitudes and prejudices to influence their understanding and statement of the law is Professor JAG Griffith. According to Griffith, bias can occur at two levels:

* *Personal bias*

  Personal bias occurs where individual judges permit their own personal prejudices to influence their judgment and, thus, the effective application of the law. It is relatively easy to cite cases where judges give expression to their own attitudes and in so doing exhibit their own prejudices. As examples of this process, two cases can be cited which consider the rule of natural justice, that a person should not be both the accuser and judge in the same case. In *Hannam v Bradford Corporation* (1970), the court held that it was contrary to natural justice for three school governors to sit as members of a local authority education disciplinary committee charged with deciding whether or not to uphold a previous decision of the governors to dismiss a teacher. This was so even though the three governors had not been present at the meeting where it was decided to dismiss the teacher. On the other hand, in *Ward v Bradford Corporation* (1971), the Court of Appeal refused to interfere with a decision by governors of a teacher training college to confirm the expulsion of a student, although they had instituted the disciplinary proceedings, and three members of the governors sat on the original disciplinary committee. What possible explanation can there be for this discrepancy? The only tenable explanation is to be found in the latter court's disapproval of the plaintiff's behaviour in that case. The truly reprehensible judgment of Lord Denning concludes that the student lost nothing as she was not a fit person to teach children in any case. Can such a conclusion be justified on purely legal grounds or is it based on individual morality? Lord Denning did his best to buttress his judgment with spurious legal reasoning, but it could be suggested that, in so doing, he merely brought the process of legal reasoning into disrepute and revealed its fallaciousness.

  Courts have also been notoriously unsympathetic to victims of rape and have been guilty of making the most obtuse of sexist comments in relation to such victims. Nor can it be claimed that depreciatory racist remarks have been totally lacking in court cases.

Such cases of bias are serious and reprehensible but the very fact that the prejudice they demonstrate appears as no more than the outcome of particular judges, who are simply out of touch with current standards of morality or acceptable behaviour, suggests that it might be eradicated by the Lord Chancellor exercising stricter control over such mavericks, and appointing more appropriate judges in the first place. Professor Griffith, however, suggests that there is a further type of bias that is actually beyond such relatively easy control.

- *Corporate bias*

Corporate bias involves the assertion that the judges *as a body* decide certain types of cases in a biased way. This accusation of corporate bias is much more serious than that of personal bias for the reason that it asserts that the problem of bias is *systematic* rather than merely limited to particular maverick judges. As a consequence, if such a claim is justified, it has to be concluded that the problem is not susceptible to treatment at the level of the individual judge, but requires a complete alteration of the whole judicial system.

Griffith claims that, as a consequence of their shared educational experience, their shared training and practical experience at the Bar and their shared social situation as members of the Establishment, judges have developed a common outlook. He maintains that they share homogeneous values, attitudes and beliefs as to how the law should operate and be administered. He further suggests that this shared outlook is inherently conservative, if not Conservative in a party political sense.

Griffith's argument is that the highest judges in the judicial hierarchy are frequently called upon to decide cases on the basis of a determination of what constitutes the public interest and that, in making that determination, they express their own corporate values, which are in turn a product of their position in society as part of the ruling Establishment. Griffith maintains that judges can be seen to operate in such a way as to maintain the status quo and resist challenges to the established authority. Underlying this argument is the implication that the celebrated independence of the judiciary is, in fact, a myth and that the courts will tend to decide cases in such a way as to buttress the position of the State, especially if it is under the control of a Conservative government.

In an attempt to substantiate his claims, Griffith examines cases relating to trade union law, personal rights, property rights and matters of national security where he claims to find judges consistently acting to support the interests of the State over the rights of the individual. Some of the concrete examples he cites are the withdrawal of trade union rights from GCHQ at Cheltenham (*Council of Civil Service Unions v Minister for Civil Service* (1984));

the banning of publishing any extracts from the *Spycatcher* book (*AG v Guardian Newspapers Ltd* (1987)); and the treatment of suspected terrorists.

Griffith, and other academics associated with the left, have expressed their reservations about the extent to which the Human Rights Act will hand power to an unelected, unaccountable, inherently conservative and unreformed body, as they claim the judiciary is. But, at the same time, they appear equally concerned that the government is delaying implementation of the Act to 3 October 2000, until the judiciary can be suitably trained: the concern would appear to be as to what is meant by the word 'suitably'.

A notable, if somewhat complacent, response to Griffith's book was provided by Lord Devlin. Lord Devlin pointed that, in most cases, and on most issues, there tended to be plurality rather than unanimity of opinion and decision amongst judges. He also claimed that it would be just as possible for a more conservatively minded person that Griffith to go through the case-books to provide a list of examples where the courts had operated in a over-liberal manner. Lord Devlin also adopted a different explanation of the judiciary's perceived reluctance to abandon the status quo. For him, any conservatism on the part of judges was to be seen as a product of age rather than class. In conclusion, he asserted that even if the judiciary were biased, its bias was well known and allowances could be made for it.

The issue of the way in which the criminal appeal procedure dealt with suspected terrorist cases is of particular relevance in the light of the Runciman Commission Report. General dissatisfaction with the trials and appeals involving suspected terrorists such as the Maguire Seven, the Birmingham Six, the Guildford Four, the Tottenham Three, Stefan Kiszko and Judith Ward helped to give rise to the widespread impression that the United Kingdom criminal justice system and, in particular, the British appeal system needed to be considered for reform.

In the light of the fact that the appeal system did not seem to be willing to consider the possibility of the accused's innocence once they had been convicted, the Runciman Commission's recommendation that a Criminal Case Review Authority be established independent of the Home Office were widely welcomed and resulted in the establishment of the Criminal Cases Review Commission in the Criminal Appeal Act 1995 (see Chapter 4 at 4.5.2). The question still remains, however, whether those earlier cases reflect an inherently and inescapably conservative judiciary or were they simply unfortunate instances of more general errors of the system which the implementation of the CCRC can overcome? And, perhaps more importantly, will the Court of Appeal give a fair hearing to the cases referred to it by the CCRC?

It is apparent from the statistics produced by the Lord Chancellor's Department cited previously that senior judges are still being appointed from the same limited social and educational élite as they always have been. This gives rise to the suspicion, if not the reality, that the decisions that this élite make merely represent values and interests of a limited and privileged segment of society, rather than society as a whole. Even if the accusations levelled by Professor Griffith are inaccurate, it is surely still necessary to remove even the possibility of those accusations.

THE JUDICIARY

The constitutional role of the judiciary

Judges play a central role in the English constitution. The doctrine of the separation of powers maintains that the judicial function be kept distinct from the legislative and executive functions of the State. The Lord Chancellor fills an anomalous situation in this respect.

The constitutional role of the Lord Chancellor

The Lord Chancellor holds an anomalous position in respect of the separation of powers within the United Kingdom Constitution, in that he is, at one and the same time; the most senior member of the judiciary and can hear cases in the House of Lords as a court; a member of the legislature as speaker of the House of Lords as a legislative assembly; and a member of the executive holding a position in the government. Although doubts have been raised about this situation, the present incumbent shows no desire to alter it, and indeed has gone on record as supporting the status quo.

The effect of the Pinochet case on the House of Lords

The recent case involving the previous dictator of Chile, General Augusto Pinochet, has brought the House of Lords into the glare on unlooked for publicity. It has raised questions as to its current role within the present constitution and even more concern has been expressed about its role under a reformed constitution with devolution and a non-hereditary House of Lords.

Judicial offices

The main judicial offices are the Lord Chancellor, the Lord Chief Justice, the Mater of the Rolls, the President of the Family Division, the Vice Chancellor and the Senior Presiding Judge. Law Lords are referred to as Lords of Appeal in Ordinary. Court of Appeal judges are referred to as Lords Justices of Appeal.

Appointment of judiciary

The Courts and Legal Services Act 1990 has opened the possibility of judicial office, even in the higher courts, to non-barristers.

All judicial appointments remain, theoretically, at the hands of the Crown. The Prime Minister advises the Crown on the appointment of senior judicial office holders and the Law Lords, and Appeal Court judges. Judges at the level of High Court judges and below, including lay magistrates, are appointed on the advice of the Lord Chancellor.

Lord Chancellor Mackay's limited steps to open up appointment procedure have been followed up by Lord Irvine, but as yet the system remains secretive, not to say mysterious, and the establishment of an independent Judicial Appointment Commission remains unlikely.

Training of the judiciary

Training of English judges is undertaken under the auspices of the Judicial Studies Board. Judges for the highest Law Lord to the lowest magistrate are subject to training. It is gratifying to note that anti-discriminatory training is a priority, although some have continued to express doubt about judicial attitudes in this regard. Special training has been instituted in relation to the Woolf reforms and the introduction of the Human Rights Act. This being said, it remains arguable that the training undergone by UK judges is not as rigorous as the training of judges on the Continent.

Removal of judges

Senior judges hold office subject to good behaviour. They can be removed by an address by the two Houses of Parliament.

Judges below High Court status can be removed by the Lord Chancellor on grounds of misbehaviour or incapacity and he can remove magistrates without the need to show cause.

Judicial immunity

To ensure judicial integrity, it is provided that judges cannot be sued for actions done or words said in the course of their judicial function.

This immunity extends to trial lawyers, witnesses and juries.

Magistrates

Magistrates have powers in relation to both criminal and civil law.

Stipendiary magistrates are professional and are legally qualified.

Lay magistrates are not paid and they are not legally qualified.

Magistrates are appointed by the Lord Chancellor.

Important issues relate to the representative nature of the magistracy.

Judicial review

Under the Constitution of the United Kingdom, and within the doctrine of the separation of powers, judges and the executive have distinct but interrelated roles.

The Rule of Law – various writers have various understandings, but see it essentially as involving a control of arbitrary power: Dicey; Hayek; Thompson; Raz; Unger; Weber.

Judicial review remedies are the prerogative remedies of *certiorari, mandamus, prohibition,* together with the private law remedies of declaration, injunction and damages. Private law remedies cannot be used in relation to public law complaints.

Increased judicial activity in relation to State programmes raises questions as to the competence and authority of judges to act as well as raising doubts as to their political views.

A recent Law Commission report has suggested various improvements to judicial review procedure to allow it operate effectively into the 21st century.

Politics of the judiciary

Judges have a capacity to make law – the question is do they exercise this power in a biased way?

Bias can take two forms: personal; and corporate.

Accusations of corporate bias suggest that, as a group, judges represent the interest of the status quo and decide certain political cases in line with that interest.

CHAPTER 7

THE CIVIL PROCESS

Bleak House, Charles Dickens:

> Jarndyce [v] Jarndyce drones on. This scarecrow of a suit has, in the course of time, become so complicated that no man alive knows what it means. The parties to it understand it least; but it has been observed that no two Chancery lawyers can talk about it for five minutes without coming to a total disagreement as to all the premises. Innumerable children have been born into the cause; innumerable young people have married into it; innumerable old people have died out of it. Scores of persons have deliriously found themselves made parties in Jarndyce and Jarndyce, without knowing how or why; whole families have inherited legendary hatreds with the suit. The little plaintiff or defendant, who was promised a new rocking horse when Jarndyce and Jarndyce should be settled, has grown up, possessed himself of a real horse, and trotted away into the other world. Fair wards of court have faded into grandmothers; a long procession of Chancellors has come in and gone out ... there are not three Jarndyces left upon the earth perhaps, since old Tom Jarndyce in despair blew his brains out at a coffee-house in Chancery Lane; but Jarndyce and Jarndyce still drags its dreary length before the Court, perennially hopeless.

......

> Many critics believe that the adversarial system has run into the sand, in that, today, delay and costs are too often disproportionate to the difficulty of the issue and the amount at stake. The solution now being followed to that problem requires a more interventionist judiciary: the trial judge as the trial manager (Lord Justice Henry, *Thermawear v Linton* (1995) CA).

The extent of delay, complication and therefore expense of civil litigation may have changed since the time of Dickens' observations about the old Court of Chancery but how far the civil process is as efficient as it might be is a matter of some debate.

A survey by the National Consumer Council in 1995 found that three out of four people in serious legal disputes were dissatisfied with the civil justice system (*Seeking Civil Justice: A Survey of People's Needs and Experiences*, 1995, NCC). Of the 1,019 respondents, 77% claimed the system was too slow, 74% said it was too complicated, and 73% said that it was unwelcoming and outdated.

According to the Civil Justice Review (CJR) 1988, delay in litigation 'causes continuing personal stress, anxiety and financial hardship to ordinary people and their families. It may induce economically weaker parties to accept unfair settlements. It also frustrates the efficient conduct of commerce and industry'. Despite some of the innovations in the five years following that CJR, the problems continued. In 1994, the Lord Chancellor set up the Woolf Inquiry to look at ways of improving the speed and accessibility of civil proceedings, and of reducing their cost.

The Heilbron Hodge Report, *Civil Justice on Trial: The Case for Change* (1993), recommended many changes in civil procedure. The Report resulted from an independent working party set up in 1992 by the Bar Council and The Law Society. The 39 member working party was chaired by Hilary Heilbron QC; its vice chair was solicitor Henry Hodge OBE. The report called for a 'radical reappraisal of the approach to litigation from all its participants'.

The Report painted a depressing picture of the civil justice system where delays are endemic and often contrived and procedures are inflexible, rule ridden and often incomprehensible to the client. It noted that incongruously for a multi-million pound operation, technology scarcely featured. All High Court and county court records, for example, were kept manually. The main plank of the report was concerned with making the operation of the courts more 'litigant-friendly'. It said that judges, lawyers and administrators should develop a culture of service to the litigant. The report made 72 recommendations for change.

7.1　The 1999 Woolf reforms – an overview

When Lord Woolf began his examination of the civil law process, the problems facing those who used the system were many and varied. His Interim Report published in June 1995 identified these problems. He noted, for example, that:

> ... the key problems facing civil justice today are cost, delay and complexity. These three are interrelated and stem from the uncontrolled nature of the litigation process. In particular, there is no clear judicial responsibility for managing individual cases or for the overall administration of the civil courts. Just as the problems are interrelated, so too the solutions, which I propose, are interdependent. In many instances, the failure of previous attempts to address the problem stems not from the solutions proposed but from their partial rather than their complete implementation (*Access to Justice*, Interim Report of Lord Woolf, 1995).

In the system that Lord Woolf examined, the main responsibility for the initiation and conduct of proceedings rested with the parties to each individual case, and it was normally the plaintiff (now claimant) who set the pace. Thus, Lord Woolf also noted:

> Without effect judicial control ... the adversarial process is likely to encourage an adversarial cultural and to degenerate into an environment in which the litigation process is too often seen as a battlefield where no rules apply. In this environment, questions of expense, delay, compromise and fairness have only a

low priority. The consequence is that the expense is often excessive, disproportionate and unpredictable; and delay is frequently unreasonable (*Access to Justice*, Interim Report, 1995, p 7).

The system has degenerated in a number of other respects. Witness statements, a sensible innovation aimed at a 'cards on the table' began after a very short time to follow the same route as pleadings, with the draftsman skill often used to obscure the original words of the witness.

The use of expert evidence under the old system left a lot to be desired:

> The approach to expert evidence also shows the characteristic range of difficulties: instead of the expert assisting the court to resolve technical problems, delay is caused by the unreasonable insistence on going to unduly eminent members of the profession and evidence is undermined by the partisan pressure to which party experts are subjected.

Historically, change has come very slowly and gradually to the legal system. The report of the Civil Justice Review was largely ignored and, with the exception of a shift in the balance of work from the High Court to the county court (under CLSA 1990), no major changes came from its recommendations. The whole process began again with the Woolf Review of the Civil Justice System. In March 1994, Lord Woolf was invited by the government to review the work of the civil courts in England and Wales. He began from the proposition that the system was 'in a state of crisis ... a crisis for the government, the judiciary and the profession'. The recommendations he formulated – after extensive consultation in the UK and in many other jurisdictions – form the basis of major changes to the system that came into effect in April 1999. David Gladwell, head of the Civil Justice Division of the Lord Chancellor's Department, stated (*Civil Litigation Reform*, 1999, LCD, p 1) that these changes represent 'the greatest change the civil courts have seen in over a century'.

Following the Civil Procedure Act 1997, the changes are effected through the new Civil Procedure Rules 1998. These have been supplemented by new practice directions and pre-action protocols. The principal parts of all of these new rules and guidelines are examined below. Thus, 'rule 4.1' refers to r 4.1 of the Civil Procedure Rules.

Leaving aside for the moment the pervasive theme of the reforms – to simplify procedure – there are three main aspects to the reforms:

Judicial case management

The judge is a case manager in the new regime. The new system allocates cases to one of three 'tracks' depending upon the complexity and value of the dispute. The small claims track deals with the simplest cases; the fast track deals with more weighty disputes; and the multi-track system allows a court to use a variety of procedures (see 7.4.6–7.4.8, below). He or she will be centre stage for the whole action, not just in David Gladwell's phrase, 'someone who is brought in for the final triumphal scene'. Litigation proceeds on a court controlled timetable. Parties can no longer agree extensions with each other. Previously, lawyers from either side were permitted to wrangle almost endlessly with each other about who should disclose what information and documents to whom and at what stage. Now, the judge is under an obligation to 'actively' manage cases. This includes:

- encouraging parties to co-operate with each other;

- identifying issues in the dispute at an early stage;

- disposing of summary issues which do not need full investigation;

- helping the parties to settle the whole or part of the case;

- fixing timetables for the case hearing and controlling the progress of the case;

- considering whether the benefits of a particular way of hearing the dispute justify its costs.

If the parties refuse to comply with the new rules, the practice directions or the protocols, the judge will be able to exercise disciplinary powers. These include:

(a) using costs sanctions against parties (that is, refusing to allow the lawyers who have violated the rules to recover their costs from their client or the other side of the dispute);

(b) 'unless' orders;

(c) striking-out;

(d) refusal to grant extensions of time;

(e) refusal to allow documents not previously disclosed to the court and the other side to be relied upon.

One of the greatest changes, however, will concern the spirit of the law. The new style of procedure which is intended to be brisk will be of paramount importance. The courts will become allergic to delay or any of the old, ponderous, long-winded techniques previously used by many lawyers. David Gladwell (*Civil Litigation Reform*, 1999, LCD, p 2) has noted that 'Strict observance of the black letter of the rules, so beloved of procedural lawyers, will no longer be enough. The courts will be adopting a more creative approach'.

Pre-action protocols

Part of the problem in the past has arisen from the fact that the courts can only start to exercise control over the progress of a case, and the way it is handled, once proceedings have been issued. Before that stage, lawyers were at liberty to take inordinate time to do things related to the case, to write to lawyers on the other side to the dispute and so forth. Now, a mechanism allows new pre-action requirements to be enforced. Two protocols have been drawn up, to apply in the largest areas of litigation: clinical negligence (including actions against doctors, nurses, dentists, hospitals, health authorities, etc); and personal injury (road accidents, work accidents, etc).

The object of the protocols is:

- to encourage greater contact between the parties at the earliest opportunity;

- to encourage a better exchange of information;

- to encourage better pre-action investigation;

- to put parties in a position to settle cases fairly and early; and

- to reduce the need for the case going all the way to court.

Alternatives to going to court

Rule 4.1 requires the court as a part of its 'active case management' to encourage and facilitate the use of Alternative Dispute Resolution (ADR) (which we examine in Chapter 8), and r 26.4 allows the court to stay proceedings (that is, halt them) to allow the parties to go to ADR either where the parties themselves request it or where the court 'of its own initiative' considers it appropriate. The Commercial Court already uses this policy with notable success. It often acts to send cases to ADR, for example, where one side applies for a lengthy extension of time for the case to be heard.

7.2   The cost of litigation – the pre-1999 problems

Many potential litigants are deterred from taking action by the high costs. It is also relevant to remember that whichever party loses the action must pay for his or her own expenses and those of the other side; a combined sum which will, in many cases, be more than the sum in issue. An appeal to the Court of Appeal will increase the costs even further (in effect, fees and expenses for another action) and the same may be true again if the case is taken to the House of Lords. There is in such a system a great pressure for parties to settle their claims. The CJR found that 90–95% of cases were settled by the parties before the trial.

The cost of taking legal action in the civil courts has been gigantic. Two cases cited by Adrian Zuckerman in an address to Lord Woolf's Inquiry illustrate the point. In one, a successful action by a supplier of fitted kitchens to stop a £10,000 a year employee from taking up a job with a competitor cost the employer £100,000, even though judgment was obtained in under five weeks from the start of the proceedings. The expense of this case was in fact double the stated amount when the cost of the legal aid fund's bill for the employee's defence is added to the total. In another case, a divorced wife had to pay

£34,000 in costs for a judgment which awarded her £52,000 of the value of the family home.

It was the spiralling costs of civil litigation, to a large extent borne by the taxpayer through legal aid, which has prompted the Lord Chancellor to move to cap the legal aid fund. The legal aid budget rose from £426 million in 1987–88 to £1,526 million in 1997–98.

The system of civil procedure entails a variety of devices. Very complex cases may require the full use of many of these devices but most cases could be tried without parties utilising all the procedures. Exorbitant costs and long delays often resulted from unduly complicated procedures being used by lawyers acting for parties to litigation. Zuckerman has argued that this problem arose from the fact that the legal system was evolved principally by lawyers with no concern for cost efficiency. In both the High Court and the county court, the system allowed parties to quarrel as much over procedural matters as the actual merits of the substantive dispute. In one case, for example, the issue of whether a writ had been properly served on the other side had to be considered by a Master (the High Court judicial officer empowered to deal with procedural matters) and then, on appeal, by a judge, and then, on another appeal, by the Court of Appeal. Thus, cost and delay could build up before the parties even arrived at the stage of having their real argument heard. If a claim or defence was amended, the fate of the amendment could take two appeal hearings to finally resolve. The pre-trial proceedings often degenerated into an intricate legal contest separate from the substantive issue.

The CJR 1988 recommended unification of the county courts and the High Court. It accepted the need for different levels of judiciary but argued that having different levels of courts was inefficient. This recommendation carried what Roger Smith, then director of the Legal Action Group, called an 'unspoken sting', namely, that a divided legal profession could hardly survive a unified court. The Bar rebelled and the judiciary was solidly opposed to such change. The recommendation was not legislated.

The CLSA 1990, following other recommendations in the CJR, legislated for large numbers of cases in the High Court being sent down to the county courts to expedite their progress. No extra resources were given to the county courts to cope with the influx of cases and so, not surprisingly, there has been a growing backlog of cases and a poorer quality of service in the county courts. This problem may well worsen rather than be helped by the introduction of the Civil Procedure Rules as more cases will be heard in the county courts.

There were tactical reasons why parties were tempted to use the full panoply of procedural rules. The rule that 'costs follow success' (that is, the losing side usually has to pay the legal costs of the other side) can operate to encourage the building up of expense. Wealthy litigants could employ protracted procedures in an effort to worry poorer opponents to settle on terms determined by the former. Conditional fee arrangements (see 12.5) have made very little impact on the system, so lawyers who are paid by the hour regardless of success are unlikely to be especially anxious about the speed and efficiency of their work.

Zuckerman has argued for the introduction of a more efficient system like the one used in Germany. There, legal fees are determined by law. A lawyer is paid for litigation in units that represent a small proportion of the value of the claim. Payment is in three stages. The first is made at the commencement of the action; the second when representation begins at a hearing; here, the judge will attempt to procure a settlement. If this fails, he will give directions for the preparation of evidence. The third payment will be made if the case goes to a full hearing. Since lawyers earn only a fixed fee, there is no systemic incentive for them to prolong any stage of the litigation; on the contrary, they have an incentive to work as expeditiously as possible so as to maximise their rate of pay at any given stage (that is, to get a reasonable return per hour). There was evidence, however, that this system encourages some lawyers to go to the final stage even where there might have been a reasonable chance of settlement at the second stage. To overcome that difficulty, it has now been regulated that a lawyer can get a full three-part fee even if the case is settled at the second stage.

In January 1995, instructions to judges from Lord Taylor, the then Lord Chief Justice, and Sir Nicholas Scott, the Vice Chancellor, may well have an effect on the length and therefore cost of High Court cases. Judges have been instructed to use their discretion to set strict time limits to lawyers' speeches and cross-examination, to limit the issues in cases and the documents to be disclosed ahead of trial, and to curb reading aloud from documents and case reports (*Practice Direction, Civil Litigation: Case Management* (1995)). Lawyers who violate these instructions will stand to lose some of their fees as the direction states that: failure by practitioners to conduct cases economically will be visited by appropriate orders for costs, including wasted costs orders (that is, some of the costs incurred will not be recoverable). Now, lawyers are no longer allowed to examine their own witnesses in court (examination-in-chief) without the express permission of the judge. These new rules apply to actions in the QBD and Chancery Division of the High Court and the county courts, and are modelled on those which have been used for some time in the Commercial Court where cases are dealt with most expeditiously.

In a statement to launch the new rules (24 January 1995), the Lord Chief Justice said that:

> The aim is to try and change the whole culture, the ethos, applying in the field of civil litigation. We have over the years been too ready to allow those who are litigating to dictate the pace at which cases proceed. Time is money, and wasted time in court means higher charges for litigants and for the taxpayer. It also means that everyone else in the queue has to wait longer for justice.

For this system to operate well, however, there is a need for judges to be better assisted with researchers and assistant lawyers so that they can be properly briefed on the contents and significance of witness statements, and so forth. So far, there has been little improvement in the provision of such services for judges.

The CJR recommended that more cases should be devolved from the county court to arbitration in the small claims procedure. Such a policy was facilitated by changes to the rule in 1992, and 1996, which raised the limit of the value of claims with which the county court small claims procedure can adjudicate to £1,000 and £3,000, respectively (now, the limit is £5,000; see 7.6, below). Cases in the small claims procedure are heard without the ordinary formal rules of evidence and procedure, the consequential informality being seen as conducive to quicker settlement of issues. The full width of jurisdiction of the court has been confirmed by the Court of Appeal's decision in *Afzal and others v Ford Motor Company Ltd* (1994). The court gave guidance on the approach to be adopted by county court judges when deciding whether small claims involving amounts below £1,000 should be tried in court instead of being automatically referred to arbitration under Ord 19 r 3 of the County Court (Amendment No 2) Rules 1992 (SI 1965). The court allowed an appeal by Ford against the decision of a judge who had declined to refer to arbitration 16 employees' claims for damages for personal injuries sustained in the workplace. The employees were supported by their trade union, and the employer's case was handled by its insurer.

The employees had argued that compulsory arbitration was unsuitable for their claims and that the issues of liability involved were too complex for summary resolution. Moreover, it was argued that the denial of the right to recover the cost of legal advice and representation at arbitration would deter trade unions from assisting claimants, who would be at a disadvantage in negotiating compensation settlements out of court. In a submission to the Woolf Inquiry in 1995, Marlene Winfield of the National Consumer Council argued that companies and insurance firms are the real beneficiaries of this law. As neither legal aid nor costs are generally available for arbitrated disputes, many people who suffer relatively minor injuries now no longer go to law because they cannot afford to get the assistance of a lawyer. How far the new system for small claims (see 7.6, below) is able to ensure greater fairness remains to be judged, but the limited costs regime in the new system and absence of legal aid do not provide for much optimism.

When Lord Woolf came to examine the system, small claims hearings played a very important part in the resolution of disputes. He noted that:

> ... in 1994, 24,219 cases where disposed of by full trial [in the county courts] while the number of small claims hearings was 87,885 (*Access to Justice*, Interim Report, 1995, p 102).

What had began life in 1973 as a new system, designed to facilitate ordinary individuals using the law, had degenerated by 1995 into a system which business and organisations played the major part. Lord Woolf noted:

... in a sample [by RDA Bowles] of 134 county court cases, in one court including a hundred small claims, only 12% of the cases were brought by private individuals, although individuals formed a large proportion of defendants. More recently, Professor John Baldwin of the University of Birmingham found that some 40% of the 109 plaintiffs in his 1994 research for the Office of Fair Trading were individuals (*Access to Justice*, Interim Report, 1995, p 106).

Professor Baldwin's research also identified some fundamental differences among district judges in the way in which they dealt with evidence and applied the substantive law to small claims. Additionally, Woolf found a real problem in the way that ordinary citizens were expected to present their cases in court (see *Access to Justice*, Interim Report, 1995, pp 102–10).

7.3   The pressure to settle claims

Most civil disputes are settled out of court. Fewer than 10% of cases where a claim form is issued actually go to court and, even of those which go to trial, many are settled before judgment. Evidence presented by the London Passenger Transport Board to the Winn Committee on Personal Injury Litigation (1968), for example, showed that, of about 5,000 claims made against it a year, about 4,900 were settled without proceedings. Of the 100 or so cases which were commenced, only about one-quarter were taken to full judgment.

The largest study of this sort was conducted by the Oxford Centre for Socio-Legal Studies (Harris *et al*, *Compensation and Support for Illness and Injury* (1984)) which examined a random sample of 1,711 accident victims who had been incapacitated for a minimum of two weeks. Of this group, only 26% had considered claiming damages, only 14% had consulted a solicitor and only 12% were awarded damages. The study looked at the level of damages obtained by the small group (8%) who gained them without the use of solicitors, and concluded that these people appeared to be under-compensated. In the 182 cases (from 1,711 in the sample) in which damages were obtained, the claimant accepted the first offer made in 104 cases. See Genn, *Hard Bargaining: Out of Court Settlement in Personal Injury Claims* (1987).

7.3.1   Costs

Many factors combine to persuade disputants to settle out of court and the fear of prohibitive costs can be a serious deterrent to taking proceedings. This is particularly so when it is remembered that the basic rule is that 'costs follow the event', that is, the successful party can expect the judge to order the loser to pay some or all of his or her solicitor's bill. Costs, however, are a discretionary matter so the whole process is beset with uncertainties. Another gamble the claimant is faced with is the procedure of 'payment into court' (now known as a 'Pt 36 payment'; see 7.12, below) where, at any stage after the commencement of proceedings, the defendant may make a payment into court in satisfaction of the claimant's claim. The claimant may accept the payment or continue the action. If the latter and the damages obtained are not greater than the amount paid in by the defendant, the claimant will be liable for the defendant's taxed costs from the time of payment in even though he or she has won the action. When the judge makes an award of damages, he will not know the amount of any payment into court, so he cannot influence the matter of whether the claimant has to suffer under the rule.

There were 80 cases in the Oxford study which involved abandoned claims and, of these, 16% were abandoned because of fear of legal expenses. Where a claimant is not legally aided, the lawyer may try to persuade him or her to accept a settlement offer plus costs rather than risk a legal action which could fail. This is better for the lawyer as it assures the payment of costs but arguably not in the best interest of many claimants because settlement awards are generally lower than damages awarded by courts for the same types of case.

A study of High Court personal injury cases by Zander (1973–74) (1975) Law Soc Gazette 680, 25 June) showed that, while costs were a relatively low proportion of damages in large claims, they were proportionately very high in small claims. Where the damages were under £1,000, 86% of cases had claimed costs for one side amounting to three-fifths of the damages or more. In 33% of cases, the total costs of both sides amounted to more than the amount in dispute. The CJR found that the average cost to the claimant in High Court personal injury actions in 1984 was £6,830 in London and £2,480 outside London. In the county court, costs were an average of 99% of the claimant's damages recovered, as opposed to about one-quarter in the High Court. When the costs of both sides were combined, it was estimated that in the county court they amounted to 125% of damages and between 50 and 75% in the High Court. Research conducted for the Woolf Report on the civil justice system threw further light on this area. The Final Report (*Access to Justice*, 1996) includes a survey of Supreme Court Taxing Office taxed bills conducted by Professor Hazel Genn of University College, London. Genn found alarming data on costs. Her findings indicate the average costs among the lowest value claims consistently represented more than 100% of the claim value. They also showed that, in cases worth between £12,500 and £25,000, average costs ranged from 40% to 95% of the value of the claim. The system provided higher benefits to lawyers than to their clients.

7.3.2 Delay

In the Oxford study, delay was another significant factor influencing people to discontinue claims; 6% of those who abandoned their actions cited it as affecting their decision. Cane (*Atiyah's Accidents, Compensation and the Law* (1993)) has shown evidence that delay and its attendant anxiety can cause a recognisable state of 'litigation neurosis', a complaint which ceases upon the resolution of the dispute. Delay generally assists the defendant and is sometimes used as a deliberate tactic against weaker opponents or to alleviate the cash flow problems of the smaller insurance companies.

7.3.3 Uncertainty

Another factor putting pressure on litigants to settle is that of the risks and uncertainties entailed in the claim. If the case goes to trial then the claimant will, to succeed, have to prove his or her case on the balance of probabilities. The process is beset with legal uncertainties. Is the defendant liable at law for the claimant's loss or injury? Even where the law is clear, there may be evidential difficulties. Genn (*Hard Bargaining: Out of Court Settlement in Personal Injury Claims* (1987)) has presented material to suggest that, in many cases, a claimant's solicitor either does not have sufficient resources to undertake proper factual investigations or does not seek out all available reports. It is also very difficult to contact all relevant witnesses and to assess how persuasive their courtroom evidence would be. Defendants, including or assisted by insurance companies, will often have resources which place them in a good position to fully investigate the circumstances of accidents. Assessing the quantum of damages is another very problematic part of litigation. In an American experiment, 20 pairs of practising lawyers negotiated on identical information about a case and were instructed to negotiate a settlement. Their resultant settlements ranged from the highest of US$95,000 to the lowest of US$15,000 with an average of just over US$47,000.

7.3.4 Other factors

The Oxford study found that many other factors contributed to the discontinuation of claims, including the fear of affecting a continuing relationship and arguments that the victim's own fault caused the accident. The most cited reason (mentioned by 45% of respondents) was problems over obtaining evidence. There have been some legal changes since the Oxford study in 1984 and it will be interesting to see if future studies detect any significant consequential changes in claimants' behaviour.

The Lord Chancellor's Department committed itself (in the CJR's *General Issues Paper*) to the use of new technology, especially for improving the system of county court debt business. The Production Centre has operated since early 1990 since when, relying on new technology, it has issued over 1.5 million summonses. Dealing more expeditiously with this sort of work could free the courts, and thus reduce delays, for other types of case.

The courts have made some progress in this area since 1996, although the challenges in the UK are considerable. Lord Justice Brooke, a leading proponent of the use of information and communications technology (ICT) in the courts, has made the following observation:

> In England, we do not have a Ministry of Justice, with masses of resources at its command. The Lord Chancellor's Department, which supports the courts, is a small department, and, over the last 10 years, its credibility with the Treasury was damaged because of the way that unbudgeted Legal Aid expenditure went on soaring. I believe that expenditure on IT suffered as a result. We have certainly not seen any of the imaginative forward investment in IT which other comparable countries have experienced. In America, for instance, the federal judiciary run the federal courts, and, in 1990, the Senate voted them US$70 million to undertake a programme of computerisation in the court process (Lord Justice Brooke, keynote speech to the 13th Bileta Conference: The Changing Jurisdiction, 'IT and the English and Welsh Courts: the Next 10 Years', Dublin, 28 March 1998).

There are only about 60 judges using computers in court, but the government is committed to achieving the transaction of 25% of all dealings with the public through ICT by 2000 (Geoff Hoon MP, then Minister of State at the Lord Chancellor's Department, speech to the Society for Computers and the Law, The Law Society, London, 25 January 1999).

7.4 The new civil process

The new Civil Procedure Rules (CPR) will be the same for the county court and the High Court. They apply to all cases except (Pt 2) to insolvency proceedings, family proceedings, and non-contentious probate proceedings. The vocabulary will be more user friendly, so, for example, what used to be called a 'writ' will be a 'claim form' and a *guardian ad litem* will be a 'litigation friend'.

Although, in some ways, all the fuss about the new CPR being so far reaching creates the impression that the future will see a sharp rise in litigation, the truth may be different. It seems likely that a fall off in litigation in the 1990s will continue. Judge John Frenkel ('On the road to reform' (1998) 95/48 Law Soc Gazette 33, 16 December) has pointed to the data. Queen's Bench Division writs were down from 50,295 in 1993–94 to 22,483 in 1997–98, and county court summonses from 2,577,704 to 1,959,958. During the same period, the number of district judges increased from 289 to 337.

7.4.1 The overriding objective

The overriding objective of the new Civil Procedure Rules (CPR) is to enable the court to deal justly with cases. The first rule reads:

> 1.1(1) These rules are a new procedural code with the overriding objective of enabling the court to deal with cases justly.

This objective will include ensuring that the parties are on an equal footing, and saving expense. When exercising any discretion given by the CPR, the court must, according to r 1.2, have regard to the overriding objective, and a checklist of factors, including the amount of money involved, the complexity of the issue, the parties' financial positions, how the case can be dealt with expeditiously and by allotting an appropriate share of the court's resources while taking into account the needs of others. In future, as Judge John Frenkel observes ('On the road to reform' (1998)), 'the decisions of the Court of Appeal are more likely to illustrate the application of the new rules to the facts of a particular case as opposed to being interpretative authorities that define the meaning of the rules'.

7.4.2 Practice directions

Practice directions (official statements of interpretative guidance) play an important role in the new civil process. In general, they supplement the CPRs, giving the latter fine detail. They tell parties and their representatives what the court will expect of them, in respect of documents to be filed in court for a particular purpose, and how they must co-operate with the other parties to their action. They also tell the parties what they can expect of the court. For example, they explain what sort of sanction a court is likely to impose if a particular court order or request is not complied with. Almost every Part of the new rules has a corresponding practice direction. They supersede all previous practice directions in relation to civil process.

7.4.3 Case control

Judges will receive support from court staff in carrying out their case management role. The court will monitor case progress by using a computerised diary monitoring system which will:

- record certain requests, or orders made by the court;

- identify the particular case, or cases to which these orders/requests refer, and the dates by which a response should be made; and

- check on the due date whether the request or order has been complied with.

Whether there has been compliance or not, the court staff will pass the relevant files to a procedural judge (a Master in the Royal Courts of Justice, a district judge in the county court) who will decide if either side should have a sanction imposed on him or her.

In the new system, the litigants will have much less control over the pace of the case than in the past. They will not be able to draw out proceedings or delay in the way that they once could have done because the case will be subject to a timetable. Once a defence is filed, the parties will get a timetable order that includes the prospective trial date. The need for pre-issue preparation is increased, and this will probably benefit litigants because, as Professor Hazel Genn's research has shown (*Hard Bargaining: Out of Court Settlement in Personal Injury Claims* (1987)), in settled personal injury actions, 60% of costs were incurred before proceedings. The court now has a positive duty to manage cases. Rule 1.4(1) states that 'The court must further the overriding objective by actively managing cases'. The rule goes on to explain what this management involves:

> 1.4(2) Active case management includes:
>
> (a) encouraging the parties to co-operate with each other in the conduct of the proceedings;
>
> (b) identifying the issues at an early stage;
>
> (c) deciding promptly which issues need full investigation and trial and accordingly disposing summarily of the others;
>
> (d) deciding the order in which issues are to be resolved;
>
> (e) encouraging the parties to use an alternative dispute resolution procedure if the court considers that appropriate ...;
>
> (f) helping the parties to settle the whole or part of the case;
>
> (g) fixing timetables or otherwise controlling the progress of the case;
>
> (h) considering whether the likely benefits of taking a particular step justify the cost of taking it;
>
> (i) dealing with as many aspects of the case as it can on the same occasion;
>
> (j) dealing with the case without the parties needing to attend court;
>
> (k) making use of technology; and
>
> (l) giving directions to ensure that the trial of a case proceeds quickly and efficiently.

We shall have to wait and see how judges use these rules and principles in practice but it is clear that what Lord Woolf identified as the misuse of rules by some lawyers (with unjust results) will be much less likely in the new environment. It is worth noting here that district judges and deputy district judges have had extensive Woolf training to promote a common approach (see 6.8.3). Training is being taken very seriously by judiciary. District judges now occupy a pivotel position in the civil process.

Part 3 of the CPR gives the court a wide range of substantial powers. The court can, for instance, extend or shorten the time for compliance with any rule, practice direction or court order, even if an application for an extension is made after the time for compliance has expired. It can also hold a hearing and receive evidence by telephone or 'by using any other method of direct oral communication'.

Part 3 of the CPR also gives the court powers to:

- strike out a statement of case;

- impose sanctions for non-payment of certain fees;

- impose sanctions for non-compliance with rules and practice directions;

- give relief from sanctions.

There is, though, a certain flexibility built into the rules. A failure to comply with a rule or practice direction will not necessarily be fatal to a case. Part 3.10 of the CPR states:

> Where there has been an error of procedure such as a failure to comply with a rule or practice direction:
>
> (a) the error does not invalidate any step taken in the proceedings unless the court so orders; and
>
> (b) the court may make an order to remedy the error.

The intention of imposing a sanction will always be to put the parties back into the position they would have been in if one of them had not failed to meet a deadline. For example, the court could order that a party carries out a task (like producing some sort of documentary evidence) within a very short time (for example, two days) in order that the existing trial dates can be met.

7.4.4 Court allocation

The new civil system works on the basis of the court, upon receipt of the claim (accompanied by duly filled-in forms giving all the relevant details of the claim including how much it is for, and an indication of its factual and legal complexity) allocating the case to one of three tracks for a hearing. These are: (a) small claims; (b) fast track; and (c) multi-track.

The new small claims limit will be £5,000, although personal injury and housing disrepair claims for over £1,000, illegal eviction and harassment claims will be excluded from the small claims procedure (for detail, see 7.6, below). The limit for cases going into the fast track system will be £15,000, and only claims for over £15,000 can be issued in the Royal Courts of Justice. Applications to move cases 'up' a track on grounds of complexity will have to be made on the new allocation questionnaire (see below).

7.4.5 Pre-action protocols

The pre-action protocols (PAPs) are an important feature of the reforms. They exist for cases of *clinical negligence* (formerly called medical negligence but now extended to cover claims against dentists, radiologists *et al*) and *personal injury* cases, and are likely to be followed, over time, with similar protocols for cases involving other specialisms like debt.

In the *Final Report on Access to Justice* (1996), Lord Woolf stated (Chapter 10) that PAPs are intended to 'build on and increase the benefits of early but well informed settlements'. The purposes of the PAPs, he said, are:

(a) to focus the attention of litigants on the desirability of resolving disputes without litigation;

(b) to enable them to obtain the information they reasonably need in order to enter into an appropriate settlement ...;

(d) if a pre-action settlement is not achievable, to lay the ground for expeditious conduct of proceedings.

The protocols were drafted with the assistance of The Law Society, the Clinical Disputes Forum, the Association of Personal Injury Lawyers, and the Forum of Insurance Lawyers. Most clients in personal injury and medical negligence claims want their cases settled as quickly and as economically as possible. The new spirit of co-operation fostered by the Woolf reforms should mean that, in future, fewer cases are pushed through the courts. The PAPs are intended to improve pre-action contact between the parties and to facilitate better exchange of information and fuller investigation of a claim at an earlier stage. Both clinical negligence and personal injury PAPs recommend:

- The claimant sending a reasonably detailed letter of claim to the proposed defendant, including details of the accident/medical treatment, a brief explanation of why the defendant is being held responsible, a description of the injury, and an outline of the defendant's losses. Unlike a 'pleading' in the old system (which could not be moved away from by the claimant), there will be no sanctions applied if the proceedings differ from the letter of claim. However, as Gordon Exall has observed ('Civil litigation brief' (1999) SJ 32, 15 January), letters of claim should be drafted with care because any variance between them and the claim made in court will give the defendant's lawyers a fruitful opportunity for cross-examination.

- The defendant should acknowledge the letter within 21 days, identifying insurers if applicable. The defendant then has a maximum of three months to investigate and tell the claimant whether liability is admitted. If it is denied, reasons must be given.

- Within that three month period or on denial of liability, the parties should organise disclosure of key documents. For personal injury cases, the protocol lists the main types of defendant's documents for different types of cases. If the defendant denies liability, then he should disclose all the relevant documents in his possession which are likely to be ordered to be disclosed by the court. In clinical negligence claims, the key documents will usually be the claimant's medical records, and the protocol includes a pro-forma application to obtain these.

- The Personal Injury PAP also includes a framework for the parties to agree on the use of expert evidence, particularly in respect of a condition and prognosis report from a medical expert. Before any prospective party instructs an expert, he should give the other party a list of names of one or more experts in the relevant specialty which he considers are suitable to instruct. Within 14 days, the other party may indicate an objection to one or more of the experts, the first party should then instruct a mutually acceptable expert. Only if all suggested experts are objected to can the sides instruct experts of their own. The aim, here, is to allow the claimant to get the defendant to agree to one report being prepared by a mutually agreeable non-partisan expert. The clinical negligence PAP encourages the parties to consider sharing expert evidence, especially with regard to quantum (that is, the amount of damages payable).

- Both PAPs encourage the parties to use ADR or negotiation to settle the dispute during the pre-action period.

At the early stage of proceedings, when a case is being allocated to a track (that is, small claims, fast track) after the defence has been filed, parties will be asked whether they have complied with a relevant protocol, and, if not, why not. The court will then be able to take the answers into account when deciding whether, for example, an extension of time should be granted. The court will also be able to penalise poor conduct by one side through costs sanctions – an order that the party at fault pay the costs of the proceedings or part of them.

7.4.6 Jurisdiction for the start of proceedings

Part 7 of the CPR sets out the rules for starting proceedings. A new restriction is placed on which cases may be begun in the High Court. The county courts retain an unlimited jurisdiction for handling contract and tort claims (that is, negligence cases, nuisance cases). Issuing proceedings in the High Court is now limited to:

- personal injury claims with a value of £50,000 or more;

- other claims with a value of more than £15,000;

- claims where an Act of Parliament requires an action to start in the High Court; or

- specialist High Court claims which need to go to one of the specialist 'lists', like the Commercial List, the Technology List, and the Construction List.

7.5 Proceedings – the CPR Pt 7 claim

One of the main aims of the Woolf reforms is to simplify court forms. Under the old system, there were various forms that needed to be completed at the outset of an action – different types including summonses, originating applications, writs and petitions. Under the new system, most claims will be begun by using a 'Pt 7' claim form – a form which has been designed for multi-purpose use. It can be used if the claim is for a *specified* amount of money (the old term was *liquidated* damages) or an *unspecified* amount (replacing the term *unliquidated* damages). The form can also be used for non-monetary claims, for example, where the claimant just wants a court order, not money. The person issuing the claim form is called a claimant (plaintiff, in old vocabulary) and the person at whom it is directed will continue to be known as a defendant.

Under the new rules, the court can grant any remedy to which the claimant is entitled even if the claimant does not specify which one he or she wants. It is, though, as Gordon Exall has observed ((1999) SJ 162, 19 February), dangerous to start an action without having a clear idea of the remedy you want. The defendant might be able to persuade the court not to allow the claimant a certain part of his or her costs if he (the defendant) finds himself having to consider a remedy which had not been mentioned prior to the trial.

How far these plainer forms simplify matters remains to be seen. In the longer term, it seems clear that a set of plain language forms designed all at one time, as a part of one coherent system, will provide a more efficient system than that afforded by a collection of outdated forms which had been generated reactively over a long period. Nonetheless, it might take a while for the new system to become fully operational in an efficient way. Around 75% of the matters received for issue at Bristol County Court in the week following the implementation of the reforms were returned, as solicitors were using either the old forms or the new ones wrongly completed ('Claims tumble in first week of Woolf as forms stymie solicitors' (1999) 96/18 Law Soc Gazette 3, 6 May). Similarly, a spokesperson for Manchester County Court said 'almost all' forms were sent back to solicitors in the week following the introduction of the new rules. Only 74 claims were received by that court that week, as opposed to a weekly average prior to the reforms of 550 claims.

7.5.1 Value

The 'value' of a claim is the amount a claimant reasonably expects to recover. Unless the amount being claimed is a specified amount, a claimant will be expected (CPR Pt 16) to state the value band into which the claim is likely to fall. The value bands reflect the values for the different tracks (for example, £1 to £5,000 for small claims). Value is calculated as the amount a claimant expects to recover, ignoring any interest, costs, contributory negligence or the fact that a defendant may make a counterclaim, or include a set-off in the defence. If a claimant is not able to put a value on the claim, the reasons for this must be given.

7.5.2 Particulars of claim

Particulars of claim, may be included in the claim form, attached to it, or may be served (that is, given or sent to a party by a method allowed by the rules) separately from it. Where they are served separately, they must be served within 14 days of the claim form being served. The time for a defendant to respond begins to run from the time the particulars of claim are served.

CPR Pt 16 is entitled *Statements of Case* (replacing the term *pleadings*). Statements of case include documents from both sides: claim forms, particulars of claims, defences, counterclaims, replies to defences and counterclaims, Pt 20 (third party) claims and any *further information* provided under CPR Pt 18 (replacing the term *further and better particulars*). Part 16 of the rules also sets out what both particulars of claim and defences should contain.

The particulars of claim must contain:

- a concise statement of facts on which the claimant relies;

- details of any interest claimed;

- specific details if exemplary, provisional and aggravated damages are claimed.

The Woolf Report was against obliging the claimant to state the legal nature of the claim as this would prejudice unrepresented defendants. If the nature of the claim is uncertain, then the court can take its own steps to clarify the matter.

Where a claimant is going to rely on the fact that the defendant has been convicted for a crime arising out of the same circumstances for which the claimant is now suing, then the particulars of claim must contain details of the conviction, the court which made it and exactly how it is relevant to the claimant's arguments.

It is optional for the claimant to also mention any point of law on which the claim is based, and the names of any witnesses which he or she proposes to call.

All statements of case must also contain a statement of truth.

7.5.3 Statements of truth

A statement of truth is a statement that a party believes that the facts or allegations set out in a document which they put forward are true. It is required in statements of case, witness statements, and expert reports. Any document which contains a statement of truth may be used in evidence. This will avoid the previous need to swear affidavits in support of various statements made as part of the claim.

Any document with a signed statement of truth which contains false information given deliberately, that is, without an honest belief in its truth, will constitute a contempt of court (a punishable criminal offence) by the person who provided the information. Solicitors may sign statements of truth on behalf of clients, but on the understanding that it is done with the clients' authority, and with clients knowing the consequences of any false statement will be personal to them.

7.5.4 Response pack

When a claim form is served, it will be served with a response pack. The response pack will contain an acknowledgment of service, a form of admission and a form of defence and counterclaim. The response pack will be served with a claim form containing the particulars of claim or which are attached to it, or, where particulars of claim are served after the claim form, with the particulars. A defendant must respond within 14 days of service of the particulars of claim. If a defendant ignores the claim, the claimant may obtain judgment for the defendant to pay the amount claimed. A defendant may:

- pay the claim;

- admit the claim, or partly admit it;

- file an acknowledgment of service; or

- file a defence.

New requirements have now also been introduced regarding the content of a defence. A defence which is a simple denial is no longer acceptable and runs the risk of being struck out by the court (that is, deleted so that it may no longer be relied upon). A defendant must state in any defence:

- which of the allegations in the particulars of claim are denied, giving reasons for doing so;

- which the defendant is not able to admit or deny but which the claimant is required to prove;

- which allegations are admitted; and

- if the defendant disputes the claimant's statement of value, the reasons for doing so and if possible, stating an alternate value.

These rules mark a significant change of culture from the old civil procedure rules. Under the old rules, a defendant could, in his defence, raise a 'non-admission' or a 'denial'. The first meant that the defendant was putting the plaintiff (now claimant) to proof, that is, challenging him to prove his case on the balance of probabilities. The second meant that the defendant was raising a specific defence, for example, a 'development risks defence' under the Product

Liability Act 1987. Defendants were allowed under the old rules to keep as many avenues of defence available for as long as possible. Under the new rules, the defendant must respond according to the choices in the four options (above). According to r 16.5(5), if the defendant does not deal specifically with each allegation, then it will be deemed to be admitted.

Writing just before the new CPR came into effect, barrister Gordon Exall observed that:

> In theory, this should lead to an enormous change in culture. In personal injury cases, for example, the defendant often denies the existence of various statutory duties owed. Often, nothing will induce the defendant to cease this denial up to the morning of the trial when the defendant's counsel, sensibly, concedes that the various duties are owed ((1999) SJ 270, 19 March).

7.5.5 Part 8 claims (CPR Pt 8)

Part 8 of the new rules introduces the *alternative procedure for claims*. This procedure is commenced by the issue of a Pt 8 claim form. It is intended to provide a speedy resolution of claims which are not likely to involve a substantial dispute of fact, for example, applications for approval of infant settlements, or for orders enforcing a statutory right such as a right to have access to medical records (under the Access to Health Records Act 1990).

The main differences between this and the Pt 7 procedure are as follows:

- a hearing may be given on issue or at same later stage if required;
- only an acknowledgment of service is served with the claim form by way of a response document:
- a defendant must file an acknowledgment of service to be able to take part in any hearing;
- a defendant must serve a copy of the acknowledgment on the other parties, as well as filing it with the court;
- no defence is required;
- default judgment is not available to the claimant; the court must hear the case;
- there are automatic directions for the exchange of evidence (in this case, in the form of witness statements);
- Pt 8 claims are not formally allocated to a track; they are automatically multi-track cases.

7.5.6   Default judgment (CPR Pt 12)

If a defendant (to a Pt 7 claim) files an acknowledgment stating an intention to defend the claim, this extends the period for filing a defence from 14 to 28 days from the date of service of the particulars. Failure to file an acknowledgment or, later, failure to file a defence can result in default judgment, that is, the court will find for the claimant so the defendant will lose the case.

If the defendant does not to reply to the claim, a claimant may apply for default judgment for the amount claimed if the amount claimed is a specified amount, or on liability, if the amount claimed is unspecified, after the 14 day period from service has elapsed.

There are a number of cases in which it is not possible to obtain judgment in default, notably, in claims for delivery of goods subject to an agreement controlled by the Consumer Credit Act 1974.

7.5.7   Service (CPR Pt 6)

Where the court is to serve any document (not just claim forms), it is for the court to decide the method of service. This will generally be by first class post. The deemed date of service is two days after the day of posting for all defendants, including limited companies. Where a claim form originally served by post is returned by the Post Office, the court will send a notice of non-service to the claimant. The notice will tell the claimant that the court will not make any further attempts at service. Service, therefore, becomes a matter for claimants. The court will return the copies of the claim form, response pack, etc, for claimants to amend as necessary, and re-serve.

Claimants may serve claim forms, having told the court in writing that they wish to do so, either personally, by post, by fax, by document exchange (a private courier service operated between law firms) or by e-mail or other electronic means. A claimant who serves a document must file a certificate of service within seven days of service with a copy of the document served attached.

7.5.8   Admissions and part admissions

The possibility of admitting liability for a claim for a specific amount and making an offer to pay by instalments, or at a later date, applies to both county court and High Court cases. Where the claim is for a specific amount, the admission will be sent direct to the claimant. However, if a claimant objects to the rate of payment offered, there are changes which affect the determination process, that is, the process by which a member of a court's staff, or a judge, decides the rate of payment.

Cases involving a specific amount where the balance outstanding, including any costs, is less than £50,000 will be determined by a court officer.

Those where the balance is £50,000 or more, or for an unspecified amount of any value, must be determined by a Master or district judge. The Master, or judge, has the option of dealing with the determination on the papers without a hearing, or at a hearing.

A defendant in a claim for an unspecified amount of money (damages) will be able to make an offer of a specific sum of money in satisfaction of a claim which does not have to be supported by a payment into court. A claimant can accept the admission and rate of payment offered as if the claim had originally been for a specific amount. The determination procedure described above will apply where a claimant accepts the amount offered but not the rate of payment proposed.

If a claimant does not accept the amount offered, a request that judgment be entered for liability on the strength of the defendant's admission may be made to the court. In the new system, this is referred to as *judgment for an amount and costs to be decided by the court* (replacing *interlocutory judgment for damages to be assessed*). Where judgment is entered in this way, the court will at the same time give case management directions for dealing with the case.

Where a request for such a judgment is received, the court file will be passed to a procedural judge. The judge may allocate the case to the small claims track and give directions if it is of appropriate value; ask that the case be set down for a *disposal* hearing, or, where the amount is likely to be heavily disputed, order a trial. Directions will be given as appropriate. A disposal hearing in these circumstances may either be a hearing at which the court gives directions, or at which the amount and costs are decided.

7.5.9 Defence and automatic transfer (CPR Pt 15)

Claims for specified amounts will be transferred automatically to the defendant's 'home court' where the defendant is an individual who has filed a defence. The defendant's home court will be 'the court or district registry, including the RCJ, for the district in which the defendant's address for service as shown on the defence is situated'. This means that, where the defendant is represented by a solicitor, this will be the defendant's solicitor's business address.

Where there is more than one defendant, it is the first defendant to file a defence who dictates whether or not automatic transfer will take place. For example, if there are two defendants to a claim, one an individual and one a limited company, there would be no automatic transfer if the limited company was the first defendant to file a defence.

7.5.10 Allocation questionnaire

The purpose of this document is to enable to court to judge in which track the case should be heard. When a defence is filed, the issuing court will send out a copy of the defence to all other parties to the claim together with an allocation questionnaire, a notice setting out the date for returning it and the name and address of the court (or district registry or the Royal Courts of Justice (that is, High Court), as appropriate) to which the completed allocation questionnaire must be returned. A notice of transfer will also be sent if the case is being automatically transferred.

When the allocation questionnaire is returned, or at the end of the period for returning it, and whether or not only some, or none, of the questionnaires (if there is more than one defendant) have been filed, the court file will be passed to a procedural judge for directions and allocation to track. If there is sufficient information, the judge will allocate the case to a track and a notice of allocation and directions will be sent out to each party. Where only one party has filed a questionnaire or there is insufficient information, the judge may make an order requesting further information, or order an allocation hearing. Where none of the parties has filed a questionnaire, the judge may also decide to impose a sanction, for example, ordering that a statement, or statements, of case be struck out unless a completed questionnaire is filed within three days of service of the order.

The questionnaire asks a number of questions, for example:

- Do you wish there to be a one month stay to attempt to settle this case?

- Which track do you consider most suitable for your case (small claims, fast track, or multi-track)? A party wishing a case to be dealt with on a track which is not the obviously suitable track must give reasons.

- At this stage, you are asked whether you have complied with any relevant protocols, and, if not, why not and the extent of the non-compliance.

- You are asked for an estimate of costs to date and the overall costs up to trial.

- You are asked if you wish to use expert evidence at the trial, whether expert reports have been copied to the other side, who the expert is, and, if the parties have not agreed upon a common expert, why not.

The purpose of this questionnaire is to make both sides have a clear overview of the case at an early stage so it becomes very difficult for lawyers to bumble along buffeted by developments in a case. To reduce delays and therefore costs, it is desirable that a lawyer should be able to purposefully stride through a case along a planned route.

7.5.11 Applications to be made when claims come before a judge

The overriding objective in Pt 1 requires the court to deal with as many aspects of the case as possible on the same occasion. The filing of an allocation questionnaire is one such occasion. Parties should, wherever possible, issue any application they may wish to make, such as an application for summary judgment (CPR Pt 24), or to add a third party (CPR Pt 20), at the same time as they file their questionnaire. Any hearing set to deal with the application will also serve as an allocation hearing if allocation remains appropriate.

7.5.12 Summary judgment (CPR Pt 24)

Summary judgment is available to both claimants and defendants. Where either party feels that the other does not have a valid claim or defence, they can apply to the court for the claim or defence to be struck out and for judgment to be entered in their favour. The applicant, either claimant or defendant, must prove to the court's satisfaction, that the other party has 'no real prospect of success' and that 'there is no other reason why the case or issue should be dealt with at trial'.

Application for summary judgment cannot be made without the court's permission (replacing the term leave), before an acknowledgment of service has been filed. Where an application is made by the claimant before a defendant files a defence, the defendant against whom it is made need not file a defence. If a claimant's application is unsuccessful, the court will give directions for the filing of a defence.

7.5.13 Allocation to track (CPR Pt 26)

Allocation will be to one of three tracks: the *small claims track*, the *fast track* and the *multi-track*. Each of the tracks offers a different degree of case management.

Directions (instructions about what to do to prepare the case for trial or hearing) will be proportionate to the value of the claim, its importance, complexity, and so on. Each track requires a different degree of case monitoring, that is, the more complex the claim, the more milestone events there are likely to be (that is, important points in the process, like the date by which the allocation questionnaire should be returned). Time for carrying out directions, no matter which track, may be extended or shortened by agreement between parties but must not, as a result, affect any of the milestones relevant to that track. The time for carrying out directions will be expressed as calendar dates rather than periods of days or weeks. Directions will include the court's directions concerning the use of expert evidence.

7.6   The small claims track (CPR Pt 27)

There is no longer any 'automatic reference' to the small claims track. Claims are allocated to this track in exactly the same way as to the fast or multi-tracks. The concept of an *'arbitration'* therefore disappears and is replaced by a *small claims hearing*. Aspects of the old small claims procedure which are retained, include their informality, the interventionist approach adopted by the judiciary, the limited costs regime and the limited grounds for appeal (misconduct of the district judge or an error of law made by the court).

Changes to the handling of small claims are:

- *an increase in the jurisdiction from £3,000 to no more than £5,000* (with the exception of claims for personal injury where the damages claimed for pain and suffering and loss of amenity do not exceed £1,000 and the financial value of the whole claim does not exceed £5,000; and for housing disrepair where the claim for repairs and other work do not exceed £1,000 and the financial value of any other claim for damages is not more than £1,000);

- *hearings to be generally public hearings* – but subject to some exceptions (CPR Pt 39);

- *paper adjudication, if parties consent* – where a judge thinks that paper adjudication may be appropriate, parties will be asked to say whether or not they have any objections within a given time period. If a party does object, the matter will be given a hearing in the normal way;

- *parties need not attend the hearing* – a party not wishing to attend a hearing will be able to give the court and the other party, or parties, written notice that they will not be attending. The notice must be filed with the court seven days before the start of the hearing. This will guarantee that the court will take into account any written evidence that party has sent to the court. A consequence of this is that the judge must give reasons for the decision reached which will be included in the judgment;

- *the introduction of tailored directions* – to be given for some of the most common small claims, for example, spoiled holidays, or wedding videos, road traffic accidents, building disputes.

Parties can consent to use the small claims track even if the value of their claim exceeds the normal value for that track, but subject to the court's approval. The limited cost regime will not apply to these claims. But, costs will be limited to the costs that might have been awarded if the claim had been dealt with in the fast track. Parties will also be restricted to a maximum one day hearing.

The milestone events for the small claims track are the *date for the return of the allocation questionnaire and the date of the hearing.*

The right to appeal under the CPR is governed by new principles. You can appeal on the basis that:

(a) there was a serious irregularity affecting the proceedings; or

(b) the court made a mistake of law.

An example of (a) (see Paul McGrath in [1999] NLJ 748) would be where an arbitrator fails to allow submissions on any crucial point upon which he hangs his judgment.

7.7 The fast track (CPR Pt 28)

In accordance with one of the main principles of the Woolf reforms, the purpose of the fast track is to provide a streamlined procedure for the handling of moderately-valued cases – *those with a value of more than £5,000 but less than £15,000* – in a way which will ensure that the costs remain proportionate to the amount in dispute. The features of the procedure which aim to achieve this are:

- standard directions for trial preparation which avoid complex procedures and multiple experts, with minimum case management intervention by the court;

- a limited period between directions and the start of the trial, or trial period, of around 30 weeks;

- a maximum of one day (five hours) for trial;

- trial period must not exceed three weeks and parties must be given 21 days notice of the date fixed for trial;

- normally, no oral expert evidence is to be given at trial; and costs allowed for the trial are fixed and which vary depending on the level of advocate.

Directions given to the parties by the judge will normally include a date by which parties must file a listing questionnaire. As with allocation questionnaires, the procedural judge may impose a sanction where a listing questionnaire is not returned by the due date. Listing questionnaires will include information about witnesses, confirm the time needed for trial, parties' availability and the level of advocate for the trial.

The milestone events for the fast track are *the date for the return of allocation* and *listing questionnaires* and the *date for the start of the trial, or trial period*.

7.8 The multi-track (CPR Pt 29)

The multi-track is intended to provide a flexible regime for the handling of the higher value, more complex claims, that is, those with a *value of over £15,000*.

This track does not provide any standard procedure, such as those for small claims or claims in the fast track. Instead, it offers a range of case management tools – *standard directions, case management conferences* and *pre-trial reviews* – which can be used in a 'mix and match' way – to suit the needs of individual cases. Whichever of these is used to manage the case, the principle of setting a date for trial, or a trial period at the earliest possible time, no matter that it is some way away, will remain paramount.

Where a trial period is given for a multi-track case, this will be one week. Parties will be told initially that their trial will begin on a day within the given week. The rules and practice direction do not set any time period for giving notice to the parties of the date fixed for trial.

7.9 Public and private hearings (CPR Pt 39)

In the new rules, the distinction between 'public' and 'private' hearings is not whether a claim, or application, is heard in a court room or the *judge's room* (formerly called *chambers*), but whether members of the public are allowed to sit in on the hearing wherever it takes place.

Courts are not required to make any special arrangements to accommodate members of the public, for example, if the judge's room is too small to accommodate more than those directly concerned with the claim. However, where a hearing is 'public', anyone may obtain a copy of the order made upon payment of the appropriate fee.

7.10 Case management conferences

Case management conferences may be regarded as an opportunity to 'take stock'. There is no limit to the number of case management conferences which may be held during the life of a case, although the cost of attendance at such hearings against the benefits obtained will always be a consideration in making the decision. They will be used, among other things, to consider:

- giving directions, including a specific date for the return of a listing questionnaire;

- whether the claim, or defence, are sufficiently clear for the other party to understand the claim they have to meet;

- whether any amendments should be made to statements of case;

- what documents, if any each party needs to show the other;

- what factual evidence should be given;

- what expert evidence should be sought and how it should be sought and disclosed; and

- whether it would save costs to order a separate trial of one or more issues.

7.11 Pre-trial reviews

Pre-trial reviews will normally take place after the filing of listing questionnaires, and before the start of the trial. Their main purpose is to decide a timetable for the trial itself, including the evidence to be allowed and whether this should be given orally, instructions about the content of any trial bundles (bundles of documents including evidence, such as written statements, for the judge to read) and confirming a realistic time estimate for the trial itself.

Rules require that, where a party is represented, a representative 'familiar with the case and with sufficient authority to deal with any issues likely to arise must attend every case management conference or pre-trial review'.

7.12 Stays for settlement (CPR Pt 26) and settlements (Pt 36)

Under the new CPR, there is a greater incentive for parties to settle their differences.

The court will take into account any pre-action offers to settle when making an order for costs. Thus, a side which has refused an reasonable offer to settle will be treated less generously in the issue of how far the court will order their costs to be paid by the other side. For this to happen, the offer, though, must be one which is made to be open to the other side for at least 21 days after receipt (to stop any undue pressure being put on someone with the phrase: 'take it or leave it, it is only open for one day then I shall withdraw the offer'). Also, if the offer is made by the defendant, it must be an offer to pay compensation and to pay the claimant's costs

Several aspects of the new rules encourage litigants to settle rather than take risks in order (as a claimant) to hold out for unreasonably large sums of compensation, or try to get away (as a defendant) with paying nothing rather than some compensation. The system of Pt 36 payments or offers does not apply to small claims but, for other cases, it seems bound to have a significant effect. Thus, if at the trial a claimant does not get more damages than a sum offered by the defendant in what is called a 'Pt 36' payment (that is, an offer to settle or a payment into the court), or obtain a judgment more favourable than a Pt 36 offer, the court will order the claimant to pay any costs incurred by the defendant after the latest date for accepting the payment or offer. The court now has a discretion to make a different order for costs than the normal order. District Judge Frenkel has given the following example:

> Claim, £150,000 – judgment, £51,000 – £50,000 paid into court. The without prejudice correspondence shows that the claimant would consider nothing short of £150,000. The claimant may be in trouble. The defendant will ask the judge to consider overriding principles of Pt 1 'Was it proportional to incur the further costs of trial to secure an additional £1,000?'. Part 44.3 confirms the

general rule that the loser pays but allows the court to make a different order to take into account offers to settle, payment into court, the parties, conduct including pre-action conduct and exaggeration of the claim ([1999] NLJ 458).

Similarly, where, at trial, a defendant is held liable to the claimant for more money than the proposals contained in a claimant's Pt 36 offer (that is, where the claimant has made an offer to settle), the court may order the defendant to pay interest on the award at a rate not exceeding 10% above the base rate for some or all of the period starting with the date on which the defendant could have accepted the offer.

Active case management imposes a duty on the courts to help parties settle their disputes. A 'stay' is a temporary halt in proceedings, and an opportunity for the court to order such a pause arises at the stage when the defence to a claim has been filed. Parties can indicate that they have agreed on a stay to attempt to settle the case and, provided the court agrees, can have an initial period of one month to try to settle the case. In order to avoid the stay being used as a delaying tactic, the order granting the stay will require the parties to report back to the court within 14 days of the end of the period of the stay to:

- inform the court if the matter has been settled either wholly or partly; or

- asking for more time for settlement; or

- reporting that the attempt to settle has failed, so that the process of allocation of court track can take place.

The court will always give the final decision about whether to grant the parties more time to use a mediator, or arbitrator, or expert to settle, even if the parties are agreed they wish to have more time. A stay will never be granted for an indefinite period.

7.13 Witness statements

In the *Final Report on Access to Justice,* Lord Woolf recognised the importance of witness statements in cases but observed that they had become problematic because lawyers had made them excessively long and detailed in order to protect against leaving out something which later proved to be relevant. He said 'witness statements have ceased to be the authentic account of the lay witness; instead they have become an elaborate, costly branch of legal drafting' (para 55).

Under the new rules, witness statements must contain the evidence that the witness will give at trial but they should be briefer than those drafted under the previous rules: they should be drafted in lay language and should not discuss legal propositions. Witnesses will be allowed to amplify on the statement or deal with matters that have arisen since the report was served, although this is not an automatic right and a 'good reason' for the admission of new evidence will have to be established.

7.14 Court fees

A new fee structure will be introduced to take account of the different procedures, a movement towards a 'pay as you go' fees regime and the need for full cost recovery. Pay as you go means that parties will be expected to contribute more in fees, the more court and judicial time they use, for example, if they do not settle and carry on to trial.

Courts will be pro-active in collecting fees, in particular, those which are payable at allocation and listing stages, but *without interrupting* a case's progress. There will be sanctions for non-payment of allocation and listing questionnaire fees which could lead to a party's statement of case being struck out.

7.15 Experts (CPR Pt 35)

New rules place a clear duty on the court to ensure that 'expert evidence is restricted to that which is reasonably required to resolve the proceedings'. That is to say that expert evidence will only be allowed either by way of written report, or orally, where the court gives permission. Equally important is the rules' statement about experts' duties. They state that it is the clear duty of experts to help the *court* on matters within their expertise, bearing in mind that this duty overrides any obligation to the person from whom they have received instructions or by whom they are paid.

There will be greater emphasis in the future on using the opinion of a single expert. Experts will only be called to give oral evidence at a trial or hearing if the court gives permission. Experts' written reports must contain a statement that they understand and have complied with their duty to the court. Instructions to experts will no longer be privileged and their substance, whether written or oral, must be set out in the expert's report. Thus, either side can insist, through the court, on seeing how the other side phrased its request to an expert.

7.16 Costs

Fixed costs (CPR Pt 45)

There are new rates for the fixed costs allowed on issue of a claim and on entry of judgment where a party is represented by a solicitor.

Assessment (CPR Pt 47)

The terms *taxed* costs and *taxation* become redundant and are replaced by assessment. Costs will either be assessed summarily, that is, there and then, or there will be a *detailed assessment* at some later stage where one party has been ordered to pay another's costs.

Summary assessment

Judges will normally summarily assess costs at the end of hearings, both interim and final, and particularly at the end of fast track trials. Parties will be expected to bring any necessary documentation to the hearing for this purpose. In this way, the need for detailed assessment of costs is avoided so far as possible.

7.17 What will the new system achieve?

The positive answer, self-evidently, is that it will achieve all or most of the reforms whose spirit is captured in Lord Woolf's *Final Report on Access to Justice*. The new system, clearly though, will not be without its problems, some minor and others more troubling.

Professor Michael Zander QC has made substantial criticism of the new civil procedure reforms. At the heart of the Woolf reforms is the mechanism of 'judicial case management'. Looking at the results of an American study about how the system operates in the United States, Zander raises serious questions about whether the Woolf reforms would be subject to similar problems ('How does judicial case management work?' (1997) NLJ 353, 7 March). The major official study that Zander examined was published by the Institute of Civil Justice at the Rand Corporation in California. The study was based on 10,000 cases in Federal Courts drawn from 16 States. It appears that a range of judicial case management techniques introduced in America had little effect on the time it took to deal with cases, litigation costs, and lawyer satisfaction. There was evidence that early judicial case management is associated with significantly increased costs to litigants because lawyer work increases in such circumstances. Zander notes that interviews with judges and lawyers in the American study suggested some reasons why tracking cases (the American divisions were Expedited/Standard/Complex) had proved problematic. One of the problems was the difficulty of deciding the correct track assignment for most civil cases using data available at or soon after the filing of the case. This would perhaps not be such a problem in the English model, as assignment to cases comes at a later stage when a defence has been entered so it is easy to evaluate the potential complexity of the case. Additionally, though, the American study showed that judges often wished to tailor case management to the needs of the case and to their style of management rather than having the track assignment provide the management structure of cases. This could equally apply to English judges.

The Rand Report explains that case management tends to increase rather than reduce costs because it generates more work by lawyer:

> ... lawyer work may increase as a result of earlier management because lawyers need to respond to a courts management – for example, talking to the litigant and to the other lawyers in advance of a conference with the judge, travelling

and spending time at the court house, meeting with the judge and updating the file after conference (Zander (1997) NLJ 353, 7 March, p 354).

Professor Zander has taken the view that the reasons for delay in civil legal process are not primarily to do with the adversarial nature of civil litigation. The only serious empirical study of the reasons for delay, argues Zander, is that done by KPMG Peat Marwick for the Lord Chancellors Department in 1994 ('Study on causes of delay in the High Court and county courts', 1994). The study was based on scrutiny of the court records in a 150 High Court personal injury cases and a 188 county court personal injury cases in nine out of London courts. The researchers also interview solicitors for both parties in 26 High Court cases and 40 county court cases from the sample. Zander has regretted that Lord Woolf did not at any time either in his Report or since cite any evidence for his view that the chief cause of delay is the way that the adversary system is played by the lawyers ('Woolf on Zander' (1997) NLJ 768, 23 May). The KPMG Report identified seven causes of delay:

- the nature of the case;

- delay caused by the parties;

- delay caused by their representatives;

- external factors such as the difficulty of getting experts' reports;

- the judiciary;

- court procedures; and

- court administration.

How the lawyers play the adversary game was not one of these factors. KPMG considered the relative important of the seven factors and found that the two factors that gave rise to the most significant delay were first, delay caused by lawyers, mainly due to pressure of work and inexperience or inefficiency in the handling of the case by the parties' solicitors, and, secondly the time taken to obtain medical or other expert reports. Zander observes ([1997] NLJ 768, 23 May):

> KMPG thought that the delay due to solicitors' inefficiency was partly remediable by better office management systems. Maybe timetabled deadlines will help some firms to brace up – but it seems improbable that the imposition of sanctions for failure to meet timetabling requirements will do much to reduce the pressure of work or the inexperience of staff which so often caused firms delay.

Zander further argues ([1997] NLJ 768, 23 May, p 769) that the enterprise of setting detailed procedural timetables, such as operate for the fast track, is doomed to failure because a huge proportion of firms, including inefficient firms, will for all sorts of reasons – some good, some bad – fail to keep to the prescribed timetables. He says 'if I am right, that will lead to enforcement procedures and sanctions on a vast scale, which in turn will lead to innumerable appeals. It will also lead to the imposition of sanctions that are disproportionate and therefore unjust and that will often work great injustice to clients for the failings of the lawyers'.

Many barristers have been following the same intricate procedures, and using the same argot for three or four decades in the civil courts. It will not be easy for them to suddenly adapt to the fundamental changes introduced by the CPR. The following opening to a report from Frances Gibb in *The Times* (27 April 1999) is worth noting. Writing about the first day in which the new CPR were applicable in court (26 April 1999), she reported:

> Within hours of the start of new reforms, part of the biggest shake-up in civil justice this century, some had already fallen foul of the rules. Michael Tillet QC, opening his case, told Mr Justice Turner: 'My Lord, I appear for the plaintiff in this action.' 'No you don't' came the judge's swift rebuke, 'You appear for the claimant'.

The following letter from Professor IR Scott, of the Faculty of Law at the University of Birmingham, appeared in *The Times* on 26 April 1999, the day the new rules came into effect. It is worth quoting in full:

From Professor IR Scott

Sir, on 26 April, the Civil Procedure Rules 1998, implementing the reforms to the administration of justice recommended by Lord Woolf, come into force. Doubtless, the Lord Chancellor's publicity machine will be putting out a considerable amount of information extolling the virtues of the new system and emphasising in particular that it will provide faster and cheaper justice.

I doubt whether one will find any hint that the implementation of the new scheme is turning out to be a shambles.

It has been asserted that the Civil Procedure Rules (CPR) constitute a 'new procedural code', written in plain English and that they will be readily understood by lawyer and lay-person alike. The truth is that, in many respects, the rules and their supplementing Practice Directions are an impenetrable mess. Errors abound. Additions and changes have been made from week to week as 'Woolf day' approached. Many appear to be very important. I say 'appear to be' because some of the material put out recently is incomprehensible. Indeed, the further supplementing Practice Direction to Pt 8 of the CPR (produced during the first week of this month) is one of the worst examples of procedural drafting I have seen.

As a result of the mismanaged implementation of the new scheme, judges, lawyers, court staff and litigants in person have been placed in an impossible position and recriminations are likely to be fierce. The civil justice system faces a long period of 'muddling through', during which much time, effort and money will be spent on trying to operate and manage a procedural system that ought to have been got right well in advance of Woolf day.

Not everyone involved in civil process will accept the view of Professor Scott. Moreover, even for those who share his pessimism, quite how long a period of 'muddling through' will have to be undergone is unclear.

For another useful and engaging overview of the reforms, we can turn to Anthony Scrivener QC. Writing in *The Independent* (26 April 1999), Mr Scrivener argued thus:

> The new procedures are more 'consumer friendly', to use the parlance of the day. The old procedures deterred litigants conducting their own cases. Before they could gather up their papers, they had failed to comply with some rule they had never heard of or, if they had, which they would not have understood. Under the new rules, this may be less likely to happen. The ability of a litigant to conduct a case personally has become more important now that the present Government is abolishing legal aid. It is rather like encouraging self-treatment under the National Health Service ...

> ... Non-compliance with time limits could have disastrous consequences for the litigant. The new procedures tend to move away from the more liberal attitude that pertained under the old regime towards dismissing a claim for non-compliance. It is said that, if you have broken the time limits, you are delaying other litigants. However, it does seem wrong to penalise the litigant for the errors of his lawyers: surely, a better consequence would have been to penalise the lawyers personally in costs but leave the action to proceed and be tried on the merits.

On the subject of the new CPR's preference for a single expert, Mr Scrivener was equally sceptical:

> Under the new system, the parties are to agree before trial on a joint expert. The idea of solicitors for the injured workman and the solicitors for the insurance company amicably agreeing on an expert whose opinion will probably determine the outcome of the case seems a little remote from reality. Litigators are resourceful and unlikely to allow, without a fight, some expert to be appointed who is likely to find against their client, and so they will obtain their own expert to advise them as to which expert should be appointed. There will then have to be a determination as to who should be the anointed expert. No doubt this will be fiercely fought since the outcome of the case may depend on it. Not only is the procedure bizarre, but it hardly advances the interest of justice, which should be directed towards getting the correct result rather than finding the most expeditious way of disposing of a case.

Another criticism of the reforms is that they will, paradoxically, complicate the legal system and cost clients money. This view has been expressed by James Diamond, a legal costs expert.

Mr Diamond, managing director of Legal Costs Services, a company which prepares figures in court costs disputes, argues that the CPR invite abuse from wealthy groups to the detriment of the less well off. The requirement that a party must pay the other side's costs 14 days after losing an interim hearing – even if it has a good chance of winning the case overall – instead of being able to set them off against final judgment winnings will, says Diamond, lead to 'a summons by warfare'.

Diamond contends that:

> Big insurance companies will just issue claim after claim, because, even if they know they're likely to lose the case, they may still win a claim on a certain point. This could leave a deserving opponent facing a £5,000 bill which they have to pay in a fortnight. Some people won't be able to afford that ('Woolf reforms hike costs' (1999) The Lawyer 2, 11 January).

The abolition of the punitive percentage fee is also open to abuse, in Diamond's view. He says that, under the old law, if a company wished to appeal, it had to pay 7.4% of the disputed figure up front. But, the reforms have introduced a fixed fee figure of £100 plus interest, so 'parties will have nothing to lose by appealing'. Even without such abuses, he asserts, appeals are likely to increase by up to 100-fold due to the need to assess every interim claim. He predicts that, in 2000, it may take up to 18 months to set a date for costs assessments. Diamond argues that the 'draconian' new time limits that require a paying party to file its objections to the receiving party's costs within 21 days will mean outfits, such as his, will have to accept fewer clients because preparing the schedule for each hearing would be so time consuming. Moreover, he observes that, since the provisions allow clients to be charged for preparation of bills of costs, they too will be out of pocket. One final point we can make here concerns the levelness of the playing field under the new system. Access to justice will, in some ways, be as unequal as it was under the old system. Those who can afford to pay for the best QC with 40 years' experience at the Bar will perhaps be given a better service than those whose purse can only run to the most junior, inexperienced and recently qualified barrister. 'There won't be an equal playing field in my case', one claimant, Dulce Maltez, insisted, 'I will be represented at trial by a junior counsel of seven years' call. My opponent will be instructing leading counsel of considerably greater call and experience. Debar him from instructing leading counsel or senior counsel'. This argument was rejected by Neuberger J in *Maltez v Lewis* (1999). There are, however, as District Judge Stephen Gold has observed, some ways in which the new CPR can help the poorer party ([1999] NLJ 718). Where the representatives could be said to be unequal, the new rules could be applied to ensure that one side was not unfairly subject to excessive costs because the other party had instructed unreasonably expensive advisers. It would also be possible to allow more time to the side engaging the smaller firm.

7.18   Appeals

The appeal system is covered in Chapter 3. The important procedural points are as follows.

From the county court, appeal lies to the Court of Appeal (Civil Division) (see Chapter 3). In almost all cases, permission is needed in order to appeal.

Appeals from the three Divisions of the High Court, and from the Divisional Courts also go to the Court of Appeal (Civil Division). Appeals are not re-trials with witnesses being called again. The appellant is limited to arguing only the narrow points of law, or law and fact, on which the appeal has been granted. The parties have four weeks from the judge's judgment in which to give notice of appeal. There are usually eight or nine courts sitting during term.

Appeals from the Court of Appeal lie to the House of Lords but the appellant must be granted leave either by the Court of Appeal or by the House of Lords. Only cases involving points of public importance reach the House of Lords and there are usually fewer than 50 civil appeals heard by the Lords each year. It is possible, under the Administration of Justice Act 1969, for the House of Lords to hear an appeal direct from the High Court, 'leapfrogging' the Court of Appeal. The agreement of both parties and the High Court judge are required. Such cases must concern a point of statutory interpretation (including the construction of a Statutory Instrument) which has been fully explored by the High Court judge or concerns a point on which he was bound by precedent to follow.

7.19   The division of work between the High Court and county courts after the Woolf reforms

In *A Programme for the Future*, the Lord Chancellor's Department's strategic plan for 1993/94–1995/96, a number of aims are set out in relation to the civil process. One of its objectives is stated to be the need 'To match fora [that is, each type of court being a different forum] and resources to different types and levels of cases'. The problem of allocating the right sort and volume of cases to the appropriate courts is a long running challenge. It is a matter of debate how far the problems highlighted by the CJR and tackled by the CLSA 1990 have been significantly reduced.

The differences in procedure between the High Court and the county court were considerable and applied from the inception of litigation until the enforcement of court judgments. The arguments for a single court were rehearsed over many years, beginning not long after the establishment of the county courts (1846) when the Judicature Commission considered the proposal in 1869. The Law Society supported the idea in 1980, arguing that: 'A one court system would lead to the expedition, standardisation and simplification of proceedings and to a saving in judicial time.'

A merger of the High Court and county court was considered by the Beeching Royal Commission in 1969, but was rejected. Instead, it recommended a more flexible use of the judiciary. Some judges are more experienced and expert than others. Clearly, it makes sense for the judges with greater expertise to preside in the more important cases, but how is 'importance' to be judged? The sum involved may not be very large but the legal point in issue may be of enormous significance. Conversely, a case where the sum claimed is very great may not raise any particularly difficult or consequential point of law. Beeching recommended that the allocation of cases to the different tiers of judges should be determined to some extent by judges rather than by simply looking at the sum claimed. Now, because there is just one set of rules (the CPR) governing both the High Court and the county courts, the courts in one sense have been unified. We now have a single procedural system.

7.20   Do we need two sorts of court after Woolf?

The introduction of the Woolf reforms in 1999 adds new impetus to the case for having only one type of civil court. With a unified set of forms and procedures applicable to both the High Court and the county courts, the question is raised as to why we need to have two sorts of venue. In an article entitled 'Why have two types of civil court?' ((1999) NLJ 65, 15 January), Richard Harrison has argued for unification.

Lord Woolf came close to recommending that the two sorts of court be merged but stopped short of that because such a suggested merger would have involved Lord Woolf in dealing with matters beyond his remit. There are three main issues:

- the need to preserve the special status of High Court judges;

- the existence of inherently specialist jurisdictions in each court;

- the problem with rights of audience.

Harrison presents cogent arguments against all three points being raised as obstacles to change. He argues:

- under the new system, cases could be allocated simply to judges 'at the right level' without levels being characterised by special conditions of service and the trappings of prestige. Now, a High Court judge is given a knighthood or a damehood and his or her tenure is under letters patent, with removal from office being only theoretically possible under address by both Houses of Parliament. Her Majesty's judges are the fount of the common law as opposed to being creatures of statute like circuit judges and district judges. Harrison states that: 'I do not think it is possible to argue sensibly that there should be a distinction between levels of the judiciary with increased prestige, respect and remuneration being afforded to an elite band';

- resistance to change relies on the view that High Court judges should not have to deal with small claims and that county court judges should not be able to judge in cases like those involving judicial review. Harrison says that specialist judges (from the High Court) could carry on, as at present, dealing with highly complex or sensitive cases without having a separate rank;

- in future, rights of audience will depend upon fitness and qualification, not on whether one is a solicitor or barrister or practising in the High Court or county court. In these circumstances, it does not appear, argues Harrison, that this will present any problem for a unified court.

Harrison recognises that unification of the civil court structure may be some time away. He therefore proposes an interim practical solution – ignoring the distinction in procedural terms. Cases could be headed 'Before the Civil Courts ...' without worrying the claimant about through which type of court his or her case is going. Case management decisions on allocation could then be made in accordance with the spirit of the Woolf reforms.

THE CIVIL PROCESS

The Woolf Inquiry into the civil justice system was set up by the government in 1994 to examine why civil litigation was generally very costly, protracted, complicated and subject to long delays.

The Inquiry published its final report in 1996 and its proposals resulted in the Civil Procedure Act 1997, and the Civil Procedure Rules 1998. The new Civil Procedure Rules (CPR) will be the same for the county court and the High Court. They apply to all cases except (Pt 2) to insolvency proceedings, family proceedings, and non-contentious probate proceedings.

The overriding objective

The overriding objective of the new CPR is to enable the court to deal justly with cases. The first rule states:

> 1.1(1) These rules are a new procedural code with the overriding objective of enabling the court to deal with cases justly.

Practice directions

Practice directions (official statements of interpretative guidance) play an important role in the new civil process. In general, they supplement the CPRs, giving the latter fine detail. They tell parties and their representatives what the court will expect of them, in respect of documents to be filed in court for a particular purpose, and how they must co-operate with the other parties to their action. They also tell the parties what they can expect of the court.

Case control

Judges will receive support from court staff in carrying out their case management role. The court will monitor case progress by using a computerised diary monitoring system.

Active case management includes:

(a) encouraging the parties to co-operate with each other in the conduct of the proceedings;

(b) identifying the issues at an early stage;

(c) deciding promptly which issues need full investigation and trial and, accordingly, disposing summarily of the others;

(d) deciding the order in which issues are to be resolved.

Court allocation

The new civil system works on the basis of the court, upon receipt of the claim (accompanied by duly filled-in forms giving all the relevant details of the claim, including how much it is for, and an indication of its factual and legal complexity), allocating the case to one of three tracks for a hearing. These are:

- small claims;
- fast track;
- multi-track.

The new small claims limit will be £5,000, although personal injury and housing disrepair claims for over £1,000, illegal eviction and harassment claims will be excluded from the small claims court. The limit for cases going into the fast track system will be £15,000, and only claims for over £15,000 can be issued in the Royal Courts of Justice. Applications to move cases 'up' a track on grounds of complexity will have to be made on the new allocation questionnaire (see below).

Pre-action protocols

The pre-action protocols (PAPs) are an important feature of the reforms. They exist for cases of clinical negligence and personal injury cases, and are likely to be followed, over time, with similar protocols for cases involving other specialisms like debt.

Jurisdiction for the start of proceedings

Part 7 of the CPR sets out the rules for starting proceedings. A new restriction is placed on which cases may be begun in the High Court. The county courts retain an unlimited jurisdiction for handling contract and tort claims (that is, negligence cases, nuisance cases). Issuing proceedings in the High Court is now limited to:

- personal injury claims with a value of £50,000 or more;
- other claims with a value of more than £15,000;
- claims where an Act of Parliament requires an action to start in the High Court; or

- specialist High Court claims which need to go to one of the specialist 'lists', like the Commercial List, the Technology List, and the Construction List.

Particulars of claim

Particulars of claim may be included in the claim form, attached to it, or may be served (that is, given or sent to a party by a method allowed by the rules) separately from it. Where they are served separately, they must be served within 14 days of the claim form being served. The time for a defendant to respond begins to run from the time the particulars of claim are served.

Part 16 of the CPR is entitled 'statements of case' (replacing the word 'pleadings'). Statements of case include documents from both sides: claim forms, particulars of claims, defences, counterclaims, replies to defences and counterclaims, Pt 20 (third party) claims and any further information provided under Pt 18 of the CPR (replacing the term 'further and better particulars'). Part 16 of the rules also sets out what both particulars of claim and defences should contain.

Statements of truth

A statement of truth is a statement that a party believes that the facts or allegations set out in a document which they put forward are true. It is required in statements of case, witness statements, and expert reports. Any document which contains a statement of truth may be used in evidence. This will avoid the previous need to swear affidavits in support of various statements made as part of the claim.

Part 8 Claims (CPR Pt 8)

Part 8 of the new rules introduces the alternative procedure for claims. This procedure is commenced by the issue of a Pt 8 claim form. It is intended to provide a speedy resolution of claims which are not likely to involve a substantial dispute of fact, for example, applications for approval of infant settlements, or for orders enforcing a statutory right such as a right to have access to medical records (under the Access to Health Records Act 1990).

Default judgment (CPR Pt 12)

If a defendant (to a Pt 7 claim) files an acknowledgment stating an intention to defend the claim, this extends the period for filing a defence from 14 to 28 days from the date of service of the particulars. Failure to file an acknowledgment or, later, failure to file a defence, can result in default judgment, that is, the court will find for the claimant so the defendant will lose the case.

Defence and automatic transfer (CPR Pt 15)

Claims for specified amounts will be transferred automatically to the defendant's 'home court' where the defendant is an individual who has filed a defence. The defendant's home court will be 'the court or district registry, including the RCJ, for the district in which the defendant's address for service as shown on the defence is situated'. This means that, where the defendant is represented by a solicitor, this will be the defendant's solicitor's business address.

Where there is more than one defendant, it is the first defendant to file a defence who dictates whether or not automatic transfer will take place. For example, if there are two defendants to a claim, one an individual and one a limited company, there would be no automatic transfer if the limited company was the first defendant to file a defence.

Allocation questionnaire

The purpose of this document is to enable to court to judge in which track the case should be heard. When a defence is filed, the issuing court will send out a copy of the defence to all other parties to the claim together with an allocation questionnaire, a notice setting out the date for returning it and the name and address of the court (or district registry or the Royal Courts of Justice – that is, High Court – as appropriate), to which the completed allocation questionnaire must be returned. A notice of transfer will also be sent if the case is being automatically transferred.

When the allocation questionnaire is returned, or at the end of the period for returning it, and whether or not only some, or none, of the questionnaires (if there is more than one defendant) have been filed, the court file will be passed to a procedural judge for directions and allocation to track. If there is sufficient information, the judge will allocate the case to a track and a notice of allocation and directions will be sent out to each party. Where only one party has filed a questionnaire or there is insufficient information, the judge may make an order requesting further information, or order an allocation hearing. Where none of the parties has filed a questionnaire, the judge may also decide to impose a sanction, for example, ordering that a statement, or statements, of case be struck out unless a completed questionnaire is filed within three days of service of the order.

Case management conferences

Case management conferences may be regarded as an opportunity to 'take stock'. There is no limit to the number of case management conferences which may be held during the life of a case, although the cost of attendance at such hearings against the benefits obtained will always be a consideration in making the decision.

Pre-trial reviews

Pre-trial reviews will normally take place after the filing of listing questionnaires, and before the start of the trial. Their main purpose is to decide a timetable for the trial itself (including the evidence to be allowed and whether this should be given orally), instructions about the content of any trial bundles (bundles of documents including evidence such as written statements, for the judge to read) and confirming a realistic time estimate for the trial itself.

Rules require that, where a party is represented, a representative 'familiar with the case and with sufficient authority to deal with any issues likely to arise must attend every case management conference or pre-trial review'.

Settlements

Under the new CPR, there is a greater incentive for parties to settle their differences.

The court will take into account any pre-action offers to settle when making an order for costs. Thus, a side which has refused a reasonable offer to settle will be treated less generously in the issue of how far the court will order their costs to be paid by the other side. For this to happen, the offer, though, must be one which is made open to the other side for at least 21 days after receipt (to stop any undue pressure being put on someone with the phrase: 'take it or leave it; it is only open for one day, then I shall withdraw the offer'). Also, if the offer is made by the defendant, it must be an offer to pay compensation and to pay the claimant's costs.

Witness statements

Under the new rules, witness statements must contain the evidence that the witness will give at trial but they should be briefer than those drafted under the previous rules; they should be drafted in lay language and should not discuss legal propositions. Witnesses will be allowed to amplify on the statement or deal with matters that have arisen since the report was served, although this is not an automatic right and a 'good reason' for the admission of new evidence will have to be established.

Court fees

A new fee structure will be introduced to take account of the different procedures, a movement towards a 'pay as you go' fees regime and the need for full cost recovery. Pay as you go means that parties will be expected to contribute more in fees, the more court and judicial time they use, for example, if they do not settle and carry on to trial.

Experts (CPR Pt 35)

New rules place a clear duty on the court to ensure that 'expert evidence is restricted to that which is reasonably required to resolve the proceedings'. That is to say, expert evidence will only be allowed either by way of written report or orally, where the court gives permission. Equally important is the rules' statement about experts' duties. They state that it is the clear duty of experts to help the court on matters within their expertise, bearing in mind that this duty overrides any obligation to the person from whom they have received instructions or by whom they are paid.

CHAPTER 8

ARBITRATION, TRIBUNAL ADJUDICATION AND ALTERNATIVE DISPUTE RESOLUTION

8.1   Introduction

Law is one method of resolving disputes when, as is inevitable, they emerge. All societies have mechanisms for dealing with such problems but the forms of dispute resolution tend to differ from society to society. In small scale societies, based on mutual co-operation and interdependency, the means of solving disputes tend to be informal and focus on the need for mutual concessions and compromise to maintain social stability. In some such societies, the whole of the social group may become involved in settling a problem; whereas in others particular individuals may be recognised as intermediaries, whose function it is to act as a go-between to bring the parties to a mutually recognised solution. The common factor remains the emphasis on solidarity and the need to maintain social cohesion. With social, as well as the geographical, distance, disputes become more difficult to deal with.

It should not be thought that this reference to anthropological material is out of place in a book of this nature. It is sometimes suggested that law itself is a function of the increase in social complexity and the corresponding decrease in social solidarity; the oppositional, adversarial nature of law being seen as a reflection of the atomistic structure of contemporary society. Law as a *formal* dispute resolution mechanism is seen to emerge because *informal* mechanisms no longer exist or no longer have the power to deal with the problems that arise in a highly individualistic and competitive society. That is not to suggest that the types of mechanisms mentioned previously do not have their place in our own society: the bulk of family disputes, for example, are resolved through internal informal mechanisms without recourse to legal formality. It is generally recognised, however, that the very form of law makes it inappropriate to deal adequately with certain areas, family matters being the most obvious example. Equally, it is recognised that the formal and rather intimidatory atmosphere of the ordinary courts is not necessarily the most appropriate one in which to decide such matters, even where the dispute cannot be resolved internally. In recognition of this fact, various alternatives have been developed specifically to avoid the perceived shortcomings of the formal structure of law and court procedure.

The increased importance of alternative dispute resolution mechanisms has been signalled in both legislation and court procedures. For example, the Commercial Court issued a practice statement in 1993, stating that it wished to encourage ADR, and followed this, in 1996, with a further direction allowing judges to consider whether a case is suitable for ADR at its outset, and to invite the parties to attempt a neutral non-court settlement of their dispute. In cases in the Court of Appeal, the Master of the Rolls now writes to the parties, urging them to consider ADR, and asking them for their reasons for declining to use it. Also, as part of the civil justice reforms, r 26.4 of the Civil Procedure Rules 1998 enables judges, either on their own account, or at the agreement of both parties, to stop court proceedings where they consider the dispute to be better suited to solution by some alternative procedure, such as arbitration or mediation.

In particular, the Family Law Act 1996, which aimed to reform the operation of divorce law, emphasises the importance of mediation in this area and provides for the possibility of legal aid to finance it in appropriate instances. This will be considered further in para 8.5.

More generally, Lord Mackay, the former Lord Chancellor, considered various ADR mechanisms in the fourth of his Hamlyn lectures, expressing the view that:

> ... the need seems to be not for further law based processes outside the courts ... but ... for processes which broaden the issues and available outcomes beyond those based in law.

The current Lord Chancellor has continued to look favourably on ADR, as is evident in his inaugural lecture to the Faculty of Mediation and ADR, in which he said:

> ADR has many supporters. But they, too, have a responsibility to proceed with care. ADR is not a panacea, nor is it cost free. But, I do believe that it can play a vital part in the opening of access to justice

> (http//www.open gov.uk./lcd/speeches/1999/27-1-99.htm).

8.2   Arbitration

The first and oldest of these alternative procedures is arbitration. This is the procedure whereby parties in dispute refer the issue to a third party for resolution, rather than take the case to the ordinary law courts. Studies have shown a reluctance on the part of commercial undertakings to have recourse to the law to resolve their disputes. At first sight, this appears paradoxical. The development of contract law can, to a great extent, be explained as the law's response to the need for regulation in relation to business activity, yet business declines to make use of its procedures. To some degree, questions of speed and cost explain this peculiar phenomenon, but it can be explained more fully by reference to the introduction to this chapter. It was stated there that informal procedures tend to be most effective where there is a high degree of mutuality and interdependency, and that is precisely the case in most business relationships. Businesses seek to establish and maintain long term relationships with other concerns. The problem with the law is that the court case tends to terminally rupture such relationships. It is not suggested that, in the final analysis, where the stakes are sufficiently high, that recourse will not be had to law; but such action does not represent the first or indeed the preferred option. In contemporary business practice, it is common, if not standard, practice for commercial contracts to contain express clauses referring any future disputes to arbitration. This practice is well established and its legal effectiveness has long been recognised by the law.

8.2.1 Procedure

The Arbitration Act (AA) 1996 repeals Pt 1 of the Arbitration Act 1950 and the whole of the Arbitration Acts of 1975 and 1979. As the Act is a relatively new piece of legislation, it is necessary to consider it in some detail.

Section 1 of the Act 1996 states that it is founded on the following principles:

(a) the object of arbitration is to obtain the fair resolution of disputes by an impartial tribunal without necessary delay or expense;

(b) the parties should be free to agree how their disputes are resolved, subject only to such safeguards as are necessary in the public interest;

(c) in matters governed by this part of the court should not intervene except as provided by this part.

This provision of general principles, which should inform the reading of the later detailed provisions of the Act, is unusual for United Kingdom legislation, but may be seen as reflecting the purposes behind the new Act, one major one of which was the wish to ensure that London did not lose its place as a leading centre for international arbitration. As a consequence of the demand driven nature of the new legislation, it would seem that court interference in the arbitration process has had to be reduced to a minimum and replaced by party autonomy. Under the new Act, the role of the arbitrator has been increased and that of the court has been reduced to the residual level of intervention where the arbitration process either requires legal assistance or else is seen to be failing to provide a just settlement.

The Act follows the Model Arbitration Law adopted in 1985 by the United Nations Commission on International Trade Law (UNICTRAL).

Whilst it is possible for there to be an oral arbitration agreement at common law, s 5 provides that Pt 1 of the new Act only applies to agreements in writing. What this means in practice, however, has been extended by s 5(3) which provides that, where the parties agree to an arbitration procedure which is in writing, that procedure will be operative, even although the agreement between the parties is not itself in writing. An example of such a situation would be where a salvage operation was negotiated between two vessels on the basis of Lloyd's standard salvage terms. It would be unlikely that the actual agreement would be reduced to written form, but, nonetheless, the arbitration element in those terms would be effective.

In analysing the Arbitration Act, it is useful to consider it in three distinct parts: autonomy of the parties; powers of the court; and appellate rights.

- *Autonomy*

  It is significant that most of the provisions set out in the AA 1996 are not compulsory. As is clearly stated in s 1, it is up to the parties to an arbitration agreement to agree what procedures to adopt. The main purpose of the Act is to empower the parties to the dispute and to allow them to decide how it is to be decided. In pursuit of this aim, the mandatory parts of the Act only take effect where the parties involved do not agree otherwise. It is actually possible for the parties to agree that the dispute should not be decided in line with the strict legal rules but rather in line with commercial fairness, which might be a completely different thing altogether.

  Powers of the arbitrator

  Section 30 provides that, unless the parties agree otherwise, the arbitrator can rule on questions relating to jurisdiction, that is, in relation to:

  (a) whether there actually is a valid arbitration agreement;

  (b) whether the arbitration tribunal is properly constituted;

  (c) what matters have been submitted to arbitration in accordance with the agreement.

  Section 32 allows any of the parties to raise preliminary objections to the substantive jurisdiction of the arbitration tribunal in court, but provides that they may only do so on limited grounds which require either: the agreement of the parties concerned; the permission of the arbitration tribunal; or the agreement of the court. Leave to appeal will only be granted where the court is satisfied that the question involves a point of law of general importance.

  Section 28 expressly provides that the parties the proceedings are jointly and severally liable to pay the arbitrators such reasonable fees and expenses as appropriate. Previously, this was only an implied term.

  Section 29 provides that arbitrators are not liable for anything done or omitted in the discharge of their functions unless the act or omission was done in bad faith.

  Section 33 provides that the tribunal has a general duty:

  (a) to act fairly and impartially between the parties, giving each a reasonable opportunity to state their case; and

  (b) to adopt procedures suitable for the circumstance of the case, avoiding unnecessary delay or expense.

Section 35 provides that, subject to the parties agreeing to the contrary, the tribunal shall have the following powers:

(a) to order parties to provide security for costs (previously a power reserved to the courts);

(b) to give directions in relation to property subject to the arbitration;

(c) to direct that a party or witness be examined on oath, and to administer the oath.

The parties may also empower the arbitrator to make provisional orders (s 39).

- *Powers of the court*

Where one party seeks to start a court action, contrary to a valid arbitration agreement to the contrary, then the other party may request the court to stay the litigation in favour of the arbitration agreement under ss 9–11 of the AA 1996. Where, however, both parties agree to ignore the arbitration agreement and seek recourse to litigation then, following the party consensual nature of the Act, the agreement may be ignored.

The courts may order a party to comply with an order of the tribunal and may also order parties and witnesses to attend and to give oral evidence before tribunals (s 43).

The court has power to revoke the appointment of an arbitrator on application of any of the parties, where there has been a failure in the appointment procedure under s 18, but it also has powers to revoke authority under s 24. This power comes into play on the application of one of the parties in circumstances where the arbitrator:

(a) has not acted impartially;

(b) does not possess the required qualifications;

(c) does not have either the physical or mental capacity to deal with the proceedings;

(d) has refused or failed (i) to properly conduct the proceedings, or (ii) has been dilatory in dealing with the proceedings or, in making an award, to the extent that it will cause substantial injustice to the party applying for their removal.

Under s 45, the court may on application by one of the parties, decide any preliminary question of law arising in the course of the proceedings.

Arbitrators

The arbitration tribunal may consist of a single arbitrator, or a panel as the parties decide (s 15). If one party fails to appoint an arbitrator, then the other party's nominee may act as sole arbitrator (s 17). Under s 20(4), where there is a panel and it fails to reach a majority decision, the decision of the chair shall prevail.

The tribunal is required to fairly and impartially adopt procedures which are suitable to the circumstances of each case. It is also for the tribunal to decide all procedural and evidential matters. Parties may be represented by a lawyer or any other person, and the tribunal may appoint experts or legal advisors to report to it.

Arbitrators will be immune from action being taken against them except in situations where they have been acted in bad faith.

- *Appeal*

  Once the decision has been made, there are limited grounds for appeal. The first ground arises under s 67 of the AA 1996 in relation to the substantive jurisdiction of the Arbitral panel, although the right to appeal on this ground may be lost if the party attempting to make use of it, took part in the arbitration proceedings without objecting to the alleged lack of jurisdiction. The second ground for appeal to the courts is on procedural grounds, under s 68, on the basis that some serious irregularity affected the operation of the tribunal. By serious irregularity is meant:

  (a) failure to comply with the general duty set out in s 33;

  (b) failure to conduct the tribunal as agreed by the parties;

  (c) uncertainty or ambiguity as to the effect of the award;

  (d) failure to comply with the requirement as to the form of the award.

Parties may also appeal on a point of law arising from the award under s 69. However, the parties can agree beforehand to preclude such a possibility and, where they agree to the arbitral panel making a decision without providing a reasoned justification for it, they will also lose the right to appeal.

8.2.2   Relationship to ordinary courts

In general terms, the courts have no objection to individuals settling their disputes on a voluntary basis, but, at the same time, they are careful to maintain their supervisory role in such procedures. Arbitration agreements are no different from other terms of a contract, and, in line with the normal rules of contract law, courts will strike out any attempt to oust their ultimate jurisdiction, as being contrary to public policy. Thus, as has been stated previously, arbitration proceedings are open to challenge through judicial review, on the grounds that they were not conducted in a judicial manner.

The Arbitration Act (AA) 1950 allowed for either party to the proceedings to have questions of law authoritatively determined by the High Court through the procedure of *'case stated'*. The High Court could also set aside the decision of the arbitrator on grounds of fact, law or procedure. Whereas the arbitration process was supposed to provide a quick and relatively cheap method of deciding disputes, the availability of the appeals procedures meant that parties could delay the final decision and in so doing increase the costs. In such circumstances, arbitration became the precursor to a court case rather than replacing it. The AA 1979 abolished the *'case stated'* procedure and curtailed the right to appeal and, as has been seen, the AA 1996 has reduced the grounds for appeal to the court system even further.

8.2.3   Advantages

There are numerous advantages to be gained from using arbitration rather than the court system:

- *Privacy*. Arbitration tends to be a private procedure. This has the twofold advantage that outsiders do not get access to any potentially sensitive information and the parties to the arbitration do not run the risk of any damaging publicity arising out of reports of the proceedings.

- *Informality*. The proceedings are less formal than a court case and they can be scheduled more flexibly than court proceedings.

- *Speed*. Arbitration is generally much quicker than taking a case through the courts. Where, however, one of the parties makes use of the available grounds to challenge an arbitration award the prior costs of the arbitration will have been largely wasted.

- *Cost*. Arbitration is generally a much cheaper procedure than taking a case to the normal courts. Nonetheless, the costs of arbitration and the use of specialist arbitrators should not be underestimated.

- *Expertise*. The use of a specialist arbitrator ensures that the person deciding the case has expert knowledge of the actual practice within the area under consideration and can form their conclusion in line with accepted practice.

It can be argued that arbitration represents a privatisation of the judicial process. It may be assumed, therefore, that of all its virtues, perhaps the greatest, at least as far as the government is concerned, is the potential reduction in costs for the State in providing the legal framework within which disputes are resolved.

8.2.4   Small claims procedure in the county court

Since 1973, an arbitration service has been available within the county court specifically for the settlement of relatively small claims. This small claims procedure, known as arbitration, is operated by county court district judges.

Under the Civil Justice Reforms, reference to arbitration will normally be automatic in cases involving sums of money up to £5,000, and arbitration proceedings may be used in situations involving more than £5,000 where the parties concerned agree. The limit with regard to personal injury cases remains at £1,000. The district judge can refuse to deal with the case in arbitration and may refer it for trial in the county court. The grounds for this action depend on:

- the case involving a difficult point of law or fact, or involving a charge of fraud;

- the agreement of the parties;

- whether the district judge considers that it would be unreasonable to decide the case in arbitration on the basis of the subject matter, or the circumstances of the parties, or the interests of any person likely to be affected by any award made. For example, in *Pepper v Healey* (1982), it was decided that it was legitimate for a registrar to use the discretion to decide that a case should be heard before the court rather than arbitration because the plaintiff required to be legally represented, as the defendant was, and could not have recovered costs in arbitration, although such cost could have been recovered in court proceedings.

In *Afzal v Ford Motor Co Ltd* (1993), the Court of Appeal held that claims from employees against their employer for personal injury damages of less than £1,000 could be suitable for decision under the county court arbitration scheme. The district judge had accepted that the case should be heard in the county court, on the basis of representations that: first, the issues of liability involved in such compensation cases were too complex for resolution in arbitration; and, secondly, the denial of the right to recover the costs of legal advice and representation at arbitration would deter trade unions from assisting claimants who would consequently be disadvantaged. In rejecting both of these grounds for not making use of the arbitration system, the Court of Appeal also considered the possibility of claimants inflating their claims above the £1,000 figure in order to avoid its operation. It stated that such action would be a misuse of process and that, in determining the financial limit, the test should be the amount that the plaintiff could reasonably expect to be awarded: if that did not exceed £1,000, then the case should be decided by arbitration procedure.

8.2.5 Procedure

Arbitration proceedings begin with an individual filing a *'statements of case'* at the county court. This document details the grounds of their dispute and requests the other party to be summonsed to appear. There may be *preliminary hearings* at which the issues involved are clarified, but it is possible for the dispute to be settled at such hearings. If no compromise can be reached at this stage, a date is set for the hearing of the arbitration.

Arbitration hearings are usually heard by the district judge, although the parties to the dispute may request that it be referred to the circuit judge or even an outside arbitrator. The arbitrator hearing the case may at any time before or after the hearing, with the agreement of the parties, consult an expert on the matter under consideration and, again with the approval of the parties, may invite an expert to sit on the arbitration in the role of *assessor*.

If one of the parties fails to appear at the hearing, the dispute can be decided in their absence. Alternatively, the parties may agree to the case being decided by the arbitrator, solely on the basis of documents and written statements.

The arbitration procedure is intended to be a less formal forum than that provided by the ordinary courts and to that end the county court rules provide that the strict rules of evidence shall not be applied. Parties are encouraged to represent themselves rather than make use of the services of professional lawyers although they may be legally represented if they wish.

The county court rules give arbitrators wide discretion to adopt any procedure they consider helpful to ensure that the parties have an equal opportunity to put their case. This discretion is not limitless, however, and it does not remove the normal principles of legal procedure, such as the right of direct cross-examination of one of the parties by the legal representative of the other party (see *Chilton v Saga Holidays plc* (1986) where the Court of Appeal held that a registrar was wrong to have refused to allow solicitors for the defendant in the case to cross-examine the plaintiff on the grounds that that person was not also legally represented).

On the basis of the information provided, the arbitrator decides the case and, if the plaintiff is successful, makes an award for appropriate compensation. A no-costs rule operates to ensure that the costs of legal representation cannot be recovered, although the losing party may be instructed to pay court fees and the expenses of witnesses. Judgments are legally enforceable.

8.2.6 Evaluation

Problems have become evident in the operation of the arbitration procedure, particularly in cases where one party has been represented whilst the other has not. In spite of the clear intention to facilitate the resolution of disputes cheaply, and without the need for legal practitioners, some individuals, particularly large business enterprises, insisted on their right of legal representation. As legal aid is not available in respect of such actions, most individuals cannot afford to be legally represented and therefore find themselves at a distinct disadvantage when opposed by professional lawyers.

One solution to this difficulty would have been to make legal aid available in the case of arbitration. Such a proposal is very unlikely ever to come to fruition, first on economic grounds, but also on the grounds that the use of professional lawyers in such cases would contradict the spirit and the whole purpose of the procedure.

Alternatively, it might have been provided that no party could be legally represented in arbitration procedures; but to introduce such a measure would have been a denial of an important civil right.

The actual method chosen to deal with the problem was to lift the restrictions on the rights of audience in small debt proceedings. Parties to the proceedings were entitled to be accompanied by a *McKenzie friend* to give them advice but such people had no right of audience and thus had no right actually to represent their friend in any arbitration (see *McKenzie v McKenzie* (1970)). In October 1992, under the Courts and Legal Services Act 1990, the Lord Chancellor extended the right of audience to lay representatives in small claims courts. This decision has the effect of allowing individuals access to non-professional, but expert, advice and advocacy. Members of such organisations as Citizens Advice Bureaux and Legal Advice Centres will now be permitted to represent their clients, although they will still not be permitted to issue proceedings. In cases involving claims of more than £1,000, they may even charge a fee.

The increase in the maximum amount to be claimed to £5,000 introduces two particular difficulties with regard to representation. The first, and by far the more serious, is the fact that the raising of the ceiling to what is a not inconsiderable sum of money, means that individuals will lose legal aid to fund their claims in such cases, and, therefore, may not have access to the best possible legal advice with respect to their case. The second, and apparently contradictory, point is that the number of lawyers appearing in small claims proceedings may actually increase as a result of the rise in the limit. Whereas it might not have been worth paying for legal representation in a £3,000 claim, it might make more economic sense to pay for professional help if the sum being claimed is that much higher. Which alternative actually happens, remains to be seen.

Perhaps the major difficulty in regard to small claims procedures is the fact that the mere winning of a case and the awarding of compensation does not actually mean that the successful party will receive any recompense if the other party chooses simply to ignore the award. A recent study concluded that 36% of those successful in the small claims procedure actually received nothing by way of recompense awarded (*Handling Small Claims in the County Courts* (1996)). More stringent and efficient mechanisms for enforcing judgments, even in relation to the comparatively small awards as are made under the arbitration procedure, is a necessity.

In evaluating the small claims arbitration procedure, regard has to be had to the Civil Justice Review of 1996 which specifically considered the arbitration procedure and concluded that it generally works in a satisfactory way to produce a relatively quick, cheap, and informal mechanism for resolving many smaller cases without the need to overburden the county courts.

The small claims procedure has not gone uncriticised. A research report from the National Consumer Council (NCC) in 1993 concluded that the civil courts were 'far from user-friendly'. It asked 819 people using 35 county courts in England and Wales about their experience. Of 12% in the survey who wanted to complain about their experience, 76% did not know there was a complaints procedure. It found that many standards in the charter were designed to assist business users rather than ordinary citizens. The 1994 report of the NCC on the courts is even more damning. It concludes that performance indicators issued by the Lord Chancellor's Department (LCD) paint a 'rosy picture' of the courts but 'do not seem to bear any relation to the experiences of court users'.

FH Pedley ([1994] NLJ 1217, 9 September), who was a magistrate for 12 years, contended that district judges are not sufficiently specialist in the areas of law they have to deal with. This would not matter so much in the ordinary courts but here, where the parties are encouraged to be unrepresented (there is no legal aid or costs for lawyers), it is critical because the judge is supposed to be active in applying his knowledge of the law.

8.2.7 Arbitration under Codes of Conduct

When it was first established in 1973, the small claims procedure was seen as a mechanism through which consumers could enforce their rights against recalcitrant traders. In reality, the arbitration procedure has proved to be just as useful for, and to have been used just as much by, traders and businesses, as consumers. There remains one area of arbitration, however, that is specifically focused on the consumer: arbitration schemes run under the auspices of particular trade associations. As part of the regulation of trade practices and in the pursuit of effective measures of consumer protection, the Office of Fair Trading has encouraged the establishment of voluntary codes of practice within particular areas. It is usual to find that such codes of practice provide arbitration schemes to resolve particularly intractable problems between individual consumers and particular members of the association. Such schemes are never compulsory and do not seek to replace the consumer's legal rights but they do provide a relatively inexpensive mechanism for dealing with problems without the need even to bother the county court. Such schemes are numerous; the most famous one is probably the travel industry scheme operated under the auspices of the Association of British Travel Agents, but other associations run similar schemes in such areas as car sales, shoe retailing, dry-cleaning, and many other areas. Again, the point of such schemes is to provide a quick, cheap means of dealing with problems without running the risk of completely alienating the consumer from the trade in question.

Although many of the trade arbitration schemes offered consumers distinct advantages, some did not and, in order to remedy any abuses, the Consumer Arbitration Act 1988 was introduced. This statute provides that, in the case of consumer contracts, no prior agreement between the parties that subsequent disputes have to be referred to arbitration can be enforced. However, consumers will be bound by arbitration procedures where they have already entered into them as a consequence of a prior agreement, or have agreed to them subsequently.

8.3   Administrative tribunals

Although attention tends to be focused on the operation of the courts as the forum within which legal decisions are taken, it is no longer the case that the bulk of legal and quasi-legal questions are determined within that court structure. There are, as an alternative to the court system, a large number of tribunals which have been set up under various Acts of Parliament to rule on the operation of the particular schemes established under those Acts. There are at least 60 different types of administrative tribunal, and within each type there may well be hundreds of individual tribunals operating locally all over the country to hear particular cases. Over a quarter of a million cases are dealt with by tribunals each year, and, as the Royal Commission on Legal Services (Cmnd 7648) pointed out in 1979, the number of cases then being heard by tribunals was six times greater than the number of contested civil cases dealt with by the High Court and county court combined. It is evident, therefore, that tribunals are of major significance as alternatives to traditional courts in dealing with disputes.

The generally accepted explanation for the establishment and growth of tribunals in Britain since 1945 was the need to provide a specialist forum to deal with cases involving conflicts between an increasingly interventionist welfare state, its functionaries, and the rights of private citizens. It is certainly true that, since 1945, the Welfare State has intervened more and more in every aspect of people's lives. The intention may have been to extend various social benefits to a wider constituency, but in so doing the machinery of the Welfare State, and in reality those who operate that machinery, have been granted powers to control access to its benefits, and as a consequence have been given the power to interfere in and control the lives of individual subjects of the State. By its nature, welfare provision tends to be discretionary and dependent upon the particular circumstance of a given case. As a consequence, State functionaries were extended discretionary power over the supply/withdrawal of welfare benefits. As the interventionist State replaced the completely free market as the source of welfare for many people, so access to the provisions made by the State became a matter of fundamental importance, and a focus for potential contention, especially given the discretionary nature of its provision. At the same time as Welfare State provisions were being extended, the view was articulated that such provisions and projects should not be under the purview and control of the ordinary courts. It was felt that the judiciary reflected a culture which tended to favour a more market-centred, individualistic approach to the provision of rights and welfare and that their, essentially formalistic, approach to the resolution of disputes would not fit with the operation of the new projects.

8.3.1   Tribunals and courts

There is some debate as to whether tribunals are merely part of the machinery of administration of particular projects or whether their function is the distinct one of adjudication. The Franks Committee (Cmnd 218, 1957) favoured the latter view, but others have disagreed and have emphasised the administrative role of such bodies. Parliament initiated various projects and schemes, and included within those projects specialist tribunals to deal with the problems that they inevitably generated. On that basis, it is suggested that tribunals are merely adjuncts to the parent project and that this therefore defines their role as more administrative than adjudicatory.

If the foregoing has suggested the theoretical possibility of distinguishing courts and tribunals in relation to their administrative or adjudicatory role, in practice it is difficult to implement such a distinction for the reason that the members of tribunals may be, and usually are, acting in a judicial capacity (see *Pickering v Liverpool Daily Post and Echo Newspapers* (1991) in which it was held that a Mental Health Review tribunal was a court whose proceedings were subject to the law of contempt. Although a newspaper was not entitled to publish the fact that a named person had made an application to the tribunal together with the date of the hearing and its decision, it was not allowed to publish the reasons for the decision or any conditions applied).

If the precise distinction between tribunals and courts is a matter of uncertainty, what is certain is that tribunals are inferior to the normal courts. One of the main purposes of the tribunal system is to prevent the ordinary courts of law from being overburdened by cases, but tribunals are still subject to judicial review on the basis of breach of natural justice or where it acts in an *ultra vires* manner or indeed where it goes wrong in relation to the application of the law when deciding cases.

In addition to the control of the courts, tribunals are also subject to the supervision of the Council on Tribunals originally established under the Tribunals and Inquiries Act 1958, as subsequently amended by the Tribunals and Inquiries Acts 1971 and 1992 which is the current legislation. Members of the Council are appointed by the Lord Chancellor and its role is to keep the general operation of the system under review.

The Annual Report of the Council of Tribunals for 1995–96 (HC 114) contained some surprisingly sharp comments aimed at the way in which the government has attempted to introduce economic imperatives into the operation of the tribunal system, as it has in all other aspects of the judicial system. As the report stated:

> We draw attention to ... a number of instances where the continued pressure on public resources is seriously eroding the quality of service which tribunals are able to deliver to the public and, in some cases, impinging on the proper exercise of the tribunal's judicial task (para 1.2),

and, later, the Council stated that their:

> ... major concern ... is the movement in the direction of fuller cost recovery. We believe that this trend is inimical to the administration of justice in tribunals (para 1.21).

The concern expressed by the Council was in relation to the introduction of fees in cases before leasehold valuation tribunals which were designed to recover the full cost of the operation. The Council, through the offices of its chair Lord Archer of Sandwell in the House of Lords, secured a reduction in the maximum fees payable to £500 for the present, but subject to alteration in the future. Equally it was concerned by the increase in fees payable for cases dealt with by the lands tribunal. The report also expressed concern at the reluctance of the government to increase the availability of legal aid in relation to tribunal hearings beyond the areas already covered which are; the land tribunal, employment appeals tribunals; the Commons Commissioners, and mental health review tribunals (para 2.85).

8.3.2   Composition of tribunals

Tribunals are usually made up of three members, only one of whom, the chair, is expected to be legally qualified. The other two members are lay representatives. The lack of legal training is not considered a drawback, given the technical, administrative, as opposed to specifically legal, nature of the provisions they have to consider. Indeed, the fact of there being two lay representatives on tribunals provides them with one of their perceived advantages over courts. The non-legal members may provide specialist knowledge and thus they may enable the tribunal to base its decision on actual practice as opposed to abstract legal theory or mere legal formalism. An example of this can be seen with regard to the tribunals having responsibility or determining issues relating to employment, which usually have a trade union representative and an employers' representative sitting on the panel and are therefore able to consider the immediate problem from both sides of the employment relationship.

The procedure for nominating tribunal members is set out in the parent statute but generally it is the Minister of State with responsibility for the operation of the statute in question who ultimately decides the membership of the tribunal. As tribunals are established to deal largely with conflicts between the general public and government departments, this raises, at least the possibility of, suspicion that the members of tribunals are not truly neutral. In response to such doubts, the 1957 Franks Committee recommended that the appointment of the chairmen of tribunals should become the prerogative of the Lord Chancellor and that the appointment of the other members should become the responsibility of a Council on Tribunals. This recommendation was not implemented and ministers, by and large, still retain the power to appoint tribunal members. As a compromise, however, the minister selects the chairperson from a panel appointed by the Lord Chancellor.

8.3.3 Statutory tribunals

There are a number of tribunals which have considerable power in their areas of operation and it is necessary to have some detailed knowledge of a selection of the most important of these. Examples of such tribunals are:

- *Employment tribunals*

  These are governed by the Employment Tribunals Act 1996 which sets out their composition, major areas of competence and procedure. In practice, such tribunals are normally made up of a legally qualified chairperson, a representative chosen from a panel representing employers and another representative chosen from a panel representing the interests of employees.

  Employment tribunals have jurisdiction in relation to a number of statutory provisions relating to employment issues. The majority of issues arise in relation to such matters as disputes over the meaning and operation of particular terms of employment, disputes relating to redundancy payments, disputes involving issues of unfair dismissal, and disputes as to the provision of maternity pay.

  They also have authority in other areas under different legislation. Thus they deal with complaints about racial discrimination in the employment field under the Race Relations Act 1976; complaints about sexual discrimination in employment under the Sex Discrimination Act 1975; complaints about equal pay under the Equal Pay Act 1970 as amended by the Sex Discrimination Act; complaints under the Disability Discrimination Act 1995; complaints about unlawful deductions from wages under the Wages Act 1986; and appeals against the imposition of improvement notices under the Health and Safety at Work Act 1974. There are, in addition, various ancillary matters relating to trade union membership and activities that industrial tribunals have to deal with.

• *Social security appeal tribunal*

Various Social Security Acts have provided for safety-net provisions for the disadvantaged in society to ensure that they at least enjoy a basic standard of living. In the pursuit of this general goal, various State functionaries have been delegated the task of implementing the very complex provisions contained in the legislation and have been granted considerable discretionary power in the implementation of those provisions. The function of the social security tribunals is to ensure that such discretion is not abused and that the aims of the legislation are being met generally. The tribunals, of which there are some 200 in England and Wales, are charged with the duty of hearing and deciding upon the correctness of decisions made by adjudication officers, who are the people who actually determine the level of benefit individuals are entitled to receive.

• *Mental health review tribunals*

These operate under the Mental Health Act 1983. The tribunals have wide powers to decide whether individuals should be detained for the purposes of compulsory treatment. They can also dispose of the property of such individuals. Given the particular area within which the mental health review tribunal operates, it is essential that there are medical experts present to decide on medical issues. This latter requirement also applies in respect of social security issues relating to the state of the individual claimant's health.

• *The lands tribunal*

Established under the Lands Tribunal Act 1949, its essential function is to determine the legality of, and the levels of compensation in relation to, compulsory purchase orders over land. It also considers matters relating to planning applications.

• *Rent Assessment Committee*

This committee deals with matters specifically relating to the rent charged for property. It resolves disputes between landlords and tenants of private accommodation, hears appeals from decisions of rent officers and has the power to fix rent in relation to furnished and unfurnished residential tenancies.

8.3.4 Domestic tribunals

The foregoing has focused on public administrative tribunals set up under particular legislative provisions to deal with matters of public relevance. The term tribunal, however, is also used in relation to the internal, disciplinary procedures of particular institutions. Whether these institutions are created under legislation or not is immaterial; the point is that domestic tribunals relate mainly to matters of private rather than public concern although at times the two can overlap. Examples of domestic tribunals are the disciplinary committees of professional institutions such as the Bar, The Law Society, or the British Medical Association; trade unions; and universities. The power that each of these tribunals has is very great and it is controlled by the ordinary courts through ensuring that the rules of natural justice are complied with and that the tribunal does not act *ultra vires*, that is, beyond its powers. Matters relating to trade union membership and discipline are additionally regulated by the Employment Rights Act 1996.

8.3.5 Advantages of tribunals

Advantages of tribunals over courts relate to such matters as:

* *Speed*

  The ordinary court system is notoriously dilatory in hearing and deciding cases. Tribunals are much quicker to hear cases. A related advantage of the tribunal system is the certainty that it will be heard on a specific date and not subject to the vagaries of the court system. This being said, there have been reports that the tribunal system is coming under increased pressure and is falling behind in relation to its caseload. Thus, in 1993, in relation to the industrial tribunal, Fraser Youlson, the Vice Chair of the Employment Lawyers Association, complained that cases which had previously taken three to five months to be heard could now take over 18 months to be heard.

* *Cost*

  Tribunals are a much cheaper way of deciding cases than using the ordinary court system. One factor that leads to a reduction in cost is the fact that no specialised court building is required to hear the cases. Also the fact that those deciding the cases are less expensive to employ than judges, together with the fact that complainants do not have to rely on legal representation, makes the tribunal procedure considerably less expensive than using the traditional court system. These reductions are further enhanced by the additional facts that there are no court fees involved in relation to tribunal proceedings and that costs are not normally awarded against the loser.

* *Informality*

  Tribunals are supposed to be informal in order to make them less intimidating than full blown court cases. The strict rules relating to evidence, pleading and procedure, which apply in courts, are not binding in tribunal proceedings. The lack of formality is strengthened by the fact that proceedings tend not to be inquisitorial or accusatorial but are intended to try to encourage and help participants to express their views of the situation before the tribunal. Informality should not, however, be mistaken for a lack of order and the Franks Committee Report itself emphasised the need for clear rules of procedure. The provision of this informal situation and procedure tends to suggest that complainants do not need to be represented by a lawyer in order to present their grievance. They may represent themselves or be represented by a more knowledgeable associate such as a trade union representative or some other friend. This contentious point will be considered further below.

- *Flexibility*

Tribunals are not bound by the strict rules of precedent although some pay more regard to previous decisions than others. It should be remembered that, as tribunals are inferior and subject to the courts, they are governed by the precedents made in the courts.

- *Expertise*

Reference has already been made to the advantages to be gained from the particular expertise that is provided by the laymembers of tribunals as against the more general legal expertise of the chairperson.

- *Accessibility*

The aim of tribunals is to provide individuals with a readily accessible forum in which to air their grievances, and gaining access to tribunals is certainly not as difficult as getting a case into the ordinary courts.

- *Privacy*

The final advantage is the fact that proceedings can be taken before a tribunal without triggering the publicity that might follow from a court case.

8.3.6   Disadvantages of tribunals

It is important that the supposed advantages of tribunals are not simply taken at face value. They represent significant improvements over the operation of the ordinary court system; but it is at least arguable that some of them are not as advantageous as they appear at first sight, and that others represent potential, if not actual weaknesses, in the tribunal system.

Tribunals are cheap, quick, flexible and informal; but their operation should not be viewed with complacency. These so called advantages could be seen as representing an attack on general legal standards; and the tribunal system could be portrayed as providing a second-rate system of justice for those who cannot afford to pay to gain access to 'real law' in the court system. Vigilance is required on the part of the general community to ensure that such does not become an accurate representation of the tribunal system.

In addition to this general point, there are particular weaknesses in the system of tribunal adjudication. Some of these relate to:

- *Appeals procedures*

  There is ground for confusion in lack of uniformity in relation to appeals from tribunals. Rights of appeal from decisions of tribunals and the route of such appeals depend on the provision of the statute under which a particular tribunal operates. Where such rights exist, they may be exercised variously, to a further tribunal, a minister or a court of law. A measure of coherence would not come amiss in this procedure.

  Prior to the Franks Committee Report, tribunals were not required to provide reasons for their decisions and this prevented appeals in most cases. Subsequent to the Franks Report, however, most tribunals, although still not all of them, are required to provide reasons for their decisions under s 10 of the Tribunals and Inquiries Act 1992. The importance of this provision is that, in cases where a tribunal has erred in its application of the law, the claimant can appeal to the High Court for an application for judicial review to have the decision of the tribunal set aside for error of law on the face of the record. All tribunals should be required to provide reasons for their decisions.

- *Publicity*

  It was stated above that lack of publicity in relation to tribunal proceedings was a potential advantage of the system. A lack of publicity, however, may be a distinct disadvantage because it has the effect that cases involving issues of general public importance are not given the publicity and consideration that they might merit.

- *The provision of legal aid*

  It was claimed previously that one of the major advantages of the tribunal system is its lack of formality and non-legal atmosphere. Research has shown, however, that individual complainants fare better where they are represented by lawyers. Additionally, as a consequence of the Franks' recommendations, the fact that chairpersons have to be legally qualified has led to an increase in the formality of tribunal proceedings. As a consequence, non-law experts find it increasingly difficult, in practice, to represent themselves effectively. This difficulty is compounded when the body which is the object of the complaint is itself legally represented; for, although the parties to hearings do not have to be legally represented, there is nothing to prevent them from being so represented.

This leads to a consideration of the major weakness in the operation of tribunals: the fact that, except for lands tribunal, employment appeals tribunals, mental health tribunals and the Commons Commissioners, legal aid is not available to people pursuing cases at tribunals. They may be entitled to legal advice and assistance under the 'green form' system but such limited assistance is unlikely to provide potential complainants with sufficient help to permit them to pursue their case with any confidence of achieving a satisfactory conclusion.

Although former Lord Chancellor Lord Mackay did not consider the operation of tribunals in his Hamlyn lecture on ADR, he did make a comment that perhaps should be considered in this context. In justifying his refusal to provide legal aid for ADR generally, he stated that:

> Legal aid pre-supposes that there is a need, so undeniable that the taxpayer should support it, for legal advice or legal services relating to legal issues.

It is suggested that the operation of the tribunal system fits within these strictures and that, on the basis of the former Lord Chancellor's own reasoning, legal aid should be available to all of those involved in and subject to the adjudication of tribunals. If tribunals are becoming increasingly important in determining individual rights and are, at the same time, becoming formalistic, then the refusal of legal aid to those seeking to use tribunals is tantamount to refusing them access to justice. The Council on Tribunals has consistently advocated the proposal that the provision of legal aid should be extended to all tribunals. Their case is unarguable on the grounds of justice; unfortunately it appears to be defensible on the grounds of economics. Unfortunately, it would appear unlikely in the extreme that the current Lord Chancellor, Lord Irvine, will disagree with his predecessor.

8.4   Ombudsman

As with tribunals, so the institution of the ombudsman reflects the increased activity of the contemporary State. As the State became more engaged in everyday social activity, it increasingly impinged on, and on occasion conflicted with, the individual citizen. Courts and tribunals were available to deal with substantive breaches of particular rules and procedures but there remained some disquiet as to the possibility of the adverse effect of the implementation of general state policy on individuals. If tribunals may be categorised as an ADR procedure to the ordinary court system in relation to *decisions taken in breach of rules*, the institution of ombudsman represents a procedure for the redress of complaints about *the way in which those decisions have been taken*. It has to be admitted, however, that the two categories overlap to a considerable degree. The ombudsman procedure, however, is not just an alternative to the court and tribunal system; it is based upon a distinctly different approach to dealing with disputes. Indeed, the Parliamentary Commissioner Act 1967, which established the position of the first ombudsman, provides that complainants with rights to pursue their complaints in either of those forums will be precluded from making use of the ombudsman procedure. (Such a prohibition is subject to the discretion of the ombudsman who tends to interpret it in a generous manner in favour of the complainant.)

The concept of the ombudsman is Scandinavian in origin, and the function of the office holder is to investigate complaints of *maladministration*; that is, situations where the performance of a government department has fallen below acceptable standards of administration. The first ombudsman, appointed under the 1967 legislation, operated, and the present ombudsman still operates, under the title of the Parliamentary Commissioner for Administration (PCA) and was empowered to consider central government processes only. Since that date, a number of other ombudsmen have been appointed to oversee the administration of local government in England and Wales, under the Local Government Act 1974. Scotland and Northern Ireland have their own local government ombudsmen fulfilling the same task. There are also Health Service Commissioners for England, Wales and Scotland, whose duty it is to investigate the administration and provision of services in the health service, and, in October 1994, Sir Peter Woodhead was appointed as the first Prisons Ombudsman. The ombudsman system has also spread beyond the realm of government administration and there are ombudsmen overseeing the operation of, amongst other things, legal services, banking, and insurance. Some schemes, such as the legal services scheme, have been established by statute but many others have been established by industry as a means of self-regulation; as regards this latter type, the newspaper ombudsman does not appear to have been a great success and it has been rumoured that it will be disbanded.

The European Parliament appointed an ombudsman under the powers extended to it by the Treaty Establishing the European Community (EC Treaty) (Art 195, formerly 138(e)). The European ombudsman has the function of investigating maladministration in all of Community institutions, including the non-judicial operation of the European Court of Justice.

8.4.1 Procedure

Although maladministration is not defined in the Parliamentary Commissioner Act 1967, it has been taken to refer to an error in the way a decision was reached rather than an error in the actual decision itself. Indeed, s 12(3) of the Parliamentary Commissioner Act 1967 expressly precludes the PCA from questioning the merits of particular decisions taken without maladministration. Maladministration, therefore, can be seen to refer to procedure used to reach a result rather than the result itself. In an illuminating, and much quoted, speech introducing the Act, Richard Crossman, the then leader of the House of Commons, gave an indicative, if non-definitive, list of what might be included within the term maladministration, and included within it: bias, neglect, inattention, delay, incompetence, ineptitude, perversity, turpitude and arbitrariness.

Members of the public do not have the right to complain directly to the PCA but must channel any such complaint through a member of Parliament. Complainants do not have to provide precise details of any maladministration. They simply have to indicate the difficulties they have experienced as a result of dealing with an agency of central government. It is the function of the PCA to discover whether the problem arose as a result of maladministration. There is a 12 month time limit for raising complaints but the PCA has discretion to ignore this.

The powers of the PCA to investigate complaints are similar to those of a High Court judge to require the attendance of witnesses and the production of documents; and wilful obstruction of the investigation is treated as contempt of court.

On conclusion of an investigation, the PCA submits reports to the member of Parliament who the raised complaint, and to the principal of the government office which was subject to the investigation. The ombudsman has no enforcement powers but, if his recommendations are ignored, and existing practices involving maladministration are not altered, he may submit a further report to both Houses of Parliament in order to highlight the continued bad practice. The assumption is that on the submission of such a report, members of Parliament will exert pressure on the appropriate Minister of State to ensure that any changes needed in procedure are made.

Annual reports are laid before Parliament and a Parliamentary Select Committee exists to oversee the operation of the PCA. The operation of the Parliamentary Commissioner for Administration is subject to judicial review (*R v Parliamentary Commissioner for Administration ex p Balchin* (1997); however, the Parliamentary Commissioner for Public Standards, established after the Nolan Inquiry into cash for questions in Parliament, is not open to judicial review (*R v Parliamentary Commissioner for Standards ex p Al Fayed* (1997)) (see 1.4.2, above).

The relationship between the PCA and the government is highlighted by three case studies:

(a) *Barlow Clowes*

The first of these concerned the Barlow Clowes group of companies. In 1988, Peter Clowes, and three others were arrested and charged with offences in connection with the Prevention of Fraud (Investments) Act 1958 and theft. The prosecution alleged an investment fraud said to have been over £115m. The main allegation was that members of the public were induced to deposit their moneys in the belief that they would be invested in gilt-edged securities; but that only £1.9m was in fact so invested. The rest was misappropriated by the defendants. Clowes alone faced charges of theft totalling some £62m. The PCA received hundreds of complaints from investors who had lost their money in relation to the Barlow Clowes affair; all alleging maladministration on the part of the Department of Trade and Industry, which had responsibility for licensing such investment companies. The PCA made five findings of maladministration against the DTI and recommended that compensation should be paid to those who had suffered as a result of it. Surprisingly, the government initially denied any responsibility for providing compensation. Subsequently, after the PCA had expressed his regret at the government's initial stance, the government agreed to pay the recommended compensation payments, amounting to £150 million; but with the rider that it still accepted no legal liability.

(b) *Child Support Agency*

The much criticised Child Support Agency (CSA) had been established in an endeavour to ensure that absent parents, essentially fathers, would have to accept financial responsibility for the maintenance of their children as determined by the Agency. The PCA's report followed complaints referred to him by 95 members of Parliament covering the time from the Agency started its operations in April 1994 until the end of 1995. Although the PCA investigated 70 complaints, the report focused on seven of those as being representative of the whole. These complaints highlighted a number of failures on the part of the CSA: mistakes as to the identity of individuals subjects to the determinations of the CSA; failure to answer correspondence; delay in assessing and reviewing maintenance assessments and delays in actually securing payments due; and the provision of incorrect or misleading advice. The conclusion of the PCA was that the CSA was liable for maladministration, inexcusable delays and slipshod service. In response to the report, the chief executive of the CSA wrote to the PCA informing him that steps were being taken to deal with the problems highlighted in the report. Such changes in the way the CSA operated has not staved off its proposed replacement by a more sympathetic, and efficient, organisation.

(c) *Channel Tunnel Rail Link*

As a consequence of the four year delay on the part of the Department of Transport in deciding on a route for the Channel Tunnel Rail Link, the owners of properties along the various possible routes found the value of their properties blighted, not to say unsaleable. The situation was not finalised until the Department announced its final selection in 1994.

According to the PCA:

> The effect of the Department of Transport's policy was to put the project in limbo, keeping it alive when it could not be funded.

As a consequence, he held that the Department:

> ... had a responsibility to consider the position of such persons suffering exceptional or extreme hardship and to provide redress where appropriate. They undertook no such considerations. That merits my criticism.

The unusual thing about this case, however, was the reaction of the Department of Transport, which rejected the findings of the PCA and refused to provide any compensation. The refusal of the Department of Transport led the PCA to lay a special report before Parliament, consequent upon a situation where an 'injustice has been found which has not or will not be remedied' (s 10(3) of the Parliamentary Commissioner Act 1967). Even in the face of the implementation of this extremely rare form of censure, the government maintained its original policy that it was not liable for the consequences of either general, or particular, blight. The matter was then taken up by the Select Committee on the Parliamentary Commissioner for Administration, which supported the conclusions of the CPS and recommended that:

> ... the Department of Transport reconsider its response to the Ombudsman's findings, accept his conclusions that maladministration had occurred ... It would be most regrettable if the department were to remain obdurate. In such an event, we recommend that as a matter of urgency a debate on this matter be held on the floor of the House on a substantive motion in government time (Sixth Report of PCA).

Such a demonstration of solidarity between the PCA and the Committee had the desired effect; leading to the government's climb down, and payments of £5,000 to those property owners who had suffered as a consequence of the housing blight.

8.4.2   Evaluation

All in all, the system appears to operate fairly well within its restricted sphere of operation, but there are major areas where it could be improved. The more important of the criticisms levelled at the PCA relate to:

• the retention of members of Parliament as filters of complaints. It is generally accepted that there is no need for such a filter mechanism. At one level, it represents a sop to the idea of parliamentary representation and control. Yet, at the practical level, PCAs have referred complaints made to them directly, to the constituent's member of Parliament in order to have them referred back to them in the appropriate form. It is suggested that there is no longer any need or justification for this farce;

- the restrictive nature of the definition of maladministration. It is possible to argue that any procedure that leads to an unreasonable decision must involve an element of maladministration and that, therefore, the definition as currently stated is not overly restrictive. However, even if such reverse reasoning is valid, it would still be preferable for the definition of the scope of the PCA's investigations to be clearly stated, and be stated in wider terms than at present;

- the jurisdiction of the PCA. This criticism tends to resolve itself into the view that there are many areas that should be covered by the PCA but which are not. For example, as presently constituted, the ombudsman can only investigate the *operation* of general law. It could be claimed, and not without some justification, that the process of *making* law, in the form of delegated legislation, could equally do with investigation;

- the lack of publicity given to complaints. It is sometimes suggested that sufficient publicity is not given either to the existence of the various ombudsmen or to the results of their investigations. The argument is that if more people were aware of the procedure and what it could achieve, then more people would make use of it leading to an overall improvement in the administration of governmental policies;

- the reactive role of the ombudsman. This criticism refers to the fact that the ombudsmen are dependent upon receiving complaints before they can initiate investigations. It is suggested that a more *pro-active* role under which the ombudsmen would be empowered to initiate investigation on their own authority would lead to an improvement in general administration as well as increase the effectiveness of the activity of the ombudsmen. This criticism is related to the way in which the role of the ombudsmen is viewed. If they are simply a problem solving dispute resolution institution, then a *reactive* role is sufficient; if, however, they are seen as the means of improving general administrative performance, then a more *pro-active* role is called for.

In his Hamlyn lecture, the former Lord Chancellor, Mackay, approvingly categorised the ombudsman as:

Popularly representing justice for the small against the great – justice that is quick, inexpensive and unfettered by legalistic procedures – acceptance of the institution of ombudsman now extends well beyond central and local government administration. The concept is widely viewed as a desirable, and even necessary, avenue to fairness wherever the individual is perceived to be at the mercy of an impenetrable administrative system.

8.5   Mediation and conciliation

The final alternative dispute mechanisms to be considered, mediation and conciliation, are the most informal of all.

8.5.1   Mediation

Mediation is the process whereby a third party acts as the conduit through which two disputing parties communicate and negotiate in an attempt to reach a common resolution of a problem. The mediator may move between the parties, communicating their opinions without their having to meet, or alternatively the mediator may operate in the presence of the parties, but, in either situation, the emphasis is on the parties themselves working out a shared agreement as to how the dispute in question is to be settled.

In his Hamlyn lecture, Lord Mackay considered three alternative systems of mediation and examined the possibility of annexing such schemes to the existing court system. One, involving lawyers advising parties as to the legal strengths of their relative positions, he rejected on the grounds that it merely duplicated, without replacing or extending, what was already available in the courts. A second, based on judges adopting the role of mediators, he rejected on the ground that it might be seen as undermining the traditional impartiality of the judiciary. The third type, and the one that found most favour with him, broadened the issues beyond the legal, to explore solutions that were not available to the court. His approval, however, did not extend to financing such a system; the implication being that public money should, and does, finance the civil justice system and that any benefits that flow from a different system should be financed privately.

In March 1998, the Lord Chancellor's Department reported that take up of the voluntary mediation procedure offered in the pilot schemes had been fairly low. As regards the pilot scheme established in the Central London County Court, a monitoring report found that only 5% of cases referred to the ADR scheme actually took it up. However, in a more positive mode, the report did find that, in cases that did go to mediation, 62% settled during the process without going on to court. The conclusion of the report was that mediation was capable of dealing with a wider range of cases than might have been expected, including personal injury cases. It also found that those who participate found the process satisfying and led to outcomes that the parties generally found acceptable.

8.5.2   Mediation in divorce

> ... in government, we have continued to encourage the use of mediation, most notably in the area of family law, where it is a central tent of divorce law reform.

> The importance of mediation and ADR in family law cases can scarcely be understated, given the high incidence of family breakdown and the appalling social consequences which result (Lord Chancellor Irvine, speech to Faculty of Mediators, 1999).

Mediation has an important part to play in family matters, where it is felt that the adversarial approach of the traditional legal system has tended to emphasise, if not increase, existing differences of view between individuals and has not been conducive to amicable settlements. Thus, in divorce cases, mediation has traditionally been used to enable the parties themselves to work out an agreed settlement rather than having one imposed on them from outside by the courts.

This emphasis on mediation was strengthened in the Family Law Act 1996, but it is important to realise there are potential problems with mediation. The assumption that the parties freely negotiate the terms of their final agreement in a less than hostile manner may be deeply flawed to the extent that it assumes equality of bargaining power and knowledge between the parties to the negotiation. Mediation may well ease pain, but, unless the mediation procedure is carefully and critically monitored, it may gloss over and perpetuate a previously exploitative relationship, allowing the more powerful participant to manipulate and dominate the more vulnerable, and force an inequitable agreement. Establishing entitlements on the basis of clear legal advice may be preferable to apparently negotiating those entitlements away in the non-confrontational, therapeutic, atmosphere of mediation.

Under the Divorce Reform Act 1969, the concept of 'no fault' divorce was introduced for those couples who had been separated for two years, and it was assumed that this would provide the main grounds for divorce applications. This has not proved to be the case and it is commonly accepted that, because of the two year delay involved, 75% of those seeking divorces still apply on the basis of adultery or unreasonable behaviour, permitting them to complete the procedure in between three and six months.

The Family Law Act 1996 proposed to introduce real 'no fault' divorce by abolishing the grounds of adultery and unreasonable behaviour, but couples will have to wait a minimum of 12 months before their divorce was confirmed. Instead of filing a divorce petition, the person seeking to be divorced is merely required to submit a statement certifying that their marriage has broken down. The process of divorce will require that the parties attend an informal meeting three months before they make their statement of marital breakdown. They will then have to wait a further nine months for their divorce, during which time they should reflect on whether the marriage could be saved, have an opportunity for reconciliation, and consider arrangements relating to finance, property and children. The Act encourages the use of mediation in appropriate cases, and allows the court, after it has received a statement of marital breakdown, to direct the parties to attend a meeting with a mediator for an explanation of the mediation process. The role of the mediator is restricted to sorting out the aspects of the divorce relating to finance and children, and should refer the case to an appropriate counsellor if it appears that the parties to the marriage might be open to reconciliation. During the 'cooling off period', State funding would be available for meetings with marriage guidance counsellors for those eligible for legal aid, and others would be encouraged to take advantage of such marriage support services.

Although the Family Law Act was passed in 1996, the proposed reforms were not implemented immediately, and trials were conducted as to the appropriateness of the new procedures. Also, the fact that the Family Law Act was passed under the previous Conservative administration, and as a consequence of the strenuous endeavours of the then Lord Chancellor, Lord Mackay, did not prevent the incoming Labour administration's continued support for the proposed reforms. As Lord Chancellor Irvine stated:

> ... in government, we have continued to encourage the use of mediation, most notably in the area of family law, where it is a central tent of divorce law reform. The importance of mediation and ADR in family law cases can scarcely be understated, given the high incidence of family breakdown and the appalling social consequences which result (Lord Chancellor Irvine, speech to Faculty of Mediators, 1999).

However, in June 1999, Lord Irvine announced that the government would not be implementing the new proposals in the Family Law Act in the year 2000 as had been previously intended. It has to be said that much academic, and legal practitioner, opinion was dubious, if not hostile, to the way in which the mediation procedure would operate. It was accepted generally that mediation might work in relation to children, but it was thought less likely to work where money was concerned and, in those circumstances, it was suggested that people would still be likely to look for their own personal legal representative rather than submit to mediation. It would appear that the results of the trials support such scepticism. Lord Irvine stated that the results of the mediation pilot schemes were disappointing, in that fewer than 10% of divorcing couples in the pilot areas were willing to make use of the preliminary information meetings, which would become compulsory under the Family Law Act proposals. Of those attending the meetings; only 7% were successfully encouraged to opt for mediation, and only 13% took up the offer to see a marriage counsellor. Almost 40% of those attending the meetings stated that they were more convinced of the need to see an independent lawyer to protect their legal rights.

Lord Irvine's announcement was merely as to the postponement of the implementation of the divorce law reforms. Many, however, believe that this postponement is merely a precursor to their future abandonment.

In March 1998, the Lord Chancellor's Department reported that take up of the voluntary mediation procedure offered in the pilot schemes had been fairly low. At least as regards the pilot scheme established in the Central London County Court, a monitoring report found that only 5% of cases referred to the ADR scheme, actually took it up. However, in a more positive mode, the report did find that in cases that did go to mediation, 62% settled during the process without going on to court. The conclusion of the report was that mediation was capable of dealing with a wider range of cases than might have been expected, including personal injury cases. It also found that those who participate found the process satisfying and led to outcomes that the parties generally found acceptable. It has to be stated, however that at least, with specific reference to the provisions of the Family Law Act, which will be fully implemented in 1999, much academic and legal practitioner opinion remains dubious, if not hostile, to the way in which the mediation procedure will operate. It is accepted that mediation may work in relation to children, but it is thought less likely to work where money is concerned, and in those circumstances, people are still likely to look for their own personal legal representative rather than submit to mediation.

In a speech at The United Kingdom Family Law Conference in London on 25 June 1999, Lord Irvine recognised that his decision to postpone the implementation of Pt 2 of the Family Law Act raised a question mark over its future, but he went on to say that the final decision depended on the outcome of the current and future research into the area

(www.open.gov.uk/lcd/speeches/1999/25.6.99.htm).

8.5.3   Conciliation

Conciliation takes mediation a step further and gives the mediator the power to suggest grounds for compromise and the possible basis for a conclusive agreement. Both mediation and conciliation have been available in relation to industrial disputes under the auspices of the government funded Advisory Conciliation and Arbitration Service. One of the statutory functions of ACAS is to try to resolve industrial disputes by means of discussion and negotiation or if the parties agree the Service might take a more active part as arbitrator in relation to a particular dispute.

The essential weakness in the procedures of mediation and conciliation lies in the fact that, although they *may* lead to the resolution of a dispute, they do not *necessarily* achieve that end. Where they operate successfully, they are excellent methods of dealing with problems, as essentially the parties to the dispute determine their own solutions and therefore feel committed to the outcome. The problem is that they have no binding power and do not always lead to an outcome. As the Heilbron Report emphasises, even if the civil law procedure is reformed to make it more litigant-friendly, ADR mechanisms will still have a very important part to play in dealing with problems in certain delicate areas that are not susceptible to resolution by the ordinary court system. Lord Mackay has recognised this in his proposal for divorce reform but he has also resisted the call to fund a wider use of mediation on the basis that for the State to fund it would lead to its use becoming compulsory and yet it is the very lack of compulsion in the procedure that makes it work successfully.

ARBITRATION, TRIBUNAL ADJUDICATION AND ALTERNATIVE DISPUTE RESOLUTION

Alternative Dispute Resolution

ADR has many features that make it preferable to the ordinary court system in many areas.

Its main advantage is that it is less antagonistic than the ordinary legal system, and is designed to achieve agreement between the parties involved.

Arbitration

This is the procedure whereby parties in dispute refer the issue to a third party for resolution, rather than take the case to the ordinary law courts. Arbitration procedures can be contained in the original contract or agreed after a dispute arises. The procedure is governed by the Arbitration Act 1996. The Act follows the Model Arbitration Law adopted by the United Nations Commission on International Trade Law (UNICTRAL). Arbitration awards are enforceable in the ordinary courts. They must be carried out in a judicial manner and are subject to judicial review.

Advantages over the ordinary court system are: privacy; informality; speed; lower cost; expertise; and it is less antagonistic.

Small claims procedure in the county court is a distinct process, although referred to as arbitration. Although still called small claims, the upper limit for such proceedings is the not inconsiderable sum of £5,000. This has raised some doubts as to the future operation of the system.

Administrative tribunals

These deal with cases involving conflicts between the State, its functionaries, and private citizens. Domestic tribunals deal with private internal matters within institutions. Tribunals may be seen as administrative but they are also adjudicative in that they have to act judicially when deciding particular cases. Tribunals are subject to the supervision of the Council on Tribunals but are subservient to and under the control of the ordinary courts.

Usually, only the chair of a tribunal is legally qualified.

Examples of tribunals are: industrial tribunal; social security appeals tribunal; mental health review tribunal; lands tribunal; Rent Assessment Committee.

Advantages of tribunals over ordinary courts relate to: speed; cost; informality; flexibility; expertise; accessibility; privacy.

Disadvantages relate to: appeals procedure; lack of publicity; the lack of legal aid in most cases.

Ombudsmen

The role of ombudsmen is to investigate complaints of maladministration in various areas of State activity. Members of the public must channel complaints through a Member of Parliament.

The powers of the PCA to investigate complaints are similar to those of a High Court judge. The ombudsman has no direct enforcement powers as such.

On conclusion of an investigation, he submits reports to the member of Parliament who raised complaint, and to the principal of the government office which was subject to the investigation. He can also report to Parliament.

Shortcomings in the procedure: the member of Parliament filter; uncertain if not narrow jurisdiction; lack of publicity; the reactive rather than proactive nature of the role.

Mediation and conciliation

Mediation: the third party only acts as a go-between. The Family Law Act 1996 proposed a greater role for mediation in relation to divorce. This proposal has been brought into doubt by the recent announcement of its postponement by the Lord Chancellor, in the light of the results of a pilot study.

Conciliation: the third party is more active in facilitating a reconciliation or agreement between the parties.

CHAPTER 9

THE CRIMINAL PROCESS:
(1) THE INVESTIGATION OF CRIME

9.1 General introduction to the criminal process

9.1.1 The criminal justice system in the 21st century

The criminal justice system has recently been the subject of widespread heated debate in Parliament, the broadcast media and the print media and in academic and professional journals. The British Crime Survey (BCS) (Home Office Statistical Bulletin, issue 21/98) estimates there were nearly 16,500,000 crimes against adults living in households in 1997. The long term trend shows that the gradual rise in BCS crime during the 1980s and the steeper rise during the early 1990s have now been reversed. Even so, the number of crimes counted by the BCS has increased by 49% since 1981.

This chapter, and the following one, refers to the 'criminal justice system'. This has been, for many years, an accepted descriptive term used by social scientists, journalists and, occasionally, lawyers. Officially, however, there is no such thing as the 'criminal justice system'. Governmental responsibilities, for example, overlap in this area. The Home Secretary is responsible for the Metropolitan Police, criminal statistics, the Probation Service, and the Crown Prosecution Service (and, more broadly, for 'law and order'), while the Lord Chancellor is responsible for all the criminal law courts, the appointment of magistrates, and the judges. Nonetheless, in recent times, there has been increasing governmental recognition of something called the 'criminal justice system'. On 30 December 1998, for example, a single official statement entitled 'Joint Press Release on the Criminal Justice System Public Service Agreement' was issued on behalf of the Home Office, the Lord Chancellor's Department, and the Attorney General's Office. It stated:

> The overarching aims, objectives and performance measures for the criminal justice system have been published for the first time in a cross departmental Public Service Agreement. The three Departments, and their respective services, will be working more closely than ever before to ensure that the criminal justice system protects the public and delivers justice. Inter-agency co-operation will be promoted at regional, local, as well as at the national level. Ministers believe that these arrangements are a good example of 'joined-up government' in practice (http://www.nds.coi.gov.uk/coi/coipress.ns).

The significance of such a pronouncement is that it reveals an attempt to make co-ordinated policy in respect of each of these branches of operation. In fact, the statement goes on to become quite explicit:

The three ministers have set two overarching aims to provide a strategic direction for the system as a whole. They have made clear that every part of the criminal justice system (including the police, courts, Crown Prosecution Service, prison and probation services) should work together so as to best serve and protect the public.

The two overarching aims are:

- to reduce crime and the fear of crime and their social and economic costs; and

- to dispense justice fairly and efficiently and to promote confidence in the rule of law.

Supporting the aims are the following eight objectives:

In support of the first aim:

(1) to reduce the level of actual crime and disorder;

(2) to reduce the adverse impact of crime and disorder on people's lives;

(3) to reduce the economic costs of crime.

In support of the second aim:

(4) to ensure just processes and just and effective outcomes;

(5) to deal with cases throughout the criminal justice process with appropriate speed;

(6) to meet the needs of victims, witnesses and jurors within the system;

(7) to respect the rights of defendants and to treat them fairly;

(8) to promote confidence in the criminal justice system.

9.2   Mistrust of the system

On the one hand, there has been an apparently growing public mistrust of the criminal justice system as a system which can convict the innocent. The number of exposed miscarriages of justice involving malpractice and disastrous errors by agencies of the criminal justice system has grown rapidly. On 19 March 1991, the day the Birmingham Six were released from prison having wrongly served 16 years in jail, the Home Secretary announced a Royal Commission on Criminal Justice to examine the system with a view to reducing the chances of wrongful conviction. The Commission published its report with 352 recommendations in July 1993. Although some of these recommendations have been implemented in subsequent legislation (like the establishment of the Criminal Cases Review Commission by the Criminal Appeal Act (CAA) 1995), great concern has been expressed by pressure groups about the government's rejection of the Royal Commission's findings in relation to the so called 'right to silence'. This right was effectively undermined by ss 34–37 of the Criminal Justice and Public Order Act (CJPOA) 1994, and this change will, arguably, increase the chances of miscarriages occurring rather than reduce them. Confidence in the criminal justice system appears to be in decline. In a national survey for the 1962 Royal Commission on the Police (Cmnd 1728, 1962, HMSO), 83% of respondents indicated that they had 'a great deal of respect' for the way the police operated. In a national poll in 1993 conducted by MORI for *The Sunday Times* and the Police Federation, under 50% of respondents indicated that they had 'a great deal of respect' for the way the police operated. The poll also showed that one in six adults (7 million people) actually distrust the police ((1993) *The Sunday Times*, 25 July). In another nationwide poll ((1993) *The Independent*, 21 June), 28% of respondents indicated that they would be 'concerned at what might be going to happen' if stopped by the police, with only 36% of respondents indicating they would be confident that they would be treated fairly.

Public confidence in the police continued to fall in the late 1990s (see, for example, 'Lack of trust at heart of attitude problem' (1999) *The Guardian*, 25 February; 'One in four say police racist' (1999) *The Guardian*, 9 February). This drop in confidence plummeted with particular sharpness after the publication of the Macpherson Report into the racist killing of the black London teenager, Stephen Lawrence. The Report identified various fundamental operational failings of the police and, more significantly, 'institutional racism'.

9.2.1 The Macpherson Report

Following the stabbing of Stephen Lawrence, a black teenager from south London, by a group of racist thugs in 1993, defects in several aspects of the English legal system failed to bring his killers to justice. There was a catalogue of profoundly incompetent errors in the way the police handled events. These included: the failure to administer proper first aid at the scene of the attack; a failure to properly search for evidence and suspects; a failure to properly log and investigate tip-offs about the identity of the killers; and a failure to treat the family of Stephen Lawrence with proper respect and sensitivity. A judicial inquiry headed by a former High Court judge, Sir William Macpherson, was set up by the government in 1997 and its report was published in February 1999 (The Stationery Office, Cm 4262-I).

The Report accuses the Metropolitan Police (in London) of 'institutional racism'. It recommends that the police and several other public services should now be brought fully within the Race Relations Act 1976 which deals with racism in the private employment sector. At present, the Act can be used only where police are operating in a service capacity but not in the course of their operational duties. For example, there is not presently any legal remedy under the Act if a black person believes he or she has been stopped in the street for reasons of racial prejudice.

Another recommendation in the Report would, if enacted, end the ancient principle against 'double jeopardy' whereby a person cannot be tried more than once for the same, or substantially the same, crime. This arose from one twist in the developments in the Lawrence case in which three suspects were sent for trial at Crown Court after a private prosecution brought by Stephen's father. The trial was stopped by the judge who ruled that there was insufficient evidence to proceed and ordered the jury to acquit the defendants. The rule of double jeopardy (*autrefois acquit* – the person has been otherwise acquitted) will now prevent any further prosecution being brought against the main suspects even if strong evidence against them is subsequently found. The feeling that the guilty have got away with such a serious and repulsive crime is widespread. One national newspaper, beneath the banner headline 'Murderers', put the names and photographs of the five chief suspects of the killings.

The Report recommends (Recommendation 38) that the Court of Appeal should have the power to permit prosecution after acquittal 'where fresh and viable evidence is presented'. The Home Secretary has said that he will refer the matter to the Law Commission. There is, arguably, a good case for change here. The rule which prevents anyone from being charged more than once in respect of the same crime arose in an ancient era when there existed none of today's multi-farious checks and balances against the abuse of official power (committal proceedings, independent magistrates and judges, random juries, stringent laws of evidence; see Chapter 10). At the time of the origin of the rule against double jeopardy, powerful aristocrats could, effectively, terrorise individual enemies with the threat of repeated prosecutions. By contrast, in today's setting, provided some form of high level and independent authorisation were to be required (Macpherson recommends the Court of Appeal) before a second prosecution could be brought, there would be no real risk that the threat of re-prosecution would constantly hang over an acquitted defendant's head. Only those fearful of new, viable incriminating evidence for serious crimes would have reason to worry.

The Report's other recommendations include:

1 That a ministerial priority be established for all police services 'to increase trust and confidence in policing among minority ethnic communities'.

   Comment: Unfortunately, only days after this report was published, it came to light that a special report commissioned 15 months ago showed that 17 out of the 43 police forces of England and Wales did not have any community and race relations policy, despite having been urged to establish one ((1999) *The Times*, 2 March).

9 That a Freedom of Information Act should apply to all areas of policing, subject only to a 'substantial harm' test for withholding information.

Comment: Both during the investigation and at various stages after the failed public prosecution, the friends and relatives of Stephen Lawrence found it impossible to get clear and accurate information from the police about how the case had been handled and was being taken forward. The more open and transparent a system, the more likely it is to carry public confidence.

11 That the Race Relations Acts should apply to police officers and that Chief Constables should be vicariously liable for the acts and omissions of their officers in this area.

Comment: This proposal would help focus police attention on what might otherwise be unconscious or unintended racist behaviour.

33 That the Crown Prosecution Service (CPS) should, in deciding whether to prosecute a racist crime, consider that, once the 'evidential test' is satisfied (that is, that there is a 'realistic prospect of conviction'), there is a rebuttable presumption that the public interest test is in favour of prosecution.

Comment: Racism in a crime is currently a factor which should strengthen the chances of a prosecution according to the Code for Crown Prosecutors; the change would make a prosecution more certain in such circumstances.

34 That the police and CPS should take particular care to recognise and to include any evidence of a racial motivation in a crime. The CPS should take care to ensure that any such motivation is referred to at trial and in the sentencing process. No plea bargaining should ever exclude such evidence.

Comment: This highlights that racism is a serious aggravating factor in any crime, as it shows that the innocent victim has been specially and vindictively selected for a reason that is irrational, and, therefore, especially terrifying.

41 That consideration be given to the proposition that victims or victims' families should be allowed to become 'civil parties' to criminal proceedings, to facilitate and to ensure the provision of all relevant information to victims and their families.

Comment: Unlike civil litigation, it is the State that prosecutes where there has been a crime; the victim neither determines whether to prosecute nor, if someone is convicted, can the victim influence the sentence for the crime. Number 41 is therefore a controversial proposal, as there has traditionally been great resistance to permitting citizens to participate in the prosecution of crimes. The essentially communicative role, suggested here, however, is arguably different from an influential role.

42 That there should be advance disclosure of evidence and documents as of right to parties who have leave from a coroner to appear at an inquest.

Comment: Presently, relatives often only discover the terrible details of the death of their loved ones at the inquest in open court as some coroners will not release any information even to bereaved next of kin before the hearing.

43 That consideration be given to the provision of legal aid to victims or the families of victims to cover representation at an inquest in appropriate cases.

Comment: This is a recommendation that has been made for many years by various bodies and committees. There is a very strong case for bereaved people in extremis, who cannot afford to have representation at the inquest of their loved one, to receive legal aid.

Britain is a multi-cultural and ethnically diverse community. Its policing is based on consent rather than sheer strength: there are 60 million citizens and only 130,000 police, so it can only work on consent. At the heart of the debate about policing, the law, and the criminal justice system in the wake of the Macpherson Report is the question of whether ethnic minorities, especially visible minorities, can quickly be made to feel confident about the way they are treated by the English legal system.

A recent report produced by the Metropolitan Police Service (MPS) entitled *Stop and Search: Reviewing the Tactic* and two Home Office research papers *Entry into the Criminal Justice System: a Survey of Police Arrests and their Outcomes* (1998) and *Statistics on Race and the Criminal Justice System* (1998) recognise the disproportionate use of stop and search powers against black people (see Cragg, 'Stop and search powers: research and extension' (1999) Legal Action 3, February). Cragg argues that, 'with the figures already showing that almost 90% of those stopped are not arrested (and, therefore, the implication must be that there were, in fact, no grounds to stop and search these people), the training and management strategy proposed by the MPS "to manage the tactic more fairly and effectively" must be rigorously imposed and monitored if it is to have any chance of success'. The exercise of stop and search powers by the police is governed by the revised Code of Practice A (see 9.3.14, below) which states that it is important these powers are used responsibly and sparingly. It warns, 'misuse of the powers is likely to be harmful to the police effort in the long run and can lead to mistrust of police in the community'.

9.2.2 Lack of confidence in the system

The rise in crime, especially certain types of offence like domestic burglary, taking and driving away (joyriding) offences, and theft of, and from, vehicles has greatly vexed large sections of the population. These crimes account for over two-thirds of all crime recorded in the Annual Criminal Statistics (1998).

In the 12 months ending March 1998, the police in England and Wales recorded a total of 4.5 million offences (Home Office Statistical Bulletin, Notifiable Offences, issue 22/98). Certain types of offence like domestic burglary, theft of, and from, vehicles and vandalism against vehicles and other household and personal property has greatly vexed large sections of the population. These offences accounted for 91% of all recorded crimes during this period. However, a large proportion of crime is unrecorded, as many offences are not reported to the police. The number of offences committed in England and Wales is double the recorded figure according to a MORI poll conducted in 1997 ((1997) *The Times*, 15 March). The poll found that 44% of victims had failed to report incidents to police because they had no confidence the offenders would be caught, or felt that the offences were too trivial or that the police would not investigate.

The survey showed that 47% of people had been a victim of crime in 1996. Of BCS crimes that can be compared to recorded offences, just a quarter ended up in police records. This is because less than half were reported to the police, and only about half of those that were reported were recorded (issue 21/98: section 4).

9.2.3 A contradiction

There is a friction between the sort of policies that these two concerns generate, that is, people seem to want the police to have greater powers to combat crime, and yet, contradictorily, want greater controls on the police and evidence so as to avoid more miscarriages of justice. It is argued that, if we wish to avoid unjust convictions like those of the Winchester Three, the Guildford Four, the Birmingham Six, the Maguire Seven, the Tottenham Three, Stefan Kiszko, Judith Ward and the Bridgewater Three ((1997) *The Guardian*, 21, 22 February), we should tighten the rules of evidence and procedure that govern the investigation and prosecution of crime. Against this, it has been argued (for example, by Charles Pollard, Chief Constable of the Thames Valley Police: letter (1995) *The Times*, 12 April; article (1995) *The Sunday Times*, 9 July) that the police should have greater powers and that the trial process should be tilted less in favour of the defendant. The rules on disclosure of evidence in criminal trials, for example, have been radically changed by the Criminal Procedure and Investigations Act 1996. In particular, the material the prosecution has to disclose to the defence is now staged and brought within a more restrictive framework and since, for the first time, the defence has a duty to disclose its case in advance of trial.

One problem, therefore, in this area of the English legal system is that as the growing problems of crime, and the fear of crime, become more important concerns of government, there are emerging two lobbies for change, lobbies which are diametrically opposed.

The criminal process is examined here in two chapters. This chapter considers the law relating to important pre-trial matters up to and including the admissibility of confession evidence in court. Chapter 10 looks at institutional and procedural aspects of prosecution and matters relating to bail, the classification of offences, trials, plea bargaining and the jury. In examining all these topics, it is important to keep in mind the various aims of the criminal justice system and the extent to which the existing law serves these aims. Amongst the aims to be borne in mind are the following:

- to detect crime and convict those who have committed it;

- to have rules relating to arrest, search, questioning, interrogation and admissibility of evidence which do not expose suspects to unfair treatment likely to lead to unjust convictions;

- to have rules as above which do not unnecessarily impede the proper investigation of crime;

- to ensure that innocent persons are not convicted;

- to maintain public order;

- to maintain public confidence in the criminal justice system;

- to properly balance considerations of justice and fair procedure with those of efficiency and funding.

9.2.4 Contemporary issues

The criminal justice system is bearing signs of strain as it tries to cope with a society in the throes of major transitions: changes in the pattern of family life, changes in the nature of employment expectations, and a revolution in information and communications technology.

In 1999, there are 67,000 people in prison with official predictions putting the figure at 83,000 at the beginning of the next century. Violent crime rose by 8% over the last year and, now that s 34 of the Crime and Disorder Act has brought 10–14 year olds within the criminal law (by abolishing the rebuttable presumption of *doli incapax* for that age range), the number of offences processed by the authorities will be likely to rise significantly over the next several years.

The Police and Magistrates' Courts Act 1994 amended the Police Act 1964, permitting Home Secretaries now to 'determine objectives for the policing of all of the areas of all police authorities'. Under this power, a new police mission statement was announced earlier this year. The purpose of the police, according to this, is 'to help secure a safe and just society in which the rights and responsibilities of individuals, families and communities are properly balanced'. This raises many contentious issues, as the determination of, for example, what is a 'just society' becomes something which is more overtly a matter for policing policy than in previous times when the police role was more simply (in the words of Robert Peel, the 19th century founder of modern policing) to 'prevent and detect crime'.

Yet, can 130,00 police officers do well enough to retain credibility in a society of 56 million people undergoing all sorts of social upheavals? In 1998, the police had to respond to 17.8 million incidents and 7.5 million 999 calls. The racist canteen culture revealed in the wake of the Stephen Lawrence Inquiry, (see 9.2.1, above) and the recognition in 1998 by the Commissioner for the Metropolitan police that he probably has 250 corrupt officers on his force did not help raise public confidence.

It is not clear yet what is the main thrust of governmental policy in relation to the criminal justice system. Thus far, we have seen an unusual cocktail consisting of several privatisation measures and a good dose of centralisation.

Criminal justice has, historically, been regarded by government as, *par excellence*, a matter for the State. Recently, however, first under the Conservative government in the early 1990s and now under Labour, various parts of the system have been privatised. Such moves have not generally been seen as runaway successes. In November 1998, there was public scandal at the extent of injury to prison officers and trainers and damage to the premises of the country's leading private institution for young offenders. It was revealed that over £100,000 of damage had been wrought by wild 12–14 year olds at the Medway Secure Training Centre in Kent. After more than one fiasco, privatised prison escort services have come in for severe criticism, and a provision of the Criminal Justice and Public Order Act of 1994 allowing for private sponsorship of police equipment has been a boon for satirical cartoonists.

By contrast, there are several ways in which aspects of the criminal justice system, historically, all independent from each other and detached from governmental control, have been drawn within the influence of central government. It has, for example, been a hallowed precept of the British Constitution that police forces are local and not governmental agencies. Yet, under Conservative legislation, the Home Secretary became allowed to 'determine objectives for the policing of the areas of all police authorities'.

More worryingly, there has been a notable governmental move to integrate different organisational functions. The Crown Prosecution Service (CPS) has been re-structured so that its erstwhile 13 regions are turned into 42 to match the 43 police forces of England and Wales. This is a remarkable swerve from previous policy. Close and often cosy relations between police officers and the lawyers who used to prosecute their cases (sometimes with atrocious malpractice) was the very reason for the establishment of the CPS.

But, moves towards criminal justice system unification go further than this. The Lord Chancellor announced in 1997 *(Ministerial Statement to the House of Lords*, 29 October 1997) that the 96 Magistrates' Courts Committees (which administer the courts dealing with 95% of all criminal cases) should enjoy much greater alignment with the police and the CPS.

Most disturbingly of all, for some, are the foundations for the Criminal Defence Service (CDS) (laid in the Access to Justice Act 1999) which will give the government greater control over legal representation. The Law Society has pointed out that campaigning lawyers like Gareth Pierce, who represented the Guildford Four, and Jim Nicol, who represented the appellants in the Carl Bridgewater case, could be avoided by the new body.

There is also reason for disquiet about the law, contained in the Criminal Justice (Terrorism and Conspiracy) Act 1998, which makes the opinion of a police officer admissible evidence in court – proof of membership of a proscribed organisation may be based upon the opinion of a senior police officer. In the wake of considerable evidence (from miscarriage of justice cases, especially those involving suspects of terrorism from Northern Ireland) that some police officers were apparently prepared to lie and falsify evidence to secure convictions, the new law has caused some people to become alarmed at the prospect that a person could be convicted of a serious offence on evidence taken mainly from the opinion of a police officer.

Other threats to the criminal justice system include plans to allow crown prosecutors to present cases in the higher courts and a public defender system, like the one being piloted in Scotland, in which defence lawyers are employed by the State.

Taken together, such moves could be seen to pose a risk to the British justice system, in which top advocates defend and prosecute in the criminal courts and appear for both sides in the civil courts; this would be lost for good were the State to take over control of all advocacy in the prosecution and defence of crimes.

Heather Hallett QC, chair of the Bar Council, has said:

> We still have a system whereby some of the best advocates in the world can be seen day in, day out, in our criminal and civil courts ... acting for the State and for the ordinary man and woman in the street, prosecuting one day, defending the next, acting for the injured plaintiff one week, the insurance company the next ((1998) *The Times*, 5 October).

She has expressed fears about increased State involvement in the criminal courts, through allowing crown prosecutors into the higher courts, and the creation of public defenders, and has said she was astonished by claims from the Scottish Legal Aid Board, which is running the pilot on public defenders, that other jurisdictions operated such a scheme successfully:

I wonder if they have spoken to the New Orleans Public Defender, Rick Tessier, who sued himself because he was being forced to take on three times more cases each year than the recommended maximum.

Many have asked why the English Bar was so concerned about the proposed changes – the answer is that the Bar does not wish to move to a system where, as in most countries, top lawyers specialised only in commercial work.

The Bar does not wish to became a small cadre of highly specialist commercial practitioners available to just the few. It has expressed a wish to remain as a body of specialist advocates and advisers available to all.

The question now is whether the peculiar current mix of privatisation and centralisation policies will satisfy some of the people some of the time or none of the people all of the time.

9.3   Arrest

Before considering the rights of the citizen and the law governing arrest and detention, what happens in the police station and what evidence is admissible in court, it is appropriate to look first at what the citizen can do if those rights are violated.

9.3.1   Remedies for unlawful arrest

Like other areas of law where the liberty of the subject is at stake, the law relating to arrest is founded upon the principle of *justification*. If challenged, the person who has attempted to make an arrest must justify his or her actions and show that the arrest was lawful. Failing this, the arrest will be regarded as unlawful.

There are three possible remedies:

- The person, or someone on his or her behalf, can bring proceedings of habeas corpus. This ancient prerogative writ used to begin with the words 'habeas corpus', meaning 'You must have the body'. It is addressed to the detainer and asks him to bring the detainee in question before the court at a specified date and time. The remedy protects the freedom of those who have been unlawfully detained in prison, hospital, police station or private custody. The writ is applied for from a judge in chambers and can, in emergencies, be made over the telephone. It must be issued if there is *prima facie* evidence that the detention is unlawful. As every detention is unlawful, the burden of proof is on the detainer to justify his conduct. If issued, the writ frees the detainee and thus allows him to seek other remedies (below) against the detainer.

- To use the illegality of the detention to argue that any subsequent prosecution should fail. This type of argument is very rarely successful as illegally obtained evidence is not, *ipso facto*, automatically rendered inadmissible. The House of Lords ruled in *R v Sang* (1979) that no discretion existed to exclude evidence simply because it had been illegally or improperly obtained. A court could only exclude relevant evidence where its effect would be 'unduly prejudicial'. This is reflected in s 78(1) of the Police and Criminal Evidence Act (PACE) 1984. This perhaps surprising rule was supported by the Royal Commission on Criminal Justice (although the argument there was chiefly focused on the admissibility of confession evidence). Professor Zander, however, in a note of dissent, contested the idea that a conviction could be upheld despite serious misconduct by the prosecution if there is other evidence against the convicted person. He states: 'I cannot agree. The moral foundation of the criminal justice system requires that, if the prosecution has employed foul means, the defendant must go free if he is plainly guilty ... the conviction should be quashed as an expression of the system's repugnance.'

- An action for damages for false imprisonment. In some cases, the damages for such an action would be likely to be nominal if the violation by the detainer does not have much impact on the detainee. Consider cases under this heading like *Christie v Leachinsky* (1947). Damages can, however, be considerable. In *Reynolds v Commissioner of Police for the Metropolis* (1982), a jury awarded £12,000 damages to the plaintiff. She had been arrested in the early hours in connection with charges of arson for gain, that is, that insured houses which had been set alight deliberately would be the subject of 'accidental fire' insurance claims. She was taken by car to a police station, a journey which took two and a half hours. She was detained until about 8.00 pm when she was told there was no evidence against her. She arrived home about 11.00 pm. The judge, Caulfield J, ruled that the police had no reasonable grounds for suspecting the plaintiff of having committed an arrestable offence and he directed the jury in relation to damages. The jury awarded £12,000 and the defendant's appeal against this sum, as excessive, was dismissed.

In a review of recent trends in actions against the police, Sadiq Khan and Mathew Ryder ((1998) Legal Action 16, September) comment on two recent cases in relation to damages. In *Goswell v Commissioner of Police for the Metropolis* (1998) CA, a jury awarded damages totalling £302,000 to Mr Goswell, comprising of £120,000 for assault, £12,000 for false imprisonment and £170,000 exemplary damages. On appeal, Simon Brown LJ held that £100 was an appropriate award for basic damages for false imprisonment for 20 minutes. He allowed for the fact that the unlawfulness of the detention was a consequence of a breach of s 28 of

PACE and expressed the opinion that the case 'does not in the fullest sense involve a wrongful deprivation of liberty'. Basic damages were assessed at £22,500, aggravated damages at £10,000 and £15,000 for exemplary damages. Overall, the figure was reduced from £302,000 to £47,500. In a second case against the police, *Commissioner of Police of the Metropolis v Gerald* (1998) CA, an initial award by a jury of £125,000 for assault, false imprisonment and malicious prosecution was reduced to £50,000 on appeal by the commissioner.

Apart from the question of civil remedies, it is important to remember:

- If the arrest is not lawful, there is the right to use reasonable force to resist it. This is a remedy, however, of doubtful advisability as the legality of the arrest will only be properly tested after the event in a law court. If a police officer was engaged in what the courts decide was a lawful arrest or conduct, then anyone who uses force against the officer might have been guilty of an offence of assaulting an officer in the execution of his duty, contrary to s 51 of the Police Act 1964.

- That, for our purposes in considering the consequences for an unlawfully arrested person faced with prosecution, s 78 of PACE 1984 states:

  78(1) In any proceedings, the court may refuse to allow evidence on which the prosecution proposes to rely to be given if it appears to the court that, having regard to all the circumstances, including the circumstances in which the evidence was obtained, the admission of the evidence would have such an adverse effect on the fairness of the proceedings that the court ought not to admit it.

9.3.2 General powers of arrest

In *Spicer v Holt* (1977), Lord Dilhorne stated:

Whether or not a person has been arrested depends not upon the legality of the arrest, but on whether he has been deprived of his liberty to go where he pleases.

So, a person detained by the police against his will is arrested. Whether this arrest is lawful will depend on whether the conditions for a lawful arrest have been satisfied.

Lawful arrests are those (1) under warrant; (2) without warrant at common law; or (3) without warrant under legislation.

9.3.3 Arrest under warrant

The police lay a written information on oath before a magistrate that a person 'has, or is suspected of having, committed an offence' (s 1 of the Magistrates' Courts Act 1980). The Criminal Justice Act (CJA) 1967 provides that warrants should not be issued unless the offence in question is indictable or is punishable with imprisonment.

9.3.4   Common law arrests

The only power to arrest at common law is where a breach of the peace has been committed and there are reasonable grounds for believing that it will be continued or renewed or where a breach of the peace is reasonably apprehended. Essentially, it requires *conduct* related to violence, real or threatened. A simple disturbance does not, in itself, constitute the offence unless it results from violence, real or threatened.

In 1981, two cases decided within months of each other offered definitions of a breach of the peace in an attempt to bring some clarification to an area of law that previously was in doubt. In *R v Howell* (1981), the defendant was arrested after being involved in a disturbance at a street party in the early hours of the morning. Watkins LJ who delivered the judgment of the court observed that there was a power of arrest for anticipated breach of the peace provided the arrestor had been witness to the earlier shouting and swearing of H, and therefore had reasonable grounds for belief, and did believe at the time, that the defendant's conduct, either alone or as part of a general disturbance, was likely to lead to the use of violence by the defendant or someone else in the officer's presence.

The court adopted the following definition of 'breach of the peace': it occurs:

> Wherever harm is actually done or is likely to be done to a person or in his presence his property or a person is in fear of being so harmed through an assault, an affray, a riot, unlawful assembly or other disturbance.

In the second of the two cases, *R v Chief Constable of the Devon and Cornwall Constabulary ex p Central Electricity Generating Board* (1981), Lord Denning MR suggested that breach of the peace might be considerably wider than this. This case involved a group of protesters who had occupied private land in order to prevent CEGB employees from carrying out a survey to assess its suitability for a nuclear power station. The protest was intended to be peaceful and non-violent. Lord Denning MR suggested that:

> There is a breach of the peace whenever a person who is lawfully carrying out his work is unlawfully and physically prevented by another from doing it ... If anyone unlawfully and physically obstructs the worker, by lying down or chaining himself to a rig or the like, he is guilty of a breach of the peace.

He appears to have been saying (Feldman, *Civil Liberties and Human Rights in England and Wales* (1993), pp 788–89) not that a breach of the peace is automatic in such circumstances but that, in the context of the *Central Electricity Generating Board* case, any obstruction or unlawful *resistance* by the trespasser could give the police a reasonable apprehension of a breach of the peace, in the sense of violence.

However, in cases that have followed (such as *Parkin v Norman* (1982); *Percy v DPP* (1995); and *Foulkes v Chief Constable of Merseyside Police* (1998) CA), it is the definition in *R v Howell* that has been preferred. Despite earlier doubts, argues Parpworth ('Breach of the peace: breach of human rights?' (1998) 152 JP 6, 7 November), the recent decision of the European Court of Human Rights in *Steel and Others v United Kingdom* (1998) brings clear and authoritative clarification to this area of law. This case represents 'a clear indorsement by a court largely unfamiliar with the common law concept of a breach of the peace that such a concept is in accordance with the terms of the European Convention on Human Rights'.

At common law, a constable may arrest a person for conduct which he genuinely suspects might be likely to cause a breach of the peace even on private premises where no member of the public is present: *McConnell v Chief Constable of Manchester* (1990). Although mere shouting and swearing alone will not constitute a breach of the peace, it is an offence under s 28 of the Town Police Causes Act 1847 and could lead to an arrest under s 25 of PACE (general arrest conditions). If it causes harassment, alarm or distress to a member of the public, it may constitute an offence under s 5 of the Public Order Act 1986.

9.3.5 Arrest under legislation

The right to arrest is generally governed by s 24 of PACE 1984 (as amended by s 85 of the CJPOA 1994). This provides that the police may arrest without a warrant for 'arrestable offences' and certain other offences. An arrestable offence is one for which the sentence is fixed by law (there are very few of these, life imprisonment for murder being the most common); any offence for which a person could be liable to a sentence of five years imprisonment or more; any one of the offences listed in s 24(2); any attempt to commit any of the above. The offences listed in s 24(2) involve Customs and Excise, the Official Secrets Acts, indecent assaults on women and taking a motor vehicle without authority and going equipped for stealing, and, since 1995, certain offences relating to obscenity and indecent photographs and pseudo-photographs of children.

There are differences between the powers of arrest given by PACE 1984 to police constables and ordinary citizens.

Section 24

(4)   Any person may arrest without a warrant:

(a)   anyone who is in the act of committing an arrestable offence;

(b)   anyone whom he has reasonable grounds for suspecting to be committing such an offence.

(5)   Where an arrestable offence has been committed, any person may arrest without a warrant:

  (a) anyone who is guilty of the offence;

  (b) anyone whom he has reasonable grounds for suspecting to be guilty of it.

(6)   Where a constable has reasonable grounds for suspecting that an arrestable offence has been committed, he may arrest without a warrant anyone whom he has reasonable grounds for suspecting to be guilty of the offence.

(7)   A constable may arrest without a warrant:

  (a) anyone who is about to commit an arrestable offence;

  (b) anyone whom he has reasonable grounds for suspecting to be about to commit an arrestable offence.

A police officer is given additional powers under s 25 which states:

> 25(1) Where a constable has reasonable grounds for suspecting that an offence which is not an arrestable offence has been committed or attempted, or is being committed or attempted, he may arrest the relevant person if it appears to him that service of a summons is impracticable or inappropriate because any of the general arrest conditions is satisfied.

The general arrest conditions are specified in s 25(3). They are that the officer does not know and cannot find out the suspect's name and address (or he has reasonable grounds to think that he has been given a false name or address), or has reasonable grounds for believing that an arrest is necessary to prevent someone causing physical harm to himself or someone else; or loss of or damage to property; or an offence against public decency; or an obstruction of the highway.

9.3.6   *G v DPP* (1989)

In *G v DPP* (1989), the appellant (G) with other juveniles, including a co-accused Gill, went to a police station to complain about being ejected from a public service vehicle. On being asked for their names and addresses by the officer, G, the appellant, refused to do so; some of the others gave false particulars but Gill gave his real name and address. The officer did not accept that Gill's particulars were correct because in his experience people who committed offences did not give correct details (even though the juveniles had only gone to the police station to complain about the way they had been treated on the bus). The juveniles would not accept the officers advice about their complaint and became threatening and abusive. Gill was arrested for 'disorderly behaviour in a police station' and he struggled and resisted; the appellant joined in, punching the officer and causing him to lose hold of Gill.

Both Gill and G were convicted of assaulting a police officer in the execution of his duty. The Divisional Court quashed their convictions. The offence of 'violent behaviour' or 'disorderly behaviour' under the Town Police Causes Act 1847 was not an arrestable offence. The only power the officer therefore had to arrest Gill was under s 25(3) of PACE 1984 if there were genuine doubts about Gill's name and address. But, the ground given by the officer – about people who commit offences not giving their proper name, etc – was not a proper ground because there was no evidence that the youths had committed any offences; they had gone to the police simply to complain. Therefore, in purporting to arrest Gill, the officer had not been acting in the execution of his duty and the appellant could not, therefore, have been guilty of obstructing him in the performance of such duty.

It should be noted in particular that, under s 24(6), no offence need actually have been committed. All that is required is that the police officer reasonably believes that an arrestable offence has been committed.

The differences in the powers of arrest in s 24 are based on whether an offence:

- *is being* committed: anyone may make the arrest; see s 24(4);

- *has been* committed: anyone may make the arrest; see s 24(5) or the wider powers of the police, s 24(6), who can arrest where they 'have reasonable grounds for suspecting that an arrestable offence has been committed' whether one has in fact been committed or not;

- is *about to be* committed: only a police officer may act here; see s 24(7).

PACE 1984 preserves an old common law distinction in respect of the powers of constables and private individuals when making such arrests. Where an arrest is being made *after* an offence is thought to have been committed, then PACE 1984 confers narrower rights upon the private individual than on the police officer.

9.3.7 *Walters v WH Smith & Son Ltd* (1914)

In *Walters v WH Smith & Son Ltd* (1914), the defendants had reasonably suspected that Walters had stolen books from a station bookstall. At his trial, Walters was acquitted as the jury believed his statement that he had intended to pay for the books. No crime had therefore been committed in respect of any of the books. Walters sued the defendants, *inter alia*, for false imprisonment, a tort which involves the wrongful deprivation of personal liberty in any form, as he had been arrested for a crime which had not in fact been committed. The Court of Appeal held that, to justify the arrest, a private individual had to show not only reasonable suspicion but also that the offence for which the arrested person was given over into custody had in fact been committed, even if by someone else. A police officer making an arrest in the same circumstances could legally justify the arrest by showing 'reasonable suspicion' alone without having to show that an offence was, in fact, committed.

This principle is now incorporated in s 24 of PACE 1984. It is worthy of note that the less prudent arrestor who acts against a suspect when the latter is suspected of being in the act of committing an arrestable offence (s 24(4)) can justify his or her conduct simply by showing that there were 'reasonable grounds' on which to base the suspicion. They need not show that an offence was in fact being committed. If the arrestor waits until he or she thinks the crime has been committed, then, whereas a police officer will only have to show 'reasonable grounds for suspecting that an arrestable offence has been committed' (s 24(6)), a citizen can only justify his behaviour if an offence 'has been committed' (s 24(5)).

9.3.8 *R v Self* (1992)

This analysis is supported by the decision of *R v Self* (1992). The defendant was seen by a store detective in Woolworths to pick up a bar of chocolate and leave the store without paying. The detective followed him out into the street and, with the assistance of a member of the public, she arrested the suspect under the powers of s 24(5) of PACE 1984. The suspect resisted the arrest and assaulted both his arrestors. He was subsequently charged with theft of the chocolate and with offences of assault with intent to resist lawful apprehension or detainer, contrary to s 38 of the Offences Against the Person Act 1861. At his trial, he was acquitted of theft (apparently for lack of *mens rea*) but convicted of the assaults. These convictions were quashed by the Court of Appeal on the grounds that, as the arrest had not been lawful, he was entitled to resist it. The power of arrest conferred upon a citizen (s 24(5)) in circumstances where an offence is thought to *have been committed*, only applies when an offence *has* been committed, and as the jury decided that Mr Self had not committed any offence, there was no power to arrest him.

9.3.9 *John Lewis & Co v Tims* (1952)

In *John Lewis & Co v Tims* (1952), Mrs Tims and her daughter were arrested by store detectives for shoplifting four calendars from the appellant's Oxford Street store. It was a regulation of the store that only a managing director or a general manager was authorised to institute any prosecution. After being arrested, Mrs Tims and her daughter were taken to the office of the chief store detective. They were detained there until a chief detective and a manager arrived to give instructions whether to prosecute. They were eventually handed over to police custody within an hour of arrest. In a claim by Mrs Tims for false imprisonment, she alleged that the detectives were obliged to give her into the custody of the police immediately upon arrest. The House of

Lords held that the delay was reasonable in the circumstances as there were advantages in refusing to give private detectives a 'free hand' and leaving the determination of such an important question as whether to prosecute to a superior official.

9.3.10 What is the meaning of 'reasonable grounds for suspecting'?

Many of the powers of the police in relation to arrest, search and seizure are founded upon the presence of reasonable 'suspicion', 'cause' or 'belief' in a state of affairs, usually that a suspect is involved actually or potentially in a crime.

In *Castorina v Chief Constable of Surrey* (1988), detectives reasonably concluded that the burglary of a company's premises was an 'inside job'. The managing director told them that she had recently dismissed someone (the plaintiff) although she did not think it would have been her, and that the documents taken would be useful to someone with a grudge. The detectives interviewed the plaintiff, having found out that she had no criminal record, and arrested her under s 2(4) of the Criminal Law Act 1967 (which has now been replaced by s 24(6) of PACE 1984). She was detained at the police station for almost four hours, interrogated and then released without charge. On a claim for damages for wrongful arrest and detention, a jury awarded her £4,500. The trial judge held that the officers had had a *prima facie* case for suspicion but that the arrest was premature. He had defined 'reasonable cause' (which the officers would have needed to show they had when they arrested the plaintiff) as 'honest belief founded upon reasonable suspicion leading an ordinary cautious man to the conclusion that the person arrested was guilty of the offence'. He said an ordinary man would have sought more information from the suspect, including an explanation for any grudge on her part. In this, he relied on the *dicta* of Scott LJ in *Dumbell v Roberts* (1944), that the principle that every man was presumed innocent until proved guilty also applied to arrests. The Court of Appeal allowed an appeal by the Chief Constable. The court held that the trial judge had used too severe a test in judging the officer's conduct.

Purchas LJ said that the test of 'reasonable cause' was objective and, therefore, the trial judge was wrong to have focused attention on whether the officers had 'an honest belief'. The question was whether the officer had had reasonable grounds to suspect the woman of the offence. There was sufficient evidence that the officer had had sufficient reason to suspect her.

Woolf LJ thought there were three things to consider in cases where an arrest is alleged to be unlawful:

- did the arresting officer suspect that the person who was arrested had committed the offence? This was a matter of fact about the officer's state of mind;

- if the answer to the first question is yes, then was there reasonable proof of that suspicion? This is a simple objective matter to be determined by the judge;

- if the answers to the first two questions are both yes, then the officer did have a discretion to arrest and the question then was whether he had exercised his discretion according to *Wednesbury* principles of reasonableness.

This case hinged on the second point and, on the facts, the Chief Constable should succeed on the appeal.

Note: The *Wednesbury* principles come from *Associated Provincial Picture Houses Ltd v Wednesbury Corporation* (1948). Lord Greene MR laid down principles to determine when the decision made by a public authority could be regarded as so perverse or unreasonable that the courts would be justified in overturning that decision. The case actually concerned whether a condition imposed by a local authority on cinemas operating on Sundays was reasonable. Lord Greene MR said:

> ... a person entrusted with a discretion must, so to speak, direct himself properly in law. He must call his own attention to matters which he is bound to consider. He must exclude from his consideration matters which are irrelevant to what he has to consider. If he does not obey those rules, he may be truly said, and often is said, to be acting 'unreasonably'.

Sir Frederick Lawton, the third judge in the Court of Appeal in *Castorina*, agreed. The facts on which 'reasonable cause' was said to have been founded did not have to be such as to lead an ordinary cautious man to conclude that the person arrested *was* guilty of the offence. It was enough if they could lead an ordinary person to *suspect* that he was guilty.

This allows quite a latitude to the police. Additionally, the House of Lords has decided in *Holgate-Mohammed v Duke* (1984) that, where a police officer reasonably suspects an individual of having committed an arrestable offence, he may arrest that person with a view to questioning her at the police station. His decision can only be challenged on *Wednesbury* principles if he acted improperly by taking something irrelevant into account. The police arrested a former lodger for theft of jewellery from the house where she had lived in order to question her at the police station. The trial judge awarded her £1,000 damages for false imprisonment. The Court of Appeal set aside the award and the decision was upheld by the House of Lords. The following passage from a judgment in the Court of Appeal in *Holgate-Mohammed* was approved in the House of Lords:

> As to the proposition that there were other things which [the police officer] might have done. No doubt there were other things which he might have done first. He might have obtained a statement from her otherwise than under arrest to see how far he could get. He might have obtained a specimen of her

handwriting and sent that off for forensic examination against a specimen of the writing of the person who had obtained the money by selling the stolen jewellery, which happened to exist in the case. All those things he might have done. He might have carried out finger print investigations if he had first obtained a print from the plaintiff. But, the fact that there were other things which he might have done does not, in my judgment, make that which he did do into an unreasonable exercise of the power of arrest if what he did do, namely, to arrest, was within the range of reasonable choices open to him.

It has been forcefully contended, however, that, in some circumstances, a failure to make inquiries before making an arrest could show that there were insufficient grounds for the arrest. See Clayton and Tomlinson, 'Arrest and reasonable grounds for suspicion' (1988) 32 Law Soc Gazette 22, 7 September.

Note, however, that the powers are *discretionary*. See *Simpson v Chief Constable of South Yorkshire Police* (1991).

9.3.11 Detention short of arrest

For there to be an arrest, the arrestor must regard his action as an arrest. If he simply detains someone to question him without any thought of arrest, the action will be unlawful. It is often reported in criminal investigations that a person is 'helping police with their inquiries'. In *R v Lemsatef* (1977), Lawton LJ said:

> It must be clearly understood that neither customs officers nor police officers have any right to detain somebody for the purposes of getting them to help with their inquiries.

There is no police power (except under the Prevention of Terrorism (Temporary Provisions) Act 1989) to detain someone against his or her will in order to make inquiries about that person. See, also, *Franchiosy* (1979). This is confirmed by s 29 of PACE 1984 which states that, where someone attends a police station 'for the purpose of assisting with an investigation', he is entitled to leave at any time unless placed under arrest. He must be informed at once that he is under arrest 'if a decision is taken by a constable to prevent him from leaving at will'. There is, however, no legal duty on the police to inform anyone whom they invite to the station to help with their inquiries that he or she may go.

9.3.12 Suspects stopped in the street

In *Kenlin v Gardiner* (1967), a police officer took hold of the arm of a boy he wanted to question about the latter's suspicious conduct. The boy did not believe the man was a policeman, despite having been shown a warrant card, and punched the officer in order to escape. The other boy behaved similarly and their convictions for assaulting an officer in the execution of his duty were quashed by the Divisional Court. The court held that the boys were entitled to act as they did in self-defence as the officer's conduct in trying to physically apprehend them had not been legal. There is no legal power of detention short of arrest. As Lawton LJ observed in *R v Lemsatef* (1977) (see 9.3.11, above), the police do not have any powers to detain somebody 'for the purposes of getting them to help with their inquiries'.

It is important, however, to examine the precise circumstances of the detaining officer's conduct because there are cases to suggest that if what the officer does amounts to only a *de minimis* interference with the citizen's liberty, then forceful 'self-defence' by the citizen will not be justified. In *Donnelly v Jackman* (1970), an officer approached a suspect to ask some questions. The suspect ignored the request and walked away from the officer. The officer followed and made further requests for the suspect to stop and talk. He tapped the suspect on the shoulder and the suspect reciprocated by tapping the officer on the shoulder and saying 'Now we are even, copper'. The officer tapped the suspect on the shoulder again which was replied to with a forceful punch. Mr Donnelly's conviction was upheld and the decision in *Kenlin v Gardiner* was distinguished as, in the earlier case, the officers had actually taken hold of the boys and detained them. The court stated that 'it is not every trivial interference with a citizen's liberty that amounts to a course of conduct sufficient to take the officer out of the course of his duties'.

In *Bentley v Brudzinski* (1982), the facts were very close to those in question. A constable stopped two men who had been running barefoot down a street in the early hours. He questioned them about a stolen vehicle, as they fitted the description of suspects in an earlier incident. They waited for about 10 minutes while the officer checked their details over a radio and then they began to leave. Another constable, who had just arrived on the scene, then said 'Just a minute' and put his hand on the defendant's shoulder. The defendant then punched that officer in the face. Unlike the decision in *Donnelly v Jackman*, the Divisional Court held, here, that the officer's conduct was more than a trivial interference with the citizen's liberty and amounted to an unlawful attempt to stop and detain him. The respondent was thus not guilty of assaulting an officer in the execution of his duty.

Note, also, that a person may be arrested for being silent or misleading under s 25 of PACE 1984 if the officer has reasonable doubts about the suspect's name and address or whether the summons procedure can be used at the address given.

9.3.13 Stop and search

PACE 1984 gives the police power to search 'any person or vehicle' and to detain either for the purpose of such a search (s 1(2)). A constable may not conduct such a search 'unless he has reasonable grounds for suspecting that he will find stolen or prohibited articles' (s 1(3)). Any such item found during the search can be seized (s 1(6)). An article is 'prohibited' if it is either an offensive weapon or it is 'made or adapted for use in the course of or in connection with burglary, theft, taking a motor vehicle without authority or obtaining property by deception or is intended by the person having it with him for such use by him or by some other person' (s 1(7)). An offensive weapon is defined as meaning 'any article made or adapted for use for causing injury to persons or intended by the person having it with him for such use by him or by some other person' (s 1(9)). This definition is taken from the Prevention of Crime Act 1953. It has two categories: things that are offensive weapons *per se* (that is, in themselves), like a baton with a nail through the end or knuckle-dusters, and things that are not offensive weapons, like a spanner, but which are intended to be used as such. If the item is in the first category, then the prosecution need prove only that the defendant had it with him to put the onus onto the accused to show that he had a lawful excuse. Stop and search powers can now also be exercised under s 8A to items covered by s 139 of the Criminal Justice Act 1988. These items are any article which has a blade or is sharply pointed except folding pocket knives with a blade of less than three inches. It is an offence to possess such items without good reason or lawful authority, the onus of proof being on the defendant. The courts will not accept the carrying of offensive weapons for generalised self-defence unless there is some immediate, identifiable threat (Broadbent, 'Offensive weapons and the Criminal Justice Act' (1989) Law Soc Gazette, 12 July).

Under s 2 of PACE 1984, a police officer who proposes to carry out a stop and search must state his name and police station, and the purpose of the search. A plain clothes officer must also produce documentary evidence that he is a police officer. The officer must also give the grounds for the search. Such street searches must be limited to outer clothing; the searched person cannot be required to remove any article of clothing other than a jacket, outer clothes or gloves. The officer is required to make a record of the search immediately, or as soon as is reasonably practicable afterwards (s 3). The record of the search should include the object of the search, the grounds of the search and its result (s 3). A failure to give grounds as required by s 2(3)(c) will render the search unlawful (*R v Fennelley* (1989)).

9.3.14 The Code of Practice for the exercise of statutory powers of stop and search

In view of the wide powers vested in the police in the exercise of stop and search, Code A has been revised to reflect the new legislation and to clarify how searches under stop and search powers are to be conducted. The revised Code came into effect on 1 March 1999 and supercedes the edition of Code A which came into effect on 15 May 1997.

The Code (1AA) restates the guidance under the previous edition and emphasises:

> It is important to ensure that the powers of stop and search are used responsibly by those who exercise them and those who authorise their use ... It is also particularly important to ensure that any person searched is treated courteously and considerately.

A person can be stopped and questioned prior to a search to discover whether the suspicion that a search is required is well founded but a person cannot be stopped in order to find grounds for a search (Code A, para 2.1). There must be a suspicion that the suspect was carrying 'articles unlawfully obtained or possessed' (para 1.5). The reasonable suspicion must be based on objective grounds (para 1.6):

> Whether reasonable grounds for suspicion exist will depend on the circumstances in each case, but there must be some objective basis for it. An officer will need to consider the nature of the article suspected of being carried in the context of other factors, such as, the time and place, and the behaviour of the person concerned or those with him.

The Code goes on to say that reasonable suspicion may exist where information has been received like a description of an article being carried or where a person is seen acting 'covertly or warily or attempting to hide something' or where a person is seen carrying something at an unusual time or in a place where a number of burglaries or thefts are known to have taken place recently.

Reasonable suspicion can never be supported on the basis of personal factors alone. For example, 'a person's colour, age hairstyle or manner of dress, or the fact that he is known to have a previous conviction for possession of an unlawful article, cannot be used alone or in combination with each other as the sole basis on which to search that person (para 1.7). The Code was amended in 1997 to provide some clarification of police powers in relation to groups and gangs who habitually carry knives or weapons or controlled drugs. The additional section (now para 1.7AA), states that, 'where there is reliable information or intelligence that members of a group or gang who habitually carry knives unlawfully or weapons or controlled drugs and wear a distinctive item of clothing or other means of identification to indicate membership of it, the members may be identified by means of that distinctive item of clothing or other means of identification'. Other means of identification might include jewellery, insignias, tattoos or other features which are known to identify members of the particular gang or group (Note 1H).

It is important to note that PACE 1984 does not apply to 'voluntary searches'. If this is given a wide interpretation, then many of the safeguards in the Act are rendered useless. Research by Dixon, Coleman and Bottomley ((1990) 17 JLS 345) has shown that the safeguards are being undermined by many police forces. If the police can get the suspect to *consent* to the search, then the search is not being made under a power but merely by agreement. Hence, if the search is not made by virtue of s 1 of PACE 1984, then Code A does not apply. The Act and, therefore, the Code would only apply if the suspect did not consent to the search so that the officer had to resort to his powers under the Act by telling the suspect that, despite the lack of consent, the officer was empowered by PACE 1984 to search the suspect. Some of the researchers' observations are controversial; they state, for instance:

> 'Consent', here, frequently consists of acquiescence based on ignorance. Many people assume that the officer who says 'What have you got in your pockets?' or 'Let's have a look in your bag' has a power to search. We asked officers how often people whom they searched knew their rights: 79% said rarely or never. Such a lack of knowledge must mean that their 'consent' has little substance. Familiar strategies are used to deal with those who do raise questions about the authority to search. As a sergeant put it: 'A lot of people are not quite certain that they have the right to say no. And then we, sort of, bamboozle them into allowing us to search.' Such 'bamboozling' is done by appealing to the willingness of the innocent to be searched, by threatening arrest, or by claiming the authority of fictional powers.

See 'Consent and legal regulation of policing' (1990) 17 JLS 345.

Code A states, in relation to the ability of an officer to search a person in the street with his consent where no search power exists, that:

> In these circumstances, an officer should always make it clear that he is seeking the consent of the person concerned to the search being carried out by telling the person that he need not consent and that, without his consent, he will not be searched (para 1D(b)).

The new Code, in addition to clarifying the procedural requirements and conduct of all searches, makes important restrictions regarding searches of non-arrested suspects in police vans. It prohibits searches in police vans that involve exposure of intimate parts of the body. Any search involving the removal of more than an outer coat, jacket, gloves, headgear or footwear, or any other item concealing identity, may only be made by an officer of the same sex as the person searched and may not be made in the presence of anyone of the opposite sex unless the person being searched specifically requests it. All searches involving exposure of intimate parts of the body shall be conducted in accordance with para 11 of Annex A to Code C (para 3.5). Every reasonable effort must be made to reduce to the minimum the embarrassment that a person being searched may experience (para 3.1).

The revised Code A includes instructions and guidance where there may be religious sensitivities about asking someone to remove a face covering using s 60 (as amended by s 25 of the Crime and Disorder Act 1998). For example, in the case of a Muslim woman wearing a face covering for religious purposes, the officer should permit the item to be removed out of public view. Where practicable, the item should be removed in the presence of an officer of the same sex as the person and out of sight of anyone of the opposite sex. In all cases, the officer must reasonably believe that the person is wearing the item in question *wholly or mainly* to conceal his or her identity (para 1AA).

Where there may be religious sensitivities about asking someone to remove headgear using a power under s 13A or 13B of the Prevention of Terrorism (Temporary Provisions) Act 1989, the police officer should offer to carry out the search out of public view (for example, in a police van or police station if there is one nearby) (para 3C).

9.3.15 Search of arrested persons

The power to search after arrest somewhere other than at the police station is governed by s 32 of PACE 1984 (searches of detained persons are dealt with by s 54 and Code C, para 4). Section 32(1) allows the police to search someone arrested where there are grounds for believing that he may present a danger to himself or to others; s 32(2) allows a search for anything that might be used to effect an escape or which might be evidence relating to any offence. Additionally, s 32(2)(b) gives the police power to enter and search premises in which he was when arrested, or immediately before he was arrested, for evidence relating to the offence for which he was arrested. Unlike the power to search under s 18, this is not limited to arrestable offences, nor do the searched premises need to be occupied or controlled by him. Such searches, however, are only lawful where there are reasonable grounds for believing that the search might find something for which a search is permitted under s 18(5) and (6). Random or automatic searching is not lawful. Section 32(4) states that a person searched in public cannot be required to take off more than outer garments like coats, jackets and gloves.

9.3.16 Search on detention

Section 54 of PACE 1984 and Code C, para 4.1 require the custody officer (a particular officer with special responsibilities in police stations) to take charge of the process of searching detainees. He must make sure a record is made of all the suspect's property unless he is to be detained for only a short time and not put in a cell. The person detained can be searched to enable this to happen but the custody officer needs to believe it to be necessary; it is not an automatic right (s 54(6)). Anything the suspect has can be seized and retained although clothes and personal effects can only be kept if the custody officer *believes* that the detained person *may* use them to escape, interfere with evidence, or cause damage or injury to himself, to others or to property. The police are not permitted, however, to retain anything protected by legal professional privilege, that is, private legal communications between the suspect and his or her legal adviser. The police can also seize things they *reasonably believe* to be evidence of an offence. A search must be carried out by a constable and only one who is the same sex as the person to be searched. Strip searches can only be made where the custody officer thinks it necessary to get some item that the suspect would not be allowed to keep; the officer must make a record of the reason for the search and its result.

9.3.17 Procedure on arrest

At common law (that is, before PACE 1984), it was necessary for the arrestor to make it clear to the arrestee that he was under compulsion either (a) by physical means, such as, taking him by the arm, or (b) by telling him, orally, that he was under compulsion. There was a danger, where words alone were used, that they might not be clear enough. Consider *Alderson v Booth* (1969). Following a positive breathalyser test, the officer said to the defendant: 'I shall have to ask you to come back to the station for further tests.' D did accompany the officer to the station. Lawful arrest was a condition precedent to anyone being convicted of driving with excess alcohol in their blood. At his trial, the defendant said he had not been arrested. He was acquitted and the prosecution appeal failed. Compulsion is a necessary element of arrest and the magistrates were not convinced that it was present in this case. The Divisional Court was not prepared to contradict the factual finding of the magistrates.

Additionally, where words alone were used, it was necessary for the arrestee to accede to the detention. There was no arrest where the arrestor said 'I arrest you' and the arrestee ran off before he could be touched (see *Sandon v Jervis* (1859)).

These principles remain good law after PACE 1984; see, for example, *Nichols v Bulman* (1985).

According to s 28(3) of PACE 1984, no arrest is lawful unless the arrestee is informed of the ground for the arrest at the time of, or as soon as reasonably practicable after, the arrest. Where a person is arrested by a constable, this applies (s 28(4)) regardless of whether the ground for the arrest is obvious.

The reasons for this rule were well put by Viscount Simon in *Christie v Leachinsky* (1947):

> ... a person is *prima facie* entitled to personal freedom [and] should know why for the time being his personal freedom is being interfered with ... No one, I think, would approve of a situation in which when the person arrested asked for the reason, the policeman replied 'that has nothing to do with you: come along with me' ... And there are practical considerations ... If the charge ... is then and there made known to him, he has the opportunity of giving an explanation of any misunderstanding or of calling attention to other persons for whom he may have been mistaken, with the result that further inquiries may save him from the consequences of false accusation ...

An arrest, however, becomes lawful once the ground is given. In *Lewis v Chief Constable of the South Wales Constabulary* (1991), the officers had told the plaintiffs of the fact of arrest but delayed telling them the grounds for 10 minutes in one case and 23 minutes in the other. The Court of Appeal said that arrest was not a legal concept but arose factually from the deprivation of a person's liberty. It was also a continuing act and therefore what had begun as an unlawful arrest could become a lawful arrest. The remedy for the plaintiffs was the damages they had been awarded for the 10 minutes and 23 minutes of illegality: £200 each.

In *DPP v Hawkins* (1988), the Divisional Court held that an exception to the rule requiring information to be given to the arrestee exists where the defendant makes it impossible (for example, by his violent conduct) for the officer to communicate the reasons for the arrest to him. In that situation, the arrest is lawful, and remains lawful until such a time as the reasons should have been given. The fact that the reasons were not given then does not invalidate the original arrest. The arrest would only become unlawful from the moment when the reasons for it should have been given to the arrested person.

In *R v Telfer* (1976), a police officer knew that the defendant was wanted for questioning about certain burglaries. The officer checked that the suspect was wanted but not for which particular burglaries. He then stopped the defendant and asked him to come back to the station; when the defendant refused, he was arrested 'on suspicion of burglary'. The arrest was held to be unlawful. The person arrested was entitled to know the particular burglary of which he was suspected.

In *Nicholas v Parsonage* (1987), N was seen riding a bicycle without holding the handlebars by two police officers. They told him twice to hold the bars and then he did so. When they drove off, N raised two fingers. They then stopped N and PC Parsonage asked him for his name, telling him it was required as he had been riding his bicycle in a dangerous manner. N refused. P then informed him of his powers under PACE 1984 and requested N's name and address. N again refused. P then arrested him for failing to give his name and address. N attempted to ride off and a struggle ensued. N was subsequently convicted of, *inter alia*, assaulting a police officer in the execution of his duty contrary to s 51(1) of the Police Act 1964. His appeal was dismissed by the Divisional Court which held that the arrest under s 25 of PACE 1984 had been lawful as a constable exercising power under s 25(3) was not required to say why he wanted the suspect's name and address. Nicholas had been adequately informed of the ground of arrest under s 28(3) of PACE 1984. N was not arrested for failing to give his name and address, he was arrested because, having committed the minor offence of 'riding in a dangerous manner', it then became necessary to arrest him because the conditions in s 25(3)(a) and (c) were satisfied, namely, that an arrest for a minor offence is possible where the officer believes that the service of a summons is impracticable because he has not been given a proper name and address.

As to the extent of the explanation that has to be given on arrest under s 28 of PACE 1984, *Christie v Leachinsky* (above) was considered in *R v Chalkley and Jeffries* (1998) CA. In this case, an arrest for an alleged credit card fraud was made for an ulterior motive, namely, to place recording equipment in the arrested defendant's house in order to record the defendants' discussions about planned robberies. The Court of Appeal held that, as there were reasonable grounds for suspecting the arrested defendant's involvement in the credit card frauds, and given that the police had informed him of this, the trial judge had been correct to rule that the arrest was lawful notwithstanding the ulterior motive.

Is it necessary for an arrestor to indicate to the arrestee the grounds on which his 'reasonable suspicion' was based? In *Geldberg v Miller* (1961), the appellant parked his car outside a restaurant in London while he had a meal. He was asked by police officers to move the car. He refused, preferring to finish his meal first. On being told that the police would remove the car, he removed the rotor arm from the distributor mechanism. He also refused to give his name and address or show his driving licence and certificate of insurance. He was arrested by one of the officers for 'obstructing him in the execution of his duty by refusing to move his car and refusing his name and address'. There was no power to arrest for obstruction of the police as no actual or apprehended breach of the peace was involved. The court held, however, that the arrest was valid for 'obstructing the thoroughfare', an offence under s 56(6) of the Metropolitan Police Act 1839, an offence the officer had not mentioned. Lord Parker CJ said:

> In my judgment, what the appellant knew and what he was told was ample to fulfil the obligation as to what should be done at the time of an arrest without warrant.

An arrest will be unlawful, however, where the reasons given point to an offence for which there is no power of arrest (or for which there is only qualified power of arrest) and it is clear that no other reasons were present to the mind of the officer: *Edwards v DPP* (1993) DC. This principle was confirmed in *Mullady v DPP* (1997) DC. A police officer arrested M for 'obstruction', an offence with the power of arrest only if the defendant's conduct amounted to a breach of the peace (for which there is a common law power of arrest) or if one of the general arrest conditions as set out in s 25 is satisfied. The police argued that the officer could have arrested M for a breach of the peace and merely gave the wrong reason. The Divisional Court held that the officer had acted unlawfully and that it would be wrong for the justices to go behind the reason given and infer that the reason for the arrest was another lawful reason.

In some circumstances, the court may infer a lawful reason for an arrest if the circumstantial evidence points clearly to a lawful reason (*Brookman v DPP* (1997) DC). However, if there is insufficient evidence to determine whether a lawful or unlawful reason was given for the arrest, then the police will fail to show that the arrest was lawful (*Clarke v DPP* (1998) DC). The issue seems to be what degree of evidence is necessary to allow the court to infer a lawful reason for arrest (see, further, Khan and Ryder (1998) Legal Action 16, September).

9.3.18 Police powers under s 60 of the Criminal Justice and Public Order Act 1994

Section 60 of the CJPOA 1994 provides for a new stop and search power in anticipation of violence, and was introduced to deal with violent conduct, especially by groups of young men. The section provides that, where authorisation for its use has been granted, a constable in uniform may:

60(4) (a) stop any pedestrian and search him or anything carried by him for offensive weapons or dangerous instruments;

(b) stop any vehicle and search it, its driver and any passenger for offensive weapons or dangerous instruments.

60(5) A constable may, in the exercise of those powers, stop any person or vehicle and make any search he thinks fit whether or not he has any grounds for suspecting that the person or vehicle is carrying any weapons or articles of that kind.

(6) If, in the course of such a search under this section, a constable discovers a dangerous instrument or an article which he has reasonable grounds for suspecting to be an offensive weapon, he may seize it.

The authorisation required by s 60 must be given by a police officer of, or above, the rank of superintendent (or a chief inspector or inspector where such an officer reasonably believes that incidents involving serious violence are imminent and no superintendent is available). The authorising officer must reasonably believe that:

(a) incidents involving serious violence may take place in any locality in his area; and

(b) it is expedient to grant an authorisation to prevent their occurrence.

Such an authorisation, which must be in writing, will permit the exercise of stop and search powers within that locality for a period up to 24 hours. The authorisation could conceivably be given in fear of a single incident, even though the CJPOA 1994 requires fear of 'incidents'. This is because s 6 of the Interpretation Act 1978 states that the plural includes the singular unless a contrary intention is shown.

There are several aspects of this section which have been drafted in what appears to be a deliberately vague way. We shall therefore have to wait and see how the courts interpret certain words in the CJPOA 1994. 'Serious violence' is not defined and this will be very much within the judgment of the senior officer concerned, provided, of course, that his view is based upon reasonable belief. Richard Card and Richard Ward, in a commentary on the Act (*The Criminal Justice and Public Order Act 1994* (1994)), have noted that the dictionary includes 'force against property' as within the definition of violence, and this may well become an important matter for decision by the courts.

The word 'locality' is left undefined in the CJPOA 1994. It could be an area outside a particular club or pub, or it might extend to a large estate. The courts have the power to declare an authorisation invalid because of an over expansive geographical area; they are unlikely to substitute their own view for that of the operational officer.

9.3.19 Other aspects of s 60 of the Criminal Justice and Public Order Act 1994

'Offensive weapon' (s 60(4), (11)) means the same as for s 1(9) of PACE 1984. It is (a) any article made or adapted for use for causing injury to persons; or (b) intended by the person having it with him for such use by him or some other person. There is no provision for reasonable excuse for the possession of such weapons.

'Dangerous instruments' (s 60(4)) will often be caught within the definition of offensive weapons but the definition extends to cover instruments which have a blade or are sharply pointed (s 60(11)).

The authorising officer must reasonably believe that it is 'expedient' to give an authorisation in order to prevent the occurrence of incidents of serious violence. Thus, the authorisation need not be the only way in which such incidents may be prevented. Various policing factors may have to be balanced including the ability of the police force to remain effective and efficient if it were to use other methods.

There is no specification about where the stop and search power may be exercised (unlike s 1 of PACE 1984) but a draft annex to Code of Practice A suggests that the power is exercisable wherever there is public access even of just a practical (rather than legal) nature. Thus, someone could not evade the powers being exercised on himself by jumping off the highway into a front garden.

There is no power to detain especially conferred on officers by s 60 in order to carry out the search but it does make failure to stop a summary offence. As it stands, there is nothing in s 60 which would permit an officer to use any force to conduct a non-consensual search. It is possible that the courts will imply such a power. When conducting the search, the officer must give the suspect his or her name, the police station to which he or she is attached, the authorisation for the search, and the reason for the search. It seems that failure to comply with these conditions will make the search unlawful (see *Fennelley* (1989), a case where the defendant was not told why he was stopped, searched and arrested in the street. Evidence from the search, some jewellery, was excluded at the trial. Evidence of drugs found on him at the police station was also excluded).

The scope of s 60 and police powers to stop and search are being incrementally extended through various Acts of Parliament. They include the following. Section 8 of the Knives Act 1997 amended s 60 to allow *initial* authorisations by an inspector or above thus obviating the need for an officer of at least the rank of superintendent; s 60(1)(b) extends the criteria under which an authorising officer may invoke this power to include reasonable belief that incidents involving serious violence may take place or that such instruments of weapons are being carried in a particular area; and s 60(3) provides that authorisations may be extended up to 24 hours instead of six although only an officer of the rank of superintendent or above may do this. A new sub-s 11A was inserted under s 60 by s 8 of the Knives Act 1997 and states that, 'for the purposes of this section, a person carries a dangerous instrument or an offensive weapon if he has it in his possession'.

'Offensive weapon' means the same as for s 1(9) of PACE 1984 (see 9.3.13, above). 'Dangerous instruments' means instruments which have a blade or are sharply pointed.

These amendments are intended to deal with anticipated violence in situations where gangs or persons may be 'tooled-up' and travelling through various police areas en route to an intended scene of confrontation. Thus, the power may be invoked even where the actual anticipated violence is believed may occur in another police jurisdiction, for example, by football hooligans travelling to and from matches.

Further amendments to s 60 have recently been made under the Crime and Disorder Act (CDA) 1998. This is mainly to deal with the problem of troublemakers deliberately wearing facial coverings to conceal their identities especially when the police are using CCTV cameras. Section 25 of the CDA 1998 inserts a new sub-s 4A under s 60 which confers a power on any constable in uniform to demand the removal of, or seize, face coverings where an authority has been given under s 60 if the officer reasonably believes that the face covering is being worn or is intended to be used to conceal a person's identity. Section 25 also extends s 60(8) and makes it a summary offence if a person fails to stop or to stop a vehicle or to remove an item worn by him when required by the police in the exercise of their powers under s 60. This is punishable by a term of imprisonment not exceeding one month and/or a maximum fine of £1,000. Section 60A inserted by s 26 of the CDA 1998 provides that things seized under s 60 may be retained in accordance with regulations made by the Secretary of State. (See Jason-Lloyd (1998) 162 JP 836, 24 October.)

9.3.20 Accountability and s 60 of the Criminal Justice and Public Order Act 1994

There are dangers that the powers under s 60 could be misused, as no reasonable suspicion is required and the requirements for authorisation are rather nebulous.

The safeguards against misuse include the fact that the admissibility of evidence gained through the use of a dubious stop and search event may be in doubt if there are serious breaches of the revised Code A. Someone charged with obstructing a police officer in the exercise of duty may raise breaches of the Code in defence. Unlawful search or seizure may also provide a basis for an application for exclusion of evidence thus obtained under s 78 of PACE 1984.

As the police have a common law power to take whatever action is necessary in order to prevent an imminent breach of the peace (*Moss v Mclachlan* (1985)), then, even if a challenge to the use of a s 60 power is technically successful, the police conduct in question may often be thus justified.

9.3.21 Section 81 of the Criminal Justice and Public Order Act 1994

Section 81 of CJPOA 1994 creates a new power of stop and search of persons and vehicles where it is expedient to do so to prevent certain acts of terrorism. This was a response to various acts of terrorism involving concealed bombs, and car bombs in 1993. The section inserts a new section (13A) into the Prevention of Terrorism (Temporary Provisions) Act 1989.

Any officer of, or above, the rank of commander or assistant chief constable may authorise a stop and search where 'it appears to him to be expedient to do so' in order to prevent acts of terrorism connected with Northern Ireland or international terrorism. There is no requirement for reasonable suspicion.

If authorisation is granted, the powers of stop and search are exercisable at any place within the area of the senior officer's force, or within a locality.

If authorisation is given, pursuant to s 13A, it confers on any police officer in uniform the power:

(a) to stop any vehicle;

(b) to search any vehicle, its driver or any passenger for articles of any kind which could be used for a purpose connected with the commission, preparation or instigation of acts of terrorism connected with the affairs of Northern Ireland or acts of international terrorism;

(c) to stop any pedestrian and search anything carried by him [but not him] for articles of a kind which could be so used.

This is thus a very wide power, and is subject to few restraints. The search could be for virtually anything, and it need not be based upon a reasonable suspicion. This power was given in the face of progressively more devastating acts of terrorism and an apparent inability of the State to deal with the threat. Any vehicle may be stopped under the section, whether or not the officer has grounds for suspecting that it contains items to be used in terrorism. It is thus unlike the power conferred under s 1 of PACE 1984 which does, to be valid, require a reasonable suspicion that the vehicle contains a proscribed item.

The powers of stop and search can only be exercised for a period specified in the authorisation, and this can be as long as 28 days (s 13A(1)). A person failing to stop for such a check, or who wilfully obstructs an officer in the exercise of these powers, is guilty of an offence (s 13A(6)).

9.3.22 The use of force to effect an arrest

The use of force by a member of the public when arresting someone is governed by the Criminal Law Act 1967. This states:

3   Use of force in making an arrest, etc

>   (1)   A person may use such force as is reasonable in the circumstances in the prevention of crime, or in effecting or assisting in the lawful arrest of offenders or suspected offenders or of persons unlawfully at large.

Reasonable force will generally mean the minimum necessary to effect an arrest.

The use of force by police officers is governed by PACE 1984. This states:

117   Power of constable to use reasonable force

Where any provision of this Act:

>   (a)   confers a power on a constable; and

>   (b)   does not provide that the power may only be exercised with the consent of some person, other than a police officer,

the officer may use reasonable force, if necessary, in the exercise of the power.

9.3.23 Duties after arrest

A person arrested by a constable, or handed over to one, must be taken to a police station as soon as is 'practicable', unless his presence elsewhere is 'necessary in order to carry out such investigations as is reasonable to carry out immediately' (s 30(1), (10)). Where a citizen makes an arrest, he 'must, as soon as he reasonably can, hand the man over to a constable or take him to the police station or take him before a magistrate', *per* Lord Denning in *Dallison v Caffery* (1965). There is no requirement, however, that this be carried out immediately: *John Lewis & Co v Tims* (1952) (see 9.3.9, above).

9.4 Entry, search and seizure

A number of statutes give police officers the powers to stop and search people and vehicles where no arrest has been made. See, for example, s 23(2) of the Misuse of Drugs Act 1971. Here, we shall concentrate on the powers given under ss 1 and 2 of PACE 1984 which relate to stolen goods, offensive weapons and articles for use in Theft Act offences. These provisions are supplemented by two new ones in s 81(1) of the Criminal Justice Public Order Act 1994 and s 60 of the 1994 Act (as amended by s 8 of the Knives Act 1997 and ss 25–27 of the Crime and Disorder Act 1998). All are, in turn, supplemented by provisions in the new Code of Practice A issued under PACE 1984, effective from 1 March 1999.

Note: PACE 1984 came into force on 1 January 1986. The Act was accompanied by four Codes of Practice: Code A on Stop and Search; Code B on Search of Premises; Code C on Detention, Questioning and Treatment of Persons in Custody; and Code D on Identification. A fifth, Code E on Tape-recording of Interviews, was added later. The Codes were produced after consultation with a wide range of interested groups and people and were debated and approved by both Houses of Parliament before being promulgated. Revised versions of these Codes came into force in 1991. The Codes are not technically law and s 67(10) of PACE 1984 states that a breach of them can lead to neither an action for damages nor a criminal prosecution against police officers. A breach of the Codes is, though, automatically a disciplinary offence (s 67(8)).

The chief significance of a breach of the Codes is that a judge may exclude otherwise relevant evidence if it has been obtained in such a way and an appeal court may quash a conviction where a trial judge has not excluded such evidence (s 67(7)).

9.4.1 Entry of premises under the common law

Premises can be searched by consent. Here, the constable must get written consent from the occupier of the premises on a special 'Notice of Powers and Rights' form before the search takes place. The officer must make inquiries to ensure that the person concerned is in a position to give that consent. Before seeking the consent, the officer in charge must state the purpose of the proposed search and inform the person concerned that he is not obliged to consent, that anything seized may be produced in evidence, and, if such is the case, that he is not suspected of any offence. These propositions come from the governing *Code of Practice (B) for the Searching of Premises by Police Officers and the Seizure of Property found by Police Officers on Persons or Premises*. An officer cannot enter and search, or continue to search premises by consent, if the consent is given under duress or is withdrawn before the search is completed (Code B, para 4.3). Consent need not be sought if this would cause disproportionate inconvenience to the occupiers of premises, for example, where the police wish to briefly check a number of gardens on a suspected escape route.

Police officers may enter premises with permission or under implied permission but then must leave when required unless remaining under some particular power. In *Davis v Lisle* (1936), Sidney Davis was a member of a firm that occupied a railway arch as a garage. Two police officers entered the garage to ask about a lorry that had been obstructing the highway. The lorry had since been moved into the garage. D, using obscene language and abuse, told the officers to leave. L was in the act of producing his warrant card when D struck him in the chest and stomach, damaging his tunic. The convictions of D for assaulting and obstructing a police officer in the execution of his duty were quashed by the Divisional Court. Lord Hewart CJ held that the officers were not acting in the course of their duty once they had remained on premises having been told in forthright terms by the occupiers to leave: 'From that moment on, while the officers remained where they were, it seems to me that they were trespassers.'

9.4.2 Entry of premises to prevent an offence being committed

There is a common law right for police officers to enter a building to deal with or prevent a breach of the peace. In *Thomas v Sawkins* (1935), the Divisional Court held that police officers were entitled to enter and remain on premises, despite being asked by the occupiers to leave, in circumstances where the officers believed that certain offences (seditious speeches, incitements to violence) would be committed if they were not present. Lord Hewart CJ said:

> I am not at all prepared to accept the doctrine that it is only where an offence has been, or is being, committed, that the police are entitled to enter and remain on premises. On the contrary, it seems to me that a police officer has, *ex virtute officii*, full right so to act when he has reasonable grounds for believing that an offence is imminent or is likely to be committed.

Section 17(5) and (6) of PACE 1984 abolishes all common law powers of entry except to deal with or prevent a breach of the peace.

Note, however, that a licensee must be given a reasonable time to leave premises before his continued presence on the land constitutes a trespass, unless he makes it clear that he will not leave voluntarily (*Robson v Hallet* (1967)).

The power has even extended to private homes. In *McGowan v Chief Constable of Kingston upon Hull* (1968), the Divisional Court held that the police were entitled to enter and remain in a private dwelling where they feared there would be a breach of the peace arising out of a private quarrel.

9.4.3 Entry and search of premises to make an arrest

This is governed by s 17 of PACE 1984 which says that a constable may enter and search premises for the purposes of arresting someone for an arrestable offence or under warrant, recapturing a person unlawfully at large whom he is pursuing; saving life or limb or preventing serious damage to property. This power can only be exercised if the constable has 'reasonable grounds' for believing that the person whom he is seeking is on the premises.

A police officer exercising his power to enter premises by the use of reasonable force to arrest a person for an arrestable offence (pursuant to ss 17 and 117 of PACE 1984) should, unless circumstances make it impossible, impracticable or undesirable, announce to the occupier the reason why he is exercising that power. In *O'Loughlin v Chief Constable of Essex* (1998), a police officer who had a lawful right to enter premises but failed to announce why he was entering when it was practicable and possible to do so was held to be acting unlawfully. In such circumstances, the occupier is entitled to use reasonable force to prevent the entry.

The relevant powers here are those discussed below under ss 18 and 32 of PACE 1984. In practice, the police act routinely under s 18 and rarely under s 32.

Section 18 of PACE 1984 gives the police power to enter and search:

> ... any premises occupied or controlled by a person who is under arrest for an arrestable offence, if he has reasonable grounds for suspecting that there is on the premises evidence other than items subject to legal privilege that relates (a) to the offence; or (b) to some other arrestable offence which is connected with or similar to that offence.

If, therefore, the police suspect that evidence of other unconnected offences is to be found at the address, then they must get a search warrant or seek the householder's consent to the search. The search of someone's address after they have been arrested normally requires the written permission from an officer of the rank of inspector or above (s 18(4)). Section 18(5) makes an exception when the arrested person is taken straight to the address rather than the police station. A search must not go beyond what is normally required to find the particular item(s) being sought; no general search is permitted (s 18(3)). The time constraint when the police use s 32 (the search has to be made at the time of the arrest) (see below) does not appear to apply to a s 18 search (see *R v Badham* (1987) (see below)). It is perhaps because of this and the comparative narrowness of s 32 in respect of searches of premises (see below) that s 18 is much more frequently used by police. Research by Ken Lidstone, for example, found that, in a survey of two city forces, s 18 accounted for 75% of searches compared with 2% for s 32: 'Entry, search and seizure' (1989) 40 NILQ 333, p 355, n 67.

Section 32(2)(b) gives the police power to enter and search premises in which the suspect was when arrested, or immediately before he was arrested, for *evidence relating to the offence for which he was arrested*. Unlike the power to search under s 18, this is not limited to arrestable offences, nor do the searched premises need to be occupied or controlled by him. Such searches, however, are only lawful where there are reasonable grounds for believing that the search might find something for which a search is permitted under s 32(5) and (6). Random or automatic searching is not lawful.

Section 32(7) states that, where a person is arrested in premises consisting of two or more separate dwellings, only the premises in which he was arrested or was in immediately beforehand and any common parts (like stairways and common corridors) can be searched.

The powers here are narrower than those given under s 18 to enter and search the premises of an arrested person. Under s 18, the police may enter and search for evidence of the offence for which the person was arrested or *any* offence which is 'connected with or similar to that offence'. Section 32 only covers searches for evidence relating to the actual offence for which the suspect was arrested. The police can, however, under s 32, search the person himself for evidence of any offence. It was held in *R v Badham* (1987) that s 32 only applies to a search made at the time of the arrest. It does not permit the police to return to the premises several hours after the arrest.

In *R v Churchill* (1989), the defendant was arrested on suspicion of burglary and placed in a police car. The police asked him to hand over the keys to the car he had been in so that they could lock it, thus keeping it safe for a later scientific examination. C was convicted of assault when, after refusing to hand over the keys, a struggle ensued and he hit an officer. On appeal, he contended that the police had no power to take the keys since they had no evidence of any crime. The court quashed the conviction, saying that the case could have been argued on the basis of the officer's duty to preserve the property but the prosecution had not used that argument. The police could, alternatively, have searched the car under s 32 as that section confers a power to search any 'premises' the defendant was in immediately before arrest and this includes a vehicle (s 23(a)).

9.4.4 Seizure of articles from searches

Seizure of articles from searches is controlled by s 19 and Code B, para 6. These state that where a constable is searching premises under statutory powers or by consent, he may seize anything on the premises (except things exempted from seizure) if he reasonably believes that it is evidence in relation to an offence which he is investigating or *any other offence* and that it is necessary to seize it in order to prevent it from being concealed, lost, altered or destroyed (s 19(3)(b)) or that it has been obtained in consequence of the commission of an offence. Items exempted from seizure are those reasonably believed to be subject to legal professional privilege (s 19(6)). The scope of the seizure rights is therefore quite wide and Zander has argued that the insistence since *Entick v Carrington* (1765) that general warrants are unlawful must now be qualified by the knowledge that, once the police have entered premises lawfully, it is difficult to hold them to a search restricted to the specific purpose of the search. The only serious restraint is the requirement in s 16(8) that a search under warrant must be carried out in a manner consistent with the items being looked for and in Code B, para 5.9 which states that 'premises may be searched only to the extent necessary to achieve the object of the search having regard to the size and nature of whatever is sought'.

9.4.5   Search warrants and safeguards

Section 8 of PACE 1984 provides for the issue of warrants by magistrates to enter and search premises for evidence of serious arrestable offences. This gives justices of the peace the power, on written application from a constable, to issue a search warrant where he or she is satisfied that there are reasonable grounds for believing that a 'serious arrestable offence' has been committed. A 'serious arrestable offence' (as distinct from an 'arrestable offence' defined by s 24) is defined by s 116 and Sched 5 of PACE 1984). The definition divides offences into two categories. One category comprises offences so serious that they are always 'serious arrestable offences'; they are listed in Sched 5 and include treason, murder, manslaughter, rape, kidnapping, incest and possession of firearms with intent to injure and attempts or conspiracies are treated as if they were completed. Any other arrestable offence is serious only if its commission has led, or is likely to lead, to any of the consequences specified in s 116(6), namely: (a) serious harm to the security of the State or public order; (b) serious interference with the administration of justice or with the investigation of offences; (c) the death of anyone; (d) serious injury to anyone; (e) substantial financial gain to anyone; (f) serious financial loss to anyone in the sense that, having regard to all the circumstances, it is serious, for the person suffering loss (the seriousness of the loss is therefore to be measured by the financial position of the potential loser).

The magistrate must also be satisfied that:

- there is material on the premises likely to be of substantial value to the investigation (s 8(1)(b));

- that it is likely to be relevant evidence (s 8(1)(c));

- that it does not include 'excluded material' (for example, human tissue taken for medical diagnosis and held in confidence); journalistic material held in confidence (see s 11), or 'special procedure material' (for example, confidential business/professional material, see s 14); or material subject to legal privilege (s 10); and

- that any of the conditions in s 8(3) applies. These are, essentially, that it is not practicable to gain entry to the premises in question without a search warrant or that the reasons for the search would be frustrated if the constable did not gain immediate entry upon arrival.

Section 15 incorporates proposals made by the Philips Royal Commission on Criminal Procedure (Cmnd 8092, 1981, HMSO) to protect against warrants being too easily obtained. Clearly, it is highly contentious at what point there is the correct, desirable balance between the State's concern to prevent and detect crime and the interests of the public at large in having the civil liberty of freedom from speculative entry into their homes by the police. If police officers could legally enter any home at any time without permission from anyone, then the detection of crime would arguably be easier than now but there would be a significant price to pay in the consequential public resentment against the police and the probably profound loss of faith in the legal and political system.

An application for a search warrant must now state the grounds for making the application, the statutory authority under which the claim is made and the object of the proposed search in as much detail as possible. Research by Lidstone (see 9.4.3, above) has shown a tendency for informations (the applications) and warrants to use very generalised terms like 'electrical goods' which he argues is not desirable. The applications are normally made *ex parte* (that is, from one side, the police, without the presence of the person whose premises are to be searched) and the information must be made in writing by an officer who must answer any questions (from the magistrate) under oath. Lidstone's research also suggests that, both before and after PACE 1984, there is evidence of reliance on formulaic informations, for example, 'As a result of information received from a previously reliable source ...', and a lack of any probative questioning by magistrates on such informations. The warrant may only be used to gain entry on one occasion; if the police find nothing relevant and wish to return, they must apply for another warrant. On each search, the occupier must be given a copy of the warrant authorising entry.

One part of s 15 has caused some difficulty for the courts. It relates to the word 'it' in s 15(1) which states that 'an entry on or search of premises under warrant is unlawful unless it complies with this section and s 16 below'.

What must comply – the warrant or the whole entry and search? In *R v Longman* (1988), Lord Lane CJ said, *obiter*:

> With some hesitation, we are inclined to think it probably refers to the warrant, but the real probability is that the intention of the framers of the Act was to provide that the warrant should comply with the terms of s 25 and the entry and search should comply with s 16. But, unhappily, that is not what it says. So, we leave that problem unresolved.

Section 16 and Code B govern the actual search of premises and seek to ensure that warrants are executed in a proper and reasonable manner. It states that any constable, not just the one named in the warrant, may execute that warrant (s 16(1)) and it must be carried out within one month of its date of issue (s 16(3)). The search must be at a 'reasonable hour' unless 'it appears to the constable executing it that the purpose of a search may be frustrated on an entry at a reasonable hour' (s 16(4)). Notice that, here, the test is subjective, it is what 'appears to the constable' which is critical, not whether such a belief is reasonable or not. If the occupier is present, he must be given a copy of the warrant (s 16(5)); if he is not there, then a copy must be left in a prominent place (s 16(7)). A constable executing a warrant must identify himself and, if he is not in uniform, he must produce documentary evidence that he is a constable, even if he is not asked (s 16(5)).

In *R v Longman* (above), a plain clothes police officer posed as a delivery girl from Interflora to gain entry to premises without alerting the occupants. She had come to the premises with other officers with a warrant to search for drugs. It was not the first time that the premises had been searched and the officers knew that entry would be very difficult. When the door was opened, the officers burst in. They did not, therefore, properly identify themselves as officers according to s 16(5), nor had they shown the householder their search warrant as required by Code B (para 5.5). The Court of Appeal held that force or subterfuge could lawfully be used for the purposes of gaining entry with a search warrant. The warrant was 'produced' for the purposes of s 16(5) when the occupier was given the opportunity of inspecting it. In this case, the occupier had not attempted to look at the warrant, he had shouted a warning to others on the premises and then tried to stab the officers with a knife. The court held that it would be prepared to overlook failures to comply with the precise provisions of ss 15 and 16 regarding production of the warrant whenever circumstances made it wholly inappropriate, such as a search for drugs or in a terrorism case. In any event, it was not necessary that the formalities set out in s 16(a)–(c), on identification of the searcher as a police officer and production of the warrant, be carried out before *entry* but only before the search begins. The revised Code B states that the officer shall first attempt to get access by asking the occupier unless (Code B, para 5.4(iii)):

> ... there are reasonable grounds for believing that to alert the occupier or any other person entitled to grant access by attempting to communicate with him would frustrate the object of the search or endanger the officers concerned or other persons.

A search under a warrant 'may only be a search to the extent required for the purpose of which the warrant was issued' (s 16(8)). In *Chief Constable of the Warwickshire Constabulary ex p Fitzpatrick* (1998), the Divisional Court disapproved of the police practice of using a warrant phrased in broad terms to seize every possible item that could broadly fall within those terms. They should ensure both that the material seized falls within the terms of the warrant and, because such a warrant is granted to search for material of evidential value, that there are reasonable grounds for believing so and to be likely to be of substantial value in the investigation. In this case, in relation to one of the warrants, the police officers went on a 'fishing expedition' and seized a large selection of documents, not on their face related to the offence under investigation. In doing so, they exceeded the ambit of the warrant. Thus, the entire search was a trespass and unlawful under ss 16(8) and 15(1) of PACE (see, further, Khan and Ryder, 'Police and the law' (1998) Legal Action 16, September).

A search warrant does not entitle the executing officers to search persons on the premises. Such persons may only be searched if arrested or if there is a specific power in the warrant, for example, as in warrants issued under s 23 of the Misuse of Drugs Act 1971 (Home Office Circular on PACE 1984, 1985, No 88/1855).

9.5 Interrogation, confession and admissibility of evidence

Before moving into the specific provisions of PACE 1984 and the Codes of Practice, it is important to be aware of the general issues at stake in this area of law. Are the rights of suspects being interrogated by the police sufficiently protected by law? Is there scope for abuse of power by the police? Are the police burdened by too many legal requirements when trying to induce a suspect to confess to a crime? What effects are likely to flow from the undermining of the right to silence (see ss 34–37 of the CJPOA 1994, 9.5.17, below)?

9.5.1 Time limits on detention without charge

Under s 42 of PACE 1984, a suspect can be held without being charged for 24 hours before any further authorisation needs to be given. At this point, the situation must be reviewed and further detention must be authorised by an officer of at least the rank of superintendent. The period is measured from arrival at the police station. If he is arrested by another force, the time runs from his arrival at the station of the area where he is wanted. If further detention is authorised, this can continue for up to the 36 hour point. After 36 hours from the beginning of the detention, there must be a full hearing in a magistrates' court with the suspect and, if he wishes, legal representation (s 43). The magistrates can grant a warrant of further detention for up to a further 60 hours – making a total of 96 hours (ss 43 and 44). However, the police could not be granted the 60 hour period as a whole because the maximum extension that a magistrates' court can grant at one time is 36 hours (ss 43(12), 44). The magistrates can only grant such extensions if the offence being investigated is a serious arrestable offence (s 116), is being investigated diligently and expeditiously and provided that the further detention is necessary to secure or preserve evidence relating to an offence for which the suspect is under arrest or to obtain such evidence by questioning him (s 43(4)).

Section 38 states that, *after being charged*, the arrested person must be released, with or without bail, unless:

- it is necessary to hold him so that his name and address can be obtained; or

- the custody officer reasonably thinks that it is necessary to hold him for his own protection or to prevent him from causing physical injury to anyone or from causing loss of or damage to property; or

- the custody officer reasonably thinks that he needs to be held because he would otherwise fail to answer bail or to prevent him from interfering with witnesses or otherwise obstructing the course of justice; or

- if he is a juvenile and ought to be held 'in his own interests'.

If the suspect is charged and not released, he will have to be brought before a magistrates' court 'as soon as practicable', and not later than the first sitting after being charged (s 46(2)).

9.5.2 Searches of detained persons

Searches of people detained at police stations are governed by s 54 and Code C. PACE 1984 has been amended by the CJPOA 1994 (ss 54–59). The rules governing the taking of intimate and non-intimate body samples have been changed. The new Act also allows 'speculative searches' in which fingerprints, samples, or information in respect thereof, can be checked against other similar data held by the police. The changes follow recommendations of the Runciman Commission Report which recommends the establishment of a national DNA database.

A person may only be searched if the custody officer considers this necessary in order to make a complete list of his property (s 54(6)). There is no automatic right to search all suspects as a matter of routine. The police can, however, search anyone to ascertain whether he has with him anything which he could use to cause physical injury, damage property, interfere with evidence or assist him to escape (s 55, as amended). Section 65 deals with intimate searches. The CJPOA 1994 repeals the old s 118 of PACE 1984 (which defined 'body orifice', including anus, vagina, mouth, nostrils and ears) and s 54(1) inserts a new definition into s 65 of PACE 1984. Section 65 of PACE 1984 now defines an intimate search as:

> ... a search which consists of the physical examination of a person's body orifices other than the mouth.

A physical examination of the mouth is therefore allowed in the circumstances where a non-intimate search of the person may occur, subject to the ordinary safeguards (Code of Practice A, para 3; Code C, para 4). A search of the mouth for drugs is not the taking of a sample as defined by s 65 of PACE 1984, so the restrictions which apply to the taking of samples do not apply here. A search of an arrested person's mouth may thus be carried out by a police officer at the station, subject to the safeguards in Code C. The officer carrying out the search must be of the same sex as the arrested person (s 54(9)). Nonetheless, an officer of either sex may search the arrested person's mouth at the time of the arrest if he has reasonable grounds to believe that the arrested person is concealing therein evidence related to the offence (s 32(2)(b)).

These searches must be authorised by an officer of the rank of superintendent or above on the basis of reasonable belief that the arrested person in police detention has concealed on him anything which could be used to cause physical injury to himself or to others and that he might so use it. Intimate searches for weapons can, if a doctor or registered nurse is not available, be carried out by a police officer of the same sex as the suspect. If the search is for drugs, it can only be carried out by a doctor or registered nurse and it cannot be carried out at a police station (s 55(4)). Intimate searches for drugs are limited to those for hard drugs, defined as Class A drugs in Sched 2 to the Misuse of Drugs Act 1971.

9.5.3 The right to have someone informed when arrested

The effect of s 56 and Code C is that, when a suspect is under arrest and is being held in custody in a police station, he is entitled, if he so requests, to have 'one friend or relative or other person who is known to him or who is likely to take an interest in his welfare' to be told as soon as practicable that he is under arrest and his whereabouts (s 56(1), Code C, para 5.1). If such a person cannot be contacted, the Code allows for two alternates to be nominated, following which any further alternates can be called at the discretion of the custody officer. Delay is only permissible in the case of a 'serious arrestable offence' (see s 116) and only if authorised by an officer of at least the rank of superintendent. The grounds for delaying appear in Annex B. They are, essentially, that there are reasonable grounds for believing that telling the named person of the arrest will lead to interference with, or harm to, evidence of witnesses or the alerting of others involved in such an offence;

or will hinder the recovery of property obtained as a result of the offence. No one, however, may be prevented from notifying someone outside the police station for longer than 36 hours after 'the relevant time' (s 41(2)), usually the time that he or she arrived at the station. Unless the reasons for a lawful delay (see Annex B) exist, Code C states that the detainee should be allowed to speak on the telephone 'for a reasonable time to one person' (para 5.6) and that this privilege is in addition to the right to phone someone under para 5.1 to inform him or her of the arrest or under para 6.1 to obtain legal advice. Children and young persons are afforded additional rights by s 57; the section says that the police should contact a person 'responsible for his welfare' to inform the person about the arrest.

9.5.4 The right to consult a solicitor

Section 58(1) of PACE 1984 states that 'A person who is in police detention shall be entitled, if he so requests, to consult a solicitor privately at any time'. The rules relating to persons held under suspicion of terrorist offences are different and will not be covered here. Where the detained person is a juvenile or is mentally handicapped or disordered, then 'the appropriate adult' (see Code C, para 3) may exercise the right to ask for legal advice.

Where the suspect has been allowed to consult a solicitor, and the solicitor is available, the solicitor must be allowed to sit in on any interview the police give the suspect (Code C, para 6.8). Normally, the request must be allowed as soon as practicable (s 58(4)).

9.5.5 Notifying the suspect of the right to free legal advice

There is clearly the danger that a person's right to legal advice can be effectively curtailed if they are not aware of it. Code C therefore goes to some lengths to ensure the suspect is aware of the right. The custody officer is required (para 3.5), when he authorises a person's detention in the police station, to make sure that the suspect signs the custody record signifying whether he wishes to have legal advice at that point. The revised Code adds the following:

> The custody officer is responsible for ensuring that the person signs the custody record in the correct place to give effect to his decision.

The Code stipulates that police stations must advertise the right to free legal advice in posters 'prominently displayed in the charging area of every police station' (para 6.3). The Code also gives precise rules concerning at what point and in what form a person should be notified of the right to get free legal advice. For example, a person who comes to the station *under arrest* must be told immediately both orally and in writing (paras 3.1, 3.2). A person who comes to the police station voluntarily (that is, someone who is helping the police with their inquiries) is to be given a leaflet if he or she requests information but, strangely, there is no police duty to notify if that person does not ask.

A person who asks for legal advice should be given the opportunity to consult a specific solicitor (for example, his or her own) or the duty solicitor (see 9.5.6, below). Alternatively, he or she should be given an opportunity to chose one from a list of those available to give advice. Ultimately, the custody officer has discretion to allow further requests if the others are unsuccessful. The revised Code C carries the provision that 'No attempt should be made to dissuade the suspect from obtaining legal advice' (para 6.4) and that reminders of the right to consult legal advice should be given at specified times, for example, on commencement and re-commencement of interviews.

The revised Code also states (para 6.15) that, if a solicitor arrives at the station to see a particular person, that person must (unless Annex B, above, applies) be informed of the solicitor's arrival and asked whether he would like to see him. This applies even if the person concerned has already declined legal advice. This would be important, for example, where the lawyer had been sent by a friend or family member.

Until the revision of Code C (effective from 1991), there was evidence that the way most police stations informed suspects of their right to legal advice meant that suspects did not realise the advice would be free and that this might well have acted as a deterrent against accepting such advice. Now, suspects must be told that 'independent legal advice is available free of charge' (para 3.1(ii)). The solicitor is paid under the legal aid scheme. At his or her discretion, a solicitor may give the advice over the telephone. The Law Society advises the solicitor when he or she is considering whether the telephone is a suitable medium to have regard to certain issues, for example, would the suspect be likely to be inhibited from speaking freely by fear of being overheard and whether the suspect has already been charged and no further police interview is proposed.

There has been notable judicial concern that the suspect's rights to be informed about the availability of legal advice is enforced. In R v Absolam (1989), the Court of Appeal quashed a conviction for the supply of cannabis and substituted one for simple possession because the defendant had not been informed of his right to see a solicitor before he had been questioned. The trial judge had held that the series of preliminary questions and answers did not amount to an 'interview', but the Court of Appeal disagreed; the questions were an 'interview' within the meaning of the Code because they were directed at a suspect with the aim of obtaining admissions on which a prosecution could be based. The reference in s 58(4) to seeing a solicitor 'as soon as practicable' was not relevant to the suspect's right to be informed of his right to legal advice from the outset of his detention.

Note: The Runciman Royal Commission Report on Criminal Justice 1993 recommends (para 38):

> The definition of an interview in Code C Note for Guidance 11A should be clarified to remove the apparent confusion as to what constitutes an interview for the purposes of the Code.

In *R v Beycan* (1990), the defendant was arrested in connection with a charge of supplying heroin. He was taken to a police station where he was asked 'Are you happy to be interviewed in the normal way we conduct these interviews without a solicitor, friend or representative?'. The Court of Appeal held that this did not amount to informing him of his right to legal advice and it quashed his conviction which was based on his subsequent confession.

9.5.6 Duty solicitors

The duty solicitor schemes at police stations and magistrates' courts are run locally but organised under the auspices of the Legal Aid Board which was set up by the Legal Aid Act (LAdA) 1988. At police stations, the duty solicitor is contacted through a special national telephone network provided by a company, Air Call plc. When a suspect asks for a duty solicitor (at any time of the day or night), a call is made to Air Call who then contact either the rota duty solicitor or telephone duty solicitors on the panel until, in the latter case, one is found who is able and willing to attend. In rota schemes, there is always (in theory) someone on duty; in panel schemes, the panellists are called one after the other on a list beginning with the name after the last solicitor to have come out. One area of concern (which has arisen from several recent cases involving poor advice to suspects in police stations) is the extent to which advice is regularly given to suspects by people who are not fully qualified solicitors but solicitor's clerks or trainee solicitors whom the duty solicitor is allowed to send as his or her 'representative'. This is permitted by the current Duty Solicitor Arrangements, Pt VI. The local committee which can approve such representation must be satisfied that the representative is in full or part time employment and has had 'experience of providing advice at a police station on behalf of the duty solicitor' on the basis of experience depending on the person's status, for example, a solicitor's clerk should have at least three years' experience of criminal defence work.

The Runciman Royal Commission on Criminal Justice noted the problem of inadequate professional advice in some cases. Its Report states (para 69):

> The Legal Aid Board should commission occasional empirical research as a means of checking on the quality of performance of legal advisers at police stations.

The inadequacy of much legal advice given to suspects was highlighted when Stephen Millar, one of the Cardiff Three, had his conviction quashed on appeal

((1992) *The Times*, 11 December). In his judgment, the Lord Chief Justice criticised the defence solicitor for not intervening to halt the questioning. In his research for the Royal Commission on Criminal Justice, Professor John Baldwin analysed 600 police interviews (see 9.5.25, below) and found that, in 66.5% of them, the advisor said nothing at all ((1993) 33 British J of Criminology 3).

9.5.7 Delaying access to legal advice

The police have no right to delay a suspect's access to legal advice except in the case of a serious arrestable offence (Annex B to Code C). Code C (para 6.2) states that 'the custody officer must act without delay to secure the provision of such advice to the person concerned'. If the suspect is being held in connection with a serious arrestable offence (s 116), he or she can be delayed access to legal advice but the delay must be authorised by an officer of the rank of superintendent and only where he has reasonable grounds for believing that the exercise of the right:

- will lead to interference with, or harm to, evidence connected with a serious arrestable offence or interference with or physical harm to other persons; or

- will lead to the alerting of other persons suspected of having committed such an offence but not yet arrested for it; or

- will hinder the recovery of any property obtained as a result of such an offence.

If a delay is authorised, the suspect must be told the reason for it and the reason must be recorded in the custody record. The maximum period of delay is 36 hours (Annex B, para 4).

9.5.8 *R v Samuel* (1988)

In *R v Samuel* (1988), the defendant was arrested on suspicion of robbery and taken to a police station. During that day and the following day, he was interviewed several times about the robbery and other offences. He asked for a solicitor during the second interview. His request was refused by a superintendent on the grounds that two of the offences under investigation were serious arrestable offences and there would be a danger of accomplices being inadvertently alerted. At the fourth interview, Samuel confessed to two burglaries. A little later, a solicitor instructed by the family was notified of the charges but he was refused access to the suspect. Shortly after that, Samuel confessed to the robbery charge. The trial judge admitted evidence of the last interview, Samuel was convicted of robbery and sentenced to 10 years' imprisonment. The Court of Appeal quashed the conviction. Two important issues were clarified:

- The police were not entitled to deny a suspect access to a solicitor after he has been charged, even if other charges are still being investigated. This follows from the plain and natural meaning of Annex B (para 1) which states the right to legal advice can be delayed where:

  ... the person is in police detention in connection with a serious arrestable offence, has not yet been charged with an offence and an officer of the rank of superintendent or above has reasonable grounds for believing ...

- The right of access to a solicitor was a 'fundamental right of a citizen' and if the police sought to justify refusing that right, they must do so by reference to specific aspects of the case; it was insufficient to suppose that giving the suspect access to a solicitor *might* lead to the alerting of accomplices. The officer had to believe that it probably would and that the solicitor would either commit the criminal offence of alerting other suspects or would be hoodwinked into doing so inadvertently or unwillingly. Either belief could only be genuinely held by an officer on rare occasions. The belief that a solicitor would commit the criminal offence had to be based on knowledge of that particular solicitor. It could not be advanced successfully in relation to solicitors generally. As to the other point, Hodgson J observed (p 626):

  But, what is said is that the detained person will be able to bring about one or more of the happenings (a) to (c) [in Annex B] by causing the solicitor to pass on unwittingly some form of coded message. Whether there is any evidence that this has or may have happened in the past we have no way of knowing. Solicitors are intelligent, professional people; persons detained by the police are frequently not very clever and the expectation that one of (a) to (c) will be brought about in this way seems to contemplate a degree of intelligence and sophistication in persons detained, and perhaps a naïveté and lack of common sense in solicitors which we doubt often occurs.

This is not perhaps a view of offenders and solicitors which would be immediately agreed with by all those whose work brings them into contact with either group. Hodgson J said there were two tests. First, did the officer have the belief? This was a subjective question. Secondly, was that belief reasonable? This is an objective matter. In this case, the solicitor was well known and highly respected. He was unlikely to be hoodwinked by a 24 year old. The suspect's mother had been informed of her son's arrest hours before the solicitor was refused access to the son. If anyone was to have been alerted, it could easily have been done already. The solicitor would have advised his client to have said nothing at that stage. Samuel would not have made his admission having been denied his 'fundamental freedom' to consult with a solicitor. The evidence of the admission should, therefore, have been excluded under s 78.

9.5.9   *R v Alladice* (1988)

In *R v Alladice* (1988), the Court of Appeal allowed the evidence of an admission made during an interview where the suspect had had access to a solicitor delayed. The decision has been regarded as based on the narrow facts of the case. Alladice had made admissions of involvement in an armed robbery and was convicted but argued on appeal that the evidence should have been excluded because there had been no valid reason for delaying his access to a solicitor. He argued that the real reason for the delay was that the police believed that a solicitor would have advised him to remain silent and that, as the Code and *Samuel* showed, this was not a valid reason. The court found that, on the facts, there had been a breach of s 58 but that this did not mean that the evidence obtained in breach of the section should automatically be excluded. There was no suggestion of oppression nor was there evidence of bad faith on the part of the police. The court took the view that it would be wrong to regard the admission has having resulted from the refusal to grant access to a solicitor. Alladice had stated that he understood the caution, that he was aware of his rights and that he was able to cope with the interview. He argued that the alleged admissions had not been made although that argument was rejected by the judge. In any event, it seemed to the Court of Appeal that the presence of a solicitor would not have made any difference to the suspect's knowledge of his rights. There was no causal link between the absence of Alladice's solicitor and the admission.

9.5.10   *R v Davidson* (1988)

In *R v Davidson* (1988), the trial judge stated that *Samuel* meant that, in order for the police to validly delay access to advice, they had to be 'nearly certain' that the solicitor granted access to a suspect would warn an accomplice or get rid of the proceeds of the crime. Davidson had been arrested for handling a stolen ring, the fruit of an armed robbery. The power to delay access to a solicitor could not be exercised until D had nominated a particular lawyer. As this had not been done when the superintendent came to consider the matter, he could not have had a reasonable fear that the lawyer would pass a message to another person involved in the crime. The suspect had already spoken to his wife twice, so the reality of the police fears that he would use the lawyer as a messenger had to be doubted. The court excluded the crucial confessions and the prosecution's case collapsed.

9.5.11   *R v Parris* (1989)

In *R v Parris* (1989), the court quashed a conviction for armed robbery because of breaches of s 58. The police arrested Parris for armed robbery and took him to the station where he was kept incommunicado (under s 56). He asked to see a solicitor at his first interview and was refused. He refused to answer any questions. During his second interview, he agreed to answer some questions provided nothing was written down. He then allegedly made oral admissions although, at trial, he denied these took place. The Crown did not deny that there had been a breach of s 58(8) as there had been no valid reason for refusing access to a solicitor; the incommunicado order under s 56 was wrongly assumed to also exclude access to a solicitor under s 58. Had there been a solicitor present at the second interview, he would probably have advised Parris not to speak; at the least, he would have discouraged the alleged fabrication of admissions. The appeal succeeded.

Code C, Annex B, B4 states:

> ... the officer may authorise delaying access to a solicitor only if he has reasonable grounds to believe that the specific solicitor will, inadvertently or otherwise, pass on a message from the detained person which will lead to any of the three results in para 1 coming about. In these circumstances, the officer should offer the detained person access to a solicitor on the Duty Solicitor Scheme.

9.5.12 Interviewing before solicitor arrives

The police have a right to start questioning suspects before a solicitor has arrived at the police station if the situation is an emergency or the solicitor is not likely to arrive for a considerable period. The power is governed by Code C (para 6.6). This says that a person who asks for legal advice may not be interviewed or continue to be interviewed until he has received it unless Annex B applies (advice delayed by superintendent, etc) or an officer of at least the rank of superintendent has reasonable grounds for believing that a delay in questioning will involve an immediate risk of harm to persons or serious loss of, or damage to, property; or where a solicitor has been contacted and is on his way but waiting 'would cause unreasonable delay to the process of investigation'. It will not normally be appropriate to begin an interview if the solicitor has said he is on his way (para 6A). Another exception is where the solicitor cannot be contacted or declines to attend and the suspect, having been told about the Duty Solicitor Scheme, declines to ask for the duty solicitor or the duty solicitor is unavailable.

9.5.13 Answering police questions and the right to silence

The police are free to ask anyone any questions. The only restriction is that all questioning is supposed to cease once a suspect has been charged. Code C, para 16.5 states that questions relating to an offence 'may not be put to a person after he has been charged with that offence, or informed that he might be prosecuted for it, unless they are necessary for the purpose of preventing or minimising harm or loss to some other person ...' or where it is in the interests of justice that the person should be given an opportunity to comment on new information which has come to light since he was charged.

Note: The Runciman Royal Commission Report 1993 recommends (para 22):

> The questioning of suspects after charge should be permissible provided that the usual caution is repeated, and that the person charged has the usual opportunity of consulting a solicitor free of charge before any interview and of having that solicitor present at the interview.

Note that this would affect the current Code C, para 16.5 (see 9.5.5, above) and 11.4.

For a good examination of the circumstances in which police questioning of a suspect may amount to a breach of Code C, see Cape, 'Police interrogation and interruption' [1994] NLJ 120.

There is no obligation on a citizen to answer police questions. A person cannot be charged, for example, with obstructing the police in the execution of their duty simply by failing to answer questions, nor can the judge or prosecutor suggest to the jury that such silence is evidence of guilt.

In *Rice v Connolly* (1966), the appellant was seen by officers in the early hours of the morning behaving suspiciously in an area where house breaking had taken place on the same evening. On being questioned, he refused to say where he was going or where he had come from. He refused to give his full name and address, though he did give a name and the name of a road which were not untrue. He refused to accompany the officer to a police box for identification purposes, saying: 'If you want me, you'll have to arrest me.' He was arrested and charged with wilfully obstructing a police officer contrary to s 51(3) of the Police Act 1964.

His appeal against conviction succeeded. Lord Parker CJ noted that the police officer was acting within his duty in inquiring about the appellant and that what the appellant did was obstructive. The critical question though was whether the appellant's conduct was 'wilful' within the meaning of s 51. Lord Parker CJ, in the Divisional Court, took that word to mean 'intentional [and] without lawful excuse'. He continued:

> It seems to me quite clear that, though every citizen has a moral duty or, if you like, a social duty to assist the police, there is no legal duty to that effect, and, indeed, the whole basis of the common law is the right of the individual to refuse to answer questions put to him by persons in authority, and to refuse to accompany those in authority to any particular place; short, of course, of arrest.

The court was unanimous although one judge, James J, cautioned that he would not go as far as to say that silence coupled with conduct could not amount to obstruction. It would depend on the particular facts of any given case.

In *Ricketts v Cox* (1982), two police officers who were looking for youths responsible for a serious assault, approached the defendant and another man in the early hours of the morning. The justices found that the officers acted in a proper manner in putting questions to the men. The defendant was abusive, unco-operative and possibly hostile to the officers, using obscene language calculated to provoke and antagonise the officers and tried to walk away. The justices were satisfied that this conduct amounted to an obstruction for the purposes of a charge under s 51(3) of the Police Act 1964. The defendant's appeal was dismissed by the Divisional Court which found that the case raised the point reserved by James J in *Rice v Connolly* – the combination of silence and hostility without lawful excuse. As Zander has observed, the state of the law here is now unclear.

9.5.14 Duties to answer

There are certain circumstances where the citizen is under a duty to answer police questions. Where a constable has reasonable grounds for believing that a vehicle has been involved in an accident and he seeks the particulars of the driver, he may arrest that person if the information is not given. With the Home Secretary's consent, and on the authority of a chief constable, coercive questioning (that is, where a suspect's silence can be used in evidence against him or her) can be used in matters under s 11 (as amended) of the Official Secrets Act 1911. There are also wide powers under the Companies Act 1985 to require officers and agents of companies to assist inspectors appointed to investigate the company. Refusal to answer questions can be sanctioned as a contempt of court (s 431) and as a criminal offence (s 447). A person can also be required to answer questions put to him or her by a liquidator of a company (*Bishopsgate Management Ltd v Maxwell Mirror Group Newspapers* (1993)).

Under s 2 of the CJA 1987, the Director of the Serious Fraud Office (SFO) (dealing with frauds worth over £5 million) can require anyone whom he has reason to think has relevant information to attend to answer questions and to provide information including documents and books. Such statements, however, cannot be used in evidence against the persons who make them unless they go into the witness box and give inconsistent testimony. Even this power, though, does not require the breach of legal professional privilege. Failure to comply with s 2 requests is a criminal offence and can result in an application for a magistrates' search warrant. These powers have been widely used. The SFO Annual Report for 1991–92 reveals that a total of 793 notices had been given during that year. In *R v Director of the Serious Fraud Office ex p Smith* (1993), the House of Lords held that the SFO could compel a person to answer questions relating to an offence with which he had already been charged. It followed that in relation to such questions the suspect did not have to be further cautioned.

Other powers to compel answers on pain of penalties for refusal exist under the Prevention of Terrorism (Temporary Provisions) Act 1989, and refusal to answer certain allegations from the prosecutor can be treated as acceptances of them under the Drug Trafficking Offences Act 1986.

The closest English law comes to creating a duty to give one's name and address is the power given to the police under s 25(3) of PACE 1984. This is the power to arrest for a non-arrestable offence where the officer cannot find out the suspect's particulars for the purpose of serving a summons on him.

There is no duty to offer information about crime to the police. However, s 11 of the Prevention of Terrorism (Temporary Provisions) Act 1989 makes it an offence for a person who has information which he knows or believes might be of material assistance in preventing an act of terrorism or to secure the arrest of anyone involved in terrorism 'to fail, without reasonable cause, to disclose that information as soon as reasonably practicable'. Additionally, s 5 of the Criminal Law Act 1967 creates the offence of accepting money or other consideration for not disclosing information that would lead to the prosecution of an arrestable offence. The House of Lords has also held that it is the duty of every citizen in whose presence a breach of the peace is being committed to attempt to stop it if necessary by detaining the person responsible. It is, however, except in the case of a citizen who is a police officer, 'a duty of imperfect obligation' (*Albert v Lavin* (1982), *per* Lord Diplock).

9.5.15 What can be said in court about silence in the face of police questioning

There is an established common law rule that neither the prosecution nor the judge should make adverse comment on the defendant's silence in the face of questions. The dividing line, however, between proper and improper judicial comment was a matter of great debate. There are many reasons why a suspect might remain silent when questioned (for example, fear, confusion, reluctance to incriminate another person) and the 'right of silence' enjoyed the status of a long established general principle in English law. Thus, in *R v Davis* (1959), a judge was ruled on appeal to have misdirected the jury when he told them that '... a man is not obliged to say anything but you are entitled to use your common sense ... can you imagine an innocent man who had behaved like that not saying anything to the police ... He said nothing'.

An exception, though, was that some degree of adverse suggestion was permitted where two people were speaking on equal terms and one refused to comment on the accusation made against him by the other. In *R v Parkes* (1976), the Privy Council ruled that a judge could invite the jury to consider the possibility of drawing adverse inferences from silence from a tenant who had been accused by a landlady of murdering her daughter. The landlady and tenant for the purposes of this encounter were regarded as having a parity of status unlike a person faced with questions from the police. It was held in *R v Chandler* (1976) that the suspect was on equal terms with the police officer where the former was in the company of his solicitor. Chandler had refused to answer some of the questions he had been asked by the police officer before the caution and the judge told the jury that they should decide whether the defendant's silence was attributable to his wish to exercise his common law right or because he might incriminate himself. The Court of Appeal quashed Chandler's conviction since the judge had gone too far in suggesting that silence before a caution could be evidence of guilt.

It was proper for the judge to make some comment on a defendant's reticence before being cautioned provided that the jury were directed that the issue had to be dealt with in two stages: (i) was the defendant's silence an acceptance of the officer's allegations?; and, if so, (ii) could guilt of the offence charged be reasonably inferred from what the defendant had implicitly accepted? The court said that it did not accept that a police officer always had an advantage over a suspect. Everything depended on the circumstances. In an inquiry into local government corruption, for example, a young officer might be at a distinct disadvantage when questioning a local dignitary. That type of interview was very different from a 'tearful housewife' being accused of shoplifting.

The Court of Appeal decision in *Chandler* asserted that silence might only be taken as acquiescence to police allegations before a caution. The court excluded silence after the caution as being something from which anything adverse can be inferred because a suspect could not be criticised for remaining silent having been specifically told of that right. This, however, seemed like an irrational dichotomy. If the suspect did, in fact, have a legal right to silence whether or not he or she has been cautioned, it is very odd that full enjoyment of the right could only be effective from the moment of it being announced by the police. Additionally, any questioning of a suspect at a police station prior to a caution being given is probably in contravention of Code C, para 10 which requires a caution to be given at the beginning of each session of questioning. Violation of the Code affords grounds for an appeal under s 78 of PACE 1984. Cautions need not be given according to para 10.1:

> ... if questions are put for other purposes, for example, to establish his identity or his ownership of any vehicle or the need to search him in the exercise of powers of stop and search.

9.5.16 Right to silence in courts

Since 1988, the right to silence was effectively abolished in Northern Ireland. It is possible for a court to draw adverse inferences from a defendant's silence when he was arrested. Adverse inferences can also be drawn from the defendant's failure to provide an explanation for any 'object, substance or mark' on his clothing, footwear or in his possession which the arresting officer found suspicious and questioned the suspect about (Criminal Evidence (Northern Ireland) Order 1988).

Similar recommendations were made by the Home Office Working Group on the Right to Silence in 1989. This question was also considered by the Runciman Royal Commission on Criminal Justice. It had to decide whether to adopt a practice like the Northern Ireland system and the one recommended by the Home Office or whether to retain the right to silence as the Philips Royal Commission on Criminal Procedure had recommended in 1981. In evidence to the Runciman Royal Commission, the proposal to retain the right to silence was supported by The Law Society, the Bar Council and the Magistrates' Association. It was opposed by the police, the Crown Prosecution Service, HM Council of Circuit Judges and senior judges.

Professor Michael Zander's research on this issue has suggested that the role of the right to silence in the real workings of the criminal justice system is in fact not as significant as is often argued. In one of his studies, 'Investigation of crime' [1979] Crim LR 211, he looked at 150 cases randomly drawn from those heard at the Old Bailey. According to police statements, of the 286 defendants (in many cases, there was more than one defendant), only 12 were said to have relied on their right of silence when confronted by police accusations. Of these, nine were convicted. Zander has also made the following points:

- most defendants plead guilty, so the right to silence is unimportant in such a context;

- common law rules permit the judge to *mention* the defendant's silence and in some limited circumstances, to comment on it;

- in any event, the jury may draw adverse conclusions about the defendant's silence to police questions, that is, whether the judge is permitted to comment on this or not.

In a study commissioned by the Lord Chancellor's Department, only 2% of 527 suspects exercised their right to silence, see Sanders *et al*, *Advice and Assistance at Police Stations and the 24 Hour Duty Solicitor Scheme*, 1989, LCD.

In a study by Stephen Motson, Geoffrey Stephenson and Tom Williamson ((1992) 32 British J of Criminology 23, pp 23–40), the researchers looked at 1,067 CID interviews carried out in nine London police stations in 1989. By carefully matching cases where the right to silence had been exercised with like cases where it had not and then comparing the outcomes, the researchers found that decisions as to whether to prosecute were based on factors like the strength of the evidence against the suspect and the seriousness of the offence; they were not correlated with whether the suspect responded to questions or not. There was no evidence that silence at the police station gave the suspect any advantage at court. They commented:

> The high proportion of silence cases who ultimately plead guilty might be taken to suggest that the use of silence is a ploy – adopted for the most part by previously convicted offenders, [it] is abandoned in favour of a guilty plea when prosecution, probable conviction and (especially) sentencing are nigh.

The Runciman Royal Commission eventually decided to recommend retaining the right to silence. Its Report (1993) states (para 82):

> The majority of us believe that adverse inferences should not be drawn from silence at the police station and recommend retaining the present caution and trial direction.

The Commission did, however, recommend (para 84) the retention of the current law regarding silence in investigations of serious and complex fraud under which adverse consequences can follow from silence (see 9.5.14, above). The Report notes that a large proportion of those who use the right to silence later plead guilty. The majority of the commission felt that the possibility of an increase in convicting the guilty by abolishing the right would be outweighed by the considerable extra pressure on innocent suspects in police stations. The commission did, however, meet the police and CPS concern about 'ambush defences' where a defence is entered late in a trial thus leaving the prosecution no time to check and rebut the defence. The Commission recommends that if the defence introduces a late change or departs from the strategy it has disclosed in advance to the prosecution, then it should face adverse comment (para 136). Professor Zander, however, issued a note of dissent that the principle must remain that the burden of proof always lies with the prosecution. He states:

> The fundamental issue at stake is that the burden of proof throughout lies with the prosecution. Defence disclosure is designed to be helpful to the prosecution and, more generally, to the system. But, it is not the job of the defendant to be helpful either to the prosecution or the system.

9.5.17 Effective abolition of the right to silence

The government ignored the recommendations of the Runciman Commission and, in ss 34–37 of the CJPOA 1994, effectively abolished the right to silence. 'Abolished' may be too strong a word because everyone still has the right to remain silent in the same circumstances as they did before the CJPOA 1994; what has changed is the entitlement of a judge or prosecuting counsel to make adverse comment on such a silence.

Notwithstanding the new Act, therefore, any person may refuse to answer questions put to him or her out of court. There are only a few exceptions to this (as with s 2 of the CJA 1987 which concerns the investigation of serious fraud, and requires certain questions to be answered under pain of punishment for refusal) and they existed before the new Act. The CJPOA 1994 does not alter the position of the accused person as a witness – he or she remains a competent but not compellable witness in their own defence (s 35), although, now, the prosecution as well as the judge may comment upon such a failure to give evidence (s 168).

Except in so far as the new law makes changes, the old law still applies.

In enacting ss 34–37 of the CJPOA 1994, the government was adopting a particular policy. The general purpose of the Act was to assist in the fight against crime. The government took the view that the balance in the criminal justice system had become tilted too far in favour of the criminal and against the public in general and victims in particular. The alleged advantage of the change in law is that it helps convict criminals who, under the old law, used to be acquitted because they took advantage of the right to keep quiet when questioned without the court or prosecution being able to comment adversely upon that silence. Introducing the legislation, the Home Secretary said that change in law was desirable because 'it is professional criminals, hardened criminals and terrorists who disproportionately take advantage of and abuse the present system'.

Section 34 states that where anyone is questioned under caution by a police officer, or charged with an offence, then a failure to mention a fact at that time which he later relies on in his defence will allow a court to draw such inferences as appear proper about that failure. Inferences may only be drawn if, in the circumstances, a suspect could reasonably have been expected to mention the fact when he was questioned. The inferences which can be drawn can be used in determining whether the accused is guilty as charged. The section, however, permits adverse inferences to be drawn from silence in situations that do not amount to 'interviews' as defined by Code C of PACE 1984, and thus which are not subject to the safeguards of access to legal advice and of contemporaneous recording which exist where a suspect is interviewed at the police station. The newly amended draft caution to be administered by police officers will read as follows (with appropriate variants for ss 36 and 37):

> You do not have to say anything. But, it may harm your defence if you do not mention when questioned something which you later rely on in court.

As Card and Ward have warned in a commentary on the CJPOA 1994 (1994), a temptation may arise for police officers to give this caution at the earliest possible stage in any situation in which they are talking to someone in connection with a crime, given that the caution may be understood (incorrectly) by some suspects as creating an obligation to speak.

The CJPOA 1994 does not affect earlier law on alibi defences. Under s 11 of the Criminal Justice Act 1967, the defence at trial on indictment cannot adduce evidence in support of an alibi defence (that is, where the accused claims to have been away from the crime at the time of its occurrence) unless notice of the details of that defence have been served on the prosecution within seven days of the transfer for trial. Nevertheless, this rule does not prevent an adverse inference being drawn by a court from a failure to have disclosed that alibi at an earlier stage (when, for instance, the accused was arrested).

Section 35 allows a court or jury to infer what appears proper from the refusal of an accused person, aged 14 or over, to testify in his own defence, or from a refusal without good cause to answer any question at trial. In the *Practice Direction (Procedure in Crown Court Trials – Right to Silence)* (1995), the Lord Chief Justice indicated that, where the accused is legally represented, the following should be said by the judge to the accused's lawyer at the end of the prosecution case if the accused is not to give evidence:

> Have you advised your client that the stage has now been reached at which he may give evidence and, if he chooses not to do so or, having been sworn, without good cause refuses to answer any question, the jury may draw such inferences as appear proper from his failure to do so?

If the lawyer replies to the judge that the accused has been so advised, then the case will proceed. If the accused is not represented, and still chooses not to give evidence or answer a question, the judge must give him a similar warning, ending: '... the jury may draw such inferences as appear proper. That means they may hold it against you.'

Section 36 permits inferences to be drawn from the failure or refusal of a person under arrest to account for any object, substances or mark in his possession, on his person, in or on his clothing or footwear, or in any place at which he is at the time of arrest. Section 37 permits inferences to be drawn from the failure of an arrested person to account for his presence at a particular place where he is found.

Thus, as the late Lord Taylor, the then Lord Chief Justice, observed, the legal changes do not, strictly speaking, abolish the right to silence:

> If a defendant maintains his silence from first till last, and does not rely on any particular fact by way of defence, but simply puts the prosecution to proof, then [ss 34–37] would not bite at all.

This is, of course, correct, but it ignores the change in the general structure of proofs. Article 6 of the European Convention on Human Rights aims to protect the rights of a suspect to a fair trial. It states that:

> Everyone charged with a criminal offence shall be presumed innocent until proved guilty in accordance with law.

The European Commission on Human Rights has already ruled as admissible a complaint that provisions in the law of Northern Ireland equivalent to those in ss 34–37 infringe Art 6. The English provisions will also be taken to Strasbourg.

Since the abolition of the court of Star Chamber in 1641, no English court has had the power to use torture or force to exact confessions from suspects.

The so called 'right to silence' really meant that a suspect could remain silent when questioned by police or in court without prosecution counsel or the judge being allowed to make adverse comment to the jury about such a silence. Traditionally, silence could not be used in court as evidence of guilt.

In support of the old rule, it could be said, that:

- people are innocent until proven guilty of a crime by the State; and that

- people should never be under force to condemn themselves; and that

- there are several reasons other than genuine guilt why someone may wish to remain silent in the face of serious accusations – he or she might be terrified, confused, retarded, wish to protect someone else or fear that the truth would get them in some other type of trouble. The 11th Report of the Criminal Law Revision Committee (1972) gives several examples. The accused might be so shocked at an accusation that he forgets a vital fact which would acquit him of blame; his excuse might be embarrassing like being in the company of a prostitute; or he may fear reprisals from another party.

The 'right' is widely protected in other aspects of society: the police, for example, when facing internal disciplinary charges, are not bound to answer questions or allegations put to them.

The change has been widely and strongly opposed by lawyers, judges and legal campaign groups. Liberty, for example, has said that drawing adverse inferences from silence would undermine the presumption of innocence. Silence is an important safeguard against oppressive questioning by the police, particularly for the weak and vulnerable.

John Alderson, former chief constable of Devon and Cornwall (1973–82) and a respected writer on constitutional aspects of policing, has written of the impending danger when police are able to 'exert legal and psychological pressure on individuals held in the loneliness of their cells'. He states ((1995) *The Independent*, 1 February) that:

> History tells us that, when an individual has to stand up against the entire apparatus of the modern State, he or she is very vulnerable. That is why, in criminal cases, the burden of proof has always rested on the State rather than on the accused. The Founding Fathers of America amended their constitution to that effect in 1791.

Another opponent of the change is the leading criminal law barrister and editor of the authoritative practitioners' text *Archbold on Criminal Evidence, Pleading and Practice*. He has described the Act as 'an ill thought-out package of expedients'. (Richardson, *Archbold*, 1995, Preface, p vii.)

Undermining the right to silence may constitute a significant constitutional change in the relationship between the individual and the State. It may be doubted whether the majority of suspects should be put under greater intimidation by the system because of the conduct of a few 'hardened criminals' – the justification for the legislation given by the Home Secretary when he introduced the legislation.

Two points should be noted, however, to put the debate in its proper historical context. First, it should not be forgotten that there were, prior to the Act, several instances in English law where there was already a legal obligation for a suspect to answer questions. These included the obligation to speak under s 2 of the CJA 1987 (see above); the obligations under ss 431–41 of the Companies Act 1985 (concerning investigations in respect of company officers and agents whose companies are being investigated by the Department of Trade and Industry); the obligations under ss 22 and 131 of the Insolvency Act 1986 (concerning inquiries upon the winding up of companies); s 18 of the Prevention of Terrorism (Temporary Provisions) Act 1989 (concerning information relating to terrorism); and the law under s 11 (as amended) of the Official Secrets Act 1911.

Secondly, in the few cases where the right to silence was used under the pre-Act law, we need to ask how far juries were genuinely sympathetic to the judge's directions that they could not assume guilt from silence. Juries convicted in half of such cases so there is evidence that jurors were suspicious and sceptical about people who exercise the right, just as they may be today where someone exercises the right (that is, remains silent from arrest until the jury retires without relying on any fact he could have mentioned earlier).

9.5.18 Directions to the jury on silent defendants

Following the enactment of the CJPOA 1994, there has been a steady stream of case law as to correct judicial practice when directing the jury about the drawing of adverse inferences under s 34 and s 35.

In *R v Cowan* (1995), the Court of Appeal considered what should be said in the summing up if the defendant decides not to testify. The jury must be directed that (as provided by s 38(3) of the CJPOA 1994) an inference from failure to give evidence could not on its own prove guilty. The jury had to be satisfied (on the basis of the evidence called by the prosecution) that the prosecution had established a case to answer before inferences could be drawn from the accused's silence. The jury could only draw an adverse inference from the accused's silence if it concluded that the silence could only be sensibly attributed to the accused having no answer to the charge or none that could stand up to cross-examination.

The difficult issue as to correct judicial practice when the accused remains silent during interview on the advice of his solicitor was considered in *R v Condron* (1997) and *R v Argent* (1997). These cases make it clear that such advice was only one factor to be taken into consideration along with all the other circumstances, in any jury determination as to whether adverse inferences could be drawn from a 'no comment' interview. In *Condron*, the Court of Appeal considered the guidelines set out in *Cowan* (above) and concluded that they were equally applicable to failure to answer questions (s 34) and failure to testify (s 35). The Court of Appeal approved the Judicial Studies Board specimen direction which states:

> If he failed to mention when he was questioned [a fact which he relied on in his defence], decide whether, in the circumstances which existed at the time, it was a fact he could have reasonably be expected then to mention.
>
> The law is that you may draw such inferences as appear proper from his failure to mention it at that time. You do not have to hold it against him. It is for you to decide whether it is proper to do so.
>
> Failure to mention such a fact at that time cannot, on its own, prove guilt, but, depending on the circumstances, you may hold that failure against him in deciding whether he is guilty, that is, take into account as some additional support for the prosecution's case. It is for you to decide if it is fair to do so.

Stuart-Smith LJ, giving the judgment of the court, went on to say that, in addition to the Judicial Studies Board direction, it was desirable to direct the jury that if, despite any evidence relied upon to explain the failure (to answer questions), or, in the absence of such evidence, they concluded that the failure could only sensibly be attributed to the accused having fabricated the evidence subsequently, they might draw an adverse inference.

More detailed guidance was given in *Argent* where Lord Bingham set out the conditions that had to be met before s 34 could operate. They include:

(a) the failure to answer had to occur before the defendant was charged;

(b) the alleged failure must occur during questioning under caution;

(c) the questioning must be directed at trying to discover whether and by whom the offence has been committed;

(d) the failure must be a failure to mention any fact relied on in the person's defence;

(e) the fact the defendant failed to mention had to be one which this particular defendant could reasonably be expected to have mentioned when being questioned, taking account of all the circumstances existing at that time (for example, the time of day, the defendant's age, experience, mental capacity, state of health, sobriety, personality and access to legal advice).

The Court of Appeal in *Argent* took a similar view to that of the Judicial Studies Board (JSB) as regards the relevance of legal advice to remain silent. This, of course, puts the solicitor who attends the interview under some difficulty, especially as The Law Society guidelines suggest that to remain silent is inappropriate when the police have made less than full disclosure of the evidence available. However, Lord Bingham in *Argent* (1997) added that the jury is not concerned with the correctness of the solicitor's advice, nor with whether it complies with The Law Society guidelines, but with the reasonableness of the defendant's conduct in all circumstances.

The court approved the trial judge's direction to the jury:

> You should consider whether or not he is able to decide for himself what he should do or having asked for a solicitor to advise him he would not challenge that advice (at p 34).

Finally, in *R v Daniel (Anthony Junior)* (1998) CA, it was held that the *dicta* of Stuart-Smith LJ in *Condron* (1997) need not be confined to a subsequent fabrication. In addition to the JSB specimen direction, it is desirable for the judge in an appropriate case to include a passage to the effect that, if the jury conclude that the accused's reticence could only sensibly be attributed to his unwillingness to be subjected to further questioning, or that he had not thought about all the facts, or that he did not have an innocent explanation to give, they might draw an adverse inference. This was upheld soon after by the Court of Appeal in *R v Beckles and Montague* (1999) when the defendant gave a 'no comment' interview on legal advice. It was held that the proper inference under s 34 was not limited to recent fabrication.

Where, however, a judge concludes that the requirements of s 34 have not been satisfied and, therefore, that it is not open to him to leave to the jury the possibility of drawing adverse inferences, he must direct the jury in terms that that they should not in any way hold against the accused the fact that he did not answer questions in interview (*R v McGarry* (1998)).

For a critical examination of the current law on the nature of inferences that may be drawn under s 34, see Turner, 'Inferences under s 34 of the Criminal Justice and Public Order Act 1994: Part One and Part Two' (1999) 163 JP, 27 March and 24 April.

9.5.19 Tape-recording of interrogations

The police were initially very hostile to the recommendation of the Philips Royal Commission on Criminal Procedure that there should be tape-recording of interviews with suspects. After a while, however, the police became more enthusiastic when it became apparent that the tape-recording of the interrogations increased the proportion of guilty pleas and reduced the challenges to prosecution evidence. Tape-recording of interviews is conducted in accordance with Code of Practice E. The tapes are time-coded so that they cannot be interfered with. It is now compulsory for all police stations to record all interviews with suspects interrogated in connection with indictable offences.

9.5.20 Confessions and the admissibility of evidence

It was long established by the common law that a confession would not be admitted in evidence if it was 'involuntary' in the sense that it was obtained by threat or promise held out by a person in authority. This would include '... even the most gentle, if I may put it that way, threats or slight inducements', *per* Lord Parker CJ in *R v Smith* (1959). In that case, a sergeant major had put the whole company on parade and told them no one would be allowed to move until one of them gave details about which of them had been involved in a fight resulting in a stabbing. A confession resulting from this incident was ruled to have been something that should not have been admitted (although the conviction was not quashed as there was other evidence against the defendant).

In *R v Zavekas* (1970), a conviction was quashed where it had resulted from an improper promise. Z was told that the police were arranging an identification parade and that he would be free to go if he was not picked out. He asked whether he could be allowed to go at once if he made a statement. The officer agreed and then Z made a statement admitting guilt. The admission was given in evidence and Z was convicted. His conviction was quashed even though the inducement had not been proffered by the police. Similarly, the Court of Appeal regarded it a 'fatal inducement' for a police officer to have agreed to a request by the defendant, in *R v Northam* (1967), for a second offence to be taken into account at a forthcoming trial rather than tried as a separate matter.

Apart from threats and promises, 'oppression' leading to a confession would render such a statement inadmissible. The Judges Rules were a set of guidelines made by Divisional Court judges for excluding unreliable evidence but they left it as discretionary whether violation of the rules should result in the exclusion of any resultant evidence.

There had been a significant change in the approach of the courts by the 1980s. The new approach was to ask, even where there had been promises or threats, as a matter of fact and causation, had there been an involuntary confession? In *R v Rennie* (1985), Lord Lane CJ stated that, even where a confession was made 'with a hope that an admission may lead to an earlier release or a lighter sentence' and the hopes were prompted by something said or done by a person in authority, the confession would not automatically be regarded as involuntary. The same applied where, as in the present case, a confession was prompted by a fear that otherwise the police would interview and perhaps charge the defendant's sister and mother. The judge should apply his 'common sense' and assume that voluntary meant 'of one's own free will'.

This approach was much criticised as it was often impossible for even trained psychologists to realise which pressures on a suspect being questioned were the ones that prompted him or her to confess.

The law is now contained in s 76 of PACE 1984 which renders inadmissible any confession obtained as a result of (i) oppression (s 76(2)(a)) or (ii) which was obtained in consequence of something 'likely in the circumstances to render unreliable any confession which might be made by the accused in consequence thereof' (s 76(2)(b)). 'Oppression' is defined by s 76(8) to include 'torture, inhuman or degrading treatment, and the use or threat of violence'.

9.5.21 Oppression

The judge rules on whether evidence is admissible on these lines; if it is admitted, then the jury decides whether to believe it. There should be a 'trial within a trial' – without the jury – to determine whether the evidence is admissible (*R v Liverpool Juvenile Court ex p R* (1988)).

The courts have not found much evidence of 'oppression' in police questioning. In *Miller* (1986), a paranoid schizophrenic had confessed to killing his girlfriend. He had admitted the killing in an interview which contained both reliable and unreliable matter. He later retracted his confession. It was argued for him at trial that the confession should be excluded under s 76(2)(a) – that it had been obtained by 'oppression of the person who made it' as it had come as the result of protracted and oppressive interviews which had caused him to suffer an episode of 'schizophrenic terror'. Medical evidence was given that the style and length of questioning had produced a state of voluntary insanity in which his language reflected hallucinations and delusion. The judge would not exclude the evidence and the defendant was convicted of manslaughter. The Court of Appeal held that the mere fact that questions triggered off hallucinations in the defendant was not evidence of oppression.

In *R v Fulling* (1987), the Court of Appeal held that it was not oppression for the police to tell the defendant that her lover had been having an affair with another woman which so affected her that she made a confession. The word 'oppression', the court held, should be given its ordinary dictionary meaning as stated in the *Oxford English Dictionary*:

> The exercise of authority or power in a burdensome, harsh or wrongful manner; unjust or cruel treatment of subjects, inferiors, etc; the imposition of unreasonable or unjust burdens.

9.5.22 Unreliability

Evidence of a confession can be excluded if it was given:

> ... in consequence of anything said or done which was likely in the circumstances existing at the time, to render unreliable any confession which might be made by him in consequence thereof ... (s 76(2)(b)).

The phrase 'anything said or done' means by someone other than the suspect. In *R v Goldenberg* (1988), G, a heroin addict, was arrested on a charge of conspiracy to supply the diamorphine. He requested an interview five days after his arrest and, during this, he gave information about a man whom he said had supplied him with heroin. It was argued for G at trial that he had given the statement to get bail and thus to be able to feed his addiction; that the words 'in consequence of anything said or done ...' included things said or done by the suspect and that the critical thing here was the things G had said and done: namely, requested the interview and given any statement that would be likely to get him out of the station. G was convicted and his appeal was dismissed. Neill LJ stated:

> In our judgment, the words 'said or done' in s 76(2)(b) of the 1984 Act do not extend so as to include anything said or done by the person making the confession. It is clear from the wording of the section and the use of the words 'in consequence' that a causal link must be shown between what was said or done and the subsequent confession. In our view, it necessarily follows that 'anything said or done' is limited to something external to the person making the confession and to something which is likely to have some influence on him.

The reasoning in cases like *Zavekas* (1970) (see 9.5.20, above) has now clearly been rejected. This view is confirmed by Code C that, if a suspect asks an officer what action will be taken in the event of his answering questions, making a statement or refusing to do either, the officer may inform him what action he proposes to take in that event 'provided that the action is itself proper and warranted' (para 11.3).

9.5.23 *R v Heaton* (1993)

In *R v Heaton* (1993), the appellant was convicted of manslaughter of his 26 day old son. The evidence of the mother, who was of limited intelligence, was that the appellant had shaken the child hard to quieten him and that he subsequently went limp and breathless. She had also said that she had given the child Calpol (a children's medicine containing paracetamol).

Due to difficulties in contacting the appellant's solicitor, he had been in custody overnight for some 15 and a half hours by the time he was able to see a solicitor. As he said he had been ill, he was examined by a doctor who said he was fit to be interviewed. He was interviewed for about 75 minutes in the presence of the solicitor and the interview was tape-recorded. The first part of the interview dealt with his background details. When asked about the events leading up to the child's death, he at first denied that he had held the child. Later, he admitted holding the child but denied holding him up in the air. Under further questioning, he admitted holding the child up in the air and finally conceded that he had shaken the child about four times to and fro to keep him quiet and that the child's head was flopping.

The defence case was that the death could have been caused solely by the administration of the wrong drug by the mother; although she claimed to have given the child Calpol, which contained paracetamol, no evidence of any paracetamol was found in the child's body on post-mortem; however, promethazine was found in the blood and was the active ingredient of Phenergen, a drug which the mother also had in the house for the older children. In his evidence, the appellant said that he come downstairs to find the baby purplish in the face and breathless and had seen the mother giving him some medicine, following which she became hysterical and shook the baby. In the interview, he had been upset and, as the police would not believe what he was saying, in the end, he had told them that he had shaken the child. He denied that he had done so violently or in order to quieten the child.

On the *voir dire* (the trial within a trial where the judge, having asked the jury to go out, decides a dispute between counsel as to whether certain evidence is admissible), the defence sought to exclude the evidence of the appellant's interview under ss 76 and 78 of PACE 1984. An application was made to call a psychiatrist, Dr Z, on the *voir dire*. The trial judge ruled against admitting Dr Z's evidence and that the interview should be admitted.

On appeal, it was argued on the appellant's behalf: that the trial judge was wrong to exclude the evidence of Dr Z; that the trial judge should have excluded the interview because the officers concerned had applied pressure to the appellant, raising their voices and repeating their questions.

9.5.24 The Court of Appeal's decision

The Court of Appeal dismissed the appeal, holding:

- The trial judge had considered Dr Z's report, which was based upon a single interview with the appellant, sight of the case papers, hearing of the interview tapes and a conversation with the probation officer. Dr Z had noted in particular: 'My impression is that he is not exceptionally bright and is possibly of dull normal intelligence and is very suggestible.' In *R v Turner* (1975), Lawton LJ said at p 83:

  ... an expert's opinion is admissible to furnish the court with scientific information which is likely to be outside the experience and knowledge of a judge or jury. If, on the proven facts, a judge or jury can form their own conclusions without help, then the opinion of an expert is unnecessary. In such a case, if it is given dressed up in scientific jargon, it may make judgment more difficult. The fact that an expert witness has impressive scientific qualifications does not, by that fact alone, make his opinion on matters of human nature or behaviour within the limits of normality any more helpful than that of the jurors themselves; but there is a danger that they may think it does.

In the more recent case of *R v Raghip, Silcott and Braithwaite* (1991), the Court of Appeal had drawn a distinction between psychiatric or psychological evidence going to *mens rea* and such evidence going to the reliability of a confession, but had not criticised the general principle laid down in *Turner*. The court had rejected a 'judge for yourself' approach by the judge in respect of the jury and, it would seem, in respect of his own task on a *voir dire*, where there was expert evidence which would have been of assistance in assessing the defendant's mental condition. In that case, Alliott J said:

> ... the state of the psychological evidence before us ... is such that the jury would have been assisted in assessing the mental condition of Raghip and the consequent reliability of the alleged confessions. Notwithstanding that Raghip's IQ was at 74 just in the borderline range, a man chronologically aged 19 years seven months at the date of the interview with a level of functioning equivalent to that of a child of nine years, and the reading capacity of a child of six years, cannot be said to be normal. It would be impossible for the layman to divide that data from Raghip's performance in the witness box, still less the abnormal suggestibility of which [the expert witness] spoke.

- There was, in *Heaton,* no suggestion of mental handicap or retardation; the appellant was within the normal range of intelligence albeit towards the duller end of it. There was nothing more than Dr Z's bare impression that the appellant was very suggestible; there was no data on which to found that assertion nor was it clear that 'very suggestible' was outside the normal range. The judge expressly indicated that he should be told if there was anything more to Dr Z's evidence than was contained in his report and he was not informed of anything else. In those circumstances, he concluded that there was nothing in the doctor's impression which complied with the tests laid down in *Turner* and illustrated by *Raghip*; in the court's judgment, he was justified in ruling as he did. Unless the medical evidence sought to be introduced on an issue of this kind was truly based on some scientific data or expert analysis outside the experience of judge and jury, a mere impression, even of a highly qualified doctor, that the defendant 'is not exceptionally bright' or was 'very suggestible' was not admissible for the reasons set out by Lawton LJ.

- The court had read the transcript of the interview and heard the tape-recordings. The appellant had a full opportunity to consult with a solicitor before the interview and the solicitor was present throughout. A doctor had examined the appellant and pronounced him fit to be interviewed. The questioning lasted in all only some 75 minutes and much of the first two tapes was concerned merely with taking the appellant's history. Voices were slightly raised but there was no shouting and no oppressive hostility; the pace of the interview was slow and the appellant was given time to consider his replies. Some questions were repeated several times but not inappropriately. In *R v Paris, Abdullahi and Miller* (1992), where similar arguments were raised, the court said:

> Of course, it is perfectly legitimate for officers to pursue their interrogation of their suspect with a view to eliciting his account or gaining admissions. They are not required to give up after the first denial or even after a number of denials.

In that case, the questioning had continued for some 13 hours and the tapes had shown hostility and bullying on the part of the interviewing officers. In the present case, the situation was wholly different, with the appellant changing his story gradually over a comparatively short period and providing further details without the police putting them in. The judge had been right to conclude that the prosecution had discharged the burden upon them to exclude oppression and the possibility that the circumstances might have rendered the admission unreliable.

In a commentary on *Heaton* in the *Criminal Law Review*, it is pointed out that the law on confessions is developing in a number of ways to prevent, as far as is possible, the conviction of weak minded and suggestible persons on the basis of their own unreliable statements. In addition to the exclusionary rule in s 76(2)(b) of PACE 1984 and the discretion in s 78, defendants labouring under a 'significant degree of mental handicap' are protected by the rule in *McKenzie* (1992), which requires an unconvincing case based solely on confessions to be withdrawn from the jury.

9.5.25 Research findings

In an interesting study of police interview techniques ('Police interview techniques: establishing truth or proof?' (1993) 33 British J of Criminology 3), John Baldwin analysed 400 videoed police interviews with suspects – 100 from each of four police stations – and 200 audio-taped interviews taken from two busy stations. As he observes, an interrogation leading to a confession can be of great importance to the police as it can provide an alternative to a time consuming investigation of the crime. Baldwin did not find much evidence of oppression but rather of deficiency in questioning technique:

> ... coercion or belligerence in police interviews strike the observer much less frequently than feebleness and ineptitude. Instances of heavy handedness were much less common than unduly timorous questioning. It must, nonetheless, be acknowledged that the boundaries between officers acting, say, upon an assumption of guilt, or failing adequately to listen to suspects' responses, and exerting undue pressures to induce a confession, are thoroughly blurred.

Baldwin concludes that, evaluated as a search for 'the truth', most police interviews are 'thoroughly deficient'. But such a judgment would be to miss the point of interrogation, a central feature of which is concerned with the future rather than past events. Interrogations are, he argues, conducted with an eye to any subsequent trial:

> A main purpose of the interrogation is thus to seek to limit, close down, or pre-empt the future options available to the subject. It will be very difficult for suspects to claim in court that, say, goods were taken by accident or that they were not at the scene when precisely the opposite was established in an earlier taped interview.

9.5.26 Evidence illegally or improperly obtained

There is an overlap between the subject of this discussion and that above because, sometimes, the illegally or improperly obtained evidence will be a confession, in which case the rules above will also apply.

There was for a long time a judicial discretion to exclude otherwise admissible evidence on the basis that it would be unfair to the defendant. The *dictum* of Lord Goddard CJ on this was often cited. He said: 'If, for instance, some admission or piece of evidence, for example, a document, had been obtained from a defendant by a trick, no doubt the judge might properly rule it out.' (See *Kuruma Son of Kaniu v R* (1955), a Privy Council case dealing with an appeal from Kenya. It held that, if evidence was relevant, it did not matter how it was obtained.)

In *R v Sang* (1979), the House of Lords took a very restrictive view of the discretion, holding that it could not be used to exclude evidence merely on the basis that it was given by an agent provocateur. The defendant claimed he had been induced to commit an offence by an informer acting on the instructions of the police. All the judges ruled that there was no defence of entrapment in English law. They were also unanimous in ruling that (except for confessions or issues of self-incrimination) no discretion existed to exclude evidence simply on the basis that it had been improperly or illegally obtained. Such illegality might lead to civil proceedings or disciplinary action within the police but not for excluding evidence. The only basis for excluding relevant evidence was if its prejudicial effect outweighed its probative value. This reasoning has been reconfirmed by the Court of Appeal in *R v Spurthwaite and Gill* (1993).

The approach of s 78 of PACE 1984 is to widen the discretion. It does not go so far as the system in the United States where improperly obtained evidence is inadmissible – the doctrine that the fruit of the poisoned tree should not be eaten. It states that the court *may* refuse to allow evidence on which the prosecution proposes to rely:

... if it appears to the court that, having regard to all the circumstances, including the circumstances in which the evidence was obtained, the admission of the evidence would have such an adverse effect on the fairness of the proceedings that the court ought not to admit it.

The courts have been persuaded on many occasions to exclude evidence using this section. In fact, Zander has suggested that 'the judges have forged the somewhat ambiguous words of s 78 into a powerful weapon to hold the police accountable for breaches of the law and the Codes of Practice'. Most cases have involved access to solicitors or the law relating to interrogations. In *R v Absolam* (1989), the Court of Appeal quashed a conviction for supplying cannabis where A, in contravention of the Code, had not been told of his right to a solicitor and rules about the tape-recording of interviews were broken.

Unlike the rule applying to s 76 (see 9.5.22, above), there does not need to be a trial within a trial under s 78 to determine whether the evidence is admissible. The admissibility of a confession can be opposed under both s 76 and s 78. The court will be less willing to exclude evidence where there were technical breaches but the defendant had experience of police stations. In *R v Dunford* (1991), the Court of Appeal refused to quash a conviction in spite of a serious breach of s 58 (see 9.5.4, above) because D, who had several previous convictions, answered 'No comment' to awkward questions of the police and refused to sign a record of the interview. The court thought it was extremely doubtful 'whether the solicitor's advice would have added anything to [his] knowledge of his rights'.

9.5.27 Runciman Royal Commission proposals

The Commission's recommendations in this area are of particular interest as it was set up in the wake of a number of grave miscarriages of justice in which people had been wrongly convicted on the basis of subsequently discredited confession evidence. The Commission was announced on the day the Birmingham Six were released from jail having served 16 years for crimes which later scientific evidence showed they could not have confessed to in the way the police alleged.

9.5.28 Confession evidence

The Commission said:

- (para 85) when PACE 1984 is next revisited, attention should be given to the fact that s 77 (judge's duty to caution the jury of the need for care in cases where mentally handicapped people have made confessions without independent witnesses) is limited to the 'mentally handicapped' and does not include the 'mentally ill' or other categories of the 'mentally disordered';

- (para 86) the law should be changed so that a judge may stop any case if the prosecution evidence is demonstrably unsafe or unsatisfactory or too weak to be allowed to go to the jury;

- (para 87) wherever a confession has allegedly been made to the police outside the police station, whether tape-recorded or not, it should be put to the suspect at the beginning of the first tape-recorded interview at the station. Failure to do this may render the alleged confession inadmissible, but, if the suspect does not confirm the confession on the tape, it should not automatically be inadmissible;

- (para 88) an alleged confession to an investigating official should be allowed to go before the jury even if not tape-recorded, provided it meets the tests contained in PACE 1984 and the judge believes the jury could safely consider it.

9.5.29 Corroboration of confessions

- (para 89) there should be a judicial warning in cases where confession evidence is involved. The precise terms of the warning should depend on the circumstances of the case. If it remains possible for a confession to be admitted without other supporting evidence, the jury should be warned that great care is needed before convicting on the basis of the confession alone;

- (para 90) the majority of the commission believed that, where a confession is credible, and has passed the tests laid down in PACE 1984, the jury should be able to consider it even in the absence of other evidence. The judge should in all such cases give a strong warning to the jury. The other evidence which the jury should be advised to look for should be supporting evidence (that is, of a different kind) in the *R v Turnbull* (1977) sense.

There was considerable disquiet among defence lawyers and civil liberty groups that the Commission had not recommended the automatic inadmissibility of uncorroborated confessions. (See, for example, (1993) *The Guardian*, 7 July.) Consider, for example, the case of the Guildford Four. Three men and a woman were jailed for life in 1975 after being convicted of bombing pubs in 1974 which killed five people. The evidence against them amounted to confessions they were alleged to have made. Fourteen years after conviction, a rough set of typed notes was discovered with handwritten addenda which matched one of the men's supposedly contemporaneously recorded interview. The Lord Chief Justice, Lord Lane, concluded that the police officers involved must have lied. The three former officers, however, were acquitted later on charges of attempting to pervert the course of justice. Alistair Logan, solicitor for two of the men, has pointed out that the men would not necessarily have been saved by Runciman's recommendations because these accept the possibility of uncorroborated confessions going to the jury.

The Commission's Report notes that it is now generally accepted that people do on occasions confess to crimes they have not committed, perhaps due to a desire for notoriety, to protect somebody else, or for immediate advantage like wanting to get out of the police station. The long held belief that people will not make false statements against themselves can no longer be sustained. The Report advocates the introduction of continuous video-recording of all police custody suites at a cost of about £9 million. The Report states (para 50):

> Continuous video-recording (including sound track) of all the activities in the custody office, the passages and stairways leading from the custody office to the cells and, if feasible, the cell passage and the doors of individual cells of all police stations designated under PACE 1984 as suitable for detaining suspects should be introduced as soon as practicable.

John Baldwin has argued ('Power and police interviews' [1993] NLJ 1194, 14 August) that the Royal Commission's Report was sadly lacking in not providing recommendations for a better legal regulation of police questioning of suspects. He says in the Report:

> There is little new thinking or analysis; rather, the emphasis is upon re-working old ideas and offering encouragement to those professional groups which are striving to improve their own procedures.

The problem needing to be addressed, argues Baldwin, is basically one of power:

> Legal advisers and their clients are bound to be relatively powerless in a situation in which it is police officers who decide when an interview takes place, how it is to be conducted and for how long. Interviews take place on police territory and on police terms. Police officers can even determine who sits where in the interview room and they may deliberately prevent eye contact between legal representatives and their clients by physically bolting the chairs to the floor. Their power to eject troublesome advisers from the interview room [Code of Practice C, para 6.9], though very infrequently exercised, underlines still further who is in charge.

It would still be open to the Home Secretary to enact changes that were not contained in the Runciman Report.

THE CRIMINAL PROCESS:
(1) THE INVESTIGATION OF CRIME

At the end of the 20th century, we can see the first governmental recognition of something of something called a 'criminal justice system'. The police, the probation service, the prison service, the magistracy, the Crown Courts and other elements have all been grouped within the system, This means that rules or policy relating to one element can be evaluated in terms of their impact in relation to another part of the system. Conflicting public desires arise in this area. On the one hand, there is a general mistrust of certain sorts of policing, and a desire for more protective civil liberties law, while, on the other hand, there is a desire for more offenders to be captured and punished, and the belief that, in order for this to succeed, civil liberties need to be reduced. The Macpherson Report following the stabbing of Stephen Lawrence has given a significant impetus for reform of the law relating to policing.

Remedies

Remedies for unlawful arrest include (1) an action for *habeas corpus*; (2) that any subsequent prosecution arising from the arrest should fail – s 78 of PACE 1984; and (3) an action for damages for false imprisonment. If the arrest is not lawful then reasonable force may be used to resist it.

Arrest

Arrest can be (1) under police warrant; (2) under common law for breach of the peace; or (3) under legislation, principally, PACE 1984. The details in ss 24 and 25 of PACE 1984 and connected cases are very important.

Detention

Detention short of arrest does not exist except under the Prevention of Terrorism (Temporary Provisions) Act 1989. Note this confirmation by s 29 of PACE 1984.

Suspects stopped in the street

Suspects stopped in the street are not legally obliged to help police with enquiries. Note the distinction between *Kenlin v Gardiner* (1967) and *Donnelly v Jackman* (1970). Note also that a person may be arrested for being silent or misleading under s 25 if the officer has reasonable doubts about the suspect's name and address or whether the summons procedure can be used at the address given. Note the newly enlarged powers of stop and search under s 60 and s 81 of the CJPOA 1994.

Procedure on arrest

Procedure on arrest involves the arrestor having to inform the suspect of the grounds for arrest (s 28(3)). Note, though, that an arrest becomes lawful from when the information is given. The extent of the required information to the suspect is important (see *Geldberg v Miller* (1961); *R v Telfer* (1976)).

The use of force

The use of force to effect an arrest must be 'reasonable in all the circumstances' (s 3 of the Criminal Law Act 1967 (citizens); s 117 of PACE 1984 (police officers)).

Stop and search

Stop and search is governed by s 1 and Code A of PACE 1984. The judge can exclude evidence obtained in breach of the Codes (s 67(7) of PACE 1984). There are legal obligations on an officer conducting a search (ss 2 and 3 of PACE 1984). Note the Code is quite specific about what indices can be grounds for reasonable suspicion and which, individually or combined, may not.

Section 60 of the Criminal Justice and Public Order Act 1994 has provided a new stop and search power in anticipation of violence. Under it, with authorisation, an officer can stop any pedestrian and search him or her for offence weapons or dangerous instruments, or even stop vehicles. The authorising officer must reasonably believe that incidents involving serious violence may take place in the area. Section 81 of the same Act creates a new power of stop and search of people and vehicles where it is expedient to do so to prevent certain acts of terrorism.

Search of arrested persons

Search of arrested persons is governed by s 32 of PACE 1984. The person arrested cannot be required to take off more than outer garments. The place where he or she was arrested, or where he or she was immediately before can also be searched under s 32. Note the differences between this power and those of s 18 regarding premises.

Search on detention

Search on detention is governed by s 54 of PACE 1984 and Code C, para 4.1 which require the custody officer to take charge of the process of searching the detained person.

Premises

Premises can be entered by police (1) with permission; or (2) to prevent a breach of the peace; or (3) pursuant to s 18 or s 32 of PACE 1984. The differences between these provisions are important. They are:

	Section 18 (entry and search after arrest)	Section 32 (Search of premises has to be at time of arrest)
Search of person:	(only s 32)	for weapons, means to escape, evidence relating to 'an offence', that is, any offence
Search of premises:	The police may enter and search the arrestee's premises to look for evidence relating to the offence for which the person was arrested or some other arrestable offence connected with that or similar to that offence for which he was arrested.	To enter and search premises where D was when or immediately before arrest for evidence relating to *the offence for which the person was arrested.* They need not be his premises but the power must be based on reasonable belief that the officer will find something for which a search is permitted.

Seizure of articles from searches

Seizure of articles from searches under s 19 and Code B, s 6 are quite wide, including items from any offence. The exemptions, like items under legal professional privilege, are important.

Search warrants and safeguards

Search warrants and safeguards issued under s 8 of PACE 1984 require the magistrate to be satisfied of four things. Note the difficulty of balancing the interests of effective policing with those of civil liberties. Note the ambiguity in s 15 and the way it was resolved in *R v Longman* (1988).

Interrogation, confession and admissibility of evidence

The main problem here is for the law to strike the proper balance between giving the police sufficient power to interrogate and protecting the interests of suspects. Too few rules governing how the police can conduct an interrogation and too few rules restricting the sort of evidence that can be put to a jury, might easily lead to oppressive behaviour by the police interviewing suspects. Too many restrictive rules, conversely, will thwart the police in their endeavours to prosecute offenders successfully.

The right to have someone informed

The right to have someone informed after arrest is given (s 56(1), Code C, para 5.1) to all suspects after arrest. It can be delayed, however, under s 116. The case must involve a 'serious arrestable offence' and it must be authorised by a superintendent on certain grounds, for example, the arrested person would alert others involved in a crime.

Access to legal advice

Access to legal advice is provided for under s 58 and Code C. The notification must accord with details set out in Code C. Note the criticisms of the Duty Solicitor scheme. Is it adequately staffed? Note also the circumstances in which legal advice can be delayed under s 116, Code C, Annex B. In an emergency, questioning can begin before the suspect's legal advisor arrives (Code C, para 6.6).

Time limits

Time limits before and after charges note ss 42 and 38 of PACE 1984. Delayed access to legal advice is possible in cases of serious arrestable offences. A suspect can be held for up to 24 hours without being charged; longer with authorisation from the superintendent and up to 96 hours with magistrates' permission.

The right to silence

The right to silence means that a person cannot be charged with obstructing the police in the execution of their duty simply by failing to answer questions. Note the important difference between *Rice v Connolly* (1966) and *Ricketts v Cox* (1982). There are some circumstances where the suspect does have to answer on pain of penalty (s 2 of the CJA 1987).

What could be said in court, before April 1995, about the defendant's silence, varied according to whether the questions were put by an officer or someone on equal terms to the questioned person. Generally, no adverse inferences could be invited although the judge could comment on reticence prior to cautioning. Most defendants did not use the right and of those who did few seemed, according to research, to benefit from it.

Now, after ss 34–37 of the CJPOA 1994, certain adverse inferences may be drawn from a suspect's failure to answer police questions, or his failure to answer them in court.

Confessions

Confessions must be voluntary and given without oppression being used to extract them; they must also not come from any circumstances likely to make them unreliable (s 76).

Evidence illegally obtained

Evidence illegally or improperly obtained is not automatically inadmissible but it may be excluded under s 78 if it appears to a court that in all the circumstances the admission of the evidence 'would have such an adverse effect on the fairness of the proceedings that the court ought not to admit it'.

Runciman Royal Commission recommendations

The Runciman Royal Commission recommendations included:

- that the law should be changed so that a judge may stop any case if the prosecution evidence is demonstrably unsafe or unsatisfactory or too weak to be allowed to go to the jury;

- that wherever a confession has allegedly been made to the police outside the police station, whether tape-recorded or not, it should be put to the suspect at the beginning of the first tape-recorded interview at the station. Failure to do this may render the alleged confession inadmissible, but if the suspect does not confirm the confession on the tape, it should not automatically be inadmissible;

- that there should be a judicial warning in cases where confession evidence is involved. The precise terms of the warning should depend on the circumstances of the case. If it remains possible for a confession to be admitted without other supporting evidence, the jury should be warned that great care is needed before convicting on the basis of the confession alone;

- that where a confession is credible, and has passed the tests laid down in PACE 1984, the jury should be able to consider it even in the absence of other evidence. The judge should in all such cases give a strong warning to the jury. The other evidence which the jury should be advised to look for should be supporting evidence of a different kind.

CHAPTER 10

THE CRIMINAL PROCESS:
(2) THE PROSECUTION

The classification of offences, and matters relating to transfers for trial, summary trial and trial on indictment are dealt with in Chapter 4.

Until 1986, England was one of only a few countries which allowed the police to prosecute rather than hand over this task to a State agency like the district attorney in the United States. The Crown Prosecution Service (CPS) was established by the Prosecution of Offences Act (POA) 1985 and the police now play no part in prosecutions beyond the stage of charging the suspect.

There have been many problems with the new system and some writers, like Zander, have argued that the change could represent a considerable setback for the criminal justice system (Michael Zander, *Cases and Materials on the English Legal System* (1996)). There used to be five different forms of prosecution, those by:

- the police, who prosecuted most offences;

- the Attorney General/Solicitor General whose permission is needed to prosecute for many serious crimes and who can enter a *nolle prosequi* to stop certain prosecutions or give a *fiat* to disallow them to begin;

- the Director of Public Prosecutions (DPP) who prosecutes in very serious cases and cases brought to him by the government;

- public bodies, like local authorities. These used to amount to about 25% of all prosecutions, most being by the Post Office for television licence offences;

- private prosecutions, which involve having to persuade a magistrate of the propriety in issuing a summons. The Attorney General and the DPP both have the power to take over a private prosecution and then drop it for reasons of public policy. Private bodies like stores and the RSPCA most regularly bring prosecutions. A study in 1980 showed that only 2.4% of prosecutions were private (Lidstone, *Prosecutions by Private Individuals and Non-police Agencies* (1980)).

10.1   The Crown Prosecution Service

The move to establish a CPS was precipitated by a report from JUSTICE, the British section of the International Commission of Jurists, in its 1970 Report, *The Prosecution Process in England and Wales*. It argued that the police were not best suited to be prosecutors because they would often have a commitment to winning a case even where the evidence was weak. They were also not best placed to consider the public policy aspects of the discretion not to prosecute. The police were firmly opposed to such a change. They argued that statistics showed that the police were not given to pursuing cases in a way which led to a high rate of acquittal. They also showed that in cases involving miscarriages of justice, the decision to prosecute had been taken by a lawyer.

The question was referred to the Philips Royal Commission on Criminal Procedure which judged the then existing system according to its fairness, openness and accountability. It proposed a new system based on several distinct features including:

- that the initial decision to charge a suspect should rest with the police;

- that thereafter all decisions as to whether to proceed, alter or drop the charges should rest with another State prosecuting agency;

- this agency would provide advocates for all cases in the magistrates' courts apart from guilty pleas by post. It should also provide legal advice to the police and instruct counsel in all cases tried on indictment.

The Crown Prosecution Act 1985 established a national prosecution service under the general direction of the DPP. The 1985 Act gives to the DPP and the CPS as a whole the right to institute and conduct any criminal proceedings where the importance or difficulty of the case make that appropriate (s 3(2)(b)). This applies to cases that could also be started by the police or other bodies like local authorities. It can also, in appropriate circumstances, take over and then discontinue cases. The CPS relies on the police for the resources and machinery of investigation.

In the period following its launch, the CPS experienced severe problems of staff shortage related to the general funding of the service. This improved over the years, and by March 1993 the full lawyer staff establishment had almost been met. It was apparently difficult to recruit staff of an adequate standard for the available pay and there has been considerable use of agents, that is, lawyers in private practice working for the CPS on a fee-for-case basis. The 1992–93 Annual Report of the CPS stated that:

> In the absence of CPS rights of audience, the presentation of all cases in the Crown Court and higher courts continues to be undertaken by counsel in private practice. In 1992–93, total expenditure was £68.5 million. The average payment in the Crown Court was £460.

The eighth annual report of the CPS (June 1994) brought much new information into the debate about how well this controversial organisation is doing its job. The new Code for Crown Prosecutors, published at the same time makes some contentious changes to the criteria used to decide whether a prosecution should be brought.

Since its inception, the CPS has been criticised for a variety of alleged faults, principally that it is inefficient and has a low success rate in prosecutions. Many police officers have expressed doubts about the rigour with which cases are handled by the CPS, and have dubbed it the 'Criminal Prosecution Society'. The Bar Council passed a motion in 1993 condemning the service for being too ready to abandon cases 'fearing defeat or cost'.

The former Director of Prosecutions, Barbara Mills QC, who headed the CPS until April 1998, laid much of the responsibility for poor conviction rates at the door of the police. In one public statement, she blamed lack of proper preparation by the police for two-fifths of the 185,824 cases dropped in the magistrates' court in 1992–93. Another 8,046 were dropped at the Crown Court. Mrs Mills claimed that in a quarter of cases that had to be dropped, CPS lawyers had no option because witnesses were missing or refused to give evidence or because the case was being considered elsewhere in the justice system so the 'double jeopardy' rule applied. Between 1994 and 1997, crime figures fell but arrest rates remained static reflecting what police claim was increasing success against offenders but the percentage of magistrate-level cases discontinued by the CPS crept up. Again, the reasoning for dropping or downgrading cases was found wanting.

To answer criticism, the CPS commissioned an analysis sample 10,000 cases that it had to drop in 1992–93. The results show that 43% were abandoned on the ground of insufficient evidence to provide a realistic prospect of conviction. In 31% of cases, prosecutors abandoned them because it was 'not in the public interest' to proceed, for example, where the defendant had already been convicted and sentenced on another matter (9%) or only a nominal penalty was likely (6%). Much criticism of the CPS has come from police officers who object to the CPS continuing not to pursue cases for these very reasons.

A highly critical report published by a review body headed by Sir Iain Glidewell in June 1998, concluded that the CPS failed to achieve the expected improvements in the prosecution system since it was set up in 1986 and became bureaucratic and over- centralised. The report depicts a service where charges are thought to be 'inappropriately downgraded' and a disproportionately large number of serious violent crimes not prosecuted. Proposals for a complete overhaul of the CPS were strongly backed by many in the criminal justice system ((1998) *The Times*, 2 June).

As a result of the Glidewell Report, the CPS underwent a major structural re-organisation in 1999. Its operation was decentralised so as to realign the CPS areas to match the boundaries of police forces – there were previously 13 CPS areas and now there are 42 to match the 43 police forces of England and Wales (there are two police forces for London, the Metropolitan Police and the City of London police). New Chief Crown Prosecutors (CCPs) for the 42 areas were appointed in 1999. As its casework load is so large, London has three CCPs. The new DPP, David Calvert-Smith QC, stated that:

The new postholders will, in effect, be local DPPs with the power to act on their own initiative and to take their own decisions. They will be placing a priority on prosecution work which will benefit the local communities they serve. (Crown Prosecution Service Official Statement, 109/99, 8 March 1999).

The CCPs will be accountable to their local communities, and the CPS contends that a localised service will enable good working relationships with the other agencies in the criminal justice system, including the police, the courts, and the judiciary (Crown Prosecution Service, Official Statement, 113/99, 12 April 1999).

In its 1997–98 Annual Report (London: HMSO), the CPS states that, in the year under review, it dealt with more than 1.4 million cases in the magistrates' courts and around 128,000 in the Crown Court. The organisation is clearly under a certain pressure as only 50.6% of committal papers were delivered to the defence within agreed timescales. The report notes that, in the magistrates' courts, the overall conviction rate was 98.1% (compared with 98.0% in 1996–97). The conviction rate in the Crown Court was 90.6% compared with 90.8% in 1996–97. These figures, though, represent cases which end up in court and they include guilty pleas. The number of discontinuances in both sorts of court is high. Discontinuances occur where witnesses fail to attend or attend and change their evidence. In 1997–98, there were 164,438 cases discontinued by the CPS in the magistrates' courts (12% of all cases brought – the same as the year before), and 8,130 cases not proceeded with in the Crown Court (7.7% of all cases brought, 1,504 more abandoned cases than the year before).

The document *Judicial Statistics 1997* (1998, LCD) notes that, of the 91,110 cases being brought to trial at Crown Court in 1997 (p 61), only 11,510 defendants who pleaded not guilty to all or some the charges against them were convicted by juries (p 65).

According to the Judicial Statistics (HMSO, 1994), the chances of being acquitted in the Crown Court seem quite high. Statistically, a defendant has three chances out of five of being acquitted if he or she pleads not guilty. Roger Smith ([1994] NLJ 1088, 5 August) has pointed to the fact that, given the choice (which they are not), defendants would be best advised to opt for trial in Newcastle, rather than Cardiff. Trial on the North East circuit, rather than Wales and Chester, increased the chance of acquittal from 55 to 65% in 1994.

According to the figures released in 1995, there was a 9% fall in the number of discontinued cases in the Crown Courts. The CPS attributed this change to a better understanding amongst police officers of tests applied by the CPS to decide whether to prosecute. In 1994, the CPS finalised 1,462,967 cases, of which 11.7% (159,803) were discontinued, compared to 12.8% in 1993.

The CPS Annual Report 1999 (ISBN 0102736 995) notes that, during the year under review, the CPS dealt with proportionally more serious crime with indictable only cases – the most serious – rising to 30% of the total Crown Court caseload.

The Report shows the proportion of indictable only offences in the Crown Court rose from 18.2% in 1991–92 to 26% in 1997–98 and 30% in 1998–99. The rise has been influenced by the Plea Before Venue procedure for either way cases, which means such cases are not unnecessarily committed to the Crown Court.

In the magistrates' courts, indictable and either way cases rose by 1.8%. The total number of cases dealt with by the CPS in 1998–99 was 1,423,200 in magistrates' courts and 124,781 in the Crown Court. In magistrates' courts, 98.3% of hearings ended in conviction and in the Crown Court the figure was 89.1%.

Pilot schemes aimed at reducing delays in criminal courts have led to more efficient and speedier justice, with more cases dealt with at the first hearing; cases which go to trial being heard more quickly and a reduction in bureaucracy.

The CPS shares key performance targets for the criminal justice system with the Home Office and Lord Chancellor's Department. These include halving the time from arrest to sentence for persistent young offenders from 142 to 71 days by 31 March 2002.

10.1.1 The Code for Crown Prosecutors

This Code (*The Code for Crown Prosecutors*, CPS, 1994) is issued under s 10 of the Prosecution of Offences Act (POA) 1985. It explains the principles used by the CPS in its work. It says that 'police officers should take account of the principles of the Code when they are deciding whether to charge a defendant with an offence'.

10.1.2 The discretion to prosecute

The police have a very significant discretion as to what to do when a crime has possibly been committed. They could turn a blind eye, caution the suspect or charge the suspect in which latter case they must decide for what. As is very cogently argued by McConville, Sanders and Leng in *The Case for the Prosecution* (1991), prosecution cases are constructed from the evidence and testimony of many people including lay witnesses, victims, the police, CPS lawyers and expert witnesses. Each of these parties is fallible and prone to perceive events in line with their own sorts of experience. The net result of this is that the prosecution case is normally nothing more than an approximation to 'the truth'. The most influential role is that of the police, as it is they who ultimately decide whether to charge anyone, if so whom and for what. Once these discretions have been exercised, there is a relatively narrow band of data on which the CPS can work.

In 1951, the Attorney General, Lord Shawcross, noted that:

It has never been the rule in this country – I hope it never will be – that suspected criminal offences must automatically be the subject of prosecution (*House of Commons Debates*, vol 483, col 681, 29 January 1951).

This *dictum* has been almost universally accepted within the criminal justice system.

There is evidence, however, that the police do (for operational or social reasons) tend to focus their attention on particular types of conduct. Research, for example, by Andrew Sanders has shown a tendency for there to be a bias in favour of prosecuting working class offenders as opposed to middle class offenders. He compared the police response to offences with that of the Factory Inspectorate's response to violation of the Health and Safety laws and found that the police were much more prone to initiate prosecutions against working class suspects than were the factory inspectors against businesses and business executives. For the police there was an institutional bias in favour of prosecution reflected in the principle 'let the court decide', whereas with the factory inspectorate prosecution was only a last resort after an attempt at negotiated compliance had failed. In 1980, there were 22,000 serious cases of tax evasion but only one in 122 cases was prosecuted. By contrast, there were 107,000 social security frauds, of which one in four were prosecuted. Tax evasion resulted in a loss to the public purse 30 times larger than that caused by social security fraud yet there was more state money spent on prosecuting people for social security fraud. See Sanders, 'Class bias in prosecutions' (1985) 24 Howard J 176.

10.1.3 Police cautioning of offenders and CPS guidelines

During 1992–93, there was a sharp increase in the number of offenders whom police chose to caution rather than prosecute (*Criminal Statistics*, 1992). The Home Office has encouraged cautioning noting that, especially in the case of juveniles, 'there may be a positive advantage to society as well as for the individual in using prosecution as a last resort' (Home Office Circular, 14/1985). The current criteria for cautioning are: the nature of the offence, the likely penalty, the offender's age and health, and his or her criminal record and attitude towards the offence. There is a presumption against prosecuting offenders with no record who are juvenile, young adults or elderly. The 1994 guidelines say that (at para 6.9):

Crown prosecutors should tell the police if they think that a caution would be more suitable than a prosecution.

The Code for Crown Prosecutors (promulgated on behalf of the DPP) sets out the official criteria governing the discretion to prosecute.

The Code, the second to be issued, retains the two previous tests which determine whether a prosecution should be brought: there must be a 'realistic prospect of conviction' (the evidential test) and the prosecution must be 'in the public interest'.

The evidential test remains the same, requiring prosecutors to predict what a jury, or bench, properly directed, would be likely to decide. The guidelines require prosecutors to assess the reliability of evidence, not just its admissibility. Thus, the question (para 5.3b): 'Is it likely that a confession is unreliable, for example, because of the defendant's age, intelligence or lack of understanding?'

As Glanville Williams ([1985] Crim LR 115)) and Andrew Sanders ([1994] NLJ 946) have argued, this test favours people who are well-respected in society like police officers and businessmen – in whose favour juries and magistrates might be biased. It also disfavours the sort of victims who are unlikely to make good witnesses. Sanders proposes a better test: whether, on the evidence, a jury or bench ought (on the balance of probabilities) to convict.

The public interest must be considered in each case where there is enough evidence to provide a realistic prospect of conviction. In cases of any seriousness, a prosecution will usually take place unless there are public interest factors tending against prosecution which clearly outweigh those tending in favour.

One innovation in the new Code is the listing of some 'public interest factors in favour of prosecution' (para 6.4) and some against (para 6.5). The former include cases where:

- a conviction is likely to result in a significant sentence;

- a weapon was used or violence was threatened during the commission of the offence;

- the offence was committed against a person serving the public, like a police officer or a nurse;

- the offence, although not serious in itself, is widespread in the area where it was committed;

- there is evidence that the offence was carried out by a group;

- the offence was motivated by any form of discrimination against the victim's ethnic or national origin, sex, religious beliefs, political views, or sexual preference.

A prosecution is less likely to proceed, we are told, where:

- the court is likely to impose a very small or nominal penalty;

- the offence was committed as a result of a genuine mistake or misunderstanding (judged against the seriousness of the offence);

- the loss or harm can be described as minor and was the result of a single incident, particularly if it was caused by a misjudgment;

- a prosecution is likely to have a very bad effect on the victim's physical or mental health, always bearing in mind the seriousness of the offence;

- details could be made public that could harm sources of information, international relations or national security.

Crown prosecutors must balance factors for and against prosecution carefully and fairly. Deciding on the public interest is, the code says (para 6.6) 'not simply a matter of adding up the number of factors on each side'.

Barbara Mills has stated that the Attorney General has commended the Code to other prosecutors. This may help to correct inconsistent approaches between the police and CPS on the one hand and, on the other, prosecutors like the Inland Revenue, and Health and Safety Executive. As Sanders (see above) has observed, if you illegally gain a fortune or maim someone, you will probably be treated more leniently than ordinary disposals for such offences if the crimes are, technically, tax evasion and operating an unsafe place of work.

10.1.4 CPS independence from the police

The CPS is institutionally separate from the police. The police are no longer in a client-lawyer relationship with the prosecutor, able to give instructions about how to proceed. The police are still, however, in the most influential position as it is only once they have taken the decision to charge a suspect that the CPS will be called on to look at the case. The CPS in practice exercises no supervisory role over the police investigation of cases; it simply acts on the file presented after the investigation by the police. The power of the CPS to discontinue prosecutions (under s 23 of the POA 1985) or the continuing power to withdraw or offer no evidence is an important feature of its independence. An argument that 'The system is dominated throughout its stages by the interests and values of the police, with the CPS playing an essentially subordinate and reactive role' is put by McConville (ed) in *The Case for the Prosecution* (1991).

The Report of the Runciman Royal Commission on Criminal Justice (1993) recommends the CPS plays a greater role in the investigative process. It states (para 93):

> The police should seek the advice of the CPS at the investigation stage in appropriate cases in accordance with guidelines to be agreed between the two services.

The Report also states (para 95):

> Where a chief officer of police is reluctant to comply with a request from the CPS to investigate further before a decision on discontinuance is taken, HM Chief Inspector of Constabulary in conjunction with the Director of Public Prosecutions should bring about a resolution of the dispute.

Oddly, however, the rationale underlying the establishment of the CPS (independence from the police) appears to have been undermined since 1998 when many police stations have has CPS liaison officers working in the stations themselves.

The following letter to *The Times* (6 August 1999) raises several noteworthy points on the other side of the argument:

From His Honour Judge Barrington Black

Sir, You report (3 August) that staff from the Crown Prosecution Service are to work with police officers in police stations to speed justice, and save £20 million a year.

Twenty years, and many millions of pounds ago, prior to the creation of the CPS, in the city where I practised, and throughout the country, the county prosecutor and his staff occupied an office above police headquarters.

They were available for consultations with police officers at any time, and they knew about the details of a case as it progressed. The police officer was responsible for the main papers and ensuing witness attendance. Defence solicitors also had direct contact with someone who could make decisions.

The words 'plea bargaining' are now forbidden but, in those days, a calculated assessment of the evidence and an indictment appropriate to that evidence were often determined to the benefit of the victim, the defendant, the public purse and justice.

I am delighted to hear that a system which was tried, tested and worked is to be revived.

Yours truly,

BARRINGTON BLACK

Harrow Crown Court

There may, however, be serious problems in developing too cosy a relationship between the police and the prosecuting authorities as, sometimes, the former have to come under the professional consideration of the latter. In August 1999, the CPS came under severe criticism in an official report into decisions not to prosecute police officers in circumstances where people had died in police custody. The report, Inquiry into Crown Prosecution Service Decision Making in relation to Deaths in Custody and Related Matters by His Honour Judge Gerald Butler QC (London, HMSO ISBN 0113412363) states that the way the CPS responded to such cases was 'inefficient and fundamentally unsound'. It lead to a 'thoroughly unsatisfactory situation' which needed to be urgently rectified. Following the criticisms in the Butler Report and further analysis by the CPS Inspectorate, the relevant decision making processes are being revised.

10.1.5 Judicial control of prosecution policy

There is a very limited way in which the courts can control the exercise of prosecutorial discretion by the police. Lord Denning MR gave the example in one case of a chief constable issuing a directive to his men that no person should be prosecuted for stealing goods worth less than £100 (over £1,000 in 1993 prices) and said 'I should have thought the court could countermand it. He would be failing in his duty to enforce the law'. More generally, the courts had no control, *per* Lord Denning MR, *R v Metropolitan Police Commissioner ex p Blackburn* (1968):

> For instance, it is for the Commissioner of Police of the Metropolis, or the chief constable, as the case may be, to decide in any particular case whether inquiries should be pursued, or whether an arrest should be made or a prosecution brought. It must be for him to decide on the disposition of his force and the concentration of his resources on any particular crime or area. No court can or should give him directions on such a matter.

Apart from this, there is the doctrine of constabulary independence, see *Fisher v Oldham Corporation* (1930), which regards the constable as an independent office holder under the Crown who cannot be instructed by organisational superiors or by governmental agency about how to exercise his or her powers. The constable is accountable only to law.

An interesting instance of the courts being used to attack a use of police discretion is *R v Coxhead* (1986). The appellant was a police sergeant in charge of a police station. A young man was brought into the station to be breathalysed and the sergeant recognised him as the son of a police inspector at that station. The sergeant knew the inspector to be suffering from a bad heart condition. In order not to exacerbate this condition, the sergeant did not administer the test and allowed the motorist to go free. The sergeant was prosecuted and convicted for conduct tending and intended to pervert the course of justice. The sergeant's defence was that his decision came within the legitimate scope of discretion exercised by a police officer. The trial judge said the matter should be left for the jury to determine; they must decide the extent of any police discretion in accordance with the facts. The jury convicted the sergeant and this was upheld by the Court of Appeal. In minor cases, the police had a very wide discretion whether to prosecute but in major cases they had no discretion or virtually none. Thus, in a serious case like drink driving, there was no discretion which the sergeant could have been exercising legitimately. It is odd, however, that this is left for the jury to decide after the event rather than be subject to clear rules.

It is a matter of contention how far the changes proposed in the Sheehy Report on the Police (Cmnd 2280, 1993, HMSO) will entail constitutional changes to the accountability of the police. Reiner has argued ('Responsibilities and reforms' [1993] NLJ 1096, 30 July) of the proposed change that:

> It will devolve responsibility downwards to local police commanders, but power will be concentrated more than ever in the hands of central government. Central government will 'set the key objectives which it expects the police to secure'.

10.1.6 State prosecutors in the Crown Courts

Much concern has been expressed about the government's plans to allow Crown Prosecution Service lawyers to conduct prosecutions in the Crown Courts ('English legal system' (1999) 26 SLR 31, Spring). The basis of the worry is that, as full time salaried lawyers working for an organisation, CPS lawyers will sometimes be tempted to get convictions using dubious tactics or ethics because their own status as employees and prospects of promotion will depend on conviction success rates. Where, as now, barristers from the independent Bar are used by the CPS to prosecute, there is (it is argued) a greater likelihood of the courtroom lawyer dropping a morally unsustainable case.

Section 42 of the Access to Justice Act 1999 tries to overcome the possible difficulties with a provision (amending s 27 of the Courts and Legal Services Act 1990) that every advocate 'has a duty to the court to act with independence in the interests of justice', in other words, a duty which overrides any inconsistent duty, for example, one to an employer. Professor Michael Zander QC has contended, however, that these are 'mere words'. He has said (letter to *The Times*, 29 December 1998) they are unlikely to exercise much sway over CPS lawyer employees concerned with performance targets set by their line managers, and that:

> The CPS as an organisation is constantly under pressure in regard to the proportion of discontinuances, acquittal and conviction rates. These are factors in the day to day work of any CPS lawyer. It is disingenuous to imagine they will not have a powerful effect on decision making.

The Bar is also very wary of this change, an editorial in *Counsel* (the journal of the Bar of England and Wales) says:

> ... we are gravely concerned about the extent to which prosecutions will be done in-house by the CPS when the need for independent prosecutors is so well established in our democracy ((1999) Counsel 3, February).

Whichever point of view you have on this, it is important in writing on the subject to set the argument in a wider context. What are the social, economic or political debates surrounding this issue of how best to run a system of courtroom prosecutors? The change to having Crown Court prosecutions carried out by salaried CPS lawyers will be more *efficient* (as the whole prosecution can be handled in-house without engaging the external service of an independent barrister), and will, ultimately, cost the State less than is currently spent on prosecutions. Some will argue that justice is being sacrificed to the deity of cost cutting. On the other hand, you could argue that justice and efficiency are not mutually exclusive phenomena.

10.2 Bail

Bail is the release from custody, pending a criminal trial, of an accused on the promise that money will be paid if he absconds. All decisions on whether to grant bail therefore involve delicate questions of balancing interests. A person is presumed innocent of a criminal charge unless he or she is proved guilty of it; this implies that no one should ever be detained unless he or she has been found guilty. For several reasons, however, it can be regarded as undesirable to allow some accused people to go back to society before the case against them is tried in a criminal court.

To refuse bail to an accused might involve depriving liberty to someone who is subsequently found not guilty or convicted but given a non-custodial sentence. Such a person will probably have been kept in a police cell or in a prison cell for 23 hours per day. Unlike the jurisdictions in The Netherlands, Germany and France, no compensation is payable in these circumstances. On the other hand, to allow liberty to the accused pending trial might be to allow him or her to abscond, commit further offences, interfere with witnesses and obstruct the course of justice. The difficulties involved in finding the proper balance have recently been highlighted by several recent cases of serious assault and rape being committed by persons who were on bail and the fleeing of Asil Nadir to Northern Cyprus in May 1993. Mr Nadir skipped his £3.5 million bail to travel to a jurisdiction which would not extradite him to England. He claimed that he would not be given a fair trial for the offences of theft and false accounting with which he was charged and went on the public record as saying that his sureties would not suffer hardship as he would repay those who had put up bail for him.

The basic way in which the law currently seeks to find the right balance in such matters is by operating a general presumption in favour of bail, a presumption which can be overturned if one or more of a number of indices of suspicion exist in respect of a particular defendant. Even where bail is granted, it may be subject to certain conditions to promote public safety and the interests of justice.

10.2.1 The Criminal Justice and Public Order Act 1994

Over recent years, the government took the view that bail was too easily granted and that too many crimes were being committed by those on bail who deserved to be in custody while awaiting trial. The Bail (Amendment) Act 1993 and the Criminal Justice and Public Order Act (CJPOA) 1994 (ss 25–30) emanate from that philosophy, their aim being to restrict the granting of bail. A case which caught public sympathy for this view involved a young man who had many convictions for car crime and joyriding. Whilst on bail, he was joyriding in a vehicle when he smashed into a schoolgirl. She clung to the bonnet but he shook her off and thus killed her. The Home Secretary commented publicly that the new legislative measures would prevent such terrible events.

Each year (prior to the Acts), about 50,000 offences are committed by people on bail. A study by the Metropolitan police in 1988 indicated that 16% of those charged by that force were already on bail for another offence. Another study, in 1993, from the same force, showed that of 537 suspects arrested in one week during a clamp-down on burglary, 40% were on bail. Some had been bailed 10 or 15 times during the preceding year. (Figures from Robert Maclennan MP, HC Committee, col 295, 1994.)

In the criminal process, the first stage at which bail is raised as an issue is at the police station. If a person is arrested on a warrant, this will indicate whether he or she is to be held in custody or released on bail. If the suspect is arrested without a warrant, then the police will have to decide whether to release the suspect after he or she has been charged. After a person has been charged, s 38(1)(a) of the Police and Criminal Evidence Act (PACE) 1984 states that a person must be released unless (a) his name and address are not known; or (b) the custody officer reasonably thinks that his detention is necessary for his own protection; or (c) to prevent him from injuring someone or damaging property or because he might abscond or interfere with the course of justice. Most arrested people are bailed by the police. In 1990, 83% of those arrested in connection with indictable offences and 88% of those arrested for summary offences (other than motoring offences) were released. This area has been amended by s 28 of the CJPOA 1994. A custody officer can now, in the case of an imprisonable offence, refuse to release an arrested person after charge if the officer has reasonable grounds for believing that the detention of that person is necessary to prevent him from committing any offence. Previously, many cases were caught by (b) (above) but some likely conduct, for example, drink driving, was not.

Section 27 of the CJPOA 1994 amends the PACE 1984 (ss 38, 47) so as to allow the police to grant conditional bail to persons charged. The conditions can be whatever is required to ensure that the person surrenders to custody, does not commit an offence while on bail, or does not interfere with witnesses or otherwise obstruct the course of justice. The new powers of the custody officer, however, do not include a power to impose a requirement to reside in a bail hostel. By amending Pt IV of PACE 1984, s 29 of the CJPOA 1994 gives the police power to arrest without warrant a person who, having been granted conditional police bail, has failed to attend at a police station at the appointed time.

The Bail Act (BA) 1976 created a statutory presumption of bail. It states (s 4) that, subject to Sched 1, bail *shall* be granted to a person accused of an offence in a magistrates' court or a Crown Court and convicted people who are being remanded for reports to be made. The court must therefore grant bail (unless one of the exceptions apply) even if the defendant does not make an application. Schedule 1 provides that a court need not grant bail to a person charged with an offence punishable with imprisonment if it is satisfied that there are substantial grounds for believing that, if released on bail, the defendant would:

- fail to surrender to custody;

- commit an offence while on bail; or

- interfere with witnesses or otherwise obstruct the course of justice.

The court can also refuse bail if it believes that the defendant ought to stay in custody for his or her own protection or if it has not been practicable for want of time to obtain sufficient information to enable the court to make its decision on bail or he has previously failed to answer to bail (Pt 1, paras 2–6).

When the court is considering the grounds stated above, all relevant factors must be taken into account, including the nature and seriousness of the offence, the character, antecedents, associations and community ties of the defendant, and his record for satisfying his obligations under previous grants of bail.

If the defendant is charged with an offence not punishable with imprisonment, Sched 1 provides that bail may only be withheld if he or she has previously failed to surrender on bail and if the court believes that, in view of that failure, he or she will fail again to surrender if released on bail.

Section 25 of the CJPOA 1994 provides that in some circumstances a person who has been charged with or convicted of murder, attempted murder, manslaughter, rape or attempted rape must not be granted bail. The circumstances are simply that the conviction must have been within the UK, and that, in the case of a manslaughter conviction, it must have been dealt with by way of a custodial sentence. The word 'conviction' is given a wide meaning and includes anyone found 'not guilty by way of insanity'.

There was debate about whether the changes wrought by s 25 are justifiable. A Home Office Minister defending the section stated that it would be worth the risk if it prevented just one murder or rape even though there might be a few 'hard cases', that is, people eventually acquitted of crime, who were remanded in custody pending trial. (David Maclean MP, Minister of State, Home Office, HC Committee, col 282, 1994.) As Card and Ward have remarked in a commentary on the CJPOA 1994, the government when pushed was unable to cite a single case where a person released on bail in the circumstances covered by s 25 re-offended in a similar way. There is no time limit on the previous conviction and there is no requirement of any connection between the previous offence and the one in question. Card and Ward suggest that there is a world of difference between a person who was convicted of manslaughter 30 years ago on the grounds of complicity in a suicide pact and who is now charged with attempted rape (of which he must be presumed innocent), and the person who was convicted of rape eight years ago and now faces another rape charge. The first person is not an obvious risk to society and it is, they argue, regrettable that bail will be denied to him. There is also argument to be had with the contents of the s 25 list. Why should some clearly dangerous and prevalent crimes like robbery be omitted from it? In any case, it may have been better had the offences in the list raised a strong presumption against bail as opposed to an absolute ban, as the former could be rebutted in cases where there was on the facts no risk.

Parliament has now made a concession on s 25. By s 56 of the Crime and Disorder Act 1998, s 25 of the 1994 Act is amended. Now, bail can be granted to people with convictions for rape or murder, but only if the court or constable considering the grant of bail 'is satisfied that there are exceptional circumstances which justify it'.

Bail can be granted as conditional or unconditional. Where it is unconditional, the accused must simply surrender to the court at the appointed date. Failure to appear without reasonable cause is an offence under the BA 1976 (s 6) and can result, if tried in a Crown Court, in a sentence of up to 12 months' imprisonment or a fine. Conditions can be attached to the granting of bail where the court thinks that it is necessary to ensure that the accused surrenders at the right time, does not interfere with witnesses or commit further offences. There is no statutory limit to the conditions the court may impose and the most common include requirements that the accused reports daily or weekly to a police station, resides at a particular address, surrenders his or her passport or does not go to particular places or associate with particular people.

Section 7 of the BA 1976 gives the police power to arrest anyone on conditional bail whom they reasonably suspect is likely to break the conditions or that he has already done so. Anyone arrested in these circumstances must be brought before a magistrate within 24 hours. The magistrate may then reconsider the question of bail.

Personal recognisances by which the suspect agreed to pay a sum if he failed to surrender to the court were abolished by the BA 1976 (s 3(2)) except in cases where it is believed that he or she might try to flee abroad. The Act did retain the court's right to ask for sureties as a condition of bail. By putting sureties in a position where they can have large sums of money 'estreated' if the suspect does not surrender to the court, a significant pressure (not using the resources of the criminal justice system) is put on the accused. The proportion of those who do not answer to bail is very small – consistently about 4% of those given bail. Section 9 of the BA 1976 strengthens the surety principle by making it a criminal offence to agree to indemnify a surety. This sort of thing could happen, for example, if the accused agreed to reimburse the surety in the event that the accused skipped bail and the surety was requested to pay.

The Crime and Disorder Act 1998 makes further changes to the law relating to bail. Section 54 provides for increased powers to require security or impose conditions (by taking away the requirement that the defendant must appear unlikely to remain in Great Britain). The 1998 Act also allows courts to be able to require defendants to attend interview with a legal representative as a condition of bail.

10.2.2 Appeals and reapplications

The rules which govern how someone who has been refused bail might re-apply and appeal have also been framed with a view to balancing the interests of the accused with those of the public and justice. The original refusal should not be absolute and final but, on the other hand, it is seen as necessary that the refusals are not reversed too easily.

If the court decides not to grant the defendant bail, then s 154 of the Criminal Justice Act (CJA) 1988 provides that it is the court's duty to consider whether the defendant ought to be granted bail at each subsequent hearing. At the first hearing after the one at which bail was first refused, he or she may support an application for bail with any arguments but at subsequent hearings the court need not hear arguments as to fact or law which it has heard before. The CJA 1982 enables a court to remand an accused in his or her absence for up to three successive one-week remand hearings provided that he or she consents and is legally represented. Such repeated visits are costly to the State and can be unsettling for the accused, especially if he or she has to spend most of the day in a police cell only to be told the case has been adjourned again without bail. If someone does not consent, they are prevented from applying for bail on each successive visit if the only supporting arguments are those that have been heard by the court before (*R v Nottingham JJ ex p Davies* (1980)).

To avoid unproductive hearings, that is, to promote courts being able to adjourn a case for a period within which reasonable progress can be made on a case, s 155 of the CJA 1988 allows for adjournments for up to 28 days provided the court sets the date for when the next stage of the proceedings should take place. What began as an experiment under this section has now by statutory order (SI 1991/2667) been extended to all courts.

The interests of the accused are also served by the variety of appeals he or she may make if bail has been refused. If bail has been refused by magistrates, then, in limited circumstances, an application may be made to another bench of magistrates. Applications for reconsideration can also be made to a judge in chambers (through a legal representative) or to the Official Solicitor (in writing). Appeal can also be made to a Crown Court in respect of bail for both pre-committal remands and where a defendant has been committed for trial or sentence at the Crown Court.

Section 3 of the BA 1976 allows for an application to vary the conditions of court bail to be made by the person bailed, or the prosecutor or a police officer. Application may also be made for the imposition of conditions on unconditional court bail. As amended by the CJPOA 1994, s 3 of the BA 1976 now allows for the same thing in relation to police bail, although the new provisions do not allow the prosecutor to seek reconsideration of the decision to grant bail itself. Under the Bail (Amendment) Act 1993, however, the prosecution does now have a right to appeal against the grant of bail by a court. This right applies to offences which carry a maximum sentence of imprisonment of five years or more, and to offences of taking a vehicle without consent (joyriding). When this right of appeal is exercised, the defendant will remain in custody until the appeal is heard by a crown court judge who will decide whether to grant bail or remand the defendant in custody within 48 hours of the magistrate's decision. Parliament was concerned that this power could be abused and has stated that it should be reserved 'for cases of greatest concern, when there is a serious risk of harm to the public' or where there are 'other significant public interest grounds' for an appeal.

Section 67(1) of the CJA 1967 states that time spent in custody pre-trial or pre-sentence can generally be deducted from the ultimate sentence. No compensation, however, is paid to people who have been remanded in custody but are subsequently found not guilty. Several European countries like France and Germany will sometimes offer compensation in similar circumstances.

Although this area of law was subject to a comprehensive revision after a Home Office special working party reported in 1974, and has been legislatively debated and modified twice since the BA 1976, it is still a matter of serious concern both by those civil libertarians who consider the law too tilted against the accused and by the police and commentators who believe it too lenient in many respects. This criticism of the law from both sides to the debate might indicate a desirable state of balance reached by the current regulatory framework.

- *Opposition to the current arrangements – civil libertarian perspective*

  It is a cause for concern that, in the 1990s, of those dealt with summarily after being remanded in custody, about 50% received non-custodial sentences and a further 25% were acquitted.

There are wide variations in the local policies of different courts; one study has shown, for instance, that the number of indictable custodial remands per 1,000 indictable proceedings was 111 in Brighton as against 313 in Bournemouth (Gibson, B, 'Why Bournemouth?' (1987) 151 JP 520, 15 August).

The last decade has seen a disturbing rise in the remand prison population. In 1980, it accounted for 15% of the average prison population. By 1990, it had risen to over 10,000 prisoners, 22% of the average prison population.

- *Opposition to the current arrangements – a police/public perspective*

There are arguments which point to the numbers of people who commit offences whilst out on bail. A study conducted in Bristol, for example, showed that over one-third of all defendants charged with burglary were on bail for another offence at the time of their arrest. Following some dreadful cases of serious offences being committed whilst the perpetrator was on bail, s 153 of the CJA 1988 required magistrates to give reasons if they decided to grant bail against police objections in cases of murder, manslaughter or rape.

The percentage of people who skip bail is too high, especially for the more minor offences. *Note*: the annual figure, however, of those who do not answer to bail is consistently under 4%.

Positive developments in recent years have been the use of Bail Information Schemes (BIS) for courts (about 100 courts now operate such schemes) and government concern to increase the number of bail hostels. The BIS resulted from pilot schemes organised by the Vera Institute of Justice of New York. They give courts verified information from the probation service about defendants' accommodation or community ties. The evidence suggests that the courts using such schemes make greater use of bail than those which do not have the schemes.

10.3 Plea bargaining

'Plea bargaining' has been defined as 'the practice whereby the accused enters a plea of guilty in return for which he will be given some consideration that results in a sentence concession' (Baldwin and McConville, *Negotiated Justice: Pressures on Defendants to Plead Guilty* (1977)). In practice, this can refer to:

- a situation either where there has been a plea arrangement for the accused to plead guilty to a lesser charge than the one with which he or she is charged (for example, charged with murder, agrees to plead guilty to manslaughter). This is sometimes called 'charge bargaining'; or

- where there is simply a sentencing discount available on a plea of guilty by the accused. This is sometimes called a 'sentence bargain'.

10.3.1 *R v Turner* (1970)

A plea of guilty by the accused must be made freely. The accused must only be advised to plead guilty if he or she has committed the crime in question. In *Turner* (1970), Lord Parker CJ set out guidelines on plea bargaining. He stated that: (1) it may sometimes be the duty of counsel to give strong advice to the accused that a plea of guilty with remorse is a mitigating factor which might enable the court to give a lesser sentence; (2) the accused must ultimately make up his or her own mind as to how to plead; (3) there should be open access to the trial judge and counsel for both sides should attend each meeting, preferably in open court; and (4) the judge should never indicate the sentence which he is minded to impose, nor should he ever indicate that on a plea of guilty he would impose one sentence but that on a conviction following a plea of not guilty he would impose a severer sentence. The judge could say what sentence he would impose on a plea of guilty (where, for example, he has read the depositions and antecedents) but without mentioning what he would do if the accused were convicted after pleading not guilty. Even this would be wrong, however, as the accused might take the judge to be intimating that a severer sentence would follow upon conviction after a guilty plea. The only exception to this rule is where a judge says that the sentence will take a particular form, following conviction, whether there has been a plea of guilty or not guilty.

10.3.2 **Court of Appeal** *Practice Direction*

These guidelines were subsequently embodied in a Court of Appeal *Practice Direction* (1976). A number of difficulties have been experienced in applying these principles. Perhaps the greatest problem has resulted from the fact that, although the principles state (No 4) that a judge should never say that a sentence passed after a conviction would be more severe than one passed after a guilty plea, it is a generally known rule that guilty pleas lead to lesser sentences. In *R v Cain* (1976), it was stressed that, in general, defendants should realise that guilty pleas attract lesser sentences. Lord Widgery said 'Any accused person who does not know about it should know about it'. The difficulty is that the trial judge must not mention it, otherwise he or she could be construed as exerting pressure on the accused to plead guilty.

In *R v Turner*, the defendant pleaded not guilty on a charge of theft. He had previous convictions and during an adjournment he was advised by counsel in strong terms to change his plea; after having spoken with the judge, which the defendant knew, counsel advised that in his opinion a plea of guilty would result in a non-custodial sentence, whereas, if he persisted with a not guilty plea and thereby attacked police witnesses, there was a real possibility of receiving a custodial sentence. The defendant changed his plea to guilty and then appealed on the ground that he did not have a free choice in changing his plea. His appeal was allowed on the basis that he might have formed the impression that the views being expressed to him by his counsel were those of the judge, particularly as it was known by the accused that counsel had just returned from seeing the judge when he gave his advice to the accused.

The advantages for the prosecution in gaining a guilty plea are obvious but, as the *Code for Crown Prosecutors* notes, 'Administrative convenience in the form of a rapid guilty plea should not take precedence over the interests of justice' (para 11, 1992–93). Justice demands that the court should be able to pass a proper sentence consistent with the gravity of the accused's actions and if a plea is accepted then the defendant can only be sentenced on the basis of the crime that he or she has admitted. It is noteworthy that the judge is not bound to accept a plea arrangement made between the sides. The Farquharson Committee on the Role of Prosecuting Counsel thought that there is a general right for the prosecution to offer no evidence in respect of any particular charge but that where the judge's opinion is sought on whether it is desirable to reassure the public at large that the right course is being taken, counsel must abide by the judge's decision. Where the judge thinks that counsel's view to proceed is wrong, the trial can be halted until the DPP has been consulted and given the judge's comments. In the notorious case of *R v Sutcliffe* (1981), the 'Yorkshire Ripper' case, the prosecution and defence had agreed that Sutcliffe would plead guilty to manslaughter on the grounds of diminished responsibility but the trial judge rejected that agreement and, after consultations with the DPP, Sutcliffe was eventually found guilty of murder.

10.3.3 *R v Pitman* (1991)

The extent of the difficulties in framing rules on plea bargaining which achieve clarity and fairness can be judged by the remark of Lord Lane CJ in the case of *R v Pitman* (1991):

> There seems to be a steady flow of appeals to this court arising from visits by counsel to the judge in his private room. No amount of criticism and no amount of warnings and no amount of exhortation seems to be able to prevent this from happening.

In this case, on counsel's advice, the appellant pleaded not guilty to causing death by reckless driving. On Cup Final day in 1989, he had driven, having been drinking all afternoon, in a car without a rear view mirror. He had crashed into another car, killing one of its passengers, whilst having double the permitted level of alcohol in his blood.

During the trial, the judge called both counsel to his room and stated that he did not think there was a defence to the charge. Counsel for the appellant explained that although the appellant had admitted that his carelessness caused the accident the advice to plead not guilty was based on the fact that the prosecution might not be able to prove the necessary recklessness. The trial judge replied that the appellant's plea was a matter for the appellant himself and not counsel and that if the appellant accepted responsibility for the accident he ought to plead guilty and if he did so he would receive 'substantial credit' when it came to sentencing.

Counsel for the appellant then discussed this with the appellant who changed his plea to guilty and was sentenced to nine months imprisonment and was disqualified from driving for four years. His appeal was allowed as the judge had put undue pressure on the appellant and his counsel to change his plea to guilty as the remarks suggested that his chances of acquittal were slight if he pleaded not guilty and that if he was found guilty he would certainly be sentenced to imprisonment. Lord Lane CJ emphasised that a judge should not initiate discussions in private and that where, at the behest of counsel, they are absolutely necessary, they should be recorded by shorthand or on a recording device.

Another problem here concerns framing the guidelines so that they are sufficiently permissive to allow counsel access to the judge in his private room in cases in deserving instances but avoiding the problems of confidentiality. As Mustill LJ said in *R v Harper-Taylor and Barker* (1988): 'The need to solve an immediate practical problem may combine with the more relaxed atmosphere of the private room to blur the formal outlines of the trial.' There is a risk that counsel and solicitors may hear something said to the judge which they would rather not hear, putting them into a state of conflict between their duties to their clients and their obligations to maintain the confidentiality of the private room. Reviewing the current state of the law, Curran has written that the effect of cases like *R v Bird* (1977) and *R v Agar* (1990) (the latter not a plea bargaining case but one which hinged on a judge's ruling in his private room as complied with by counsel to the appellant's detriment) is that defence counsel has a duty to disclose to his client any observations made by the judge in his room which significantly affect the client's case, whether or not the judge expresses them to be made confidentially.

The difficulties in this area of law stem, largely, not from deficient rules but rather from the wish that the rules should achieve diverse aims. As Zander has observed, the fundamental problem is that the Court of Appeal wants to have it both ways: 'On the one hand, it wants defendants to appreciate that, if they plead guilty, they will receive a lesser sentence. On the other hand, it does not want judges to provide defendants with solid information as to how great the discount will be.'

10.3.4 Royal Commission recommendations

A more open system of plea bargaining was advocated by the Runciman Royal Commission on Criminal Justice (para 156). The report argues that this would do much to alleviate the problem of 'cracked trials' in which defendants do not plead guilty until the last moment, wasting the time of witnesses, the police, the CPS and the court. In a system where the vast majority of cases in the Crown Court and magistrates' courts result in guilty pleas (79% and 81.5%, respectively), the operation of the plea bargain becomes very important.

The Commission research indicated that 'cracked trials' accounted for more than one-quarter of all cases. The Commission also noted that sentence discounts of between 25% and 30% for guilty pleas have been long established practice in the Crown Court. The Commission suggested that higher discounts should be available for those who plead guilty earlier in the process. The Report states:

> The most common reason for defendants delaying a plea of guilty until the last minute is a reluctance to face the facts until they are at the door of the court. It is often said too that a defendant has a considerable incentive to behave in this way. The longer the delay, the more the likelihood of witnesses becoming intimidated or forgetting to turn up or disappearing.

It recommends (para 157):

> At the request of defence counsel on instructions from the defendant, judges should be able to indicate the highest sentence that they would impose at that point on the basis of the facts as put to them.

On the issue of charges, it recommends (para 161):

> Discussions on the level of charge (charge bargaining) should take place as early as possible in order to minimise the need for cases to be listed as contested trials.

Requests made to the judge could be made at a preparatory hearing, at a hearing called specially for the purpose, or at the trial itself. The Report denies that such a system is at all near the American scheme which is widely regarded as promoting injustice as it acts as a wholesale plea bargaining system in which the prosecution can suggest the appropriate sentence. Lord Runciman states that: 'We agree that to face defendants with a choice between what they might get on an immediate plea of guilty and what they might get if found guilty by the jury does amount to unacceptable pressure.'

Research conducted by Professor Zander for the Royal Commission on Criminal Justice (Zander and Henderson, *The Crown Court Study*, Royal Commission on Criminal Justice Study 19, 145, 1993) found that, in a study of 900 Crown Court cases, 90% of barristers and two-thirds of judges were in favour of formalising plea bargaining based on sentence discounts. The study suggests that 11% of those who pleaded guilty in fact maintained their innocence but wanted to secure a reduction in sentence.

The Court of Appeal has consistently indicated that the information should not be given to defendants because that might put undue pressure on them to plead guilty, but sentence discounts are legally recognised: in Thomas, DA (ed) *Current Sentencing Practice*, para A8 2(b) says: a guilty plea attracts a lighter sentence, the extent of the reduction is usually between one-quarter and one-third of what would have otherwise been the sentence. Moreover, Lord Widgery has stated (see 10.3.2, above) that defendants should know about them. The pressure could scarcely be increased by informing a defendant with details rather than leave it to his or her general knowledge. If anything, Zander has argued, it would diminish the pressure by making it clear that the defendant's fears about the penalty for pleading not guilty are exaggerated.

In a detailed research report on this issue, the reform group JUSTICE has cast serious doubt on many aspects of the system which could soon be adopted if the Runciman Royal Commission proposals are enacted. In *Negotiated Justice: a Closer Look at the Implications of Plea Bargaining* (1993), it is argued that, although favoured in some form by 90% of barristers and 60% of judges, plea bargaining can not only lead to unjust convictions but also inaccurate and unfair sentences. The latter occur because when the trial judge is making an offer of a reduced penalty, the defendant is still at that stage formally protesting his innocence so it is extremely difficult for his lawyer to present a plea in mitigation of sentence.

The reform body JUSTICE argues that the earlier withdrawal of weak prosecution cases; better liaison between defence and prosecution; and earlier contact between defendant and barrister would result in greater efficiency and fairness.

There is, though, reason for anxiety with such a call for more openness. Sanders and Young ([1994] NLJ 1200, 9 September) regard it as 'an idealistic notion' that one can improve the effectiveness of the system in convicting the guilty without also increasing its effectiveness in convicting the innocent. They say that one simply has to make a 'value choice' about the weight to be given to protecting the innocent relative to other important values such as repressing crime, and economy in the use of scarce resources. In one Home Office study (*Magistrates' Court or Crown Court? Mode of Trial Decisions and Sentencing*, Home Office Study No 125, 1992), Hedderman and Moxon found that 65% of those pleading guilty in Crown Court cases said that their decision had been influenced by the prospect of receiving a discount in sentence, and nearly one-third claim to have pleaded guilty as a direct result of a charge bargain. Even the Royal Commission recognised that not all those pleading guilty are, in fact, guilty; some may have just capitulated to the pressure of taking the reduced sentence rather than run the risk of the full sentence. As Sanders and Young contend, this issue goes to the heart of constitutional principles. Only if the State acts properly in collecting and presenting evidence can punishment be justified according to commonly accepted principles. Even the guilty are entitled to due process of law. A system of plea bargaining may undermine such principles as it allows the state to secure convictions based on unproven allegations.

10.4   The jury

It is generally accepted that the jury of '12 good men and true' lies at the heart of the British legal system. The implicit assumption is that the presence of 12 ordinary lay persons, randomly introduced into the trial procedure to be the arbiters of the facts of the case, strengthens the legitimacy of the legal system. It supposedly achieves this end by introducing a democratic humanising element into the abstract impersonal trial process, thereby reducing the exclusive power of the legal professionals who would otherwise command the legal stage and control the legal procedure without reference to the opinion of the lay majority.

According to EP Thompson:

> The English common law rests upon a bargain between the law and the people. The jury box is where the people come into the court; the judge watches them and the jury watches back. A jury is the place where the bargain is struck. A jury attends in judgement not only upon the accused but also upon the justice and humanity of the law (*Writing by Candlelight*).

Few people have taken this traditional view to task but, in a thought-provoking article in the *Criminal Law Review* ([1991] Crim LR 740), Penny Darbyshire did just that. In her view, the jury system has attracted the most praise and the least theoretical analysis of any component of the criminal justice system. As she correctly pointed out, and as will be shown below, juries are far from being either a random or a representative section of the general population. In fact, Darbyshire goes so far as to characterise the jury as 'an anti-democratic, irrational and haphazard legislator, whose erratic and secret decisions run counter to the rule of law'. She concedes that while the 20th century lay justices are not representative of the community as a whole, neither is the jury. She points out that jury equity, by which is meant the way in which the jury ignores the law in pursuit of justice, is a double-edged sword which may also convict the innocent; and counters examples such as the *Clive Ponting* case with the series of miscarriages of justice relating to suspected terrorists in which juries were also involved.

Darbyshire is certainly correct in taking to task those who would simply endorse the jury system in an unthinking, purely emotional, manner. With equal justification, she criticises those academic writers who focus attention on the *mystery* of the jury to the exclusion of the hard reality of the magistrates court. It is arguable, however, that she goes to the other extreme. Underlying her analysis and conclusions is the idea that 'the jury trial is primarily ideological' and that 'its symbolic significance is magnified beyond its practical significance by the media, as well as academics, thus unwittingly misleading the public'. Whilst one might not wish to contradict the suggestion that the jury system operates as a very powerful ideological symbol, supposedly grounding the criminal legal system within a framework of participative democracy and justifying it on that basis, it is simply inadequate to reject the practical operation of the procedure on that basis alone. Ideologies do not exist purely in the realm of ideas, they have real concrete manifestations and effects; and, in relation to the jury system, those manifestations operate in a such a way as to offer at least a vestige of protection to defendants. In regard to the comparison between juries and the summary procedure of the magistrates' courts, Darbyshire puts two related questions. First, she asks whether the jury system is more likely to do justice and get the verdict right than the magistrates' courts; then, she goes on to ask why the majority of defendants are processed through the magistrates' courts. These questions are highly pertinent; it is doubtful, however, whether her response to them is as equally pertinent. Her answers would likely be that the jury does not perform any better than the magistrates and, therefore, it is immaterial that the magistrates deal with the bulk of cases. Her whole approach would seem to be concentrated on denigrating the performance of the jury system. A not untypical passage from her article admits that, in relation to the suspect terrorist miscarriages of justice, juries 'were not to blame for these wrongful convictions' but then goes on in the same sentence to accuse the juries of failing 'to remedy the lack of due process at the pre-trial stage', and thus blames them for not providing 'the break on oppressive state activity claimed for the jury by its defenders'.

Although there is most certainly scope for less a romantic view of how the jury system actually operates in practice, Darbyshire's argument seems to be that the magistrates are not very good but then neither are the juries; and as they only operate in a small minority of cases anyway, the implication would seem to be that their loss would be no great disadvantage. Others, however, would maintain that the jury system does achieve concrete benefits in particular circumstances and would argue further that these benefits should not be readily given up. Amongst the latter is Michael Mansfield QC who, in an article in response to the Runciman Report, claimed that the jury 'is the most democratic element of our judicial system' and the one which 'poses the biggest threat to the authorities'.

(These questions will be considered further in relation to the Report of the Runciman Commission.)

Having defended the institution of the jury generally, it has to be recognised that there are particular instances which tend to bring the jury system into disrepute. For example, in October 1994, the Court of Appeal ordered the re-trial of a man convicted of double murder on the grounds that four of the jurors had attempted to contact the murder victims using a Ouija board in what was described as a 'drunken experiment'. A second convicted murderer appealed against his conviction on the grounds of irregularities in the manner in which the jury performed its functions. Amongst the allegations levelled at the jury is the claim that they clubbed together and spent £150 on drink when they were sent to a hotel after failing to reach a verdict. It is alleged that some of the jurors discussed the case against the express instructions of the judge and that on the following day the jury foreman had to be replaced because she was too hung-over to act. One female juror is alleged to have ended up in bed with another hotel guest.

Another example of the possible criticisms to be levelled against the misuse of juries occurred in Stoke on Trent, where the son of a court usher, and another six individuals, were found to have served on a number of criminal trial juries. Whilst one could praise the public spirited nature of this dedication to the justice process, especially given the difficulty in getting members of jury panels (see 10.6 and 10.7, below), it might be more appropriate to condemn the possibility of the emergence of a professional juror system connected to court officials. Certainly, the Court of Appeal was less than happy with the situation, and overturned a conviction, when the Stoke practice was revealed to it.

10.5   The role of the jury

It is generally accepted that the function of the jury is to decide on *matters of fact*, and that *matters of law* are the province of the judge. Such may be the ideal case, but most of the time the jury's decision is based on a consideration of a mixture of fact and law. The jury determines whether a person is guilty on the basis of their understanding of the law as explained to them by the judge.

The oath taken by each juror states that they 'will faithfully try the defendant and give a true verdict according to the evidence', and it is contempt of court for a juror subsequent to being sworn in to refuse to come to a decision. In 1997, Judge Anura Cooray, sentenced two women jurors to 30 days in prison for contempt of court for their failure to deliver a verdict. One of the women, who had been the jury foreman, claimed that the case, involving an allegation of fraud, had been too complicated to understand, and the other had claimed that she could not ethically judge anyone. Judge Cooray was quoted as justifying his decision to imprison them on the grounds that:

> I had to order a re-trial at very great expense. Jurors must recognise that they have a responsibility to fulfil their duties in accordance with their oath.

The women only spent one night in jail before the uproar caused by Cooray's action led to their release and the subsequent overturning of his sentence on them.

10.5.1 The jury's function in trials

Judges have the power to direct juries to acquit the accused where there is insufficient evidence to convict them, and this is the main safeguard against juries finding defendants guilty in spite of either the absence, or the insufficiency, of the evidence. There is, however, no corresponding judicial power to instruct juries to convict (*DPP v Stonehouse* (1978)). There is nothing to prevent the judge summing up in such a way as to make it evident to the jury that there is only one decision that can reasonably be made, and that it would be perverse to reach any other verdict but guilty.

What judges must not do is, overtly, put pressure on juries to reach guilty verdicts. Finding of any such pressure will result in the overturning of any conviction so obtained. The classic example of such a case is *R v McKenna* (1960) in which the judge told the jury, after they had spent all of two and a quarter hours deliberating on the issue, that, if they did not come up with a verdict in the following 10 minutes, they would be locked up for the night. Not surprisingly, the jury returned a verdict; unfortunately for the defendant, it was a guilty verdict; even more unfortunately for the judicial process, the conviction had to be quashed on appeal, for clear interference with the jury.

In the words of Cassels J:

> It is a cardinal principle of our criminal law that in considering their verdict, concerning, as it does, the liberty of the subject, a jury shall deliberate in complete freedom, uninfluenced by any promise, unintimidated by any threat. They stand between the Crown and the subject, and they are still one of the main defences of personal liberty. To say to such a tribunal in the course of its deliberations that it must reach a conclusion ... is a disservice to the cause of justice ... (*R v McKenna* (1960)).

Judges do have the right, and indeed the duty, to advise the jury as to the proper understanding and application of the law that they are considering. Even when the jury is considering its verdict, they may seek the advice of the judge. The essential point, however, is that any such response on the part of the judge must be given in open court, so as to obviate any allegation of misconduct (*R v Townsend* (1982)).

In criminal cases, even perversity of decision does not provide grounds for appeal against acquittal. There have been occasions where juries have been subjected to the invective of a judge when they have delivered a verdict with which he disagreed. Nonetheless, the fact is that juries collectively, and individual jurors, do not have to justify, explain, or even give reasons for their decisions. Indeed, under s 8 of the Contempt of Court Act 1981, it would be a contempt of court to try to elicit such information from a jury member in either a criminal or a civil law case. (See below for the Runciman Commission's proposal to amend s 8.)

These factors place the jury in a very strong position to take decisions that are 'unjustifiable' in accordance with the law, for the simple reason that they do not have to justify the decisions. Thus, juries have been able to deliver what can only be described as perverse decisions. In *R v Clive Ponting* (1985), the judge made clear beyond doubt that the defendant was guilty, under the Official Secrets Act 1911, of the offence with which he was charged: the jury still returned a not-guilty verdict. Similarly, in the case of *Pat Pottle and Michael Randall*, who had openly admitted their part in the escape of the spy George Blake, the jury reached a not guilty verdict in open defiance of the law.

In *R v Kronlid* (1996), three protestors were charged with committing criminal damage, and another was charged with conspiracy to cause criminal damage, in relation to an attack on Hawk Jet aeroplanes that were about to be sent to Indonesia. The damage to the planes allegedly amounted to £1.5 million, and they did not deny their responsibility for it. They rested their defence on the fact that the planes were to be delivered to the Indonesian State, to be used in its allegedly genocidal campaign against the people of East Timor. On those grounds, they claimed that they were, in fact, acting to prevent the crime of genocide. The prosecution cited assurances, given by the Indonesian Government, that the planes would not be used against the East Timorese, and pointed out that the UK Government had granted an export licence for the planes. As the protestors did not deny what they had done, it was apparently a mere matter of course that they would be convicted as charged. The jury, however, decided that all four of the accused were innocent of the charges laid against them. A government Treasury minister, Michael Jack, subsequently stated his disbelief at the verdict of the jury. As he stated:

> I, and I am sure many others, find this jury's decision difficult to understand. It would appear there is little question about who did this damage. For whatever reason that damage was done, it was just plain wrong ((1996) *The Independent*, 1 August).

It is perhaps just such a lack of understanding, together with the desire to save money on the operation of the legal system, that has motivated the government's expressed wish to replace jury trials in relation to either way offences (see 10.8.6).

A non-political example of this type of case can be seen in the jury's refusal to find Stephen Owen guilty of any offence after he had discharged a shotgun at the driver of a lorry that had killed his child. The tendency of the jury occasionally to ignore legal formality in favour of substantive justice is one of the major points in favour of its retention, according to its proponents.

10.5.2 Appeals from decisions of the jury

In criminal law, it is an absolute rule that there can be no appeal against a jury's decision to acquit a person of the charges laid against him.

Although there is no appeal as such against acquittal, there does exist the possibility of the Attorney General referring the case to the Court of Appeal to seek its advice on points of law raised in criminal cases in which the defendant has been acquitted. This procedure was provided for under s 36 of the CJA 1972 although it is not commonly resorted to. It must be stressed that there is no possibility of the actual case being reheard or the acquittal decision being reversed, but the procedure can highlight mistakes in law made in the course of Crown Court trial and permits the Court of Appeal to remedy the defect for the future. (See *Attorney General's Reference No 1* (1988) for an example of this procedure in the area of insider dealing in relation to shares on the Stock Exchange. This case is also interesting in relation to statutory interpretation.)

In civil law cases, the possibility of the jury's verdict being overturned on appeal does exist, but only in circumstances where the original verdict was perverse, that is, no reasonable jury properly directed could have made such a decision.

10.5.3 Majority verdicts

The possibility of a jury deciding a case on the basis of a majority decision was introduced by the CJA 1967. Prior to this, the requirement was that jury decisions had to be unanimous. Such decisions are acceptable where there are:

- not less than 11 jurors and 10 of them agree; or

- there are 10 jurors and nine of them agree.

Where a jury has reached a guilty verdict on the basis of a majority decision, s 17(3) of the Juries Act (JA) 1974 requires the foreman of the jury to state in open court the number of jurors who agreed and the number who disagreed with the verdict. See *R v Barry* (1975), where failure to declare the details of the voting split resulted in the conviction of the defendant being overturned. In *R v Pigg* (1983), the House of Lords held that it was unnecessary to state the number who voted against where the foreman stated the number in favour of the verdict and thus the determination of the minority was a matter of simple arithmetic. There is no such requirement in respect of a not guilty verdict.

10.5.4 Discharge of jurors or the jury

The trial judge may discharge the whole jury if certain irregularities occur. These would include the situation where the defendant's previous convictions are revealed inadvertently during the trial. Such a disclosure would be prejudicial to the defendant. In such a case, the trial would be ordered to commence again with a different jury. Individual jurors may be discharged by the judge if they are incapable of continuing to act through illness 'or for any other reason' (s 16(1) of the JA 1974). Where this happens the jury must not fall below nine members.

10.6 The selection of the jury

In theory, jury service is a public duty that citizens should readily undertake. In practice, it is made compulsory, and failure to perform one's civic responsibility is subject to the sanction of a £1,000 fine.

10.6.1 Liability to serve

The JA 1974, as amended by the CJA 1988, sets out the law relating to juries. Prior to the Juries Act, there was a property qualification in respect to jury service which skewed jury membership towards middle class men. Now, the legislation provides that any person between the ages of 18 and 70 who is on the electoral register and who has lived in the UK for at least five years is qualified to serve as a juror.

The procedure for establishing a jury is a threefold process:

- an officer of the court summons a randomly selected number of qualified individuals from the electoral register;

- from that group, panels of potential jurors for various cases are drawn up;

- the actual jurors are then randomly selected by means of a ballot in open court.

As has been pointed out, however, even if the selection procedure were truly random, randomness does not equal representation. Random juries, by definition, could be: all male, all female, all white, all black, all Conservative or all members of the Raving Loony Party. Such is the nature of the random process; the question that arises from the process is whether such randomness is necessarily a good thing in itself, and whether the summoning officer should take steps to avoid the potential disadvantages that can result from random selection.

As regards the actual random nature of the selection process, a number of problems arise from the use of electoral registers to determine and locate jurors:

- electoral registers tend to be inaccurate. Generally, they misreport the number of younger people who are in an area simply because younger people tend to move about more than older people and therefore tend not to appear on the electoral role of the place they currently live in;

- electoral registers tend to under-report the number of members of ethnic minorities in a community. The problem is that some members of the ethnic communities, for a variety of reasons, simply do not notify the authorities of their existence;

- the problem of non-registration mentioned above was compounded by the disappearance of a great many people from electoral registers in order to try to avoid payment of the former poll tax. It is a matter of some doubt whether such people have registered with the passing of that particular tax or whether they will simply cease to exist for the purpose of jury service. The Runciman Commission, not surprisingly, suggested that every endeavour should be made to ensure that electoral registers are accurate.

10.6.2 Exceptions, excusals and disqualifications

The general qualification for serving as a juror is subject to a number of exceptions.

A number of people are deemed to be *ineligible* to serve on juries on the basis of their employment or vocation. Amongst this category are judges; justices of the peace; members of the legal profession; police and probation officers; and members of the clergy or religious orders. The reason for excluding those involved in the administration of justice is understandable, but less so is the exclusion of clergy. The Runciman Report recommends that the clergy and members of religious orders should be eligible to serve on juries, but that members of such orders which have beliefs that are incompatible with jury service should be excused. The latter recommendation was introduced by s 42 of the CJA 1994.

In an endeavour to maintain the unquestioned probity of the jury system, certain categories of persons are *disqualified* from serving as jurors. Amongst these is anyone who has been sentenced to a term of imprisonment, or youth custody, of five years or more. In addition, anyone who, in the past 10 years, has served a sentence, or has had a suspended sentence imposed on them, or has had a community service order made against them, is also disqualified. Finally, with respect to people with criminal records, anyone who has been placed on probation within the previous five years is also disqualified. Those on bail in criminal proceedings are disqualified from serving as a juror in the Crown Court. (See the recommendations of the Runciman Commission, below.) The final category of people disqualified from serving as jurors are the mentally ill.

Certain people are *excused as of right* from serving as jurors on account of their jobs. Amongst these are members of the medical professions, members of Parliament and members of the armed forces. Others may be excused from current jury service on the basis of past service. There is additionally a *discretionary power* given to the court to release a person from jury service, or alternatively to defer their service to some time in the future, if they show grounds for such treatment. Grounds for such excusal or deferral are supposed to be made only on the basis of good reason but there is at least a measure of doubt as to the rigour with which such rules are applied.

A Practice Note issued in 1988 stated that applications for excusal should be treated sympathetically and listed the following as good grounds for excusal:

(a) personal involvement in the case;

(b) close connection with a party or a witness in the case;

(c) personal hardship;

(d) conscientious objection to jury service.

10.6.3 Physical disability and jury service

It is to be hoped that the situation of people with disabilities has been altered for the better by the CJPOA 1994 which introduced a new section, 9B, into the JA 1974. Previously, it was all too common for judges to discharge jurors with disabilities, including deafness, on the assumption that they will not be capable of undertaking the duties of a juror. One notorious case occurred in January 1994 when Judge John Binns discharged a deaf woman from jury service in King's Lynn Crown Court even though there were interpreting facilities in the court.

Under the new provision, where it appears doubtful that a person summoned for jury service is capable of serving on account of some physical disability, that person, as previously, may be brought before the judge. The new s 9B, however, introduces a presumption that people should serve and provides that the judge must affirm the jury summons unless he or she is of the opinion that the person will not be able to act effectively. Whether such a presumption is sufficient to displace preconceptions remains to be seen.

10.6.4 Challenges to jury membership

That juries can be 'self-selecting' provides grounds for concern as to the random nature of the jury; but the traditional view of the jury is further, and perhaps even more fundamentally, undermined by the way in which both prosecution and defence seek to influence their constitution.

Under s 12(6) of the JA 1974, both prosecution and defence have a right to challenge the array where the summonsing officer has acted improperly in bringing the whole panel together. Such challenges are rare, although an unsuccessful action was raised in *R v Danvers* (1982) where the defendant tried to challenge the racial composition of the group of potential jurors.

10.6.5 Challenge by the defence

Until the CJA 1988, there were two ways in which the defence could challenge potential jurors:

- *Peremptory challenge*

  The defence could object to any potential jury members, up to a maximum number of three, without having to show any reason or justification for the challenge. Defence counsel used this procedure in an attempt to shape the composition of the jury in a way they thought might best suit their client, although it has to be said that it was an extremely inexact process, and one that could upset or antagonise rejected jurors. In spite of arguments for its retention on a civil liberties basis, the majority of the Roskill Committee on Fraud Trials (HMSO, January 1986) recommended that the right be abolished, and abolition was provided for in the CJA 1988.

- *Challenge for cause*

  The defence retains the power to challenge any number of potential jurors *for cause*, that is to say that there is a substantial reason why a particular person should not serve on the jury to decide a particular defendant's case. A simple example would be where the potential juror has had previous dealings with the defendant or has been involved in the case in some way. There may be less obvious grounds for objection, however, which may be based on the particular juror's attitudes, or indeed political beliefs. The question arises whether such factors provide grounds for challenge. In what is known as *The Angry Brigade* case in 1972 (see (1971) *The Times*, 10–11 December; (1972) *The Times*, 12–15 December), a group of people were charged with carrying out a bombing campaign against prominent members of the Conservative government. In the process of empanelling a jury, the judge asked potential jurors to exclude themselves on a variety of socio-political grounds, including active membership of the Conservative Party. As a consequence of the procedure adopted in that case, the Lord Chief Justice issued a Practice Direction in which he made it clear that potential jurors were not to be excluded on account of race, religion, politics or occupation. Since that Practice Direction, it is clear that the challenge for cause can only be used within a restricted sphere, and this makes it less useful to the defence than it might otherwise be if it were to operate in a more general way.

It has been argued that the desire of civil libertarians to retain the right of the defence to select a jury that might be more sympathetic to its case is contradictory, because although in theory they usually rely on the random nature of the jury to ensure the appearance of justice, in practice they seek to influence its composition. When, however, the shortcomings in the establishment of panels for juries is recalled it might be countered that the defence is attempting to do no more than counter the in-built bias that ensues from the use of unbalanced electoral registers.

10.6.6 Challenge by the prosecution

If the defence attempts to ensure that any jury will not be prejudiced against its case, if not predisposed towards it, the same is true of the prosecution. However, the prosecution has a greater scope to achieve such an aim. Whilst the prosecution has the same right as the defence to challenge for cause, it has the additional option of excluding potential jury members by simply asking them to *stand by* until a jury has been empanelled. The request for the potential juror to stand by is only a provisional challenge and, in theory, the person stood by can at a later time take their place on the jury if there are no other suitable candidates. In practice, of course, it is unlikely in the extreme for there not to be sufficient alternative candidates, to whom the prosecution do not object, and prefer to the person stood by.

When the Roskill Committee recommended the removal of the defence's right to pre-emptive challenge, it recognised that, in order to retain an equitable situation, the right of the Crown to ask potential jurors to stand by should also be withdrawn. Unfortunately, although the government of the day saw fit to follow the committee's recommendation in relation to the curtailment of the defence rights, it did not feel under the same obligation to follow its corresponding recommendation to curtail the rights of the prosecution. Thus, the CJA 1988 made no reference to the procedure and, in failing to do so, established a distinct advantage in favour of the prosecution in regard to selecting what it considered to be suitable juries.

The manifest unreasonableness of this procedure led to the Attorney General issuing a *Practice Note* (1988) to the effect that the Crown should only exercise its power to stand by potential jurors in the following two circumstances:

- to prevent the empanelment of a 'manifestly unsuitable' juror, with the agreement of the defence. The example given of manifest unsuitability is an illiterate person asked to sit in a highly complex case. It is reasonable to doubt the ability of such a person to follow the process of the case involving a number of documents, and on that basis they should be stood by;

- in circumstances where the Attorney General has approved the vetting of the potential jury members and that process has revealed that the particular juror in question might be a security risk. In this situation, the Attorney General is also required to approve the use of the 'stand by' procedure.

10.6.7 Jury vetting

Jury vetting is the process in which the Crown checks the background of potential jurors to assess their suitability to decide particular cases. The procedure is clearly contrary to the ideal of the jury being based on a random selection of people; but it is justified on the basis that it is necessary to ensure that jury members are not likely to divulge any secrets made open to them in the course of a sensitive trial, or, alternatively, on the ground that jurors with extreme political views should not be permitted the opportunity to express those views in a situation where they might influence the outcome of a case.

The practice of vetting potential jurors developed after the *Angry Brigade* trial in 1972 but it did not become public until 1978. In that year, as a result of an Official Secrets Act case, known by the initials of the three defendants as the ABC trial, it became apparent that the list of potential jurors had been checked to establish their 'soundness'. As a consequence of that case, the Attorney General published the current guidelines for vetting jury panels. Since that date, the guidelines have been updated and the most recent guidelines were published in 1988. These guidelines maintain the general propositions that jury members should normally be selected at random from the panel and should be disqualified only on the grounds set out in the JA 1974. The guidelines do, however, make reference to exceptional cases of public importance where potential jury members might properly be vetted. Such cases are broadly identified as those involving national security, where part of the evidence may be heard in camera, and terrorist cases.

Vetting is a twofold process. An initial check into police criminal records and police Special Branch records should be sufficient to reveal whether a further investigation by the security services in required. Any further investigation requires the prior approval of the Attorney General.

In addition to vetting, properly so called, the Court of Appeal in *R v Mason* (1980) approved the checking of criminal records to establish whether potential jurors had been convicted of criminal offences in the past and therefore were not eligible to serve as jurors. The Runciman Commission recommended that this process of checking on those who should be disqualified on the basis of previous criminal conviction should be regularised when the collection and storage of criminal records is centralised.

10.6.8 The racial mix of the jury

In *R v Danvers* (1982), the defence had sought to challenge the array on the basis that a black defendant could not have complete confidence in the impartiality of an all-white jury. And the question of the racial mix of a jury has exercised the courts on a number of occasions. In *R v Ford* (1989), the trial judge's refusal to accept the defendant's application for a racially mixed jury was supported by the Court of Appeal, on the grounds that 'fairness is achieved by the principle of random selection' as regards the make up of a jury, and that to insist on a racially balanced jury would be contrary to that principle, and would be to imply that particular jurors were incapable of impartiality. A similar point was made in *R v Tarrant* (1997), in which a person accused of drug related offences was convicted by a jury that had had been selected from outside the normal catchment area for the court. The aim of judge had been to minimise potential jury intimidation, but, nonetheless, the Court of Appeal overturned the conviction on the grounds that the judge had deprived the defendant of a randomly selected jury.

To deny people of colour the right to have their cases heard by representatives of their own race, on the basis of a refusal to recognise the existence of racial discriminatory attitudes, cannot but give the appearance of a society where such racist attitudes are institutionalised. This has particular resonance given the findings of the Macpherson Inquiry that the police force were 'institutionally racist'. Without suggesting that juries as presently constituted are biased, it remains arguable that if, in order to achieve the undoubted appearance of fairness, jury selection has to be manipulated to ensure a racial mix then it should at least be considered.

An interesting case study in this respect is the trial in 1994 of Lakhbir Deol, an Asian who was accused of the murder of a white youth in Stoke on Trent in 1993. Mr Deol's lawyers sought to have the case moved from Stafford to Birmingham Crown Court on the grounds that Stafford has an almost completely white population whereas Birmingham has an approximately 25% ethnic minority population. Mr Justice McKinnon repeatedly refused the request and the trial was heard in Stafford as scheduled. Mr Deol was acquitted, so his fears were proved groundless but, surely, the worrying fact is that he had those fears in the first place.

It is heartening to note that the Runciman Commission fully endorsed the views expressed above and recommended that either the prosecution or the defence can insist that up to three jury members be from ethnic minorities, and that at least one of those should be from the same ethnic minority as the accused or the victim. (This will be considered in more detail immediately below.)

It is of interest, if not concern, to note that the former Lord Chief Justice, Lord Taylor, whilst recognising that the criminal justice system was:

> ... failing blacks and Asians, by tolerating racist attitudes and allowing ethnic minorities to believe that they were beyond the protection of the law ...,

was equally sure that proposals for ethnically balanced juries, and, indeed, the new offence of racially-motivated attacks, were:

> ... Attractive sounding, but deeply flawed proposals.

He went on to criticise the Runciman proposals as:

> ... the thin edge of a particularly insidious wedge ...,

and, somewhat ironically, given subsequent proposals by the current Home Secretary, he asserted that:

> We must on no account introduce measures which allow the State to start nibbling away at the principle of random selection of juries (speech to NACRO reported in *Guardian*, 1999).

10.7   The decline of the jury trial

The resistance to the Runciman proposal to reduce the scope of jury trials (see Chapter 4) has to be placed within the context of the general decline in the use of jury trials that has occurred in the fairly recent past. Perhaps the heat engendered in the current debate is a consequence of the fact that the continued existence of the jury as it is presently constituted cannot be taken for granted.

10.7.1 The jury trial in civil procedure

Under s 69 of the Supreme Court Act 1981, the right to a jury trial is limited to only four areas: fraud; defamation; malicious prosecution; false imprisonment. (Similar provisions are contained in the County Courts Act 1984.)

Even in these areas, the right is not absolute and can be denied by a judge under s 69(i) where the case involves: 'any prolonged examination of documents or accounts or any scientific or local investigation which cannot conveniently be made with a jury'. (See *Beta Construction Ltd v Channel Four TV Co Ltd* (1990) for an indication of the factors that the judge will take into consideration in deciding whether a case should be decided by a jury or not.)

The question of whether or not juries should be used in libel cases gained wider consideration in the case involving McDonalds, the fast-food empire, and two environmentalists, Dave Morris and Helen Steel. McDonalds claimed that their reputation was damaged by an allegedly libellous leaflet issued by members of an organisation called London Greenpeace including Morris and Steel, which linked McDonalds' products to heart disease and cancer as well as the despoliation of the environment and the exploitation of the Third World. In a preliminary hearing, later confirmed by the Court of Appeal, it was decided that the evidence to be presented would be of such scientific complexity that it would be beyond the understanding of a jury. (See (1997) *The Times*, 10 June.)

The right to jury trial in defamation cases has been the object of particular criticism. In 1975, the Faulks Committee on the Law of Defamation recommended that the availability of jury trial in that area should be subject to the same judicial discretion as all other civil cases. In its conclusions, the Faulks Report shared the uncertainty of the Court of Appeal in *Ward v James* (1965) as to the suitability of juries to determine the level of damages that should be awarded. Support for these views has been provided by a number of defamation cases decided since then, such as *Sutcliffe v Pressdram Ltd* (1990), in which the wife of a convicted serial killer was awarded damages of £600,000. She eventually settled for £60,000 after the Court of Appeal stated that it would re-assess the award. In *Aldington v Watts and Tolstoy* (1989), damages of £1.5 million were awarded.

This huge award was subsequently held by the European Court of Human Rights to be so disproportionate as to amount to a violation of Tolstoy's right to freedom of expression under Art 10 of the Convention (*Tolstoy Miloslavsky v UK* (1995). Domestic law has also sought to deal with what could only be seen as excessive awards of damages in defamation cases, even prior to the Human Rights Act 1998 which makes the ECHR *Tolstoy* decision, and Art 10 of the Convention, binding in UK law.

Section 8 of the Courts and Legal Services Act 1990 gave appeal courts the power to alter damages awards made by juries to a level that they felt to be 'proper'. Nonetheless, the question of what actually constitutes a proper level of damages continued to present problems for juries, which continued to award very high damages. The problem arose from the limited guidance that judges could give juries in making their awards. In *Rantzen v Mirror Group Newspapers* (1993), the Court of Appeal stated that judges should advise juries, in making their awards, to consider the purchasing power of the award, and its proportionality to the damage suffered to the reputation of the claimant, and should refer to awards made by he courts under s 8 of the CLSA (Rantzen's original award of £250,000 was reduced to £110,000). Still, extremely large awards continued to be made, and, in *John v MGN Ltd* (1996), the Court of Appeal stated that past practice should be altered to allow juries to refer to personal injury cases to decided the level of award and that the judge could indicate what sort of level would be appropriate (John's awards of £350,000 for the libel and £275,000 in exemplary damages were reduced to £75,000 and £50,000 respectively).

In 1996, statute law intervened in the form of the Defamation Act, which was designed to simplify the procedure of defamation cases. The main provisions of the Act are:

(a) a new one year limitation period for defamation actions;

(b) a new statutory defence based on responsibility for publication. This replaces the common law defence of innocent dissemination;

(c) an updating of defences in relation to privilege; that is, reporting on the proceedings and publications of, for example, the courts and government;

(d) a new streamlined procedure for dealing with a defendant who has offered to make amends. This would involve paying compensation, assessed by a judge, and publishing an appropriate correction and apology.

(e) new powers for judges to deal with cases without a jury. Under this provision, the judge can dismiss a claim if he considers it has no realistic prospect of success. Alternatively, if he considers there to be no realistic defence to the claim, he can award summary relief. Such relief can take the form of a declaration of the falsity of the statement; an order to print an apology; an order to refrain from repeating the statement; and damages of up to £10,000.

Although enacted in July 1996, the procedure relating to the new defence of making amends and the, more controversial, summary disposal of claim procedure have not yet been implemented. In April 1999, the Lord Chancellor's Department announced its intention to issue a consultation paper before bringing all the rules into effect on 1 January 2000.

It is a matter of constitutional interest that s 13 of the Defamation Act 1996 altering the operation of s 9 of the Bill of Rights 1689, was specially introduced to allow the former Conservative MP, Neil Hamilton, to take a defamation action against the *Guardian* newspaper, which had accused him of accepting money for asking question in the House of Commons. The Bill of Rights had granted qualified privilege to MPs, but the *Guardian* had successfully argued that, as they could not sue Hamilton in regard to parliamentary matters, he, in turn, could not sue them. Unusually, as Law Lords are not supposed to involve themselves in party political matters, s 13 of the Defamation Act, which allowed MPs to waive their privilege, was moved by Lord Hoffman, apparently at the behest of the then Lord Chancellor, Lord Mackay. Hamilton's action against the *Guardian* subsequently collapsed and he lost his parliamentary seat in the 1997 election. Lord Hoffman went on to demonstrate his lack of political grasp in the infamous Pinochet case (see Chapter 6).

If the extent of damages has been a particular problem in relation to defamation actions, especially when they are compared to the much smaller awards made in relation to personal injury, it should also be noted that legal aid is not normally available in defamation cases, although it is available in relation to malicious falsehood. This effectively has made defamation a rich person's action. As a consequence, people without the necessary wealth to finance a legal action find it extremely difficult to gain redress when they have suffered from what subsequently turns out to be false and damaging press coverage of their affairs. It is to be hoped that the new summary procedure, under the Defamation Act 1996, will redress this situation. But of equal concern is the way some wealthy people were able and allowed to abuse the system. One example was the late, and notorious publisher, Robert Maxwell who often used libel proceedings or the threat of them to silence critics. As it turned out, much of what Mr Maxwell sought to prevent from becoming public knowledge was, in fact, illegal and harmful business conduct.

In all other civil cases, there is a presumption against trial by jury although, under s 69(3), the judge has the discretion to order a trial by jury. (See *Ward v James* (1965) where the court decided that a jury should be used in civil cases only in 'exceptional circumstances', although no exhaustive list as to what amounted to exceptional circumstances was provided.)

10.7.2 Criminal juries

This issue was central to the Runciman Report and detailed consideration will be postponed till later. It has to be borne in mind, however, that the criminal jury trial is essentially the creature of the Crown Court, and that the magistrates' courts deal with 97% of criminal cases. In practice, juries determine the outcome of less than 1% of the total of criminal cases for the reason that, of all the cases that are decided in the Crown Court, 72% of defendants plead guilty on all counts and therefore have no need of jury trial, and a further 2% plead guilty to some counts. In all, there were only a total of 26,117 contested cases in the Crown Court in 1990 (*Judicial Statistics,* 1990 Cmnd 1573). It can be seen, therefore, that, in absolute and proportional terms, the jury does not play a significant part in the determination of criminal cases.

If trial by jury is not statistically significant, it cannot be denied that it is of major significance in the determination of the most serious cases. Even this role, however, has not gone without scrutiny and, in 1986, the Roskill Committee on Fraud Trials critically examined the operation of the jury in complex criminal fraud cases. Its report recommended the abolition of trial by jury in such cases. The Roskill Committee did not go as far as to recommend that all fraud cases should be taken away from juries, only the most complex, of which it was estimated that there were about two dozen or so every year. It was suggested that these cases would be better decided by a judge assisted by two lay persons drawn from a panel with specialist expertise. The government declined to implement the recommendations of the Roskill Committee and, instead, introduced procedures designed to make it easier to follow the proceedings in complex fraud cases. It is interesting to note, given the controversy relating to the accusation that the Runciman Report represented an attack on the jury system, that it did not follow Roskill in its recommendations.

After being found not guilty of a £19 million fraud charge, George Walker, the former chief executive of Brent Walker, said: 'Thank God for the jury. It would be madness to lose the jury system.' This enthusiastic endorsement of the jury system is in no little way undercut, however, by the fact that Walker is reported as going on to state that he was sure the jury had not properly understood much of the highly detailed material in the trial, as he admitted: 'I didn't understand a lot of it, so I can't see how they could.'

Mr Walker's enthusiasm perhaps was not shared by his co-accused, Wilfred Aquilina, who was found guilty, on a majority verdict, of false accounting.

In February 1998, the Home Office issued a Green Paper entitled *Juries in Serious Fraud Trials*. The consultation paper suggested the need for a new procedure in relation to complex fraud trials, due to the fact that 'the detection, investigation and trial of serious criminal fraud offences have presented certain difficulties not commonly found amongst other types of offences'. A variety of possible alternatives were put forward:

- *special juries*: these would be made up of qualified people and might be drawn from a special pool of potential jurors. Alternatively, ordinary jurors would have to be assessed as to their competency to sit on the case;

- *judge run trails*: specially trained judges, either singly or in a panel, and possibly with the help of lay experts;

- *fraud tribunals*: following Roskill, these would be made up of a judge and qualified lay members with the power to question witnesses;

- *verdict-only juries*: in this situation the judge would hear the evidence and sum up the facts leaving the jury simply to vote on guilt or innocence;

- *a special juror*: here, 11 of the jury would be selected as normal, but the 12th would be specially qualified in order to be able to assist the others on complex points.

With respect to these alternatives, the government stated that it had no particular preference.

Under the proposals, a judge would decide at a pre-trial hearing if the case would be heard by an ordinary jury, or under whichever of the possible new procedures is finally selected. The Green Paper estimated that, at most, 85 cases per year would be subject to the new procedure, but, significantly, it was also estimated that costs of adopting the new procedures would cut costs by up to 25%.

Subsequently, in April 1998, the Home Secretary requested the Law Commission to carry out a review of fraud trials focusing particularly on whether the existing law is:

- readily comprehensible to juries;

- adequate for effective prosecution;

- fair to defendants; and

- able to cope with changes in technology.

It should not be forgotten that the right to jury trial has been abolished in Northern Ireland since 1973. In response to the problem of the intimidation of jury members, the Report of the Commission to Consider Legal Procedures to

Deal with Terrorist Activities in Northern Ireland, headed by Lord Diplock, recommended that cases be decided without juries in particular situations. The so called Diplock courts operate in relation to certain 'scheduled offences', particularly, but not exclusively, associated with terrorism.

10.8 The Runciman Commission

The Report of the Royal Commission on Criminal Justice made numerous recommendations relating to juries. Indeed, the very first recommendation made by it was that s 8 of the Contempt of Court Act 1981 should be repealed to enable research to be conducted into juries' reasons for their verdicts. At present, s 8 makes it an offence to obtain, disclose or solicit any particulars of statements made, opinion, expressed, arguments advanced or votes cast by members of a jury in the course of their deliberations in any legal proceedings.

In *Attorney General v Associated Newspapers* (1994), the House of Lords held that it was contempt of court for a newspaper to publish disclosures by jurors of what took place in the jury room while they were considering their verdict, unless the publication amounted to no more than a republication of facts already known. It was decided that the word 'disclose' in s 8(1) applied not just to jurors but to any others who published their revelations.

10.8.1 General points about jury selection

In relation specifically to the selection of juries, the Commission addressed itself to many of the problems that were considered above and made the following recommendations.

- *Every endeavour should be made to ensure that the electoral rolls are comprehensive and include everybody who ought to be included.*

  Such a recommendation is certainly worthy, but it is difficult to see how electoral registration officers will succeed in overcoming the problems, considered previously, of people's failure to appear on the register through conscious design or mere accident.

- *Clergymen and members of religious orders should be eligible; but practising members of religious sects which object to jury service should be excluded.*

  Alterations should be made to the list of people liable to serve on juries. This sensible measure to increase the pool of potential jurors was enacted by s 92 of the CJA 1989.

- *Potential jurors should be given alternative dates if they cannot sit on the date originally suggested.*

  This recommendation is aimed at accommodating people who have difficulty attending for jury service at a particular time, whilst at the same time it does not simply let them disappear if they cannot make that date. It thus aims at preventing certain individuals from opting out of the duty to serve on juries.

- *The rates of financial allowances for those on jury service should be reviewed as a matter of urgency.*

This is a clear recognition of the fact that it costs people money to serve on juries and that, as a consequence, people try to avoid their social and legal duty to serve. The Commission is clearly of the opinion that this should not be the case and that to avoid this occurrence, the levels of allowance should be raised.

- *Jury-summoning officers should try to make sure that potential jury members do not know each other or the accused.*

Clearly, such occurrences, but especially the latter one, are to be avoided wherever possible.

10.8.2 Disqualification

The Commission made some recommendations designed to improve the operation of the existing disqualification procedure, and as such no great exception can be taken to them:

- when the national criminal record system is fully operational courts should arrange for that agency to screen jurors on a routine basis to discover any disqualifying convictions they might have;

- jurors should be required to positively affirm that they have no disqualifying convictions, and should be open to conviction if they provide false information.

There are, however, some recommendations that are less obviously justified or needed and which give some cause to suspect the underlying purpose of the Commission's report in general. These are:

- *People currently on bail should be disqualified from serving.*

One is immediately prompted to ask why such people should be disqualified. By definition, they have not been convicted of the offence of which they stand charged, and may not be. Is disqualifying them, on no other ground than they have been charged with an offence, not tantamount to pre-judging the case against them? It may be argued that if such people are later found guilty of the offence in relation to which they were granted bail, then their previous disqualification was clearly justified; and if they are later found innocent then they would not have been in the right frame of mind to decide any cases they would have been involved in an objective manner. The former argument is at best a *post hoc* justification for an action that has no inherent justification; the latter is even more objectionable in that it assumes that objectivity cannot encompass scepticism of the case presented by the prosecution with its underlying assumption that the purpose of the trial process is simply to convict the accused.

In any case, the proposal was effected by s 40 of the CJA 1994 and consequently any person on bail in criminal proceedings is disqualified from serving as a juror in the Crown Court. The disqualification does not cover service in civil proceedings.

- *Once s 8 of the Contempt of Court Act is repealed, it is recommended that research be carried out into the possible influence of jurors with criminal records on the decisions of juries.*

It would appear to be an implicit assumption that such people have a deleterious effect on the operation of juries. The further implication is that such research would be conducted to prove the point, as the first step to disqualifying them as potential jurors. Thus, the apparently praiseworthy procedure of opening up the jury process to investigation may have the ulterior motive of intending to discredit its operation.

10.8.3 The ethnic origin of jurors

The Runciman Commission addressed the difficulties looked at above (see 10.6.8) and made the following recommendations:

- in exceptional cases, it should be possible for either the prosecution or the defence to apply to the trial judge to have the jury selected in such a way as to ensure that it contains three people from ethnic minority communities;

- it should also be open for the prosecution or defence to argue the need that one of these three be of the same ethnic minority as the defendant or the victim.

It should be noted that these two measures would not just operate in cases where the accused was a member of an ethnic minority but could also be used in relation to trials involving white accused, perhaps charged with racist offences. In either situation, the intention would be to provide a signal indication of the impartiality of the procedure.

10.8.4 The conduct of trials

Most of the proposals made in this section relate to ensuring that jurors are fully aware of what is going on in the court and what is expected of them. There are a couple of recommendations that are worthy of closer consideration:

- Every effort should be made to protect jurors from intimidation. Guidance should be given to jurors on what to do if they feel intimidated and in sensitive cases the public gallery should be sited in such a way as to preclude the possibility of intimidation of the jury.

  In the context of this chapter, it is worth noting that claims about intimidation have been used to justify the removal of jury trials in Northern Ireland. This proposal, however, appears to be a reasonable and practical suggestion designed to curtail the problem without undermining the jury system. Section 51 of the CJPOA 1994 introduced the offence of jury intimidation in furtherance of this aim.

- In long trials lasting weeks or months, judges should consider staggering the courts' normal hours to enable jurors to keep in touch with their employment. Once again, this is a sensible proposal recognising and attempting in some way to deal with one of the problems that arise for jurors from involvement in long trials.

  With specific regard to fraud trials, it is recommended that:

- Section 10(3) of the CJA 1988 should be amended to permit judges to put the issues before the jury at the outset of the trial.

  This proposal recognises the particular difficulties faced by jurors in fraud trials but, in the light of the controversy considered below in cases triable 'either way', it is interesting to note that the Commission does not suggest the removal of the jury from such cases.

10.8.5 The rights to jury trial

The general proposals of the Runciman Commission in relation to juries were not without an element of controversy but it was, without doubt, the Commission's proposal to limit the role of the jury in the criminal process that generated the most controversy. This particular recommendation, number 114 out of a total 352, stimulated more response than any other single proposal; and, by and large, that response was hostile.

In order to understand the full implications of the recommendation, it is necessary to reconsider points that have been discussed previously in Chapters 4 and 6.

It is essential to appreciate the distinction, established in the Criminal Law Act 1977, between offences to be tried *only* by summary procedure, offences to be tried *only* on indictment and offences triable '*either way*'. Summary offences are those which are triable only in the magistrates' courts and cases which, as has been noted previously, magistrates decide on their own without the assistance of a jury. There are literally hundreds of summary offences; given the limitations on the sentencing powers of magistrates, they are by necessity the least serious of criminal acts, such as road traffic offences, and minor assault.

The most serious offences, such as major theft, serious assault, rape, manslaughter and murder have to be tried on indictment before a jury in the Crown Court. There is, however, a third category, offences triable 'either way' which, as the name suggests, may be tried either summarily or on indictment. It was the Runciman Commission's recommendation in relation to this third category that gave rise to most controversy.

The current way of determining how an offence triable 'either way' is actually heard is set out in the Magistrates' Courts Act (MCA) 1980. Under s 19 of that Act, the magistrates' court has to decide whether the offence is more suitable for summary trial or trial on indictment. In reaching that decision, the magistrates must take into account the nature of the case, its seriousness, and whether the penalty they could impose would be adequate, and any other circumstances which appear to the court to make it more suitable for the offence to be tried one way rather than the other. (Guidelines are set out in *Practice Note* (1990).) If the magistrates decide that the case is suitable for summary hearing, they are required by s 20 of the MCA 1980 to inform the defendant of their decision and also to inform him that, if he is found guilty on the summary hearing, he may still be committed to the Crown Court for sentencing if the magistrates are of the opinion that their powers of sentencing are inadequate. If the accused agrees to a summary hearing, the trial goes ahead in the magistrates' court. If, however, the defendant objects to the summary procedure, the case goes on indictment to the Crown Court and the magistrates merely act as examining justices. It is this latter right, the right of the defendant in cases triable 'either way' to elect for/insist on a trial by jury, that the Runciman Commission recommended should be removed. It is not inappropriate to cite the recommendation in full:

> In cases involving 'either way' offences, the defendant should no longer have the right to insist on a trial by jury. Where the CPS (the Crown Prosecution Service) and the defendant agree that the case is suitable for summary trial, it should proceed to trial in a magistrates' court. The case should go to the Crown Court for trial if both the prosecution and defence agree that it should be tried on indictment. Where the defence do not agree with the CPS's proposal on which court should try the case, the matter should be referred to the magistrates for a decision (Royal Commission Report on the Criminal Justice System, 1993, Cm 2263, London: HMSO).

This recommendation supports the view of the former Director of Public Prosecution, Barbara Mills, who, in an interview in *The Times* on 21 April 1993, suggested that the right to opt for trial by jury should be removed from a greater number of defendants who should be dealt with in a summary manner. If accepted, according to the report it would affect more than 35,000 cases per year.

The declared aim of the recommendation is the achievement of 'a more rational division of "either way" cases between the magistrates' courts and the Crown Court' (see para 6.13 of the Report) and it is claimed that this rationalisation would bring about 'significant benefits for the overall efficiency of the criminal justice system ... without the quality of justice being diminished thereby' (see para 6.15 of the Report). If efficiency is defined in relation to the parameter of economic cost then the first half of this claim may well be true, for as the Commission itself pointed out 'A trial in a magistrates' court is many times cheaper than a trial at the Crown Court'. It is greatly to be doubted, however, if the second part of that claim is as accurate; and it is on the need to maintain the quality of justice that much of the attack on Runciman focused.

In support of its recommendation, the Runciman Commission cited statistics drawn from various research projects and although some of the statistics did not actually support the argument of the Commission, the main problem with its recommendation was that there was a fundamental flaw at the heart of its apparent logic. As pointed out in Chapter 6 of this book, the Commission referred to empirical research that found that for offences that could be tried 'either way', the chances of acquittal were substantially higher in the Crown Court with a jury (57%) than in the magistrates' courts without a jury (30%). The Commission commented, with what can only be taken as irony, on the fact that, although most defendants opt for the Crown Court on the basis of an expectation of an acquittal, by the time their trial comes on, 70% of them plead guilty to all charges and a further 13% plead guilty to at least some of the charges of which they are accused. The Commission, however, also provided the answer for this apparent paradox in the conclusions of another research project. This one found that of a sample of defendants who elected to have their case decided in the Crown Court, 50% did so in the belief that even if the jury decided they were guilty their sentence would be lighter in the Crown Court than it would have been in the magistrates' court. The same research proved the fallacy of that belief, for it found that in practice, in matched cases, judges were three times more likely to impose immediate custody and their sentences were on average two and a half times longer than those delivered by magistrates. That latter finding in no way undermines the former point relating to the defendants' subjective perception of the two courts; indeed it strengthens it. A further point in relation to subjective opinions about the operation of the Crown Court is provided by a research study produced for the Commission. It was stated that the police and the Crown Prosecution Service found nearly half of all jury acquittals surprising; but as Michael Mansfield has suggested such an opinion might well be predicated on an arrogant assumption that they know best who is guilty in the first place.

The Commission's Report stated that defendants should not 'be able to choose their court of trial solely on the basis that they think that they will get a fairer hearing at one level than another' (see para 6.18 of the Report). The conclusion of the Commission seems to be that because defendants do not trust the magistrates' court, and there is some justification for this in respect of the rates of acquittal, and do have more faith in the Crown Court than is warranted in terms of sentencing, then they should be *forced* to use the magistrates' court.

As the report stated: 'Magistrates' courts conduct over 93% of all criminal cases and should be trusted to try cases fairly' (see para 6.18 of the Report). It is at least arguable that in this conclusion the Commission is missing the point. Put starkly, the evidence supports the conclusion that defendants do not trust magistrates' courts. Indeed, the evidence as to the number of people changing their plea to guilty in the Crown Court would seem to support the conclusion, not so much that defendants trust juries but more that they do not trust magistrates. This lack of trust in the magistracy is further highlighted by the fact that those who do not plead guilty would rather have their guilt or innocence determined by a jury.

Simply forcing such people to use the magistrates' courts does not address the underlying problem let alone solve it.

It would have been possible for the Commission to have achieved its end by simply recommending that particular offences, that are defined as triable 'either way' at present, should be re-categorised as offences only open to summary procedure. That it did not do so further indicates the weakness of the underlying logic of its case for removing the right to insist on trial on indictment. The Commission rejected the reclassification of offences partly because of the difficulty and uncertainty inherent in the task. Additionally, and more importantly, however, it rejected this approach because it wished to leave available the possibility of the defendant successfully insisting on trial on indictment in the case of first offenders, where the consequences of loss of reputation would be significant. In the words of the Commission: 'Loss of reputation is a different matter, since jury trial has long been regarded as appropriate for cases involving that issue. But, it should only be one of the factors to be taken into account and will often be relevant only to first offenders' (see para 6.18 of the Report).

There are two assumptions in this proposal. First, there is the, surely objectionable, assumption that the reputation of anyone with a previous conviction is not important. But, of even more concern is the fact that it is recognised that in the cases of first offenders they *should* be permitted access to the jury. The question has to be asked: why should this be the case if juries do no more than magistrates do? It appears that in the instance of first offenders it is recognised that juries *do* offer more protection than magistrates. Again, this demands the question: why should the extra protection not be open to all? Thus, once more, the economic imperative that motivated the Commission comes into question, and once again the pursuit of lower cost takes over from the need *to be clearly seen to provide justice*.

It has been claimed that this proposal comes dangerously close to advocating a two-tier system of criminal justice, with the cheaper version being reserved for the punishment of the 'criminal classes'. Opposition to it has been voluble and former Lord Chief Justice Taylor stated his personal disapprobation. Also, the Vice President of The Law Society, Charles Elly, stated the Society's strong opposition to this particular proposal and expressed the view that it 'can only have been based on the interests of cost-cutting, not of justice'. The then Chairman of the Criminal Bar, whilst approving of the rest of the report, was equally outspoken about this proposal. As he saw it, the abolition of the right to jury trial in such cases was: '... likely to involve unequal treatment of defendants, favouring those whom society views as more respectable than others'. Or, as Michael Mansfield QC put the matter: 'If the Commission has its way we are racing towards middle class justice.'

10.8.6 Proposals for change

In May 1999, the government announced its intention to introduce legislation to curb the right to jury trial. In essence, it wishes, in cases triable either way, to disallow a defendant from insisting upon trial by jury in circumstances where magistrates believe that they are well-suited to hear the case ((1999) *The Times*, 19 May). More than 18,500 defendants a year would lose their right to trial by jury under these plans. The plans were advanced by the government to, according to its own contentions, speed up the hearing of criminal cases. The proposed reform was widely condemned by civil rights groups, the Bar and other lawyers.

The Home Secretary, Mr Straw, decided to push ahead with the change after finding that many people who opt in the early stages of their cases for trial by jury change their plea to guilty before the trial is heard. Home Office research shows that more than 70% of those who opt for jury trial plead guilty by the day their Crown Court case opens. The average cost of a jury trial is £13,500, compared with £2,500 for a hearing by magistrates. Mr Straw has been convinced of the need for change in spite of opposing a similar plan when it was floated by Michael Howard, as Conservative Home Secretary. Mr Straw attacked the idea then as 'unfair, short-sighted and likely to prove ineffective' ((1999) *The Times*, 19 May).

One Home Office paper (*Jury Trials*, 1998, Home Office) suggested that defendants elect for trial by jury at the Crown Court in an attempt to put pressure on the Crown Prosecution Service to accept a plea to a less serious charge; to make it more likely that witnesses do not turn up or be vague in their recollections; or simply to put off the day of conviction and sentence.

One problem for those who support such a change is that if, for serious crimes, you support the rigmarole of jury trials because so much is at stake for the defendant, how then can you justify removal of the defendant's right to a jury trail in cases which manifestly threaten life-ruining results for a defendant? Offences like indecent assault and theft are cases in point.

In earlier times, judges would often fine or imprison jurors who persisted in returning verdicts at variance with the preference of the Bench. In 1671, *Bushell's Case* established that juries should be immune from punishment for their verdicts. Such meddling, however, might be seen by some as of modest significance in contrast to a plan to rule out the right to jury trial for several types of serious offence.

10.8.7 Conclusion

It has been repeatedly suggested by those in favour of abolishing, or at least severely curtailing, the role of the jury in the criminal justice system that the general perception of the jury is romanticised and has little foundation in reality. Runciman did not actually make this point explicitly but it is implicit in his assessment of the jury system as against the magistrates' courts. Others have been more explicit; thus, the Roskill Committee expressed the view that:

> Society appears to have an attachment to jury trial which is emotional or sentimental rather than logical (para 8.21).

A similar point had been made previously by the Faulks Committee, but that report also recognised the source of the public's opinion and was careful not to dismiss it as unimportant:

> Much of the support for jury trials is emotional and derives from the undoubted value of juries in serious criminal cases where they stand between the prosecuting authority and the citizen (para 496).

The ideological power of the jury system should not be underestimated. It represents the ordinary person's input into the legal system and it is at least arguable that in that way it provides the whole legal system with a sense of legitimacy. It is argued by some civil libertarians that the existence of the non-jury Diplock Courts in Northern Ireland brings the whole of the legal system in that province into disrepute.

As Lord Devlin noted (*Trial By Jury*, 1966):

> The first object of any tyrant in Whitehall would be to make Parliament utterly subservient to his will; and the next to overthrow or diminish trial by jury, for no tyrant could afford to leave a subject's freedom in the hands of 12 of his countrymen.

THE CRIMINAL PROCESS:
(2) THE PROSECUTION

The Crown Prosecution Service

The Crown Prosecution Service was introduced in 1986 and it is important to understand the five types of prosecution which existed before this time and how the CPS was supposed to improve the old system's criticisms. What sort of biases can occur in the use of prosecutorial discretion and why? Why were the police regarded as not the most suitable agency to exercise the prosecutorial discretion? What were the police defences to those criticisms? The police argued that conviction rates vindicated the way they exercised their discretion. The new Code for Crown Prosecutors (1994) introduces factors which should weigh for and against a prosecution.

Cautioning offenders

Cautioning offenders has recently increased as a proportion of the ways police respond to crime. Why is this? The CPS guidelines on prosecution require a 'realistic prospect of conviction' and that the 'public interest' is served by any prosecution. What difficulties are entailed by such formulae?

Judicial control

Judicial control of prosecution policy is very limited and amounts to being able to correct only flagrantly irrational decisions by senior officers (*R v Metropolitan Police Commissioner ex p Blackburn* (1968)).

Bail

Bail is the release from custody, pending a criminal trial, of an accused on the promise that money will be paid if he or she absconds. The important issue raised here is how best the regulations should be framed so as to balance the conflicting interests of public safety and civil liberty. Public safety would perhaps be best served by keeping in custody everyone accused of a crime until their trial; this, though, would clearly be unnecessarily draconian. Conversely, civil liberty might be best served by allowing every suspect to remain free however heinous the crime they have been accused of and whatever their past record. The important statutory provisions are s 38 of PACE 1984 and ss 3, 4, 6 and Sched 1 of the BA 1976. Changes made by the Bail (Amendment) Act 1993, and the CJPOA 1994, allow prosecutors to appeal against the granting of bail, restrict some aspects of it being granted, and afford greater opportunities for police bail.

Plea bargaining

Plea bargaining is the practice where the accused enters a plea of guilty in return for which he will be given a sentence concession. It can also refer to 'plea arrangements' where the accused agrees to plead guilty to a lesser charge than the one with which he or she is or is to be charged. Note the recommendation of the Runciman Commission to introduce sentence discounting as a means to avoid 'cracked trials'. Dangers arising from such procedures include innocent persons being pressurised to 'take a plea' and serious offenders being processed for minor offences. In a system where the vast majority of cases in the Crown Court and magistrates' courts result in guilty pleas (79% and 81.5%, respectively), the operation of the plea bargain becomes very important.

The jury

The jury has come under close public scrutiny since the Runciman Commission's recommendation to curtail the right to jury trial. It is important to know the standard arguments in favour of the jury and also the arguments showing it to be not truly random and representative. The detail of the jury's function in a trial and the extent to which its verdict can be appealed against are important. In what ways can the membership of the jury be challenged? What arguments were adopted by the Runciman Commission when recommending fewer jury trials? Juries lie at the heart of the English criminal justice system. There is debate about whether juries provide any better justice than magistrates' courts or whether the role is purely symbolic.

The role of the jury

To decide matters of fact – judges decide matters of law. Judges can instruct juries to acquit but not to convict. Juries do not have to give reasons for their decision. There is no appeal against an acquittal verdict, although points of law may be clarified by an Attorney General's reference. Civil cases can be overturned if perverse – but not criminal cases. Verdicts can be delivered on the basis of majority decisions. The use of juries has declined in relation to criminal and civil law.

Selection of juries

Random in theory – selective in practice. All on the electoral register are liable to serve but the registers tend to be inaccurate. Service is subject to exemption, excusal and disqualification. Defence and prosecution can challenge for cause. Prosecution can ask jurors to stand by. Jury vetting is checking that jurors are suitable to hear sensitive cases. If Runciman is followed, juries may be required to have a racial mix.

The Runciman Report

Section 8 of the Contempt of Court Act 1981 should be amended. Attempts should be made to improve the representative nature of juries. The operation of disqualification procedures should be tightened and extended to those on bail. The ethnic mix of a jury should be open to adjustment. In complex fraud trials, judges should be permitted to explain the matters involved at the outset of the trial. Magistrates should have the final say in where offences triable 'either way' are heard.

CHAPTER 11

LEGAL SERVICES

11.1   Introduction

We are concerned here with a number of issues related to the provision and organisation of legal services, and the problem of access to legal services. This is a period of great change for all of these matters. The legal profession has undergone a series of major changes as a result of the Courts and Legal Services Act (CLSA) 1990; the provision of legal aid, advice and assistance has been drastically altered as a result of changes introduced in 1999. The introduction of the 'conditional fee arrangement' in 1995 was another contentious issue in this area.

The former Lord Chancellor, Lord Mackay, saw his primary objective as improving access to justice by making the environment of legal services more competitive. He was also very concerned at the costs of providing free and subsidised legal aid, advice and assistance. Speaking in October 1992 at The Law Society Conference, Lord Mackay said:

> My task is to secure a balance between my responsibilities to the public to provide the means for reasonable access to justice and my responsibility to the public as taxpayers in controlling what is now a very high level of expenditure [then over £1.1 billion gross]. That task is not an easy one, but I am convinced that I can achieve it. To do so, however, will involve some radical re-thinking of some elements of the present system. In the short term, it may involve measures which will be uncomfortable and, perhaps to some of you, unwelcome. But, if the future of the legal aid scheme is to be put on a firm base ... changes are inevitable.

It is important when considering all the elements of this chapter to ask yourself questions about the aims of all the systems and proposed changes to them. What is their immediate aim? Is such an immediate aim part of a wider legal or social objective? How does the funding of any given component operate and what do its critics say is wrong or undesirable about it or the way it works?

11.2   The legal profession

The English legal system is one of only three in the world to have a divided legal profession where a lawyer is either a solicitor or a barrister. Each branch has its own separate traditions, training requirements and customs of practice. It is important to remember that not only lawyers regularly perform legal work. As one text notes (Bailey and Gunn, *Smith & Bailey on The Modern English Legal System*, 1991, p 105):

> ... many non-lawyers perform legal tasks, some of them full time. For example, accountants may specialise in revenue law, trade union officials may appear regularly before industrial tribunals on behalf of their members, and solicitors may delegate work to legal executives. Conversely, many of the tasks performed by lawyers are not strictly 'legal'.

11.3 Solicitors

The solicitor can be characterised as a general practitioner: a lawyer who deals with clients direct and when a particular specialism or litigation is required will engage the services of counsel, that is, a barrister. Looking at the solicitor as a legal GP and the barrister as a specialist, however, can be misleading. Most solicitors, especially those in large practices, are experts in particular areas of law. They may restrict their regular work to litigation or commercial conveyancing or revenue work. Many barristers on the other hand might have a quite wide range of work including criminal, family matters and a variety of common law areas like tort and contract cases. The origins of the solicitor go back to the *attornatus*, or later the 'attorney', a medieval officer of the court whose main function was to assist the client in the initial stages of the case. One group of people practising in the Court of Chancery came to be known as 'solicitors'. Originally, they performed a variety of miscellaneous clerical tasks for employers such as land owners and attorneys. Their name was derived from their function of 'soliciting' or prosecuting actions in courts of which they were not officers or attorneys. Eventually, neither of these groups were admitted to the Inns of Court (where barristers worked); they merged and organised themselves as a distinct profession.

It was not, however, until 1831 that 'The Society of Attorneys Solicitors Proctors and Others not being Barristers Practising in the Courts of Law and Equity in the United Kingdom' was given its Royal Charter. This body emerged as the governing body of solicitors, the term 'attorney' falling from general use.

According to the latest Law Society figures available (June 1999), there are 95,521 solicitors on the Roll, an annual increase of 4.1% on the previous year. Of these, 75,072 had practising certificates. Of those holding practising certificates, Law Society statistics (*Trends in the Solicitors' Profession*, Annual Statistical Report 1998) show that 81% work in private practice. The remaining 19% work in commerce, industry or the public sector. Of those currently holding practising certificates, 33.9% are women and 52% are aged under 40. Overall, membership of The Law Society has increased by 230% since 1968.

One very significant area of development and concern for solicitors at the beginning of the 21st century is the extent to which their monopolies of certain sorts of practice have been eroded. They have already lost their monopoly on conveyancing (although only a solicitor is authorised to give final endorsement to such work if carried out by a licensed conveyancer). Then, in 1999, the Access to Justice Act (see Chapter 12) introduced the provision that the Lord Chancellor will in future be able to authorise bodies other than The Law Society to approve of their members carrying out litigation. This, however, should be seen in the wider context of the policy to break down the historical monopolies of both branches of the legal profession. Thus, we can note the growth, since the Courts and Legal Services Act 1990, of solicitors rights of audience in court, and a corresponding anxiety at the Bar when these rights were granted.

The 1999 Act provides that every barrister and every solicitor has a right of audience before every court in relation to all proceedings. The right, however, is not unconditional. In order to exercise it, solicitors and barristers must obey the rules of conduct of the professional bodies and must have met any training requirements that have been prescribed like the requirement to have completed pupillage in the case of the Bar, or to have obtained a higher courts advocacy qualification in the case of solicitors who wish to appear in the higher courts.

11.3.1 Training

The standard route to qualification is a law degree followed by a one year Legal Practice Course (LPC) and then a term as a trainee solicitor which, like the barrister's pupillage, is essentially an apprenticeship. Non-law graduates can complete the Common Professional Examination in one year and then proceed as a law graduate. All newly admitted solicitors must now undergo regular continuing education which means attendance at non-examined legal courses designed to update knowledge and improve expertise. After completion of the LPC and traineeship, a trainee solicitor may apply to The Law Society to be 'admitted' to the profession. The Master of the Rolls will add the names of the newly qualified to the roll of officers of the Supreme Court. To practise, a solicitor will also require a practising certificate (currently £420) issued by The Law Society and will be required to make a contribution to the compensation fund run by The Law Society to pay clients who have suffered loss through the misconduct of a solicitor. Additionally, solicitors have to pay an annual premium for indemnity insurance.

11.3.2 The Law Society

This is the profession's governing body controlled by a council of elected members and an annually elected President. Its powers and duties are derived from the Solicitors Act 1974. Complaints against solicitors used to be dealt with by the Solicitors' Complaints Bureau and the Solicitors' Disciplinary Tribunal, the latter having power to strike from the rolls the name of an offending solicitor. It had been sometimes seen as worrying that the Society combined two roles with a possible conflict of interests: maintenance of professional standards for the protection of the public and as the main professional association to promote the interests of solicitors. Consider a rather basic example. Acting for its members, The Law Society should perhaps try to ensure that insurance policies against claims for negligence are always available for solicitors even if they have been sued for this several times. For such insurance to be granted to someone with such a questionable professional record is, however, clearly not in the best interests of the public who use solicitors.

Office for the Supervision of Solicitors

From 1 September 1996, the solicitors' disciplinary tribunal continued to work as before, but the Office for the Supervision of Solicitors (OSS) took over the work of the Solicitors' Complaints Bureau, and the old organisation was abolished. The new organisation, based in Leamington Spa, has more than 200 staff and employs solicitors, accountants, qualified mediators and administrative support staff. The Office is divided into two parts, one of which deals with client-related matters and the other with regulation. All new cases are examined upon arrival and directed to one or other of them. Staff work in small teams, and one member of staff will follow a complaint through from start to finish.

A Remuneration Certificate Department carries out free reviews of solicitors' bills to ensure that they are fair and reasonable. The Office for Professional Regulation (a part of OSS) ensures that solicitors comply with the regulations that govern them like the Solicitors' Investment Business Rules.

The Compensation Fund was set up in 1941 by The Law Society to protect the clients of dishonest solicitors. The fund is supervised by the OSS. In matters of professional misconduct, OSS can either impose an internal disciplinary sanction or prosecute the most serious cases before the solicitors' disciplinary tribunal. In cases of inadequate professional service, the OSS can order compensation of up to £1,000. The mission statement of the OSS states that 'our aim is to work for excellence and fairness in guarding the standards of the solicitors' profession'. How far that aim is achieved must be judged in the light of developments over the next couple of years.

Members of the public with criticisms about solicitors' work will receive an initial response within 24 hours under the new practice of OSS. Staff have been asked to be more open with the public, make greater use of telephones in contacting complainants and to write letters in plain English rather than in legalistic language. Advertisements were placed in the media for 10 lay people to join a committee dealing with the supervision of the profession.

The major problem for OSS is delay in responding to complaints (Office for the Supervision of Solicitors, *Annual Report 1997–98*) – a point which irks many solicitors as the complaint against them often involves allegations of delay ('Best practice and the OSS' [1999] NLJ 589, 23 April). According to the 1997–98 Report, the extent of complaints against solicitors is considerable. Approximately 950 firms out of the 8,500 practices in England and Wales are responsible for 80% of the problems brought to OSS.

A new strategy to deal with complaints was announced in 1999 by Philip Hamer, Chairman of the OSS Review Task Force ([1999] NLJ 959, 25 June).

It followed publication by The Law Society of an independent review of its complaints handling. The review, conducted by management consultants Ernst and Young, outlined a series of steps that must be taken if the OSS is to clear its backlog and end the delays which have beset the organisation for so long. The Report has concentrated on client complaints, currently rising at 16% per year, although, of course, other regulatory matters are also dealt with by the OSS.

Mr Hamer said:

> The problems at the OSS are well known and often repeated. There are unacceptable delays in resolving cases and those delays have led to a growing backlog of untouched complaints. This is causing serious damage to the credibility of the profession and, unless something radical is done, the situation can only get worse ([1999] NLJ 959, 25 June).

The Report by Ernst and Young indicates that the necessary improvements needed – to establish an efficient and effective complaints handling system, clear the backlog of 17,000 complaints, and to deal with all complaints within three months – are achievable by December 2000.

The Review recommends improved systems of management and case filtering, and that an extra 23 permanent and 82 temporary caseworkers be recruited by OSS, together with support and supervisory staff, as well as an increase in the number of additional senior management posts. Estimates of likely costs, excluding overheads, are expected to be in the region of £1.4 million for 1999 and a further £4.3 million in 2000. This sum needs to be considered in context, since the Society has already invested some £5 million in a new computer system for the OSS, which went live at the end of 1998.

OSS is, however, funded by The Law Society, so a serious question arises as to whether the new body will be seen as sufficiently independent by the public.

In *Wood v Law Society* (1995), the plaintiff (W) alleged that she was the victim of continuing misconduct by a firm of solicitors. She complained that H, a partner in a law firm, wrongly acted for both sides when arranging a series of loans for W on the security of W's home, and that H failed to disclose that H's husband was a director of one of the lenders. H's firm acted for the lenders in issuing court proceedings and obtained possession of the cottage for them. After many complaints to them by W, The Law Society conceded, after much delay, that it had been 'unwise' for H's firm to act for the lenders and that this was 'conduct unbefitting a solicitor'. The Society issued a formal rebuke. W sought damages from The Law Society, arguing that as a result of the Society's incompetence and delay, she lost the chance of avoiding repossession of her home and suffered anxiety and distress.

The Court of Appeal held that if there was a duty owed to W by the Society it did not include a duty to provide peace of mind or freedom from distress. Even though the Society appeared not to have lived up to the standards reasonably to be expected of it, there was no prospect of establishing that its failure properly or timeously to investigate her complaints could have any sounding in damages. The loss suffered by W was not directly caused by The Law Society's incompetence and delay.

Another recent case dealing with the liability of solicitors is *White v Jones* (1995). This decision arguably widens the liability of solicitors. The House of Lords decided that a solicitor owes a duty of care to the intended beneficiary of a will when instructed by the testator to draw up that will. A firm of solicitors had been instructed by a client to change his will so that his daughters (whom he had previously cut out of an inheritance) should each receive £9,000. The firm did not act promptly on these instructions and the father eventually died before the will had been changed. Thus the daughters received nothing. The person actually acting in the matter was a legal executive, not a solicitor, but it was the liability of the firm which was in issue. The Court of Appeal allowed an appeal by the plaintiffs, and granted that they should be awarded damages from the firm of solicitors to cover the loss, that is, the amounts they would have inherited had the firm acted professionally. The House of Lords upheld this decision.

The case is an interesting illustration of the judicial development of the common law. There was no obvious way in which the plaintiffs had an action. They could not sue the firm in contract because they had made no contract with the firm; only their father had done so. The daughters were outside of the arrangements between their father and his solicitors; they were third parties and the law does not recognise a *ius quaesitum tertio* (a contractual right for the benefit of a third party). The precedents in the tort of negligence did not provide much assistance because unlike the facts of those cases, the daughters here were not people who had relied upon the firm (as in a case like *Ross v Caunters* (1979)).

The leading opinion was given by Lord Goff who decided that there was a need to give people like the plaintiffs a remedy in this sort of situation, a remedy which was not available according to technical rules of law. He thus favoured 'practical justice', recognising that:

> ... cases such as these call for an appropriate remedy and that the common law is not so sterile as to be incapable of supplying that remedy when it is required (at p 777).

By a majority of three to two, the Lords extended the duty of care owed by professionals as it had been expressed in *Hedley Byrne v Heller* (1963). They said that, where the loss suffered by the victim was purely economic, it would be possible to bring an action not only where the professional had given negligent advice or made negligent statements, but it extended to the general principle that the provider of professional services could be liable for pure economic loss where his or her skills were being relied upon.

11.3.3 The Institute of Legal Executives

The Institute of Legal Executives represents senior persons employed in solicitors' offices. There are currently over 20,000 legal executives. They are legally trained (the Institute runs its own examinations) and carry out much of the routine legal work which is a feature of most practices. Changes made to the law by the Access to Justice Act 1999 (see 11.8.3, below) mean that the Institute will apply for limited rights of audience for those of its members who pass certain examinations.

11.3.4 British Standard 5750

The Law Society has launched a scheme whereby firms of solicitors can prove the quality of the services they offer by the award to the firm of British Standard 5750. Applicant firms are judged on their administrative and legal systems and the efficiency and professionalism with which their clients are handled.

11.4   Barristers

The barrister is often thought of as primarily a court advocate although many spend more time on drafting, pleadings and writing advices for solicitors. Professional barristers are technically competent to perform all advocacy for the prosecution or defence in criminal cases and for a plaintiff or defendant in a civil action. More generally, however, established barristers tend to specialise in particular areas of work. Over 60% of practising barristers work in London.

According to the latest figures (*Annual Report 1998*, 1999, The General Council of the Bar, London), there were 9,698 barristers in independent practice in England and Wales in 1998, of whom 7,288 were men and 2,410 were women. There were 1,006 Queen's Counsel, of whom 974 were men and 72 women.

The Bar had been organised as an association of the members of the Inns of Court by the 14th century. Today, there are four Inns of Court (Inner and Middle Temples, Lincoln's Inn and Gray's Inn) although there were originally more including Inns of Chancery and Sergeants' Inns, the latter being an association of the King's most senior lawyers. Until the CLSA 1990, the barrister had a virtual monopoly on advocacy in all the superior courts (in some cases, solicitors could act as advocates in the Crown Court). Barristers, known as 'counsel' when acting in the course of their profession, number about 8,935, of whom 2,115 are women. They cannot deal direct with clients but must be engaged by solicitors.

11.4.1 Training

Entry to the Bar is now restricted to graduates and mature students. An aspirant barrister must register with one of the four Inns of Court in London. Commonly, a barrister will have a law degree and then undertake professional training for one year leading to the Bar Examinations. Alternatively, a non-law graduate can study for the Common Professional Examination for one year and, if successful in the examinations, proceed to the Bar Examinations. The successful student is then called to the Bar by his or her Inn of Court. It is also a requirement of being called that, during study for the vocational course, the student attends his or her Inn to become familiar with the customs of the Bar. A Bar student must attend to eat a certain number of dinners over the course. The student then undertakes a pupillage, essentially, an apprenticeship to a junior counsel. Note that all barristers, however senior in years and experience, are still 'junior counsel' unless they have 'taken silk' and become Queen's Counsel (QCs). Barristers who do not intend to practise do not have to complete the pupillage.

11.4.2 The Inns of Court

The Inns of Court are administered by their senior members (QCs and judges) who are called Benchers. The Inns administer the dining system and are responsible for calling the students to the Bar.

11.4.3 The General Council of the Bar

The General Council of the Bar of England and Wales and of the Inns of Court (the Bar Council) is the profession's governing body. It is run by elected officials. It is responsible for the Bar's Code of Conduct, disciplinary matters and representing the interests of the Bar to external bodies like the Lord Chancellor's Department, the government and The Law Society. According to its own literature, this Council:

> ... fulfils the function of what might be called a 'trade union', pursuing the interests of the Bar and expanding the market for the Bar's services and is also a watchdog regulating its practices and activities.

11.4.4 The Council of Legal Education

The Council of Legal Education is responsible for the educational programme of prospective barristers, their examination and admission.

11.4.5 Queen's Counsel

Queen's Counsel are senior barristers of special merit. There are currently over 1,006 QCs in practice, the status being conferred on about 45 barristers each year. They are given this status (known as 'taking silk', as a part of the robe they are entitled to wear is silk) by the Queen on the advice of the Lord Chancellor. There are annual invitations from the Lord Chancellor for barristers to apply for this title. Applicants need to show at least 10 years successful practice at the Bar. If appointed, the barrister will become known as a 'Leader' and he or she will often appear in cases with a junior. The old 'Two Counsel Rule' under which a QC always had to appear with a junior counsel, whether one was really required or not, was abolished in 1977. He or she will be restricted to high level work (of which there is less available in some types of practice) so appointment can be financially difficult but in most cases it has good results for the QC as he or she will be able to considerably increase fee levels.

11.4.6 The barrister's chambers

Barristers are not permitted to form partnerships (except with lawyers from other countries); they work in sets of offices called chambers. Most chambers are run by barrister's clerks who act as business managers, allocating work to the various barristers and negotiating their fees. Imagine the situation where a solicitor wishes to engage a particular barrister for a case on a certain date and that barrister is already booked to be in another court three days before that date. The clerk cannot be sure whether the first case will have ended in time for the barrister to be free to appear in the second case. The first case might be adjourned after a day or, through unexpected evidential arguments in the early stages in the trial, it might last for four days. If the barrister is detained, then his brief for the second case will have to be passed to another barrister in his chambers very close to the actual trial. This is known as a late brief. Who will be asked to take the brief and at what point is a matter for the clerk. The role of the barrister's clerk is thus a most influential one.

11.5 Professional etiquette

The CLSA 1990 introduced a statutory committee with responsibilities in the regulation of both branches of the profession. It is the Lord Chancellor's

Advisory Committee on Legal Education and Conduct and comprises a chairman and 16 members appointed by the Lord Chancellor. The chairman is to be a Lord of Appeal or judge of the Supreme Court. The membership must comprise another judge, two practising barristers; two practising solicitors; two law teachers and nine lay members. The committee is under a general duty (s 20) of 'assisting in the maintenance and development of standards in the education, training and conduct of those offering legal services'. It has some specific functions, including giving advice to the General Council of the Bar and The Law Society on all aspects of their qualification regulations and rules of conduct.

The Law Society and the Bar Council exercise tight control over the professional conduct of their members. Barristers can only meet the client when the solicitor or his or her representative is present. This is supposed to promote the barrister's detachment from the client and his or her case and thus lend greater objectivity to counsel's judgment. Barristers and solicitors must dress formally for court appearances although solicitors, when appearing in the Crown, county or High Court, are required to wear robes but not wigs. A barrister not wearing a wig and robe cannot be 'seen' or 'heard' by the judge.

Traditionally, lawyers were not permitted to advertise their services although this area has been subject to some deregulation in the light of recent trends to expose the provision of legal services to ordinary market forces. Solicitors can, subject to some regulations, advertise their services in print and on broadcast media.

11.5.1 Immunity from negligence claims

Barristers cannot be sued by their clients for negligent performance in court or for work which was preparatory to court work (*Rondel v Worsley* (1969)); this immunity has also been extended to solicitors who act as advocates (*Saif Ali v Sidney Mitchell* (1980)). The client of the other side, however, may sue for breach of duty (*Kelly v London Transport Executive* (1982)).

The immunity is justified on the grounds that advocacy could not be executed to the desired standards if its practitioners were always worried about being sued for negligence. Their performance would be impaired by such anxiety and this could lead to too many decisions prompted by a desire to play things safely rather than as well as they might be played. There are also public policy considerations. Lord Wilberforce addressed this problem in *Saif Ali*. He said the immunity was justified:

> ... mainly on the grounds that a barrister owes a duty to the court as well as to his client and should not be inhibited through fear of an action by his client, from performing it; partly on the undesirability of relitigation as between barrister and client of what was litigated between the client and his opponent.

The immunity has been extended to other advocates under s 62 of the CLSA 1990. It has never extended, however, to negligent advice. In *Saif Ali,* the House of Lords held that the immunity only extended to pre-trial work which was:

> ... so intimately connected with the conduct of the cause in court that it can fairly be said to be a preliminary decision affecting the way that cause is to be conducted when it comes to a hearing.

In *Saif Ali,* it was alleged that a barrister had given negligent advice which led to the wrong person being joined as defendant in an action. The House of Lords held that the immunity did not apply here as the decision in question had effectively prevented the plaintiff's claim from coming to court.

Smith and Bailey (Bailey and Gunn, *The Modern English Legal System,* 1991) have characterised the arguments by which the immunity is defended as follows:

- the barrister's duty to the court transcends the duty to the client so the necessary confidence between the Bar and Bench would be undermined if barristers were afraid of being sued;

- rules should promote openness in court and the administration of justice would be badly affected if participants in cases could be sued;

- the 'cab rank rule' (by which barristers are obliged to take the next case irrespective of its desirability in their opinion; the same rule applies to cab drivers picking up passengers) would be difficult to apply properly if barristers had to take on clients who could pursue actions against them;

- that relitigation of cases is undesirable and the correct method of challenge is *via* an appeal.

It could be argued that rules, very protective as they are to barristers, have been contrived by judges (senior barristers who have spent their working lives in that profession) with a particular sympathy for the work, worries and economic interests of advocates. The judges who have been responsible for framing the law in cases like *Rondel v Worsley* and *Saif Ali v Sidney Mitchell* have been in an unusual position. Surgeons and plumbers do not make the law concerning the circumstances in which they can and cannot be sued. Barristers do (if one accepts that a judge, whilst no longer practising as counsel, is by training, custom company and working life a barrister) have a say.

Zander has argued against the immunity. He has doubted whether barristers would be influenced to do their work much differently by the thought that they might be sued for negligence; he has contended that re-opening a case is not necessarily a bad thing, for example, if someone has been wrongly imprisoned because of a lawyer's negligence; and that there is little prospect of a huge wave of litigation in view of the other existing barriers facing a potential litigant. See *Legal Services for the Community,* 1978.

There would not be a barrage of litigation if the immunity was abolished, nor is there any evidence that the performance of barristers would weaken as alleged. There is, though, every good reason to believe that their performances would improve (JUSTICE, *Professional Negligence and the Quality of Legal Services – An Economic Perspective* (1983)). The studies mentioned above also show the significance of the rule that barristers are only liable for negligence, not errors of judgment. If the immunity rule were abolished, it would not entail aggrieved litigants being able to successfully sue their barristers for any error made in the course of handling their cases. It would have to be the sort of mistake that no reasonably competent barrister would have made in identical circumstances.

The immunity was, however, supported by the Benson Royal Commission on Legal Services in 1979 and is preserved by s 62 of the CLSA 1990.

A new system of dealing with complaints against barristers was introduced in 1997. It is operated by the Professional Conduct and Complaints Committee (PCCC), and a Complaints Commissioner, who is not a lawyer. The Commissioner oversees the investigation of complaints. Conduct which is not serious enough to amount to professional misconduct is judged against a concept of 'inadequate professional service'. If there is a *prima facie* case of such wrong then the Commissioner will refer the matter to the PCCC. Panels, summary hearings and disciplinary tribunals are now able to require barristers to repay fees or, in certain circumstances, pay compensation up to £2,000 to a lay client in cases involving inadequate professional service. The Commissioner is able to encourage barristers and complainants to resolve their differences by means of conciliation in appropriate cases. Powers to disbar or suspend a barrister will remain with the Disciplinary Tribunals of the four Inns of Court. The new system meets criticisms of the earlier model of insufficient lay involvement, lack of opportunity for conciliation, and redress for inadequate service.

11.6 Fusion

The division of the legal profession into two branches can be seen as problematic in some respects. Even before the changes wrought by the CLSA 1990, solicitors did a reasonable amount of advocacy in the lower courts and in tribunals. On the other hand, barristers quite often give advice to clients, albeit through solicitors. Both barristers and solicitors do pleadings and drafting work. One article contends that 'solicitors and barristers are now seeing the lines of distinction between them blurred': see MacErlean (1993) 7 *The Lawyer* 30, 27 July. For many years, there was a strong movement for fusion of the two branches. Submissions made to the Benson Royal Commission on Legal Services argued that the necessity of a member of the public employing a barrister as well as a solicitor for certain work (for example, litigation) was like insisting on a taxi traveller hiring two taxis at once when one would be sufficient to get him to his destination. The legal need to hire two lawyers when one will do causes inefficiency (failures in communication, delay, return of briefs by barristers who are fully booked), damages the client's confidence in the legal process as barristers are regarded as too remote and often insufficiently prepared, and is more expensive than simply engaging a single lawyer.

Fusion was strongly opposed by The Law Society and the Senate of the Inns of Court (now the Bar Council) in their submissions to the Benson Commission. It was argued that fusion would lead to a fall in the quality of advocacy. The leading barristers in a single-profession environment would simply join the major law firms and thus be unavailable for general engagement. Smaller firms would be unlikely to generate enough litigation to keep a barrister as a partner and then find it increasingly challenging to brief counsel of equal standing with that of an opponent. This would create an overall pattern of larger firms expanding and smaller ones – those serving small towns, etc – going out of business.

There would be a reduced number of specialist advocates because whereas with the divided profession a specialist barrister could 'sell' his specialism to a queue of solicitors from different firms, under the fused profession he would be pressured into working at one firm. Another opposition hinges on two features of the English court process: orality and single, continuous hearings designed to make the best use of judicial time but at the expense of practitioners. It has been argued that barristers are better placed organisationally to meet both such requirements.

Additionally, unlike the American system, judges do not have researchers or much time to prepare themselves for cases. The judge relies on the parties to present the case thoroughly. In such circumstances, it is argued, there is a critical need for the judge to have confidence in the competency of the advocates appearing in the case. This can only be properly achieved in the system which cultivates the barrister as a separate professional branch.

The Benson Royal Commission on Legal Services unanimously rejected the idea of fusion. The report concedes that fusion might lead to some saving but only in the smaller cases and in larger cases the expense could be even greater. Using two lawyers did not necessarily entail duplicated work.

It is arguable now that fusion has effectively been organised covertly and gradually. Solicitors' monopolies over conveyancing and the right to conduct litigation have been technically removed (by the Courts and Legal Services Act 1990, and the Access to Justice Act 1999, respectively), and the Bar's monopoly over rights of audience, even in the higher courts, has also been removed (by the same legislation, see below). Specialism thus becomes a *de facto* matter more than an automatic function of one branch of the profession. We begin the new century with specialist criminal law solicitor advocates operating from dedicated offices in some cities (a sort of solicitors 'chambers'), and barristers who are effectively working as in-house lawyers in companies doing work which seems very like the traditional work of solicitors.

11.7 The Courts and Legal Services Act 1990

In December 1983, a second reading was given to the House Buyers Bill, a Private Members' Bill introduced by Austin Mitchell MP. It proposed the introduction of a system of licensed conveyancers who would be permitted to undertake the conveyancing of houses with registered title. This was hitting at the solicitors' cherished monopoly of this type of work. They had sometimes even justified the high fees charged for such work as their 'bread and butter' money which enabled them to undertake the more unusual types of work from most high streets. The government responded by indicating its intention to introduce legislation establishing a system of licensed conveyancers and to allow solicitors employed by building societies and banks to undertake conveyancing for their employers' clients whether the land was registered or not. The government wanted to engender more competition and to reduce prices. The Administration of Justice Act (AJA) 1985 went some way to these ends but the government was persuaded by The Law Society that the banks and building societies could not offer the conveyancing if they were the lending institution; to allow otherwise might be to cause conflicts of interest. The provisions, however, were never brought into effect.

The Law Society was alarmed by the potential loss to its members if the mainstay of revenue for many practices (conveyancing) was to become something which non-solicitors could also perform. In attempts to increase business opportunities for its members it quickly relaxed the rules on solicitors being able to advertise; it also revived its opposition to the Bar's monopoly on High Court advocacy. As Zander has charted (*A Matter of Justice*, 1989), there then followed an acrimonious dispute between the two branches. The Marre Committee was established to look into the extent to which the needs and demands of the public were being met by the current structure of the legal profession. It was asked to examine how the services of the profession could be made readily available to meet public needs and those areas where changes in the education, structure and practices of the legal profession might be in the public interest. The Committee's 1988 report offered no radical remedies and largely supported the *status quo*. Significant change became more likely with the appointment of Lord Mackay of Clashfern as Lord Chancellor. He came to the position from the Scottish Bar and with a particular enthusiasm for opening up the legal process to market forces.

On 25 January 1989, Lord Mackay published three Green Papers: *The Work and Organisation of the Legal Profession; Contingency Fees;* and *Conveyancing by Authorised Practitioners*. The first paper contained a statement of the government's overall objective (para 1.1):

... to see that the public has the best possible access to legal services and that those services are of the right quality for the particular needs of the client.

These, it stated, would be best achieved by ensuring that:

- a market providing legal services operates freely and efficiently so as to give clients the widest possible choice of cost effective services; and

- the public can be certain that those services are being supplied by people who have the necessary expertise to provide a service in the area in question.

After a four month consultation period, the Lord Chancellor published a White Paper, *Legal Services: A Framework for the Future*, which took up many of the proposals from the 1987 Civil Justice Review. This formed the basis of the CLSA 1990. The main changes of Pts II to IV of the Act are:

- the establishment of the Lord Chancellor's Advisory Committee on Education and Conduct;

- the establishment of the Legal Services Ombudsman;

- the extension of rights of audience, rights to conduct litigation and undertake probate work to suitably qualified persons, even to non-lawyers;

- the removal of the restriction preventing banks and building societies offering conveyancing services to borrowers, subject to safeguards like the Conveyancing Ombudsman Scheme;

- new regulations and codes setting qualification standards and practice requirements for advocacy and litigation;

- the ending of restrictions on multi-disciplinary and multi-national partnerships;

- changes in rules of eligibility for judicial appointment to reflect the enjoyment of advocacy rights rather than status as barrister or solicitor.

11.8   The effects of the CLSA 1990

Both branches of the legal profession have traditionally enjoyed monopolies in the provision of certain legal services. The Lord Chancellor argued that these monopolies did not best serve the users of legal services as they entailed unnecessarily limited choice and artificially high prices.

Two principal questions examined by the Benson Royal Commission on Legal Services (1979) were (1) whether barristers should retain their monopoly of the right of audience in the higher courts; and (2) whether solicitors should retain their monopoly over conveyancing work. The Commission recommended in favour of the *status quo* on each point.

The government at first accepted these proposals but later changed its mind and in the AJA 1985, it broke the solicitors' conveyancing monopoly in allowing licensed conveyancers to practise (above). There was, initially, evidence that this increased competition resulted in benefits to the consumer. From 1985, The Law Society permitted solicitors to sell property, like estate agents, so as to promote 'one-stop' conveyancing. The Consumers' Association estimated that solicitors' conveyancing prices fell by a margin of 25–33% before licensed conveyancers actually began to practise.

Under the CLSA 1990, apart from allowing the Bar Council and The Law Society to grant members rights of audience as before, The Law Society is able to seek to widen the category of those who have such rights. Applications are made to the Lord Chancellor who refers the matter to his Advisory Committee. If the Committee favours the application it must also be approved by four senior judges (including the Master of the Rolls and the Lord Chief Justice) each of whom can exercise a veto. The Director General of the Office of Fair Trading must also be consulted by the Lord Chancellor. All those who consider applications for extended rights of audience or the right to conduct litigation, must act in accordance with the 'general principle' in s 17.

11.8.1 Section 17

The principle in s 17 states that the question whether a person should be granted a right of audience or to conduct litigation is to be determined only by reference to the following four questions:

- is the applicant properly qualified in accordance with the educational and training requirements appropriate to the court or proceedings?;

- are applicants members of a professional or other body with proper and enforced rules of conduct?;

- do such rules have the necessary equivalent of the Bar's 'cab rank rule', that is, satisfactory provision requiring its members not to withhold their services on the ground that the nature of the case is objectionable to him or her or any section of the public; on the ground that the conduct, opinions or beliefs of the prospective client are unacceptable to him or her or to any section of the public; on any ground relating to the prospective client's source of financial support (for example, legal aid)?;

- are the body's rules of conduct 'appropriate in the interests of the proper and efficient administration of justice'?

Subject to the above, those who consider applications must also abide by s 17's 'statutory objective' of 'new and better ways of providing such services and a wider choice of persons providing them, while maintaining the proper and efficient administration of justice'.

Applications have been made by The Law Society, the Head of the Government Legal Service and the Director of Public Prosecutions (DPP). The Advisory Committee, whilst rejecting the idea of an automatic extension of solicitors' rights of audience upon qualification (for example, guilty plea cases in Crown Courts), accepted the principle that they should qualify for enlarged rights after a course of advocacy training. The Committee rejected the idea that employed lawyers like those in the Crown Prosecution Service (CPS) should be granted extended rights of audience. It was thought that such employed lawyers would not have the necessary detachment and objectivity to carry out the work properly and, in any event, the CPS was still experiencing difficulties in coping with its current workload.

Non-lawyers can also apply for rights of audience in the courts. The Chartered Institute of Patent Agents is applying for rights to conduct litigation in the High Court. Under s 11 of the CLSA 1990, the Lord Chancellor will use his power to enable lay representatives to be used in cases involving debt and housing matters in small claims procedures. Similarly, under ss 28 and 29 of the CLSA 1990, the right to conduct litigation is thrown open to members of any body which can persuade the Advisory Committee, the Lord Chancellor and the four senior judges that its application should be granted as the criteria set out in s 17 (above) are satisfied.

The historic monopoly of barristers to appear for clients in the higher courts was formally ended in 1994 when the Lord Chancellor approved The Law Society's proposals on how to certify its members in private practice as competent advocates. The innovation is likely to generate significant change in the delivery of legal services, especially in the fields of commercial and criminal cases. The prospective battle between solicitors and barristers for advocacy work can be simply characterised. The 1995 figures show that there are 63,600 solicitors with practising certificates, and about 7,000 barristers. To the extent that solicitors qualify as certified advocates (solicitor advocates) and take up work in the magistrates' courts, Crown Courts, county courts and the High Court, barristers will be forced out of work, as most cannot survive on opinion and non-contentious work alone. One Bar Council member estimates that up to 50% of practising barristers may be casualties of such a change. The results for the consumers of legal services may be a cheaper, more efficient service. On the other hand, the quality of advocacy work might deteriorate. It is important to be aware of the brief history of developments leading to this change.

11.8.2 Employed solicitors' rights of audience

In February 1997, the Lord Chancellor, Lord Mackay, and the four designated judges (Lord Bingham, Lord Woolf, Sir Stephen Brown, and Sir Richard Scott; see s 17 of the CLSA 1990) approved The Law Society's application for rights of audience in the higher courts for employed solicitors, but subject to certain restrictions.

Following the approval (see 11.8.1, above) for solicitors in private practice to apply for rights of audience in the higher courts, there are (1 March 1997) now 438 solicitors in private practice with such rights, with a further 170 in the process of application. The number of employed solicitors expected to apply is likely to be greater. Although the new right has been granted to a category of solicitor, solicitors will, individually, have to apply to be granted the rights of audience. They will have to take the established tests and show relevant court experience (see below).

Under Law Society proposals now approved by the Lord Chancellor's Department, some solicitors (those who are also barristers or part time judges) will be granted exemption from the new tests of qualification for advocacy. Others will need to apply for the grant of higher courts qualifications, either in civil proceedings, criminal proceedings or in both. A holder of the higher courts (criminal proceedings) qualification will have rights of audience in the Crown Court in all proceedings (including its civil jurisdiction) and in other courts in all criminal proceedings. A holder of the higher courts (civil proceedings) may appear in the High Court in all proceedings and in other courts in all civil proceedings. Applicants for these qualifications must have practised as a solicitor for at least three years. The qualifying scheme is designed only for solicitors who are already lower court advocates. The three elements which must be demonstrated by an applicant are:

- two years' experience of advocacy in the lower courts and experience of the procedures of the relevant higher court;

- competency in a written test on evidence and procedure; and

- satisfactory completion of an advocacy training course.

Large, city firms of solicitors are already having their litigation lawyers trained to qualify for advocacy in the High Court. Three of the biggest commercial firms in England and Wales have held a one week course for partners and fee earners, run by the National Institute of Trial Advocacy, an American body with a good reputation for its methods of training. Investment in training is heavy – one major firm estimated the cost of the course, which trained 24 lawyers, at about £100,000 – but the rewards to be reaped in future are potentially great if solicitors can offer a one-stop service in major commercial work. Continental and American clients are often perplexed by the need to brief an outside barrister.

One problem, however, for these large firms is that they will find it very difficult for their applicants (for audience rights) to meet The Law Society's requirement for county court advocacy experience. Although the expansion of this court's jurisdiction under the CLSA 1990 (in particular, commercial litigation involving sums up to £50,000) has given more county court work to large firms, they generally do very little of this. Large firms are worried that they will have to take on perhaps hundreds of county court cases just to get the ones that will go to trial, and even then these would only be a means to an end, namely the qualification to appear in the High Court.

One benefit for law firms is that those which offer advocacy training are likely to attract the best graduates. Julian Wilson, a litigation partner in Herbert Smith, has said that this is a major worry for the commercial Bar, as graduates will see articles with advocacy as a better option than the insecure Bar pupillage. The Bar is determined that it will not lose any significant ground in the face of this new competition. Its representatives claim that solicitors will not be able to compete with barristers because of their much higher overheads. Peter Goldsmith QC, former Vice Chairman of the Bar Council, has stated that: 'Barristers will remain the pre-eminent advocates. They are the only professionals who are fully trained for advocacy and practise it full time.' Solicitors have replied that their fees are now much more competitive because of the recession, and that cost savings will be made because time will not be spent briefing barristers.

The take-up rate for solicitors opting to try and qualify for rights of audience has, so far, not been high. There are now 170 solicitor advocates with rights of audience in the higher courts. In the first generation of those seeking qualification (that is, those who had not been granted exemption) only 34 out of 72 passed the criminal and civil evidence and procedure tests. Nevertheless, the phenomenon of the solicitor advocate may well expand significantly. An eight-strong solicitor advocate chambers in Birmingham called Midlands Solicitor Chambers is already a model for such developments elsewhere. The larger firms may soon find it propitious to create general or specialist advocacy units, a point whose significance is best seen when the influence of the large firms is appreciated. There are currently 8,524 solicitor firms of which no more than 420 have 10 or more partners, yet this small group of firms employ the vast majority of the workforce: 34% of all principals, and 56% of all assistant solicitors.

Many barristers are very worried about the threat to their traditional work. In 1994, a the Bar Council rejected a proposal to allow its members to deal directly with the public. If it had succeeded, the change would have put those barristers specialising in criminal, family, personal injury, and commercial work in a better position to compete with solicitor advocates. Neil Addison, a member of the Bar Council, has argued that an exclusively referral Bar is only practicable if the Bar becomes, in effect, a branch of the solicitors' profession as in Australia and New Zealand. If the Bar wishes to remain totally independent with separate recruiting and training, it must act accordingly. Young barristers will now be in open competition with solicitor advocates and, Addison argues, it is unrealistic to expect them to fare well in such competition while they remain completely dependent on solicitors for their work. They must, therefore, he argues, be allowed direct access to the public, and be allowed to form partnerships with each other and with solicitors.

11.8.3 The Access to Justice Act 1999 and rights of audience

Lawyers' rights of audience before the courts are covered in Pt III of the Access to Justice Act 1999. It replaces the Lord Chancellor's Advisory Committee on Legal Education and Conduct with a new Legal Services Consultative Panel.

- It provides that, in principle, all lawyers should have full rights of audience before any court, subject only to meeting reasonable training requirements.

- It reforms the procedures for authorising further professional bodies to grant rights of audience or rights to conduct litigation to their members; and for approving changes to professional rules of conduct relating to the exercise of these rights.

The Act also contains sections which:

- simplify procedures for approving changes to rules and the designation of new authorised bodies;

- give the Lord Chancellor power, with the approval of Parliament, to change rules which do not meet the statutory criteria set out in the Courts and Legal Services Act 1990 as amended by these sections;

- establish the principle that all barristers and solicitors should enjoy full rights of audience; and

- establish the primacy of an advocate's ethical duties over any other civil law obligations.

The legislation enables employed advocates, including Crown Prosecutors, to appear as advocates in the higher courts if otherwise qualified to do so, regardless of any professional rules designed to prevent their doing so because of their status as employed advocates.

Background

The background to these proposals is set out in a consultation paper issued by the Lord Chancellor's Department in June 1998 – *Rights of Audience and Rights to Conduct Litigation in England and Wales: The Way Ahead.*

Rights to appear as an advocate in court (rights of audience) and rights to do the work involved in preparing cases for court (rights to conduct litigation) are governed by the Courts and Legal Services Act 1990. The 1990 Act leaves it to 'authorised bodies' (currently, the Bar Council, The Law Society and the Institute of Legal Executives) to set the rules which govern the rights of their members, subject to a statutory approval process in which new or altered rules must be submitted for the approval of the Lord Chancellor and the four 'designated judges' (the Lord Chief Justice, Master of the Rolls, President of the Family Division and Vice Chancellor). Before making their decisions, the Lord Chancellor and designated judges receive and consider the advice of the Lord

Chancellor's Advisory Committee on Legal Education and Conduct (ACLEC) and of the Director General of Fair Trading. Applications for the designation of new authorised bodies are subject to a similar procedure, but the designation of the new body is made by Order in Council subject to approval by both Houses.

The government argued that the old approval procedures were convoluted and slow, and that rights of audience were too restrictive. Some applications for approvals took several years to be processed, in part, due to the need for applications to meet the approval of several parties. Rights of audience in the higher courts (the House of Lords, Court of Appeal, High Court and Crown Court) remain restricted to barristers and a small number of solicitors in private practice.

The Act simplifies and expedites the approval procedure. ACLEC will be replaced by a smaller and less expensive committee, the Legal Services Consultative Panel. The functions of the new Panel are not prescribed in detail in the statute, and its composition will be left to the Lord Chancellor to determine, although, in appointing members, he will be required to have regard to specified criteria setting out appropriate knowledge and experience. This will enable the Panel to develop flexibly, in response to the matters on which the Lord Chancellor requires expert independent advice, and will leave the Lord Chancellor free to appoint the best candidates to the Panel. The Act will also give the Lord Chancellor a new power to call in and if necessary replace professional rules affecting rights of audience or rights to conduct litigation, which he considers unduly restrict the exercise of those rights. The exercise of this power will be subject to Parliamentary approval.

The Act makes the Bar Council and the Institute of Legal Executives authorised bodies for the purpose of granting rights to conduct litigation to their members. At present, The Law Society is the only body able to grant these rights; so currently only solicitors are able to conduct litigation. It will also put into statutory form the principle that an advocate's or litigator's first duties are to the court to act with independence in the interests of justice, and to his profession's ethical standards and that these duties cannot be overridden by any other civil law obligations, such as a contract of employment.

The Act provides that every barrister and every solicitor has a right of audience before every court in relation to all proceedings. These general rights were not present for solicitors in the 1990 Act. The Act also restates the current position, that all solicitors have rights to conduct litigation before all courts. These rights are not unconditional; in order to exercise them, solicitors and barristers must obey the rules of conduct of the professional bodies and must have met any training requirements that may be prescribed (such as the requirement to complete pupillage in the case of the Bar, or to have obtained a higher courts advocacy qualification in the case of solicitors who wish to appear in the higher courts).

Section 38 of the Access to Justice Act 1999 provides that advocates and litigators employed by the Legal Services Commission can provide their services to members of the public. Without this clause, they might be prevented from doing so by professional rules.

Section 40 of the 1999 Act gives the General Council of the Bar and the Institute of Legal Executives the power to grant their members rights to conduct litigation. There will be no requirement to grant such rights and it would be a matter for the authorised bodies to propose, subject to approval under the provisions contained in Scheds 5 and 6 of the 1999 Act, whether and in what form such rights might be granted.

The new procedures do not contain the old requirement for each of the designated judges to approve an application (for a body to become an authority to grant rights of audience or rights to conduct litigation), although the Lord Chancellor must seek, and have regard to, their advice. An applicant body will first submit its application to the Lord Chancellor. In the case of an application to become an authorised body, the Lord Chancellor must consult the Legal Services Consultative Panel (ACLEC's replacement body, established by s 35), the Director General of Fair Trading (DGFT), and the designated judges.

Schedule 5, cl 17(1) of the 1999 Act confers on the Lord Chancellor a controversial new power to amend the qualification regulations or rules of conduct of an authorised body by order, if he considers that they place unreasonable restrictions on rights of audience or rights to conduct litigation, or the exercise of those rights. He will be required to consult the Panel, the DGFT and the designated judges before doing so; and his order will be subject to Parliamentary approval by the affirmative resolution procedure.

Section 42 of the 1999 Act gives statutory force to the existing professional rules which make it clear that the overriding duties of advocates and litigators are their duty to the court to act with independence in the interests of justice; and their duty to comply with their professional bodies' rules of conduct. Those duties override any other civil law obligation which a person may be under, including the duty to the client or a contractual obligation to an employer or to anyone else. A barrister, solicitor or other authorised advocate or authorised litigator must refuse to do anything required, either by a client or by an employer, that is not in the interests of justice (for example, suppress evidence). The purpose of this clause is to protect the independence of all advocates and litigators.

11.8.4 Accelerating legal argument

In an effort to reduce the cost of High Court cases, a new measure was introduced in 1995 to put limits on the time lawyers spend addressing the judge. Lawyers who are long winded, or call unnecessary witnesses, can be financially penalised by not being awarded their full costs. The *Practice Direction (Civil Litigation)* (1995) allowed judges to use their discretion to set limits for lawyers' speeches and cross-examination, to limit the issues in cases, and to curb the reading aloud of documents and case reports. Lawyers became unable to examine their own witnesses in court without the permission of the judge. Such an 'examination-in-chief' is normally replaced by the courts' acceptance of a written statement. The *Direction* stated that:

> The paramount importance of reducing the cost and delay of civil litigation makes it necessary for judges sitting at first instance to assert greater control over the preparation for and conduct of hearings than has hitherto been customary. Failure by practitioners to conduct cases economically will be visited by appropriate orders for costs, including wasted order costs.

The *Direction* also instructed judges to ensure that the parties have tried and failed with alternative dispute resolution before the case goes to trial.

The *Practice Direction* has now been superseded by the new Civil Procedure Rules 1998 (see Chapter 7), but the principles have been retained within the new Rules.

11.8.5 Partnerships

By virtue of s 66 of the CLSA 1990, solicitors are enabled to form partnerships with non-solicitors (multi-disciplinary partnerships or MDPs) and confirms that barristers are not prevented by the common law from forming such relationships. They are, however, prohibited from doing so (unless with a foreign lawyer) by the Bar. Solicitors are able, under s 89 of the CLSA 1990 (Sched 14) to form multi-national partnerships (MNPs). The arrival of MNPs over the coming years will raise particular problems concerning the maintenance of ethical standards by The Law Society over foreign lawyers. MDPs also raise potentially serious problems as even in arrangements between solicitors and others, it will be likely that certain work (for example, the conduct of litigation) would have to be performed by solicitors.

11.8.6 Monopoly conveyancing rights

Historically, barristers, solicitors, certified notaries and licensed conveyancers enjoyed statutory monopolies making it an offence for any other persons to draw up or prepare documents connected with the transfer of title to property for payment. The CLSA 1990 seeks to break this monopoly by allowing any person or body not currently authorised to provide conveyancing services to make an application to the Authorised Conveyancing Practitioners Board (established by s 34) for authorisation under s 37. The Board must be satisfied, before granting authorisation, that the applicant's business is, and will be, carried on by fit and proper persons, and must believe that the applicant will establish or participate in the systems for the protection of the client specified in s 37(7) including, for example, adequate professional indemnity cover and regulations made under s 40 concerning competence and conduct. Banks and building societies are in a privileged position (s 37(8)) since they are already regulated by statute. These institutions did not initially appear enthusiastic to compete with solicitors by establishing in-house lawyers. They have preferred instead to use panels of local practitioners. Because of this lack of interest, the Lord Chancellor has postponed the making of new regulations (under s 40). David Tench, director of legal affairs for the Consumers Association, has stated that it was appropriate for the regulations to be postponed in the current depressed market.

Mr Tench has also observed that the way solicitors have responded to the threat of competition – by becoming more competitive in terms of price and service – has diminished the need to broaden the market. Another factor reducing the urgency of the matter is the change in Law Society rules which allows solicitors to contract with lenders to provide conveyancing for lenders' customers thus, in effect, permitting one-stop house transfer packages.

The solicitors' monopoly on the grant of probate has also been abolished. Under ss 54–55 of the CLSA 1990, probate services were opened to be available from approved bodies of non-lawyers. Grant of probate is the legal proof that a will is valid, which is needed for a person to put the will into effect. New probate practitioners directly compete with solicitors for probate work. The grant of probate is only a small part of the probate process but when it was restricted as business which only a solicitor could perform it effectively prevented others, except some banks, from being involved in probate. The banks seem best placed to take up work in this area as they already have trustee and executor departments. Like the slow take-up to do conveyancing work (there are still only relatively few commercial licensed conveyancers), enthusiasm to break into the probate business has been hard to detect.

In its Green Papers published in 1989, the government stated that the means it favoured to produce the most efficient and effective provision of legal services would be 'the discipline of the market'. This technique, however, has not been without its problems. There was not a rush to use the conveyancing services of solicitors who had made their prices very competitive in the wake of competition from licensed conveyancers. In one survey, The Law Society found that only 8% of clients had opted for cheaper services ((1993) The Lawyer, 12 October). More worrying is the allegation that a significant number of those offering 'cut-price' conveyancing are not producing a respectable quality of service. Tony Holland, a former president of The Law Society, has argued that this is a result of a rush of inadequately trained persons to make money from that part of solicitors' erstwhile monopoly which has been thrown open to non-lawyers ([1994] NLJ 192, 11 February). He notes that, at the time of writing the article, he was engaged in giving expert testimony in no fewer than 19 actions for negligence arising from incompetent conveyancing.

Nevertheless, recent research published by the Department of the Environment, Transport and the Regions showed that conveyancing in England and Wales was the cheapest of the 10 European countries surveyed, even though it was the slowest. It takes an average of six to eight weeks for a contract to be exchanged in England and Wales while, in the USA and South Africa, the average is a week. Even so, while the legal fee for conveyancing on a £60,000 house in England and Wales is about £1,500, the same service in France costs about £3,600 and, in Portugal, it is about £6,000 (see News in Brief, 'Cheap conveyancing' [1998] NLJ 8, 9 January).

Various reports by consumer associations have attacked aspects of the delivery of legal services in the years following the implementation of the CLSA 1990. In 1994, Dr Neville Harris of the University of Liverpool surveyed 60 firms of solicitors and 301 clients. He found that 40% of privately paying clients were not told at the outset of cases how much they would be likely to have to pay. One in four of the firms did not operate the internal complaints procedure required by The Law Society, and only one firm in 10 said that it actively sought feedback from clients ('Solicitors and client care: an aspect of professional competence', February 1994, National Consumer Council).

11.8.7 The Legal Services Ombudsman

This position was created by s 21 of the CLSA 1990 to reinforce the existing system with more effective measures for dealing with complaints. The Legal Services Ombudsman (LSO), currently Ann Abraham, is empowered by s 22 to 'investigate any allegation which is properly made to him and relates to the manner in which a complaint made to a professional body with respect to an authorised advocate, authorised litigator, licensed conveyancer, recognised body or notary who is a member of that professional body; or any employee of such a person, has been dealt with by that professional body'. The LSO cannot normally investigate any complaint whilst it is being investigated by a professional body nor if it has been dealt with by a court or the solicitors' disciplinary tribunal or the disciplinary tribunal of the Council of the Inns of Court, since the procedures in such tribunals satisfy the need for public accountability.

Upon completing an investigation, the LSO must send a copy of his reasoned conclusions to the complainant and the person or body under investigation. The report can make any of the following recommendations:

- that the complaint be reconsidered by the professional body;

- that the professional body should consider its powers in relation to the person who was the subject of complaint;

- that the person complained about, or any person connected to him or her, should pay compensation to the complainant for loss suffered or inconvenience or distress caused;

- that the professional body concerned should pay such compensation;

- that a separate payment be made to the complainant in respect of costs related to the making of the allegation.

The person or body to whom these recommendations are sent must reply within three months explaining what action has been or is proposed to be taken to comply with the recommendation(s) made.

The 1998–99 Annual Report of the Legal Services Ombudsman states that 1998 saw a continuing increase in the number of complaints handled by all the professional bodies – the Office for the Supervision of Solicitors (OSS), the General Council of the Bar (GCB), and the Council for Licensed Conveyancers (CLC). Complaints against the Institute of Legal Executives (ILEX) are included for the first time in the annual report (*Modernising Justice ... Modernising Regulation?*, the 8th Annual Report of the Legal Services Ombudsman, 1998–99, London: HMSO).

The Ombudsman conducted 1,658 investigations in the 15 months from January 1998 to March 1999. In 1998, the Report notes: one complaint was made to the professional body for every 24 practising solicitors, for every 18 practising barristers; and one complaint for every five practising licensed conveyancers. In each case, the figures represent an increase in the number of complaints per lawyer since 1997.

The Ombudsman states in the Report that, in 67% of cases, she was satisfied with the way the complaint had been handled by the professional body, and thus made no formal recommendation or criticism. This, however, represents an overall decrease in the Ombudsman's level of satisfaction with the handling of complaints by the professional bodies since 1997 when the relevant figure was 70%.

The total number of recommendations made was 510. These comprised 192 recommendations that the professional body reconsider; 206 recommendations for payment of compensation by the professional body; and 112 recommendations for payment of compensation by the individual lawyer. Compensation awards for loss ranged from £10 to £6,850.

LEGAL SERVICES

The main area of debate on this theme is the best approach to supplying the highest number and widest range of people with legal services appropriate to what citizens need. How can the legal profession become more user friendly? Have the changes made under the CLSA 1990 to increase competition in the provision of legal services been successful? Have the restrictive professional monopolies been properly broken and if so will the quality of services offered by non-lawyers (for example, conveyancing, probate, litigation) be reduced? Will the exclusion of millions of people from legal aid eligibility have any serious consequences?

The impact of the conditional fee arrangements, the 1995 Green Paper on legal aid, and franchising are of special importance, but to deal with these issues properly you need to be familiar with the details of how legal services are delivered in general.

The legal profession

The legal profession, although not fused, comprises solicitors and barristers whose work is becoming increasingly similar in many respects. Additionally, the ending of monopolies on litigation, probate and conveyancing have meant that lawyers' traditional work is increasingly becoming blurred with that of other professionals. The liabilities of lawyers for errors and negligence is a key issue. Another is the way in which complaints are handled by the professions.

The Courts and Legal Services Act 1990

The CLSA 1990 was passed 'to see that the public has the best possible access to legal services and that those services are of the right quality for the particular needs of the client'. The detail by which the Act sought to do this is very important, especially s 17 (general principle, litigation and rights of audience); s 11 (lay representatives); ss 28–29 (right to conduct litigation); s 66 (multi-disciplinary partnerships); s 89 (multi-national partnerships); ss 34–37 (conveyancing); ss 21–26 (the Legal Services Ombudsman); and s 58 (conditional fee arrangements).

The Access to Justice Act 1999

The 1999 Act makes many changes which will have an impact upon the professions. It articulates the principle that all lawyers should have full rights of audience before all courts, provided they have passed the relevant examinations. Also, by reforming the procedures for authorising further professional bodies to grant rights of audience, it signals a widening of those rights in the future.

CHAPTER 12

THE FUNDING OF LEGAL SERVICES

12.1 Introduction

Legal aid was introduced after the second world war to enable people who could not otherwise afford the services of lawyers to be provided with those services by the state. The system grew and extended its reach and range of services enormously over the decades. Costs to the government were gigantic. The system underwent various restrictions and cut-backs during the late 1990s and was almost abolished in 1999. In this chapter, we sometimes refer to the 'current' system of legal aid. This is because parts of the system will still be operational for much of 2000, until it is entirely replaced by the new amendments we describe.

Two factors combined in the early 1990s to cause great change in the way that legal services are funded. The first factor was the spiralling cost of legal aid to the State during a period of recession. The money available to government was insufficient to meet the rising cost of maintaining the level and extent of legal services previously available. The second factor (and some people would directly link these in a causational way) was the professed aim of the government in general and Lord Mackay, the then Lord Chancellor, in particular, to reduce the State's role in the provision of legal services.

Over 10 million people have been taken out of the bracket of legal aid eligibility as a result of governmental changes of the eligibility criteria (see Smith, *Shaping the Future: New Directions in Legal Services*, 1995). To try to compensate for this exclusion of millions of people from the effective right to use the law, other schemes have been promoted and developed. These include the use of 'no win, no fee' arrangements, the use of non-lawyer legal services, and legal services private insurance.

The legal aid budget for 1996–97 was £1.48 billion. It was in this context that the White Paper (proposed legislation) *Striking the Balance: the Future of Legal Aid in England and Wales* (HMSO) was published in 1996. The paper proposed the most radical changes to the legal aid system since its launch in 1951. The main aims of the White Paper in relation to funding legal services were: (a) to impose cash limits on the legal aid scheme (instead of allowing it to have a demand-led budget); (b) to require some form of payment from all users; and (c) to operate a separate budget for major, expensive cases.

There are several State funded schemes to facilitate the provision of aid and advice. Each scheme has different rules relating to its scope, procedures for application and eligibility. Because of the importance of justice and access to the legal machinery, the idea behind legal aid is to give people who could otherwise not afford professional legal help the same services as more wealthy citizens. This raises important social, political and economic questions. Do poorer people deserve the same quality of legal advice as that which can be afforded by wealthy people? If so, how should such schemes be funded?

12.1.1 A brief historical overview

The legal aid system was introduced under the Legal Aid and Advice Act 1949 by a Labour government after the Second World War to allow poor people to have access to the justice system. Before this time, such people had to rely on charity if they went to court. The system was seen by the government as the 'second arm of the Welfare State' (the first one being the National Health Service). The system expanded throughout the 1950s and 1960s. It moved from just covering the higher courts to covering the lower courts; and from just civil courts to criminal courts.

A number of historical and economic factors combined to reduce the scope of the system from the mid-1970s. By the 1990s, the system applied to a much smaller section of the community than it had done in previous decades. In the 1950s, about 80% of the population was covered by the legal aid system, whereas, by 1998, less than 40% of the population is covered.

The scope of eligibility had expanded quickly in the 1970s. As a result, more lawyers were setting up practices catering for legal aid clients. Divorces were becoming much more common (as the result of social factors and legislation which made divorce easier), and divorce accounts for a very large part of civil legal aid. Alongside all this, the economy was going into recession, and this had two effects: (a) it resulted in there being less money in government funds from which to finance legal aid; and (b) it generated waves of economically related problems (unemployment, family break-ups, welfare problems) which needed legal services for people who could not afford to pay for them.

From the mid-1980s, successive Lord Chancellors have been engaged in a series of measures to try to reduce public expenditure on the legal system. They have been particularly concerned to curb expenditure on legal aid which almost doubled to £1.4 billion over a four year period to 1995. The system of paying lawyers for legal aid work has been changed, the eligibility criteria have been changed to exclude millions of people from the scheme, and control of the funds has been moved from The Law Society to the Legal Aid Board and now much power has been devolved to regional centres and particular firms through 'franchising'.

Since 1950, the system has been 'demand-led'. This meant that a person needing a service could get it, provided that he or she satisfied the appropriate 'means test' and appropriate 'merits test'. From 1996, the then Lord Chancellor, Lord Mackay, proposed that the system will be financially capped, that is, that regional authorities of the Legal Aid Board be given a single lump sum at the beginning of the financial year for expenditure that year and when that sum is spent on legal services, no more becomes available for any applicant, no matter how urgent and deserving his or her case. Lord Mackay said that 'legal aid is not, and cannot be, an unconditional blank cheque from the taxpayer'.

In an address to The Law Society in October 1992, Lord Mackay, the then Lord Chancellor, made the following comment:

> Expenditure on legal aid is now over £1.1 billion gross. That figure is the amount paid from legal aid to the legal profession (including VAT and other outgoings). The net cost to the taxpayer in 1991–92, after allowing for legal aid contributions and costs recovered, was more than £900m. The net figure ... will exceed £1bn during [1992–93], more than double what it was a mere four years ago ... This rate of growth, and that's what I'm speaking of, cannot be allowed to continue. Every extra pound for legal aid means a pound less for the NHS, for schools, for social security, or for the infrastructure of the economy.

It is this thinking which prompted major changes in the provision of legal aid in 1993 and 1995. In particular, the financial eligibility criteria were changed so that only the very poorest people qualify for free aid. Additionally, the Lord Chancellor changed the way that solicitors are paid for criminal legal aid and assistance, with the result that the pay will be worse and many practitioners currently offering the service are expected to withdraw from the scheme as they would be losing money by continuing to do such work.

Speaking to the Social Market Foundation in 1995, the Lord Chancellor traced the geometric growth in legal aid expenditure since 1949. The scheme cost £685 million in 1990–91 and, in the year 1995–96, cost around double that sum. The number of people now being assisted is high: around 4.5 million in 1997–98. Nonetheless, as a result of recent significant financial cut-backs and changes in eligibility regulations, it can be argued that the original ideal is now quite remote from current practice.

The cuts were intended by Lord Mackay to make savings of £43 million during 1993–94, £110 million the following year and £170 million during 1995–96. During the financial year 1996–97, the legal aid budget of £1.48 billion was £150 million less than an original government estimate after savings of £240 million over three years.

The last government had been particularly keen to reduce fraud on legal aid funds by the 'apparently wealthy'. Lord MacKay, the former Lord Chancellor made new regulations changing eligibility following a period of consultation about this problem in 1995. The Civil Legal Aid (Assessment of Resources) (Amendment) Regulations 1996, and the Legal Aid in Criminal and Care Proceedings (General) (Amendment) Regulations 1996 address this issue. The most important change concerns the treatment of an assisted person's dwelling house which has previously been wholly exempt for eligibility purposes. Since June 1996, for both advice and assistance, and legal aid, it has been possible to take into account the market value of the applicant's property in so far as it exceeds £100,000 when calculating the applicant's capital. Where there is equity in the property (that is, the property is worth more than the mortgage), then the equity can count as capital in so far as it exceeds £100,000.

Lord Justice Steyn once observed (*Lwch* (1994)) that 'it is a principle of our law that every citizen has a right of unimpeded access to a court'. Taken with the recent doubling of many civil court fees, the radical reduction of legal aid introduced in 1999 will not, despite the various alternative measures to be established, further the principle enunciated by Lord Steyn. The changes will, if anything, confirm the observation of Mr Justice Darling that 'the law courts of England are open to all men, like the doors of the Ritz Hotel'.

According to one theory of law and government, the justice system has a pre-eminent claim on resources. This is because, however important are social services like health and education, if people do not have the effective citizen's right to take and defend legal action (including actions concerning health and education), then they are not properly incorporated into society. A society without the majority feeling they could, if necessary, participate in the legal process is an unstable society.

Today, however, it is arguable that the principles of ordinary market economics have superseded theories of social incorporation and 'stake holding' in determining who gets access to lawyers and courts.

The dangers of social exclusion

The new systems for allowing citizens to participate in the legal system, and the dramatic reduction in legal aid provision demonstrate that nothing is sacred within the legal system. In a parliamentary debate in 1997, Earl Russell reminded the government of what can happen in societies where people *en masse* are denied access to the courts. He urged that we consider 'the cost of not spending money as well as the cost of spending it'. He was speaking about the obstacles posed to the prospective litigant by high court fees but his observations are equally applicable to debate about dismantling civil legal aid.

12.1.2 Types of legal aid

Although the term 'legal aid' is used to cover a wide range of subsidised or free services, in strict language it only refers to one sort of help: representation in court. Legal Advice and Assistance (also known as the Green Form scheme) covers advice and help with any legal problem; and, in some cases, under what is called 'assistance by way of representation' (ABWOR), it also covers going to court, for example, with the permission of the local Legal Aid Board Director, a solicitor can represent a client in court in most civil proceedings in magistrates' courts. It is available for cases where advice or letter writing has not solved a problem and the matter has to go to court. Civil legal aid is available for many types of action but not, notably, for proceedings in coroners' courts, tribunals (except the lands tribunal and the employment appeal tribunal) nor for proceedings involving libel or slander. Criminal legal aid covers the cost of case preparation and representation in criminal cases. In addition to these schemes, some solicitors are prepared to give a free or fixed-fee interview without giving any means test related to the interviewee's income or capital. Duty Solicitor Schemes are available at most magistrates' courts and police stations. Solicitors can give *free* legal advice to someone who is being questioned by the police whether or not such a suspect has been arrested; advice and free representation can also be given for someone's first appearance for a particular offence at a magistrates' court.

12.1.3 Legal advice and assistance

Under the Green Form scheme, a solicitor can undertake ordinary legal work (excluding court work) up to a limit, initially, of two hour's worth of work for a client who passes the relevant means test. The amount of work done can be extended with the permission of the local Legal Aid Area Committee. Undefended divorce cases have not been eligible for legal aid since 1977 but the Green Form scheme is available and extends now to a limit of three hours worth of work. The work which a solicitor may undertake includes assistance with certain hearings to which the client may be a party; this is ABWOR. In 1998–99, there were 1,592,722 Green Form acts of assistance and 58,123 acts of Assistance by Way of Representation. Most solicitors participate in this scheme. It is within the solicitor's discretion as to what sort of work he or she undertakes. An argument for presentation in a court or tribunal could be prepared, letters written, documents drafted; negotiation with another party may even be undertaken.

The Green Form scheme and ABWOR were the most widely used of the legal aid schemes prior to the Access to Justice Act. At the beginning of the 1990s, the take-up was stable at around one million acts of assistance per year, but then the scheme began to grow, reaching a peak of 1.6 million acts of assistance in 1993–94. This growth was principally fuelled by increased demand for advice on social and economic matters, such as housing, debt and welfare benefits, although advice on personal injuries, employment and immigration matters also grew during that period (Legal Aid Board, *Annual Report*, 1998–99, section 3, p 117). Since 1996, the volume of Green Form cases paid for by the Legal Aid Board started to rise again. The introduction of standard fees for criminal legal aid in the magistrates' courts in 1993 produced a steady growth in demand for advice and assistance on criminal matters, but, more recently, another factor has been renewed demand for advice on civil, non-matrimonial matters. In 1998, demand in this area reached its 1994 peak. (*Annual Report*, 1998–99, p 120). The most rapidly growing areas of advice have been immigration and nationality and welfare benefits.

The means test for the applicant is administered by the solicitor. The upper limit for Green Form assistance, from April 1999, is a disposable income of £83 per week and a disposable capital of £1,000 for those without dependants (moving up with each additional dependant, for example, £1,335 for those with one dependant).

ABWOR allows representation to be undertaken without a legal aid certificate. It applies to domestic proceedings in magistrates' courts, proceedings before mental health review tribunals, representations under the Police and Criminal Evidence Act (PACE) 1984 for warrants of further detention and representation in certain child care proceedings. The scheme covers the cost of a solicitor preparing a case and representing a client in most civil cases in magistrates' courts, now known as Family Proceedings Courts. These cases include separation, maintenance (except child maintenance where the Child Support Agency has jurisdiction) residence/contact, paternity and defended adoption proceedings. The income and capital conditions for ABWOR are different from those applying in Legal Advice and Assistance (LAA) cases. Here, applicants will qualify if their weekly disposable income is £172 or less and they have savings of no more than £3,000. The same dependant's allowances apply as for the LAA scheme. Unlike LAA, the applicant might have to make a contribution for ABWOR. If the applicants disposable income is between £72 and £172, he or she will have to make a contribution of one-third of the amount by which the income exceeds £72. Someone, for example, whose disposable income is £102 per week (£30 over the lower limit) will have to pay a contribution of £10 per week, payable to the solicitor.

12.1.4 Civil legal aid

Since 1989, civil legal aid has been run by the Legal Aid Board. An applicant must satisfy two tests. Under the 'merits test', now governed by the Legal Aid Act (LAdA) 1988, the applicant must show the Board that he or she has reasonable grounds for taking, defending or being party to an action (s 15) but the applicant can be refused aid if it appears to the Board unreasonable to grant representation. The *Legal Aid Handbook* (published by the Board) states that, although financial benefit set against the costs of an action will be the normal criterion, there might be cases involving the applicant's status, reputation or dignity (for example, sex or race discrimination) where legal aid would be appropriate even though the financial benefit to be gained from any action was small.

Means test

The other test is a means test. This uses the concepts of 'disposable capital' and 'disposable income'. The former includes savings, jewellery, etc, but not the value of a house nor of a car unless it is especially valuable; the latter involves actual income less income tax, national savings, money for dependants, necessaries, travel to work, etc. From April 1999, to qualify for free legal aid, an applicant must have a disposable income of not more than £2,680 a year and a disposable capital of not more than £3,000. If disposable income is more than £2,680 but less than £7,940 (£8,751 for personal injury cases), or disposable capital is between £3,000 and £6,750 (or £8,560 for personal injury cases), then an applicant can qualify for legal aid subject to a contribution. An applicant with more than £7,940 disposable income (£8,751 in personal injury cases) or disposable capital of more than £6,750 (£8,560 in personal injury cases) will not be eligible for aid. Where applicants have to make a contribution because of their income, it is an ongoing monthly contribution from the applicant's income, and is $\frac{1}{36}$ of the excess over £2,680 for the life of the certificate. A contribution from the applicant's disposable capital (in excess of £3,000) may also be required. Where contributions are payable owing to capital, the payment will be all of the disposable capital over £3,000.

In 1993–94, 359,000 civil legal aid certificates were issued. Over the last two years, this has been the area of most rapid growth within the Legal Aid Board's responsibility. Under s 17 of the LAdA 1988, a legally aided person can, if he or she loses the case, be liable to meet some of the opponent's costs. This is known as the Indemnity Rule. Usually, the legally aided person is asked to pay the same amount again as that already paid in respect of his or her own contribution. When a legally aided party wins the case, the Legal Aid Fund recoups its costs from costs paid by the loser, from the winner's contribution and from any damages awarded to him or her or property won or recovered in the action. Some awards, like maintenance, are exempt from this 'statutory charge'.

There is now much evidence to show that the eligibility for legal aid has fallen dramatically over recent years. Glasser (a solicitor and former consultant to the Lord Chancellor on Legal Aid) has argued that the numbers eligible for legal aid fell by 13 million between 1979 and 1989 ((1988) Law Soc Gazette, 9 March, p 11; (1989) 5 April, p 9). Murphy, a statistician at the London School of Economics, has put the figure closer to 14 million ((1989) Legal Action, 7 October). In 1991, in a report on legal aid undertaken for the Lord Chancellor, figures were given which were the basis of the Lord Chancellor's concern to control legal aid expenditure. In the five years to 1990, whilst the number of legal aid certificates had risen by 22%, gross expenditure rose by 120% from £70 million to £153 million and net expenditure (cost to the taxpayer) had risen from £31 million to £76 million.

The review showed a marked decline in eligibility for legal aid: 74% of the population were eligible in 1979 whereas only 66% were eligible in 1990. The review was, however, critical of the notion that a particular proportion of the population 'should' be eligible for legal aid. Such a notion presupposed that the distribution and level of means in the population remained constant in relation to legal costs, that is, that, for example, the poorest 70% of the population would always be too poor to afford legal representation.

12.1.5 Criminal legal aid

The decision as to whether to grant legal aid is made by the court clerk according to criteria in the LAdA 1988. In the event of a refusal, there is a statutory right to criminal legal aid committees run by The Law Society. As with civil legal aid, the applicant must pass a merits and a means test. The merits test is simply whether it would be in the 'interests of justice' (s 21). This is usually satisfied by defendants in the Crown Court – the success rate has been about 98% in recent years. Section 22 of the LAdA 1988 lists some factors to be taken into account by any court which is deciding whether granting legal aid would be in the interests of justice. The factors are: (a) whether the offence is such that if proved it is likely that the court would impose a sentence which would deprive the defendant of his liberty or lead to his loss of livelihood or serious damage to his reputation; (b) the determination of the case may involve consideration of a substantial question of law; (c) where the defendant has linguistic difficulties or other disability; (d) the defence will require expertise like cross-examination; or (e) it is in the interests of another party that the accused be represented.

The means test is normally carried out by court clerks. Until 1982, there was a discretion as to whether the defendant should make any contribution and, if so, how much. Under current Regulations (which came into force on 10 April 1995), the courts question the defendant to determine his or her disposable income and capital. The income limit for free criminal legal aid is £51 a week disposable income. The capital limit for free legal aid is £3,000. The contribution system here requires a person to pay anything above £3,000 disposable capital, and weekly contributions from income of £1 for every £3 or part of £3 by which disposable income exceeds £51. Anyone receiving the State benefits of income support, family credit or disability working allowance is automatically eligible for criminal legal aid without having to make any contribution.

In 1983, an official survey of the granting of criminal legal aid confirmed earlier research in finding a distinct lack of uniformity in the decisions of different courts when refusing aid in similar cases. Research published by the Legal Aid Board (September 1992) also confirms the discrepancies between the approaches of both court clerks and area committees. In dummy applications for aid in a range of typical criminal cases, one court granted 10 out of 12 whilst two courts refused aid in seven cases. The Lord Chancellor referred to these as 'alarming inconsistencies'. Clearly, inadequate training of clerks and committees in this area may have resulted in a number of applicants being refused aid, thus adding to the numbers who have been, in effect, cast out of the system of protection.

12.1.6 Legal franchising

Since October 1993, following a pilot scheme in the Birmingham area, solicitors who meet certain management criteria have been devolved certain administrative powers previously exercised by the Legal Aid Board, thereby reducing the administrative costs to the Board and increasing the speed with which legal aid can be obtained. In return for meeting the management efficiency criteria, the practices receive certain fiscal benefits such as a lump sum payment from the Legal Aid Board on account immediately upon the approval of a case.

The devolved powers the solicitors receive are approval of Green Form extensions and grant of emergency certificates, 'where the interests of justice demand the immediate taking or defending of proceedings' – issued in circumstances such as the urgent need for orders preventing domestic violence. The old system will continue for firms which do not obtain a franchise, that is, applications for aid will still be made to the Board but clearly, in time, franchised firms will obtain a competitive advantage. The Board, soon to be superseded by the Legal Services Commission will then move from being an approving body to a quality control organisation. The fear amongst many lawyers and commentators is that this trend will lead to seriously reduced access to legal services because the smaller firms which find it too difficult to satisfy the management criteria will become uncompetitive and a number will go out of business.

Over 2,500 offices were franchised by July 1999, with over 2,000 more applications being processed. The emerging picture of future practice is one in which law firms and advice agencies bid for part of a fixed regional civil legal aid budget. The work to be covered by the franchised firms will include family, housing, debt, employment, welfare benefits, immigration, consumer, and mental health. Personal injury and medical negligence work will be handled by specialist franchised firms.

One real danger here is the expected move away from paying lawyers for the time they take to do the necessary work and towards paying set sums for particular sorts of work. In a strong editorial against such changes, the *New Law Journal* ([1998] NLJ 577, 24 April) reflects The Law Society view that these changes could 'pave the way to a bureaucratic and inflexible system for rationing legal advice to people on low incomes and that the bureaucrats will pay for what they perceive is needed rather than what is actually required'. The Criminal Law Solicitors' Association and the Legal Aid Practitioners' Group have both expressed fears that the proposals would lead to a breach of a basic principle of practice: that lawyers should be able to provide fearless representation for clients. By entering into contracts with the Legal Aid Board (soon to be superseded by the Legal Services Commission), lawyers might well end up compromising or impairing their independence as they will be under pressure to retain favour with the Board or Commission in order to ensure renewal of the contract.

12.1.7 Modernising justice

The White Paper, *Modernising Justice: the Government's Plans for Reforming Legal Services and the Courts,* was published at the end of 1998. It proposed the most fundamental changes in the English legal system for over 40 years.

The paper stated:

> A fair and efficient justice system is a vital part of a free society. The criminal justice system exists to help protect us from crime, and to ensure that criminals are punished. The civil justice system is there to help people resolve their disputes fairly and peacefully. This government has a radical programme of reform for the whole country. The justice system cannot be left out. We want a clearer, fairer, better system, that will make justice available to all the people.

The paper asserted that many people are put off getting help with legal problems, because the legal system is slow, expensive and difficult to understand. It proposed a new Community Legal Service that will ensure that 'people's needs are properly assessed, and that public money is targeted on the cases that need help most.'

Providing value for money in law is identified as a key aim of reform. The paper argued that taxpayers have, year on year been paying heavily for legal aid, while fewer people have been helped. By introducing contracting for legal services (the franchise system) and abolishing restrictive practices, the government aims to increase competition among lawyers and help keep costs down. It committed itself to create new avenues to justice by extending conditional fees, and modernising court procedures. References to statute sections below are to the Access to Justice Act 1999 (the 1999 Act).

The Community Legal Service

Until recently, about £800 million a year was spent on lawyers' fees under the civil legal aid system. Another £150 million a year from local government, central government, charities and businesses is spent on the voluntary advice sector, including Citizens' Advice Bureaux, law centres and other advice centres. The Legal Services Commission (to replace the Legal Aid Board) will take the lead in establishing a Community Legal Service to co-ordinate the provision of legal services in every region (s 1 of the 1999 Act). The plan is to achieve control over the legal aid budget and to gradually change over to a system in which the governmental spending on legal aid and voluntary sector advice is managed from one fund.

The Legal Services Commission will manage the Community Legal Service fund (s 4 of the 1999 Act), which will replace legal aid in civil and family cases.

Why replace civil legal aid?

The government argues as follows. Taxpayers spend £800 million a year through the civil legal aid system on buying legal services from lawyers for those who cannot afford to pay for themselves, and this system now needs radical change:

- it is too heavily biased towards expensive court based solutions to people's problems;

- despite a merits test, legal aid is sometimes used to fund cases that appear to be undeserving;

- it is not possible to control spending effectively. From 1992–93 to 1997–98, spending on civil and family legal aid grew by 35% from £586 million to £793 million; but, at the same time, the number of cases funded actually fell by 31% from 419,861 to 319,432;

- in the ordinary legal aid system, lawyers were paid according to the amount of work claimed for, so there is no incentive to handle cases quickly or work efficiently.

Who will do the work and who will qualify for help?

The Legal Services Commission will buy services for the public under contracts. Only lawyers and other providers with contracts will be able to work under the new scheme. This will enable budgets to be strictly controlled, will help to ensure quality of service, and will provide a basis for competition between different providers. The fund will be targeted on those people who are most in need of help, and on high-priority cases. There will be no absolute entitlement to help, and the fund will not be spent on cases which could be financed by other means, such as conditional fees (see 12.5, below). The government does, however, intend to increase the number of people potentially eligible for advice and assistance under the scheme, to bring this into line with eligibility for representation. At the same time, those who can afford to contribute towards their legal expenses will be required to do so.

How will the government help people who do not qualify for help from the Community Legal Service fund?

It is clear that not everyone will benefit from the new scheme. In this context, the government states that it will work with the insurance industry to widen cover (it says that 17 million people are already covered by one sort of legal insurance or another, although this figure includes people entitled to legal services in respect of only one type of situation like a traffic accident or holiday disasters). It is also intended to widen the scope of the conditional fee system.

Criminal Defence Service

The government states that it will maintain the fundamental principle that those facing a criminal trial should not be afraid that lack of resources and proper representation might lead to their wrongful conviction. However, serious weaknesses in the current criminal legal aid system are identified:

The cost has risen from £507 million in 1992–93 to £733 million in 1997–98 – an increase of 44%. At the same time, the number of cases dealt with increased by only 10%. Although standard fees are now paid in many cases, the most expensive cases are paid in the traditional way by calculating the fee after the event. The White Paper stated that the system gave lawyers an incentive to boost their fees by dragging cases out, and that such cases took up a disproportionate amount of money. The system for means testing defendants to see whether they should contribute to the costs of their case was seen as a waste of time and money. The test has not stopped some apparently wealthy defendants from receiving free legal aid, and 94% of defendants in the Crown Court pay no contribution.

The government will replace the current criminal legal aid scheme with a new Criminal Defence Service (CDS). To begin with, the CDS will be run, by the Legal Services Commission, but it will be an entirely separate scheme from the Community Legal Service, with a separate budget. The Commission will develop contracts for different types of criminal defence services and implement them following pilot schemes. All contracts for criminal defence services will include quality requirements, and, wherever possible, prices for the contracts will be fixed in advance. Fixed prices create an incentive to avoid delay, and reward efficient practice. Eventually, contracts with solicitors firms will cover the full range of defence services, from advice at the police station to representation in court. If a case requires the services of a specialist advocate in the Crown Court, this is likely to be covered by a separate contract. Opponents of this move argue that fixed price work is not conducive to justice as such a system of payment encourages corner-cutting and work of an inferior standard.

Very complex and expensive cases – where the trial is expected to last 25 days or more – will not be covered by ordinary contracts. A defendant's choice of solicitor will be limited to firms on a specialist panel, and a separate contract will be agreed in each case.

One key question here was to what extent a defendant's choice of lawyer in a criminal matter would be restricted under the new scheme. Many lawyers expressed worry that if the legislation allowed the government (through the Lord Chancellor's Department) to choose the defendant's lawyer, then famous campaigning lawyers, such as Gareth Peirce (who helped release the Guildford

Four and the Birmingham Six) and Jim Nicol (who acted for the appellants in the Carl Bridgewater case), might be shunned by the Criminal Defence Service ((1998) *The Independent*, 25 November). The right to choose a defence lawyer has historically been regarded as a precious right in the UK. As prosecutions are brought in the name of the Crown, there is an appreciable danger in permitting the Crown (albeit a different branch of government) to have an influence over who represents the defendant. In the end, the Access to Justice Act 1999 offers a compromise in s 15. The section says that, where a defendant has been granted the right to representation, he may choose any representative and the LSC must fund that representation. However, s 15(2) explains that regulations can be made which do restrict the defendant's choices in some ways. In some types of cases, for example, the right might be excluded – the government has mentioned complex fraud trails as an example. The right will not include a right to choose only a lawyer of a particular description, for example, a defendant on a simple theft charge could not insist on representation by a QC. Section 15(4) provides that the regulations made to determine the details of how the system will work 'may not provide that only a person employed by the Commission, or by a body established and maintained by the Commission, may be selected'. Thus, there will always be the right to select a lawyer from the independent field, rather than (as some lawyers feared) a choice only of lawyers employed directly or indirectly by a governmental agency.

Who will decide whether to grant criminal representation, and how? As now, it will be for the court to decide whether to grant a defendant representation at public expense, according to the interests of justice (Sched 3, cl 5(1) of the 1999 Act). But the current requirement for a means test will be abolished. Instead, after a case is over, a judge in the Crown Court will have the power to order a convicted defendant to pay some or all of the costs of his defence. This will mean that assets frozen during criminal proceedings, and any assets which only come to light during proceedings, will be taken into account, so some wealthy criminals will pay much more than they do now.

12.1.8 The Access to Justice Act 1999 – a summary

We address the main provisions of the Act where relevant throughout this chapter. Here, for convenience, we present an overview of the main changes made by the Act and related regulations.

Under the new system, legal aid will no longer be available for:

- those seeking personal injury compensation (except clinical negligence cases);
- disputes about inheritance under a will or an intestacy;
- matters affecting the administration of a trust or the position of a trustee;

- matters relating to the position of directors of companies, restoring a company to the Register or dealing with the position of minority shareholders;

- matters affecting partnerships;

- matters before the Lands Tribunal;

- cases between landowners over a disputed boundary of adjacent property; and

- cases pursued in the course of a business.

The hope is that the extension of conditional fees in these areas will provide increased public access to lawyers.

The government is now committed to:

(a) allowing conditional fee agreements (no-win, no-fee agreements) to be used in all except family and criminal cases;

(b) transferring to conditional fees most money and damages claims currently supported by legal aid;

(c) removing most personal injury actions from the scope of legal aid;

(d) ensuring that medical negligence cases are to be conducted only by practitioners who are experienced in this field of litigation;

(e) the setting up of a limited transitional fund which would provide support in cases where there are high investigative costs in establishing the merits of a case or where the costs of carrying the case are very high.

Since 1995, 45,000 people have taken advantage of conditional fee arrangements (CFAs) to bring personal injury claims. The government has noted that many of these people would have been unable to afford to pursue their claims at all without conditional fees – people only just above the legal aid limit, people who are far from well off. These people, the Lord Chancellor has argued, are the great majority of the population who are in work – with families, mortgages, savings, or other assets, which mean that they are not eligible for legal aid, but who cannot contemplate the open-ended commitment of meeting lawyers' fees.

Lord Irvine stated that the government had been listening carefully to the comments received in relation to medical negligence cases, and accepted that many lawyers practising in this area needed time to modernise the way they run their firms so that they can take cases on regardless of their financial standing. That is why State funding of representation will be retained for the time being. There is currently not a good record of claims in this area. The net cost of medical negligence cases to the taxpayer last year was £27 million. Looking at the cases closed by the Legal Aid Board in 1996–97, 32 cases recovered £500,000 or more. Leaving these cases aside, the average cost of cases was £4,122 to recover average damages of £4,107. In only 17% of cases was £50 or more recovered (and 1996–97 was a good year: closed case data from previous years shows recovery rates between 13% and 17%). Medical negligence cases are a specialist area of litigation. It can be difficult to identify at the outset whether a case has merit, and, even as the medical evidence unfolds, whether the negligence alleged has caused the ailment or injury. The government believes that part of the reasons for the high failure rate is that cases are being pursued by lawyers who are insufficiently experienced in this area of litigation.

The Lord Chancellor stated that:

> The government does not, therefore, propose to remove these cases from the scope of legal aid for the present. We do, however, intend to do what we can to reduce the high failure rate of these cases. It cannot be right that it is only in as few as 17% of all the cases that are supported by a legal aid certificate that more than £50 is recovered in damages. Medical negligence cases should be conducted by practitioners who are experienced in this field of litigation. We cannot any longer allow inexperienced practitioners to take cases. We propose that the Legal Aid Board should establish contracts only with lawyers of sufficient experience. Anyone who is granted legal aid to pursue a medical negligence case will be required to use a lawyer who holds a contract with the Board (Lord Chancellor's Department, Official Statement, 57/98, 4 March 1998).

12.2 The Access to Justice Act 1999

12.2.1 Background

The old scheme was contained in the Legal Aid Act 1988.

A common feature of the civil and criminal legal aid schemes was that expenditure on them was demand-led. Any lawyer could do legal aid work for a client who passed the relevant means test (if any), and whose case passed the statutory merits test (in the case of civil legal aid), or the interests of justice test (in the case of criminal legal aid). Lawyers were (and will continue to be under the transitional arrangements) paid on a case by case basis for each individual case or other act of assistance, usually at rates or fees set in regulations, but in some cases on the same basis as a privately-funded lawyer.

This, in the government's view, meant that there were few mechanisms or incentives for promoting value for money or assuring the quality of the services provided; and that neither the government nor the Legal Aid Board was able to exert adequate control over expenditure or determine the priorities for that expenditure.

During 1992–1998, expenditure on legal aid overall increased from £620m in 1991–92 to £1,526m in 1997–98, a rise of 68%. In comparison, GDP rose by

18% over the same period. Meanwhile, the number of people helped overall increased by 18% to 3.6m. In civil and family legal aid, expenditure rose from £330m to £634m, an increase of 92%, while the number of people helped fell by almost 10%. Average payments in civil and family cases rose by almost 90%, from £1,598 in 1991–92 to £3,018 in 1997–98. The cost of criminal legal aid rose by 50% between 1991–92 and 1997–98, from £397m to £597m, while the numbers helped remained at around 615,000. Over the period average payments to defence lawyers went up by 11% and 66% in the magistrates' courts and the Crown Court respectively.

Since August 1994, the Legal Aid Board operated a voluntary quality assurance scheme, known as franchising. Currently, some 2,500 solicitors' firms have franchises in one or more of the 10 subject categories in which they are awarded (criminal, family, personal injury, housing, etc). A further 2,030 applications for franchises were pending in July 1999. The Board is continuing to develop the franchising scheme, and to introduce new categories, in order to underpin the move to a generally contracted scheme under the reforms in this Act.

In Autumn 1994, the Board set up a pilot scheme which showed that non-profit making advice agencies could provide legally aided advice and assistance which the government argued were to the same standard as those provided by solicitors' firms. In October 1996, a second pilot was established, involving a larger number of agencies, to develop systems for contracting for advice and assistance work.

In November 1996, the Board began to pilot contracts with solicitors' firms to provide advice and assistance in civil matters. A pilot of contracts to provide mediation in family cases under the legal aid scheme commenced in May 1997. A pilot covering advice and assistance in criminal cases began June 1998, and was extended to cover representation in the youth court in February 1999. Since October 1997, the Board has set up a Regional Legal Services Committee in each of its 13 areas to advise it about future priorities for contracting.

In 1999, the government announced that all civil advice and assistance, and all family work will be provided exclusively under contract from January 2000. Only organisations with a relevant franchise will be eligible to bid for these contracts. Also, a new clinical negligence franchise came into effect in February 1999; and from July 1999 only firms with that franchise will be able to take these cases under the legal aid scheme.

12.2.2 The advice sector

There are over 1,500 non-profit making advice agencies in England and Wales. They receive their funding – over £150 million a year in total – from many different sources, mainly local authorities, but also charities, including the National Lottery Charities Board, Central Government, the Legal Aid Board, and business.

The provision of advice services is not spread consistently across the country. Some areas appear to have relatively high levels of both legal practitioners and voluntary outlets, while others have little or none. For example, the Legal Aid Board's South East Area has one Citizens Advice Bureau per 46,000 people, but, in the East Midlands, 138,000 people share a Citizens Advice Bureau. The government believes that the fragmented nature of the advice sector obstructs effective planning, and prevents local needs for legal advice and help from being met as rationally and fully as possible.

12.3 Overview of the Act

The 1999 Act replaces the legal aid system with two new schemes; and makes provisions about rights to supply legal services, appeals (we look at these in Chapter 11) and court procedure (we look at these in Chapter 7), magistrates and magistrates' courts (see Chapter 4).

The provisions in the Act form part of the wide ranging programme of reforms to legal services and the courts, described in the government's White Paper, *Modernising Justice*, published on 2 December 1998. Except where noted, the Act only affects England and Wales. There is currently very little literature on the Act as it has only just been promulgated so, aside from our own views and the viewpoints of other commentators, we rely heavily here, for official interpretations, on governmental guidance provided when the legislation was in draft form, that is, a Bill.

12.3.1 Funding of legal services (Pts I and II)

Part I of the 1999 Act provides for two new schemes, replacing the legal aid scheme, to secure the provision of publicly funded legal services for people who need them. It establishes a Legal Services Commission to run the two schemes; and enables the Lord Chancellor to give the Commission orders, directions and guidance about how it should exercise its functions.

It requires the Commission to establish, maintain and develop a Community Legal Service. A new Community Legal Service fund will replace the legal aid fund in civil and family cases. The Commission will use the resources of the fund, in a way that reflects priorities set by the Lord Chancellor and its duty to secure the best possible value for money, to procure or provide a range of legal services. The Commission will also have a duty to liaise with other funders of legal services to facilitate the developments of co-ordinated plans for making the best use of all available resources. The intention is to develop a network of legal service providers of assured quality, offering the widest possible access to information and advice about the law, and assistance with legal problems.

The Commission will also be responsible for running the Criminal Defence Service, which replaces the current legal aid scheme in criminal cases. The new scheme is intended to ensure that people suspected or accused of a crime are properly represented, while securing better value for money than was possible under the legal aid scheme.

Some of Pt III relates to privately funded litigation. It amends the law on conditional fee agreements between lawyers and their clients, and the recovery of insurance premiums as costs between the parties to litigation.

Lawyers' rights of audience before the courts are also covered in Pt III and we look at this in Chapter 11.

Part IV of the Act deals with aspects of reforms for the system for appeals in civil and family cases, and we look at these in Chapter 3.

12.3.2 The Legal Services Commission

Section 1 of the 1999 Act establishes the new Legal Services Commission, and makes provision for appointments to it. The Commission will replace the Legal Aid Board. It was considered necessary to establish a new body to reflect the fundamentally different nature of the Community Legal Service (CLS) compared to civil legal aid. Within the broad framework of priorities set by the Lord Chancellor, the Commission will be responsible for taking detailed decisions about the allocation of resources. It will also be required to liaise with other funders to develop the CLS more widely. The Commission will also have a wider role in respect of the Criminal Defence Service than the Legal Aid Board did in respect of criminal legal aid. The Board had very limited responsibilities for legal aid in the higher criminal courts. Membership of the Commission will differ from that of the old Legal Aid Board, to reflect a shift in focus from the needs of providers to the needs of users of legal services. Also, the Commission is smaller than the Board: 7–12 members rather than 11–17. This is intended to facilitate 'focused decision making'.

Schedule 14 of the 1999 Act makes transitional provisions for the replacement of the Legal Aid Board by the Commission. Briefly, it provides that, on an appointed day (probably some time in 2000), the Commission shall take over all the property, rights and liabilities of the Board. Staff of the Board will automatically become staff of the Commission. The intention is that the provisions of the 1988 Act will remain in force for any cases that have already started when the new schemes come into effect.

Section 2 of the 1999 Act gives the Lord Chancellor the power to replace the Commission with two bodies: one responsible for the Community Legal Service and the other for the Criminal Defence Service. The intention is to allow for the possibility that, because of the different nature and objectives of the two schemes, it may prove more effective in the longer term to administer them separately. It would not be practicable to set up two bodies from the outset.

This is because of the need to retain, in substance, the existing infrastructure and expertise of the Legal Aid Board to manage the transition from legal aid to the two new schemes. This involves both administering existing cases under the old scheme and developing contracting as the principal means of procuring services under the new schemes.

The government indicated in 1999 that it had no definite intention to split the administration of the two schemes in future. Rather, the intention is to review the situation once the new schemes are firmly established, probably after about five years.

12.3.3 The Community Legal Service

The Legal Services Commission will have two main duties in respect of the Community Legal Service (CLS):

- First, it will manage a Community Legal Service fund (ss 4–11), which will replace legal aid in civil and family cases. The CLS fund will be used to secure the provision of appropriate legal services, within the resources made available to it, and according to priorities set by the Lord Chancellor and by regional and local assessments of need. A Funding Code, drawn up by the Commission and approved by the Lord Chancellor, will set out the criteria and procedures for deciding whether to fund individual cases. As spending is brought under better control, the government says, it will be possible to expand the scope of the fund over time into areas that are not covered by legal aid. In particular, the intention is to extend the availability of alternatives to lawyers and courts, like mediation and advice agencies. Mediation is already a requirement in family matters (see Pt III of the Family Law Act 1996).

- Secondly, as part of a wider CLS, the Commission will, in co-operation with local funders and interested bodies, develop local, regional and national plans to match the delivery of legal services to identified needs and priorities.

The development of the CLS at a local level is dependent in practice on the formation of Community Legal Service Partnerships (CLSPs) in each local authority area. (These do not require specific provisions in the Act.) The CLSP will provide a forum, in each local authority area, for the local authority and the Legal Services Commission, and if possible other significant funders, to come together to co-ordinate funding and planning of local legal and advice services, to ensure that delivery of services better matches local needs. There have, however, been warnings from some lawyers that government plans are so vague as to how the CLS will work that the credibility of the entire new system is in question. According to the one view, the CLS is in danger of becoming a 'leafleting service' (News,

'The legal profession and the Community Legal Service' [1999] NLJ 1195, 6 August.

Even at early stages of the launch of this project, the government's plan has been attacked by sections of the legal community. In May 1999, the Lord Chancellor faced calls for an imposition of a duty on local authorities to fund legal services after a long-awaited consultation paper on the CLS was published (Irvine, 'Community vision under fire' (1999) Law Soc Gazette, 26 May, pp 1, 5). Michael Mathews, the then Law Society President, said it was 'baffling that after so many months there should be such a lack of information on this important service ... Sadly, this consultation paper is more government waffle on legal aid'.

The Commission will develop a system of kitemarking, on the basis of common quality criteria. This is designed to reinforce public confidence that the voluntary sector is a provider of good quality legal advice and help.

The Commission and the CLSPs will encourage innovation by the voluntary sector in the delivery of advice through increased use of information technology and mobile 'outreach' services providing help to people in remote communities.

Overall, the intention is to:

- make best use of all the resources available for funding legal services, by facilitating a co-ordinated approach to planning;

- improve value for money through contracting and the development of quality assurance systems;

- establish a flexible system for allocating Central Government funding, in a rational and transparent way within a controlled budget, so as to provide legal services where they are judged to be most needed; and

- ensure that the scheme is capable of adapting to meet changing priorities and opportunities.

Section 4 of the 1999 Act describes the services which may be provided under the CLS. These range from the provision of basic information about the law and legal services, to providing help towards preventing or resolving disputes and enforcing decisions which have been reached. The scheme will encompasses advice, assistance and representation by lawyers (which have long been available under the legal aid scheme), and also the services of non-lawyers. It will extend to other types of service, including, for example, mediation in family or civil cases where appropriate.

Section 4(3) of the 1999 Act provides that the CLS does not cover services funded as part of the Criminal Defence Service, in order to avoid any overlap between the two schemes. Under Sched 2, also excluded is any help (beyond the provision of general information about the law and the legal system') relating to company matters, defamation and malicious falsehood, conveyancing and the making of wills.

Under s 5 of the 1999 Act, the CLS fund is established and the mechanisms by which the Lord Chancellor will provide the resources to the fund are defined. Each year, as part of the general public expenditure planning process, the Lord Chancellor will set a budget for the CLS. This will take account of the receipts from contributions (for example, from local authorities) with the balance of the budget provided by Lord Chancellor from money voted by Parliament. The CLS fund will therefore not be an open-ended fund, as was the legal aid fund.

The Lord Chancellor will be able to direct the Commission to use specified amounts within the fund to provide services of particular types (s 5(6)). The intention is that the Lord Chancellor will divide the fund into two main budgets, for providing services in (i) family and (ii) other civil cases, while allowing the Commission limited flexibility to switch money between the two areas. The Lord Chancellor may set further requirements within these two budgets, by specifying the amount, or the maximum or minimum amount, that should be spent on, say, services from the voluntary advice sector, mediation, or cases involving a wider public interest. The idea here is that, in this way, it will be possible to ensure that resources are allocated in accordance with the government's priorities.

A duty is placed on the Commission to aim to obtain the best value for money – a combination of price and quality – when using the resources of the fund to provide services.

Section 6(3) of the 1999 Act sets out the ways in which the Commission may use the CLS fund to provide services. These include making contracts with or grants to service providers, or employing staff to provide services directly to the public. These flexible powers are intended to give effect to one of the principal objectives of the reform of publicly funded legal services: that is the ability to tailor the provision of services, and the means by which services are to delivered, to the needs of local populations and particular circumstances. They will also allow the Commission to test new forms of service provision through pilot projects.

Schedule 2 of the 1999 Act excludes from the scope of the CLS fund specified types of service which would otherwise fall within the broad definition of cases covered by the scheme, and says that the Lord Chancellor can make directions bringing other cases within the provisions of the act in exceptional circumstances. For example, the Lord Chancellor may direct that for personal injury cases (which are generally excluded by Sched 2, because most such cases are suitable for conditional fees) funding by the CLS fund should nonetheless be possible where exceptionally high investigative or overall costs are likely to be necessary, or where issues of wider public interest are involved. The consultation paper, *Access to Justice with Conditional Fees*

(LCD, 1998), notes (para 3.31) that it will be necessary to decide what should constitute public interest. For example, a test case about a novel point of law might have no more than a 50% chance of success, but the decision could impact on numerous future cases (in the way that recent cases involving sporting injuries have extended the duty of care owed by officials wider than was previously accepted). Or a claim for a relatively small sum in damages might benefit a large number of other people with a similar claim. Examples might be claims arising out of the use of pharmaceutical products, and pollution of water supplies or the atmosphere. Very expensive cases often include this type of public interest aspect: they are expensive because they are novel and complex, or because their wide potential impact means that they are hard fought.

Under Sched 2, people (but not corporate bodies) will be able to receive information on any matters of English law. Schedule 2 provides for restrictions on the more substantial services that will be available in different categories of case. For some categories, a full range of services will be available (subject to priorities). For some others, all services except representation at court by a lawyer will be available. Finally, for some categories, only the provision of information and basic advice will be possible.

The intention is that the scope of the CLS fund should initially mirror the previous scope of civil legal aid; but that it may change over time. In particular:

- as conditional fees, legal expenses insurance and other forms of funding develop more widely, it may be possible to exclude further categories which can generally be funded privately;

- as resources become available through the greater control of spending and value for money provided by the new scheme and the development of private alternatives, it may be possible to extend the scheme's scope to cover services that are excluded now because, although they would command some priority, they are unaffordable.

The following changes to the scope of the legal aid scheme were given immediate effect. In future, subject to any exceptions that the Lord Chancellor may make by direction, only basic information and advice will be available for:

- disputes involving allegations of negligent damage to property or the person ('personal injury'), apart from those about clinical negligence. These cases are generally considered suitable for conditional fees;

- allegations of defamation or malicious falsehood. Generally, legal aid was not currently available for representation in defamation, but it was sometimes possible to get legal aid by categorising the case as one of malicious falsehood. The government's view is that these cases do not command sufficient priority to justify public funding; and, in any event, they may often be suitable for a conditional fee;

- disputes arising in the course of business. Legal aid was not available for firms and companies, but a sole trader could get legal aid to pursue a business dispute. Businessmen have the option of insuring against the possibility of having to take or defend legal action. The government does not believe that the taxpayer should meet the legal costs of sole traders who fail to do so;

- matters concerned with the law relating to companies or partnerships; matters concerned with the law of trusts or trustees; boundary disputes. The government does not consider that these command sufficient priority to justify public funding. In addition, funding for representation at proceedings before the Lands Tribunal or Commons Commissioners will no longer be available. Other services, including assistance with preparing a case, will continue to be available.

Section 7 of the 1999 Act allows the Lord Chancellor, using regulations, to set financial eligibility limits for people to receive services funded by the CLS fund. It allows him to set different conditions, or no conditions, for different circumstances or types of case or service.

There are, however, no immediate plans to make any substantive changes to the present financial eligibility limits, although the government has stated it will continue to uprate them each Spring as it did with the legal aid eligibility criteria. The government has said that, in due course, it intends to expand the availability of advice and assistance to people who can afford to make a contribution.

The Commission will, under s 8, prepare a Code setting out the criteria for determining whether services funded by the CLS fund should be provided in a particular case, and if so what services it is appropriate to provide. The Code will also set out the procedures for making applications.

The funding assessment under the Code will replace the merits test for civil legal aid. Section 8 (its first three sub-sections) of the 1999 Act is the relevant provision. It says:

8 (1) The Commission shall prepare a Code setting out the criteria according to which it is to decide whether to fund (or continue to fund) services as part of the Community Legal Service for an individual ... and ... what services are to be funded for him.

(2) In settling the criteria to be set out in the Code, the Commission shall consider the extent to which they ought to reflect the following factors:

(a) the likely cost of funding the services and the benefit which may be obtained by there being provided;

(b) the availability of sums in the Community Legal Service Fund for funding the services and (having regard to the present and likely future demands on that Fund) the appropriateness of applying them to fund the services;

(c) the importance of the matters in relation to which the services would be provided for the individual;

(d) the availability to the individual of services not funded by the Commission and the likelihood of his being able to avail himself of them;

(e) if the services are sought by the individual in relation to a dispute, the prospects of his success in the dispute;

(f) the conduct of the individual in connection with services funded as part of the Community Legal Service (or an application for funding) or in, or in connection with, any legal proceedings;

(g) the public interest; and

(h) such other factors as the Lord Chancellor may by order require the Commission to consider.

(3) The criteria set out in the code shall reflect the principle that, in many family disputes, mediation will be more appropriate than court proceedings.

The new assessment is intended to be more flexible than the existing merits test. It will be possible to apply different criteria in different categories according to their priority. It will also be possible to take account of factors, such as a wider public interest, which attach to particular cases, rather than those whole categories of case for which contracts might be let. The reform of the merits test, which regulates the demand that qualifies for help, is said by the government to complement the reforms of the supply of services – with the intention of creating a flexible system for deploying resources to meet a range of priorities within a controlled budget.

The criteria for funding the various types of service in different categories of case will be defined by considering these factors. The Code will define which factors are relevant in a given category, how they should be taken into account, and what weight should be given to them. For example, prospects of success will not be a relevant factor in cases about whether a child should be taken into local authority care.

The Code is required to reflect the principle that in many family disputes mediation is more appropriate than court proceedings. This is intended to reinforce the development, under the Family Law Act 1996, of mediation as a means of resolving private law family disputes in a way that promotes as good a continuing relationship between the parties concerned as is possible in the circumstances. The government has argued that mediation is more constructive than adversarial court proceedings, and that litigation in these cases usually serves only to reinforce already entrenched positions and further damage the relationship between the parties. In addition, the cost of court proceedings is higher than that of mediation, and additional costs have to borne by the property of the family, reducing the amount available to the parties and their children in future. The credibility of mediation as an appropriate forum for family matters in general took a blow in 1999, when the government abandoned plans to introduce the scheme related to divorce after pilot studies failed to produce good results.

Sections 7 and 8 of the 1999 Act enables the Lord Chancellor to set financial conditions to apply to people receiving services funded by the CLS fund. Subject to two additions, the effect of the Act is generally to replicate the provisions of the old Legal Aid Act 1988.

As before, it will be possible to make regulations requiring people to contribute towards the cost of the services they receive by way of flat rate fees, contributions related to disposable income and capital, and from any property recovered or preserved as a result of the help given. In general, the intention is to replicate the old regulations.

The 1999 Act, though, extends the potential scope of financial conditions in two ways, although there are no immediate plans to use either of these powers:

- It will be possible to make the provision of services in some types of cases subject to the assisted person agreeing to repay an amount in excess of the cost of the services provided in the event that their case is successful (s 10(2)). This might make it possible to fund certain types of case on a self-financing basis, with the additional payments from successful litigants applied to meet the cost of unsuccessful cases. It would also be possible to mix public funding with a private conditional fee arrangement, subject to the same conditions about the uplift to the costs in the event of a successful outcome. The government has suggested that this might be appropriate, for example, where a case could not be taken under a wholly private arrangement, because the solicitors' firm was not large enough to bear the risk of the very high costs likely to be involved.

- It will be possible (s 10(3), (4)) to require the assisted person to repay, over time and with interest, the full cost of the service provided (for example, through continuing contributions from income). This will make it possible to provide services in some categories of case in the form of a loan scheme.

Section 11 of the 1999 Act establishes limits on the liability of the person receiving funded services to pay costs to the unassisted party. The costs he must pay cannot go above what is 'reasonable' (s 11(1)), taking into account the financial resources of all parties. It also provides that regulations may specify the principles that are to be applied in determining the amount of any costs awarded against the party receiving funded services and the circumstances in which a costs order may be enforced against the person receiving funded services.

Henceforward, those regulations which limit the circumstances in which the costs order may be enforced against the person receiving funded services, or the liability of the Commission to meet any costs order on behalf of the person receiving funded services, will be made on a more flexible basis. Previously, protection from costs was seen by governments to create too great an advantage in litigation for the person receiving legal aid.

12.3.4 The Criminal Defence Service

The purpose of the CDS is to secure the provision of advice, assistance and representation, according to the interests of justice, to people suspected of a criminal offence or facing criminal proceedings (s 12).

The Commission will be empowered to secure these services through contracts with lawyers in private practice, or by providing them through salaried defenders, employed by non-profit-making organisations. All contractors will be expected to meet quality-assurance standards and contracts will, where possible, cover the full range of services from arrest until the case is completed. (The old arrangements for criminal legal aid were widely seen as fragmented: a person could receive assistance in respect of the same alleged offence under several separate schemes, each resulting in a separate payment for the lawyers involved.)

There will be a transitional period while contracts are developed and extended to cover the full range of services. The Commission will therefore be able to pay lawyers on a case by case basis for representation provided on a non-contractual basis, according to remuneration scales set in regulations (that is, broadly on the same basis as the current criminal legal aid scheme).

As under the old system, the courts will grant representation under the scheme to defendants according to 'the interests of justice'. However, the courts will no longer have to conduct a means test as well before granting representation. Instead, at the end of a case in the Crown Court, the trial judge will have power to order a defendant to pay some or all of the cost of his or her defence. The Commission may investigate the defendant's means in order to assist the judge. The intention is to abolish the system of means testing every defendant, which the government considers an ineffective and wasteful aspect of the current scheme, while ensuring that in the more expensive cases defendants continue to pay towards the cost of their defence when they can afford to do so.

Section 12(2) of the 1999 Act defines 'criminal proceedings'. These include criminal trials, appeals and sentencing hearings, extradition hearings, binding over proceedings, appeals on behalf of a convicted person who has died, and proceedings for contempt in the face of any court. The Act allows the Lord Chancellor to add further categories by regulation. This power will be used, for example, to prescribe Parole Board reviews of discretionary life sentences.

The Legal Services Commission will gradually take over the functions currently undertaken by the higher courts in respect of criminal legal aid. At first, Court Service staff will continue to determine costs in many Crown Court cases but the numbers will diminish as the Commission increases the proportion of cases covered by contracts. Staff at the Court of Appeal (Criminal Division) and the House of Lords will continue to determine costs in cases before those courts, although the scope for the Commission to contract for these cases as well will be considered in due course.

Section 13(1) of the 1999 Act places the Legal Services Commission under a duty to provide such advice and assistance as it considers appropriate in the interests of justice for individuals who are arrested and held in custody, and in other circumstances to be prescribed by the Lord Chancellor in regulations.

Initially, it is intended that regulations will provide for advice and assistance in broadly the categories for which it is currently available to people subject to criminal investigations or proceedings. These categories include advice and assistance provided by duty solicitors at a magistrates' court, at a solicitor's office, and to a 'volunteer' at a police station.

Section 13(2) also enables the Commission to comply with this duty by securing advice and assistance through entering into contracts; by making payments to persons or bodies; by making grants or loans to persons or bodies; by establishing and maintaining bodies; by making grants to individuals; or by doing anything else which the Commission considers appropriate for funding advice and assistance except providing it itself. It also enables the Commission to secure the provision of advice and assistance by different means in different areas in England and Wales and in relation to different descriptions of cases.

The aim of this part of the Act is to provide the Commission with a range of options for securing advice and assistance in criminal matters. Contracting with quality assured suppliers, the government contends, should provide greater control over both expenditure and the quality of the service provided; and better value for money.

Section 13(2)(f) of the 1999 Act also contains powers to enable the Commission to provide services through lawyers in its own employment. These powers are intended to provide flexibility if, for example, there is limited coverage by private lawyers in rural areas. Using employed lawyers should also, the government has argued, provide the Commission with better information about the real costs of providing these services.

Section 14 places a duty on the Commission to fund representation for individuals granted a right to representation. It enables the Commission to comply with this duty in the same ways as for advice and assistance. The power to make direct case by case payments to representatives will allow the Commission to continue to pay non-contracted lawyers to provide representation during the transitional period while contracting develops; and possibly thereafter where that proves to be the best means of securing the necessary services.

The legislation provides that defendants granted a right of representation can choose their representative, restricted only as provided in regulations (s 15). In due course, it is intended that regulations will, in particular, provide that a defendant's choice of representatives is limited to those holding contracts with the Commission. In time, the Commission will provide all, or nearly all, representation exclusively through contracted representatives, who it will require to meet defined quality standards.

In certain types of cases – such as serious fraud trials – defendants' choice may be further limited to representatives from a panel of firms or individual advocates who specialise in a particular type of case. Membership of a panel will depend on meeting pre-determined criteria. In this way, the Commission can ensure that defendants facing charges in these exceptional cases are represented by those with the necessary expertise, experience and resources.

Section 15(2)(a) of the 1999 Act enables the Lord Chancellor to make regulations defining circumstances where a defendant will not have a right to a choice of representative, but will instead have a representative assigned to them. This power might be used, for example, to assign an advocate to a previously unrepresented defendant charged with serious sexual offences where the victim/witness is a child. (Unrepresented defendants may not cross-examine child witnesses directly when charged with violent or sexual offences.)

Schedule 3 deals with the grant of a right to representation and, in particular:

- the individuals to whom a right of representation may be granted;

- the extent of the right;

- which courts and other bodies are competent to grant representation;

- appeals against the refusal of a right to representation; and

- the criteria for granting the right.

Schedule 3 of the 1999 Act provides for rights to representation to be granted to defendants or appellants in criminal proceedings where the interests of justice require it. The factors to be considered in assessing the interests of justice mirror s 22(2) of the Legal Aid Act 1988. Other provisions in the Schedule also reflect provisions in the 1988 Act.

Section 16 of the 1999 Act will ensure that salaried defenders employed by the Legal Services Commission – are subject to a code guaranteeing minimum standards of professional behaviour. The Code is to include duties: to avoid discrimination; to protect the interests of the individuals for whom services are provided; to the court; to avoid conflicts of interest; and of confidentiality. Before preparing or revising the Code, the Commission is required to consult. The Code will be approved by a resolution of each House of Parliament, and published.

The Act enables the Lord Chancellor to make regulations setting out how the new power should be applied.

Under the criminal legal aid scheme, most defendants (about 95%) were not required to make a contribution to their defence costs. Those who did contribute and were acquitted usually had their contributions returned. The cost of means testing and enforcing contribution orders was high in relation to the contributions recovered. In 1997–98, criminal legal aid contributions totalled £6.2 million, while the direct cost of administering the system was about £5 million. Means testing also led to delays in cases being brought to court, because cases had to be adjourned when the evidence required to conduct the test was not produced.

The new law (s 18) requires the Lord Chancellor to provide the necessary funding of criminal defence services secured by the Commission. As a result, like legal aid, the Criminal Defence Service will be a demand-led scheme. The Act also enables the Lord Chancellor to determine the timing and way in which this money should be paid to the Commission, and requires the Commission to seek to secure the best possible value for money in funding the Criminal Defence Service.

12.3.5 Conditional fees

We look at conditional fees more fully at the end of this chapter. For now, it is enough to observe that the Act (ss 27–31) reforms the law relating to conditional fees to enable the court to order a losing party to pay, in addition to the other party's normal legal costs, the uplift on the successful party's lawyers' fees; and in any case where a litigant has insured against facing an order for the other side's costs, any premium paid by the successful party for that insurance. The intention is to:

- ensure that the compensation awarded to a successful party is not eroded by any uplift or premium. The party in the wrong will bear the full burden of costs;

- make conditional fees more attractive, in particular to defendants and to claimants seeking non-monetary redress. (These litigants can rarely use conditional fees now, because they cannot rely on the prospect of recovering damages to meet the cost of the uplift and premium);

- discourage weak cases and encourage settlements;

- provide a mechanism for regulating the uplifts that solicitors charge. In future, unsuccessful litigants will be able to challenge unreasonably high uplifts when the court comes to assess costs.

12.4 Unmet legal need

Since the early 1970s, there have been many published research papers and texts which cast doubt on how effectively the legal profession provides for the needs of the whole community. It has been argued that whilst presenting itself as available to give service to everyone on the full range of matters which are capable of being effectively resolved by law, the truth is that lawyers are generally only used by a narrow social group for a narrow range of services. Many problems people suffer which are susceptible of legal resolution are not taken to lawyers for their advice and assistance. The reasons for this appear to be multifarious but are broadly to do with (a) the inaccessibility of lawyers; (b) the failure of sufferers to perceive their problem as something a lawyer could help to solve; (c) the failure of lawyers to market themselves as being able to help with as wide a range of problems as the law could help solve; and (d) financial barriers (real or apparent).

Early American research by Mayhew and Reiss ('The social organisation of legal contacts' (1969) 34 American Sociological Rev 311) surveyed American residents and found that while seven out of 10 had seen a lawyer at least once, and one in four had visited one in the last five years, only 39% had ever sought advice on a matter other than property. They concluded:

> The association between income and legal contacts is in part an organisational effect. The legal profession is organised to serve business and property interests. The social organisation of business and property is highly legalised. Out of this convergence emerges a pattern of citizen contact with attorneys that is heavily orientated to property ...

The results of a mass observation study in England in which the legal experiences of 2,004 people were examined showed similar results to the Detroit study. Eighty one per cent of respondents said they had never come into contact with a solicitor. Of those who did consult solicitors, 45% went about a property matter (see Zander, 'Who goes to solicitors?' (1969) 16 Law Soc Gazette 174, March).

It is appropriate first to consider the nature of a 'legal' problem. The basic premise of pioneering research on this subject is that it is wrong to define as 'legal problems' simply those predicaments which are usually taken to lawyers to solve. Such a definition excludes problems which could be solved by legal means but are not dealt with by lawyers. Solicitors have been criticised for the restricted view they have of their work but there is evidence to suggest that the public has an even narrower perception of the sort of thing a solicitor could help them with than do solicitors themselves (Morris, White and Lewis, 1973). As far as the solicitors themselves are concerned, some of their narrow-minded approaches might be attributable to their legal education. Subjects like welfare law, for example, are only optional and are not widely available to undergraduates. In any event, the subjects which offer more lucrative career paths, like revenue law or company law, have always been more popular than welfare subjects. The Marre Report on the future of the legal profession (*A Time for Change*, 1988) made a specific call for a better response from lawyers to problems involving housing and immigration law.

The largest survey of what lawyers do and for whom was conducted for the Benson Royal Commission on Legal Services (Survey of Users and Non-users of Legal Services in England and Wales, *RCLS*, Vol 2). The sample was based on 2,026 consultations in 1977 which involved 1,770 people out of 7,941 households interviewed. It found that some 15% of adults used a lawyer's service in 1977. It also found that of 27 categories of work used by the survey, just seven accounted for over 80% of all the work taken to solicitors: domestic conveyancing, probate, wills, divorce and matrimonial, motoring and other offences, personal injury cases and property matters. A survey conducted for The Law Society in 1989 confirmed this general pattern.

There has been much debate as to the true significance of these research findings. Do they reflect a restricted public perception of what solicitors deal with or simply a failure to approach solicitors for other reasons like, for example, perceived costs? The Commission found that, during 1977, a solicitor was used by 25% of the professional class, 21% of employers and managers but only 10% of unskilled workers. Michael Zander has argued that the results of the survey demonstrate that the use of lawyers is 'problem connected' even more than it is 'type-of-person connected'. That is that although people from different socio-economic backgrounds use solicitors to a different extent, it is not simply their background that provides the best explanation. In fields of work involving property (for example, conveyancing, probate), those with property use lawyers much more than those who do not. As this is the largest single source of work for the solicitors' profession, it explains why lawyer-use appears to reflect the differences between classes. Zander has argued that this impression is misleading: 'If one looks at non-property types of work, the use of lawyers is relatively even as between members of different socio-economic backgrounds.'

One main reason for people not using solicitors is ignorance that the lawyer could be useful. Genn ('Who claims compensation', in Harris *et al*, *Compensation and Support for Illness and Injury*, 1984) has shown how many people fail to pursue proper claims because their first line of inquiry to another body (for example, employers, police, trade union) gives misleading advice. Apathy in prospective litigants is also a significant factor. The rules permitting solicitors to advertise, made in 1983, and their further relaxation in 1987, will perhaps bring more people into solicitors' offices. This will only help, however, to the extent that the apathy is not as a result of fear of costs. All research on the matter, including that of Genn (1984) and the Marre Committee (1988) has demonstrated that costs have a deterrent effect on seeking legal advice. Widespread ignorance of the legal aid schemes must also be relevant to this point.

The image of lawyers has sometimes been identified as a barrier to a greater range of customers. The Marre Committee (1988) focused on the facts that most solicitors' offices are inaccessible and unwelcoming and they do not cater for many needs like those of linguistic minorities. The results of the most recent population census, published in 1992, show that 5.5% of the population is from ethnic minorities (*Britain 1998*, 1998, Office for National Statistics, p 39) and whilst that figure does not represent those who are not conversant in English, it suggests that there might be a real problem for many people – who are perhaps likely to have problems that lawyers could help to solve. The Law Society survey (1989) found that the image of solicitors amongst the general public is 'good but not outstanding'. Compared with bank managers, accountants, NHS doctors and estate agents, although they were found to be easier to talk to than all the others bar doctors, solicitors were regarded as 'after your money' only less than estate agents. In 1999, it found its image was poor enough in the public eye to warrant spending £60,000 on a public relations exercise to improve the way lawyers are perceived.

In *Rethinking Legal Need: the Case of Criminal Justice* (1991), Paul Robertshaw rejects normative definitions of need, arguing that these rely too heavily on the assumptions of whoever is doing the defining; tend to be lawyer orientated and result in other people's problems being redefined by experts. He also rejects self-defined notions of 'legal need' as it is too uncertain and subject to methodological difficulties. Instead, he uses a concept of comparative need and tries to establish a negative definition of need by comparing outcomes: '... if those in receipt of the [legal] service are not significantly better off than those without them, there can be no need.' He analyses existing research data on the outcomes of legally aided representation and non-legally aided cases and concludes that the general assumption that people assisted by representation need it because they get a better outcome by using it is not proven. There are several problems with such reasoning, as Ed Cape has demonstrated (1994). Basically, Robertshaw equates the provision of legal services with 'representation', whereas in fact representation is only a part of any legal service. If one just measures the outcome of representation as opposed to the whole legal service, the result is likely to be very misleading. A suspect may well need legal advice at a police station, and such advice may well result in the police deciding not to charge the suspect.

12.4.1 Does it matter if such needs remain unmet?

In the Dimbleby Lecture 1992, the late Lord Chief Justice Taylor observed that there may be very serious social problems even resulting in 'unrest' if the law did not become more accessible.

The true extent of unmet need might be less than is apparent simply by asking questionnaire respondents whether they have consulted solicitors about certain matters. This is because people might be making use of other sources of advice, for example, Citizens Advice Bureaux, accountants, building societies, licensed conveyancers, in circumstances where they might otherwise have consulted lawyers.

The greater the level of unmet need the worse the social implications. It is, though, notoriously difficult to ascertain the extent of the unmet need. Similar problems affect different people to different degrees. When does a person *need* legal advice? The pioneering research by Abel-Smith, Zander and Brooke adopted a partly subjective test of 'need'. They used a test of what would constitute 'a risk of substantial loss or disadvantage which would be important for the individual concerned'. This standard differed for each category of problem. Zander, writing five years later, acknowledged that these tests for need were highly artificial.

On the whole, poor people use lawyers much less than do rich people. Although, as Zander has argued, the current picture of unmet need has come from researchers who have concentrated on the poor, not the whole population; and Genn has found that people from the higher socio-economic groups are less likely to make a claim consequent upon personal injury (Genn, 1984), it is not difficult to see that the poor are legally disadvantaged by their lack of legal awareness, influence and resources like energy and time.

12.4.2 Law Centres

There are 52 Law Centres in England and Wales, staffed by salaried solicitors, trainee solicitors and non-lawyer experts in other areas like debt management. They are funded by local and central government and charity. They have 'shop front' access and aim to be user-friendly and unintimidating. They are managed by committees and represented by the Law Centres Federation. The report of the Rushcliffe Committee on Legal Aid and Advice (1945) had recommended a nationwide network of State salaried lawyers providing advice for a low, fixed fee. There was provision in the Legal Aid and Advice Act 1949 for this but it was never implemented. The first centre was established in England in North Kensington in July 1970 in the face of great opposition from The Law Society. Since then, the Society has developed a more tolerant stance to the centres as it acknowledges that they can confer benefits to local law firms through the referrals of clients.

Law Centres take on individual cases, providing, for example, advice on landlord and tenant matters and representing people at tribunals. Some centres also take on group work since quite often the problems of one client are part of a wider problem. This sort of work is controversial.

How far is it correct for lawyers to become involved in socio-legal problems in an effort to combat the disadvantages of the poor? In 1974, in a collective statement of purpose, the Law Centres supported American statements such as one which claimed that effective solution of the problems of the poor may require the lawyer '… to direct his attention away from the particular claim or grievance to the broader interests and policies at stake …'. Such campaigns could deal, for example, with slum clearance or matters concerning roads and pavements. The Benson Commission rejected this sort of work for its proposed Citizens' Law Centres (CLCs), taking the view that community action tends to involve only one section of the community and that the independence of a centre can be compromised if it becomes a base for campaigns.

The commission's proposed CLCs seemed to be an attempt to win back for private practitioners the large number of clients who were being assisted by Law Centres, as the CLCs would have been operated under the control of The Law Society and Bar Council and users would pay on the same basis as legally aided clients of private practitioners. This would have increased the burden on the legal aid fund, though, when the government was keen to make retrenchments, so the proposal was rejected.

12.4.3 Other voluntary advice

There are now 709 Citizens Advice Bureaux with 1,313 outlets in total. They deal with a high number of cases (over six million a year) and a very wide range of problems of which between one third and one half are legal problems. There are, however, very few trained lawyers working for the bureaux.

The Bar Council supports a Free Representation Unit for clients at a variety of tribunals for which legal aid is not available. Most of the representation is carried out by Bar students supported and advised by full time case workers. A special Bar unit based in London was formed in 1996 through which more senior barristers provide representation.

Some colleges and universities also offer advice. For example, The College of Law in London operates a free advice service in which vocational students give advice on such matters as personal injury cases and employment law.

12.5 Conditional fee arrangements

As part of the scheme to expose the provision of legal services to the full rigour of market forces, the then Lord Chancellor chose to devote an entire Green Paper in 1989 to *Contingency Fees*. Following a recommendation from the Civil Justice Review, the paper had sought opinion on the funding of litigation on a contingent fee basis. This provides that litigation is funded by the claimant only if he or she wins, in which event the lawyer claims fees as a portion of the damages payable to the claimant. The response to this idea was largely hostile although there was a reasonable support for a system based on the Scottish model of the 'speculative fee' whereby the solicitor can agree with his client that he would be paid his ordinary taxed costs only if he won the case. Section 58 of the Courts and Legal Services Act (CLSA) 1990 permitted the Lord Chancellor to introduce conditional fee arrangements, although these cannot apply to criminal cases, family cases or those involving children (s 58(10)). Conditional fees can be based on an 'uplift' from the level of fee the lawyer would normally charge for the sort of work in question. Originally, the maximum uplift was to be 20% in order to induce lawyers to take on potentially difficult cases and to help finance the lawyers' unsuccessful conditional fee cases. This would have meant they could charge the fee that they would normally charge for a given type of case, plus an additional fifth.

In August 1993, after a long process of negotiation with the profession, Lord Mackay, the then Lord Chancellor, finally announced that he would allow the conditional fee to operate on a 100% uplift. Thus, solicitors receive no fee if they lose a case but double what they would normally charge if they win the case. The Law Society had campaigned vigorously against the proposed 20% uplift, arguing that such risks as the no-win, no-fee arrangement entailed would not be regarded as worth taking by many solicitors simply on the incentive that their fee for winning the case would be 20% more than they would normally charge for such a case. The Lord Chancellor's Department originally decided to restrict the scheme to cases involving personal injury, insolvency and the European Court of Human Rights.

The system came into effect in June 1995. Such agreements are legal now, provided that they comply with any requirements imposed by the Lord Chancellor and are not 'contentious business agreements'. These are defined under s 59 of the Solicitors Act 1974 as agreements between a solicitor and his client made in writing by which the solicitor is to be remunerated by a gross sum, or a salary, at agreed hourly rates or otherwise, and whether higher or lower than that at which he would normally be remunerated.

The traditional opposition to contingency fees in the English legal system was that they were 'maintenance' (the financial support of another's litigation) and 'champerty' (taking a financial interest in another's litigation). Champerty occurs when the person maintaining another takes as his reward a portion of the property in dispute. It taints an agreement with illegality and renders it void (for a recent discussion of the principle, see *Grovewood Holding plc v James Capel & Co Ltd* (1995)). Section 14 of the Criminal Justice Act 1967 abolished maintenance and champerty as crimes and torts but kept the rules making such arrangements improper for solicitors.

English litigation uses the Indemnity Rule by which the loser pays the costs of the winner and thus puts him, more or less, in the position he enjoyed before the damage was done. Objectors to contingency fee agreements pointed out that such things were incompatible with the Indemnity Rule because although the winner's costs would be paid for him by the other side, he would still have to pay for his lawyer from his damages (calculated to put him in the position he would have enjoyed if no wrong had been done to him) so he would not really be 'made whole' by his award. The position is different in the United States where contingency agreements are common in personal injury cases because there each side bears his own costs.

It was further contended by objectors to the contingency fee that the legal aid system adequately catered for those who were too poor to afford an ordinary private action. Even if there were people who were just above the legal aid financial thresholds, but still too poor to pay for an action, this should be dealt with simply by changing the threshold.

The Green Paper indicated that the government favoured some form of deregulation. Two forms of contingency fee were rejected during the consultation period as being unsuitable. The first was a restricted contingency fee system in which the fee payable in the event of a successful action would be a *percentage of the damages* but where the actual levels of recovery would be governed by rules. The second was an unrestricted contingency arrangement, similarly based on a percentage of damages, but at uncontrolled levels. These plans were rejected because it was thought that to give the lawyer a stake in the claimant's damages would be likely to create an unacceptable degree of conflict of interests.

12.5.1 The Conditional Fees Order 1998

The right to use 'no-win, no-fee' agreements to pursue civil law claims was extended by the Conditional Fees Order 1998 which came into effect on 30 July.

The Order allows lawyers to offer conditional fee agreements to their clients in all civil cases excluding family cases. Speaking in the House of Lords on 23 July, the Lord Chancellor, Lord Irvine, said:

> These agreements will result in a huge expansion of access to justice. Today, only the very rich or the very poor can afford to litigate. In future, everyone with a really strong case will be able to secure his rights free of the fear of ruin if he loses. They will bring the majority of our people into access to justice.

Conditional fees have been the means by which at least 45,000 personal injury cases have been brought, and many, in all likelihood, would not have been brought but for the existence of conditional fees. The new Order retains the old rule that the maximum uplift on the fees lawyers can charge is 100%, that is, a lawyer may take on an action against an allegedly negligent employer whose carelessness has resulted in the client being injured. The lawyer, who might normally charge £2,000 for such a case, can say 'I shall do this work for nothing if we lose, but £3,000 if we win'. In fact, as the price uplift can be up to 100% of the normal fee, he or she can stipulate for up to £4,000 in this example. The Law Society has recommended an additional voluntary cap of 25% of damages, and this has been widely accepted in practice over the last two years.

The real problems here continue to be:

(a) that the new system, designed really to help the millions who have been regulated out of the legal aid system, does not help people whose cases stand only a limited chance of success – as lawyers will not take their cases; and

(b) the difficulties of a claimant getting insurance to cover the costs that he will have to pay, if he loses the action, for the other side's lawyers. Where a personal injury action arises from a road traffic incident, it is almost always clear to a solicitor where blame and legal liability probably lie. Risks are therefore calculable by insurance companies so one can presently insure against having to pay the other side's costs in the event of losing an action on an insolvency case for about £100 in a 'no-win, no-fee' arrangement. There are, however, many areas, and medical negligence cases are good examples, where the chances of success are notoriously difficult to predict. Thus, insurance against having to pay the other side's costs is prohibitively high, running into many thousands of pounds in some cases. It is quite unrealistic to assume that all such cases arising often from highly distressing circumstances, will be dealt with in future on a 'no-win, no-fee' basis. Lawyers will generally not want to take on such cases on such a basis, and, even where they do, clients will often not be able to afford the necessary insurance. As insurance to cover client costs in medical 'no-win, no-fee' cases has proven so expensive, the government has decided for the time being not to end legal aid for such cases.

In its response to the 1998 Lord Chancellor's consultation paper *Access to Justice with Conditional Fees*, The Law Society made several interesting points. The Lord Chancellor had proposed that insurance premiums supporting conditional fee arrangements should be recoverable between the parties. The Legal Aid Board was in favour of this change. It said in its response document (para 2.7) that 'this would make conditional fee agreements more viable and more attractive for clients and lawyers without unduly penalising opponents.'

There is, though, still a risk of a 'perverse incentive' operating – defendants with meritorious defences might end up paying higher premiums than those with no real defence. This is because an insurance company backing a defendant with a good defence will realise that the case will last longer than one where the defendant only has a mediocre defence. If the defendant then loses after a long case, he or she will have a bigger bill to pay for the other side's costs than in a shorter case. This leads to the paradox that the stronger the case you have as a defendant, the higher the premium you will have to pay, as your case will last longer. Weak defendants get defeated early on in proceedings. If a losing defendant has to pay not only the other side's lawyer's fee but also the other side's insurance premium, the paradox above is worsened because a strong defendant will mean that a claimant's premium will be high, and if the claimant's premium is high, and the defendant might end up having to cover that cost if he loses, then the defendant's premium will also be raised!

'Pursuit' is the name of a legal expenses insurance policy offered by the Royal Sun Alliance. Under the policy, the premium is only paid if the case is won although there is a £200 non-refundable assessment fee. The government has endorsed this policy although The Law Society and the Bar have been more reserved. The Law Society Vice President, Robert Sayer, said: 'No insurance product, this included, will provide a solution to the removal of legal aid' ((1999) Law Soc Gazette 12, 24 March).

12.5.2 The advantages

For claimants, the advantages can be summarised as being:

- that lawyers acting in any case will be confident (they will have had to weigh carefully the chances of success before taking the case as their fee depends on winning) and determined;
- there will be freedom from the anxiety of having to pay huge fees;
- there will be no need to pay fees in advance; and
- there will be no delays or worries with legal aid applications.

For defendants, there will be advantages too as the contingency fee system will probably reduce the number of spurious claims. In a period where legal aid is being cut-back so drastically, preventing so many people from going to law, this system can be seen as a way of preserving at least some limited access to the legal process. Losing parties will still be liable to pay the other side's costs, so it will be unlikely that people will take action unless they consider they have a good chance of success.

The taxpayer can also be given the advantage in the form of a significant reduction in the funding of the legal aid system. Furthermore, practitioners who are competent to assess and willing to take the risks of litigation, will arguably enjoy a better fee-paying basis, increased fee income and overall business, fewer reasons for delay and more satisfied clients with fewer complaints.

Consider two examples. A middle class couple consult their solicitor about injuries received in a road accident. Their joint income and savings puts them outside the legal aid scheme. The proposed litigation is beset with uncertainties as the other driver's insurers have denied liability. The couple have to worry about their own expenses and the possibility under the Indemnity Rule of paying for the defendant's costs. Again, a young man has been injured at work wants to sue his employer. The case will turn on some difficult health and safety law on which there are currently conflicting decisions. He is eligible for legal aid but he will have to make substantial contributions because of his level of income and if his claim fails he will have to pay the same sum again towards the expenses of his employers. In both cases, the prospective litigants might well drop any plan to litigate. Both cases, however, might proceed expeditiously if they could find a lawyer to act on a no-win, no-fee basis.

12.5.3 The disadvantages

Critics of the system argue that it encourages the sort of speculative actions that occur frequently in the United States, taken up by the so called 'ambulance chasing' lawyers. It can be argued that the system of contingency fees creates a conflict of interest between the lay client and the lawyer, with a consequential risk of exploitation of the client. Where a lawyer's fee depends on the outcome of a case, there is a greater temptation for him or her to act unethically. When the Royal Commission on Legal Services (1979) rejected the idea of contingent fees, it stated that such a scheme might lead to undesirable practices by lawyers including '... the construction of evidence, the improper coaching of witnesses, the use of professionally partisan expert witnesses, especially medical witnesses, improper examination and cross-examination, groundless legal arguments designed to lead the courts into error and competitive touting'. If the case was won, the lawyer claimed a significant part of the damages, but there was also a real danger that lawyers would be pressured to settle too readily to avoid the costs of preparing for a trial that could be lost and therewith the fee. An example would be where an insurance company admits liability but contests the level of damages. The claimant might stand to get substantially higher compensation by contesting the case. Under the new system, however, his solicitor will have a strong interest in advising him to settle. A settlement would guarantee the solicitor's costs and the agreed 'mark up' (up to 100% more than a normal fee for such work), both of which would be completely lost if the case was fought and lost. This would not occur outside of a conditional fee arrangement. Although the conventional system of payment was not without problems, as Walter Merricks, then of The Law Society, has stated:

> ... when a lawyer is being paid by the hour, he may have a financial interest in encouraging his client to go on with an open-and-shut case, increasing his own fees.

The Law Society has argued that the system, if not properly regulated, could promote some of the 'ambulance chasing' like that of American lawyers in the wake of the 1984 Bhopal disaster in which over 2,500 people were killed by escaping gas from a UCC plant in India. American lawyers flew out to act for victims and their relatives and some were reported to be taking fees of 50% of the claimant's damages.

It was argued by some that, by allowing lawyers to *double* their normal fee for certain cases, the Lord Chancellor risked eliminating any benefit speculative fees may bring. If the successful client was not be able to recover the *uplift* from the other side, he would have to fund it himself out of the damages he was been awarded. In effect, this often resulted in his damages being halved. The uplift can now be recovered, subject to taxation (that is, court official approval), following changes made by the Access to Justice Act 1999.

It is not even clear that the main claim made for the system – that it increases access to the courts – is correct. The Scottish experience is that speculative cases do not exceed 1% of the cases in the caseload of the Faculty of Advocates. One firm opponent of the system is Mr Justice Auld. He has argued that the system will eventually endanger the esteem in which lawyers are held by the public. He has doubted whether the scheme will produce greater commitment by lawyers to their cases: 'There is a distinction to be drawn between the lawyer's commitment to the case and his anxiety to recover his fees. The two do not always correspond.'

Opinion within the legal profession about the desirability of the changes is mixed. A useful juxtaposition of opposite views (those of George Pulman QC and Michael Napier) appear in the *Law Society Gazette* ((1995) 92/16 at 1626).

12.5.4 The English system – recent changes

The only major study of the conditional fee system (Yarrow, 1997), commissioned by the Lord Chancellor's Advisory Committee on Legal Education and Conduct, assessed how widely, and in what ways, conditional fees were being used. The research was based on a survey of 120 firms of solicitors and an analysis of 197 conditional fee cases begun in the personal injury field. The research found evidence of considerable inconsistency in the size of the 'success fee' calculated for cases with similar chances of success. Moreover, the fee appeared to be too high in up to six cases in 10 which had 'very good' chances of winning.

Yarrow found that a surprisingly high proportion of cases were regarded as having relatively low chances of success, given that personal injury cases usually have an extremely high success rate. This could indicate that some solicitors could be over estimating the chances of failure and, therefore, charging a higher 'success fee'. Yarrow concludes that such concerns could cast doubt over the entire scheme. Overall, the average 'success fee' charged by solicitors was 43% but, for one in 10 cases, it was close to the maximum of 100%. However, the voluntary 25% cap on the proportion of damages that can be swallowed up by the 'success fee', recommended by The Law Society, is used by almost all solicitors.

Since the introduction of conditional fees, the common law has been developed in two recent decisions by the courts (in *Thai Trading Co (A Firm) v Taylor* (1998) and *Bevan Ashford v Geoff Yeandle (Contractors) Ltd* (1998)). In the first of these cases, the Court of Appeal held that there were no longer public policy grounds to prevent lawyers agreeing to work for less than their normal fees in the event that they were unsuccessful, provided they did not seek to recover more than their normal fees if they were successful. (The latter was only permissible in those proceedings in which conditional fee agreements were allowed.) In *Bevan Ashford*, the Vice Chancellor held that it was also lawful for a conditional fee agreement to apply in a case which was to be resolved by arbitration (under the Arbitration Act 1950), even though these were not court proceedings, provided all the requirements specified by regulations as to the form and content of the agreement were complied with.

There are also available insurance policies which can be taken out when someone is contemplating litigation to cover the costs of the other party and the client's own costs (including, if not a conditional fee case, the client's solicitor's fees) if the case is lost. Some of them were developed to support the use of conditional fee agreements but others are used to meet lawyers' fees charged in the more traditional way. For the same reason that the success fee under a conditional fee is being made recoverable, it is also proposed to make any premium paid for protective insurance recoverable too. The principles behind the government's desire to see an expansion in the use of conditional fee arrangements were set out in a consultation paper, *Access to Justice with Conditional Fees*, Lord Chancellor's Department, March 1998.

The Access to Justice Act 1999 further reforms the law on conditional fees (see 12.3.5) to allow the courts to order that a successful litigant should recover the success fee payable under the conditional fee arrangement from the losing party. Section 27 of the 1999 Act does this by inserting a new s 58A(7) into the CLSA 1990. By s 27, the 1999 Act also allows the cost of any insurance against the risk of losing the case to be recovered in the same way, and it makes it easier, by s 28, for membership organisations, such as trade unions or motoring organisations, to underwrite litigation on behalf of their members. These changes are likely to make the conditional fee arrangement a more attractive and practicable option for many prospective claimants.

THE FUNDING OF LEGAL SERVICES

Legal aid

The scheme prior to the Access to Justice Act 1999 was contained in the Legal Aid Act 1988. A common feature of the civil and criminal legal aid schemes was that expenditure on them was demand-led. Any lawyer could do legal aid work for a client who passed the relevant means test (if any), and whose case passed the statutory merits test (in the case of civil legal aid), or the interests of justice test (in the case of criminal legal aid). Lawyers were (and will continue to be under the transitional arrangements) paid on a case by case basis for each individual case or other act of assistance, usually at rates or fees set in regulations, but, in some cases, on the same basis as a privately funded lawyer.

This, in the government's view, meant that there were few mechanisms or incentives for promoting value for money or assuring the quality of the services provided.

The Access to Justice Act 1999

The Act replaces the legal aid system with two new schemes, and makes provisions about rights to supply legal services, appeals, and court procedure, magistrates and magistrates' courts.

The provisions in the Act form part of the wide ranging programme of reforms to legal services and the courts, described in the government's White Paper, *Modernising Justice*, published in 1998.

Funding of legal services

The 1999 Act provides for two new schemes, replacing the legal aid scheme, to secure the provision of publicly funded legal services for people who need them. It establishes a Legal Services Commission to run the two schemes and enables the Lord Chancellor to give the Commission orders, directions and guidance about how it should exercise its functions.

It requires the Commission to establish, maintain and develop a Community Legal Service. A new Community Legal Service fund will replace the legal aid fund in civil and family cases. The Commission will use the resources of the fund, in a way that reflects priorities set by the Lord Chancellor and its duty to secure the best possible value for money, to procure or provide a range of legal services. The Commission will also have a duty to liaise with other funders of legal services to facilitate the developments of co-ordinated plans for making the best use of all available resources. The intention is to develop a network of legal service providers of assured quality, offering the widest possible access to information and advice about the law, and assistance with legal problems.

The Commission will also be responsible for running the Criminal Defence Service, which replaces the current legal aid scheme in criminal cases. The new scheme is intended to ensure that people suspected or accused of a crime are properly represented, while securing better value for money than is possible under the legal aid scheme.

The Legal Services Commission

The 1999 Act establishes the new Legal Services Commission and makes provision for appointments to it. The Commission will replace the Legal Aid Board. It was considered necessary to establish a new body to reflect the fundamentally different nature of the Community Legal Service (CLS) compared to civil legal aid. Within the broad framework of priorities set by the Lord Chancellor, the Commission will be responsible for taking detailed decisions about the allocation of resources.

The Community Legal Service

The Legal Services Commission will have two main duties in respect of the CLS.

First, it will manage a CLS fund, which will replace legal aid in civil and family cases. The CLS fund will be used to secure the provision of appropriate legal services, within the resources made available to it, and according to priorities set by the Lord Chancellor and by regional and local assessments of need. A Funding Code, drawn up by the Commission and approved by the Lord Chancellor, will set out the criteria and procedures for deciding whether to fund individual cases.

Secondly, as part of a wider CLS, the Commission will, in co-operation with local funders and interested bodies, develop local, regional and national plans to match the delivery of legal services to identified needs and priorities.

Overall, the intention is to:

- make best use of all the resources available for funding legal services, by facilitating a co-ordinated approach to planning;

- improve value for money through contracting and the development of quality assurance systems.

The Access to Justice Act 1999 describes the services which may be provided under the CLS. These range from the provision of basic information about the law and legal services, to providing help towards preventing or resolving disputes and enforcing decisions which have been reached. The scheme will encompasses advice, assistance and representation by lawyers (which have long been available under the legal aid scheme) and also the services of non-lawyers. It will extend to other types of service, including, for example, mediation in family or civil cases where appropriate.

This sets out the ways in which the Commission may use the CLS fund to provide services. These include making contracts with or grants to service providers, or employing staff to provide services directly to the public. These flexible powers are intended to give effect to one of the principal objectives of the reform of publicly funded legal services, that is, the ability to tailor the provision of services, and the means by which services are to be delivered to the needs of local populations and particular circumstances. They will also allow the Commission to test new forms of service provision through pilot projects.

In future, subject to any exceptions that the Lord Chancellor may make by direction, only basic information and advice will be available for:

- disputes involving allegations of negligent damage to property or the person ('personal injury'), apart from those about clinical negligence. These cases are generally considered suitable for conditional fees;

- allegations of defamation or malicious falsehood. Generally, legal aid is not currently available for representation in defamation, but it is sometimes possible to get legal aid by categorising the case as one of malicious falsehood. The government's view is that these cases do not command sufficient priority to justify public funding and, in any event, they may often be suitable for a conditional fee.

The 1999 Act allows the Lord Chancellor, using regulations, to set financial eligibility limits for people to receive services funded by the CLS fund. It allows him to set different conditions, or no conditions, for different circumstances or types of case or service.

The funding assessment under the Code will replace the merits test for civil legal aid The new assessment is intended to be more flexible than the existing merits test. It will be possible to apply different criteria in different categories according to their priority.

The Code is required to reflect the principle that, in many family disputes, mediation is more appropriate than court proceedings. This is intended to reinforce the development, under the Family Law Act 1996, of mediation as a means of resolving private law family disputes in a way that promotes as good a continuing relationship between the parties concerned as is possible in the circumstances.

The 1999 Act extends the potential scope of financial conditions in two ways, although there are no immediate plans to use either of these powers:

- it will be possible to make the provision of services in some types of cases subject to the assisted person agreeing to repay an amount in excess of the cost of the services provided in the event that their case is successful. This might make it possible to fund certain types of case on a self-financing basis, with the additional payments from successful litigants applied to meet the cost of unsuccessful cases;

- it will be possible to require the assisted person to repay, over time and with interest, the full cost of the service provided (for example, through continuing contributions from income). This will make it possible to provide services in some categories of case in the form of a loan scheme.

The Act establishes limits on the liability of the person receiving funded services to pay costs to the unassisted party.

The Criminal Defence Service

The purpose of the Criminal Defence Service (CDS) is to secure the provision of advice, assistance and representation, according to the interests of justice, to people suspected of a criminal offence or facing criminal proceedings.

The Commission will be empowered to secure these services through contracts with lawyers in private practice, or by providing them through salaried defenders, employed by non-profit making organisations. This will necessarily mean that suspects' and defendants' choice of representative is limited to contracted or salaried defenders, although the intention is to maintain an element of choice in all but exceptional cases.

There will be a transitional period while contracts are developed and extended to cover the full range of services. The Commission will therefore be able to pay lawyers on a case by case basis for representation provided on a non-contractual basis, according to remuneration scales set in regulations.

The Access to Justice Act 1999 places a duty on the Commission to fund representation for individuals granted a right to representation. It enables the Commission to comply with this duty in the same ways as for advice and assistance. The power to make direct case by case payments to representatives will allow the Commission to continue to pay non-contracted lawyers to provide representation during the transitional period while contracting develops and, possibly, thereafter where that proves to be the best means of securing the necessary services.

Conditional fees

The Act reforms the law relating to conditional fees to enable the court to order a losing party to pay, in addition to the other party's normal legal costs, the uplift on the successful party's lawyers' fees and, in any case where a litigant has insured facing an order for the other side's costs, any premium paid by the successful party for that insurance. The intention is to ensure that the compensation awarded to a successful party is not eroded by any uplift or premium. The party in the wrong will bear the full burden of costs. It is also the intention to make conditional fees more attractive, in particular, to defendants and to claimants seeking non-monetary redress.

CHAPTER 13

THE EUROPEAN CONTEXT

13.1 Introduction

As was stated in Chapter 2, it is unrealistic and, indeed, impossible for any student of English law and the English legal system, to ignore the UK's membership of the European Union and European Communities. Nor can the impact of the European Court of Human Rights be ignored, especially now that the Human Rights Act 1998 has made the Articles of the European Convention on Human Rights directly applicable in the UK. However, it has to be recognised that placing the English legal system in its European context does make some demands on the individual. For one thing, although the Treaty on European Union 1992 (the Maastricht Treaty) established the Union of its title, it did not dissolve its constituent communities which therefore continue in existence, distinct from that Union. There are said to be three pillars to the European Union:

(a) European Community consisting of not only its treaties but wider aspects relating to citizenship and, indeed, economic and monetary union;

(b) common foreign and security policy;

(b) home affairs and justice.

It is particularly important to note, however, that the European Union does not share the same legal institutional form as the European Community and that it is, therefore, still appropriate to talk about Community law rather than Union law.

It is also essential to distinguish between the two different courts that operate within the European context: the European Court of Justice, which is the court of the European Community, sitting in Luxembourg; and the European Court of Human Rights, which deals with cases relating to the European Convention on Human Rights and sits in Strasbourg.

The long term process leading to the, as yet still to be attained, establishment of an integrated European Community was a response to two factors: the disasters of the Second World War; and the emergence of the Soviet Bloc in Eastern Europe. The aim was to link the separate European countries, particularly France and Germany, together in such a manner as to prevent the outbreak of future armed hostilities. The first step in this process was the establishment a European Coal and Steel Community. The next step towards integration was the formation of the European Economic Community under the Treaty of Rome in 1957. The UK joined the EEC in 1973. The Treaty of Rome has subsequently been amended in the further pursuit of integration as the Community has expanded. Thus, the Single European Act (SEA) 1986 established a single economic market within the European Community and widened the use of majority voting in the Council of Ministers. The Maastricht Treaty further accelerated the move towards a federal European supranational State in the extent to which it recognised Europe as a social and political – as well as an economic – community. Previous Conservative governments of the UK have resisted the emergence of the European Union as anything other than an economic market and have objected to, and resiled from, various provisions aimed at social as opposed to economic affairs. Thus, the UK was able to opt out of the Social Chapter of the Treaty of Maastricht. The present Labour administration in the UK has had no such reservations and, as a consequence, the Treaty of Amsterdam 1997 incorporated the European Social Charter into the EC Treaty which, of course, applies to the UK. One of the consequences of the Amsterdam Treaty was a renumbering of all the Articles in the various EC Treaties. This book will adopt the new numbering, but list the old numbers in brackets.

As the establishment of the single market within the European Community progressed, it was suggested that its operation would be greatly facilitated by the adoption of a common currency, or at least a more closely integrated monetary system. Thus, in 1979, the European Monetary System (EMS) was established, under which individual national currencies were valued against a nominal currency called the ECU and allocated a fixed rate within which they were allowed to fluctuate to a limited extent. Britain was a member of the EMS until 1992, when financial speculation against the pound forced its withdrawal. Nonetheless, other members of the EC continued to pursue the policy of monetary union, now entitled European Monetary Union (EMU) and January 1999 saw the installation of the new European currency, the Euro, against which all currencies within the scheme are allocated fixed values. Thereafter, the newly created European Central Bank will oversee the replacement of national currencies by the Euro. The UK did not join the EMU at its inception and the question as to whether or not it should join is one of the most pressing of current political issues.

The general aim of the EU is set out in Art 2 (number unchanged) of the Treaty of Rome, as amended by the Maastricht Treaty, as follows:

> The Community shall have as its task, by establishing a common market and an economic and monetary union and by implementing the common policies or activities referred to in Article 3, to promote throughout the Community a harmonious and balanced development of economic activities, sustainable and non-inflationary growth respecting the environment, a high degree of convergence of economic performance, a high level of employment and of social protection, the raising of the standard of living and quality of life, and economic and social cohesion and solidarity among Member States.

Amongst the policies originally detailed in Art 3 (number unchanged) were included:

- the elimination, between Member States, of custom duties and of quantitative restrictions on the import and export of goods;

- the establishment of a common custom tariff and a common commercial policy towards third countries;

- the abolition, between Member States, of obstacles to the freedom of movement for persons, services and capital;

- the adoption of a common agricultural policy;

- the adoption of a common transport policy;

- the harmonisation of laws of Member States to the extent required to facilitate the proper functioning of the single market;

- the creation of a European Social Fund in order to improve the employment opportunities of workers in the community and to improve their standard of living.

Article 3 has subsequently been extended to cover more social, as opposed to purely economic, matters and now incorporates policies relating to education, health, consumer protection, the environment and culture generally. In 1989, the Community adopted a Charter of Fundamental Social Rights of Workers, although the UK Government under the leadership of the then Prime Minister, Margaret Thatcher, declined to sign it, seeing it as representing an unacceptable interference in the free operation of the market. The Treaty on European Union, the Maastricht Treaty, had originally contained a 'Social Chapter', based on the earlier Social Charter, and designed to further the 'promotion of employment, improved living and working conditions, proper social protection, dialogue between management and labour, the development of human resources with a view to lasting high employment and the combating of exclusion'. Once again, the UK Government, this time under the leadership of John Major, refused to accede to such provisions, and, in order to save the rest of the Treaty, the Social Chapter had to be removed and appended as a protocol binding on the then other 11 Members of the Community but not the UK. It is of perhaps signal importance that one of the very first measures taken by the new Labour administration, led by Prime Minister Tony Blair, was to declare its intention to sign up to the Social Chapter.

Consequent upon the agreement of the UK Government, the Treaty of Amsterdam 1997 was able to incorporate the European Social Charter into the EC Treaty.

Article 10 (formerly, Art 5) requires:

Member States to take all appropriate measures, whether general or particular, to ensure fulfilment of the obligations arising out of this Treaty or resulting from action taken by the institutions of the Community. They shall facilitate the achievement of the Community's tasks. They shall abstain from any measure which could jeopardise the attainment of the objectives of this Treaty.

This Article effectively means that UK courts are now Community law courts and must be bound by, and give effect to, that law where it is operative. The reasons for the national courts acting in this manners are considered by John Temple Lang, Director in the Competition Directorate General, in an article entitled 'The duties of national courts under Community constitutional law' ([1997] EL Rev 22). As he writes:

> National courts are needed to give companies and individuals remedies which are as prompt, as complete and as immediate as the combined legal system of the Community and of Member States can provide. Only national courts can give injunctions against private parties for breach of Community law rules on, for example, equal pay for men and women, or on restrictive practices. Private parties have no standing to claim injunctions in the Court of Justice against a Member State, they can do so only in a national court. In other words, only a national court could give remedies to individuals and companies for breach of Community law which are as effective as the remedies for breach of national law.

Before the UK joined the EU, its law was just as foreign as law made under any other jurisdiction. On joining the EU, however, the UK and its citizens accepted, and became subject to, European Community law. This subjection to European law remains the case even where the parties to any transaction are themselves both UK subjects. In other words, in areas where it is applicable, European law supersedes any existing UK law to the contrary.

An example of European Community law invalidating the operation of UK legislation can be found in the *Factortame* case. The Common Fishing Policy established by the EEC had placed limits on the amount of fish that any member country's fishing fleet was permitted to catch. In order to gain access to British fish stocks and quotas, Spanish fishing boat owners formed British companies and re-registered their boats as British. In order to prevent what it saw as an abuse and an encroachment on the rights of indigenous fishermen, the British Government introduced the Merchant Shipping Act 1988, which provided that any fishing company seeking to register as British would have to have its principal place of business in the UK and at least 75% of its shareholders would have to be British nationals. This effectively debarred the Spanish boats from taking up any of the British fishing quota. Some 95 Spanish boat owners applied to the British courts for judicial review of the Merchant Shipping Act 1988 on the basis that it was contrary to Community law. The case went from the High Court, through the Court of Appeal, to the House of Lords who referred the case to the European Court of Justice (ECJ). There, it was decided that the Treaty of Rome required domestic courts to give effect to the directly enforceable provisions of Community law and, in doing so, such courts are required to ignore any national law that runs counter to Community law. The decision gave rise to some heated responses in the UK where it was attacked on the basis that it effectively undermined parliamentary sovereignty.

13.2   Sources of European Community law

Community law, depending on its nature and source, may have direct effect on the domestic laws of its various members; that is, it may be open to individuals to rely on it, without the need for their particular State to have enacted the law within its own legal system (see *Factortame*).

There are two types of direct effect. Vertical direct effect means that the individual can rely on EC law in any action in relation to their government, but cannot use it against other individuals. Horizontal direct effect allows the individual to use the EC provision in an action against other individuals. Other EC provisions only take effect when they have been specifically enacted within the various legal systems within the Community.

The sources of Community law are fourfold:

- internal treaties and protocols;
- international agreements;
- secondary legislation;
- decisions of the ECJ.

13.2.1   Internal treaties

Internal treaties govern the Member States of the EU and anything contained therein supersedes domestic legal provisions. The primary treaty is the Treaty of Rome as amended by such legislation as the SEA 1986; or the Maastricht Treaty on European Union and the Amsterdam Treaty. Upon its joining the Community, the Treaty of Rome was incorporated into UK law by the European Communities Act 1972.

As long as treaties are of a mandatory nature and are stated with sufficient clarity and precision, then they have both vertical and horizontal effect (*Van Gend en Loos* (1963)).

13.2.2   International treaties

International treaties are negotiated with other nations by the European Commission on behalf of the EU as a whole and are binding on the individual members of the EU.

13.2.3 Secondary legislation

Secondary legislation is provided for under Art 249 (formerly, Art 189) of the Treaty of Rome. It provides for three types of legislation to be introduced by the European Council and Commission. These are:

- *Regulations* apply to, and within, Member States generally without the need for those States to pass their own legislation. They are binding and enforceable from the time of their creation and individual States do not have to pass any legislation to give effect to regulations. Regulations must be published in the *Official Journal* of the EU. The decision as to whether or not a law should be enacted in the form of a regulation is usually left to the Commission, but there are areas where the Treaty of Rome requires that the regulation form must be used. These areas relate to: the rights of workers to remain in Member States of which they are not nationals; the provision of State aid to particular indigenous undertakings or industries; the regulation of EU accounts and budgetary procedures.

- *Directives*, on the other hand, state general goals and leave the precise implementation in the appropriate form to the individual Member States. Directives, however, tend to state the means as well as the ends to which they are aimed and the ECJ will give direct effect to directives which are sufficiently clear and complete. See *Van Duyn v Home Office* (1974). Directives usually provide Member States with a time limit within which they are required to implement the provision within their own national laws. If they fail to do so or implement the directive incompletely, then individuals may be able to cite, and rely on, the directive in their dealings with the State in question. Further, *Francovich v Italy* (1991) has established that individuals who have suffered as a consequence of a Member State's failure to implement Community law may seek damages against that State.

  The provisions in the Unfair Terms in Consumer Contracts Regulations 1994 is an example of UK law being introduced in response to EU directives.

- *Decisions* on the operation of European laws and policies are not intended to have general effect but are aimed at particular States or individuals. They have the force of law under Art 249 (formerly, Art 189).

- Additionally, Art 211 (formerly, Art 155) provides for the Commission to issue recommendations and opinions in relation to the operation of Community law. These have no binding force although they may be taken into account in trying to clarify any ambiguities in domestic law.

13.2.4 Judgments of the European Court of Justice

The ECJ is the judicial arm of the EU and, in the field of Community law, its judgments overrule those of national courts. Under Art 234 (formerly, Art 177), national courts have the right to apply to the ECJ for a preliminary ruling on a point of Community law before deciding a case.

The mechanism through which Community law becomes immediately and directly effective in the UK is provided by s 2(1) of the European Communities Act 1972. Section 2(2) gives power to designated ministers or departments to introduce Orders in Council to give effect to other non-directly effective Community law.

13.3 The institutions of the European Union

The major institutions of the EU are: the Council of Ministers; the European Parliament; the European Commission; the ECJ.

13.3.1 The Council of Ministers

The Council is made up of ministerial representatives of each of the 15 Member States of the EU. The actual composition of the Council varies depending on the nature of the matter to be considered. When considering economic matters, the various States will be represented by their finance ministers or, if the matter before the Council relates to agriculture, the various agricultural ministers will attend. The organisation of the various specialist councils falls to the President of the Council and that post is held for six monthly periods in rotation by the individual Member States of the EU. The Presidency of the Council is significant to the extent that the country holding the position can, to a large extent, control the agenda of the Council and thus can focus EU attention on areas that it considers to be of particular importance.

The Council of Ministers is the supreme decision making body of the EU and, as such, it has the final say in deciding upon EU legislation. Although it acts on recommendations and proposals made to it by the Commission, it does have the power to instruct the Commission to undertake particular investigations and to submit detailed proposals for its consideration.

Council decisions are taken on a mixture of voting procedures. Some measures only require a simple majority; in others, a procedure of qualified majority voting is used; and, in yet others, unanimity is required. Qualified majority voting is the procedure in which the votes of the 15 Member countries are weighted in proportion to their population from 10 down to two votes each. There are a total of 87 votes to be cast and, in order to pass a vote on the basis of a qualified majority, a minimum of 62 votes in favour is required. The corollary of this is that it requires a total of 26 votes to block any proposal that can be decided on by qualified majority voting. It can be seen, therefore, that even qualified majority voting requires a substantial degree of agreement across the EU.

Prior to approving the enlargement of the EU, by the accession of Austria, Finland and Sweden on 1 January 1995, both the UK and Spain insisted on what is known as the Ioannina Compromise. The Compromise states that:

> ... if members of the Council representing a total of 23 to 25 votes indicate their intention to oppose the adoption by the Council of a decision by qualified majority, the Council will do all in its power to reach within a reasonable time and without prejudicing obligatory time limits laid down in the Treaties and by secondary law, such as Arts 251 and 252 [formerly, Arts 189B and 189C] of the Treaty establishing the European Community, a satisfactory solution that could be adopted by at least 65 votes.

The effectiveness of this Compromise is a matter of some doubt, especially given the Commission's subsequent declaration that it would call for a vote on the new basis, as soon as it considered that a reasonable time had elapsed.

The SEA (a European Treaty legislated into UK law as the European Communities (Amendment) Act 1986) extended the use of qualified majority voting but unanimity is still required in what can be considered as the more politically sensitive areas, such as those relating to the harmonisation of indirect taxation, or the free movement of individuals. In addition to the need for unanimity in such sensitive areas, there is also the ultimate safeguard of what is known as the Luxembourg Compromise. This procedure, instituted at the behest of the French Government in 1966, permits individual Member States to exercise a right of veto in relation to any proposals which they consider to be contrary to what they consider to be a 'very important interest' of theirs.

As the format of particular council fluctuates, much of its day to day work is delegated to a committee of permanent representatives which operates under the title of Coreper.

Article 2 of the SEA 1986 provided that:

> The European Council shall bring together the Heads of State or of government of the Member States and the President of the Commission of the European Communities. They shall be assisted by the Ministers for Foreign Affairs and by a member of the Commission. The European Council shall meet at least twice a year.

The European Council, now known as the Council of the European Union, can be seen, therefore, as a form of EU summit meeting. It is chaired by the head of government currently holding the presidency of the Council. Although not originally recognised in the Treaty of Rome, the function of the European

Council was clarified by Art D of the Treaty on European Union which stated that it 'shall provide the union with the necessary impetus for its development and shall define the general political guidelines thereof'.

13.3.2 The European Parliament

The European Parliament is the directly elected European institution and, to that extent, it can be seen as the body which exercises democratic control over the operation on the EU. As in national Parliaments, members are elected to represent constituencies, the elections being held every five years. There are a total of 626 members divided amongst the 15 members approximately in proportion to the size of their various populations. Members of the European Parliament do not sit in national groups but operate within political groupings.

The European Parliament's general secretariat is based in Luxembourg and, although the Parliament sits in plenary session in Strasbourg for one week in each month, its detailed and preparatory work is carried out through 18 permanent committees which usually meet in Brussels. These permanent committees consider proposals from the Commission and provide the full Parliament with reports of such proposals for discussion.

13.3.3 Powers of the European Parliament

The powers of the European Parliament (the Parliament), however, should not be confused with those of national Parliaments, for the European Parliament is not a legislative institution and, in that respect, it plays a subsidiary role to the Council of Ministers. Originally, its powers were merely advisory and supervisory.

In pursuance of its advisory function, the Parliament always had the right to comment on the proposals of the Commission and, since 1980, the Council has been required to wait for the Parliament's opinion before adopting any law. In its supervisory role, the Parliament scrutinises the activities of the Commission and has the power to remove the Commission by passing a motion of censure against it by a two thirds' majority.

The legislative powers of the Parliament were substantially enhanced by the SEA 1986. Since that enactment, it has had a more influential role to play particularly in relation to the completion of the internal market. It can now negotiate directly with the Council as to any alterations or amendments it wishes to see in proposed legislation. It can also intervene to question and indeed alter any 'joint position' adopted by the Council on proposals put to it by the Commission. If the Council then insists on pursuing its original 'joint position', it can only do so on the basis of unanimity.

The SEA 1986 also required the assent of Parliament to any international agreements to be entered into by the EU. As a consequence, it has ultimate control, not just in relation to trade treaties, but also as regards any future expansion in the EU's membership.

The European Parliament is, together with the Council of Ministers, the budgetary authority of the EU. The budget is drawn up by the Commission and is presented to both the Council and the Parliament. As regards what is known as 'obligatory' expenditure, the Council has the final say but, in relation to 'non-obligatory' expenditure, the Parliament has the final decision whether to approve the budget or not. Such budgetary control places the Parliament in an extremely powerful position to influence EC policy, but perhaps the most draconian power the Parliament wields is the ability to pass a vote of censure against the Commission, requiring it to resign en masse.

The events of 1998–99 saw a significant shift in the relationship between the Parliament and the Commission. In December 1998, as a result of sustained accusations of mismanagement, fraud and cover ups levelled against the Commission, the Parliament voted not to discharge the Commission's accounts for 1996. Such action was, in effect, a declaration that the Community's budget has not been properly handled and was tantamount to a vote of no confidence in the Commission. In January 1999, the Community's Court of Auditors delivered what can only be described as a devastating report on fraud, waste and mismanagement and maladministration on the part of the Commission. It was found that the Commission had understated its financial obligations by £3.3 billion, and was so lax in its control that it had not even noticed that its banks were not paying any interest on huge amounts of money they were holding. The report of the Court of Auditors led to a vote of no confidence in the Commission in early January 1999 and, although the Commission survived the vote by a majority of 293 to 232, it had to accept the setting up of a 'committee of wise persons' to investigate and report on its operation. At the time, the appointment of this committee was thought to be a diplomatic fudge, allowing the Commission to carry on under warning as to its future conduct. However, when the committee submitted its report, it was so damning that it was immediately obvious that the Parliament would certainly use its power to remove the Commission. To forestall this event, the Commission resigned en masse. Somewhat ironically and certainly anti-climactically, however, as this book is being written, the previous President of the Commission, Jacques Santer, has actually gone, to be replaced by Romano Prodi; but the same commissioners, including the ones who were particularly picked out as the objects of blame, are still in place; on a temporary basis of course, simply ensuring the continuing smooth operation of the Commission.

The Europe wide selection of a new Parliament in June 1999 saw the election of a centre-right majority which will have a significant role to play in approving a new Commission.

As this book was being written, the previous President of the Commission, Jacques Santer, had gone, to be replaced by Romano Prodi; but the same commissioners, including the ones who were particularly picked out as the objects of blame, remained in place; on a temporary basis of course, simply ensuring the continuing smooth operation of the Commission. However, by the first week of July 1999, a new Commission had been proposed and gained the approval of the European Parliament later that month. In what President Prodi has said was to be a reforming Commission, the senior United Kingdom commissioner, Neil Kinnock, has been appointed as vice president with the specific remit of reforming the EU.

13.3.4 Economic and Social Committees

If the Parliament represents the directly elected arm of the EU, then the Economic and Social Committee represents a collection of unelected but, nonetheless, influential interest groups throughout the EU. This committee is a consultative institution and its opinion must be sought prior to the adoption by the Council of any Commission proposal. The Economic and Social Committee represents the underlying 'corporatist' nature of the EU to the extent that it seeks to locate and express a commonality of view and opinion on proposals from such divergent interests groups as employers, trade unions and consumers. It is perhaps symptomatic of the attitude of recent British governments to this underlying corporatist, essentially Christian Democratic, strand within the EU that it dispensed with its own similar internal grouping, the National Economic Development Council in 1992.

13.3.5 The European Commission

The European Commission is the executive of the EU and, in that role, it is responsible for the administration of EU policies. There are 20 Commissioners chosen from the various Member States to serve for renewable terms of four years. Commissioners are appointed to head departments with specific responsibility for furthering particular areas of EU policy. Once appointed, Commissioners are expected to act in the general interest of the EU as a whole rather than in the partial interest of their own home country.

In pursuit of EU policy, the Commission is responsible for ensuring that Treaty obligations between the Member States are met, and that Community laws relating to individuals are enforced. In order to fulfil these functions, the Commission has been provided with extensive powers both in relation to the investigation of potential breaches of Community law and the subsequent punishment of offenders. The classic area in which these powers can be seen in operation is in the area of competition law. Under Arts 81 and 82 (formerly, Arts 85 and 86) of the Treaty of Rome, the Commission has substantial powers to investigate and control potential monopolies and anti-competitive behaviour and it has used these powers to levy what, in the case of private individuals, would amount to huge fines where breaches of Community competition law have been discovered. In February 1993, the Commission imposed fines totalling more than £80 million on 17 steel producers for what was described as 'a very serious, illegal price fixing cartel'. The UK company British Steel suffered the greatest individual imposition of £26.4 million.

The Commission also acts, under instructions from the Council, as the negotiator between the EU and external countries.

In addition to these executive functions, the Commission also has a vital part to play in the EU's legislative process. The Council can only act on proposals put before it by the Commission. The Commission, therefore, has a duty to propose to the Council measures that will advance the achievement of the EU's general policies.

13.3.6 The European Court of Justice

The ECJ is the judicial arm of the EU and, in the field of Community law its judgments overrule those of national courts. It consists of 15 judges, assisted by nine advocates general, and sits in Luxembourg. The role of the advocate general is to investigate the matter submitted to the Court and to produce a report together with a recommendation for the consideration of the Court. The actual Court is free to accept the report or not as it sees fit.

The SEA 1986 provided for a new Court of First Instance to be attached to the existing Court of Justice. The jurisdiction of the Court of First Instance is limited mainly to internal claims by employees of the Community and to claims against fines made by the Commission under Community competition law. The aim is to reduce the burden of work on the Court of Justice but there is a right of appeal, on points of law only, to the full Court of Justice.

The Court of Justice performs two key functions:

(a) it decides whether any measures adopted, or rights denied, by the Commission, Council or any national government are compatible with treaty obligations. Such actions may be raised by any EU institution, government or individual. A Member State may fail to comply with its Treaty obligations in a number of ways. It might fail or, indeed, refuse to comply with a provision of the Treaty or a regulation; or, alternatively, it might refuse to implement a directive within the allotted time provided for. Under such circumstances, the State in question will be brought before the ECJ, either by the Commission or another Member State or, indeed, individuals within the State concerned;

(b) it provides authoritative rulings, at the request of national courts under Art 234 (formerly, Art 177) of the Treaty of Rome, on the interpretation of points of Community law. When an application is made under Art 234, the national proceedings are suspended until such time as the determination of the point in question is delivered by the ECJ. Whilst the case is being decided by the ECJ, the national court is expected to provide appropriate interim relief, even if this involves going against a domestic legal provision, as in the *Factortame* case.

This procedure can take the form of a preliminary ruling where the request precedes the actual determination of a case by the national court.

Article 234 (formerly, Art 177) provides that:

The Court of Justice shall have jurisdiction to give preliminary rulings concerning:

(a) the interpretation of treaties;

(b) the validity and interpretation of acts of the institutions of the Union and of the European Central Bank;

(c) the interpretation of the statutes of bodies established by an act of the Council, where those statutes so provide.

Where such a question is raised before any court or tribunal of a Member State, that court or tribunal may, if it considers that a decision on the question is necessary to enable it to give judgment, request the Court of Justice to give a ruling thereon.

Where any such question is raised in a case pending before a court or tribunal of a Member State against whose decision there is no judicial remedy under national law, that court or tribunal shall bring the matter before the Court of Justice.

It is clear that it is for the national court and not the individual parties concerned to make the reference. Where the national court or tribunal is not the 'final' court or tribunal, the reference to the ECJ is discretionary. Where the national court or tribunal is the 'final' court, then reference is obligatory. However, there are circumstances under which a 'final' court need not make a reference under Art 234 (formerly, Art 177). These are:

• where the question of Community law is not truly relevant to the decision to be made by the national court;

• where there has been a previous interpretation of the provision in question by the ECJ so that its meaning has been clearly determined;

• where the interpretation of the provision is so obvious as to leave no scope for any reasonable doubt as to its meaning. This latter instance has to be used with caution given the nature of Community law; for example, the fact that it is expressed in several languages using legal terms which might have different connotations within different jurisdictions. However, it is apparent that, where the meaning is clear, no reference need be made.

Reference has already been made, in Chapter 5, to the methods of interpretation used by courts in relation to Community law. It will be recalled that, in undertaking such a task, a purposive and contextual approach is mainly adopted, as against the more restrictive methods of interpretation favoured in relation to UK domestic legislation. The clearest statement of this purposive contextualist approach adopted by the ECJ is contained in its judgment in the *CILFIT* case:

> Every provision of Community law must be placed in its context and interpreted in the light of the provisions of Community law as a whole, regard being had to the objectives thereof and to its state of evolution at the date on which the provision in question is to be applied.

It can be appreciated that the reservations considered previously in regard to judicial creativity and intervention in policy matters in the UK courts apply *a fortiori* to the decisions of the ECJ.

Another major difference between the ECJ and the court within the English legal system is that the former is not bound by the doctrine of precedent in the same way as the latter is. It is always open to the ECJ to depart from its previous decisions where it considers it appropriate to do so. Although it will endeavour to maintain consistency, it has, on occasion, ignored its own previous decisions, as in *European Parliament v Council* (1990) where it recognised the right of the Parliament to institute an action against the Council.

The manner in which European law operates to control sex discrimination, through the Equal Treatment Directive, is of significant interest and, in *Marshall v Southampton and West Hampshire Area Health Authority* (1993), a number of the points that have been considered above were highlighted. Ms Marshall had originally been required to retire earlier than a man in her situation would have been required to do. She successfully argued before the ECJ that such a practice was discriminatory and contrary to Community Directive 76/207 on the equal treatment of men and women.

The present action related to the level of compensation she was entitled to as a consequence of this breach. UK legislation, the Sex Discrimination Act 1975, had set limits on the level of compensation that could be recovered for acts of sex discrimination. Marshall argued that the imposition of such limits was contrary to the Equal Opportunity Directive and that, in establishing such limits, the UK had failed to comply with the Directive.

The House of Lords referred the case to the ECJ under Art 234 (formerly, Art 177) and the latter determined that the rights set out in relation to compensation under Art 6 of the Directive were directly effective, and that, as the purpose of the Directive was to give effect to the principle of equal treatment, that could only be achieved by either reinstatement or the awarding of adequate compensation. The decision of the ECJ, therefore, overruled the financial limitations placed on sex discrimination awards and effectively overruled the domestic legislation.

P v S and Cornwall County Council (1996) extended the ambit of unlawful sex discrimination under the directive to cover people who have undergone surgical gender reorientation (sex change). However, in *Grant v South West Trains Ltd* (1998), the ECJ declined to extend the directive to cover discrimination on the grounds of sexual orientation (homosexuality), even though the Advocate General had initially supported the extension of the directive to same sex relationships. Whilst *Grant* was in the process of being decided in the ECJ, a second case, *R v Secretary of State for Defence ex p Perkins (No 2)*, had been brought before the English courts arguing a similar point, that discrimination on grounds of sexual orientation was covered by the Equal Treatment Directive. Initially, the High Court had referred the matter, under Art 234 (formerly, Art 177), to the ECJ for decision, but, on the decision in *Grant* being declared, the referral was withdrawn. In withdrawing the reference, Lightman J considered the proposition of counsel for Perkins to the effect that:

> ... there have been a number of occasions where the ECJ has overruled its previous decisions; that the law is not static; and, accordingly, in a dynamic and developing field such as discrimination in employment there must be a prospect that a differently constituted ECJ may depart from the decision in *Grant* ... But, to justify a reference, the possibility that the ECJ will depart from its previous decision must be more than theoretical: it must be a realistic possibility. The decision in *Grant* was of the full Court; it is only some four months old; there has been no development in case law or otherwise since the decision which can give cause for the ECJ reconsidering that decision ... I can see no realistic prospect of any change of mind on the part of the ECJ.

It could be pointed out that there could be no change in case law if judges, such as Lightman J, refused to send similar cases to the ECJ; but there may well be sense, if not virtue, in his refusal to refer similar cases to the ECJ within such a short timescale.

13.3.7 The Court of Auditors

Given the part that the Court of Auditors played in the 1998–99 struggle between the Parliament and the Commission, the role of this body should not be underestimated.

As its name suggests, it is responsible for providing an external audit of the Communities' finances. It examines the legality, regularity and soundness of the management of all the Communities' revenue and expenditure. The following passage, from its statement of assurance relating to the budget for the year 1996–97, provides a flavour of its findings:

> ... as in previous years, the incidence of errors affecting the transactions underlying the Commission's payments is too high for the Court to provide assurance about their legality and regularity.

> Many of the errors found in the payments provide direct evidence of failure to implement the control mechanisms foreseen in the regulations or to apply requisite checks before payments are made ... there were, again, many formal errors affecting payments. These are, essentially, cases where there was a failure to comply with the applicable regulations ... in many cases, formal errors involve specific systems weaknesses, notably failure to implement the control procedure required to ensure the eligibility of the recipients and the accuracy of the amounts paid [www.eca.eu.int.EN/notinf/dasra97.htm].

From this passage may well be seen the reason why the Parliament sought to establish some control over the operation of the Commission.

13.4   The European Convention on Human Rights

It has to be established, and emphasised, from the outset that the substance of this section has absolutely nothing to do with the EU as such; the Council of Europe is a completely distinct organisation and, although membership of the two organisations overlap, they are not the same. The Council of Europe is concerned not with economic matters but with the protection of civil rights and freedoms.

It is gratifying, at least to a degree, to recognise that the Convention and its Court (the ECHR) are no longer a matter of mysterious external control; the Human Rights Act 1998 having incorporated the European Convention on Human Rights into UK law and placing the ECHR as the supreme court in matters related to its jurisdiction. Much attention was paid to the Convention and the Human Rights Act in Chapter 1 (see 1.7), so it only remains to consider the structure and operation of the ECHR.

The Convention originally established two institutions:

(a) the European Commission of Human Rights. This body was charged with the task of examining, and if need be investigating the circumstances of, petitions submitted to it. If the Commission was unable to reach a negotiated solution between the parties concerned, it referred the matter to the Court of Human Rights;

(b) the European Court of Human Rights (ECHR). The European Convention on Human Rights provides that the judgment of the Court shall be final and that parties to it will abide by the decisions of the Court. This body, sitting in Strasbourg, was, and remains, responsible for all matters relating to the interpretation and application of the current Convention.

However, in the 1980s, as the Convention and its Court became more known and popular as a forum for asserting human rights, so its workload increased. This pressure was exacerbated by the break up of the old Communist Eastern Bloc and the fact that the newly independent countries, in both senses of the words, became signatories to the Convention. The statistics support the view of the incipient sclerosis of the original structure.

Applications registered with the Commission

Year	Number of applications registered
1981	404
1993	2,037
1997	4,750

Cases referred to the Court

Year	Number of cases referred
1981	7
1993	52
1997	119

As a consequence of such pressure, it became necessary to streamline the procedure by amalgamating the two previous institutions into one Court. In pursuit of this aim, Protocol 11 of the Convention was introduced in 1994. The new ECHR came into operation on 1 November 1998, although the Commission continued to deal with cases which had already been declared admissible for a further year.

The ECHR consists of 40 judges, representing the number of signatories to the Convention, although they do not have to be chosen from each State and, in any case, sit as individuals rather than representatives of their State. Judges are elected, by the Parliamentary Assembly of the Council of Europe, generally for six years, but arrangements have been put in place so that one half of the membership of the judicial panel will be required to seek renewal every three years.

It has to be recognised that the UK does not have a good record in relation to cases taken against it in the ECHR; in fact, currently, it comes second only to Turkey in the league of offenders. A number of case studies may highlight the way in which the ECHR deals with cases. It must not be forgotten, however, that these previous decisions of the ECHR are now binding precedents in UK law.

In *Malone v UK* (1984), the ECHR decided that telephone tapping by the police, authorised by the UK Government, and condoned under common law powers by the High Court, was in breach of Art 8 of the European Convention on Human Rights which guarantees the right to privacy. The Article holds:

> There shall be no interference by a public authority with the exercise of this right except such as is in accordance with the law and is necessary in a democratic society in the interests of national security ...

The ECHR held that the tapping was against the Convention because it was not 'in accordance with law' but rather governed by an unregulated discretion. It could not be 'necessary in a democratic society' as there were no constitutional safeguards against misuse of the power. The government reacted by introducing legislation to control telephone tapping by the police. The Interception of Communications Act 1985 limits telephone tapping to cases where the Home Secretary has issued a warrant and, to safeguard against arbitrary use, the warrant can only be issued in three specified circumstances, one of which is the prevention of serious crime. Further safeguards are provided by a tribunal to investigate complaints about the use of these powers and by the establishment of a commissioner to review annually how the Home Secretary has exercised his powers.

Another example of the way in which the system operates may be seen in the case of Earnest Saunders, one of the original defendants in the *Guinness* fraud trial of 1990. Prior to his trial, Saunders had been interviewed by Department of Trade and Industry inspectors and was required, under the provisions of the companies legislation, to answer questions without the right to silence. It was claimed that interviews under such conditions, and their subsequent use at the trial leading to his conviction, were in breach of the Convention on Human Rights. In October 1994, the Commission decided in Saunders' favour, and the Court confirmed that decision in 1996, although Saunders was not awarded damages. As a result, the Government has recognised that the powers given to DTI inspectors, breach the Convention, and has declared an intention to alter them, but not in a retrospective way that would benefit Mr Saunders.

Nor should one forget the potentially crucially important decision in *McGonnell v UK* (1995), in which the Commission has placed the situation of the Lord Chancellor in doubt.

In deciding cases before it, the ECHR applies what is known as the 'margin of appreciation'. This means that Member States have a measure of national discretion in the way they give effect to general standards set out in the Convention. An example of this may be seen in the 1996 decision on the ECHR in favour of the UK's decision to ban the film, *Visions of Ecstasy*, under its blasphemy law, in spite of the director's claim that the ban was contrary to his right to freedom of speech. The court decided that such delicate decisions as those relating to issues such as blasphemy should be decided at the local level and should not be imposed centrally. This particular decision may have pleased the UK Government, but it has been less than pleased with a number of other controversial cases in which the decisions have gone against it. Notable amongst these was the decision that the rights of the suspected IRA terrorists had been violated by their summary execution in Gibraltar.

Equally, the concerns of the government cannot but have been strengthened by the recent decision of the High Court to effectively take the impact of the Human Rights Act into consideration immediately (see 1.7).

13.5   The European Convention and the European Union

Having started this section by stressing the fundamental distinction between the ECJ and the ECHR, it is necessary to finish it by blurring it and pointing out the various ways in which the European Community, and then Union, have expressly recognised the rights provided in the Convention and the decisions made by the ECHR. Thus, in a joint declaration delivered in 1997, the European Parliament, the Council, and the Commission emphasised the prime importance they attached to the protection of fundamental rights:

> ... as derived particularly from the constitution of the Member States and the European Convention for the Protection of Human Rights and Fundamental Freedoms [(1977) OJ C103].

Article 6 (formerly, Art F(2)), which was introduced by the Maastricht Treaty, expressly states that:

> The Union shall respect fundamental rights, as guaranteed by the European Convention for the Protection of Human Rights and Fundamental Freedoms ...
> as general principles of Community law.

The ECJ, in the same way as English courts, has equally been guided by the Convention where Community law is silent. It still remains possible, however, for cases to be brought to either or both judicial forums. Issues relating to discrimination are an ideal case in point by being potentially both in breach of employment law regulated by the EC, and fundamental human rights regulated by the ECHR. It is also an unfortunate fact that it is possible for at least a degree of incompatibility between the decisions of the two courts in relation to very similar matters (for example, see *SPUC v Grogan* (1991); and *Open Door and Well Women v Ireland* (1992)). Such possibilities would be precluded if, following the recent action of the UK, the European Union, as a body, were formally to incorporate the Convention.

THE EUROPEAN CONTEXT

The European Union

UK law is now subject to Community law in particular areas.

In practice, this has led to the curtailment of parliamentary sovereignty in those areas.

Sources of European Union law

The sources of EC law are:

- internal treaties and protocols;
- international agreements;
- secondary legislation; and
- decisions of the European Court of Justice.

Secondary legislation takes three forms:

- regulations which are directly applicable;
- directives which have to be given statutory form;
- decisions are directly applicable.

Major institutions

The major institutions of the European Union are:

- the Council of Ministers;
- the European Parliament; the Commission; and
- the European Court of Justice.

The European Court of Human Rights

The European Council, the European Commission of Human Rights and the ECHR are distinct institutions whose purpose is to regulate the potential abuse of human rights. They are not part of the EU structure.

Since the enactment of the Human Rights Act 1998, the European Convention on Human Rights has been incorporated into United Kingdom law. It remains to see what effect this has on domestic UK law but it cannot but be significant.

BIBLIOGRAPHY

Alderson, J, 'Modern policing' (1995) The Independent, 1 February

Allen, T, Aikenhead, H and Widdison, R, 'Computer simulation of judicial behaviour', www.webjcli.ncl.ac.uk/1998/issue3allen3.html

Bailey, SH and Gunn, MJ, *Smith & Bailey on The Modern English Legal System*, 1991, London: Sweet & Maxwell (see, also, 3rd edn, 1996)

Baldwin, J, 'Police interview techniques: establishing truth or proof?' (1993) 33 British J of Criminology 3

Baldwin, J, 'Power and police interviews' [1993] NLJ 1194, 14 August

Baldwin, J, and Hill, S, *The Operation of the Green Form Scheme in England and Wales*, 1988, London: LCD

Baldwin, J and McConville, M, *Negotiated Justice: A Closer Look at the Implications of Plea Bargaining*, 1993, London: Martin Robertson

Baldwin, J and McConville, M, *Negotiated Justice: Pressures on Defendants to Plead Guilty*, 1977, London: Martin Robertson

Barnard, M, 'All bar none' (1999) 96/26 Law Soc Gazette 20, 30 June

Bennion, F, 'A naked usurpation?' [1999] NLJ 421

Bennion, F, 'Statute law obscurity and drafting parameters' (1978) British JLS 235

Bennion, F, *Statutory Interpretation*, 2nd edn, 1992, London: Butterworths

Bindaman, D, 'Crown duals' (1999) 96/13 Law Soc Gazette 22, 31 March

Bindman, G, 'Lessons of Pinochet' [1999] NLJ 1050

Broadbent, G, 'Offensive weapons and the Criminal Justice Act' (1989) Law Soc Gazette, 12 July

Burrow, J, 'Pre-committal custody time limits' [1999] NLJ 330

Cane, P (ed), *Atiyah's Accidents, Compensation and the Law*, 5th edn, 1993, London: Butterworths

Cape, E, 'Police interrogation and interruption' [1994] NLJ 120

Card, R and Ward, R, *The Criminal Justice and Public Order Act 1994*, 1994, Bristol: Jordans

Clayton, R and Tomlinson, H, 'Arrest and reasonable grounds for suspicion' (1988) 32 Law Soc Gazette 22, 7 September

Cragg, S, 'Stop and search powers: research and extension' (1999) Legal Action 3, February

Craig, P and de Búrca, G, *EU Law: Text, Cases and Materials*, 2nd edn, 1998, Oxford: OUP

Crawford, L, 'Race awareness training and the judges' (1994) Counsel 11, February

Croall, H, *Crime and Society in Britain*, 1998, London: Longman

Darbyshire, P, 'The lamp that shows that freedom lives – is it worth the candle?' [1991] Crim LR 740

Devlin (Lord), *Trial by Jury*, 1966, London: Stevens

Diamond, D, 'Woolf reforms hike costs' (1999) The Lawyer 2, 11 January

Dicey, AV, *An Introduction to the Study of the Law of the Constitution* (1885), 10th edn, 1959, London: Macmillan

Dixon, D, Coleman, C and Bottomley, K, 'Consent and legal regulation of policing' (1990) 17 JLS 345

Exall, G, 'Civil litigation brief' (1999) SJ 162, 19 February

Exall, G, 'Civil litigation brief' (1999) SJ 270, 19 March

Exall, G, 'Civil litigation brief' (1999) SJ 32, 15 January

Feldman, D, *Civil Liberties and Human Rights in England and Wales*, 1993, Oxford: OUP

Frenkel, J, 'Offers to settle and payments into court' [1999] NLJ 458

Frenkel, J, 'On the road to reform' (1998) 95/48 Law Soc Gazette 33, 16 December

Genn, H, *Hard Bargaining: Out of Court Settlement in Personal Injury Claims*, 1987, Oxford: OUP

Genn, H and Genn, Y, *The Effectiveness of Representation at Tribunals*, 1989, London: LCD

Gibb, F, 'Plaintiff cries as law goes native' (1999) The Times, 27 April

Gibb, F, 'Rude judges must mind their language' (1999) The Times, 29 June

Gibb, F, 'Thatcher furious at "vindictive" Pinochet decision' (1999) The Times, 16 April

Gibson, B, 'Why Bournemouth?' (1987) 151 JP 520, 15 August

Glasser, C, 'Legal aid and eligibility' (1988) Law Soc Gazette 11, 9 March

Glasser, C, 'Legal services and the Green Papers' (1989) Law Soc Gazette 9, 5 April

Gold, S, 'Woolf watch' [1999] NLJ 718

Goodhart, A, 'The *ratio decidendi* of a case' (1959) 22 MLR 117

Goodrich, P, *Reading the Law*, 1986, Oxford: Basil Blackwell

Grainger, I and Fealy, M, *An Introduction to the New Civil Procedure Rules*, 1999, London: Cavendish Publishing

Griffith, JAG, *The Politics of the Judiciary*, 5th edn, 1997, London: Fontana

Griffiths, C, 'Jury trial' (1999) Counsel 14, April

Hamer, P, 'Complaints: a new strategy ' [1999] NLJ 959, 25 June

Harris, D *et al, Compensation and Support for Illness and Injury*, 1984, Oxford: Clarendon

Harrison, R, 'Cry Woolf' [1999] NLJ 1011

Harrison, R, 'Why have two types of civil court?' [1999] NLJ 65, 15 January,

Hart, H, *The Concept of Law*, 1961, Oxford: OUP

Hayek, FA, *The Road to Serfdom* (1971), 1994, London: Routledge and Kegan Paul

Hedderman, C and Moxon, C, *Magistrates' Court or Crown Court? Mode of Trial Decisions and Sentencing*, Home Office Study No 125, 1992, London: HMSO

HM Magistrates' Courts Service Inspectorate, *Annual Report 1997–98*, London: HMSO

Holdsworth, W, *A History of English Law*, 1924, London: Methuen

Holland, T, 'Cut price conveyancing' [1994] NLJ 192, 11 February

Jason-Lloyd, L, 'Section 60 of the Criminal Justice and Public Order Act 1994' (1998) 162 JP 836, 24 October

JUSTICE, *Professional Negligence and the Quality of Legal Services – An Economic Perspective*, 1983, London: JUSTICE

Kairys, D, *The Politics of Law: A Progressive Critique*, 1982, New York: Pantheon

Keating, D, 'Upholding the Rule of Law' [1999] NLJ 533

Khan, S and Ryder, M, 'Police and the law' (1998) Legal Action 16, September

Irvine (Lord), 'Community vision under fire' (1999) 96 Law Soc Gazette 1, 26 May

Lee, S, *Judging Judges*, 1988, London: Faber & Faber

Lidstone, K, 'Entry, search and seizure' (1989) 40 NILQ 333

Lidstone, K (ed), *Prosecutions by Private Individuals and Non-police Agencies*, 1980, London: HMSO

Lidstone, K and Palmer, C, *The Investigation of Crime*, 1996, London: Butterworths

Lord Chancellor's Department, *Judicial Statistics 1998*, Cm 3980, London: HMSO

MacCormick, N, *Legal Rules and Legal Reasoning*, 1978, Oxford: Clarendon

Mackay (Lord), *The Administration of Justice*, 1994, Hamlyn Lectures, London: Sweet & Maxwell

Malleson, K, *The New Judiciary – The Effect of Expansion and Activism*, 1999, Aldershot: Ashgate

Mansell, W and Meteyard, B, *A Critical Introduction to Law*, 2nd edn, 1999, London: Cavendish Publishing

McConville, M, Sanders, A and Leng, R, *The Case for the Prosecution*, 1991, London: Routledge

Mayhew, L and Reiss, A, 'The social organisation of legal contacts' (1969) 34 American Sociological Rev 311

McGrath, P, 'Appeals against small claims track decisions' [1999] NLJ 748

Money-Kyrle, R, 'Advocates' immunity after *Osman*' [1999] NLJ 945 and 981

Montesquieu, C, *De l'Esprit des Lois* (1748), 1989, Cambridge: CUP

Morris, P, White, R and Lewis, P, *Social Needs and Legal Action*, 1973, London: Robertson

Motson, S, Stephenson, G and Williamson, T, 'The effects of case characteristics on suspect behaviour during police questioning' (1992) 32 British J of Criminology 23

Murphy, M, 'Civil legal aid eligibility' (1989) Legal Action 4, October

Napier, M, 'Conditional fees' (1995) 92/16 Law Soc Gazette 1626

News, 'The legal profession and the Community Legal Service' [1999] NLJ 1195, 6 August

News in Brief, 'Cheap conveyancing' [1998] NLJ 8, 9 January

Pannick, D, *Advocates*, 1992, Oxford: OUP

Pannick, D, *Judges*, 1987, Oxford: OUP

Parker, C, 'Judicial decision making' [1999] NLJ 1142

Parpworth, N, 'Breach of the peace: breach of human rights?' (1998) 152 JP 6, 7 November

Payne, R, 'To counsel, not confront: the law on ADR' (1999) Counsel 30, February

Pedley, FH, 'The small claims process' [1994] NLJ 1217, 9 September

Purchas, F (Sir), 'What is happening to judicial independence' [1994] NLJ 1306, 30 September

Raz, J, 'The Rule of Law and its virtue' (1977) 93 LQR 195

Reid (Lord), 'The judge as law maker' (1972) 12 JSPTL 22

Reiner, R, *Crime, Order and Policing*, 1994, London: Routledge

Reiner, R, 'Responsibilities and reforms' [1993] NLJ 1096, 30 July

Reiner, R, *The Politics of the Police*, 1995, Hemel Hempstead: Wheatsheaf

Richardson, J (ed) *et al*, *Archbold on Criminal Evidence, Pleading and Practice*, 1995, London: Sweet & Maxwell

Robertson, G, 'The Downey Report: MPs must realise they are not above the law' (1997) The Guardian, 4 July, p 18

Robertshaw, P, *Rethinking Legal Need: the Case of Criminal Justice*, 1991, Aldershot: Dartmouth

Rutherford, A, 'Judicial training and autonomy' [1999] NLJ 1120

Rutherford, A, 'Preserving a robust independence' [1999] NLJ 908

Sanders, A, 'Class bias in prosecutions' (1985) 24 Howard J 176

Sanders, A, 'The silent code' [1994] NLJ 946

Sanders, A, and Young, R, *Criminal Justice*, 1995, London: Butterworths

Sanders, A and Young, R, 'Plea bargaining and the next Criminal Justice Bill' [1994] NLJ 1200, 9 September

Sanders, A *et al*, *Advice and Assistance at Police Stations and the 24 Hour Duty Solicitor Scheme*, 1989, London: LCD

Scrivener, A, 'The birth of a new language in the court room: English' (1999) The Independent, 26 April

Sedley, S (Sir), 'A right to law' (1995) The Guardian, 11 May, p 18

Sedley, S (Sir), 'Human rights: a 21st century agenda' [1995] PL 386

Simpson, A, 'The *ratio decidendi* of a case' (1957) 20 MLR 413

Skordaki, E, *Judicial Appointments*, Law Society Research Study No 5, 1991, London: HMSO

Slapper, G, 'English legal system' (1999) 26 SLR 31, Spring

Smith, JC, 'Criminal appeals and the Criminal Cases Review Commission' [1995] NLJ 534

Smith, R, 'Judicial statistics: questions and answers' [1994] NLJ 1088, 5 August

Smith, R, 'Politics and the judiciary' (1993) 143 NLJ 1486

Smith, R (ed), *Achieving Civil Justice*, 1996, London: LAG

Smith, R (ed), *Shaping the Future: New Directions in Legal Services*, 1995, London: LAG

St Luce, S, 'Cutting the lifeline' [1999] NLJ 398

Steyn (Lord), 'The weakest and least dangerous department of government' [1997] PL 84

Temple Lang, J, 'The duties of national courts under Community constitutional law' [1997] EL Rev 22

Thomas, DA (ed), *Current Sentencing Practice*, 1999, London: Sweet & Maxwell

Thompson, P (ed), *The Civil Court Practice*, 1999, London: Butterworths

Turner, AJ, 'Inferences under s 34 of the Criminal Justice and Public Order Act 1994: Part One' (1999) 163 JP, 27 March

Turner, AJ, 'Inferences under s 34 of the Criminal Justice and Public Order Act 1994: Part Two' (1999) 163 JP, 24 April

Trent, M, 'ADR and the new Civil Procedure Rules' [1999] NLJ 410

Twining, W and Meirs, D, *How To Do Things With Rules*, 4th edn, 1999, London: Butterworths

Unger, R, *In Law and Modern Society*, 1976, New York: Free Press

Verkaik, R, 'Opinions on counsel' (1998) 95/04 Law Soc Gazette 22, 28 January

von Hayek, FA, *The Road to Serfdom* (1971), 1994, London: Routledge and Kegan Paul

Wadham, J and Arkinstall, J, 'Human rights and crime' [1999] NLJ 703

Watson, A, 'The right to elect trial by jury: the issue reappears' (1998) 163 JP 636, 15 August

Weber, M, *Economy and Society (Wirtschaft und Gemeinschaft)*, 1968, Roth, G and Widttich, C (trans), Berkeley: California UP

Wendel Holmes, O, *The Common Law* (1881), 1968, London: Macmillan

Williams, G, 'Letting of the guilty and presecuting the innocent' [1985] Crim LR 115

Wolchover, D and Heaton-Armstrong, A, 'Jailing psychopaths and prison cell confessions' [1999] NLJ 285

Woolf (Lord), 'Judicial review – the tensions between the executive and the judiciary' (1998) 114 LQR 579

Yarrow, S, *The Price of Success*, 1997, Grantham: Grantham

Zander, M, *A Matter of Justice*, 1989, Oxford: OUP

Zander, M, *Cases and Materials on the English Legal System*, 7th edn, 1996, London: Butterworths

Zander, M, 'Costs of litigation – a study in the Queen's Bench Division' (1975) Law Soc Gazette 680, 25 June

Zander, M, 'How does judicial case management work?' [1997] NLJ 353, 7 March

Zander, M, 'Investigation of crime' [1979] Crim LR 211

Zander, M, *Legal Services for the Community*, 1978, London: Temple Smith

Zander, M, 'The trouble with fast track fixed costs' [1997] NLJ 1125

Zander, M, 'The Woolf Report: forwards or backwards for the new Lord Chancellor' (1997) 16 Civil Justice Quarterly 208

Zander, M, 'Who goes to solicitors?' (1969) 66 Law Soc Gazette 174

Zander, M, 'Woolf on Zander' [1997] NLJ 768, 23 May

Zander, M and Henderson, P, *The Crown Court Study*, Royal Commission on Criminal Justice Study 19, 145, 1993, London: HMSO

FURTHER READING

Many of these articles and reports are excerpts from Slapper, G and Kelly, D, *Sourcebook on English Legal System*, 1996, London: Cavendish Publishing.

Chapter 1   Law and Legal Study

Barnett, H, *Constitutional and Administrative Law*, 2nd edn, 1998, London: Cavendish Publishing

Bradney, A *et al*, *How to Study Law*, 3rd edn, 1995, London: Sweet & Maxwell

Clinch, P, *Using a Law Library*, 1992, London: Blackstone

Fitzpatrick, P (ed), *Dangerous Supplements*, 1991, London: Pluto

Holmes, N and Venebles, D, *Researching the Legal Web*, 1997, London: Butterworths

Social and legal order

Mansell, W and Meteyard, B, *A Critical Introduction to Law*, 2nd edn, 1999, London: Cavendish Publishing

Roberts, S, *Order and Dispute*, 1979, Harmondsworth: Penguin

Legal language

Friedman, L, 'On interpretation of laws' (1988) 11(3) Ratio Juris 252, December, pp 252–62

Goodrich, P, *Reading the Law*, 1986, Oxford: Basil Blackwell

Jackson, B, *Making Sense in Law*, 1995, London: Deborah Charles

Law, politics and the Rule of Law

Bennion, F, 'A naked usurpation?' [1999] NLJ 421, pp 421–26

Dicey, AV, *Introduction to the Law of the Constitution*, 1897, London: Macmillan

Feldman, D, 'The Human Rights Act and consitutional principles' (1999) 19(2) JLS, June

Fine, R, *Democracy and the Rule of Law*, 1984, London: Pluto

Hill, C, *Liberty Against the Law*, 1996, Harmondsworth: Penguin

Horowitz, MJ, 'The Rule of Law: an unqualified good?' (1977) 86 Yale LJ 561

Kairys, D (ed), *The Politics of Law: A Progressive Critique*, 1990, London: Pantheon

Keating, D, 'Upholding the Rule of Law' [1999] NLJ 533, pp 533–34

Laws, J (Sir), 'Law and democracy' [1995] PL 72

Locke, J, *The Treatises of Government*, 1988, Cambridge: CUP

Raz, J, 'The Rule of Law and its virtue' (1972) 93 LQR 195

Sedley, S (Sir), *Freedom, Law and Justice*, 1998, Hamlyn Lectures, London: Sweet & Maxwell

Sedley, S (Sir), 'Human rights: a 21st century agenda' [1995] PL 386

Steiner, H and Alston, P, *International Human Rights in Context*, 1996, Oxford: Clarendon

Thompson, A, 'Taking the right seriously: the case of FA Hayek', in Fitzpatrick, P (ed), *Dangerous Supplements*, 1991, London: Pluto

Thompson, E, *Whigs and Hunters*, 1977, Harmondsworth: Penguin

von Hayek, F, *The Road to Serfdom*, 1962, London: Routledge

Young, J, 'The politics of the Human Rights Act' (1999) 26(1) JLS 27, pp 27–37

Chapter 2   Sources of Law

Boulton, C (ed), *Erskine May's Treatise on the Law, Privileges, Proceedings and Usage of Parliament*, 1989, London: Butterworths

Cross, R, *Cross, Harris and Hart, Precedent in English Law*, 4th edn, 1991, Oxford: Clarendon

Goodhart, A, 'The *ratio decidendi* of a case' (1959) 22 MLR 117

Holdsworth, W, 'Case law' (1934) 50 LQR 180

Jenkins, C, 'Helping the reader of Bills and Acts' [1999] NLJ 798, pp 798–99

MacCormick, N, *Legal Rules and Legal Reasoning*, 1978, Oxford: Clarendon

Simpson, A, 'The *ratio decidendi* of a case' (1957) 20 MLR 413; (1958) 21 MLR 155

The following are also relevant to the issues in Chapter 5:

Bates, T, 'The contemporary use of legislative history in the United Kingdom' (1995) 54(1) CLJ 127, March, pp 127–52

Bell, J and Engle, G (Sir), *Cross: Statutory Interpretation*, 3rd edn, 1995, London: Butterworths

Bennion, F, *Statutory Interpretation*, 2nd edn, 1992, London: Butterworths

Bennion, F, 'Statute law: obscurity and drafting parameters' (1978) 5 British JLS 235, Winter, pp 235–45

Committee on the Preparation of Legislation, *Renton Committee Report*, 1975, Cmnd 6053, London: HMSO

Eskridge, W, *Dynamic Statutory Interpretation*, 1994, Cambridge MA: Harvard UP

Friedman, L, 'On interpretation of laws' (1988) 11(3) Ratio Juris 252, December, pp 252–62

Chapter 3 The Civil Court Structure

Barnard, D and Houghton, M, *The New Civil Court in Action*, 1993, London: Butterworths

Greenslade, R, *Civil Court Practice*, 1997, London: Butterworths

Harrison, R, 'Why have two types of civil court?' [1999] NLJ 65, pp 65–70

Judicial Statistics Annual Report 1996, Government Statistical Service, 1997, London: HMSO

Pedley, FH, 'The small claims process' [1994] NLJ 1217

Pershad, R, 'Delay, listing and the county court' (1994) Counsel 16, February

Fage, J and Whitehead, G, *Supreme Court Practice and Procedure*, 1992, London: Fourmat

Smith, R, 'Judicial statistics' [1995] NLJ 1364

Woolf (Lord), *Access to Justice – Final Report to the Lord Chancellor on the Civil Justice System in England and Wales*, 1996, London: HMSO

Chapter 4   The Criminal Court Structure

Carlen, P, *Magistrates' Justice*, 1976, Oxford: Martin Robertson

Fallon, P and Bursell, R, *Crown Court Practice (Trial)*, 1978, London: Butterworths

Malleson, K, 'The Criminal Cases Review Commission: how will it work?' [1995] Crim LR 928

Matthews, P and Foreman, J (eds), *Jervis: On the Office and Duties of Coroners*, 1993, London: Sweet & Maxwell

Moxon, D and Hedderman, C, 'Mode of trial decisions and sentencing differences between courts' (1994) 33(2) Howard J of Criminal Justice 97, pp 97–103

Smith, JC, 'The Criminal Appeal Act 1995: appeals against conviction' [1995] Crim LR 921

Richardson, PJ (ed), *Archbold on Criminal Pleading, Evidence and Practice*, 1997, London: Sweet & Maxwell

Chapter 5   Judicial Reasoning

Bell, J and Engle, G (Sir), *Cross on Statutory Interpretation*, 1995, London: Butterworths

Bennion, F, *Statutory Interpretation*, 1992, London: Butterworths

Bindman, G, 'Lessons of Pinochet' [1999] NLJ 1050, pp 1050–51

Denning (Lord), *Due Process of Law*, 1980, London: Butterworths

Denning (Lord), *The Discipline of Law*, 1979, London: Butterworths

Parker, C, 'Judicial decision making' [1999] NLJ 1142, pp 1142–44

Pickles, J, *Straight from the Bench*, 1987, London: Hodder and Stoughton

Reid (Lord), 'The judge as law maker' (1972) 12 JSPTL 22

Chapter 6   The Judiciary

Baldwin, J, 'The social composition of magistrates' (1976) 16 British J of Criminology 171

Browne-Wilkinson, N (Sir), 'The independence of the judiciary in the 1980s' [1988] PL 4

Crawford, L, 'Race awareness training and the judges' (1994) Counsel 11, February

Griffith, JAG, *The Politics of the Judiciary*, 5th edn, 1997, London: Fontana

Hailsham (Lord), 'The office of Lord Chancellor and the separation of powers' (1989) 8 Civil Justice Quarterly 308, pp 308–18

Lee, S, *Judging Judges*, 1988, London: Faber & Faber

MacCormick, N, *Legal Rules and Legal Reasoning*, 1978, Oxford: Clarendon

Mackay (Lord), *The Administration of Justice*, 1994, London: Sweet & Maxwell

Malleson, K, *The New Judiciary – The Effect of Expansion and Activism*, 1999, Aldershot: Ashgate

McLachlin, B, 'The role of judges in modern Commonwealth society' [1994] LQR 260, April, pp 260–69

Pannick, D, *Judges*, 1987, Oxford: OUP

Parker, H *et al*, *Unmasking the Magistrates*, 1989, Milton Keynes: OU

Royal Commission on Criminal Justice, *Runciman Report*, Cm 2263, 1995, London: HMSO

Rutherford, A, 'Judicial training and autonomy' [1999] NLJ 1120, pp 1120–22

Skordaki, E, *Judicial Appointments*, Law Society Research Study No 5, 1991, London: HMSO

Stevens, R, *The Independence of the Judiciary*, 1993, Oxford: OUP

See, in addition, reading for Chapter 2.

Chapter 7   The Civil Process

Baldwin, J, *The Small Claims Procedure and the Consumer*, 1995, London: Office of Fair Trading

Genn, H, *Hard Bargaining: Out of Court Settlements in Personal Injury Claims*, 1987, Oxford: OUP

Grainger, I and Fealy, M, *An Introduction to the New Civil Procedure Rules*, 1999, London: Cavendish Publishing

Harrison, R, 'Cry Woolf' [1999] NLJ 1011, pp 1011–13

Lawton, F, 'Court experts' (1995) SJ 793

Miller, F, 'The adversarial myth' [1995] NLJ 743

Thompson, P (ed), *The Civil Court Practice*, 1999, London: Butterworths

Trent, M, 'ADR and the new Civil Procedure Rules' [1999] NLJ 410, pp 410–11

Woolf (Lord), *Access to Justice – Final Report to the Lord Chancellor on the Civil Justice System in England and Wales*, 1996, London: HMSO

Zander, M, 'Are there any clothes for the emperor to wear?' [1995] NLJ 154

Zander, M, 'The trouble with fast track fixed costs' [1997] NLJ 1125

Zander, M, 'The Woolf Report: forwards or backwards for the new Lord Chancellor' (1997) 16 Civil Justice Quarterly 208, pp 208–27

Zuckerman, AAS, 'A reform of civil procedure – rationing procedure rather than access to justice' (1995) 22 JLS 156

Chapter 8   Arbitration, Tribunal Adjudication, and Alternative Dispute Resolution

Abel, R, 'The comparative study of dispute institutions in society' (1973) 8 Law and Society Rev 217

Baldwin, J, *The Small Claims Procedure and the Consumer*, 1995, London: Office of Fair Trading

Beale, H and Dugdale, T, 'Contracts between businessmen: planning and the use of contractual remedies' (1975) 2 British JLS 45

Committee on Administrative Tribunals and Inquiries, *Franks Report*, Cmnd 218, 1957

Genn, H and Genn, Y, *The Effectiveness of Representation at Tribunals*, 1989, London: LCD

JUSTICE, *Industrial Tribunals*, 1987, London: JUSTICE

Mackay (Lord), *The Administration of Justice*, 1994, London: Sweet & Maxwell

Payne, R, 'To counsel, not confront: the law on ADR' (1999) Counsel 30, February, pp 30–32

Pedley, FH, 'The small claims process' [1994] NLJ 1217

The Annual Report of the Council on Tribunals, 1995–96, HC 114, London: HMSO

The Annual Report of the Council on Tribunals, 1996–97, London: HMSO

Chapter 9   The Criminal Process: (1) The Investigation of Crime

Baldwin, J, *The Conduct of Police Investigation*, 1992, London: HMSO

Baldwin, J and McConville, M, *Jury Trials*, 1979, Oxford: Clarendon

Bevan, V and Lidstone, K, *The Investigation of Crime*, 2nd edn, 1996, London: Butterworths

Brown, D, Ellis, T and Larcombe, K, *Changing the Code: Police Detention under the revised PACE Codes of Practice*, Home Office Research Study No 129, 1993, London: HMSO

Burrow, J, 'Pre-committal custody time limits' [1999] NLJ 330, pp 330–32

Committee on Fraud Trials, *Roskill Report*, 1986, London: HMSO

Darbyshire, P, 'The lamp that shows that freedom lives – is it worth the candle?' [1991] Crim LR 740

Dennis, I, 'The Criminal Justice and Public Order Act 1994: the evidence provisions' [1995] Crim LR 4

Devlin, P, *Trial by Jury*, 1956, London: Stevens

Dixon, D, Coleman, C and Bottomley, K, 'PACE in practice' (1991) 141 NLJ 1586

Doran, S and Jackson, J, 'The case for jury waiver' [1997] 155 Crim LR

Findlay, M and Duff, P, *The Jury Under Attack*, 1988, London: Butterworths

Greer, S, 'The right to silence: defence disclosure and confession evidence' (1994) 21 JLS 103

Herbert, P, 'Racism, impartiality and juries' [1995] NLJ 146

Royal Commission on Criminal Justice, *Runciman Report*, Cm 2263, 1995, London: HMSO

Wadham, J and Arkinstall, J, 'Human rights and crime' [1999] NLJ 703, pp 703–06

Wolchover, D and Heaton-Armstrong, A, 'Jailing psychopaths and prison cell confessions' [1999] NLJ 285, pp 285–314

Zander, M, *The Police and Criminal Evidence Act 1994*, 3rd edn, 1995, London: Sweet & Maxwell

Chapter 10   The Criminal Process: (2) The Prosecution

Ashworth, A and Fionda, J, 'The new code for crown prosecutors: prosecution, accountability and the public interest' [1994] Crim LR 894

Baldwin, J and McConville, M, *Negotiated Justice: Pressures on Defendants to Plead Guilty*, 1977, Oxford: Martin Robertson

Bindaman, D, 'Crown duals' (1999) 96/13 Law Soc Gazette 22, 31 March, pp 22–28

Cockburn, JS and Green, TA, *Twelve Good Men and True*, 1988, Guilford: Princeton UP

CPS, *The Code for Crown Prosecutors*, rev edn, June 1994, London: CPS

Devlin, P, *Trial by Jury*, 1956, London: Stevens

Griffiths, C, 'Jury trial' (1999) Counsel 14, April, pp 14–16

Henderson, P and Nicholas, T, *Offending While on Bail*, Home Office Research Bulletin 32, 1992, London: Home Office Research Unit

Hucklesby, A, 'The use and abuse of conditional bail' (1994) 33 Howard J 258

Findlay, M and Duff, P, *The Jury Under Attack*, 1988, London: Butterworths

Mills, B, 'The prosecution code' (1994) SJ 709

Rutherford, A, 'Preserving a robust independence' [1999] NLJ 908, pp 908–10

Rose, D, *In the Name of the Law – The Collapse of Criminal Justice*, 1996, London: Jonathan Cape

Sanders, A, 'Class bias in prosecutions' (1985) 24 Howard J 176

Thompson, EP, *Writing by Candlelight*, 1980, London: Merlin

Watson, A, 'The right to elect trial by jury: the issue reappears' (1998) 163 JP 636, 15 August, pp 636–40

Chapter 11 Legal Services

Abel, R, *The Legal Profession in England and Wales*, 1988, Oxford: Basil Blackwell

Barnard, M, 'All bar none' (1999) 96/26 Law Soc Gazette 20, 30 June, pp 20–24

Boxer, C, 'Conditional fees: lawyers courting disaster' (1995) 145 NLJ 1069

Cocks, R, *Foundations of the Modern Bar*, 1983, London: Sweet & Maxwell

Editorial, 'Rights of audience' (1998) 162 JP 193, pp 193–95

Genn, H and Genn, Y, *The Effectiveness of Representation at Tribunals*, 1989, London: LCD

Holland, A, 'Cut price conveyancing' (1994) 144 NLJ 192

Jackson, R, 'Disappointed litigants and doubtful actions'(1995) Counsel 16, May

Law Society Consultation Paper, *Supervision of Solicitors – The Next Decade*, July 1995

Money-Kyrle, R, 'Advocates' immunity after *Osman*' [1999] NLJ 945, pp 945–50 and 981–82

Powell, JL, 'Barristers' immunity – time to go' (1995) Counsel 11, March

St Luce, S, 'Cutting the lifeline' [1999] NLJ 398, pp 398–99

Verkaik, R, 'Opinions on counsel' (1998) 95/4 Law Soc Gazette 22, 28 January

Chapter 12   The Funding of Legal Services

Bean, D, 'Surveying the new landscape' (1999) Counsel 8, June, pp 8–10

Knafler, S, 'Litigation for the poor' (1994) SJ 256

Law Commission Consultation Paper, *Legal Aid – Targeting Need: The Future of Publicly Funded Help in Solving Legal Problems and Disputes in England and Wales*, Cm 2854, London: HMSO

Morris, P *et al*, *Social Needs and Legal Action*, 1973, Oxford: Martin Robertson

Peysner, J and Balen, P, 'Conditional fees' (1995) Law Soc Gazette 20, 31 August; (1995) Law Soc Gazette 16, 13 September

Zander, M, 'Access to justice and legal aid: 12 reasons for rejecting the Legal Aid Green Paper' (1995) 145 NLJ 1098

Zander, M, *Legal Services for the Community*, 1978, London: Temple Smith

Chapter 13   The European Context

Benoetvea, J, *The Legal Reasoning of the European Court of Justice: Towards a European Jurisprudence*, 1993, Oxford: Clarendon

Borgsmit, K, 'The Advocate General at the European Court of Justice: a comparative study' (1988) 13 EL Rev 106

Craig, P and de Búrca, G, *EU Law: Text, Cases and Materials*, 2nd edn, 1998, Oxford: OUP

Dickson, B, *Human Rights and the European Convention*, 1997, London: Sweet and Maxwell

Foster, N, *EC Legislation*, 9th edn, 1998, London: Blackstone

Harris, DJ *et al*, *Law of the European Convention on Human Rights*, 1995, London: Butterworths

Kennedy, T, *Learning European Law: a Primer and* Vade-mecum, 1998, London: Sweet and Maxwell

Lasok, D, *Law and Institutions of the European Union*, 6th edn, 1994, London: Butterworths

Neville Brown, L and Kennedy, T, *The Court of Justice of the European Communities*, 4th edn, 1994, London: Sweet & Maxwell

Shaw, J, *European Community Law*, 2nd edn, 1996, London: Macmillan

Ward, I, *A Critical Introduction to European Law*, 1996, London: Butterworths

Weatherill, S and Beamont, P, *EC Law*, 1993, London: Penguin

INDEX